THE MAKING

OF

CENTRAL AND EASTERN

EUROPE

THE MAKING

OF

CENTRAL AND EASTERN

EUROPE

BY

FRANCIS DVORNIK

D.D., D. ès Lettres (Sorbonne), Hon.D.Lit.(London)
Corresponding Fellow of the British Academy.
Associate of the Royal Academy of Belgium.
Hon. Member of the Academy of Rumania.
Member of the Czech Academy and of the Slavonic Institute.
Professor in Charles IV University.

Second Edition

With a New Introduction and Notes to the Text

by the Author

ACADEMIC INTERNATIONAL PRESS

1974

A volume in **The Central and East European Series** under the editor-
ship of Professor *Joseph Frederick Zacek*, State University of New
York at Albany.

Volume 3

Francis Dvornik **The Making of Central and Eastern Europe**. Second
edition, with a New Introduction and Notes to the Text, by the Author. First edition published London, 1949.

Library of Congress Catalog Card Number: 73-90780
ISBN: 0-87569-023-8
A Catalog Card follows the Index

Printed in the United States of America

ACADEMIC INTERNATIONAL PRESS
Box 555 Gulf Breeze, Florida 32561

ABOUT THE AUTHOR

Francis Dvornik is one of the world's leading Byzantinists. Born in Moravia in 1893, he holds the D.D. of the University of Olomouc (1920), the Diploma of the École des Sciences Politiques of Paris (1923), the D. Litt. of the Sorbonne (1926), and an honorary D. Litt. from the University of London (1946). He has taught at Charles University (Prague), the Collège de France, the École des Hautes Études, and Cambridge, and since 1949 has been Professor of Byzantine History at the Dumbarton Oaks Research Library of Harvard University. A prolific writer, he is a recognized senior authority on Byzantine church history and early Slavic history, specializing in Byzantine political philosophy, the ecumenical councils, and particularly in Byzantine cultural and religious influences on the Slavs and on Western Europe in the ninth century. Perhaps the best known of his other publications are: *Les Slaves, Byzance, et Rome au IX siècle* (1926); *Les Légendes de Constantin et de Méthode vues de Byzance* (1933); *The Photian Schism: History and Legend* (1948); *The Slavs: Their Early History and Civilization* (1956); *The Slavs in European History and Civilization* (1962); *Byzantium and the Roman Primacy* (1966); and *Byzantine Missions among the Slavs: SS. Constantine - Cyril and Methodius* (1970). There is a biographical sketch and a knowledgeable appreciation of Father Dvornik by Dimitri Obolensky and a detailed bibliography of his publications to 1954 in *Harvard Slavic Studies*, Vol. II (Cambridge, Mass., 1954). In 1972, Professor Francis Dvornik received the Award for Distinguished Contributions to Slavic Studies of the American Association for the Advancement of Slavic Studies.

J. F. Z.

INTRODUCTION TO THE SECOND EDITION
WITH NOTES TO THE TEXT

The Making of Central and Eastern Europe is in some ways the continuation of my book *Les Slaves, Byzance et Rome au IXe siècle*, published in Paris in 1926 and in a second edition, with a new introduction in English by Peter Charanis, by Academic International Press in 1970. This book was my main thesis presented to the University of Paris, with another work containing the edition of the Greek life of Gregory the Decapolite, to obtain the degree of Docteur ès Lettres of the Sorbonne. When preparing this thesis I wanted to extend my research to the tenth century, but the late Professor Charles Diehl, who supervised my research, advised me to limit myself to the ninth century and to devote a special study to the tenth and eleventh centuries. The problems touched upon in the thesis led me to a more profound study of Constantine and Methodius, which was published in 1933 under the title *Les Légendes de Constantin et de Méthode vues de Byzance*. Academic International Press reissued this work in 1969, with my own new introduction and notes to the text.

Upon the publication of my book *The Photian Schism: History and Legend*, printed by Cambridge University Press in 1948 (French edition, 1950; Italian edition, 1951) and reprinted in 1970, I closed my studies of the problems of that important period in Slavic and Byzantine history. So it came about that I could start my research on the following period, characterized by the appearance of new factors in European history such as the rise of Germany and the birth of new Slavic states only in 1939, when on leave in London from Charles University.

The present work was written wholly during the war at the British Museum, sometimes in difficult circumstances. The Polish Research Centre in London undertook publication of the book in spite of obstacles to book printing in the post-war period, when it was difficult to find printers familiar with Slavic characters. This explains the many inaccuracies in the printing of Slavic names in the bibliography.

Scholarly books published during the post-war era very often escaped the attention of scholars in countries recovering from the war, and I am therefore very much indebted to Academic International Press for initiating this new edition of *The Making of Central and Eastern Europe*.

More than twenty years have passed since this work was first published. The number of new contributions touching the problems discussed in my book published in the interval has been enormous. In my introduction to the present second edition, I will attempt to quote at least the main studies which concern these problems and which show new findings and offer new material for their study. Most of the further progress in the analysis of these problems we owe to German scholars, whose contributions deserve both respect and esteem. I will endeavor as well to quote works by Slavic scholars, although it is difficult in the United States to find many post-war Polish and Czech publications, in many of which new views are expressed. Newer points of view notwithstanding, it appears necessary to change only a few of my conclusions. Often, however, the choice must be left to the reader! Many issues, as will be seen, are still far from a definite solution. While the main printing errors have been noted, specialists will easily discover and, I hope, will understand, the typographical errors in the Slavic names in the bibliography.

CHAPTER I. DAWN OF SLAVONIC HISTORY AND THE RISE OF GERMANY.

Pages 11-17. ORIGINS AND MIGRATION OF THE SLAVS   A more detailed sketch of these problems will be found in F. Dvornik, *The Slavs: Their Early History and Civilization* (Boston, 1956), pages 3-45, the most important bibliography being listed on pages 344-347, and in the French edition, *Les Slaves* (Paris, 1970), on pages 19-39 and 475-477, respectively.

In his book, *Rukovět slovanské archeologie* [Handbook of Slavic Archeology] (Prague, 1966), J. Eisner lists the results of his most recent researches on the origin of the Slavs, indicating to what extent Czech, Polish, Soviet and other specialists have participated in the solution of these problems (pp. 17-40). On pages 87-136 he discusses the expansion of the Slavs towards the West, South, and East, adding an extensive bibliography on the migration of the Slavs. On pages 40-50 he reviews the problems concerning the origin and nature of the Lusatian culture. According to him, the Venedian culture had developed from the Lusatian. The greatest part of his work is devoted to the description of Slavic material culture, based on recent archeological finds.

Eisner's study is more detailed and more documented than that of the Polish specialist, W. Hensel (2nd. ed., Warsaw, 1956), which was translated into German by E. Epperlein under the title *Die Slawen im frühen Mittelalter: Ihre materielle Kultur* (Berlin, 1965). A short introduction to early Slavic history is given by Z. Vaňa, *Einführung in die Frühgeschichte der Slawen* (Neumünster, 1970), with a good bibliography. The most recent study on the origins of the Lusatian culture is offered by E. Plesl in *Vznik a počátky Slovanů*, 5 (Prague, 1969), 149-164.

Page 14. THE AVARS   Recent works: H. Preidel, "Awaren und Slawen," *Südostdeutsche Forschungen*, 11 (1946-1952), 33-45; A. Kollautz, "Die Awaren," *Saeculum*, 5 (1954), 129-178; B. Zástěrová, "Avaři a Slované" [Avars and Slavs], in *Vznik a počátky Slovanů* [The Origin and Early Development of the Slavs], J. Eisner, ed., 2 (Prague, 1958), 19-54. The latter is a review of modern works on the Avars. The newest account of the Avars is by A. Kollautz and Hisayuki Miyakawa, *Geschichte und Kultur eines Völkerwanderungszeitlichen Nomadenvolkes* (Klagenfurt, 1970), Vol. I. (History). See especially pages 199-238. Compare further B. Zástěrová, *Les Avares et les Slaves dans la Tactique de Maurice* (Czech Academy *Rozpravy*: Prague, 1971).

Page 15. SAMO   Here the most important study is G. Labuda's *Pierwsze Państwo słowiańskie — Państwo Samona* [Samo: The First Slavic State] (Poznań, 1949). This contribution states that Samo was not of Czech, but of Celtic origin. The revolt against the Avars probably started in Moravia. The Slavs of the Alps do not seem to have been included in the political structure outlined by the author. On Labuda's work consult the detailed French summary by V. Chaloupecký in *Byzantinoslavica* (11 (1952)). Compare as well the work by A. Kollautz and Hisayuki Miyakawa cited above (pp. 225 ff.).

Page 17. GREAT MORAVIA   Two works deserve attention: M. Hellman, *et al.*, *Cyrillo-Methodiana* (Köln, Graz, 1964) and *Symposium Magna Moravia* (Brno, 1965). The most modern work dealing with all problems concerning Great

Moravia and Constantine-Cyril and Methodius, with a complete bibliography, is my book, *Byzantine Missions Among the Slavs* (Rutgers University Press: New Brunswick, N.J., 1970).

Although Great Moravia had flourished as a state only for a few decennia, the Moravian mission of the two Byzantine brothers, albeit short, had a lasting importance for the whole of Christianity. This fact, generally overlooked, is stressed by Professor John Meyendorff in his review of *Byzantine Missions Among the Slavs* in *St. Vladimir Theological Quarterly* (14 (1970), 233) with these words: "The remarkable missionary expansion of the Byzantine Church in the ninth and tenth centuries is one of the crucial events of European history. If this expansion had not taken place, the Greek Church, which was during the same period engaged in competing with Rome and which had lost control, since the fifth century, over the non-Greek speaking Christians of the Middle East, would have entered modern history as a purely ethnic Church. Thus, historically, the Slavic mission of Byzantium preserved the universality of Orthodoxy and secured its effectiveness as a world religious body."

On Great Moravia and the two Greek brothers, refer also to A.P. Vlasto's *The Entry of the Slavs into Christendom* (Cambridge, 1970), pages 20-85. The author mostly agrees with the deductions contained in my book.

Page 22 - 24. ORIGINS OF THE GERMAN KINGDOM M. Lintzel has dated the birth of the German Kingdom from the year 887, when Arnulf of Caranthania became king, thus breaking the old Carolingian order of dynastic succession *(Die Anfänge des Deutschen Reiches. Über den Vertrag von Verdun und die Erhebung Arnulfs von Kärnten* (Munich, Berlin, 1942)). His thesis is disputed, especially by G. Tellenbach's *Die Entstehung des Deutschen Reiches* (4th ed., Munich, 1947). Compare the review of Lintzel's book by M. Mitteis in *Historische Zeitschrift* [hereafter *H.Z.*] (164 (1944), 119-121). W. Schlesinger's "Die Anfänge der deutschen Königswahl" *(Zeitschrift der Savigny Stiftung für Rechtsgeschichte, German. Abt.,* 66 (1948), 381-440) agrees with Lintzel.

From these contributions, it appears that the formation of a national German state went through a long process dating from the Pact of Verdun in 843. The election of Arnulf in 887 and that of Conrad in 911 were two important phases in this development. The final breakthrough was the appointment of Henry of Saxony by the dying Conrad as his successor in 918, confirmed by Henry's election at Fitzlar in May, 919.

On the Pact of Verdun turn to Th. Mayer's *Der Vertrag von Verdun, 843* (Stuttgart, 1943). G. Baescke, one of the nine scholars whose studies Mayer included in this work, points out that German national feeling in the Carolingian Empire can be traced in the use of the name *theotiscus, germanicus* and so forth (pp. 116-136). In addition, consider M. Lintzel's review (*H. Z.,* 172 (1951), 343-346) as well as G. Tellenbach's "Germanentum und Reichsgedanke im frühen Mittelalter" *(Historisches Jahrbuch* [hereafter *H. J*], 62-69 (1949), 109-139) and H. J. Bartmuss, *Die Geburt des ersten deutschen Staates* (Berlin, 1966). G. Labuda's study "Uwagi o genezie sredniowiecznego państwa niemieckiego" [Studies of the Origin of the German Medieval State], published in *Kwartalnik historyczny* (76 (1969), 117-130), dates the embryonic origin of the first German state from 843, its birth from 911, and its full growth after 936.

Page 23 ff. *HENRY I* On this ruler consult the following: M. Lintzel, "Heinrich I. und die fränkische Königsalbung," *Berichte, Sächsische Akademie. Philosofisch-historische Klasse,* 102 (Berlin, 1955), Heft 3; W. Metz, "Die Abstammung König Heinrich I.," *H.J.,* 84 (1964), 271-287; M. Lintzel, "Miszellen für die Geschichte des zehnten Jahrhunderts," *Berichte, Sächsische Akademie. Philosofisch-historische Klasse,* 100 (1953), Heft 2, pp. 34-65. W. Mohr in his *König Heinrich I. (919-936). Eine kritische Studie zur Geschichtsschreibung der letzten Hundert Jahren* (Saarlouis, 1950), depreciates wrongly the work of Henry I, as W. Schlesinger correctly states in his review (*H.Z.,* 174 (1952), 106-110).

Page 29. *HENRY I AND ST. WENCESLAS OF BOHEMIA* The generally accepted date of Wenceslas' death (929) is again questioned by Z. Fiala in his study "Dva kritické příspěvky ke starým dějinám českým [Two Critical Contributions to the Early History of Bohemia] in *Sborník historický* (6 (Prague, 1962), 5-40). He interprets Widukind's statement in the sense that Wenceslas, not Boleslas, had remained faithful to the German king, Henry I, until the king's death (936). If this reading is accepted, Wenceslas' death should be dated in 936, and Boleslas' reign should have started at that date. The clash between the Czechs and Germans under Henry I also should be dated from this year. Nonetheless the date of 929, indicated by the oldest source, the Old Slavonic Legend on Wenceslas, should be accepted, as has been shown definitely by F. V. Mareš in his study "Das Todesjahr des hl. Wenzel in der kirchenslawischen Wenzelslegende" in *Wiener slawistisches Jahrbuch* (17 (1972), 192-208).

Page 30 ff. *HENRY I AND THE WESTERN SLAVS* Since 1950 German scholars have made great progress in their studies on the Slavic tribes that settled on the soil which eventually became parts of modern Germany. An extensive résumé of the results achieved in historical, archaeological, and political research concerning the Slavs in Germany is given in a handbook published by Joachim Herrmann, with the collaboration of numerous specialists, entitled *Die Slawen in Deutschland. Geschichte und Kultur der slawischen Stämme westlich von der Oder und Neisse vom 6. bis 12. Jahrhundert,* and published under the auspices of the German Academy (East Berlin, 1970).

The main part of this handbook is devoted to the material culture of the Slavs in Germany, on the basis of new archaeological discoveries. In the first chapter the specialists outline a clear picture of the expansion of Slavic tribes in Germany, listing the names of tribes and their seats. At the end of the publication is append-ed a short account of the conquest of these Slavs by feudal Germany. An extensive bibliography, together with maps, closes the handbook.

Among many studies the following works deserve to be consulted for their new notions on the history, culture, and political organization of the Slavs in Germany: E. Schwarz, "Das Vordringen der Slawen nach Westen," *Südostforschungen,* 15 (1956), 86-108; M. Hellmann, "Grundlagen slawischer Verfassungsgeschichte des frühen Mittelalters," *Jahrbücher für Geschichte Osteuropas,* N. F., 2 (1954), 387-404; H. Ludat, *Vorstufen und Entstehung des Staatswesens in Osteuropa* (Köln, 1955).

See the following studies in H. Ludat et al., *Siedlung und Verfassung der Slawen zwischen Elbe, Saale und Oder* (Giessen, 1960): W. Schlesinger, "Die Verfassung der Sorben," pp. 75-102; M. Hellman, "Grundzüge der Verfassungsstruktur de Liutizen," pp. 103-113; and W. Fritze, "Probleme der Abodritischen Stammes- und Reichsverfassung," pp. 141-219. W. Brüske's *Untersuchungen zur*

Geschichte des Liutizenbundes: Deutschwendische Beziehungen des 10.-12. Jahrhunderts (Münster, 1955) has shown that this coalition was organized not on democratic, but on an aristocratic basis. For this reason the Redariers who were the most energetic tribe of the coalition could not obtain the leading role in it.

W. Schlesinger's book, *Mitteldeutsche Beiträge zur deutschen Verfassungsgeschichte des Mittelalters* (Göttingen, 1961), contains a reprint of his *Verfassung der Sorben* (1960), and also includes his *Bäuerliche Gemeindebildung in den mittelelbischen Landen im Zeitalter der deutschen Ostbewegung* (212-275). Another work by Schlesinger is "Die deutsche Kirche im Sorbenland und die Kirchenverfassung auf westslawischem Boden" in *Zeitschrift für Ostforschung* (1 (1952), 345-371). Consult also H.D. Kahl, *Slawen und Deutsche in der brandenburgischen Geschichte des 12. Jahrhunderts* (Köln, Graz, 1964); Y. Brankačik, *Studien zur Wirtschafts- und Sozialstruktur der Westslawen zwischen Elbe, Saale und Oder aus der Zeit vom 9. bis zum 12. Jahrhundert* (Bautzen, 1964).

The Czech archaeologist, V. Procházka, published a general study, "Die Stammesverfassung der Erbslawen," in *Zeitschrift für Archeologie* (3 (1969), 36 ff.). Another Czech scholar, H. Bulín, studied the beginnings of the states of the Obodrites and Veletzians in *Právněhistorické studie* (4 (Prague, 1958), 5 ff.; 5 (1959), 5 ff.). Bulín reviewed Polish contributions to this subject in *Vznik a počátky Slovanů* (4 (Prague, 1963), 49 ff.).

A short sketch of the history of the Baltic and Polabian Slavs will be found in my *The Slavs: Their Early History and Civilization* (Boston, 1956), pages 293-311. M. Hellmann in his review "Zur Problematik der slawischen Frühzeit" (*Jahrbücher für Geschichte Osteuropas, N. F.*, 7 (1959), 196-203) rightly stressed that the bibliography given to this chapter in my book was too short, while forgetting that most of the important studies on this subject appeared during and after the publication of the book. His review resounds the echoes of anti-Slavic sentiments prevailing in pre-war Germany. F. Dölger's review of my book (*H. J.*, 78 (1959), 204-206) is fair. A more complete bibliography will be found in the French edition (*Les Slaves*) of my work. On the conversion of the Wends, see also P. Vlasto's work cited above (pp. 142-154). For the Slavs in Thuringia there is H. Bach and S. Dušek, *Slawen in Thüringen* (Weimar, 1971), with interesting recent archaeological findings and anthropological studies.

Page 27 ff. THE SO-CALLED "Drang nach Osten" The push towards the East which Henry I is believed to have reopened following the period of the Carolingian rulers, is rather a modern expression which was unknown to medieval Germans. Their expansion towards the Slavic lands of modern Germany displayed different incentives. The feudal German aristocracy was looking for more land. Their domains, primitively cultivated, were not producing enough to supply their needs. Overpopulation in certain regions caused the colonization of less populated lands. There was need to defend the existing boundaries against the inroads of hostile neighbors and, above all, there was the stimulus of spreading Christianity among pagan populations. This was regarded as a sacred duty by German kings and lords.

Henry I's main preoccupation was the consolidation and expansion of his dukedom — Saxony — and this explains why he concentrated his military expeditions against the Slavs between the rivers Oder and Elbe. National sentiments among German and Slav historians influenced their dissertations on this struggle. In this respect the perceptive judgement of the eastern movement offered by M. Schlesinger under the title "Die geschichtliche Stellung der mittelalterlichen deutschen Ostbewegung" (*H.Z.*, 183 (1957), 517-542) deserves special attention. It is a brilliant survey of this centuries-old process and, even though all his explanations and justifications may not be accepted, it should be read by all scholars interested in the struggle between Germans and Western Slavs. It is reprinted in his *Mitteldeutsche Beiträge* (*op. cit.*, pp. 447-469). For the Slavic point of view consult G. Labuda, *Historiograficzna analiza tzw. niemieckiego "Naporu na Wschód"* [Historical Analysis of the So-called "Drang nach Osten"], published in Poznań in 1963.

Pages 26, 31. **HENRY I AND THE MAGYARS** The Magyar incursions into Germany before and during Henry's reign, and into France and Italy after their establishment in Hungary, are discussed by Szabolcz de Vajav in his book *Der Eintritt des Ungarischen Stämmebundes in die europäische Geschichte, 862-933* (Studia Hungarica, 4 (Mainz, 1968)). His thesis that the invaders acted mostly at the invitation of their allies in these lands is exaggerated, and it is rightly rejected in R.T. Coolidge's review in *Speculum* (45 (1970), 666-667).

Pages 27-29. WIDUKIND On this topic there is the book by H. Beumann, *Widukind von Korvei. Untersuchungen zur Geschichtschreibung und Ideengeschichte des 10. Jahrhunderts* (Weimar, 1950). Find also the review by M. Lintzel in *H. Z.* (176 (1953), 112-116).

CHAPTER II. EMPEROR OTTO I, POLAND, BOHEMIA AND RUSSIA

Pages 32-48. OTTO I A general study is R. Holtzmann's *Geschichte der sächsischen Kaiserzeit* (4th ed., Munich, 1961). For Otto's biography and reign: M. Lintzel, *Die Kaiserpolitik Ottos des Grossen* (Munich, Berlin, 1943); H. Günther, *Kaiser Otto der Grosse* (2nd ed., Stuttgart, Berlin, 1943); C. Erdmann, *Ottonische Studien*, H. Beumann, ed. (Darmstadt, 1969); H. Beumann, *Das Kaisertum Ottos des Grossen. Zwei Vorträge von H. Beumann und H. Büttner* (Constance, 1963).

The following works deal with Otto's coronation: H. Aubin, "Otto der Grosse und die Erneuerung des abendländischen Kaisertums im Jahre 962," *Historisch-politische Hefte der Ranke-Gesellschaft* (Göttingen, 1962); H. Grundmann, "Betrachtungen zur Kaiserkrönung Ottos I.," *Bayerische Akademie, Sitzungsberichte, Philosophisch-historische Klasse* (Munich, 1962); H. Löwe, "Kaisertum und Abendland in Ottonischer und Frühsalischerzeit," *H.Z.*, 196 (1963), 529-562; W. Ohnsorge, "Die Anerkennung des Kaisertums Ottos I. durch Byzanz," *B. Z.*, 56 (1963), 165; H. Zimmermann, "Otto und das Papstum," *Mitteilungen des Instituts für Österreichische Geschichte*, 69 (1961), 243-264; G. Lukas, *Die deutsche Politik gegen die Elbslawen vom Jahre 982 bis zum Ende des Polenkrieges Heinrich II.* (Halle, 1940).

Further contributions include: H. D. Kahl, "Zum Geist der deutschen Slawenmission des Hochmittelalter," *Zeitschrift für Ostforschung*, 4 (1955), 1 ff., H.J. Freytag, *Die Herrschaft der Billungen in Sachsen* (Göttingen, 1951); M. Uhlirz, "Die italienische Kirchenpolitik der Ottonen," *Mitteilungen des Instituts für Österreichische Geschichte*, 48 (1954), 201-321; W. Kölmel, "Die kaiserliche Herrschaft im Gebiet von Ravenna (Exarchat und Pentapolis) vor dem Investiturstreit," *H. J.*, 88 (1968), 257-299; *Festschrift zum Jahrausendfeier der Kaiserkrönung Ottos des Grossen* (2 vols., Graz, Köln, 1962-63), Volume I:

L. Santifaller, "Otto I., das Imperium und Europa" (19-30); E. Schramm, "Die Kaiser aus dem Sächsischen Hause im Lichte der Staatssymbolik" (31-52); E. Dupré-Theseida, "Otto I. und Italien" (53-70); H.F. Schmid, "Otto I. und der Osten" (70-106); W. Ohnsorge, "Otto I. und Byzanz" (107-120); H. Zimmerman, "Ottonische Studien. I: Frankreich und Reims in der Politik der Ottonenzeit" (122-190); Volume II: H. Zimmerman, "Das Privilegium Ottonanum von 962 und seine Problemgeschichte" (147-190).

In addition: H. Beumann, "Das Kaisertum Ottos des Grossen. Ein Rückblick nach tausend Jahren," *H. Z.,* 195 (1962), 529-573; H. Büttner, "Die christliche Kirche ostwärts der Elbe bis zum Tode Otto I.," *Festschrift für F. Zahn. Mitteldeutsche Forschungen* 50/I (Köln, Graz, 1968), pp. 145-181. Useful also are these more general studies: H. Löwe, "Kaisertum und Abendland in Ottonischer- und Frühsalischerzeit", *H. Z.,* 196 (1963), 529-562; W. Seegrün, "Kirche, Papst und Kaiser," *H. Z.,* 207 (1968), 4 - 41. The article by G. Koch, "Die mittelalterliche Kaiserpolitik im Spiegel der bürgerlichen deutschen Historiographie" *(Zeitschrift für Geschichtswissenschaft,* 10 (1962), 1850 ff.), is a critical review.

Page 41 ff. CHARLEMAGNE: RECENT BIBLIOGRAPHY Noteworthy are L. Halphen, *Charlemagne et L'empire Carolingien* (2nd. ed., Paris, 1949) and W. Braunfels, ed., Unter Mitwirkung von H. Beumann, B. Bishoff, H. Schnitzler, P. E. Schramm, *Karl der Grosse: Lebenswerk und Nachleben* (5 vols., Düsseldorf, 1965-68). In the latter work Volume I treats Charlemagne's personality and history and Volume II his spiritual life. Volume III covers Carolingian art and Volume IV deals with Charlemagne's tradition in history. Further there are A. Waas, "Karls des Grossen Frömmigkeit" *(H.Z.,* 203 (1966), 265 - 279) and P.E. Schramm's *Karl der Grosse* (Düsseldorf, 1951).

For Charlemagne's imperial ideas turn to F.L. Ganshof, *The Imperial Coronation of Charlemagne: Theories and Facts* (Glasgow, 1949); P. Classen, "Romanum gubernans imperium. Zur Vorgeschichte der Kaisertitulatur Karls des Grossen," *Deutsche Archiv für Erforschung des Mittelalters,* 9 (1951), 103-121; P.E. Schramm, "Die Anerkennung Karls des Grossen als Kaiser," *H. Z.,* 172 (1951), 436-551; Idem., "Karl der Grosse: Denkart und Grundauffassungen. Die von ihm bewirkte Correctio (Rennaissance)," *H. Z.,* 198 (1964), 306-345; R. Folz, *Le Couronement impérial de Charlemagne* (Paris, 1964); H. Beumann, "Nomen imperatoris: Studien zur Kaiseridee Karls des Grossen," *H. Z.,* 185 (1958), 515-549; P.A. van den Baar, *Die kirchliche Lehre der Translatio Imperii Romani* (Rome, 1956); W. Goez, *Translatio Imperii* (Tübingen, 1958); H. Fichtenau, *Das karolingische Imperium: Soziale und geistige Problematik eines Grossreiches* (Zurich, 1949); Th. Mayer, "Staatsverfassung in der Karolingerzeit," *H. Z.,* 173 (1952), 467-485; W. Mohr, *Die karolingische Reichsidee* (Münster, 1967).

Works dealing with Charlemagne and Alcuin include J. Kleinclausz, *Alcuin* (Paris, 1948); E.S. Duckett, *Alcuin, Friend of Charlemagne: His World and His Work* (New York, 1951); L. Wallach, *Alcuin and Charlemagne. Studies in Carolingian History and Literature* (Ithaca, N.Y., 1959); H. Hürten, "Alcuin und Episkopat im Reiche Karls des Grossen," *H. J.,* 82 (1963), 22-49; J. Fleckenstein, *Die Hofkapelle der deutschen Könige. I. Grundlegung. Die Karolingische Hofkapelle* (Stuttgart, 1959).

Page 49 ff. The problem of the imperial policy of Otto I, especially his involvement in Italy, which was followed by his successors, was subjected by M. Lintzel to a very lively and even sharp criticism in his book *Die Kaiserpolitik*

Ottos des Grossen (Munich, Berlin, 1943), which became accessible outside Germany only after 1949. It was reprinted in Volume 2 of his *Ausgewählte Schriften* (Berlin, 1961). After examining the internal state of the German kingdom under Henry I and Otto I, he rightly observes that the Italian policy was necessary neither for the domestic strengthening of the kingdom, nor for its defense from outside threat.

Lintzel's statement that Otto did not necessarily need the Pope's help in order to toughen his authority over his bishops should be accepted because Otto, in any case, was master of the German Church. His position in the world of the tenth century was sufficiently strong for him to have no need of papal authority to bolster it. Nor were the Roman and Carolingian traditions, or the eschatological expectations general among the population of the tenth century, strong enough to force Otto into his Italian adventures. Lintzel concedes, however, that these traditions and general expectations may have influenced Otto's decision, and that the annexation of Lombardy may have helped to strengthen the ties of Bavaria with Saxony and prevent any adventures by other German duchies into Italy.

It is pointed out that expeditions in Italy may have curtailed the German advance in the East. The author rightly criticizes Otto's expeditions beyond Rome into Byzantine possesions, which could not succeed and which weakened German influence elsewhere. Rightly he weighs the advantages of the conquests in Italy from the economic and cultural view. It is admitted that the prestige of the German kingdom had been enhanced in contemporary Europe without, however, giving the new Emperor any visible supremacy over other Christian kings.

How these sobering statements have influenced German historians can be measured by H. Beumann's "Das Kaisertum Ottos des Grossen. Ein Rückblick nach tausend Jahren" (*H. Z.*, 195 (1962), 529-573). In this connection the following may be consulted also: R. Folz, *Le souvenir et la légende de Charlemagne dans l'Empire Germanique médiéval* (Paris, 1950); L. Santifaller, *Zur Geschichte des ottonischen Reichskirchensystems* (Wien, 1964); G. A. Bezzolea, *Das ottonische Kaisertum in der französischen Geschichtsschreibung des 10. und Beginn des 11. Jahrhunderts* (Graz, Köln, 1956)); W. Schmidt, *Deutsches Königtum und deutscher Staat des hohen Mittelalters während und unter dem Einfluss der italienischen Heerfahrten* (Wiesbaden, 1964). Further, H. Kämpf's review in *Historische Zeitschrift* (207 (1968), 641-643) may be examined.

Page 54 ff. MIESZKO I The Slavic origin of the first known Polish ruler is now generally accepted. See H. Łowmiański, *Zagadnienie roli Normanów w genezie państw słowiańskich* [Problems of the Norman Role in the Origin of Slavic States] (Warsaw, 1957). After asserting the Slavic origin of the Polish dynasty, this author admits (pp. 13-35) that Normans may have reached Mieszko's lands by reason of their commercial relations with the Slavs. Note as well W. Kowalenko's "Ekspansja Polski na Bałtyk za Mieszka I" in *Liber Josepho Kostrzewski octogenario* (Warsaw, Cracow, 1968), pages 410 ff.

Mieszko's relations with Germany and the Polabian Slavs are discussed in "Die Slawen in Deutschland" (*op. cit.*, pp. 279-291), by S. Epperlein.

J. Bakala in his paper "K uloze českých zemí při počátcích christianizace Polska" [On the Role Played by the Czech Lands during the Christianization of Poland], published in *Práce i materiály* of the Łodz Archaeological Museum (No. 14 (1967), 35-53), posed the theory that Mieszko was not baptized by the Bishop of Regensburg nor by a German missionary, but by a Czech bishop of Moravia who had survived the catastrophic events in his country. This theory can be accepted if it is kept in mind that the Moravian hierarchy, ordained in 900, had taken refuge, after the destruction of Moravia, in the land of the Vistulanians, which was part of the Great Moravian state and which was not invaded by the Magyars. On the survival of the Moravian Slavonic hierarchy and liturgy in Poland, consult F. Dvornik, *Byzantine Missions Among the Slavs* (pp. 198-204). Thus, Mieszko could have been baptized by one of the hierarchy residing in modern Galicia, a part of which Mieszko seems to have occupied after 955.

Page 54 ff. THE ORIGIN OF THE POLISH STATE. STUDIES ON SOURCES One such study is J. Dobrowski, *Dawne dziejopisarstwo polskie (do roku 1480)* [Early Polish Historiography] (Warsaw, Cracow, 1964). M.Z. Jedlicki, "Kronika Thietmara" (*Biblioteka tekstów historycznych, Vol. 3* (Poznań, 1953)), is a new edition of Thietmar's chronicle with a commentary and quotations from works of other Polish specialists. Another relevant work is G. Labuda, *Źródła, sagi i legendy do najdawniejszych dziejów Polski* [Sources, Sagas and Legends Concerning the Earliest History of Poland] (Warsaw, 1960).

The following are accounts of early Polish history: G. Labuda, *Studia nad początkami państwa polskiego* [Studies on the Origin of the Polish State] (Poznań, 1946); S. Kętrzyński in *The Cambridge History of Poland* (Cambridge, 1950), pp. 16 ff.; J. Widajewicz, *Państwo Wiślan* [The Vistulanian State] (Cracow, 1947); Idem., *Początki Polski* [Origins of Poland] (Warsaw, 1948). Volume I of H. Łowmiański's *Początki Polski* (2 vols., Warsaw, 1963) treats the early history of the Slavs, and their culture, while Volume II surveys the expansion of the Slavs. Volumes III (1968) and IV (1970) treat the early history of Poland. For the formation of the Polish state there is A. Gieysztor, *Podania nad genezą państwowości Polskiej* [Studies on the Development of Polish Statecraft] (Poznań, 1950).

In addition, *Początki państwa polskiego* (2 vols., Warsaw, 1962) contains studies by different Polish scholars. Further consult A. Gieysztor, "Aspects territoriaux du premier état polonais (IX-XI siècles)," *Revue historique,* 226 (1961), 357 ff.; G. Labuda, "Zagadnienie suwerenności Polski wczesnofeudalnej w X-XII wieku" [Problems Concerning Polish Sovereignty During the Early Feudal Period of the Tenth to Twelfth Centuries], *Kwartalnik Historyczny,* 67 (1960), 1035-1068; K. Żurowski, *Les Origines des villes polonaises* (Paris, La Haye, 1960); J. Widajewicz, *Polska i Niemcy w dobie panowania Mieszka I.* [Poland and the Germans During the Reign of Mieszko I.] (Lublin, 1953).

Other studies are P. Bogdanowicz, "Uwagi nad panowaniem Mieszka I." [Studies on the Reign of Mieszko I], *Roczniki Historyczne,* 26 (1960), 80 ff.; W. Dziewulski, "Postępy chrystianizacji za Mieszka I i Bolesława Chrobrego" [Progress of Christianization under Mieszko I and Boleslas Chrobry], *Zeszyty Naukowe, Historia,* II (Opole, 1961), 53-128; Idem., *Postępy chrystianizacji i proces likwidacji pogaństwa w Polsce wczesnofeudalnej* [Progress of the Christianization and the Process of the Liquidation of Paganism in Early Feudal Poland] (Wroclaw, Warsaw, Cracow, 1964).

Page 61 ff. THE RUSSO-SCANDINAVIAN PROBLEM The controversy between the normanists and anti-normanists, the latter denying any role to the Normans in the formation of the first Russian state, still goes on. Soviet historians are outspoken anti-normanists. See V. Mavrodin, *Bor'ba s normanizmom v russkoi istoricheskoi nauke* [The Struggle with Normanism in Russian Historical Science] (Leningrad, 1951).

A very useful review of Soviet historical works on the problems of medieval Russia is given by G. Stökl in "Russisches Mittelalter und sowjetische Mediavistik" (*Jahrbücher für Geschichte Osteuropas, N. F.,* 3 (1955), 1-40), which includes a bibliography of anti-normanist literature (p. 23).

Recently the whole history of this controversy has been outlined by H. Łowmiański in "Zagadnienie roli Normanów" (*op. cit.,* p. 62-124). According to him, the Normans appeared in Russia as merchants and mercenary warriors. S. Stender-Peterson described the role of the Normans in early Russia in his *Varangica* ((Aarhus, 1953), pp. 26 ff.), and also wrote "Die vier Etappen der russisch-warängischen Beziehungen" (*Jahrbücher für Geschichte Osteuropas,* 2 (1954), 137-157). In his latest study, "Der älteste russische Staat" (*H. Z.,* 191 (1961), 1-17), he theorizes that the Swedes were settling among the Slavic and Finnish population as peasants and peaceful colonists. The pressure coming from the two Volga states — Bulgaria and Khazaria — forced them and their Slavic neighbors to form a common political unit organized on the political principles of the Bulgars and Khazars. The author's hope that this theory will be accepted by the anti-normanists has little chance of fulfillment.

According to Stender-Peterson, this first political formation of the Swedes with the Finns and Slavs slowly extended its supremacy over Novgorod and from there over the Slavic tribes on the Dnieper as far as Kiev. The messengers who in 838 appeared at the court of Emperor Theophilus were sent by the ruler of this Ladoga Rhôs state in order to open commercial relations with Byzantium. The Emperor sent them to Louis the Pious in 839 (see page 63 of the present book).

This combination, however, has its weakness. First, the research of Russian archeologists has demonstrated that Novgorod did not yet exist in the ninth century. Kiev was occupied by another Scandinavian expedition led by Skold and Dir. As I have explained in the introduction to the reimpression of my *Les Légendes de Constantin et de Méthode* (Academic International Press, 1969), page xix, the embassy was dispatched by the new rulers of Kiev for the purpose of assuring the Emperor of friendly relations after the occupation by the former of Kiev, previously subject to the sovereignty of the Khazars, allies of the Emperor. Łowmiański (*Zagadanie,* pp. 151 ff.) is of the same opinion. Consult further M. I. Artamonov, *Istoriia Khazar* [History of the Khazars] (Leningrad. 1962), page 366. Both authors agree that the expedition against Constantinople in 860 could have been organized only from the new Rhôs state of Kiev. Refer also to my book, *Byzantine Missions Among the Slavs* (p. 266) and to F. I. Kaplan, "The Decline of the Khazars and the Rise of the Varangians," in *American Slavic and East European Review* (13 (1954), 1-10). G. Vernadsky and M. von Ferdinandy in their *Studium zur ungarischen Frühgeschichte* (Südosteuropäische Arbeiten, 47 (Munich, 1957)) asserted that the Magyars became masters of Kiev in the ninth century. This thesis is rightly rejected by A.V. Soloviev in his study, "Die angebliche ungarische Herrschaft in Kiew im 9. Jahrhundert" (*Jahrbücher für Geschichte Osteuropas,* 8 (1960), 123-129).

Page 65. On the attack of the Rhôs on Constantinople, see the English translation of *The Homilies of Photius, Patriarch of Constantinople* by C. Mango (Cambridge, Mass., 1958), with a detailed commentary (pp. 82-110).

Page 66. For Igor's expedition see K. Bártova, "Igorova výprava na Cařihrad" [Igor's Expedition Against Constantinople] in *Byzantinoslavica* (8 (1946),

87-108) and A. A. Vasiliev, "The Second Russian Attack on Constantinople" (*Dumbarton Oaks Papers*, 6 (1951), 161-225) as well as G. Ostrogorsky's *History of the Byzantine State* (J. Hussey, trans. (Oxford, 1968), pp. 259-277).

Page 66. Footnote 65. There is a new edition of S.H. Cross' translation of the Russian Primary Chronicle by O.P. Sherbowitz-Wetzor (Cambridge, Mass., 1953), with an extensive introduction and commentary.

Page 70 ff. On the ecclesiastical organization of Poland in the tenth century, refer to the new edition of H. Abraham's *Organizacja Kościoła w Polsce* (Poznań, 1962).

Page 77 ff. H. Łowmiański's *Początki Polski* (*op. cit.*, IV (1970), 478-487) provides a complete bibliography — especially Polish — on the document of 1086 concerning the bishopric of Prague.

THE ORIGINS OF BOHEMIA Works to be consulted include R. Turek, *Čechy na úsvitě dějin* [Bohemia at the Dawn of History] (Prague, 1963); R. Wenskus, *Die slawischen Stämme in Böhmen* in *Siedlung und Verfassung Böhmens in Frühzeit* (F. Graus und H. Ludat, eds. (Wiesbaden, 1967), pp. 32 ff.); W. Wostry, "Die Ursprünge der Přemysliden" in *Prager Festschrift für Th. Mayer* (R. Schneider, ed. (Salzburg, 1953), pp. 156 ff.); F. Graus, "Die Entstehung der mittelalterlichen Staaten in Mitteleuropa," *Historica*, 10 (1965), 5 ff.; Idem., "Die Bildung eines Nationalbewusstseins im mittelalterlichen Böhmen," *Historica*, 13 (1966), 5-49; Z. Fiala, *Přemyslovské Čechy: Český stát a společnost* [Bohemia Under the Przemyslides. The Czech State and Social Relations in Bohemia] (Prague, 1965).

A treatment of historical development from 995 to 1310 is Z. Fiala's "Hlavni problémy politických a kulturnich dějin českých v 10. a 11. století podle dnešních znalostí," *Československý Časopis Historický* [hereafter ČČH], 14 (1966), 54-65.

For a résumé of Czech historical literature on problems concerning Great Moravia, Bohemia, and Poland in the tenth and eleventh centuries turn to Z. Fiala's "Die Organisation der Kirche im Přemysliden-Staat des 10.-13. Jahrhunderts" in *Siedlung und Verfassung Böhmens in der Frühzeit* (F. Graus, H. Ludat, eds. (Wiesbaden, 1967), pp. 133-147) and his article "Vztah českého státu k německé říši do počátku 13. stoleti [Relations of the Czech State with the German Reich to the Beginning of the 13th Century] (*Sborník historický*, 6 (1959), 23-95), which includes a summary in German.

The relations of Bohemia with the Polish state under Mieszko I are treated in the study by H. Bulín, "Polský stát Měška I a Čechy," *Slovanské historické studie*, 4 (Prague, 1962).

OTTO II, POLAND AND BOHEMIA A new contribution is M. Hellmann, "Die Ostpolitik Kaisers Ottos II." in *Syntagma Friburgense* (Lindau, Konstanz, 1956), pages 49-67. Otto II followed the Eastern policy of his father. On the relations of Mieszko of Poland and Boleslas II of Bohemia with the Veletians during the reign of Otto II, follow G. Labuda, "Polska, Czechy, Niemcy: Związek wielecki w X w." in his *Fragmenty dziejów Słowiańszczyzny zachodniej* (Poznań, 1960).

Concerning the conflict between Mieszko and Boleslas II of Bohemia, G. Labuda tried to date with more precision the loss of the "regnum" by the

Czech duke to the Poles. Correcting the dating of Cosmas, which often is not reliable, in his "O rzekomej utracie Krakowa przez Czechów w r. 999" [The Presumed Loss of Cracow by the Czechs in 999] (*Slavia Occidentalis*, 26 (1961), 79-93) he concludes that Mieszko occupied Little Poland including Cracow in 989, and Silesia in 990. In the present book (pp. 106-108) I agree that Labuda's dating is acceptable.

Page 67 ff. On the beginning of Christianity in Kiev and on Olga's conversion, refer to my *Byzantine Missions* (pp. 267 ff., 416-417) where new details are discussed. Also: D. Obolensky's paper, "Byzantium, Kiev, and Moscow," *Dumbarton Oaks Papers*, 11 (1957), 23-78; C. von Rauch, "Frühe christliche Spuren in Russland," *Saeculum*, 9 (1956), 40-67; K. Rose, *Grund und Quellort des russischen Geisteslebens: Von Skythien bis zur Kiewer Rus* (Berlin, 1956). E. Erikson's "The Earliest Conversion of the Rus' to Christianity" (*The Slavonic and East European Review*, 44 (1966), 98-121) wrongly attributes the first conversion of the Rhôs to the Emperor Theophilus and his iconoclastic Patriarch, John the Grammarian. E. Winter, "Die Christianisierung der Russ in der Diplomatik des Papsttums und der Byzantiner" (*Aus der byzantinischen Arbeit der DDR*, 1 (1957), 147-157), confirms our thesis that Rome had no share in the Christianization of Russia.

Page 89. For a more detailed bibliography on Svyatoslav, the Bulgars and the Byzantines, see G. Ostrogorsky, *History of the Byzantine State*, pages 292-296.

Page 90. On the Red City there is H. Łowmiański, "Problematyka historyczna Grodów Czerwieńskich" [Historical Problems Concerning the Red Cities], *Kwartalnik Historyczny*, 60 (1953), 58 ff..

CHAPTER III.   THE PRZEMYSLIDES AND THE SLAVNIKS IN BOHEMIA

Page 95 ff. The problems of the origins, the formation and the expansion of the second Bohemian dukedom of the Slavnik dynasty are still being discussed by Czech historians. The study by Z. Fiala, *Přemyslowské Čechy*, noted above, is the most serious of this kind. It was published in Prague in 1965. The author describes the Slavnik dukedom as a solid political entity, independent of the Przemyslide dukedom, although both dynasties collaborated in affairs of common interest. The Slavnik domination extended over more than half of Bohemia — from the boundary of Moravia and modern Austria toward the East and North. Its main centers were Kouřim and Libice.

F. Graus, reviewing Fiala's study in *ČČH* (14 (1966), 228-230), disagrees with Fiala's central thesis, namely that the Slavnik dukedom was independent of the Przemyslide rulers. His chief argument revolves on the fact that in the oldest literary sources, from the tenth century, the Slavniks are never called *dux*, which should mean an independent ruler. It was the chronicler Cosmas, not a contemporary source, who gave the Slavniks this title. Graus admits, however, that towards the end of the tenth century, the Slavniks had displayed a tendency to act as independent rulers. Graus' argument is not conclusive, and hence I still follow my own interpretation of the situation.

It is not true to say that Moravian cultural influences had not penetrated into Bohemia. It is logical to suppose that at least a few Slavonic priests had found refuge in Bohemia during the persecution by Bishop Wiching following the death of Methodius, and after the destruction of Great Moravia by the Magyars. Recent archaeological discoveries in Bohemia rather confirm this supposition. Moreover, it appears that the territory under Slavnik supremacy experienced pronounced Moravian cultural influences. Most of the archaeological discoveries have been made in eastern Bohemia. The excavations undertaken at Kouřim, the residence of the Slavnik chief, and in cemeteries in its neighborhood, show that this region was in lively commercial contact with the industrial centers of Great Moravia.

The results of these excavations were published recently by M. Šolle as *Stará Kouřim a projevy velkomoravské hmotné kultury v Čechách* [The Ancient Castle of Kouřim and the Influence of Great Moravian Material Culture in Bohemia] (Prague, 1966). Many objects, such as battle-axes and jewelry, were imported from Moravian workshops. Other finds reveal that this location had become a prominent industrial center producing its own wares on Moravian models. The workshops described were probably erected by Moravian artisans who had escaped the catastrophe and who taught their techniques to Bohemian artisans. These the latter improved, and produced objects of surprising quality. This is demonstrated by silverware found in the tomb of a princess of Kouřim dating from the tenth century.

The cultural influences in question also reached the lands of the Przemyslides either directly from Moravia, or from Slavnik territory. Included in Šolle's work is a complete list of, and documentary evidence for, archaeological discoveries made in the lands of the Slavniks and Przemyslides (pp. 35 ff., 126 ff., 147 ff., 156 ff.,). A short account of these discoveries is offered by R. Turek in his paper "Die grossmährische Epoche in Böhmen" (in *Das grossmährische Reich* (Prague: Academy, 1966), pp. 85 ff.) and in his book *Čechy na úsvitu dějin* [Bohemia at the Dawn of History] (Prague, 1963, pp. 149 ff.). Also consult Turek's *Libice* (Prague, 1966-1968). See as well my *Byzantine Missions* (pp. 207 ff., 398), with reproductions of some of these findings. For a short history of the Slavniks and their relations with the Przemyslides, consult my *The Slavs: Their Early History* (pp. 113 ff., 151, 170, 264) and, in the French edition (*Les Slaves*), pages 101-107, 137, 155, 235, 236.

On Libice, its fortifications as revealed by new excavations, and on the role it played during the relations between Bohemia and Poland, consider R. Turek, "Der Burgwall Libice und seine Bedeutung im Rahmen der polnisch-böhmischen Beziehungen des 10.-11. Jahrhunderts" (*Slavia Antiqua*, 10 (1963), 207 ff.). The foundation of the episcopal see in Prague is studied in L. Hauptmann, "Das Regensburger Privileg von 1086 für das Bistum Prag," *Mitteilungen des Instituts für Geschichte Österreichs* (Vienna, 1954), pp. 146-154.

ST. ADALBERT (VOJTĚCH) Studies and biographies may be listed as follows: R. Holinka, *Svatý Vojtěch* [Saint Adalbert] (Brno, 1947); F. Dvornik, *Svatý Vojtěch* (Chicago, 1950; 2nd ed., Rome, 1968); Z. Biernacki et al., eds., *Św. Wojciech, 997-1947. Księga pamiątkowa* (Gniezno, 1947); J. Karwasińska, "Studia krytyczne nad żywotami św. Wojciecha" [Critical Studies of the Lives of St. Adalbert], *Studia źródłoznawcze*, Vol. 2 (Poznań, 1959).

M. Uhlirz, in her *Die älteste Lebensbeschreibung des hl. Adalbert* (Göttingen, 1957), sought to demonstrate that the oldest description of Adalbert's life is the versified panegyric of this bishop called *Quatuor immensi*, composed in the years 997-999. This legend, according to Uhlirz, was the main source for J. Canaparius' *Vita et Passio s. Adalberti*, which is preserved in three redactions and was republished in 1962 by J. Karwasińska. Uhlirz' argumentation is, however, not convincing, as has been shown by H. Löwe in his review of Uhlirz' book in *Historische Zeitschrift* (188 (1959), 114-116). Compare as well R. Wenskus' review in *Zeitschrift für Ostforschung* (10 (1961), 357-358). The first *Vita* of St. Adalbert is that written by J. Canaparius. W. Meysztowicz, in "Sylvestre II, auteur de la *Vita prima sancti Adalberti*" (*Mélanges Eugene Tisserant*, Vol. 5 (Citta' del Vaticano, 1964), 155-164), after resuming discussion of the authorship, attributed the *Vita* to Pope Sylvester II. His line of reasoning is not compelling.

The *Passio s. Adalberti* written by Bruno of Querfurt, of which J. Karwasińska is preparing a new edition, was the subject of critical commentary most recently in W. Meysztowicz's "Szkice o świętym Brunie-Bonifacym" in *Sacrum Poloniae Millenium* (5 (Rome, 1958), 445-501). The most important study on Bruno is the work by R. Wenskus, *Studien zur historisch-politischen Gedankenwelt Brunos von Querfurt* (Münster, 1956). Note also: H.L. Mikoletzky, "Zur Charakteristik Brunos von Querfurt," *Festschrift des Haus, Hof und Staatsarchives*, I (Vienna, 1949), 378-391.

The Czech literary historian, O. Králík, has devoted several studies to the biographies of Adalbert, to Cosmas, and to other sources from the tenth and eleventh centuries. He has searched for fresh solutions to the problems concerning the Slavniks and St. Adalbert, and frequently he has disagreed with views generally accepted by specialists. His principal work, *Slavníkovské interludium* (Ostrava, 1966), deals with Czecho-Polish cultural relations around the year 1000. He has accepted Uhlirz' thesis that the first *Vita* of St. Adalbert is the versified panegyric, which he has wrongly ascribed to Adalbert's half-brother, Radim. He has placed the destruction of the Slavniks in the autumn of 996. Králík identifies Adalbert's tutor, Radla, as a son of Boleslas I, called Strachkvas. Radim is considered to have been the author of the Legend of Wenceslas and Ludmila, usually attributed to Christian, and he has been promoted by Králík to the rank of a most prominent defender of the Old Slavonic liturgy. The *Life of the Five Hermits*, who were assassinated in Poland in 1003, is also attributed to Radim. In consequence he is regarded by Králík as the first Slavic writer.

Králík's ideas have been criticized severely by two young Czech, historians, Z. Fiala and D. Třeštík, in *Československý Časopis Historický* (9 (1961), 515-531). They dealt critically with Králík's views concerning St. Wenceslas, St. Ludmila, and St. Adalbert. While all of their opinions, sometimes inspired by Marxist tendencies, cannot be accepted, they have shown that Králík went too far and that some of his interpretations of the legends are rather fantastic.

The suggestion advanced by Králík that Adalbert's principal idea was to achieve a great synthesis of Latin and Slavic cultures, and that Radim-Gaudentius was the main propagator of this concept, which was to be realized in his Polish ecclesiastical province, is interesting, but far-fetched and illusory.

My reading of this new literature has convinced me that the best approach to these problems is to follow the conservative conclusions of the pre-war Czech and German historians. Although some issues concerning St. Adalbert demand further serious analysis, I see no reason at this time to change my present interpretation of this period of Bohemian and Polish history.

The studies now listed are useful for a better understanding of the first Czech historians, Christian and Cosmas: J. Ludvíkovský, "Crescente fide, Gumpold a Kristián," *Sborník of the Philosophy Faculty of Brno University,* 3 (Brno, 1955), 48 ff.; Idem., "Nový zjištěný rukopis legendy Crescente Fide a jeho význam pro datování Kristiána" [The Discovery of a New Manuscript of Crescente Fide and its Importance for the Dating of Christian's Legend], *Listy filologické,* 6 (1958), 56-68. D. Třeštík's "Kosmas a Regino," (*ČČH,* 8 (Prague, 1960), 369-486) shows that Cosmas used in his composition the work of Regino to a great extent.

Pages 131-133. ST. ADALBERT AND HIS MISSION IN PRUSSIA S. Mielczarski in his *Misja pruska świętego Wojciecha* [The Prussian Mission of St. Adalbert] (Gdańsk, 1967) brings new details illustrating better the brief activity of St. Adalbert in Prussia. Adalbert reached Danzig (Gdańsk) by land, not by sea. From Danzig he went not to Samland (Sambia), but to Pomezania, to the locality called Truso. A conspiracy among some Prussian tribes complicated his work. The conspiracy was discovered and Adalbert was arrested and judged by the Prussians. He was banished and forbidden to revisit the district under penalty of death. Nevertheless, upon reaching the Polish territory of Sulan he returned to Prussia, whereupon he was arrested and executed near the fort of Chodin.

Pages 157-176. ST. ADALBERT AND THE CHRISTIANIZATION OF HUNGARY R. Holinka, the author of the Czech biography of St. Adalbert mentioned above, devoted a special study to the activity of St. Adalbert in Hungary — *K činnosti sv. Vojtěcha v Uhrách* [Concerning the Activity of St. Adalbert in Hungary] (Brno, Prague, 1941-1942). He assumes, rightly I think, the existence of a Life of Adalbert, written in Hungary, which is more informative of the activities of the Bishop of Prague in Hungary than is Bruno's *Vita.* This Hungarian Life has not survived, but it was used by the author of the *Vita Maior* of St. Stephen of Hungary. The earlier *Vita* was composed shortly before 1083 by a Benedictine monk who, according to some Hungarian specialists, may have been of Czech origin. Holinka dates the composition of the lost Life of Adalbert soon after the martyrdom of St. Adalbert, but certainly before 1010, the year of the foundation of the "major church" in Ostergom by St. Stephen, dedicated to St. Adalbert.

Holinka discovered traces of the lost Life in the thirteenth-century *Chronicon Hungarico-Polonicum,* quoted in the present work (pp. 194, 214). Although the latter source mostly contains legendary accounts, it does mention some details of Adalbert's undertakings which are not contained in the *Vita Maior.* The author may have taken them from a Polish *Vita,* whose author had at hand the lost Hungarian *Vita.* Even Pulkava, the author of the fourteenth-century *Chronica Boemorum,* seems to have used information about Adalbert contained in sources now lost. Holinka thinks that this knowledge was preserved by the monks of the monastery of Břevnov, near Prague, who had been in touch with Hungarian Benedictines and may have known the lost Hungarian *Vita.* These new observations should be studied more thoroughly by Hungarian specialists. The *Chronicon Hungarico-Polonicum,* little appreciated by its editor, L. Deér, because of its many legendary accounts, deserves better and more serious study.

Those wishing to pursue the topic of Magyar Christianization may consult the following publications. A general account is by A. L. Gabriel, *The Conversion of Hungary to Christianity* (New York, 1962). The book by D. Sinor, *History of Hungary* (New York, 1959), is a popular compilation. More important is L. Deér, *Die Entstehung des ungarischen Königstums* (Budapest, 1942). An interesting study is that by Th. von Bogay: "Der Eintritt des Ungarentums in die christlich-europäische Kulturgemeinschaft im Lichte der Kunstgeschichte," *Südostforschungen*, 18 (1959), 6-26. On the Christianization of the Magyars by the Byzantines refer to J. Macůrek, *Dějiny Maďarů a uherského státu* [History of the Magyars and the Hungarian State] ((Prague, 1934), pp. 37 ff.), and especially to Gy. Moravcsik, "The Role of the Byzantine Church in Medieval Hungary" (*Studia Byzantina* (Budapest, 1967), pp. 326-340).

Pages 124-128, 250 ff. ST. ADALBERT AND GRECO-SLAVONIC CULTURE. SLAVIC LITURGY IN POLAND This topic is treated in my *Byzantine Missions*(pp. 198-203, 215, 220, 395 ff.). In addition, please consult these works: K. Lanckorońska, "Studies on the Roman-Slavonic Rite in Poland," *Orientalia christiana periodica*, 161 (Rome, 1961), 21-56, 71 ff., 111 ff.; J. Golos, "Traces of Byzantino-Slavonic Influence in Polish Medieval Hymnology," *The Polish Review*, 9 (1963), 73-81; H. Paszkiewicz, *The Origin of Russia* (London, 1954), pp. 390 ff..H. Łowmiański's *Początki Polski* (*op. cit.*, IV (1970), 495-515) reviews studies on Adalbert and on the Slavonic liturgy in Poland not easily obtainable in the West. His presentation of the role of Adalbert is inexact. The idea that the Slavonic liturgy penetrated into Poland from Bulgaria cannot be accepted.

CHAPTER IV. OTTO'S Renovatio imperii

Page 136 ff. A modern investigation is by H. Beumann and W. Schlesinger: "Urkundenstudien zur deutschen Ostpolitik unter Otto III.," *Archiv für Diplomatik*, 1 (1958), 132 ff.. The following research efforts may be consulted with profit: in *Jahrbücher des Deutschen Reiches unter Otto II. und Otto III."* (Berlin, 1954) see "Otto II." by Karl Uhlirz and "Otto III." by Mathilde Uhlirz. The latter contribution supplies a rich commentary and an extensive bibliography (pp. 599-633). Later studies are P.E. Schramm, *Kaiser, Rom und Renovatio* (Vol. I, 2nd ed., Darmstadt, 1957) and W. Meysztowicz, "La vocation monastique d'Otto III" in *Antemurale* (4 (Rome, 1968), 26-75).

Theophano, Otto's mother, is the subject of several portrayals: M. Uhlirz, "Studien über Theophano," *Deutsches Archiv*, 6 (1943), 442-474; F. Dölger, "Wer war Theophano?," *H. J.*, 62-69 (1942-1949), 646-658; Idem., "Nochmals: Wer war Thephano?," *Byzantinische Zeitschrift*, 43 (1950), 338-339. Dölger seems to have the problem definitely solved. Thephano was no more than a relative of Emperor John Tzimisces.

OTTO III, ROME AND IMPERIAL IDEOLOGY The following are essential recent analyses: M. Uhlirz, "Das Werden des Gedankens des *Renovatio imperii* bei Otto III." in *Centro Italiano di Studi sull'alto Medievo* (Spoleto, 1955); M. Sedlmayer, "Rom und Romgedanke im Mittelater," *Saeculum*, 7 (1956), 395-412; M. Fuhrmann, "Die Romidee der Spätantike," *H.Z.*, 207 (1968), 529-561. The contribution by Th. Mayer, "Papsttum und Kaisertum in hohem Mittelalter" (*H. Z.*, 187 (1959), 1-53), contains a useful bibliography. Further see: P. E. Schram, "Die Geschichte des mittelalterlichen Herrschertums im Lichte der Herrscherzeichen," *H. Z.*, 178 (1954), 1-24; R. Folz, *L'idee de l'empire en Occident* (Paris, 1953); H. Focillon, *L'An mil* (Paris, 1952); H. Erdmann, *Forschungen zur politischen Ideenwelt des Frühmittelalters* (Berlin, 1951); R. Bezzola, *La Tradition Imperiale de la Fin de l'antiquité an XIe s.* (Paris, 1958); C. Brühl, "Die

Kaiserpfalz bei St. Peter und die Pfalz Ottos III. auf dem Palatine," *Quellen und Forschungen aus italienischen Archiven,* 34 (1954), 1 ff.; W. Ullmann, *The Growth of Papal Government in the Middle Ages* (London, 1955); G. Tellenbach, "Kaisertum, Papsttum und Europa in hohem Mittelalter," *Historia Mundi,* Vol. VI (Bern, 1958), 1-104.

Page 141. On the origin of the Gelasian theory, see F. Dvornik, *Early Christian and Byzantine Political Philosophy* (2 vols., Washington, 1966): Vol. II: pp. 803-812, 829, 847, 848. The role of St. Augustine in the introduction of this theory into Western Christendom is discussed in the work just named (pp. 840--850).

OTTO III AND POLAND A.W. Czajkowski, "The Congress of Gniesno and the Year 1000," *Speculum,* 24 (1949), 339-356; Z. Wojciechowski, "*La Renovatio imperii* sous Otto III et la Pologne," *Revue historique,* 201 (1949), 30 ff.; Idem., "Le Patrice Boleslas le Vaillant," *Revue belge d'histoire,* 29 (1959), 33 ff.; R. Wenskus, "Bruno von Querfurt und die Stiftung des Erzbistums von Gnesen," *Zeitschrift für Ostforschung,* 5 (1950), 526 ff.; H. Appelt, "Die angebliche Verleihung der Patriciuswürde an Boleslaw Chrobry," *Festgabe H. Aubin* (Hamburg, 1951), pp. 65-81; W. Dzieciot, *Imperium i państwa narodowe około r. 1000* [The Empire and National States Around the Year 1000] (London, 1962); P. Bogdanowicz, "Zjazd Gnieźnieński w roku 1000" [The Congress of Gniesno in the Year 1000], *Nasza Przeszłość,* 16 (1962), 5-151; H. Ludat, *Piasten und Ottonen* in *L'Europe aux IXe - XIe siècle. Aux origines des Etats Nationaux* (Warsaw, 1968); L. Koczy, "The Holy Roman Empire and Poland," *Antemurale, 2* (Rome, 1955), 50-65; H. Ludat, *An Elbe und Oder um das Jahr 1000* (Böhlau, 1972), with rich bibliography (pp. 177-197).

The problem of what kind of honorific title Otto III granted to Boleslas the Brave in Gniesno is not yet definitely solved and remains in dispute among Polish specialists. W. Meysztowicz in his "Koronacje pierwszych Piastów" [Coronation of the First Piasts] (*Sacrum Poloniae Millenium,* 3 (Rome, 1956), 283-341) asserts that Otto III crowned Boleslas as Caesar or co-emperor. Certainly this seems to be a very far-fetched theory. An interesting solution to this problem has been offered by V. Wasilewski in "Bizantyńska symbolika zjazdu gnieźnieńskiego i jej prawno - polityczna wyzmowa" (*Przegląd Historyczny,* 87 (1966), 1-14). Recalling the example of the Byzantine Emperor, Heraclius, who, in 626-627 laid his imperial crown on the head of the Khazar Khagan, accepting him in this manner into the family of kings, the author considers that Otto III's gesture — that of decorating the head of Boleslas with his own crown — should be interpreted in a similar way. Boleslas was solemnly accepted into the family of national kings, "friends and allies of the Empire." The theory, so far generally acknowledged, that Otto conferred upon Boleslas the dignity of a Patricius is, nonetheless, characterized by too many weaknesses. This has been shown, for example, by Appelt, quoted above, and by other specialists.

Pages 160-166. OTTO AND HUNGARY The report of Thietmar and of other sources that Otto III presented a royal crown to Stephen of Hungary should be explained in the fashion resembling that of the ceremony between Boleslas the Brave and Otto at Gniezno depicted on the tomb of St. Adalbert. Otto was inspired by the overriding concept of the *renovatio imperii* in Christian form. As emperor and head of the Christian commonwealth, he solemnly accepted Stephen, an independent ruler, into the renovated empire, extending to him a royal crown. In this connection it should be stressed that Otto displayed an active interest in the Christianization of Hungary. M. Uhlirz rightly reminded L. Deér of this fact when interpreting the sources relating the coronation of Stephen (Excursus XXIII of her "Die Krönung Stephens von Ungarn zum König" in *Jahrbücher* (pp. 572-582), quoted above). See her monograph, *Die Krone des heiligen Stephens* (Graz, Wien, 1951).

M. Uhlirz has further demonstrated that consent for the building up of an ecclesiastical hierarchy in Hungary was obtained from Silvester II and from the Emperor, whom Stephen's envoy met in Ravenna. Her identification of this envoy as Ascheriscus, the future Bishop of Hungary and Archbishop of Gran, is correct. Also most probably correct is her establishment of August 15, 1001 as the approximate date of the solemn coronation of Stephen by Ascheriscus. With regard to Ascheriscus, I continue to hold to my own interpretations. In her Excursus XXII, "Die Weihe des Ascheriscus zum Erzbischof von Sobottin" (pp. 566-571), M. Uhlirz follows the information contained in the *Passio Adalberti,* which she wrongly regards as the first Life of Adalbert. It is difficult to imagine why Ascheriscus should have been named a bishop at Zobten in Poland when accompanying Otto on his pilgrimage to Gniezno.

Brackmann's studies quoted in the present book were republished in his *Gesammelte Aufsätze* (Weimar, 1941): pp. 108-139, 154-187, 188-210, 242-258. Brackmann has also written "Die Entstehung des ungarischen Staates," which appeared in the *Abhandlungen* of the Prussian Academy (1940). Further: L. Deér, *Die Entstehung des ungarischen Königstums* (Budapest, 1942); M. Uhlirz, "Otto III. und das Papsttum," *H. Z.,* 162 (1940), 258-268. On Stephen's crown compare M. Uhlirz in *Jahrbücher (op. cit.,* pp. 371 ff.), E. Molnar, *Osnovanie vengerskogo gosudarstva* [The Formation of the Hungarian State] (Budapest, 1952) and Sz. de Vajay, "Grossfürst Geyza von Ungarn: Familie und Verwandschaft" (*Südostforschungen,* 21 (1962), 45-101).

CHAPTER V. A POLISH-CZECH OR A CZECH-POLISH STATE

Pages 185-235. The most important new contribution to the history of the emperor, Henry II, and the Polish duke, Boleslas Chrobry, is the work by H.F. Grabski, *Bolesław Chrobry. Zarys dziejów politycznych i wojskowych* [Boleslas the Brave. A Political and Military History] (2nd. ed., Warsaw, 1966). Beginning with a short history of the reign of Mieszko I, the author then describes the main events in Gniezno in the year 1000, and continues with the election of Henry II and the first acts of Boleslas. The chief concern of this book is to offer a detailed portrayal of the military conflicts between the Polish duke and the German emperor.

Grabski's account is descriptive in character and is divided into three chapters. The first is devoted to the beginning of the massive conflict (1003-1005), characterized by Boleslas' military successes in Lusatia, Milsko and Bohemia, and by the alliance of Henry II with the pagan confederation of the Veletians. The occupation of Bohemia by Boleslas is not presented by the author as an attempt to create a Slavic empire. Mistakenly, Grabski holds that Boleslas did not pursue the ideas of Otto III. Rather, he believes that Boleslas's principal goal was that of finding allies among the German feudal lords opposed to Henry II. This phase of the hostilities culminated with the making of peace in Poznań.

The second period of the conflict, outlined in detail on pages 162-205, concluded with the Peace of Merseburg in 1013. The final phase of the war, covered in Chapter VI, involves events spanning the period from 1013 to the Peace of Budzisyn in 1018. Appended is a special chapter (pp. 243-272) devoted to the relations of Boleslas with Russia.

Grabski's picture of the Polish-German hostilities contains many new details which depict more graphically than hitherto the famous struggle and which, in addition, delineate Boleslas' great political and military talents. Neverthless, this book does not replace in Polish historical literature S. Zakrzewski's *Bolesław Chrobry Wielki* (Warsaw, 1925) despite the fact that Grabski considers some of Zakrzewski's views to be outmoded. To be sure, in his introduction Grabski stresses that his chief interest lies in the military aspects of the contest. Earlier he published a long military study of this conflict with the title *Polska sztuka wojenna w okresie wczesnofeudalnym* [Polish Military Ingenuity During the Early Feudal Period] (Warsaw, 1959). He is also the author of "Geneza wojen polsko-niemieckich na początku XI wieku" [Genesis of the Polish-German Wars at the Beginning of the Eleventh Century], *Studia i materiały,* 5 (1960), 453-476.

A brief and clear history of the Polish-German struggle under Henry II and Boleslas Chrobry is given by S. Epperstein in die *Slawen in Deutschland (op. cit.,* pp. 289-299). He accords special attention to the role of the Lutizi and in addition sketches the wars of Konrad II (1024-1039) with them.

MIESZKO I AND BOLESLAS CHROBRY See S. Kętrzyński, *Polska X-XI wieku* [Poland in the Tenth and Eleventh Centuries] (Warsaw, 1961); Z. Wojciechowski, "Boleslas le Vaillant et la crise des relations polono-allemandes," *Revue occidentale,* 1 (1948), 215-230.

On the Polabian Slavs, Henry II and Konrad II, turn to the following works: W. Fritze, "Die Datierung des Geographus Bavarus und die Stammensverfassung der Abodriten," *Zeitschrift für slawische Philologie,* 21 (1952), 32 ff.; G. Lukas, *Die deutsche Politik gegen die Elbslawen von dem Jahre 982 bis zum Ende des Polenkrieges Heinrichs II.* (Halle, 1940); Th. Schieffer, "Heinrich II. und Konrad II.," *Deutsches Archiv zur Erforschung des Mittelalters,* 8 (1951), 384 ff.; H. L. Mikoletzky, *Kaiser Heinrich II. und die Kirche* (Vienna, 1946); C. Pfaff, *Kaiser Heinrich II. Sein Nachleben und sein Kult* (Basel, 1963); V. D. Koroliuk, "O poslednem periode pravleniia Boleslava Khrabrago" [The Final Period of the Reign of Boleslas Chrobry], *Istoricheskie zapiski,* 19 (1946), 146 ff..

On the coronation of Boleslas there is Grabski's *Bolesław Chrobry (op. cit.,* pp. 288 ff.), with bibliographical notices, as well as W. Meysztowicz, "Koronacje pierwszych Piastów," cited above.

POLAND IN THE ELEVENTH CENTURY Deserving of attention are: D. Borawska, *Kryzys monarchii wczesnopiastowskiej w latach trzydziestych XI w.* [The Crisis of the Early Piast Monarchy in the Third Decade of the Eleventh Century] (Warsaw, 1964); G. Labuda, "Utrata Moraw przez państwo polskie w XI wieku" [Poland's Loss of Moravia in the Eleventh Century], *Studia z dziejów polskich i czechosłowackich,* 5 (1960), 97-124. Labuda corrects Cosmas' date of the reconquest of Moravia by the Czechs. It is his reasoning that Moravia was conquered not in 1021 by Brzetislas, but in 1031 by Odalrich. The latter profited by the crisis in Poland when Mieszko II was for some time his prisoner. Review pages 214 and 220-224 of the present work. Labuda's dating must be accepted.

THE GENERAL SITUATION IN POLAND On this question see: G. Rhode, *Die Ostgrenze Polens* (Cologne, Graz, 1955); F. Bujak, *Państwo i naród polski w XI wieku* [The Polish State and Nation During the Eleventh Century] (Warsaw, 1947); H. Ludat, "Soziale und politische Strukturprobleme des früh-piastischen Polen," *Agrar-, Wirtschafts- and Sozialprobleme* (Wiesbaden, 1965), pp. 371-392; J. Cticrowski, "Du Pologne medievale. Problemés du régime politi-que et l'organisation administrative du Xe au XIIIe s.," *Annali della Fondazione Ita-liana per la storia administrativa,* 1 (1964), 135-156. Also G. Labuda, "Początki diecezjalnej organizacji kościelnej na Pomorzu i na Kujawach w XI a XII wieku" [Beginning of the Diocesan Ecclesiastic Organization in Pomerania and Kujavja in the Eleventh and Twelfth Centuries], *Zapiski Historyczne,* 33 (1968), 19-60. For Günther the Hermit turn to pages 199, 220, 228 of the present work. Related studies include the following: G. Lang, "Günther der Eremit in Geschichte, Sage und Kultur," *Studien und Mitteilungen aus dem Benediktiner und Zisterziener-orden,* 59 (Munich, 1941-1942), 1-83; E. Hanfelder, *1000 Jahre St. Günther. Festschrift* (Cologne, 1955). For Casimir refer to Ř. Kaczmarczyk, *Kazimierz Wielki (Casimir le Grand)* (Warsaw, 1948) and to his *Polska czasów Kazimierza Wielkiego* [Poland under Casimir the Great] (Cracow, 1964).

Pages 215 ff. and 237 ff. POLAND AND KIEVAN RUSSIA In particular see A. F. Grabski's "Studia nad stosunkami polsko-ruskimi w początkach XI wieku" [Studies on Polish-Russian Relations at the Beginning of the Eleventh Century] (*Slavia Orientalis,* 6 (1957), 164-211), with a detailed bibliography, and his "Bolesław Chrobry" (pp. 243-269). In addition: F. Persowski, *Studia nad pograniczem polsko-ruskim w X-XI wieku* [Studies on Polish-Russian Boundaries During the Tenth and Eleventh Centuries] (Wroclaw, 1962); B. Widera, "Brun von Querfurt und Russland," *Jahrbuch für Geschichte der UdSSR und der volks-demokratischen Ländern Europas,* 3 (Berlin, 1950), 365 ff.; A.F. Grabski, "Po povodu polsko-vizantiiskikh otnoshenii v nachale XI v." [Concerning Polish-Byzan-tine Relations at the Beginning of the Eleventh Century], *Vizantiiskii vremennik,* 14 (Moscow, 1958), 175-184.

Page 249 ff. See F. Dvornik, *Byzantine Missions,* pages 194-205 and 395-398 (notes and bibliography), and pages 109 ff. and 364 ff. (new findings on *The Leaflets or Fragments of Kiev*).

CHAPTER VI. KIEVAN RUSSIA AND CENTRAL EUROPE

Pages 236-261. A more detailed account of the cultural achievements of Kievan Russia and of the penetration of Western Slavonic literature into Kiev is offered on pages 218-225 of my book, *The Slavs: Their Early History and Civilization* (Boston, 1956) and in the French edition *(Les Slaves),* pages 171-228, 982-987. Further bibliographical evidence on this subject will be found in my "Les Benedictins et la Christianisation de la Russie" (*L'Église et les Églises* (Chevetogne, 1954), pp. 323-349). The German translation is "Die Benediktiner und die Christianisierung Russlands" (*Erbe und Auftrag,* 35 (1959), 292-310). See also my "Byzantine Political Ideas in Kievan Russia" (*Dumbarton Oaks Papers,* 9-10 (1956), 73-121), with bibliography on Kievan jurisprudence, and my study "The Kiev State and its Relations With Western Europe," reprinted in *Essays in Mediaeval History* (R. W. Southern, ed. (London, 1968), pp. 1-23). A more popular treatment will be found in my contribution to *The Root of Europe* (M. Huxley, ed. (London, 1952), pp. 85-106).

An important study is that of N. K. Gudzy, *History of Early Russian Literature,* translated by S. W. Jones (New York, 1949). Further, consult K. J. Conant, "Novgorod, Constantinople, and Kiev in Old Russian Church Architecture," *The Slavonic and East European Review,* 22 (American Series) (1944), 75-92; K. G. Conant and S. H. Cross, *Medieval Russian Churches* (Cambridge, Mass., 1949); B. D. Grekov and M. L. Artamanov, *Geschichte der Kultur der alten Rus',* translated by B. Widera (Berlin, 1960); B. A. Rybakov, *Kultura drevnei Rusi* (Moscow, 1956); A. Poppe, "Le Recit sur le martyre et les miracles des St. Boris et Gleb," (in Polish) *Slavia Orientalis,* 18 (1960), 367-376; D. Oljančyn, "Zur Regierung des Grossfürsten Izlaslav-Demeter von Kiew (1054-1078)," *Jahrbücher für Geschichte Osteuropas,* 8 (1960), 397-410.

THE KIEVAN CHURCH   D. Obolensky, "Russia's Byzantine Heritage," *Oxford Slavonic Papers,* 1 (1950), 37-63; A. V. Kartashov, *Ocherki po istorii russkoi tserkvi* [Studies on the History of the Russian Church] (Paris, 1950). According to the latter author, Kiev — the metropolis of Russia — had eleven dioceses about the middle of the eleventh century. Additional recent studies include: L. Müller, *Zum Problem des hierarchischen Status und der jurisdiktionellen Abhängigkeit der russischen Kirche von 1039* (Köln, Braunsfeld, 1959); A. Poppe, *Państwo i kościół na Rusi w XI wieku* [State and Church in Russia During the Eleventh Century] (Warsaw, 1969); Idem., "L'organisation diocesaine de la Russie aux XIe-XIIe siecles," *Byzantion,* 40 (1970), 165-217. Consult further D. Obolensky's paper, "The Relations Between Byzantium and Russia (Eleventh to Fifteenth Centuries)," for the XIII International Congress of Historical Sciences in Moscow, 1970.

For more detailed bibliography on Kievan and Muscovite Russia see, in addition to G. Stöckl's *Russisches Mittelalter* cited above, K. Meyer, "Literaturbericht über die Geschichte Russlands und der Sowjetunion" (*H. Z.,* Sonderheft 1 (1962). The author reviews publications which appeared outside of the USSR between 1953 and 1959.

THE ORIGIN AND FORMATION OF THE RUSSIAN STATE   Among newer studies are: G. Stöckl, "Die Wurzeln des modernen Staates in Osteuropa," *Jahrbücher für Geschichte Osteuropas,* 1 (1953), 255-269; Idem., "Die Begriffe Reich, Herrschaft und Staat bei den orthodoxen Slawen," *Saeculum,* 5 (1954), 104-118; Idem., "Russisches Mittelalter und sowjetische Mediaevalistik," *Jahrbücher für Geschichte Osteuropas,* 3 (1955), 1-40 (bibliography); M. Hellmann, "Staat und Recht im Altrussland," *Saeculum,* 5 (1954), 41-61; Idem., "Slawisches, insbesondere ostslawisches Herrschertum des Mittelalters," *Das Königtum* (Maimanvorträge) (Konstanz, 1963), 243-277; H. Paskiewicz, *The Origins of Russia* (London, 1954); Idem., *The Making of the Russian Nation* (London, 1963). V. T. Pashuto's *Vneshnaia politika drevnei Rusi* [Foreign Policy of Ancient Russia] (Moscow, 1968) contains a rich Russian and Western bibliography. Compare also A.V. Soloview, "Der Begriff 'Russland' im Mittelalter," *Wiener Archiv,* 2 (Köln, Graz, 1956), 143-168.

ST. VLADIMIR   M. Hellmann, "Wladimir der Heilige in der zeitgenössischen abendländischen Überlieferung," *Jahrbücher für Geschichte Osteuropas,*

7 (1959), 379-412; L. Müller, *Des Metropoliten Ilarion Lobrede auf Wladimir den Heiligen und Glaubensbekenntnis* (Wiesbaden, 1962).

Pages 268-297   APPENDIX I AND II   New editions of sources noted are as follow: J. Widajewicz, *Studia nad relacją o Słowianach Ibrahima Ibn Jakuba* [Studies on the Account of the Slavs by Ibrahim Ibn Jakub] (Cracow, 1946); T. Lewicki, *Źródła arabskie do dziejów Słowiańszczyzny* [Arabic Sources on Slavic History] (Wrocław, Cracow, 1956; Vol. 2, 1969); F. Kupfer and T. Lewicki, *Źródła hebrajskie do dziejów Słowian* [Hebraic sources on Slavic History] (Wrocław, 1956); G. Flusser, "Zpráva o Slovanech v hebrejské kronice z X století," *ČČH*, 48-49 (1947-1948), 238-241; G. Labuda, *Źródła skandynawskie i anglosaskie do dziejów Słowiańszczyzny* [Skandinavian and Anglo-Saxon Sources on Slavic History] (Warsaw, 1961); The Bavarian Geographer, "Descriptio civitatum ad septemtrionem Danubii," B. Horák and D. Trávníček, eds., *Rozpravy of the Czech Academy,* 66 (Prague, 1956); Constantine Porphyrogenitus, *De administrando imperio,* G. Moravcsik and R.J.H. Jenkins, eds. (Budapest, 1949); Second edition, *Dumbarton Oaks Texts* I (Washington, 1968).

My own detailed commentary on Constantine Porphyrogenitus' report on White Croatia and White Serbia, with bibliographical notices, will be found in Volume 2 of his *De administrando imperio —Commentary* (R.J.H. Jenkins, ed. (London, 1962), pp. 93-142). Deeper study of his report has confirmed my conclusions, given in Appendix I, on the existence of White Croatia and White Serbia, and has verified Constantine's report of the migration of White Croatians and White Serbs during the reign of the Emperor Heraclius. In my *Byzantine Missions,* I devoted a chapter to the Christianization of the Croats and Serbs (pp. 1-48) and reached the conclusion that the first attempts at the conversion of the two nations must be attributed to Heraclius, with the collaboration of Rome, as is attested by the imperial writer. It appears that Split (Spalato) had become the heir of the metropolis of Salona, destroyed by the Avars.

On the meaning of color designation in ancient geography, consult H. Ludat, "Farbenzeichnungen in Völkernamen. Ein Beitrag zur asiatisch-europäischen Kulturbeziehungen," *Saeculum,* 4 (1953), 138-155.

The Polish historian H. Łowmiański, in Volume III of his *Początki Polski,* devoted a long study to the problem of the White Serbs (pp. 53-83) and White Croats (pp. 114-200). While accepting the theory of the Sarmatian origin of the primitive Serbs, he rejects the theory of T. Lewicki ("Litzike Konstantyna Porfyrogenety," *Roczniki Historyczne,* 22 (Poznań, 1956), 9-34) that the Serbs were originally settled in Poland. He thinks that many place names apparently indicating the existence of Serbian settlements in Great Poland — the main argument of Lewicki's theory — are of later date. Boleslas Chrobry seems to have resettled Serbs in Poland from modern Saxony. Many of them served in his army and found new homes in Polish lands.

On pages 114-142 the author gives a very detailed history of the problem concerning the origin of the Croats, quoting the opinions of every Slavic philologist and historian. On pages 142-182 he examines all written documents which place the seats of the Croats in the East, north of the Carpathian Mountains, especially the reports given by Constantine Porphyrogenitus. At the end of his long discussion Łowmiański gives toponymic items indicating the settlements of Croats in Little Poland in the past.

Łowmiański only knew my book, *The Early History,* which he quoted. It is regrettable that he was unable to refer to my present study, as it would have facilitated his research. He uses the same sources, interpreting them mostly in the same sense as I have done. It is rather gratifying that, independently and in almost all the main details, he arrived at the same conclusions as the present writer.

On the Avars and their relations with the Slavs, especially the Antes, see Łowmiański's book (ibid., pp. 340-360). On the Avars and the Dulebians (pp. 282, 283), consult the study by B. Zástěrová, "Avaři a Dulebové" (Vznik a počátky Slovanů, 1 (1960), 15-37), which contains a résumé in French. It appears that the report of the Russian Primary Chronicle on the Dulebians and the sufferings they endured at the hands of the Avars cannot mean the Russian Dulebians-Volynians, but rather a tribe of the same name living in Pannonia, in the vicinty of the Avars.

On the Sarmatians there is a new book by T. Sulimirski, The Sarmatians (London, 1970). On page 167, Sulimirski agrees with my thesis that the territory of the Antes included Silesia and Little Poland, through which the Langobards passed on their way south (my present book, pp. 284, 285).

APPENDIX III. THE POLISH AND RUSSIAN CONFLICT   Consult A. F. Grabski, Bolesław Chrobry, pp. 244 ff.. It is generally admitted by Polish historians that in 981 Vladimir occupied the territory of the Red Cities, including Przemyśl, an important commercial center giving him access to the Western market. A Polish-Russian conflict, at that date, did not take place. The report of the Hildesheim Annals that in 992 Poland was threatened by Russia, does not mean that a military conflict occurred between the two countries. The relations between Poland and Russia during the eleventh century have been studied by A.F. Grabski in a special paper published in Slavia Orientalis (6 (1957), 164-211). See also S.M. Kuczyński, "Stosunki polsko-ruskie do schyłku wieku XII" [Polish-Russian Relations to the Twelfth Century (ibid., 7 (1958), 223-255), with a detailed bibliography.

APPENDIX IV. THE PRIMITIVE RUSSIANS   G. Vernadsky has treated the same problems in his later publication, The Origins of Russia (New York, 1959), with many new suggestions and daring etymologies. For details, see my review of this book in The American Historical Review (65 (1960), 347-349). On these problems consult also H. Łowmiański's Zagadnienie (op. cit., pp. 124-161). with a detailed bibliography. In addition: T.J. Arne, "Die Warägerfrage und die sowjetrussische Forschung," Acta Archaeologica, 23 (Copenhagen, 1952), 138-147; R. Ekblom, "Roslagen-Russland," Zeitschrift für slawische Philologie, 26 (1957), 47 ff.; H. Łowmiański, "O znaczeniu nazwy Ruś w wieku X-XIV" [The Meaning of the Name Rus' in the Tenth to Fourteenth Centuries], Kwartalnik Historyczny, 64 (1957), 84-101.

APPENDIX VI.   Dagome iudex   There are several new studies on the document and the name Dagome: G. Labudá, "Znaczenie prawno-polityczne dokumentu Dagome Iudex" [Legal and Political Importance of the Document Dagome Iudex], Nasza Przeszłość, 4 (1948), 33 ff.; P. Bogdanowicz, "Geneza aktu zwanego Dagome Iudex" [The Genesis of the Document Dagome Iudex], Rocznik Historyczny, 25 (1959), 1-33; S. Kętrzyński, "Dagome Iudex," Przegląd Historyczny, 41 (1950), 133-151. A. Steffen in his "Greckie ślady w regeście Dagome Iudex" ([Greek Traces in the Document Dagome Iudex], Antemurale, 3 (Rome, 1956), 95-116) searched without success for traces of Greek words in the document. His critic W. Meysztowicz (*ibid.,* pp. 95, 96), interpreted the name as Tugumir, known to the Havelans, a Slavic tribe. So far, no other satisfactory solution has been found, and therefore I uphold my own interpretation.

FRANCIS DVORNIK, *Professor Emeritus*

Dumbarton Oaks, Washington, D.C.
November 1972

TABLE OF CONTENTS

between the Emperor and the Pole—The Emperor's alliance with the pagan Veletians deals death blow to Ottonian ideology—Bruno of Querfurt's mission to Hungary and Poland and his defence of Boleslas—Boleslas' bid for a Western Slavonic empire and his sympathisers in Germany—Henry II and Boleslas before the bar of history—Polish King succeeds to the role relinquished by the Emperor—Poland, Bohemia, Hungary and Russia—Mieszko II and Conrad II— Last bid for a Przemyslide State—Conrad's " Divide et impera "—Abortive Czech-Polish State—Poland and Bohemia at the close of a period.

PREFACE

My first intention was to write a History of Central and Eastern Europe and to follow the growth of its States throughout the length of the medieval period. Such a study, giving a complete survey of their cultural constituents—Roman, Byzantine, Germanic and Slavonic—seems to be desirable. Historians who have dealt with the nations that live between the Rhine, the Adriatic and the Ural Mountains, too often choose their own particular nationality as their central point of observation and present a confusing, sometimes even a biassed picture of that part of Europe. They overlook the common trends that should lend order and logic to otherwise bewildering and chaotic conflicts.

But when I started my researches in this field, I soon came to the conclusion that before any attempt of this kind could be made, a thorough study of the tenth and eleventh centuries was essential. That period was vital, for it was then that national interests began to assert themselves and to clash, as they still do in the historical works of the scholars of different nations. I therefore concentrated on that period, and the present work is the result. It is in many aspects a continuation of my book "Les Slaves, Byzance et Rome au IXe siècle," published in Paris in 1926.

As the subject is highly controversial, I have taken care to produce all available documentary evidence. Unfortunately, I have not found all the support I had looked for and I am afraid that my original plan will have to be abandoned. But as the present fate of Central and Eastern Europe is being decided on the basis of factors which originated in the period covered by this book, I felt prompted to publish the results of my researches such as they are. The solutions I propose may help students in further investigation.

Western European and American readers may possibly find some of my discussions too lengthy and some topics too remote from Western interests. But these problems should be viewed from the point of view of the nations concerned. To them, the medieval period means much more than it means to Western nations. It was then that most of them came nearest to their ideals of national independence and that some of them played their part in the work of civilising Europe. And when their national individuality was absorbed into the neighbouring empires of Germany, Austria, Muscovite Russia and Ottoman Turkey, it was from those memories that they drew comfort and strength. To-day, their past is their only inspiration in carrying on the struggle to preserve their national identity. Nowhere more than in Central and Eastern Europe is it true to say that modern development can only be understood in the light of medieval history.

It was in the period I am dealing with, that Medieval Germany was born and that a great Slavonic State was rising between Germany and

iii

Russia ; then also, under Otto III, Germany was on a fair way to become the leading civilising agent in the West. But the premature death of this offspring of Saxony and Byzantium spoiled the development and set Germany on the fatal course of the " Drang nach Osten," the results of which are costing her so dear to-day.

I have tried to place these events in a new light. I am conscious of the deficiencies of my work, but the task was not easy. The book was written at the British Museum, when London was in the front line ; many books that would have facilitated research, were destroyed by enemy action ; others were unobtainable. The book was ready by the end of 1944, but had to wait for more than three years for a publisher. I am therefore most grateful to the Polish Research Centre and especially to its director, Professor A. Żółtowski, for having undertaken its publication.

I would like to express my sincere thanks to all who have helped me in my task. I would like to thank the Superintendents and the staff of the British Museum Reading Room, who, in constant danger of air raids, did their utmost to assure the library service and were most helpful to me. I thank my colleagues, Professor M. Jedlicki, of the Jagellon University of Cracow and Professor Roman Jakobson, of Columbia University, for reading the MS., and giving me most valuable advice, the one on Polish history, the other, on Old Slavonic letters. I am grateful to Captain Stary for drawing the maps. Without pretending to be absolutely accurate, as the frontiers up to the Xth century were so fluid, they will help the reader to find his bearings in the history of the period.

My friend, the Rev. A. Gille gave me valuable literary and secretarial help, while the index was compiled by Princess Sophy Sapieha. I owe many excellent suggestions to Professor A. Żółtowski, to Mr. Robert Threlfall, to Mr. J. R. Carey and to Mr. Godfrey Scheele. I also owe sincere thanks to Mr. A. Mazzucato, director of the Alma Book Co. Ltd. in London, who undertook the printing of the book in spite of the difficulties which attend the making of a scholarly book under existing conditions.

I much regret I was only able to a limited extent to make use of the publications that appeared in Central Europe during the war, as many of them, chiefly those that came out in Prague, were unobtainable. Among these, I wish to mention the third volume of the Anthology of S. Wenceslas.

Deficiencies notwithstanding, I trust that my work may be of help to all those who look for a common ground on which the various nations of Central Europe could meet and forget the old quarrels which so often led them to servitude.

F. DVORNIK.

Dumbarton Oaks, Washington, May, 1948.

INTRODUCTION

Few periods in Europe's history were as portentous as the ninth and tenth centuries, for it was in those eventful years that the foundations of continental Europe were finally laid. In the ninth century, the last rumblings of the distressing migrations died down, after spending themselves in the eighth. From the ruins and destruction wrought by the Germanic and Slavonic tribes in the majestic structure of the Roman Empire there gradually emerged the renovated features of a new Europe.

No power on earth could have hindered the romanising process which was transforming the Goths in Spain, the Lombards in northern and southern Italy, the Franks and Burgundians in Gaul. Already, when these Germanic tribes, driven by blind instinct, settled in the south, on imperial territory, amongst cultured and romanised populations, their fate was sealed. The notion of one single empire uniting all nations and embracing the whole world, or at least the whole of Europe—an idea born in pagan Rome and readily adopted by Christian Rome—had revealed extraordinary vitality, and the new invaders were so awed by the glories of the capital of the world that they long refrained from touching its unifying principle; they were proud to be looked up to as the Empire's standing army and their kings gloried in ruling Rome and the occupied provinces in the name of the Emperor. To this glamour, the notion of the Empire's unity owed its survival in the worst crises, and it enabled Constantine the Great's successors to maintain for centuries, their fictitious authority over the West.

But not even Justinian's heroic endeavour to lend substance to those illusions and to reconvert the Mediterranean into a Roman sea could save the ideal that had inspired generations of Romans and overawed masses of barbarians, and it was in the ninth century that the Franks and their Charlemagne gave it the *coup de grâce*.

It is true that contemporaries did not fully realise the implications of this revolution and in blissful ignorance went on for some generations nursing the old fiction of Empire unity as the only possible political entity that suited the world they knew. But neither their illusions nor the protests from the distant city on the Bosphorus could halt the process. Europe finally broke into two fragments; the lengthy operation of raising new national kingdoms in East and West had started. Such was, among other implications, the true meaning of Charlemagne's coronation in Rome by Leo III on the Christmas night of A.D. 800.

With all the energy of youthful enthusiasts and the ruthlessness of semi-civilised barbarians, the Franks began expanding their empire and imposing their rule on neighbouring nations ; they penetrated to the Adriatic, conquered Friuli and Istria, extended their dominion over Croatia and even tried to push as far as Bulgaria. Their colonists and missionaries crossed the Alps and descended on Pannonia. Thence they crossed the Danube to reach the north-eastern limit of their penetration at Nitra, in modern Slovakia, about the year 835, after Charlemagne's victorious armies had cleared the way and annihilated the Avars, the Turco-Tartar invaders of modern Hungary. It looked as though a new imperial era, in the best Roman imperial tradition, had dawned on western Europe. By a strange coincidence, the Roman legions also, in their north-eastern drive, had come to rest not far from Nitra. This is recorded by a Roman inscription under the castle of Trenchin to the effect that about the year 179, under Marcus Aurelius, Roman legions had camped at the foot of the Carpathian Mountains. But by claiming supremacy over Moravia and Bohemia, the Franks outstripped the Romans, whose outposts never got beyond Brno, the modern capital of Moravia. The Elbe, whose waters had so often mirrored the eagles of the Roman legions under Drusus and Tiberius, also fell to Charlemagne's troops, as they made the eastern borders of his Empire safe against invasions by the pagan Slavs settled on its banks. Even Spain, or what was left of it after the Arab conquest, looked to Charlemagne as the only man able to set it free and make it a Christian country once more.

When we consider the many possible lines along which development could have taken place, we are bound to wonder how the history of Europe would have shaped had Charlemagne's empire survived and had his successors been able to complete this immense political structure, erected on the debris of an old universalism and held together by the new Christian faith. The Frankish Empire revealed a striking process of formation. Its centre of gravity lay originally in the West and in the South where romanised elements predominated and only a chance event prevented this preponderance from leaving its mark. The severance of the commercial routes between Marseilles, Sicily, Byzantium and Africa by the Arabs, who since the seventh century had gained control over the Mediterranean, brought about the economic decadence of Southern France and prevented this cultured portion of the Frankish Empire from taking a lead in its development. But though the centre of gravity shifted and the initiative passed to the north, the romanised element of the south lost none of its prestige in the new-born Empire. But for an accident it would have had sufficient vitality to cross the Rhine and to romanise, or at least to leaven with Latin, French and Italian culture the Germanic tribes whose civilisation fell so short of Western and Southern standards.

It was Charlemagne himself who unwittingly arrested this development. Historians still comment with bitterness on the brutality displayed by that great admirer of S. Augustine, the builder of the City of God on earth, in subjugating the proud Saxons who lived between the lower and the middle Elbe, modern Holland and Franconia, crushing their repeated revolts and forcing them to embrace Christianity. Charlemagne no doubt had only the interests of his empire and of Christianity in mind, but without intending to do so, he rendered a great service to the German nation as such, for it was due to his brutal treatment that a vigorous Germanic tribe was prevented from isolating itself and forming a separate nation and state as did the Danes, the Scandinavians and the Anglo-Saxons. The Saxons remained Germans whilst the forcible diffusion of many Saxons among neighbouring Germanic tribes powerfully contributed to their amalgamation and stiffened their resistance to non-Germanic infiltration from south and west of the Rhine and of the Alps. The Saxons were a martial race, but as they had only recently emerged from their pagan and primitive civilisation, the whole of Francia suffered in consequence a cultural set-back.

Charlemagne's policy mainly contributed to the breaking of his Empire into two portions—the Romanised and the Germanic parts—the split that heralded the second phase in the work of reconstruction. But disintegration went on. Complications in Italy, where the Papacy was engrossed in territorial claims and where memories of the imperial period still lingered in idle regrets, restricted the extension of the Lombard kingdom; France went on disintegrating, whilst maintaining the fiction of a unity that was no longer effective. In Spain, the Romanised Iberians and Goths, the backbone of the proud Spanish race, despairing of the help they expected from Western Christendom, went their own way and started almost single-handed their heroic struggle against the Mussulmans, which ended in the liberation of Spain in the fifteenth century. Even Croatia shook herself free and Bulgaria grew into a State and a menace to Byzantium, the last and sole heir to ancient Rome.

Further east, on the periphery of the Frankish Empire, there rose on the left bank of the middle Danube and on its affluents, from the Morava in the direction of the Tisza, a new power known as Great Moravia which under the native dynasty of the Moimirs finally barred the way to the Franks in their drive to the Carpathians. It gathered round itself the Slavonic tribes of the Upper Vltava, its affluents and the Upper Vistula, and threatened to impose its rule on the whole of former Pannonia or that part of modern Hungary which lies between the Danube bend, the Alps and the Drava river. Further to the north, the many Slavonic tribes, on the right bank of the Elbe and between the Elbe and the Baltic, soon recovered from the fright which the armies of Charlemagne and his successors had given them and set about crossing the river and doing what damage they could on the territory of East Francia or future Germany.

With the Norman invasions which spread terror over the European coastlands on the Atlantic Ocean and paralysed Europe's economic life, Charlemagne's work steadily went to pieces. Yet it was at that very moment that a power made its appearance on the Danube and the Morava, so rich in promise for Central and Western Europe that it still baffles many scholars. The new State found access to Constantinople, the storehouse of the old classical and Hellenistic culture, and received from there its knowledge of the Gospel. This sudden reversal broke the eastward drive of Frankish culture and opened the Slavonic East to Byzantium. The invention of Slavonic letters by SS. Cyril and Methodius and the introduction of Slavonic into the liturgy—an innovation unheard of in the West—threatened to undo the cultural life-work of Charlemagne who had made it his business to enforce the use of Latin and of the Roman rite on the whole West, including the non-Latin populations of Germanic stock.

At any rate, Charlemagne's ambition gave strong proof of the fascination which Roman culture had exercised on the Germans. With nothing to return in exchange for the gifts which Rome had to offer, they appropriated them wholesale and insisted that the language of the Romans was the only medium sufficiently dignified to convey the thoughts of the intellectuals to the mob and the prayers of the faithful to God. They failed to see the disparity between their own position and that of the romanised nations and never for a moment considered that such acceptance would for centuries place their own tongue at a disadvantage. These considerations should help one to appreciate the statesmanship of the Moravian dukes. But at that time Latin institutions were so firmly embedded in Frankish life as to be part and parcel of West and East Francia's national character and, instead of copying their eastern neighbours, the Franks, scenting danger, struck out for themselves. What brought the danger home to them was that the Papacy, alarmed by the growing power of the Frankish hierarchy, took sides with Moravia and its Byzantine missionaries.

It was East Francia—what is Germany to-day—that set the ball in motion. With characteristic Germanic tenacity, Louis gave his Moravian neighbours no rest and Arnulf, his successor, feeling unable to crush them single-handed, did not scruple to call in the next invaders of Central Europe, the Finno-Ugrian Magyars. After their defeat by the Bulgarian Tzar Simeon and his allies the Pechenegs (Patzinaks)—their mortal enemies—and after their expulsion from their seat in Southern Russia, the Magyars were only too anxious to cross the Carpathians to overthrow the Moravian Empire and set up their home on the Danubian plains. Arnulf was certainly not aware of what he was doing. He did secure his object, but in effect cut the line of communication which the Moravian princes were building to link Byzantium with Central Europe and which would have poured on the West the treasures of Greek and Hellenistic culture. With the Moravian way barred by the uncultured Magyars and other ways of access to Byzantium all but cut by the Arab sea power, Western Europe had to wait four centuries before her military and economic expansion to the Middle East at the time of the Crusades restored contact with Greek and Hellenistic culture, saved by Byzantium, and which was to culminate in the intellectual stir of the western Renaissance.

No less disastrous was the immediate consequence of this move. The new invaders became the scourge of Europe and their forays into Bavaria and the rest of Germany, Burgundy, West Francia and even Italy left her no peace. Instead of the Moravian problem, there rose the Magyar problem, one far worse and needing another Charlemagne to cope with it.

4

In the meantime, another Germanic tribe, the Scandinavians of Sweden, were about to establish the greatest among Nordic creations, the Russia of Novgorod and of Kiev, among the Slavonic and Finnish tribes in the north and east of Europe. This was a region that had so far been scarcely known to the Romans or their successors in the West, the Franks, and was a closed book for the rest of mankind. This new political formation, which Igor consolidated round Kiev, made contact not only with Byzantine civilisation, but also with the Arabs of Bagdad across the Turco-Tartar Empire of the Khazars on the lower Volga, and across the Empire of the Bulgars on the middle reaches of that stream.

There was serious danger that the civilisation of the Khalifs would outshine that of Christian Byzantium—the Scandinavians were pagans and felt equally attracted by both. Then instead of Christianity in either its western or eastern form, it would be Islam that would cross the Dnieper, the Dniester, the Carpathian Mountains, and obtain a footing among the Magyars. In their wandering over the steppes of Russia, then under Khazarian rule, they were probably acquainted to some extent with Mohammed's easy faith and like all nomads would have fallen under its spell in preference to the austere doctrine of Christianity.

That danger was averted by Byzantium. Svyatoslav, the pagan Duke of Kiev, was driven towards the Danube and instead of settling on the Volga among the Mussulman Bulgars, he made war on the Danubian Bulgars to the advantage of Byzantium. The Magyar peril was overcome by the youngest Germanic tribe, the latest acquisition of East Francia, the Saxons. It was again due to the invasions of the Norsemen and the Magyars that none but the Saxons, of all the Germanic tribes the least affected by the incursions, the most vigorous, the least permeated by the spirit of old Roman Christianity, could take serious action against the invaders. And when the last scions of the Carolingian dynasty had died, the Germanic tribes reverted to their old practice of electing their national kings. After the death of their first choice, Conrad of Franconia, they handed the royal crown to the Duke of Saxony, Henry the Fowler.

It was this forcible ruler and his successor Otto I who in several expeditions liquidated the Magyar peril, and finally quelled their nomadism at the battle of Lechfeld in 955. But Otto I did not follow the example set by Charlemagne who so thoroughly massacred the Avars that they vanished from history for ever. Instead he preferred to leave the Magyars alone, made sure of the Czechs' submission and their military support and then turned against the Slavs on the Elbe. The river was crossed and the first wave of what the Germans were pleased to call their *Drang nach Osten*, or drive to the East, swept over Slavonic land, ravaging with fire and sword the territory that was destined to be the future site of Berlin, Prussia and the new Germany.

It was in the course of this drive that the Germans for the first time came up against the Poles and were surprised at the existence between the Bober, the Warta, the Vistula and the Oder rivers of a vigorous confederation of Slavonic tribes, possessed of all the features of a solid political organisation and ruled by a gallant prince, Mieszko I. In point of fact, it was the race to the Baltic through Pomerania, occupied at the time by Slavonic tribes belonging to the Polish group, and coveted by Germans and Poles alike, with Mieszko I as easy first, that brought the Poles to the fore and into the orbit of German interests. From that time, the German annalists reported on the Poles and their ruler in terms sufficiently expressive of the anger felt by contemporary Saxons at the unexpected obstacle; but unfortunately they were too vague and sometimes deliberately reticent about facts that would interest us. Their studied discretion gave rise to a number of problems on the origin of Mieszko, the building of his State and his relations with the Ottonian Empire that have been hotly debated by German and Polish scholars during the last decades, more especially in the years preceding the last conflict. These discussions will interest future historians, because, whether by accident or design, they served as an ideological introduction to a world conflict.

But memories of the faded glories of the Frankish Empire still haunted the German tribes, now federated into a new German kingdom, and the temptation to revive the past proved too strong for Otto I. Saxons and other Germans resurrected the Empire of Charlemagne with Otto I as its first Emperor, successor of Charles the Great and heir to all his ambitions. The Roman Empire of the German nation was born, but the designation is of a much later date. So deeply was the name of the Franks venerated by the Germans that, in donning his royal robes, Otto I actually imagined himself to have become a Frank.

It proved, however, impossible to realise Charlemagne's full ambition and to extend the new Empire according to this plan. West Francia stayed outside. But it was essential to bring Lombardy under control and to lend support to the popes and their tottering Patrimony of St. Peter. Byzantium was blocking all further progress towards the south, and in the end Otto was only too glad to come to a compromise with a state the power of which inspired respect as far as Italy, and to marry his son to a Byzantine princess. Croatia was too strongly entrenched in its new position and Bulgaria was again in Byzantium's power. But there were immense possibilities in the eastern territories between the Elbe, the Gulf of Finland and the Dnieper, which teemed with numerous Slavonic tribes, mostly pagan and not sufficiently coherent to offer serious resistance to any systematic penetration. Otto I seized his opportunity with both hands and in obedience to his imperial mission as champion and propagator of the Christian faith, he founded the archbishopric of Magdeburg, intending to make that city the metropolis of all Slavonic lands. He did not forget even distant Russia of Kiev and included it in his imperial schemes, undaunted by the lamentable failure of his first attempt to christianise that pagan State.

Otto's plans provoked an unexpected reaction in Poland. To avert the danger of being absorbed with his lands into this scheme, Mieszko hastened to get his first missionaries, not from the Germans, but from the Czechs—the only Christian Slavonic nation in the West then in existence.

6

This was a clever move which the Emperor could not parry, since the Czechs were subjects of the Empire. Mieszko also found an unexpected ally in the Papacy which instinctively resented Otto's experiments in the religious field. The Pole thus succeeded in wrecking Otto's plans, considerably slowing up Germany's cultural and political infiltration towards the Slavonic East and, without knowing it, acting as a shield for the protection of Russia against German encroachments. Poland's first contact with the Holy See created a tradition in Polish history, which, owing to the need for both parties to have an ally against German claims, and to other circumstances, held firm throughout the Middle Ages and was a feature of Polish national life and foreign policy.

Otto I was thus able to realise his ambition only to a limited extent. He did not enjoy the satisfaction of surpassing Charlemagne, but he and his father Henry the Fowler are considered to be the co-founders of Germany's power in Europe. With the imperial notion which he revived, he bequeathed to Germany a valuable possession, as it gave the Germans the consciousness of a certain preponderance over all rising States, France and England not excluded. This conviction later turned out to be a dangerous weapon which Otto's successors learned to handle with skill in their drive to the Slavonic East.

But the bequest carried a liability—Italy, and Otto II learned more about it than he would have wished when he died in Calabria fighting Saracens and Byzantines. He was the first of a long series of German kings, dukes, knights and warriors who in the following centuries were to obey the call of the South and to drench with their blood and strew with their bones the fertile plains of Lombardy and the sunburnt fields of Southern Italy. There seemed to be something uncanny which allured the sons of the Germanic North to the blue skies of the South, where Lombards, Goths and Vandals had paid the penalty of extinction and the Germans only ventured at their cost.

Otto II's misfortune in Italy all but wrecked his father's life work. The subjugated Slavs on the Baltic and on the right bank of the Elbe revolted and in a few years undid the work of two Saxon kings. Of all the Slavonic nations subject to Henry I and Otto I, only the Slavs living between the Saale and the Elbe, and the Czechs, remained in the Empire. The Czechs, who had been Christians since the Moravian period and already boasted two saints—Wenceslas and his grandmother Ludmila, succeeded under Otto I's protection in annexing a substantial portion of the old Moravian Empire after the defeat of the Magyars. After Wenceslas' time, they supported, except for a short period, the Saxon dynasty and assisted Saxony in eliminating Bavaria from the direction of affairs in Germany. They still treasured remnants, saved from Great Moravia, of the Graeco-Slavonic culture which gave them a certain cultural level, superior in many respects to the Saxon standard of the time; but because of their geographical position, they found it impossible to form a rallying centre for the Slavonic tribes that remained independent. Thi task devolved on the Poles who were more numerous and were safely isolated

7

from Germany by the Czechs and the Slavs who occupied the right bank of the Elbe. Already Mieszko I was grouping round him all the Polish tribes, including the Pomeranians and the Silesians, and a great Slavonic empire was in the course of formation, incorporating the lands lying between the Elbe and the frontiers of Russia of Kiev.

Such was the position when Otto III came to power. This Graeco-Saxon half-breed displayed, in spite of the romantic dreams of his youth, astounding realism. Brought up in an atmosphere of Roman imperialism, with an instructor—Gerbert of Aurillac—who did all he could to feed his pupil on the glories of classical Rome, Otto fell under the spell of the medieval ideology that depended on the close partnership between the secular and spiritual powers to realise S. Augustine's ideal of the City of God on this earth. With his learned associate, Gerbert, now Pope Sylvester II, and with the encouragement of his friend Adalbert, Bishop of Prague, a commanding figure, unfortunately forgotten, of the imperial circle that gathered the best minds of the period round the Emperor, Otto III devised a new imperial conception.

He planned to give to all new nations and States in Europe the freedom to regulate their own affairs in return for their membership of his renovated Roman and Christian Empire. The conception was at once idealistic and realistic; it was the only scheme ever conceived by a German King for Central Europe and one that could have been accepted without fear by any new State, whilst to the German element in that part of Europe it allotted the place it deserved at the time as being the most vigorous and cultural power in Central Europe.

The plan met with enthusiastic response in Poland where in A.D. 1000 Boleslas the Great and his Poles greeted the Emperor as the head of Christendom. The foundation of the Polish national hierarchy, with Gniezno as its metropolis, was the reward for Poland's adherence to the renovated Roman Empire, and plans were drawn up in Rome and in Poland for the conquest for Christ of the Slavonic tribes dwelling between the Elbe and the Oder. Centres for the training of missionaries were opened in Rome, Ravenna and Gniezno, the whole venture bidding fair to become an international Christian crusade of German, Italian, Czech and Polish missions.

Hungary followed Poland's example when the Duke Stephen applied for admission to the new Christian Empire. Stephen was made King and received from the Emperor and the Pope permission to create bishoprics wherever he should consider it necessary. It was Adalbert of Prague and his disciples who deserved the credit for having paved the way for Christianity and the Emperor's ideology in Hungary. Even the Croats showed a willingness to join this universal Christian confederation. A new era dawned on Europe with Germany and the new States as the leading actors.

But the whole construction collapsed at the death of Otto III and the Pope, and with them vanished an interesting attempt to realise the ideal of the Middle Ages before it had time to mature. Henry II, Otto's successor, had not the mind for such lofty conceptions and was more interested in the expansion of German power over Central and Eastern Europe.

Then the first conflict, so often repeated since, broke out between Germany and Poland. Henry II jettisoned Otto's schemes and with characteristic German stubbornness concentrated all his energies on Poland's destruction. To the scandal and the indignation of contemporary Europe, he made an alliance with the pagan Slavs against the Christian Duke, thereby wrecking in the eyes of many the conception of the Emperor's ideal mission as head of Western Christendom and propagator of the faith.

The gallant Pole, on realising that Otto's ideals had been abandoned, broke away from the Empire and in the course of his struggle with Henry II, started building a Slavonic Empire extending as far as the Elbe. This created the possibility of a new political formation which, had it lasted, would have ended for good all notion of a Roman Empire under German leadership and blocked for ever the Germans' eastern drive beyond the Elbe. As such a Polish-Czech combination would have raised a power able to deal with Germany on equal terms and would have drawn other political units in Central Europe, chiefly Hungary, into its sphere, the whole course of Europe's history would have been altered. But the plan was wrecked. The Czech dynasty refused to look beyond its own immediate interests and, with the assistance of Henry II, recovered possession of Bohemia. The goal was lost and the Germans won the first great battle of Central Europe.

Such was the background, hastily sketched, to one of the most eventful periods in the history of Central Europe, the consequent results reaching stability in the tenth and the beginning of the eleventh century: Central Europe remained divided for centuries, with Germany as the dominant factor. As the foundations of the following centuries were laid at this stage, it deserves special examination. If a structure cracks under the pressure of a storm, the architects would be well advised to probe the foundations before planning new erections.

But the study of this period is none too easy, as its problems bristle with national jealousies, and information is meagre. No historical record gives us commentaries on the events in any systematic and historical order. The close of the sixth century saw the last of the Greek and Latin historians trained in the old classical school, and times did not favour the survival of their tradition. The last Roman writers of the old Latin stock had died out by the beginning of the ninth century and their methods were tried by sons of barbarians who only learned half of what their masters knew. Hence chroniclers instead of historians set out to report on events which they considered of moment to the abbots, bishops, kings and emperors they were interested in, omitting facts of the utmost importance on which genuine historians would have lingered with delight. To make matters worse, the chroniclers are few, their information is often as jejune as their Latin, and as chancelleries were only in their infancy and directed by men

9

not grounded in the old Roman tradition, it is extremely difficult to find the necessary materials to complete our knowledge. Byzantium unfortunately offers little to fill in the gaps, not being interested in so distant a theatre of events; only the imperial writer, Constantine Porphyrogennetos, managed to save such information about those far-away countries, as was in the possession of the Byzantine Foreign Office, but his materials must be treated with caution. As the Slavonic nations, with the exception of the Czechs, had not yet developed their own literature, we have in most cases to fall back upon German data which, in the matter of a German struggle with pagan Slavs, could scarcely be considered to be detached. By a stroke of good luck, Arab writers have left us some data to supplement knowledge gathered elsewhere. It all goes to explain why this period has not yet received the attention it deserves and why many of the events are treated so differently by different historians. A closer examination would therefore seem necessary for a better understanding of the evolution of Central and Eastern Europe.

CHAPTER I

DAWN OF SLAVONIC HISTORY AND RISE OF GERMANY

ORIGIN AND EXPANSION OF THE SLAVS—BYZANTIUM AND MORAVIA—
BOHEMIA AND BAVARIA—BIRTH OF MEDIEVAL GERMANY—WENCESLAS OF
BOHEMIA, HENRY I OF SAXONY AND ARNULF OF BAVARIA—THE FIRST WAVE
OF THE DRANG NACH OSTEN—HENRY I, BAVARIA AND LOMBARDY—OTTO I
AND THE GERMAN DUKES—GERMAN INTERVENTION IN FRANCE AND
LOMBARDY—OTTO'S SUCCESS IN BOHEMIA AND HIS VICTORY OVER THE
MAGYARS.

The leading feature of Central and Eastern Europe's evolution at the
vital period between the IXth and XIth centuries was the political
début of the Slavs. Not that they were newcomers to Europe's history,
but from that time onward they played their part on equal terms with
the Franks, the Germans and Byzantium, the heir of Rome. The reason
for the Slavs' late entry on the political stage, at a time when Italy, Spain
and Gaul had lived their normal lives for centuries, when even Britain
had made her contribution to Europe's progress, lay mainly in the remote-
ness of the Slav countries from Rome and from Byzantium, the main
centres of European civilisation. They were in this respect less favoured
than the ancient inhabitants of Western Europe and Britain and than
the Germans.

The original seat of the Slavs was situated further east, beyond that
of the Germans who originated from Scandinavia, Denmark and the
adjacent isles, whence they gradually overran, during the last millenary B.C.,
the countries later called Germania, and then started on their migrations.
Whereas there never was much uncertainty about the pre-historic home
of the Germans, problems concerning the cradle of the Slav race have been
a topic of debate among specialists since the beginning of the XIXth
century. In the general opinion of scholars, the birthplace of the Slavs
is to be found in the basin of the Pripet river(1), mainly on the plea that
this region lies outside the habitat of the beech tree, for which the
primitive Slavonic language lacks a term. But the modern Polish school of
Slavonic archeologists(2) has invalidated the argument by proving that at that

---

(1) I have discussed the main theories on the Slavs' origins in my book *Les Slaves,
Byzance et Rome au IXe siècle*, (Paris, 1926), pp. 1sq., Cf. especially L. Niederle's *Manuel
de l'Antiquité Slave*, Paris, 1923, I, pp. 13-26, which is a summary of this authority's great
work on Slavonic archeology published in Czech.

(2) Especially J. Czekanowski, *Introduction to the History of the Slavs* (in Polish), Lwów,
1927 ; id. The ethnographical differentiation of Poland in the Light of the Past, (in Polish)
Proceedings of the Polish Academy vol. XI, Cracow, 1935, pp. 64-67. See also : "The Racial
Structure of Silesia," by the same author, in *Baltic and Scandinavian Countries*, vol. III,
Toruń-Gdynia, 1937pp. 227-237, Kozłowski L., "Lusatian Culture and the problem of the
Origin of the Slavs," (in Polish) *Memorial of the* IVth *Congress of Polish Historians held at
Poznań ;* Lwów, 1925 ; do. Maps of Lusatian Culture), *Kwart. Histor.* XL, Lwów, 1926; do.
The Venedae in Historical Sources and in the Light of Prehistoric Cartography, Lwów,
1937. These works are all in Polish, without summaries in other languages.
Reports on important excavations made by another specialist, Prof. J. Kostrzewski

early pre-historic period, climatic conditions were different in this part of Europe, and also that the region lying between the Elbe and the Oder, the Vistula and the Bug lay outside the beech area. Since excavations in the marshy Pripet region have yielded no tangible results, so that any dense settlements in this area in prehistoric times, are by implication excluded, we must locate the Slavs' place of origin nearer to that of the Germans and the Balts *i.e.* between the Elbe, the Vistula, the Oder and the Bug rivers. If such be the case, the culture of high level, the remnants of which archeologists have discovered in this region and creators of which have so far remained unknown, should be attributed to the primitive Slavs.

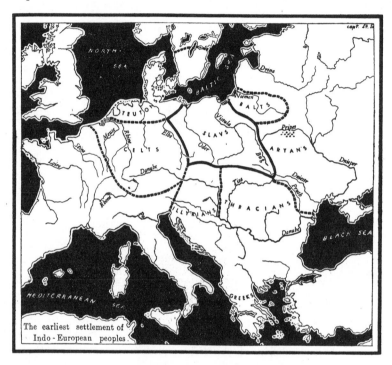

The earliest settlement of Indo-European peoples.

That this primitive civilisation, called by archeologists " Lusatian culture," should have suddenly vanished about B.C. 500 could only be explained by the hostile intrusion of a strong invader, apparently the Scythians, who were probably an Iranian people living in the south of modern Russia and well known to Greeks and Romans(3). Their destructive irruption must have encouraged neighbouring tribes also to encroach on territory so far occupied by the Slavs. Bohemia, Moravia and the territory of the

may be found in English in *Antiquity*, vol. XII, 1938, pp. 311-317 ; and by the same author in *Baltic Countries*, vol. I, Torun, 1935, pp. 228-232. Prof. T. Sulimirski summarised his colleague's findings in a booklet published in Polish in 1941, *The Oldest History of the Polish Nation* (in Polish), and in his *Germany and Poland*, London, 1943, pp. 7-17.

(3) That is how Prof. T. Sulimirski explains the numerous relics of Scythian civilisation found in the area of Lusatian culture. His arguments, as detailed in his study " Scythian Antiquities in Central Europe" *The Antiquaries' Journal*, vol. XXV, 1945, pp. 1-2 seem convincing.

Upper Vistula, with part of Silesia, were occupied by Celts, whilst the territory extending to the Oder was occupied by Germanic tribes. These Germanic conquerors must have been living for a long while in close contact with the Slavs to be in some instances absorbed and assimilated by their prolific subjects(4). As may be gathered from the relics of civilisation found in this territory, the Slavs gradually recovered from the blows and better days dawned for them in the first century B.C., when they developed a new type of culture called by archeologists Venedian, which mainly flourished in the first century of our era. Not till then did the movement of expansion towards the West and the South recommence among the Slavs.

Slavonic infiltration from the Upper Vistula and the Upper Bug into the modern Ukraine must have started as early as 500 B.C., or before the Scythian invasion. It gathered momentum in the direction of the Dniester and the basin of the Dnieper after the Slavs had recovered. But the main invasion of the Russian plains must have taken place in the first centuries of our era. Before those Slavs who had moved eastward coalesced into the eastern group of Russians, Ukrainians and White Russians, they were divided into many tribes—Dulebians, Tivercians, Ulichians, Polianians, Derevlians, Dregovichians, Severians, Radimichians, Krivichians, Viatichians and Slovianes—whose home was on the Upper Dvina. Some of these came under the influence of Sarmatian tribes that had been driven there, probably by the Huns. Outstanding among them was the tribe of the Antes, its ranks swelled by those Slav subjects who adopted their name in the fifth and sixth centuries, as recorded by the Byzantine writers who dealt with this period. Two other Sarmatian tribes akin to the Antes, the Croats and the Serbs, penetrated even further. The Croats seem to have gathered the Slavonic tribes of Galicia, Silesia and part of Bohemia into a sort of State, the White Croatia of Constantine Porphyrogennetos, whilst the Serbs imposed their rule on the Slavonic tribes between the Elbe and the Saale rivers(5).

Previous to this, from the third century of our era onwards, Slavs had started migrating through the Carpathian Mountains into what is now Hungary, in the direction of the Danube and of the Roman frontiers. The troubles created in those regions by the Asiatic invaders, especially the Huns and the Avars, only accelerated the transformation, chiefly in the fifth and sixth centuries. The Avars, probably a Turkish tribe (Uigurs) that had adopted the name of its masters, destroyed the empire of the Antes and forced the Slavonic tribes to swarm southwards either on their own initiative or under Avar leadership. They broke through the

---

(4) The influence of the Goths was particularly noticeable at the early period of the Slavs belonging to the Polish group, but it is not established that the Goths stayed in this territory before they set out towards the Lower Danube. They may also have reached that country from their new settlement in southern Russia, and the Gothic element may have been reinforced among the Polish Slavs after the Goths had been defeated and scattered by the Huns.

(5) For further details, see *infra*, Appendix II, pp. 277 seq.

Roman outer defences, crossed the Danube, the Sava and the Drava, swept over the ancient Roman provinces of Pannonia and Illyricum, finally to halt at the gates of Constantinople(6).

Slavonic expansion also struck out towards the west and to the south. These Slavs must have occupied parts of the Baltic coast from the beginning, which would explain why Pliny the Elder (7), Tacitus (8) and Ptolemy (9) located them (they called them Venedi) near the mouth of the Vistula and why Ptolemy spoke of "the Baltic sea of the Venedi." Their expansion to west and south must have been slowed down by the Scythian invasions and their aftermath ; but on recovering, the Slavs set out again towards the Elbe and the Saale rivers, forded them at several points and came up against German tribes which were also on the move. The tribes of the Wagiri and of the Obodrites occupied the whole region from the Danish border, along the Baltic Sea and the Elbe, to the lower Oder ; the Veletians took possession of the country between the middle Elbe and the middle Oder, while the Lusatians, the Daleminzi and other tribes known as the Sorabs or Serbs swarmed and settled between the Saale and the Bober rivers. Some tribes pushed on further to settle along the whole length of the Elbe from Magdeburg to Hamburg. Slavonic settlements are known to have existed round Brunswick, near the sites of Fulda, Gotha and Erfurt, being particularly numerous between Bamberg on the upper Main and Regensburg on the Danube.

Whilst the southern Slavs were taking possession of the Balkans, those known to-day as Czechs and Slovaks hailing from the north—the Elbe, the Oder and the Vistula—were already in occupation of the land of the old Celtic Boii (whence the name of Bohemia), which the Germanic Marcomans and the Quades had only just vacated. Only the tribes belonging to the Polish branch clung to their original habitat.

The Slavs' migration to Central and Eastern Europe was completed in the seventh century, the only possible time when they were in a position to take a hand in the making of Europe. Naturally, only those Slavonic tribes that were nearest to the cultural centres of the Europe of those days could be expected to transmit to other Slavs less favourably situated the cultural inheritance of Europe. Unfortunately for them, they were forced to mark time for two centuries by the arrival of the Avars. These, after laying waste the province of Illyricum, settled in what is now Hungary and imposed their rule thence on all the Slavonic tribes living in the Balkans, the Alps, Bohemia, Moravia, on the Drava and the Sava. As long as these nomads remained in occupation of the Danubian basin, geographically the pivot of Central Europe, it was impossible for the Slavs to contribute to the shaping of Europe's destiny. Avar domination was

(6) For more details on the Slavonic and Avar invasions of the Byzantine Empire, see my book, *Les Slaves, Byrance et Rome*, pp. 3—19.

(7) *Naturalis Historia*, IV, 97 ; ed. L. Janus, Leipzig (Teubner), 1870, I, p.177.

(8) *De Origine et Situ Germanorum*, ch. 46 ; ed. E. Koestermann, Leipzig (Teubner), 1936, II, pp.247 seq.

(9) *Geographica* III, ch. 5, 7, 8 ; ed. C. Müller, *Claudii Ptolomaei Geographia* (Paris, 1883), vol. I, pp. 419, 421, 423. Cf. also E. L. Stevenson, *Geography of Claudius Ptolemy*, Translated into English (with an introduction by I. Fisher), New York, 1932.

not such as to crumble at a touch, but the Byzantines struck the first blow when they defeated the Avars with their Slavonic subjects and auxiliaries under the walls of Constantinople (A.D. 626). Then the ·Bulgarians, a Turanian race akin to the Huns and the Avars, hailing from the Volga and established north of the Danube, freed themselves from their Avar masters, crossed the Danube in 679 and settled among the Slavs of the Lower Danube. They offered them protection against the Avars and the Byzantines and set up in their midst the State that was to be Bulgaria.

The Slavs of the old province of Illyricum apparently emancipated themselves, as we shall see later in detail(10), with the help of the Croats and the Serbs. According to information recorded by the imperial writer Constantine VII " Porphyrogennetos "(11), the Emperor Heraclius befriended these two Sarmatian tribes, who were already Slavicised to a great extent but were as eager as ever for new adventures and, with their assistance, he liberated the province of Illyricum There again the Croats and the Serbs succeeded to the Avars and brought within their own rule, under Byzantine suzerainty, the Slavonic tribes they had set free. That is how of all the Slavonic tribes settled in the south between the Alps, the Lower Danube and the Black Sea, only the Slovenes kept their name, all the others adopting the names of their masters—Sarmatian Croats, Serbs and Turkish Bulgars.

An interesting attempt to group the Slavs of the Alps, of Bohemia and Moravia into a semblance of a State was made by the legendary Samo. He is often taken for a Frank. At any rate, he had freed his subjects from the Avar yoke, but his work did not survive him(12).

All this explains why the Slavs failed to make themselves felt in the councils of Europe between the sixth and ninth centuries, and why their neighbours in Central Europe, the Germanic tribes of Tacitus' *Germania*, had got the start of them. But whereas the Slavs of Central Europe found themselves cut off from all cultural centres(13), their brethren in the south were more lucky, being near Byzantium, the only centre of civilisation that was in advance of Rome. Despite the onslaughts delivered by the invading Slavs, the Byzantine Empire remained faithful to its Christian and cultural mission—so much so that rather than call back its legions from the East, where the fiercest enemies of Christian civilisation, the Persians and after them the Moslem Arabs, were trying to force the defences, it preferred to suffer the loss of its western provinces. This gave the Southern Slavs a respite of two or three centuries to consolidate their positions. Bulgaria was the first to step into prominence under its Khagans, who put up a strenuous defence to safeguard the political independence of their State against Byzantium. But the Bulgars succumbed

---

(10) See pp. 286 seq.
(11) *De Administrando Imperio*, chs. 30-33, Bonn, pp. 140-61. Cf. J. B. Bury's edition of the main passages in his " Slavonic Settlements " *Texts for students*, No. 18, (London, 1920).
(12) I have been unable to consult the latest study on Samo, published by C. Vanderlinden in *Revue Belge de Philologie et d'Histoire*, (1933), t. XII. The author seems to favour the opinion that Samo was a Czech.
(13) Cf. for further details the first chapters of my book, *Les Slaves, Byzance et Rome au IXe siècle*, (Paris, 1926).

to Byzantine cultural superiority when in the middle of the ninth century Boris-Michael, the first Christian Khagan, opened Bulgaria to Christianity and Greek culture. So, at the beginning of the tenth century, when in the original Slavonic home on the Oder and the Vistula, Ziemomysl, the legendary ancestor of the first Polish Duke known to history, Mieszko, was gathering the Polish tribes into some sort of a political unit which Mieszko I developed into a State, Bulgaria had already reached the summit of its power and its greatest Khagan, Tsar Simeon, was hammering at the gates of Constantinople with his warlike boyars, making a bid for the imperial crown.

*   *   *

The position of the Western Slavs was less fortunate. In their expansion towards the west and south-west, they did not find themselves confronted by a secular tradition and a deeply rooted Christian culture such as that of Byzantium. Instead, they came up against the young Frankish Empire, which had dared to usurp the title of heir to Rome. This State was vigorous and dynamic, half barbarian, lacking every kind of tradition, only recently christianised, but intensely proud of its Christianity. Charlemagne had extended its power as far as the rivers Sava, Danube and Elbe, and that way lay the direction of its future thrust.

The danger threatening the Western Slavs was made even more menacing by their contact with the eastern part of the Empire— the future Germany—the part least affected by the influences of Roman and Christian culture. The Saxons, the most powerful of the German tribes and the latest to be converted to Christianity, had been forced by Charlemagne to join the Empire. And their own tastes encouraged them to think of expansion in terms of force of arms ; and indeed, in the newly embraced Christian faith they found a ready pretext for such instincts, for all Europe in those days was prepared to consider aggression as justifiable proselytising zeal.

It looked, however, as though Byzantium would be able to confine this expansion to definite limits. The Croats, in fact, owed their national existence to their proximity to Byzantium. Frankish culture did not have the same fascinating effect on them, since they possessed on the Adriatic coast some scattered remnants of the old Roman tradition in the cities of Zara, Spalato, Doclea, Ragusa and Dyrrhachium (Durazzo) which had survived under Byzantine rule. Coveted by both sides, these Latin centres served to sustain what culture was left in Illyricum. This gave the Croats sufficient self-reliance to withstand the pressure of the Franks, and the Dalmatian Croats the strength to win and maintain their complete independence.

The Franks attempted to penetrate through Croat territory between the rivers Sava and Drava as far as Bulgaria ; but there they were too near Byzantium to feel comfortable. Furthermore, when in the first half of the ninth century, after the destruction of the Avar Empire by

Charlemagne, Prince Moimir succeeded in uniting the Moravian tribes and showed a determination to resist Frankish penetration, Byzantium was presented with an unexpected opportunity for extending its rule to the remote regions of Central Europe and thus checking, at least temporarily, the programme of Frankish expansion.

Rastislav, the successor of Moimir, eventually brought to a halt the push of the Franks towards the Tatras, the high peaks of the Carpathian Mountains. About A.D. 835, the archbishop of Salzburg consecrated a church at Nitra, the place that marks the north-easterly limit which the Franks reached. Shortly after this date, Rastislav expelled Prince Privina from Nitra and joined his territory, which included the major part of modern Slovakia, to Moravia. By thus removing for ever the danger of a Frankish attack from the south upon the Polish tribes, he rendered Poland a signal service.

Some time later, Louis the German, endeavouring to smash Rastislav's growing power, made an alliance with the Bulgars whose empire touched the territory of Rastislav on the Tisza river. But Rastislav warded off the danger by a surprising counter move. In 862 his envoys arrived in Byzantium to offer the Emperor Michael III a military and cultural pact. The offer was accepted and the new alliance directed against the Bulgars. Its provisions were carried into effect in the year 864 when the Bulgarians, moving towards Moravia in order to help Louis the German's army, were surprised by a Byzantine military force and obliged to capitulate.

The cultural part of the treaty with Byzantium was to be sealed by a special mission headed by two brothers from Thessalonica, Constantine-Cyril and Methodius, both distinguished representatives of the cultural renascence in Byzantium in the ninth century. The move was important. If the mission could be adequately fulfilled, it would have a decisive influence not only on the destiny of the Slavs, but also on the whole future evolution of the West and of the Western Church. What these Greek missionaries actually did was to found in Moravia a Slavonic Church with Roman rites, but in the Slavonic language, and to compose for the benefit of the Slavs a special alphabet called *Glagolitsa*, which later, in the tenth century, was replaced by a new alphabet called *Cyrilitsa*, the medium still used to-day by the orthodox Slavs. Their activities in Moravia provoked the keenest interest even in Rome where Popes Hadrian II and John VIII perceived that such a work provided them with the best possible means to check the dangerous expansion of the German Church, which was then coming to a realisation of its strength. So they accepted and confirmed the innovation and even went so far as to revive for the benefit of Methodius the ancient diocese of Sirmium (Sriem in Croatia), and join to it the whole of ancient Pannonia and Moravia(14).

The sensational innovation marked a break with the usual practice of the Roman See. Even the territory which at a later period formed

---

(14) I have treated this subject in detail in my book *Les Légendes de Constantin et de Méthode vues de Byzance*, (Prague, 1933), pp. 249-83.

part of Poland came in some measure under this new ecclesiastical redistribution. Svatopluk, the successor of Rastislav, extended his empire not only over Bohemia and towards the Elbe, but also further east. The Old Slavonic Legend of S. Methodius(15) has left us the account of how Svatopluk overpowered a certain prince on the Vistula river. This is a record of some interest, since it reveals what was happening at this time among the Slavonic tribes adjoining the Czechs and Slovaks of Bohemia, Moravia and northern Hungary, who then formed a single group with a common language. The political combination of the Vistulanians could be nothing but the remnants of the empire once founded by the Croats on the northern slopes of the Carpathians, surviving somehow, though weakened by the emigration of a substantial portion of the Sarmatian upper class, until in the ninth century it was forced to submit to the ruler of Moravia. Svatopluk at last succeeded in gathering the remnants of this empire under his sway, and as the easternmost frontiers of his empire must have touched the Upper Bug and the Styr(16), he annexed all the territories between these rivers and Cracow and Silesia, which had very probably formed the bulk of White Croatia.

The above should be borne in mind, if we wish to understand European developments in the centuries that followed. It explains the first entry into recorded history of the territory destined later to form the southern part of Poland, and entitles us to infer that the Greco-Slavonic culture and the Slavonic liturgy, once introduced into Moravia by Constantine-Cyril and Methodius, found their way into future Polish territory.

This was the Slavs' first great contribution to the making of Central Europe, here only recorded in brief(17). Great possibilities were thrown open. Had Great Moravia and the Church of Constantine-Cyril and Methodius only endured longer, the shaping of Central and Eastern Europe would have run along different lines. A great Slavonic Empire was rising to claim its place by the side of the Frankish Empire which was then, though past its zenith, still strong enough ; and what was even more important, this new empire based on a Slavonic adaptation of Greco-Byzantine culture had a contribution to make to the education of ninth-century Europe. Such a power would have provided a convenient centre around which all the western and some of the southern Slavonic tribes would have developed. East Francia, or later Germany, would have found it difficult to move its frontiers far beyond the Elbe river, and this great waterway might possibly have kept the Germanic and the Slavonic worlds apart for ever, as it did in the ninth century.

Promising as they were, these possibilities were never fully realised : Arnulf, the ruler of East Francia, frustrated them with his Magyar alliance.

(15) Chapter XI. See the French translation of the Legend in my book *Les Légendes* . . . p. 389.

(16) For more details, see *infra* Appendix II, pp. 277 seq.

(17) I have dealt with it in full in my previous works *Les Slaves, Byzance et Rome* (Paris, 1928), and *Les Légendes de Constantin et de Méthode* (Prague, 1933).

When the hordes of nomadic invaders had swept over the Carpathians, Velehrad, the capital of the last ruler of Moravia, Moimir II, was so thoroughly destroyed that to-day its very site is still a topic of controversy among archeologists. Yet the work of Moimir I and Svatopluk was not as utterly annihilated as is generally believed. We shall see later that the rising Czech State boldly claimed the succession of the Moravian Empire and that the Przemyslide princes considered themselves to be the heirs of the Moimir dynasty, a claim which the Polish Piasts disputed in the eleventh century. It will then appear how much the introduction of Christianity into Hungary owed to the remnants of the Moravian Church.

The cultural work of the two Greek missionaries survived the political disaster of Moravia and continued for centuries to leaven the life of Bohemia. It took over two centuries to stamp out the Slavonic liturgy introduced by the Greeks and even so, the Czechs never forgot the Slavonic origin of their Christian faith. The Slavonic liturgy as used in Moravia still survives in Dalmatia, whilst the Bulgarians adapted it to the eastern rite and transmitted it to the Russians and the Serbs. The case is unique in history. This cultural survival would seem to prove that the political possibilities for Great Moravia were less purely utopian than is generally believed. However, as things turned out, the first Slavonic attempt to organise Central Europe was defeated by the Magyar invasion. The next attempt was to come not from the Slavs, but from East Francia, the forerunner of Germany.

* * *

The Magyars took good care not to let Arnulf and his successor Louis the Child clamp East Francia's hegemony on the remains of the Moravian Empire ; they held fast to the Danubian plain, which suited their nomadic instincts and, little as they felt interested in the hilly regions at the foot of the Carpathians where religious and cultural life apparently suffered nothing worse than a set-back. They held modern Slovakia and Moravia under strict political control; they also made an end of Bulgarian supremacy over the lands between the river Tisza and the southern part of the Carpathians—modern Transylvania—and showed little regard for Frankish possessions in Pannonia which extended between the Alps, the Danubian bend and the Sava river. The flourishing Frankish colonies in this region were the first to fall a prey to the Magyar hordes as they moved out on their devastating raids. East Francia had good reasons to regret opening the door of Central Europe to such uncouth allies, and contemporary chronicles of East and West Francia in reporting the devastations wrought by the new scourge of Western Europe call Arnulf by some very hard names(18). What little profit the Franks had derived from the destruction of the Moravian Empire was soon outweighed by the damage inflicted on Frankish interests. The Magyars were as difficult to handle as

---

(18) For more details on the Magyar invasions, see the book by R. Lüttich, " Ungarnzüge in Europa im 10. Jahrhundert " (Berlin, 1910), *Historische Studien*, Heft 84.

the Moravians and their first contact with European life proved disastrous to the whole West, whilst their occupation of the Danubian basin hastened, the disintegration of the West into a multiplicity of national units and drafted the first outline of Central Europe's present pattern.

Only one corner of the Moravian Empire definitely stayed under Frankish supremacy—Bohemia. This country had been occupied by the Bavarians after they had ousted the Celtic Boii, before the arrival of the Czechs ; and when they took possession of the lands between the Bohemian Forest, the upper Danube and the northern slopes of the Alps, their western neighbours called them " the men from the country of the Boii "— Baiuvari(19). Thus the names " Marcomans " and " Quades " of the Germanic tribes that settled in those territories were forgotten and both the country the Bavarians left—Bohemia—and the country they occupied— Bavaria—received names that recalled the Celtic Boii who once were the occupants of Central Europe.

The country that fell to the Bavarians benefited by the preservation to a certain extent of Roman civilisation. Many a cultural monument still recorded the presence of the Roman legions on the Danube in the former province of Rhaetia and kept Roman tradition alive, faintly recalling its survival on the Rhine and in Gaul. The Bavarians had been evangelised by Irish, Scots and Anglo-Saxon missionaries, and a first contact with them opened the Czechs' eyes to the high degree of civilisation which Roman Christianity had to offer, prompting them to share in the same benefits. Bavarian missionaries must have been active in Bohemia during the first half of the ninth century and this with satisfactory results. Some of the missionaries certainly knew the Slavonic language, as Slav settlements were still numerous in Bavaria at the time, and the Slavs in Bavaria had been baptised under Charlemagne(20). We learn from the Annals of Fulda that in 845 fourteen chiefs of the Slavonic tribes living in Bohemia made their appearance in Regensburg, surrounded by their primitive followers, and applied for baptism(21). This step, apparently the result of free decision, proves that the Slavs of Bohemia were not only, as pictured by early Frankish chronicles, fierce and redoubtable warriors, but also possessed an appreciable degree of political wisdom.

But Bavarian Christian influence was doomed to be short-lived, for soon after 845, political relations between Bavaria and Bohemia must have deteriorated, as we hear of bloody encounters between Bavarians and Bohemians. The Annales Xantenses place the clash in the year 849(22) and suggest that the Bavarians were to blame for the rupture. But the Slavs

---

(19) On the nature and organisation of the life of the Baiuvari from their first occupation of Bavaria till the days of Charlemagne, cf. S. Riezler, " Die Landnahme der Baiuwaren," Sitzungsber. d. Bayer. Akad. d. Wissensch., Phil. Hist.. Kl. (München, 1921).

(20) On the Christianisation of the Slavs of the left bank of the Elbe, cf. A. Hauck, Kirchengeschichte Deutschlands (Leipzig, 1900-1920), vol. II (2d ed. 1900), pp. 339-43). Vol. I by the same author deals with the Christianisation of the Germans.

(21) M.G.H.S., I, p. 364 : Hludovicus quatuordecim ex ducibus Boemanorum cum hominibus suis Christianam religionem desiderantes suscepit et in octavis theophaniae baptizari jussit.

(22) M.G.H.S., II, p. 229.

got the better of the fight and the annalist deplores the consequences of a misunderstanding so detrimental to Christianity. But the subject was too unpleasant for a Bavarian to enlarge on it.

It is justifiable to infer that, in consequence of the Bavarian attack and the Czech victory, the Bohemians severed relations with the Franks and that the breach facilitated the penetration of Moravian influence into Bohemia. What encouraged this country's orientation to the Moravian Empire was the fact that the Moravians had something more than the Bavarians to offer the Bohemian Slavs—the Slavonic liturgy, Slavonic letters and the much higher culture derived from Byzantium with which not even Rome dared to compete. As this novel form of Christianity proved much more popular and attractive to the Slavs, those of Bohemia embraced it with eagerness and soon forgot the first sample of Christianity hailing from Bavaria. Of this, the national tradition in Bohemia knows nothing and only the Bavarian historical sources have kept the record of the Bavarian missionaries' first promising successes in that country.

It thus came about that Borzivoy, the first known Christian Duke of Bohemia, together with his wife Ludmila, received baptism at the hands of S. Methodius. On his return from the court of Svatopluk to his own residence at Levy Hradec and Prague, he was accompanied by Slavonic priests carrying with them Slavonic liturgical books. At that moment, Bohemia stepped into the sphere of Byzantine influence and Greco-Slavonic culture.

Contact with Bavaria was resumed by Bohemia at the end of the ninth century, when that country drifted away from the Moravian Empire, torn as it was by dissensions between Svatopluk's successor Moimir II and his brothers. Of this new orientation towards the Franks we learn some details from the Annals of Fulda. In the year 895, so we read there, the Bohemians appeared again at the Reichstag of Regensburg, led by Spytihniev and Vitislav, the first belonging to the Przemyslide ducal family which claimed some sort of suzerainty over all the Bohemian princes, and the latter probably belonging to the family of the Slavniks, the second reigning dynasty of that country. They were received with full honours by the King and renewed with the customary handshake their allegiance to the Frankish Empire as represented by the Duchy of Bavaria, their next-door neighbour(23). Bohemia's submission to the Franks naturally implied, at least in the eyes of the Bavarians, severance of all religious ties with the Moravian ecclesiastical organisation. She was incorporated into the diocese of Regensburg.

The final destruction of Great Moravia following soon after put an end to Bohemia's further fluctuations between the Franks and the Moravians. The Magyar danger naturally concerned Bohemia as well ; Vratislav, who succeeded to the Duke Spytihniev (915) presumably died in 920 or 921 in defending Bohemia against a Magyar invasion. Sharing the same danger, Bohemia and Bavaria drew closer together. As the ecclesiastical framework created in Moravia by archbishop Methodius and, after his death, by

(23) M.G.H.S., I, p. 411. For more particulars, see Appendix II, p. 277 seq.

Pope John IX's legates, was broken up, the jurisdiction of Regensburg over Bohemia remained uncontested. Yet, in spite of efforts to the contrary made by German priests, Bohemia clung to the Slavonic liturgy and letters and remained bi-liturgical for two centuries, the first half of the tenth century being the period when Slavonic liturgy and culture were at their best.

*　　*　　*

Such was the position in that part of Central Europe at the beginning of the tenth century. As Bohemia was unable single-handed to put up a serious defence against the Magyar menace, the task devolved on East Francia. A slow transformation had taken place in the Frankish Empire. Royal power had steadily declined under the last Carolingians and, with no central authority to organise common resistance to the invaders—Norsemen, Magyars and Slavs—the various provinces and tribes had to fall back on their own resources. Some nobles, mostly margraves, so impressed their tribesmen with their prowess and their capacity for organising military defence that they rose to prominence from the ranks of the German nobility, became the *de facto* military leaders and were acknowledged as the Dukes of the tribes of East Francia—Franks, Saxons, Suabians, Bavarians, Lotharingians and Thuringians—without, however, claiming descent from the old genuine tribal chiefs, since the Franks, on receiving their submission to the Empire, had pulled down their political and tribal framework(24). A similar modification went on in West Francia and in Italy, but only in East Francia did it reach its culminating point, as there the tribes, after the death of their Carolingian King, Louis the Child (899-914), instead of acknowledging the Carolingian king who still ruled in the West, preferred to break with the dynastic tradition and, using their ancestral right, elected in 911 Conrad, Duke of the Franks, to royal honours.

That was the year of medieval Germany's birth. The offer of the royal title to Conrad, Duke of Franconia, was but a sign of the old Frankish tradition overshadowing the cradle of Germany, and, powerful as they were, the Saxons willingly acknowledged it, since their choice of Conrad in Forchheim (10, 11, 911) (25) had been prompted by their own Duke Otto of Saxony. This magnate had annexed Thuringia where Saxon

---

(24) The rise of "stem-duchies" is a problem keenly debated among the historians of medieval Germany and among the best contributions to its solution are the following works : W. Varges, " Das Herzogtum," published in the collection dedicated to G. v. Below (*Aus Politik und Geschichte. Gedächtnissschrift für Georg von Below*, (Berlin, 1928), pp. 17-31) ; G. Läwen, " Stammesherzog und Stammesherzogtum " (Berlin, 1935), *Neue Deutsche Forschungen. Abteilung Mittelalterliche Geschichte*, Bd. I. ; E. Klebel, " Herzogtümer und Marken bis 900," *Deutsches Archiv für Geschichte des Mittelalters* (1938), vol. II, pp. 1-53 A good outline of the problem is to be found in G. Barraclough, " Medieval Germany," (*Studies on Medieval Germany*), vol. I, (Oxford, 1938), pp. 27-46. Cf. also his book on *The Origins of Modern Germany* (Oxford, 1946), pp. 16-46.

(25) On Conrad I, by F. Löher (König Konrad I und Herzog Heinrich von Sachsen, *Abhandl. d. Bayr. Akad.*, München, 1857) will still be found useful. The more recent work by Heidman, *König Konrad I*, Dissert. (Jena, 1922), I found unobtainable.

influence prevented the election of a new Duke in succession to Burchard, slain in battle with the Magyars in 908, and the combined pressure by the Duke and his Saxons steered the new course of events. The Suabians and the Bavarians accepted the King, whilst Lotharingia and Frisia, where the prestige of West Francia outbalanced that of the four prominent German tribes, remained faithful to the Carolingian tradition and acknowledged the authority of the King of West Francia, Charles III.

The new King's position was awkward from the outset. In vain did he try and force the Lotharingians to submit to his authority, and with the assistance of the Church, to undermine the position of the Bavarian duchy, where Arnulf (907-937), son of Liutpold, was in power. He did not interfere in the Suabian duchy and his endeavours to keep Thuringia as a unit separate from Saxony brought him into conflict with the powerful Duke Henry, successor of Otto.

Conrad saw that his failure was due to the weakness of his own duchy. As duchies spontaneously grew into independent units at the expense of royal authority, Frankish tradition proved inadequate as a centralising power, and on his return, fatally wounded, from his campaign against Arnulf of Bavaria, Conrad appointed as his successor the Duke of Saxony and instructed his brother Eberhard, his legitimate heir, to hand over the royal insignia to Henry of Saxony and make peace with him. With the consent of the Franks and the Saxons, Henry I thus became King of Germany, his appointment being confirmed by an election at Fritzlar in 918(26). By this decision Conrad gave evidence of good statesmanship and the year 918 stands out in history as another landmark in Germany's and Central Europe's coming of age.

The election was, however, repudiated by the Suabians and the Bavarians. The Duke Burchard II, who nursed ambitions to extend Suabia's sphere of influence across the Alps into Lombardy, was ready, with his eye on this goal, to accept Henry I as King on condition of being given a free hand in his manipulation of churchmen and their possessions. But the Bavarians were adamant and elected their own Duke as King of the *Regnum Teutonicorum*. This we learn from an important and newly discovered source, the *Annales Juvavensium Maiores*, where incidentally we find the first intimation that the designation for the German kingdom as *Regnum Teutonicorum* was already current at that early period(27). Unable to come to any agreement with the Bavarians, Henry I tried the sword and in 921 lay siege to Regensburg, to little purpose, as he had to mollify his opponent with important concessions, including full powers over the Bavarian Church and the exclusive right of coining money in his own dukedom. Arnulf agreed

---

(26) For details Cf. H. Heimpel, "Bemerkungen zur Geschichte König Heinrichs des Ersten," *Berichte über die Verhandlungen der Sächs. Akademie der Wissenschaaften Leipzig,* (1937), Bd. 88, Heft 4.

(27) Latest edition in 1937 by H. Bresslau, *M.G.H.S.*, XXX, pars 2, p. 742 : Bavari sponte se reddiderunt Arnolfo duci et regnare eum fecerunt in regno teutonicorum.—On Arnulf and his relations with Henry I, cf. Riezler, *Geschichte Baierns*, (Gotha, 1878,) vol. I, pp. 313-35. On Henry I and Arnulf's successes, *ibid.*, pp. 336-49. Cf. also M. Doeberl, *Entwicklungsgeschichte Bayerns* (München, 1906), vol. I, pp. 99 seq..

to relinquish his royal title, but continued to behave almost as the sovereign of his own territory.

Bavaria's attitude was such as to make royalty uneasy and Henry I, who was well aware of it, took every precaution to strengthen his own position, reduce the power of the other dukes, enforce his royal authority and thereby reduce the potential danger of Arnulf's quasi-independence. In this he was luckier than his predecessor, since Saxony could afford to be more helpful to him than Franconia was to Conrad. He secured recognition from Charles III, King of West Francia, then took advantage of the troubles that eventually ended in the rise of a new rival House in France founded by Hugh Capet and destined in course of time to eclipse the dynasty of the Carolingians(28). The Frisians made their submission and Giselbert, whose father Reginar had refused to give way to Conrad I, was confirmed in his ducal dignity(29). Henry was equally successful in Suabia(30). The Duke of the Suabians, Burchard II, in his anxiety to add northern Italy to his dominions, backed up his son-in-law Rudolph II, King of Burgundy, in his struggle with Count Hugh of Provence for the mastery of the Lombard kingdom; but the Duke fell in battle and Henry I promptly forced his own candidate and loyal supporter Hermann, cousin of the Duke of Franconia, on the unsuspecting Suabians. This was killing two birds with one stone, for the King's intervention not only made for his own security, but effectively nipped the duchies' tendency to grow into stem-duchies at the expense of his central power. It was the first instance of a king imposing on a duchy a duke of a different tribe. At the same time, Suabia formed an important link between Saxony, Burgundy and Italy, so that a tighter hold on this duchy gave Henry I or his successor every chance to take over the part which Burchard II was planning to play in Northern Italy. To improve matters, Henry recovered his royal supremacy over the Suabian Church which he had relinquished in exchange for Burchard's recognition.

* * *

But this left Bavaria's position untouched. Far from surrendering his quasi-independence, Arnulf had his eyes on his neighbourhood and only waited for the chance to claim Burchard's succession in northern Italy. In the meantime, he proceeded to take action in Bohemia without the least

(28) On the last Carolingian Kings in West Francia, cf. F. Lot, *Les derniers Carolingiens* (Paris, 1891), Bibliothèque de l'Ecole des Hautes Etudes, vol. 87.

(29) Cf. H. Holtzmann, *Kaiser Otto der Grosse* (Berlin, 1936), pp. 11-26., *Ibid.* pp. 206-8, detailed bibliographical indications on the reign of Henry I. Of the more recent publications on Henry I and his work, we may quote in particular : F. Lüdtke, *Heinrich I der Deutsche* (Leipzig, 1934), and *König Heinrich I* (Berlin, 1936) ; A. Cartellieri, *Die Weltstellung des Deutschen Reiches* 911-1047 (München, Berlin, 1932) ; A. Thoss, *Heinrich I, der Gründer des Ersten Deutschen Volksreichs* (Goslar, 1936), pp. 207-19 give an exhaustive bibliography ; on Henry's architectural activities, W. Radig-Elbing, *Heinrich I, der Burgenbauer und Reichsgründer* (Leipzig, 1937). Cf. also W. v. Giesebrecht, *Geschichte der Deutschen Kaiserzeit* (Braunschweig, 1873, 1875), vol. I, pp. 205 seq ; H. v. Sybel, *Entstehung des Deutschen Königtums* (Frankfurt, 1881) ; E. Rosenstock, *Königshaus und Stämme in Deutschland zwischen 911 und 1250* (Leipzig, 1914), G. Waitz, *Jahrbücher des Deutschen Reiches unter Heinrich I*, (Leipzig, 1885), Henry I and Lotharingia, *ibid.*, pp. 923 seq.

(30) On Suabia, see Lintzel, " Heinrich I und das Herzogtum Schwaben," *Hist. Vierteljahrschrift* (1929).

reference to the King. This country had been governed, after the death of Vratislav, by his wife Drahomira, a convert Veletian princess, who with some nobles carried on the Regency for her son Wenceslas I (920-929). Finding her influence undermined by her mother-in-law Ludmila, who had trained her grandson in the principles and practice of piety and wielded great authority over the young Duke and the country, Drahomira decided to gather the reins of government into her own hands and in 920 or 921 murdered her with the connivance of some semi-pagan reactionaries. The game was, however, not worth the candle, for her husband's party over-threw the murderess and proclaimed young Wenceslas the reigning Prince.

This palace revolution must have given Arnulf the chance he sought for a Bavarian coup, as some annalists refer to an expedition against Bohemia by Arnulf round about 922(31). The only plausible explanation of the puzzle, which has worried many a Czech and German historian, is the assumption that Arnulf still looked upon Bohemia as his own sphere of influence and was not going to allow anybody to meddle with Bohemian affairs, not even the Saxon duke, whom he had recently accepted as King of the *regnum Teutonicorum*. If that country was to be considered part of East Francia, *alias* Germany, it had to be linked to it *via* Bavaria and be attached to Arnulf's duchy.

It is also possible that the opponents of Drahomira's secular policy and of her party found support in Bohemia on the territory of another Bohemian dukedom, which was governed by the second ducal family, the Slavniks. On this supposition Bavarian intervention may have been provoked by the opposition, with Drahomira's dethronement and exile as the result. There is one detail that seems to point to this possibility: it appears that the reigning Duke of the Slavniks had married a daughter of the Bavarian Duke Arnulf, since, according to Bruno of Querfurt, the biographer of S. Adalbert, bishop of Prague and a Slavnik, this Saint's grandmother was Arnulf's daughter(32). So, it may have been on the pretext of this matrimonial connection with the second ducal family in Bohemia that Arnulf took a hand in Bohemia's domestic affairs.

Wenceslas's reign started thus under Bavarian auspices and the young Duke must have submitted to the patronage which Arnulf intended to exercise over Bohemia, if we may credit the evidence found in one version of the Slavonic Legend of S. Wenceslas(33). It attributes to the young prince the intention of building in Prague a cathedral church dedicated to S. Emmeran, a Patron of Bavaria and Arnulf's favourite saint. This version did attract the attention of experts, but since the church which Wenceslas started building was eventually dedicated to S. Vitus instead, the statement

---

(31) Cf. the discussion on the dates and the sources in V. Novotny's *Czech history* (in Czech, Prague, 1912), vol. I, p. 468. The short accounts of Auctarium Garstense (*M.G.H.S.*, IX, p. 565), in the Annales S. Rudberti Salisburgensis (*ibid.*, p. 771) and in the Annales Ratispo-nenses (*ibid.* XVII,, p. 583) are particularly striking, as all those sources place Arnulf's expedition in 922 and clearly differentiate it from Henry's and Arnulf's combined expedition in 929.

(32) J. Emler, *Fontes Rerum Bohemicarum*, vol. I, p. 267 (Prague, 1871).

(33) Latest edition by J. Vajs, *Collection of Old Slav. Literary Records of S. Wenceslas and S. Ludmila* (in Czech) (Praha, 1929), Cf. *F. R. B.* vol. I, p. 130.

M.   B

was generally put down to a copyist's error. But what if Wenceslas original intention was intended as a compliment to Arnulf?

How then did Wenceslas come to change his plan and dedicate his church to the Patron Saint of Saxony, S. Vitus? Very probably we should read the change as a pointer to what happened in Germany after Arnulf's successful Bohemian experiment. One may imagine that Henry I did not relish it and it certainly never had been his intention to let Bavaria's power grow out of all proportion or to countenance Arnulf's policy of a Bavaria taking Bohemia in tow in Germany's hypothetical interest. We have seen that Conrad had already tried to prevent the formation of duchies that would outstrip their neighbours, and Henry I was too realistic a statesman not to scent danger to his royal power, which it was his intention to identify with the Duchy of Saxony. Hence his efforts to bring Bohemia under the direct allegiance to the King of Germany and to Saxony.

The moment looked propitious about the years 926 and 927. Whereas the Magyars' persistent raids into Germany prevented Arnulf from consolidating his gains, Saxony had found protection in the nine-year armistice which Henry I concluded with the Magyars in 924 without including any other duchy in the stipulations. This gave him the necessary respite to take in hand the military re-organisation of his own duchy and of Thuringia and to introduce the *Burgwarde* system, consisting of fortresses commanding strategic points in various districts. Saxony's military importance grew apace, so that other dukes, less fortunately placed, began to take notice, not excluding Arnulf, who gradually began to appreciate the necessity for closer contact with Saxony. In fact, we hear that in 928 he attended the *Hoftag* at Ingelheim(34). Measures concerning the whole kingdom were then decided upon, the old system of popular military service was revived and thenceforth the military leadership of Saxony and the King was taken for granted.

We may then surmise that the ground was thus prepared for Henry I to show a bold front and approach Bohemia without arousing Bavarian suspicions. He must then have asked the Bohemian Duke to acknowledge his royal authority, a request Arnulf could not object to, since he himself had done the same; and Wenceslas was only too eager to oblige, as he and his counsellors considered it better for Bohemia to be under the supremacy of the King, whose duchy was more remote from Bohemia than Bavaria. Distance spelled safety. They even went further than Arnulf expected by exchanging Bavarian overlordship for the Saxon. All this may have happened about the year 926, Wenceslas not having started building his church previous to that date. As devotion must comply with politics, the Saxon Patron Saint S. Vitus (Guy) became the Patron of the cathedral of Prague and of Bohemia in preference to the Patron Saint of Bavaria.

Another important source may be quoted in support of our reading of the facts. By far the best Latin biography of S. Wenceslas was written by Christian, uncle of S. Adalbert and a Slavnik, in 992-994. There we read

---

(34) Annales Juvavensium Maiores, *M.G.H.S.*, XXX, 2, p. 743, Cf. G. Waitz, *Jahrbücher*, pp. 118 seq.

that Wenceslas was bound to Henry I by ties of close friendship(35). If this statement is true, we are left to suppose that the association was of some duration, a conclusion the chronicler Thietmar also points to when he writes that Wenceslas was loyal to Henry I and to God(36).

These facts are too often overlooked by Czech and German historians. Czech experts were slow in admitting Christian's authority and few dared to look for the solution of these puzzles of early Czech history in the history of Germany and the rivalry between Bavaria and Saxony. They deemed it more convenient to assume that Wenceslas' submission to Henry's rule had been forced on him in 929, when Henry I defeated and subjugated the Slavs between the Elbe and the Saale(37). Only a vague reference by the Saxon Chronicler Widukind might favour that explanation, as he mentions the submission of Prague after that of the Slavonic tribes on the middle Elbe, though his account should be taken cautiously, as his information on Wenceslas is of the scantiest. Though Widukind refers to Wenceslas on two different occasions(38), he does not even know his name. The expedition he mentions was aimed, as we shall see, not at Wenceslas but at his brother Boleslas. Our reading tallies better with the sources and throws additional light on the rivalry between Henry I and Arnulf in the new *Regnum Teutonicorum*. Bohemia did make a not inconsiderable contribution to Saxony's victory, since Wenceslas' ready acceptance of Henry's supremacy raised her status in the new German Empire, much to the detriment of Bavaria, whose decline, as subsequent events were to show, started with Bohemia's change of allegiance(39).

*   *   *

If we are right, then it must be assumed that Henry I started his victorious drive for the subjugation of the Slavonic nations adjoining the eastern frontiers of his kingdom from the south-east. For the Slavs of Bohemia were not the last, but the first Slavonic nation to acknowledge his authority before 928, the only difference being that the dukes of Bohemia, as Christian princes who since Charlemagne's time had looked upon their

---

(35) J. Pekař, *Die Wenzels—und Ludmila Legenden und die Echtheit Christians* (Prag, 1906), p. 111 ; Cui felix isdem amicus iungebatur assidue. In this work the author definitely established the authenticity of the Legend.

(36) Thietmar, Chronicon, II, ch. I, *M.G.H.S.*, N.S.IX, p. 38 : Nam Boemiorum ducem Wentizlavum Bolizlavus nefandus fratrem Deo ac regi perimens fidelem, restitit multo tempore audacter, et postea devictus est a rege viriliter.

(37) Cf. V. Novotný, *Czech history*, vol. I, pp. 467 seq.

(38) Widukind, Chronica Saxonum, I, ch. 35 ; II, ch. 3. *M.G.H.S.* in us. schol. (ed. P. Hirsch, A. E. Soliman) pp. 50, 51, 68.

(39) It was the merit of the greatest modern Czech historian J. Pekař, to put the history of Wenceslas in an entirely new light. His work, published in Czech in the *Antho ogy of S. Wenceslas* (Prague, 1934), pp. 1-101, especially pp. 18 seq., 38 seq., 71, is the best study on S. Wenceslas. Cf. also J. Cibulka's study in the same *Anthology*, "Wenceslas' Rotunda," pp. 232, seq., 342 seq. I think, however, it is erroneous to place Bohemia's change over to Saxony in the year 921, when Henry was trying to reduce Arnulph by force of arms. This struggle had nothing to do with Bohemia, or else Arnulph's intervention in Bohemia in 922 would be left without an explanation. Pekař omitted to follow up the parallel evolution in Germany with all its consequences, where alone the key to the solution of these problems is to be found.

allegiance to East Francia and the Frankish Empire as the logical concomitant of one single Christian Empire, voluntarily submitted to the new German King who in their estimation was the legitimate successor of the Frankish Empire.

In preparing for the defence of his kingdom against possible Magyar invasions, Henry I was bound to make sure of his eastern frontiers before risking the main attack. The Slavs on the right bank of the Elbe were worse than merely pagans, they were the determined allies of the Magyars, whom they often joined in their raids into Germany. In 928, Henry I felt confident and ready for his big campaign. Undaunted by winter conditions, his army crossed the Elbe and the frozen marshes of the Havel river, fell upon the Slavonic tribe of the Hevelians and captured their principal town Brunabor. Hunger and cold, says the Saxon chronicler Widukind (40), proved to be the best allies of the German sword in this campaign. Brunabor was then erected into a German burg and strengthened into an important Saxon outpost to keep watch and ward over the right bank of the Elbe, the corner stone of the history of Brandenburg and the first land mark of the German push to the east and the Polish lands. Followed the conquest of the Veletians, alternatively called Ljutici or Vilci, a powerful confederation (41) of Slavonic tribes settled between the middle course of the Elbe and the Baltic Sea, who were given no choice but to pay tribute. The same fate rapidly overtook the Obodrites and those Slavonic tribes whose home lay between the lower course of the Elbe and the Baltic, or modern Schleswig Holstein and Mecklenburg.

The Saxon army pursued its triumphal march up the Elbe towards the territory of the Sorabs or Serbs, occupants of the triangle formed by the Elbe and Saale rivers and the Bohemian Mountains (42). Henry had fought them in his youth. This time he completed his work, probably in the spring of 929, and forced them under his authority. Their capital Jahna was captured and a new city founded, to become the second important Saxon outpost, Meissen, on the territory of the Sorabian tribe of the Daleminzi.

Shortly after the submission of the Serbs between the Saale and the Elbe. Henry I was once again called upon to intervene in Bohemia. Wenceslas's reign is extolled by his numerous biographers as the reign of a saintly man, keen on the material, and especially, the spiritual welfare of his people as he was bent on raising its cultural level (43). But his policy must have provoked a certain amount of resentment and, though Bohemia had been a Christian country for several generations, the clergy's growing influence over the young Duke and the country must have been resented by the same party as had previously enlisted Drahomira's sympathies. There was no question

(40) I, ch. 35, *M.G.H.S.* in us. schol., p. 50.
(41) The name Ljutici or Vilci means " sons of the wolf." Vilk or vlk, *i.e.* wolf, was a common Slav synonym for ljuty or ferocious beast. On the character of the Veletian Confederation cf. K. Wachowski, Western Slavdom (in Polish), *Studia Hist.* vol. I (Warsaw, 1902), pp. 132 seq.
(42) Here we only touch on facts that are relevant to a clear picture of the rise of Germany. Of the origin and expansion of the Serbs there will be more to say in Appendix 2, p. 277.
(43) See my booklet on *S. Wenceslas, Duke of Bohemia* (Prague, 1929), where the reader will find an appreciation on numerous legends and a bibliography on S. Wenceslas.

this time of Drahomira's collaboration, since Wenceslas had recalled the lady from exile and lived with his mother on the best of terms; but the party had interested itself in Wenceslas' younger brother Boleslas, an impetuouss youth who was jealous of the Prince. When Wenceslas married and had a son(44), Boleslas lost all hope of succession and listened too readily to complaints. A plot was hatched which ended in tragedy. Wenceslas was on a visit to his brother Boleslas at his residence in Stara Boleslav, when in a quarrel and a scuffle between the two, Boleslas' over-zealous accomplices joined in and murdered Wenceslas at the entrance of the church.

The news of the murder spread like wildfire and reached the ears of the German King, Henry I, who must have gathered the impression that the new Duke intended to change his attitude to Saxony and the German Empire. Widukind's report, confirmed by many others, of a clash between the Saxons and the Czechs should most probably be dated, not from Wenceslas's days, but from the first year of Boleslas's reign. On realising that Boleslas was harbouring no such intentions and that the murder and the change on the Czech throne were merely a matter of private jealousy and internal policy, Henry I turned against the Slavs on the Elbe where his interests were in greater danger. This is how we can best explain Widukind's statement that Boleslas continued to live on good terms with Saxony as long as Henry I was alive (936) (45). Not till then did a clash occur between the Czechs and the Germans, and the war ended only in 950, when Boleslas I, as will be explained presently, made his submission to Otto I.

Although the motive of Wenceslas' murder was not altogether religious, Wenceslas was venerated by his contemporaries as a martyr to the Christian cause to which he had consecrated his life. By his death, the young Duke rendered a signal service to his nation and his country. News of miracles spread quickly through Bohemia and abroad. His first biography was written in Slavonic, but others, written in Latin, followed in Bohemia, Germany and Italy. The fact that the Przemyslides could count a saint among their relatives contributed to enhancing the importance of the Czech tribe and rendered possible the work of unification under his successors. The Christianity of the Czech State was thus fully recognised.

There remains one observation to make on the 929 expedition. Whereas Arnulf's participation in it, as mentioned by several Bavarian

---

(44) Such is the account of the Slavonic Legend mentioned above and recently published by J. Vajs. According to the Legend, Wenceslas was urged by his counsellors to marry and when he had a son, decided to live with his wife as brother and sister. For her being intimate with another man, Wenceslas had his marriage dissolved and made her marry her lover. This account has been generally rejected by Wenceslas' historians; but I consider it to be reliable, as it does not seem possible at that early period that any reigning prince could have been encouraged to be without issue. The legend that Wenceslas was unmarried and remained single originated later in the second half of the tenth century, when reformist ideas had penetrated into the circle that produced Wenceslas's biographers.

(45) Widukind, Chronica Saxonum, I, ch. 35, M.G.H.S. In us. schol., p. 50 : With the whole army he marched on Prague, city of the Bohemians, and received the king's submission. About him, some extraordinary things are told, but as we do not approve them, we prefer to pass them over in silence. He was, in any case, the brother of Boleslas, who remained faithful and useful to the Emperor the whole of his life. So, having made Bohemia into a tributary State, the King returned to Saxony. Cf. my study, " The First Wave of the Drang Nach Osten," published in the Cambridge Historical Journal (1943), vol. VII, No. 3, pp. 129-45.

sources, is beyond question, it yet appears that an armed clash occurred between the Czechs and the Germans before Boleslas had cleared up matters. How is one to reconcile this with what was said about the jealousy between Bavaria and Saxony over Bohemia ? But we should not forget that the Duke of Bavaria was under feudal obligation to the King and that, unable to prevent the growth of Saxon influence in Bohemia, he was certainly not going to let the Saxons act alone in Bohemia to the detriment of Bavarian prestige in that country. Placed in this light, his participation in the Bohemian expedition is in keeping with the course of events in Germany.

Henry's lightning mobilisation against Boleslas I, probably at the end of 929, will be better understood if we bear in mind what happened at the time of Wenceslas's murder, on the Elbe, in Bohemia's immediate neighbourhood. To face the growing menace of the dreaded Saxons, the threatened Slavonic tribes—Obodrites, Veletians and Sorbians (Serbs)—decided to form a coalition under the leadership of the Ratarians, the warlike clan of the Veletian confederation, who were the custodians of the Rethra, the Slavonic religious centre and shrine of the Slavonic pagan faith. It was this coalition which faced Henry at Lenzen on the right bank of the Elbe on September 4, 929. All contemporary and many subsequent German chroniclers have something to say of this great battle. The coalition was broken and its armies scattered and hunted down with a ruthlessness which then surpassed all precedents. According to the chroniclers, who often had but a sentimental conception of numbers, between 120,000 and 200,000 fugitives were slaughtered by the infuriated Saxons. No wonder then that Henry was seriously alarmed at the news reaching him from Bohemia and felt tempted to think that Boleslas's coup was of a piece with the Slavonic rebellion.

As a matter of fact, the Slavs were anything but pacified after their defeat in 929, and in 932 Henry had to send another expedition against the Slavs who lived between the Elbe and the Saale(46). His troops made their way up the Elster, engaged and routed them at Lebusa. This completed the subjugation of the Slavs between the two rivers and extended the sphere of German influence for the first time in history on the right bank of the Elbe towards the Oder.

The Obodrites lost their last hope of foreign support in their struggle with the Germans when Henry crushed the pagan Danes and established the tiny march of Schleswig in 934 for the protection of Saxony against further assaults from that quarter. After the defeat of the Danes the bishop of Hamburg set to work to convert them(47). The consequence was that the Duke of the Obodrites had to follow the Danes' example and accept Christianity. They also had to refuse the alliance offered to them by the Magyars. But the moment had come for Henry to deal with these. It had been, indeed, his life's ambition to rid the country of those fierce and dreaded

---

(46) For details, see W. Bogusławski, *History of the North-Western Slavs* (in Polish, Poznań, 1892), vol. III, pp. 235-48. G. Waitz, *Jahrbücher des Deutschen Reichs unter der Herrschaft König Heinrichs I* (Berlin, 1837), pp. 90 seq. ; Thompson, *Feudal Germany*, pp. 479 seq.

(47).Cf. A. Hauck, *Kirchengeschichte Deutschlands*, vol. III, pp. 80 seq.; F. E. Dahlmann, *Geschichte von Dänemark*, vol. I (Hamburg, 1840), pp. 73-87.

invaders, and his victory on the river Unstrut in 933 dealt them the first serious blow.

Henry's achievements in the lands of the Slavs, as German historians describe them, actually were *eine Weltgeschichtliche Tat*, for they inaugurated a policy which Germany was to pursue for the next thousand years. It was Henry who gave the first impetus to the Drive to the East, which opened the gateway to lands that were, centuries later, to become the centre of German power.

           *   *   *

By subjugating the Slavs of the right bank of the Elbe, Henry I meant to resume building where Charlemagne had left off. By a singular irony of fate, this " slayer of the Saxons " saw a Saxon duke enter upon his inheritance, and inspired him to carry on the conquests along lines which his own ambition had traced. But there still remained another part of Charlemagne's legacy to be claimed, the conquest of the kingdom of Lombardy. Henry never overlooked it, but there he had to proceed warily and bide his time

Two other German dukes happened to share the same designs and they were geographically better placed to operate across the Alps and steal a march on the Saxons on the River Po: the Duke of Suabia and the Duke of Bavaria. It will be remembered how the attempt by the Suabian Duke Burchard II ended. But when Rudolph of Burgundy put up his candidature to the throne of Lombardy in 934, Arnulf of Bavaria thought the moment had come for him to step in and see what he could do for himself on the other side of the Alps(48). His chances were fair; there was, besides his geographical advantage, the racial affinity between the Lombards and his Bavarians. He did so well that with the help of his backers in Lombardy his son Eberhard was elected king. There only remained for him to get his kingdom, and this he lost in a contest with Hugh of Provence, the rival candidate, who defeated him and forced him to leave Italy in 935. Without giving up all hopes, Arnulf, at any rate, made sure of Bavaria's independence and freedom from royal interference by appointing his son co-regent with right of succession.

Thus the race between Bavaria and Saxony which set them by the ears in Bohemia started all over again in Italy. After the defeat of the Magyars in 933, Arnulf, feeling less dependent on royal assistance, resumed his old competitive game; but this time, Henry I was first to put in his claim. Probably in 935 Rudolph II of Burgundy passed over to Henry's camp and sent him the famous Holy Spear, believed to contain the nails of the Holy Cross and to have been the treasured possession of Constantine the Great.(49)

(48) Now we know more of the part played by Arnulf in the struggle for Lombardy from the recently discovered *Annales Juvavensium Maiores*, latest ed. by H. Bresslau, 1934, in *M.G.H.S.* XXX, 2, pp. 732-44. Passage concerning Arnulf's rôle in Lombardy, p. 743.

(49) On the Holy Spear and its function in the first period of the German Empire, cf. the study by A. Hofmeister, "Die Heilige Lanze ein Abzeichen des Alten Reichs" in O. Gierke's *Untersuchungen für Deutsche Staats-und Rechtsgeschichte*, Heft. 96 (Berlin, 1908). I have been unable to consult this study. Cf. also R. Poupardin, "Le Royaume de Bourgogne (888 1038)" (Paris, 1907), *Biblioth. de l'Ecole des Hautes Etudes, Sc. Hist. et Philol.*, vol. 163, pp. 375-83. On the reign of Rudolph II and his relations with Henry I, *ibid.*, pp. 28-65. On the older relations between Burgundy and France, cf. Ph. Lauer, " Robert I et Raoul de Bourgogne, Rois de France (923-936)," *Biblioth. de l'Ecole des Hautes Etudes* (Paris, 1910), *Sc. Hist. et Philol.* vol. 188.

It was regarded as the symbol of power over Italy, giving its holder the right to canvass for the imperial crown. It is also admissible that Rudolph II acknowledged the suzerainty of the German King after the example of his own father who had sworn fealty to Arnulf, King of East Francia.

Henry I was now holding a trump card which might have set the seal on his life's work. Widukind(50), the best Saxon chronicler, was well aware of it with many of his contemporaries when he wrote that after subjugating all neighbouring nations, the King decided to march on Rome. However, fate decided otherwise and, after conferring on his son Otto I the right to succeed to the throne, Henry I died on the 2nd July, 936.

Henry's achievement was remarkable. He laid the foundations of medieval Germany and opened avenues which the Germans were to follow for centuries to come. But there remained a good deal to be done and Henry, who knew it, selected from amongst his sons Otto for the succession as the best qualified to carry on his work, however much his second wife Matilda and many nobles would have preferred her second son Henry. None but a ruler conscious of his royal power and dignity, and determined to maintain them, would be able to cope with the menace coming from the dukes, from Bavaria whose junction with Lombardy would have threatened the unity and the very existence of the Empire, from the Slavs on the Elbe, who were only waiting for a chance to regain their freedom, and from the Magyars, whose warlike spirit was still unbroken. The new kingdom still lacked compactness, royal authority, glamour and strength. Even Henry's plan for the annexation of Lombardy might have been wrecked, as France, after the loss of her non-Carolingian king and the election of Louis IV, a descendant of Charlemagne, was making a bid for the revival of her claims on Charlemagne's legacy in Italy and what was once East Francia.

Otto(51) and his nobles must have scented danger from that quarter. Otto was not a Carolingian, but to make up for the deficiency and to lend weight to his father's appointment he had himself solemnly elected in the presence of all the dukes and many nobles at Aix-la-Chapelle, Charlemagne's residential city. Unlike his father who refused to be crowned by the representatives of the Church, Otto insisted on being anointed and crowned

(50) I, ch. 40. *M.G.H.S.* in us. schol., p. 59.

(51) The latest monograph on Otto I, written by R. Holtzmann (*Kaiser-Otto der Grosse*, Berlin, 1936) gives on pp. 168 seq. all the sources for Otto's reign and a valuable bibliography. Cf. also M. Lintzel, " Zur Geschichte Otto des Grossen." *Mitteil. d. Österr. Institutes für Geschichte*, vol. 48 (1934), pp. 423 seq. ; K. Hampe, *Herrschergestalten des Deutschen Mittelalter* (3d. ed. Leipzig, 1939). Of the older works on Otto's times the following should be consulted W. v. Giesebrecht, *Geschichte der Deutschen Kaiserzeit* (Braunschweig, 5th ed., 1881) ; E. Dümmler, *Kaiser Otto der Grosse*, (München, 1876). On questions relating to ecclesiastical history : A. Hauck, *Kirchengeschichte Deutschlands*, vol. 3 (Leipzig, 4th ed., 1906). See also W. von der Steinen, " Kaiser Otto d. G." *Heilige und Helden des Mittelalters*, vol. V, (Breslau, 1928) ; F. M. Fischer, " Politiker um Otto d. G.", *Hist. Studien*, Heft 329 (Berlin, 1938) ; L. A. Winterswyl, *Otto d. G. und das Erste Reich der Deutschen* (Berlin, 1937) ; Gerd Tellenbach, " Otto d. G." *Die Grossen Deutschen, Neue Deutsche Biographie*, edited by W. Andreas and W. v. Scholz, vol. I, 1935, pp. 58 seq. For a detailed account of Otto's activities, see S. W. Doenniges, *Jahrbücher des Deutschen Reichs unter Otto I* (Berlin, 1839). On the sources bearing on the reign of Otto I, see W. Wattenbach-R. Holtzmann, *Deutschlands Geschichtsquellen im Mittelalter*, vol. I (Berlin, 1938), where all bibliographical indications on the editions of the sources in connection with the period of the Ottos will be found. Cf. also R. Holtzmann's remarks on the Saxons and the Empire under Otto, *ibid.*, pp. 4-10.

by the archbishop of Mainz according to the old Carolingian ritual, and on the tomb of Charlemagne. The ceremony was meant to provide royal authority with an historical background and the German claims to the Duchy of Lotharingia with legal justification ; also, to forestall any claim the western portion of the former Carolingian Empire might lay to the East, and to pave the King's way to Italy, as heir of Charlemagne.

Otto lost no time in organising the conquered territory and making ready for eventualities in the East. In 936 he erected the region between the rivers Trave and Peene, near the Danish border, into a March and presented it to his friend Hermann Billung with a watching brief over the Slavonic tribes of the Wagiri and the Obodrites. To link up Saxony, Bavaria and Bohemia, the region between the Saale and the Elbe was converted into the Thuringian March, which Otto called Reichsland and jealously reserved to his personal control. Into this land he introduced the military system which his father had set up in Saxony and Thuringia—a network of Burgwards or districts, each grouped around a fortified castle, mostly on the three rivers Saale, Mulde and Elbe which flowed across the territory, and entrusted the defence of this area to the notorious Count Gero, a grim and heartless campaigner whose memory was cursed by the Slavs on the Elbe for generations.

Otto's re-organisation of the conquered Slavonic lands must have made an impression on some tribal chiefs of the Bohemian Slavs, since one of them, as reported by Widukind(52), transferred his allegiance from Boleslas to the Saxon king. Neither his name nor the seat of his tribe is known, but it appears that it hailed from the northern or north-western borders of Bohemia(53). When Boleslas threatened his vassal with reprisals, the chieftain appealed to Otto for assistance and the King despatched to Bohemia two armies of Saxons and Thuringians together with the notorious regiment of Merseburg, recruited from among ex-prisoners and outlaws who had obtained king's pardon in return for military service—the original idea of a practical minded king. Defeated by one of the two armies Boleslas re-organised his forces, and perceiving that the Saxons were relaxing after their victory whilst the redeemed criminals, by sheer force of habit, were busy stripping the dead bodies of their fallen comrades of their earthly possessions, Boleslas fell on them with lightning speed and cut the royal armies to pieces, ex-prisoners and all. He then stormed the chief castle of his unfaithful vassal and levelled it to the ground.

According to Widukind, this incident provoked a war between the King and Boleslas I of Bohemia that lasted fourteen years ; but he should not be taken too literally. Otto I, during those fourteen years, had business to attend to in Germany too serious to leave much time for minding what was little worse than a nuisance. And as to Boleslas, we can scarcely suppose that he would stand up to Germany in earnest. Otto I for the time being con-

---

(52) Chronica Sax. III., ch. 35. *M.G.H.S.* in us. schol., p.68.

(53) Cf. V. Novotný, *Czech History* (in Czech), vol. I (Prague, 1912) p. 482, and V. Šimák " Vicinus Subregulus r. 936", *Czech Hist. Rev.* (1912), vol. XXVII, pp. 413-15 : the " Sub-regulus " could be identified with the Duke of the Croats.

tented himself with ordering the neighbouring counts to keep a look-out on the Bohemian Duke's movements, and if there was any action at all, it must have been limited to local raids. Nor is there a word in the sources to suggest that Boleslas plotted with the King's enemies or federated with other Slavs against the Empire.

One need not wonder that Otto I should have had to hold over the settlement of the Bohemian incident for so long. The first years of his reign were exceptionally eventful and more than once the future of both Otto and Germany were hanging in the balance. It was the King's misfortune to alienate his half-brother Thankmar by singling out Gero for appointment, Count Wichman, by giving preference to Hermann, Wichman's brother, and the Duke of Franconia, by intervening in favour of some of Eberhard's vassals in Saxony. This created enmities that might have been fatal when in 938 Otto attempted to interfere with Bavaria's independence and failed in his attempt. After Arnulf's death, on the 14th July, 937, Otto asked his son to surrender his rights over the Bavarian Church as the price for his recognition and on the young Duke Eberhard's refusal, Otto took the offensive. It miscarried. This was the signal for all the discontented dukes and counts to conspire against the King. However, he was well able to deal with them and his half-brother Thankmar paid with his life for his audacity. When later Otto defeated Eberhard of Bavaria and handed over his Duchy to Arnulf's brother Berchtold on his own conditions, the crisis blew over and things began to look more hopeful.

At any rate, for some time; for his brother Henry, disappointed at his failure in obtaining Bavaria, soon gave trouble and with the concurrence of the Dukes of Franconia and Lotharingia, raised the standard of revolt. When Otto had stood up to the first impact, though not without difficulty, the allied rebels turned to France and obtained the support of Louis IV in return for the transfer of Lotharingia to French suzerainty. But Otto countered the move by an alliance with his brother-in-law and Louis's rival, Hugh the Great, Duke of the Franks and Count of Paris. The revolt would have spread (even the archbishop of Mainz and the bishop of Strassburg had joined the coalition) had it not been for Otto's determination. The Duke of Franconia fell in battle; the Duke of Lotharingia perished in flight and the prelates were taken prisoner. It was Otto's greatest triumph. The Dukedom of Franconia was suppressed; its counts were made directly subject to the King, and Lotharingia was made safe against any further French claims. The whole position was reversed when Hugh,the Duke of the Franks, and Heribert of Vermandois paid their homage to Otto at Attigny on the river Aisne(54). It looked as though instead of the King of the Carolingian dynasty becoming a danger to the native dynasty of East Francia, it would be the Saxon King, once anointed on Charlemagne's tomb, who would claim the inheritance of the founder of the Frankish Empire and impose his supremacy on the better part of Western Francia.

But Otto I had no such intention; nor did he mean to substitute one brother-in-law—Hugh—for another—Louis IV. All he insisted on was the

---

(54) Cf. R. Holtzmann, *Kaiser Otto der Grosse*, pp. 26-44.

incorporation of Lotharingia into the *Regnum Teutonicorum* and the maintenance of a certain balance of power between the King and his opponents. He made peace with Louis IV in 942 and induced his rivals to submit to the King's authority. When in 945 the French King tried to subjugate the Duchy of Normandy, was captured by the Normans and handed over to Hugh the Great, Otto I demanded the King's release; but when Hugh so restricted the King's power as to make it almost illusory, Otto marched with his Saxons on Paris and went in pursuit of Hugh as far as Rouen. The peace which after many vicissitudes was concluded in 950 between the two French rivals was mainly due to Otto's active interest(55).

Otto's French experiment shows that feelings common to Charlemagne's subjects were hard to kill. Even after complete separation, the two kingdoms were still believed to share interests in common, the one considering it its duty to intervene whenever things went wrong in the other. Otto's competence increased his ascendancy, so that when the German kings blossomed into emperors, they were readily accepted as leaders of Western Christendom and invested with a certain amount of moral authority over other Christian kings and princes, even in France and England.

Further addition to the German King's power came from another quarter. By 950 Otto I had rendered the dukes apparently powerless to harm royalty: he was holding Saxony and Franconia under his personal control; he made his brother Henry who had repented of his misdeeds, Duke of Bavaria after Berchtold's death (947), and his son, Liudolf, Duke of Suabia in 949 in succession to the faithful Duke Hermann; finally, the Duke of Lotharingia, Conrad the Red, was his own son-in-law. With his rear thus sufficiently protected, Otto set out to carry out his father's last wishes: the conquest of Lombardy and the vindication of the imperial crown. He first made sure of Burgundy where he supported Rudolph's son Conrad, as that country commanded the strategic passes over the Alps. He then found the chance to have his say in Italian affairs, when Count Berengar of Ivrea took refuge at his court, seeking protection from the vengeance of Hugh of Lombardy, promising to become Otto's faithful vassal, and promptly forgetting his promise, directly he ascended the royal throne of Lombardy after the death of Hugh and of his son Lothar. Liutprand, bishop of Cremona, the learned chronicler, who left such interesting accounts of Italy and Byzantium in the tenth century, has some very hard

(55) For details see A. Heil, " Die Politischen Beziehungen zwischen Otto dem Grossen und Ludwig von Frankreich (936-954)," *Hist. Studien*, Heft 46 (Berlin, 1904) ; Kawerau, " Die Rivalität Deutscher und Französicher Macht im 10 Jh.", *Jahrbuch der Gesellschaft für Lothringische Geschichte und Altertumskunde* (1910). Cf. also W. Sante, " Die Deutsche Westgrenze im 9. und 10. Jhrh.", *Hist. Aufsätze A. Schulte gewidmet* (Düsseldorf, 1927), pp.99-112 ; J. Haller, *Tausend Jahre Deutsch-Französicher Beziehungen*, 4th ed. (Stuttgart, 1939), p. 5 (English translation by Dora von Beseler, *France and Germany. The History of a Thousand Years*, London, 1932). For details on the dukes' revolt, see F. M. Fischer, "Politiker um Otto d. G.", *Hist. Stud.*, Heft 329, pp. 7-60. On Louis IV, King of France, see Ph. Lauer, " Le Règne de Louis IV d'Outre-Mer " (Paris, 1900), *Bibl. de l'Ec. des Hautes Et. Sc. Hist. Phil.*, vol. 127, pp. 50-188 ; also F. Lot, "Les Derniers Carolingiens, Lothaire, Louis IV, Charles de Lorraine (954-991) " (Paris, 1891), *Bibl. de l'Ec. des Hautes Et. Sc., Hist. Phil.*, vol. 87, pp. 3 seq.; C. Schoene, *Die Politischen Beziehungen zwischen Deutschland und Frankreich in den Jahren 953-980* (Berlin, 1910) ; P. E. Schramm, *Der König von Frankreich* (Weimar, 1938), pp. 80-90.

things to say about Berengar(56). He had his own reasons for disliking the King, that would probably have left Otto unmoved but for one thing. The late King Lothar's young widow, the beautiful and wealthy Adelheid, numbered many admirers in Northern Italy, and whereas Berengar's wife was jealous of her looks and her jewels, Berengar was jealous of her political influence, and he deprived her of both. The widowed queen lost her possessions and her freedom. But she was the sister of Conrad, the King of Burgundy and a protégé of Otto I(57). This was too much for the German monarch and he marched into Italy. Berengar fled from Pavia; Otto occupied the city (20th August, 951), proclaimed himself King of Lombardy and lent his successful military campaign a romantic touch by marrying the pretty widow Adelheid. It was the height of his ambition (58). He was not so successful in Rome, where his ambassador, Frederick archbishop of Mainz, who had hastened thither to prepare the imperial coronation, could not convince the Pope: Agapet II was too much under the influence of the Senator Alberich, who had no use for emperors at any time.

Not until Otto had made sure of his position in the German kingdom could he devote attention to the East, and his first pre-occupation was to force Bohemia to reiterate her submission. Like Henry I he must have attached some importance to Bohemia's attitude, since he decided to take personal command of the army. He marched against Boleslas in 950(59). Widukind is again our best informant about this campaign which must have been run on a sufficient scale to receive publicity in so many chronicles. The King's brother Henry, Duke of Bavaria, as was to be expected, was singled out for special mention. The attack was concentrated not on Prague but on a new fortified place of some importance, probably Boleslav, then under the command of the Duke's son, his father's namesake. Widukind's account does not seem to imply that Otto's campaign was a complete military success, since Boleslas I made his submission to Otto before the fortress was captured. The old ties were then restored between Germany and Bohemia, the Duke had to pay tribute and promise the King military aid whenever summoned to do so, while the Duke of Bavaria was charged with the task of supervision over Bohemia(60). It was the part

---

(56) Liutprand of Cremona, *Antapodosis*, II, ch. 33. English translation by F. A. Wright. *The Works of Liutprand of Cremona* (London, 1930), p. 86, II, chs. 56 seq., loc. cit., pp. 96 seq., III, I, loc. cit., p. 109, IV, 8, p.147, V, 10-12, pp. 182 seq., V, 26-32, loc. cit., pp. 194 seq., VI, 2-6, pp. 206 seq. Liber de Rebus Gestis Ottonis, chs. 1-3, loc. cit., pp. 215 seq.

(57) On the history of Burgundy and its relations with Germany at the time of the Ottose cf. R. Poupardin, *Le Royaume de Bourgogne*, pp. 66-86 ; also A. Hofmeister, *Deutschland und Burgund im Früheren Mittelalter* (1914), especially pp. 31 seq., 65 seq. ; *ibid.*, pp. 9-18, a useful bibliography of works and sources bearing on the history of Burgundy and its relations with Germany. On the history of Burgundy previous to this period, see the interesting remarks by L. Poole, " Burgundian Notes," in *English Historical Review*, (1911), vol. XXVI, pp. 310-7 ; (1912), vol. XXVII, pp. 299-309 ; (1913), vol. XXVIII, pp. 106-12. Cf. also C. W. Previté Orton, " Italy and Provence, 900-950," *Engl. Hist. Rev.* (1917), vol. XXXII, pp. 335-47.

(58) For details on the struggle for the Kingdom of Italy, cf. L. M. Hartmann, *Geschicht. Italiens im Mittelalter*, Bd. III, 2, (Gotha, 1911), pp. 175-242 ; on Otto I and Adelheid, *ibid.*, pp. 243-66.

(59) Widukind, III, ch.8 ; *M.G.H.S.* in usum schol., p. 108. Cf. V. Novotný, loc. cit., vol. I, p. 485, where all the chroniclers who make reference to the expedition are quoted.

(60) Thietmar, Chronicon, II, ch. 2, *M.G.H.S.* N.S. IX, p. 40.

36

Bavaria had played before the formation of the *Regnum Teutonicorum*, but circumstances had altered now that Bavaria was no longer under Arnulf but under the King's own brother. It was obviously in the interest of the Saxon dynasty to place Bohemia under the chaperoning care of a member of the reigning house.

A parallel case occurred in the political life of Italy at the time. When in 952 Otto I received the submission of Berengar and his son and confirmed him in his dignity as King of Lombardy under German suzerainty, Berengar had to cede the March of Verona with Aquileia and Istria to Henry of Bavaria. This territory represented a third of Lombardy and the King joined it to Henry's dukedom not merely to meet the Duke's wish for territorial extension but because it gave him control over the Brenner Pass. This strategic advantage would keep Berengar up to the mark and the Magyars at arm's length from Lombardy; and as he could not find a more reliable agent than his own brother, he placed him in charge of that valuable key position. The analogy sufficiently explains Otto's policy in Bohemia.

After this, Boleslas I remained faithful to Otto and refrained from meddling with the internal affairs of the kingdom. At the last conspiracy which was headed by the King's son Liutpold, Duke Conrad and the archbishop of Mainz(61), and which more than once forced Otto into a tight corner, nothing was heard of Boleslas I of Bohemia. He seemingly preferred to live his own life and mind his own business. Not even the conspirators went out of their way to solicit his help or elicit his interest. Bohemia was not considered then to stand on the same footing as other duchies with Germany. The national character of the *Regnum Teutonicorum* must have meant more than specialists have been ready to admit.

The disorders following the insurrection against Otto's rule time and again brought the kingdom to the brink of confusion, but Otto's stubbornness stood him in good stead and saved the monarchy. It was when the Magyars chose their moment and took advantage of Germany's embarrassment to invade and devastate Bavaria and Suabia that the necessity for common leadership was brought home to the Germans. Otto I promptly responded to the general feeling and made up his mind to be done with the Magyar menace. He gathered his forces and with the support of a strong Czech detachment commanded by Boleslas of Bohemia, marched against the Magyars and met them at Lechfeld on the 10th August, 955. It was a massacre(62); the Magyars had their lesson and lost their taste for invasion for good. Their way back to the South Russian steppes being blocked by other nomads and would-be invaders, the defeated Magyars settled down in

---

(61) For particulars on the Duke's revolt and the part played by the archbishop of Mainz in the evolution of Germany under Otto I see W. Norden, " Erzbischof Friedrich von Mainz und Otto d. G. Zur Entwicklung des Deutschen Staatsgedankens in der Ottonenzeit," *Hist Studien*, Heft 103 (Berlin, 1912).

(62) For details on this memorable battle see D. Schäfer, " Die Ungarnschlacht von 955," *Sitzungsberichte der Preuss. Akad., Phil. Hist. Kl.* (Berlin, 1905), pp. 552 seq., where an exhaustive bibliography will also be found ; H. Breslau, " Die Schlacht auf dem Lechfelde," *Hist. Zeitschrift* (1906), vol. XCVII ; R. Lüttich, " Ungarnzüge in Europa im 10 Jh.," *Hist. Studien*, Heft 84 (Berlin, 1910), pp. 150-70.

the Hungarian plains where time and common sense gradually made them amenable to their neighbours' cultural influence.

The effect of this victory on the German soul was overwhelming. It had been the joint effort of the whole *Regnum Teutonicorum* and it rallied all the tribes to the authority of the King. Even Conrad the Red, who had lost his Duchy of Lotharingia for his recent participation in the rebellion, fought under the King's orders and his heroic death on the battle-field was commended by every German as sufficient atonement for past misdeeds. Otto was again the mighty King, the central figure in all Germany.

The victory also redounded to Otto's honour outside Germany. The Magyars had for the last fifty years been the nightmare of Western Europe and the monarch who rid the continent of that scourge was naturally looked up to as Europe's mightiest ruler. Even the Byzantines felt awed by Otto's growing power, for Constantine VII sent him an embassy as early as 945, presumably in connection with the Magyar danger. Italy also rejoiced and the imperial crown, Otto's life-long ambition, fell within his grasp.

CHAPTER II

THE EMPEROR OTTO I, POLAND, BOHEMIA AND RUSSIA

OTTO I EMPEROR—POLITICAL THEORIES OF CHARLEMAGNE AND OTTO I—
OTTO'S PLAN FOR EASTERN EXPANSION AND THE CHURCH—MIESZKO I—
HIS ALLEGED VIKING DESCENT—HIS RELATION TO THE EMPIRE—HIS
STRUGGLE FOR POMERANIA—THE VARYAGS AND THE ORIGIN OF RUSSIA
OTTO I AND OLGA OF KIEV—BOLESLAS I OF BOHEMIA AND THE CONVER-
SION OF POLAND—OTTO I, MAGDEBURG, ROME AND POSEN—A FAMOUS
FOUNDATION CHARTER—THE MORROW OF QUEDLINBURG REICHSTAG—
SLAVONIC INSURRECTION—SLAVONIC DUKES AND THE SUCCESSION OF
OTTO II—EXPANSION OF POLAND, BOHEMIA AND RUSSIA—THEY MEET ON
THE CARPATHIANS.

Contemporaries must have been alive to the fact that Otto I by his achievement well deserved the supreme honour of Europe's leadership, since we read in Widukind's chronicle how after the battle of Lechfeld the victorious army acclaimed Otto as Augustus(1). For us, it is difficult to-day to appreciate how Otto, his Germans and Western Europe felt about the revival of the Roman Empire, and how eagerly the princes surrendered to the binding force of the imperial tradition founded by Charlemange. It literally dominated the minds of the Western Christians for more than a century, until the Roman elements which had contributed to the birth of his *Imperium* were under Charlemagne's successors, almost completely sub-merged by the ideal of Christian universality. This ideal took the place, in Western Europe, of the old notion of an universal *orbis Romanus* and postulated, besides a pope, an emperor as the natural protector of the Church and of the Holy City.

In this light, Otto's contemporaries must have taken it to be the Christians' inherited duty to raise the Christian Roman Empire from the state of decadence to which it had sunk ever since the death of the two last candidates to imperial honours, Berengar of Friuli (d. 924) and Louis of Burgundy (d. 928), as well as the responsibility of the rulers of Germany, France, Burgundy and Italy, the four main countries that had formed the Empire of Charlemagne. Since France, or what was once Western Francia, had been outpaced by Germany, or Eastern Francia of days gone by, and since in the light of recent experience Burgundy and Italy had been unable to make such dreams come true, the feeling gradually matured that the task devolved on the King of the *Regnum Teutonicorum*. Two of its Kings, Charles III and Arnulf, had already worn the imperial crown and now Otto I had the whole West in his debt for the signal service of defeating the Magyars.

It is difficult to see how Otto could have shirked the obligation and disappointed public opinion. His environment was not ours and he had not

---

(1) Widukind, III, ch. 49, *M.G.H.* in usum schol., p. 128. The criticism of the account and the explanation of how it may have been invented by Widukind is given by E. E. Stengel, *Den Kaiser macht das Heer* (Weimar, 1910), pp. 17-30.

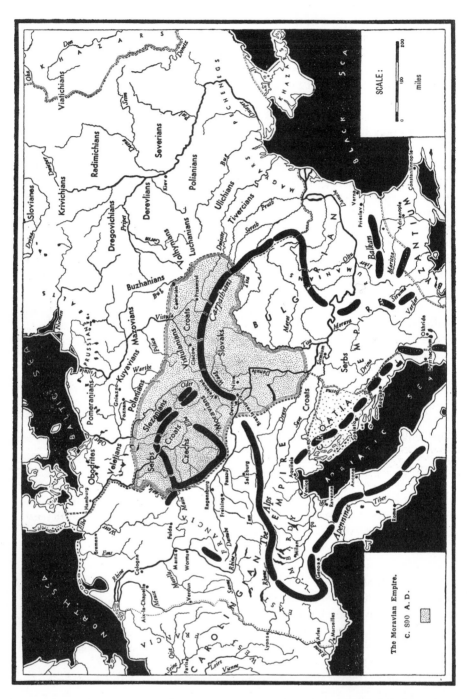

The Moravian Empire. C. 890 A.D.

SCALE: miles

our historical reasons to suspect that the liabilities he was incurring in Italy would one day prove Germany's worst handicap. Uppermost in his mind, as the first Prince of the West, was the duty to revive the glories of an undying Christian Roman Empire, and if that implied any contingencies,

40

they had to be accepted in the interest of the whole Christian community of which the Germans were members.

There were other considerations urging Otto to active participation in the life of Italy. Berengar of Ivrea had proved unreliable and Liudolf, whom his father Otto had intended to take over his succession in northern Italy, had died suddenly after defeating Berengar. Besides, there was always the potential danger of the renovation of Charlemagne's Empire being attempted outside Germany. Having, moreover, erected the fabric of his royal authority on the support of the German Church, Otto saw the necessity of having a more direct influence on the Papacy such as only the imperial status could give him. So, when Pope John XII asked him for assistance against Berengar of Ivrea and his son Adalbert, who had regained control over Lombardy and were trying to get at the Duchy of Spoleto across territory that belonged to St. Peter's patrimony, Otto decided that the moment had come for him to realise his plan and do what was expected of him: he marched his forces into Italy in 961 and the following year, on February 2, was crowned Emperor by the Pope.

Thus, the Christian Roman Empire came to life again, this time through the instrumentality of a Saxon, a King of Germany. The old Carolingian tradition which Otto, on taking over his father's succession, had made his own and introduced into his kingdom, was now resurrected with all its implications. The idea was embodied in the so-called *Privilegium Otto-nianum*(2), a historic document in which Otto I confirmed the gift made to the Pope by Pippin, Charlemagne's father, of St. Peter's *Patrimonium*.

Otto I was now supreme master of Italy, inclusive of papal territory; the Pope did him homage. He became the official Protector of the Church and the Papacy. The *de facto* ascendancy over other rulers which Otto had gained by his intervention in France now rested on a legal basis. Without its being able to claim, like Charlemagne, any direct authority over Western Europe, there still remained to Germany the very substantial advantage that its emperor was looked upon abroad as the natural leader of all Western Christians, to the obvious benefit of Germany's central authority and at the expense of the dukes' centrifugal tendencies.

*   *   *

Thus a vital element was introduced into the history of Germany, one destined to leave its impress on the future of Central Europe. Otto's decision to revive Charlemagne's imperial ideology undoubtedly steered the fate of Central Europe into new channels. What was that tradition? How did it come to be transformed under Charlemagne's successors? And to what extent was it adopted by Otto I?

First of all, classical considerations had little to do with Charlemagne's

(2) *M.G.H.* Diplomata, I, pp. 322 seq. The best study dealing with the Privilegium comes from Th. Sickel, *Das Privilegium Otto I. für die Römische Kirche vom Jahre* 962 (Innsbruck, 1883). A more recent study with bibliographical indications is by E. E. Stengel, " Der Entwurf des Kaiserprivilegs für die Römische Kirche, 817-962," *Histor. Zeitschr.* (1926), vol. 134. For details see K. Hampe, "Die Bedeutung Ottos des Grossen nach Rom durch den Papst., *Hist. Aufsätze, Festgabe K. Zenmer* (Weimar 1910) pp. 153-67.

rise to power. Nor could the coronation ceremony have been intended, as historians would have it, to symbolise a renovation of the Western Roman Empire, such as Charles and his contemporaries would have been pining for(3). Constantinople was at the moment governed by a woman, Irene, and the thought that imperial power had fallen into abeyance may have served as a welcome pretext and justified the Pope's initiative; but from the Byzantine standpoint the crowning was nothing less than the proclamation of an anti-emperor for the purpose of ousting the legal holder of the title at least from Rome and the Italian imperial possessions.

Charlemagne was aware of it and this may have been one of the reasons for his displeasure at the Pope's action, as recorded by his biographer Eginhard(4). He had no wish to be drawn into a quarrel with the lawful heirs of the Roman Emperors in Byzantium, and immediately started negotiations with Irene with a view to regularise his position. They proved difficult and the war that followed ended in a compromise, Charlemagne handing over Istria and Venice in return for the recognition of his title. The year before his death, he had the satisfaction of being greeted by the ambassadors of Michael I as Emperor(5). True to the old Roman tradition which made room for the existence of co-emperors, the Byzantines were ready to put up with one in the interest of their western possessions, provided he were acknowledged as such by the supreme Basileus. The Aachen ceremony of homage was designed to give satisfaction in this respect.

Such was the origin of the western medieval imperial tradition. Charlemagne must have been aware of it, since he took care not to usurp the official titles of the Roman Emperors—*Imperator Romanorum* or *Semper Augustus*, but simply called himself *Imperator*, *Romanorum gubernans imperium*, adding the titles that really mattered—*Rex Francorum et Langobardorum*.

But fear of complications with Byzantium was not the main reason for Charlemagne's irritation. Pope Leo III had grown weary of the incessant Lombard menace and disappointed with Roman emperors who from their distant city on the Bosphorus were unable to give effective support to the bishops of Rome. All that was expected of the Popes was to help them in saving the antiquated notion of an undying Roman Empire that embraced the whole Christian world and in keeping up the semblance of their supremacy over the West. It was all so far away, whilst palpable realities were ever present on the other side of the Alps. To Leo III it seemed preferable to raise an efficient ruler among the Franks, one able to deal with the Lombard menace, and to set a new tradition going, in closer

---

(3) Such was the opinion of leading historians in the XIXth century. See also J. Bryce, *The Holy Roman Empire* (8th edition, London, 1887), pp. 34-75. Like theories were discarded by K. Heldmann, *Das Kaisertum Karls des Grossen* (Weimar, 1928). His arguments were summed up by H. Dannenbauer, " Zum Kaisertum Karls des Grossen und seiner Nachfolger," *Zeitschrift für Kirchengeschichte* (1930), vol. XLIX, pp.301-6. See also J. Haller, *Der Eintritt der Germanen in die Geschichte* (Berlin, 1939), pp. 82 seq., and the observations by Pirenne in his *Mahomet and Charlemagne* (London, 1939), pp. 227 seq. For general views on Charlemagne's work, see D. Woodruff, *Charlemagne* (London, 1934), especially pp. 72-94 and Ch. Dawson, *The Making of Europe* (London, 1932), pp. 214 seq., where he discusses the restoration of the Western Empire.

(4) Einhardi Vita Karoli M., ch. 28, *M.G.H.S.* II, p. 458.

(5) Einhardi Annales ad a. 812, *M.G.H.S.* I, p. 199. Annales Fuldenses, *ibid.*, p. 355.

association with the Church and the Papacy. It would prove more helpful than a tradition that dated back to pagan days and allowed the Church but an insignificant share in the selection of future emperors. Leo III and the Curia succumbed to the temptation and started an innovation which in Byzantine eyes amounted to a revolt against the lawful rulers.

There was also the danger, not to be overlooked, of the cure growing worse than the disease ; of the new Emperor's influence expanding to a size that would dwarf both the turbulent Roman nobility and Byzantium into minor evils. But the Curia's self-protecting instinct conjured up the legendary figure of Constantine the Great, which was held up to the barbarous Franks as the Roman embodiment of a great tradition. The notorious *Donatio Constantini*(6) was designed to incorporate the main features of this tradition. The document was forged by some obscure Italian cleric in the second half of the eighth century for the purpose of assisting the Papacy in the recovery of Italian territories that belonged to the Byzantine Empire, especially the Exarchate of Ravenna. The forger invented the story of the Christian Emperor solemnly declaring before leaving Rome for Constantinople that he surrendered to the Pope of Rome all his imperial insignia, together with supreme domination over Rome, the provinces of Italy and all Western lands.

To some extent, the *Donatio* was also the Roman rejoinder to the Decree of the iconoclastic emperor Leo III, who, to punish Pope Hadrian I for rebuking him for heresy, wrenched the Byzantine territories in South Italy, together with Sicily, from the Roman patriarchate and confiscated the papal patrimony in those parts. The document, which exalts the Pope as the supreme judge of the whole Church, the representative of Christ on earth and the Emperor's advocate before the throne of God, was at the same time designed to impress the Franks and clip their aspirations to the desired length. It would, so it was hoped, keep the Franks on their best behaviour, piously reverent at a respectable distance from Rome and ever ready on the first alert to rush to its rescue(7).

Charlemagne knew of the Curia's feelings and had no wish to have to thank them for his crown. It looked to him as though the Pope were using the power he had received over Italy and Rome from Constantine the Great to make his own imperial appointments. He had his own ideas about the functions of a Roman Patricius, even in the guise of an Emperor, and of the Pope, and in 796 told Leo III what he thought about them. When the Pope sent him the standard of Rome with the invitation to come to the city and receive the homage of the Romans, Charles in a letter(8) defined his

---

(6) On the history of this forgery and the hold it had on medieval minds, see G. Laehr, " Die Konstantinische Schenkung in der abendländischen Literatur des Mittelalters bis zur Mitte des 14. Jhs.," *Historische Studien* (Berlin, 1926), H.166, especially pp. 1-22. Cf. also R. Cessi, "Il Costituto di Constantino," *Rivista Stor. Ital.* (1931), vol. 48, pp. 155-76.

(7) Already L. Duchesne (*Beginning of the Temporal Sovereignty of the Popes*, London, 1908), pp. 119 seq., p. 60 in the French original text, saw the connection between the document and the papal view of Charlemagne's coronation. This was further elaborated by A. Brackmann in " Die Erneuerung der Kaiserwürde im Jahre 800," *Geschichtliche Studien für A. Hauck* (Leipzig, 1916), pp. 126 seq.

(8) Epistolae Carolinae, Jaffe, *Bibliotheca Rerum Germanicarum* (Berlin, 1867), vol. IV, p. 356.

own part as that of the defender of the Church against all attacks—the part of the Pope as that of Moses praying for the success of his arms. This clearly excluded the Pope from politics. He meant to be Emperor after his own ideas, not the Curia's.

As a matter of fact, Charlemagne's political notions had little in common with those of either the forger of the *Donatio* or of the Curia. He visualised himself as the Priest-King charged with the supreme control over all secular and spiritual matters and the builder of the City of God, an ideal he had borrowed from S. Augustine. The concept was Merovingian. Already Chlodwig in 511 was praised(9) by the bishops assembled in Orleans for his priestly spirit; S. Gregory of Tours compared the Frankish King(10) to the good priest, and Venantius Fortunatus(11) addressed Childebert I as " our Melchisedech, verily King and Priest."

Charlemagne's theory only summarised a political system of thought the origin of which went back to the day of Constantine. At that time the Church, in her delight at last to meet an Emperor who was willing to be a Christian, agreed to adopt the principles on kingship as they had grown up in the East, been transformed by the Hellenistic period and further adapted by the Roman Caesars from Augustus to Constantine the Great. All she did was to cut them to the size of her own doctrine by divesting the emperor of his divine character. Instead, she made him the representative of God, the vice-Christ charged with the mission of bringing the world back to God. He kept his priestly character, as easterners had bestowed it on their kings, with the right and the obligation to see that God's interests on earth were properly safeguarded, to look after the material welfare of the Church and to police the faithful(12).

This notion travelled from East to West, where the idea of the Rex-Sacerdos received ready welcome among the Germanic tribes, whose pagan teaching had conferred divine powers on royal families and made them descendants of the gods(13). On these two concepts, the Franks erected their own native monarchism. It recalled in many ways the system that governed the relations between the emperors and the Church in Byzantium. Only the fact that western kings needed their bishops and priests, the only cultured profession in their realms, in their chancelleries and councils

---

(9) *M.G.H.* Concilia I, p. 2. cf. also p. 196.

(10) Historia Francorum, IX, ch. 21, *M.G.H.S.* Rer. Merov. I, p. 379.

(11) Carmina, *M.G.H.* Auct. Antiq. IV, p. 40 (Liber II, carm. 10, vers. 21).

(12) The classical work on this subject has been A. Gasquet's *De l'Autorité Impériale en Matières Religieuses à Byzance* (Paris, 1879), but it would need radical revision. I have treated the subject in my Birkbeck Lectures in Cambridge, March, 1946, which have been enlarged and will appear in book form. Cf. my booklet, *National Churches and the Church Universal* (London, 1944), pp. 33 seq.

(13) Cf. H. von Schubert, " Der Kampf des Geistlichen und Weltlichen Rechts," in *Sitzungsberichte der Akad. Heidelberg, Hist. Philol. Kl.* (1927), pp. 25 seq. On German customs and the influence of the Roman imperial tradition on the Germans, see F. Kern, Gottesgnadentum und Widerstandsrecht im Früheren Mittelalter, *Mittelalt. Studien*, vol. I (Leipzig, 1914), pp. 14-140. Kern's work was translated into English by S. B. Chrimes and published in *Studies on Medieval History* (vol. I : Kingship and Law in the Middle Ages, Oxford, 1939). The German edition has an exhaustive bibliography and much valuable information omitted in the English translation.

helped the western Church to keep a modicum of freedom and influence on State affairs(14).

It was then only natural that Charlemagne should not view with favour the new Roman spirit as revealed in forged documents. He went on ruling Church and State in his own way. In 813, he settled the question as to whose business it was to make emperors when he designated his son as co-Emperor with every Roman formality of designation, acclamation and coronation ; but this time the Frankish nobles replaced the Romans and the Pope was left out of it.

Charlemagne's imperial idea, however, soon underwent transformations. The classical renascence provoked by his encouragement of culture was responsible' for a wider knowledge of Roman history among Frankish intellectuals and for the growing prestige of classical Rome. The author of the Annals of Lorch(15) defended the legitimacy of Charlemagne's imperial coronation on the ground that he was the master of Rome and of all imperial residences in Italy, Gaul and Germany. His successor Louis the Pious went further, dropped his royal title and called himself Imperator Augustus and gathered under his Imperium all the possessions of the Roman Empire. He later adopted the title of *Imperator Francorum* and made his realm the *Imperium Francorum*. It was the first step towards the foundation of a Western Roman Empire, unknown to the Romans and their heirs, the Byzantines. All they knew was the *Imperium Romanum*.

The Franks overlooked Roman antiquities in one particular. Instead of following the Roman usage of the emperors' election by the senate or army and their acclamation by the people, the Germans laid the emphasis on the coronation ceremony by the head of Christendom and considered essential what the Byzantines only looked upon as a secondary part of the emperor's accession. By this change of method did the curial notions of the forged *Donatio* take root in Western minds; how rapidly, we can guess from the way Louis II countered the protest by Basil I of Byzantium against his assumption of the imperial title. He retorted that he had been crowned and appointed by the Pope(16), a plea which the Byzantines were not likely to appreciate. Such an association with the Popes and with Christian Rome forced classical reminiscences into the background to the benefit of the Church's universality and made the emperor the Defender of the Church and the head of the Christian Empire. Thence it was but a step to the mediaeval assumption that through the instrumentality of Leo III imperial power had passed from the Greeks to the Germans.

Such was the concept of the Christian Roman Empire which Otto I decided to rebuild. The move was well timed. After the disintegration of the Frankish Empire, signs were not wanting to show that Frankish

---

(14) Cf. A. Gasquet, *L'Empire Byzantin et la Monarchie Francque* (Paris, 1888), where the author tries to show how the monarchism of Byzantium found its way to the Franks. Cf. also F. Kampers, " Rex et Sacerdos", *Histor. Jahrbuch*, vol. 45 (1925), pp. 495 seq. The subject is treated more fully by K. Voigt, *Staat und Kirche von Konstantin d. Gr. zum Ende der Karolingenzeit* (Stuttgart, 1936), pp. 236 seq.

(15) Annales Laureshamenses ad a. 801, *M.G.H.S.* I, p.38.

(16) Chronicon Salernitanum, ch. 106, *M.G.H.S.* III, p. 522.

traditions were losing ground in Germany; that under Conrad I and chiefly under Henry I the *Regnum Teutonicorum* was going to stand on its own feet and follow its own lines of growth. The die was cast when Otto accepted ecclesiastical coronation on the tomb of Charlemagne at Aix-la-Chapelle. One has but to read the old coronation rite of Mainz(17) dating from this period and modelled on the coronation ritual designed by Otto I, to realise that the Frankish political ideology in relation to kingship had been bodily adopted by Otto I. Here again, after Charlemagne, the king was regarded as Rex-Sacerdos, King and Priest, the secular head of the Church and her Protector. Kingship is adorned with a sacramental character clearly discernible in the similarity between the liturgy of royal anointment and coronation and the corresponding rite of episcopal consecration(18).

There is then sufficient evidence that Otto I meant to revive in his kingdom the Carolingian theocracy in all its bearings and likewise to follow Charlemagne as his imperial pattern. But he found it more difficult of execution than he had expected. Things had altered since Charlemagne's death. Otto had to deal with the powerful opposition of the dukes, whose ambitions were always to be reckoned with. There only remained the Church over which Otto found it possible to lord it even more absolutely than Charlemagne had done.

This was due to conditions which had already obtained under Charlemagne, but had been aggravated under his successors; they arose from the special social conditions that prevailed among Germanic nations. For instance, in their conception of personal property, so much more comprehensive than that of the Romans, any structure erected on a German's land legally belonged to him. In pagan days, sanctuaries built by rich landowners were considered to be and remain their property(19). It was the owner who claimed the management of the buildings, provided the things necessary for worship, supported the priests and, of course, claimed the offerings of the faithful as well as all rights and properties attached to the place of worship concerned. On becoming Christian, the Germanic tribes kept the custom and resisted every inducement by the Roman missionaries to

(17) See P. E. Schramm's " Die Krönung in Deutschland bis zum Beginn des Salischen Hauses (1028)," *Zeitschrift der Savigny Stiftung für Rechtsgeschichte*, vol. 55, Kanon. Abt. XXIV (Weimar, 1935), pp. 184-332. On Otto's coronation, *ibid.*, pp. 196-215 ; edition with analysis of the Ordo of Mainz, *ibid.*, pp. 228-332.

(18) On this subject, see the important study by E. Eichmann, "Königs und Bischofsweihe," *Sitzungsber. d. Bayer. Ak. Phil. Hist. Kl.* (München, 1928), Cf. also G. Tellenbach, " Römischer und Christlicher Reichsgedanke in der Liturgie des Frühen Mittelaters," *Sitzungsber. der Ak. Heidelberg, Phil. Hist. Kl.* (1934), and E. Erdmann, " Der Heidenkrieg in der Liturgie und die Kaiserkrönung Otto I," *Mitteilungen des Oester. Instituts für Geschichtsforschung* 1932), vol. 46, pp. 129-42.

(19) Traces of this Germanic, pagan and tribal practice are still extant in various countries. For England, cf. F. M. Stenton's *Anglo-Saxon England* (Oxford History of England, 1943); especially pp. 101 seq., on the proprietary sanctuaries in the pagan Anglo-Saxon period : Cusan weoh near Farnham in Surrey and the weoh or shrine that belonged to a man named Paeccel, a name that still survives under the disguise of Patchway, near Staumer in Sussex. The greatest authority on proprietary churches is the German scholar Ulrich Stutz. One of his studies, " The Proprietary Church as an element of Medieval German Ecclesiastical Law," appeared in G. Barraclough's *Studies in Medieval Germany* (Oxford, 1938), vol. II, pp. 35-70. Stutz' main work on the problem is *Die Eigenkirche als Element des Mittelalterlich-Germanischen Kirchenrechtes* Berlin, 1895).

substitute the old Roman practice whereby the representatives of the Church were the legal owners of all places of worship, disposed of them, supplied all necessaries and controlled the priests in charge. With notions of such a primitive character, the Germans could never conceive the possibility of any property being vested in a society or organisation. An owner had to be a person and legal bodies did not exist. There thus grew up in all Western lands inhabited or ruled by a Germanic tribe—Franks, Lombards, Germans, Burgundians, Vandals, Anglo-Saxons and Goths—the system by which churches were considered to be the property of their founders. The practice extended to bishoprics and rich abbeys, as in West Francia, where whole dioceses became the property of powerful nobles, who claimed cathedrals as their possessions. Only in countries such as Spain, North Africa, and to some extent Burgundy, where the Roman hierarchy had gained complete ascendancy among Germanic conquerors, did the system of proprietary churches or *Eigenkirchen* fail to supersede the old pre-Germanic and Roman practice of early Roman canon law.

So it happened that the king of a Germanic tribe, for being the richest landowner, also owned the greatest number of proprietary churches and consequently wielded paramount influence within the Church. The kings of East Francia succeeded in putting a stop to the practice which had developed in West Francia. It was Otto I who was mostly responsible for preventing its introduction into Germany.

Otto I considerably improved upon a custom which armed him with such authority by exempting churches and abbeys from the jurisdiction of the counts and placing them under special advocates who were acting as his representatives. All this helped him to make of the Church a *Reichskirche* absolutely devoted to the King and Emperor(20).

*　　　*　　　*

In one respect, Otto I stood to gain particularly by the theory of Empire as it developed under Charlemagne and his successors. It was the general belief that the Emperor's first duty was to propagate the faith amongst pagan nations. Otto I had his plans ready for the spread of his power and influence over the East. We have seen what attention he devoted to the Slavonic territories conquered by this father, detailing two of his best counts, Hermann Billung and Gero, for their supervision. Billung's task on the right bank of the Elbe was not made any easier by the support which the Slavonic tribes of the Wagiri and the Obodrites received in their resistance to German overlordship from the Danes and their occasional raids on German territory, and it took the margrave four years of stiff fighting before he was able to break their stubborn resistance and to pacify the region under his command. The Danes then paid tribute to Otto and

---

(20) Otto I mostly chose his bishops from among his chaplains, who as members of the Royal Chancellery and charged with the composition of Royal Charters were well trained in political matters. On the *Hofkapelle*, see the latest publication by S. Görlitz, " Beiträge zur Geschichte der Königl. Hofkapelle im Zeitalter der Ottonen und Salier," *Hist. Dipl. Forschungen* (Weimar, 1936), vol. I.

to keep the Germans out of Denmark, King Harald called the Blue Tooth, built a wall along the sector of his frontier that touched the Reich.

In preference to scaling walls, Otto discovered an alternative way for Saxon influence to get into Denmark—the propagation of the Christian faith, and for this purpose he found a good agent in the person of Adaldag, archbishop of Hamburg-Bremen, an enterprising prelate who felt at home in ecclesiastical as well as in political matters and whose interest in the venture was stimulated by the prospect of expanding the jurisdiction of his metropolis by the addition of new bishoprics(21).

Germany's internal troubles, besides encouraging Slavonic resistance, made Count Gero's task even more difficult than Hermann Billung's ; but the Count was not fastidious in his selection of methods. On one occasion, he is reported to have invited about thirty Slav chiefs to a friendly banquet and slaughtered every one of them. The struggle went on none the less and the Saxon Widukind(22) has some interesting things to say about the protracted hostilities and the Slavs' irreducible attitude :—" Nevertheless, the Slavs preferred war to peace, valuing dear liberty above comfort (*omnem miseriam carae libertati postponentes*). That kind of people is tough (*durus*), hardworking (*patiens laboris*), abstemious, and the Slavs find delicious what would revolt others. Many days thus passed, one side fighting with varying fortunes for glory and imperial expansion, the other, for freedom and escape from the direst servitude." In this clumsy imitation of Sallust, Widukind gives an idea of what the unfortunate Slavonic tribes had to suffer at the hands of Gero.

Things altered in 939 when Gero made use of the treachery of a captured Slavonic prince of the Hevelianes, a tribe of the Veletian confederation, called Tugumir, to annex the whole of its territory besides Brandenburg, which was lost on another occasion so far unknown. "By this feat," says Widukind(23), " all the barbaric nations as far as the Oder submitted to royal authority and paid tribute." But this was not the end of hostilities between Gero's Saxons and the Slavs, and not until Otto I succeeded in crushing the revolts of the dukes were the Germans able to subdue, at least temporarily, the rebellious Serbs and Veletians.

To pacify the conquered regions in the East, Otto I decided to use the method that served him so well in Denmark—evangelisation; but instead of first sending the priests to convert the pagans and prepare the ground for the ecclesiastical administrative structure, he started by founding the bishoprics. This procedure was not anything like the methods used by the primitive Church nor by the Roman Church in the conversion of the new settlers of the Western provinces of the Roman Empire, but it suited German mentality

---

(21) On this interesting personality, consult F. M. Fischer,"Politiker um Otto den Grossen", loc. cit. pp. 61-74. Cf. also F. E. Dahlmann, *Geschichte von Dänemark*, vol. I, pp. 78 seq.

(22) L. II, ch. 20, *M.G.H.S.* in us. schol., p.84. Cf. also on the struggle between the Slavs and the Saxons L. Giesebrecht, *Wendische Geschichten* (3 vol., Berlin, 1834), vol. I, pp. 140 seq. Though published a century ago, this book has still its value.

(23) L. II, ch. XXI, *ibid.*, p. 85.

and fitted into the fabric of the renovated Christian Roman Empire as Otto conceived it(24).

For such an undertaking, he needed the Pope's collaboration. The assumption of the imperial title would give him a distinct advantage in his eastward expansion, a useful hold on the Pope and, in Christian eyes, the juridical and religious justification of his drive to the East.

Here we are touching on an important problem that has for several decades preoccupied the minds of German historians : Was the expansion of the German Empire, after its first spirited start, inspired by the imperial idea, or did it merely draw its momentum from the innate vigour of the *Regnum Teutonicorum* which happened to be superior to that of its neighbours and grew in proportion to their incapacity to withstand its relentless pressure ? Ever since Roman times, the imperial notion had stood for world domination, and since the days of Charlemagne for a universal Christian community cast in the mould of the City of God on earth under the leadership of the emperor, backed by the highest religious authority, the Pope. On becoming emperors the German kings thus naturally adopted these two leading motives and drew from them the main incentive for their political expansion. Committed by their office to the spread of Christianity and finding in the newly converted nations willing materials for a universal Christian Empire, the German Kings posed as Roman Emperors and Charlemagne's heirs and found the ground conveniently cleared for their political aggrandisement. Such is the theory that has been adopted by the majority of German historians, foremost among them being H. v. Sybel, W. v. Giesebrecht, O. v. Gierke, L. v. Ranke, G. Waitz, and followed by most of their contemporaries and by many modern historians such as K. Hampe, L. Hahn, K. Burdach, H. Finke, E. Bernheim, A. Cartellieri, F. Schneider, E. E. Stengel, A. Brackman and others(25).

But the exponents of the " imperial theory " found a worthy opponent in F. X. Wernz who looked for reasons to account for medieval Germany's expansion in the nature and strength of the *Regnum*. Others followed suit : D. Schäfer, F. L. Ganshof, H. Günter, J. Haller, H. Heimpel and to some extent A. Hauck, arguing that the imperial idea is too slight to

---

(24) On the missionary notion of the Ottos, cf. I. Kirchberg, "Kaiseridee und Mission unter den Sachsenkaisern und den Ersten Saliern von Otto I bis Heinrich III", *Histor. Studien*, (Berlin, 1934), Heft 259 (full bibliography of the subject on pp. 159-63). Cf. also C. Erdmann, *Der Heidenkrieg in der Liturgie und die Kaiserkrönung Otto I*, pp. 129-42 and A. Brackmann, " Die Anfänge der Abendländischen Kulturbewegung in Osteuropa und deren Träger," *Jahrbücher für Geschichte Osteuropas* (1938), vol. III, pp. 185-215.

(25) It is not within the scope of the present book to go more into detail. Exhaustive bibliographical information is given by Th. E. Mommsen, *Studien zum Ideengehalt der deutschen Aussenpolitik im Zeitalter der Ottonen und Salier* (Berlin, 1930), pp. 8 seq.; and his indications are completed by M. Z. Jedlicki, " Poland's Legal Relations with the Empire till the year 1,000." *Poznańskie Towarz. Przyj. Nauk, Kom. Hist.* (Poznań, 1937), t. XII (in Polish). The same opinion concerning the imperial idea has also been defended by I. Bryce, *The Holy Roman Empire* (London, 1887), VIIIth ed., pp. 89 seq., and by A. Luchaire, " Les Premiers Capétiens," in E. Lavisse's *Histoire de France*, vol, II, 2 (Paris, 1901), pp. 151 seq., 205. Cf. also R.W. A. J. Carlyle, *A History of Medieval Political Theory in the West*, vol. III (London, 1928), pp. 170 seq., and Westfall Thompson, *Feudal Germany* (Chicago II., 1928), p. 361. A review of the controversy is found in A. Brackmann's, "Der Streit um die deutsche Kaiserpolitik des Mittelalters", *Vekhagen Klassings Monatschefte* (1929), vol. 43.

account for Germany's expansion(26). The controversy will go on, as long as it remains impossible to draw a clear demarcation line between the two notions in the history of medieval Germany. There were emperors who looked for their political inspiration almost exclusively to the imperial idea, and there were kings who pursued a purely German and national policy of expansion ; yet there can be no doubt that Christian imperialism did influence the political evolution of Germany and that even the kings who refused to be interested in this ideology and only believed in national expansion benefited by it to a very large extent.

All this must be borne in mind, if we wish to understand the import-ance of the missions founded by the German kings and the particular method which Otto I and his successors followed in their endeavour to convert the nations bordering on Germany. The missions were their own personal undertakings, the bishops their chosen agents representing their interests, and the new ecclesiastical foundations in some way their proprietary churches. It is easy to see how this system benefited Germany, but it unfortunately eliminated to a large extent the free collaboration of the native would-be converts. The native nobility could only see its dangers, and it was not till a later stage of Christianisation that some of the nobles perceived the economic advantages which the system of proprietary churches offered to their own interests.

Otto I seemingly had his plans ready for the erection of bishoprics in Denmark and in subjugated Slavonia as early as 946, for the next year he sent the abbot of Fulda to Rome to obtain the consent of Pope Agapetus II and the foundation was carried into effect in 947 for Denmark, and for Slavonia in 948 after a synod, held in the presence of a papal legate at Ingelheim(27). Otto's Danish foundations characteristically revealed his intention to gain control over Denmark by diocesan extension ; only one of the new Danish dioceses, namely Schleswig, was situated on territory which could be claimed to belong to Otto's kingdom, whereas the two others, Ribe and Aarhus, lay definitely outside Germany. Yet the three dioceses were placed under the jurisdiction of the metropolis of Hamburg-Bremen, which of course was under Otto's authority. King Harald must have seen through Otto's politico-religious subtleties and scented danger that needed checking, obviously the reason why he decided to become a Christian, with the result that Otto had to relax his grip on the Danish bishoprics and renounce the taxes the Danish bishops were expected to pay him. Being a Christian, the King of Denmark could, in accordance with current practice, claim certain rights over the Church in his country. He did continue to pay tribute to Otto I till the latter's death, but the set-back suffered by Germany in Denmark impaired her control over the Danish Church.

(26) For the complete bibliography, see M. Z. Jedlicki, loc. cit., p. 10. The same author gives a clear and terse summary of the whole controversy.

(27) On this, cf. M.G.H. Const. I, pp. 8-16. On the foundation of the Danish and Slavonic bishoprics, cf. Synod of Ingelheim, A. Hauck, Kirchengeschichte Deutschlands, vol. III, pp. 93-104. On the erection of a March against Denmark, cf. H.I. Dahlmann, loc, cit., vol. I, pp. 70 seq.

Different as conditions were in Slavonic lands, Otto had hopes that the ecclesiastical organisation would forge a link strong enough to bind the Slavs to Germany. He founded the diocese of Brandenburg for the territory of modern Lower Lausitz, Havelberg, for the territory of the warlike clan of the Redarii and Oldenburg for the Obodrites and the Wagiri, leaving out the territory lying between the Black Elster and Bohemia for reasons that are not clear(28).

However, for the time being, Otto I could not take full advantage of his foundations, as Germany's internal troubles, aggravated by Magyar attacks, had given the Slavs the stimulus to revolt. The years 954 and 955 were the worst, in spite of Gero's victory over the Ukeri tribe. The son of Wichmann, the disgruntled count who never forgave Otto the preference given to his brother Hermann Billung, inherited his father's grudge and incited the Obodrites to insurrection. The situation looked desperate, but Otto remained firm and refused the Slavonic chieftain's offer to accept German overlordship in return for administrative autonomy; he insisted on unconditional submission. Here again the Lechfeld victory reversed the whole position. Straight from the Lech, Otto marched against the Slavs, accompanied by the Czechs, and defeated the rebels. Wichmann fled to France, tried his luck again in 957 and in 958, but eventually was only too pleased to use Gero's mediation and obtain Otto's pardon. We hear of another expedition by Otto against the Slavs and that is all. They were so thoroughly pacified that when Wichmann, who was too undisciplined even for a Saxon, broke his word and made trouble again, he got no support from the Slavs. On the Danish King Harald's refusal to take common action against Hermann Billung and after some desultory fighting and plundering, Wichmann once more took refuge at Gero's court(29).

*　　*　　*

Such successes reinforced German power on the right banks of the Elbe whence Germany's influence crept as far as the Oder, gradually bringing her to a territory which for centuries had been left to itself and was occupied by a solid mass of Slavonic tribes of the same linguistic group, emerging into history under the name of one of its units, the tribe that gradually came out on top, the Poles.

It fell to the notorious Gero's lot to be the discoverer of the Poles. In his drive to the Oder he happened to make contact with the Polish Duke Mieszko (962-992)(30), who likewise happened to be bent on the conquest

(28) As German influence seemed to be firmly rooted in this region and as there could scarcely exist any difficulties with Bohemia, the most likely reason for the decision must have been, as suggested by I. Kirchberg, loc. cit., p. 28, some differences of opinion between the King and the archbishop of Mainz on the future of this territory.

(29) The main source for all these happenings is again Widukind, III, chs. 42, 53-55, 59, 60; *M.G.H.S.* in us. schol., pp. 122, 132, 136 seq., 138 seq. For details, cfr. O. von Heidemann, *Markgraf Gero* (Brunswick, 1860), pp. 87 seq. ; J. Widajewicz, " Wichmann," *Poznańskie Towarzystwo Przyjaciół Nauk, Kom. Hist.* (Poznań, 1933), t. VIII, pp. 394 seq.

(30) There exists a monograph on Mieszko written by H. Zeisberg (" Miseco der Erste Polnische Christliche Beherscher," *Sitzungsber. d. Akad., Hist. Phil. Kl.*, Wien, 1867), which though published in 1867, still repays consulting. I have been unable to come across the more recent monograph by St. Zakrzewski—Mieszko I, Builder of the Polish State (Warszawa, 1921), (in Polish).

of parts of the territory held by the Polabian Slavs and other Slavonic tribes on the Baltic coast. He had even stolen a march upon the German count who much to his regret was made to realise that the German eastward drive had at last, after the first rush over the Elbe and the victorious submersion of Slavonic lands, come upon a snag and been brought to a standstill.

To many historians, the appearance of Mieszko on the scene of history has seemed a somewhat incomprehensible phenomenon. He was indeed the first ruler of the Polish tribes to have had his name and his achievements put on record by contemporary historians and chroniclers, whilst the names of his predecessors—Ziemomysl, Leszek, Ziemovit and Piast, the legendary founder of the first Polish national dynasty—are barely mentioned by the earliest Polish chronicler known as *Anonymus Gallus*, who flourished at the beginning of the twelfth century(31). The only non-German contemporary writer to give us some interesting accounts of Mieszko and his Slavonic neighbour, the Czech Duke Boleslas I, is Ibrahim ibn Jacub, a Jewish Arabian traveller, who on his trading expeditions visited some Slavonic countries and in 965 or 973 spent some time at the Germanic court at Merseburg(32). Ibrahim must have been impressed by all he heard about Mieszko to lavish such praise on his realm as being the largest of all Slavonic lands, overflowing with honey, wheat, fish and meat.   He describes at some length Mieszko's standing army of three thousand well-armed men, who received their regular pay ``in minted money.''

The last detail prompted many historians to see there an indication that the ruling Polish dynasty of the Piasts was of Germanic, Norse or Viking origin and that Mieszko's standing army was composed of Norsemen, who with their chief were holding the conquered Slavonic countries in subjection. But this claim has no reasonable ground to stand on.   Nothing entitles us to identify Mieszko's army with Viking warriors and conquerers.   Mieszko, by sheer weight of personality, was the absolute leader of his men, paid their salaries and took individual care of their families, though it is possible that the Polish chieftain had enlisted into his service a band of Viking auxiliaries. The Norsemen, who at this period were making frequent incursions along the coasts of England and France, were not likely to neglect the nearer shores of the Baltic Sea.   There they settled not only in the lands later to be called the land of the Rhos or Russia—Novgorod and Kiev—but also at Wollin at the mouth of the Oder.

---

(31) Historia Polonorum, I, chs. 1-3 ; *S.R.P.*, I, pp. 395-398.

(32) The most recent edition of Ibrahim's text was issued by G. Jacob in *Arabische Reise-berichte* (Berlin, 1927), where the older bibliography of the same passage is also to be found-Cfr. also an extract from this book with some original observations by the same in P. Hirsch's German translation of Widukind " Widukinds Sächsische Geschichten " (Leipzig, 1931), *Die Geschichtschreiber der Deutschen Vorzeit* (Bd. 33), pp. 177-95.   Cf. also the remarks made by B. Spuler, " Ibrahim ibn Ja'Qub", in " Orientalische Bemerkungen," *Jahrbücher für Geschichte Osteuropas*, vol. III (1938), pp. 1-10, where the writer pointedly states that the Arabian Jew meant Polish Cracow, and he rejects every other reading of this text.   But he is less emphatic about Ibrahim's sojourn at Otto's court.   Although inclined to date it 973, as the date favoured by most of the German writers on the subject, he is not so categorical on the point, as the Arab seems to assume the existence of the Khazarian Empire whose collapse occurred in 969.

The country which Mieszko was governing had not been conquered by him and his warriors alone, nor was his empire set up by conquest in the true Viking manner: it was rather the result of a long process of alternating spasms of war and peace which remained anonymous, because Mieszko's forefathers had not had the advantage of contact with any civilised country whose chroniclers would have been ready with their pens to perpetuate the erection of the Polish State by the Piast dynasty(33). We must not forget that the Polish tribes had for many decades been protected against all possible German attacks by the Slavs of Bohemia and the Slavonic tribes settled along the Elbe and that their consolidation may have been achieved by other than military means. The Moravians had also been blessed at the dawn of their existence with some very able rulers—Mojmir, Rastislas, Svatopluk—and nobody is going to pretend that their leading family was of Germanic-Scandinavian descent. There is therefore no positive reason why the dynasty of the Piasts should have been less Slavonic than the dynasties of the Moravians(34).

At the outset of Mieszko's reign, two big Polish tribes, the Polanians and the Masovians, were living under the acknowledged supremacy of the Piast dynasty, whose centre was at Gniezno (Gnesen). The Polanians occupied a central position among the Polish tribes from the middle Oder along the whole length of the Warta, in the direction of the Vistula and Prussia, whereas the Masovians were settled on the middle Vistula and the lower reaches of the Bug as far as the Prussian territory to the north and the Russian country to the east. South of them was the seat of the Polish tribes of the Vistulanians on the middle and upper Vistula. Probably after the collapse of the Moravian Empire, the Piasts succeeded in obtaining supremacy over the greater part of their territory, with its centre in Sandomierz. The rest of the Vistulanians, centring on Cracow, were incorporated, as we shall have occasion to see, into the state of the Czech Przemyslides. The latter also succeeded in imposing their rule on the

---

(33) On the origins of the Piast dynasty cf. Z. Wojciechowski *Polish organisation of Polish Lands in the times preceding the Rise of the Piast Dynasty* (Lwów, 1927), pp. 17-64 (in Polish).

(34) The history and bibliography of this controversy was summarised by Z. Wojciechowski in his book—*Mieszko and the Rise of the Polish State* (Toruń-Gdynia-London, 1936), pp. 5-38, (Origin and Rise of the Piast Dynasty). The first German scholar to advocate this theory was R. Holtzmann in his study " Böhmen und Polen im 10. Jahrhundert " (*Zeitschrift des Vereins für Geschichte Schlesiens*, vol. 52, 1918, pp. 34-7). Historians who would deny the Polish Slavs the capacity to produce statesmen of Mieszko's standard, at such an early stage of their existence, allow themselves to be influenced by the theory, now out of date, which locates the primitive Slavs' original seat in the Pripet Basin ; since the poor conditions of those swampy lands were not such as to stimulate the cultural development of any people living on them, the sudden emergence of an able ruler among the Poles who had been severed from all contact with the civilised world seems difficult to explain on the assumption that the Slavs moved into this region only a few centuries before and there remained in their stagnation. But, as already stated, this theory is untenable. The problem ceases to offer any difficulty once it is admitted that the primitive seat of the Slavs was situated on the very lands that composed Mieszko's empire. Their culture was on a high level and they were in commercial contact with the civilised world. Although Germanic, and especially Gothic influence did touch them, there is no reason for assuming that, after centuries of occupation, the Slavs should not be able to produce one competent statesman. We can also assume that, though Mieszko's forefathers were not directly dependent on the Carolingian Empire, some cultural influence may yet have reached them from that quarter. Frankish methods of building a State may have inspired them to some extent.

numerous clans of the Polish tribe of the Slezanians. The Slavonic tribe of the Pomeranians or sea coast settlers, which occupied modern Pommern on the Baltic coast between the lower Oder, the lower Vistula, the Baltic and the Warta and Notec rivers, also belonged to the Polish group and was still independent. It was Mieszko's task to gather into his empire those Polish tribes that were still living either in independence or under the rule of another dynasty. This object inspired the whole political work of this great Pole, and it was in the course of his struggle for Pomerania that Mieszko rose to the surface as one of Poland's greatest historical figures.

*　　　*　　　*

Mieszko was ushered into Central Europe's history by Widukind of Corvey who for the first time mentioned him in his Saxon history(35) in connection with an armed conflict between him and Count Wichmann in 963. According to Widukind's statement, " Count Gero, who, remembering his (Wichmann's) oath and seeing him arraigned, knew him to be guilty, sent him back to the Slavs from whom he had got him. They welcomed him and in many a battle did Wichmann harass the barbarians in distant lands. In two actions he defeated King Misica (Mieszko), under whose rule the Slavs called Licicaviki were living, killed his brother and secured rich booty."

It seems evident from this statement that Gero, seeing the risk he ran in keeping among his followers a rebel who had perjured himself and broken his word to the King to be of good behaviour, sent him back to the Slavonic tribe on whose territory he had been staying after his defection from Otto I. The tribe concerned was that of the Ratarians, the most powerful clan of the tribal federation of the Veletians, and coastal settlers of the Baltic, in the neighbourhood of modern Stettin, on the western bank of the mouth of the Oder. Taking command of the Ratarians and aided probably by other tribes, Wichmann defeated Mieszko in battle and gathered immense booty for his reward. Mieszko's own brother was killed in one of the two encounters. This report by the Saxon chronicler is completed by another Saxon chronicler, Thietmar, who states(36) that in the same year Mieszko made his submission to Count Gero, that he remained faithful to the Emperor (*fidelis imperatori*) and was paying tribute about the year 972(37) for lands as far as the Warta river which he held in his possession. The meaning of these extracts has raised a controversy between German and Polish historians(38). What did they mean and where were the lands for which Mieszko had to pay tribute ?

---

(35) III, ch. 66, 67, *M.G.H.S.* in us. schol., p. 141.

(36) Chronicon, II, ch. 14, *M.G.H.S.*, N.S. IX, p. 54 : Gero Orientalium marchio Lusizi et Selpuli, Miseconem quoque cum sibi subjectis imperiali subdidit dicioni.

(37) Thietmar II, ch. 29. *M.G.H.S.*, N.S. IX, p. 74 : Interea Hodo, venerabilis marchio, Miseconem imperatori fidelem tributumque usque in Vurta fluvium solventem, exercitu petivit collecto . . . .

(38) A full account of the controversy is to be found in a recent publication on the legal relations between Poland and Germany by M. Z. Jedlicki, *Poland's Legal Relations*, loc. cit., pp. 21 seq.

Widukind's report on the clash between Mieszko and the Ratarians under Wichmann suggests that Mieszko's expansion movement was at that time aimed at the mouth of the Oder and the Baltic coast, where those Pomeranians had settled. This expansion, the Ratarians, who were settled on the left bank of the lower Oder and were anxious about their freedom and independence, naturally resented. They therefore blocked Mieszko's advance by a powerful counter attack and for the time being called a halt to his drive towards the mouth of the Oder.

This failure evidently upset the Pole's plans, for he found the unification of the Polish tribes in the neighbourhood of the Veletians jeopardised by the Ratarians and other tribes of the Veletian confederacy in support. Widukind expressly states that Wichmann's attack had been aimed at one of them—the Licicaviki; but Mieszko must have been aware of the fact that Gero could not but regard his drive towards the mouth of the Oder with suspicion. No doubt Gero himself coveted the same prize and wished to get the estuary under German control, but circumstances handicapped him for the moment. Mieszko knew that Gero had sent Wichmann to the Slavs for a purpose; not only would he keep Wichmann from harassing Saxony, but knowing the Ratarians' apprehension at Mieszko's approach, Gero could expect Wichmann to make things very uncomfortable for Mieszko and enable Gero's warriors to complete the subjugation of the other Slavs(39).

In consideration of all these facts, Mieszko took a decision typical of his statesmanship: he approached Gero with a view to combine forces and made a pact of which details have not been reported by the chroniclers, but stray references to it by Widukind and Thietmar will help us to piece together its main stipulations.

Thietmar of Merseburg (973-1018),(40) in the fourteenth chapter of the second book of his chronicle quoted above, states that in 963 Gero brought the Lusacians, the tribe of the Selpuli on the river Spree, and Mieszko with his subjects under the Emperor's authority. His reference further on, in the twenty-ninth chapter of the second book quoted previously in connexion with events of the year 972, to Mieszko paying tribute for lands as far as the river Warta is responsibe for the general opinion, held till recently, that Thietmar had in mind the lands adjoining the left bank of the river. Mieszko was thus, in the light of this reading, tributary to the Reich for a great portion of his lands from the Oder to the Warta. At a first glance this interpretation, which has found favour with all German and even some Polish scholars, would seem to be the only possible one; but a more detailed examination would show that the problem is not so simple as it looks.

First of all, if Mieszko paid tribute for all his lands from the Oder to the left bank of the Warta, he must have suffered a major defeat at the hands of Gero, or been at least in fear of a dangerous attack from that quarter, for nothing else would have induced him to submit to such a

---

(39) Cfr. what M. Z. Jedlicki recently wrote on this subject in his book already quoted, on the *Legal Relations with the Empire till the year* 1,000 pp. 24 seq.

(40) On this first-rate Saxon Chronicle, cf. W. Wattenbach, R. Holtzmann, *Deutschlands Geschichtsquellen*, vol. I, pp. 52-8.

sacrifice. Thietmar's report, indeed, hints at such a defeat, but the surprising thing is that Widukind, a contemporary writer, whose chronicle constitutes the best source for the history of this period, mentions nothing of the kind, though such a sensational event could hardly have escaped the notice of a writer who was out to glorify the Saxons. It is true that it was Gero's plan to push his way as far to the east as possible beyond the Oder, but Gero did not feel he was in a position to carry it out, much less to start any serious drive beyond the Oder. The Serbs between the Saale and the Elbe had not yet been completely crushed, and at the very moment Mieszko was fighting Wichmann, Gero was busy preparing a new expedition against the Lusacians, the most powerful Serbish tribe that needed his attention. The expedition was by no means a comfortable parade, for, as Widukind reports(41), Gero lost his own nephew and many of his valiant nobles, he himself being seriously wounded. There was little chance after this for Gero being a menace to the Pole before the complete pacification of the Slavonic tribes between the Saale and the Elbe.

Mieszko must evidently have known the position. He also knew that he was screened against any possible German attack, after the Serbs' defeat by the Czechs who at that time were still holding the whole of Silesia under their sway. Count Hermann Billung had for the moment, as stated by Widukind, his hands full in trying to deal with the princes of the Vagrians and the Obodrites, his subjects, and to make matters worse, the inevitable Wichmann again appeared on the scene as an ally of the prince of the Vagrians. This makes it all the more difficult to understand why Mieszko, without a defeat, should have been reduced to the condition of a mere vassal paying tribute for so large a territory, which extended from the Oder to the Warta i.e. almost to the heart of the Polish realm and the cradle of the Polish race. We must bear in mind that Gero was not even in a position seriously to threaten him, let alone worry him with an expedition. In that case there must have been some other motive to account for Mieszko's submission.

*　　　*　　　*

Everything seems to point to the conclusion that the pourparlers had for their one object to find ways and means for dealing with the common enemy, the Veletians. This being admitted, Mieszko had offered to keep them in check by the conquest of their neighbours on the right bank of the lower Oder ; and in order to allay any anxiety on the part of Gero as well as to protect his own flank against any possible German attack whilst he was busy elsewhere, he undertook to pay tribute to the Empire for the country he proposed to conquer, known later by the name of Western Pomerania. This was after all not such a bad bargain, even for the Germans. The territory in question had its importance, enabling its holder to keep the Veletians in check. Since neither Hermann Billung nor Gero were in a position to subdue them, the wisest course was to let

---

(41) L.III, ch. 67, *M.G.H.S.* In us. schol., p. 142.

somebody else do the work, and here was one ready even to pay tribute for the service(42).

This explanation would be much more in keeping with Thietmar's account. Widukind mentions Mieszko only as a friend of the Emperor, suggesting the existence of some sort of an alliance between the two. He also writes at some length(43) about another expedition led by Count Wichmann against Mieszko in 967, Wichmann being this time ally and leader of the Volinians—a Slavonic tribe settled on the Baltic coast on the right bank of the lower Oder—probably supported by the Ratarians. This suggests that Mieszko had not relinquished his plan to conquer the Pomeranians' territory and that his slow penetration in the direction of the mouth of the Oder had once more alarmed the tribes in occupation. With the help of Wichmann's supporters and under his leadership they renewed the attempt to bar the Polish Duke's progress.

It was characteristic of Mieszko not to appeal to the Germans, his allies, for help, but to the Czech Duke Boleslas I, who presented him, according to Widukind, with two regiments of cavalry. This time, Mieszko was successful and with Czech assistance defeated the Volinians and slew Count Wichmann. After this victory we may suppose that the mouth of the Oder fell into Polish hands and that the conquest of the whole of Pomerania was soon completed. Eastern Pomerania, from Danzig on the mouth of the Vistula, must have been captured before 963, since that same year Mieszko, as mentioned previously, tried hard to advance towards the mouth of the Oder, an attempt that would have been futile, if his right flank had been under threat from the unsubdued Pomeranian tribes.

Unfortunately, Widukind's chronicle stops dead at the year 973, and in the last chapter, which takes us from 968 to 973, the author is only interested in the doings of the Emperor Otto I in Italy, and in his death. The greater pity, as Widukind's information is generally reliable(44). Thietmar of Merseburg (973-1018), our best informant for the next period, is in comparison with Widukind's historical work very inaccurate on the events of 963. We know that Mieszko was not defeated by Gero, the Emperor's general, as Thietmar has it, but by Wichmann, a rebel. The distinction is of some importance and it is certainly wrong to conclude, as has too often been done on Thietmar's authority, that Mieszko was the Emperor's tributary on a par with the defeated Sorbs.

Another reference to Mieszko's exploits by Thietmar—in the twenty-ninth chapter of the same book—is more accurate and completes what we know of Mieszko's progress toward the mouth of the Oder. In 972 the margrave Hodo, who after Gero's death (965) obtained possession of part of his territory, i.e., Nordthüringen, made an attack on Mieszko, the " Emperor's faithful liege and tributary for territory extending as far as

---

(42) The tribute could only be intended as compensation to the Empire for having written off the conquest of the country in question. On this point, M. Z. Jedlicki (*Poland's Legal Relations*, pp. 119 seq.), is right as against his German opponents.

(43) L.III, ch. 69, *M.G.H.S.* in us. schol., pp. 143 seq.

(44)—Thietmar and Widukind, cf. W. Wattenbach, R. Holtzmann, *Deutschlands Geschichtsquellen*, pp. 25-34. Cf. also L. Koczy Thietmar and Widukind, *Kwart. Hist.* vol. 50 (1936), pp. 656-76 (in Polish).

M.   C

the Warta river." But the attack, successful as it was at the outset, ended in disaster. The German army suffered defeat near the modern locality of Zehde and all its officers were slain.

Zehde lies on the right bank of the Oder, not quite half-way between the mouth of the Warta and Stettin. It shows that Mieszko had by this time conquered the greater part of the Western Pomeranian territory, the battle being fought north of the Warta river. Hodo's attack proved Mieszko's wisdom in concluding an alliance with the Germans in 963, before embarking on the conquest of Western Pomerania, and incidentally revealed the fact that the Germans were as keen as Mieszko on gaining control over the Oder delta. In relating the event, Thietmar could scarcely conceal his regret, though his own father had been fighting on Hodo's side, that the margrave should have joined battle with a *fidelis* and tributary of the Emperor.

Viewed in this light, the tribute paid for lands as far as the Warta seems to concern the country in which the fighting took place and which it was Hodo's ambition to bring under his control. It came to this, that Mieszko, the Emperor's friend, was paying tribute for the country north of the Warta, which Hodo actually invaded. The invasion was therefore not only unjustifiable but futile, since the Empire had renounced the conquest and indemnified itself with a tribute and because the country was being held by a friend and faithful ally of the Emperor. In this respect, Thietmar was not looking at the Warta river from the Merseburg angle, but from the standpoint of Western Pomerania where his father was fighting side by side with Hodo, and from the north, where the German army had penetrated deep in its victorious progress before being smashed up at Zehde. This interpretation seems to be the right one(45) : Hodo, not content with the tribute which Mieszko was paying, tried to bring this important territory under direct German influence and, killing two birds with one stone, to enlarge his own possession in the same process. His defeat should have convinced him that Count Gero knew the position far better when, satisfied with the promised tribute, he gave Mieszko free rein to conquer a country which at that moment he was unable to tackle himself(46).

---

(45) It was first suggested by Professor Z. Wojciechowski, loc. cit., pp. 38-69.
(46) J. Widajewicz in his studies " The Licicaviki in Widukind's Chronicle" (in Polish), *Slavia Occidental.*, vol. VI (Poznań, 1927), pp: 148 seq. and *Wichman*, loc. cit., pp. 74 seq., limited the territory for which Mieszko paid tribute to Germany to the lands of the tribe of the Licicaviki, where the conflict between the Polish Duke and Wichmann had taken place in 963. His arguments are, however, not convincing, as was again lately demonstrated by M. Z. Jedlicki, *Poland's Legal Relations*, pp. 45 seq. What German scholars consider to be the last word in favour of the theory of Mieszko being tributary for all his lands on the left bank of the Warta is the study by H. Ludat, " Mieszkos Tributpflicht bis zur Warthe," *Archiv für Landes und Volksforschung* (1938), pp. 380 seq., in which he tries to prove that according to German texts of the thirteenth century, the Warta is called Noteć from the point where it meets the Noteć river to its confluence with the Oder. But his evidence is not conclusive, as J. Widajewicz has shown in his critique of Ludat's study in *Kwartalnik Historyczny* (1938), pp. 442-8. Ludat overlooked a text of St Otto's biography of the beginning of the twelfth century published by A. Hofmeister " Das Leben des Bischofs Otto von Bamberg von einem Prüfeninger Mönch" (Leipzig, 1928), p. 30 (*Die Geschichtschreiber Deutscher Vorzeit*, vol. 96), which calls this section of the Warta by its usual name. Cf. Jedlicki, loc. cit., pp. 43 seq. The variations in the nomenclature of the river in later years can be explained by the influx from the end of the twelfth century of colonists who were not familiar with the local topography.

CAMROSE LUTHERAN COLLEGE
LIBRARY

With regard to the extent of the territory for which Mieszko promised to pay tribute to the German kingdom, I feel inclined to take Thietmar more literally than specialists dealing with this problem have done so far, and to locate it between the Baltic Sea, the lower Oder as far as the mouth of the Warta and the Warta river down to the point where it makes a sharp turn to the south-south-east. From this bend the frontier of that territory ran in the direction of the Baltic Sea along a line that later divided Western from Eastern Pomerania. It was probably due to the fact that Mieszko paid for only a part of Pomerania to indemnify the Emperor that we find this country divided into two in its subsequent evolution.

The only objection to this geographical reconstruction is that the frontier of Pomerania is believed to have followed the Noteć river in the south and that the territory between the Noteć and the Warta is supposed to have formed part of Poland proper ; but it is quite possible that in Mieszko's time the frontier had not yet been traced along the Noteć and that the territory between the Noteć and the Warta was annexed to Poland only much later. We know that the frontier between Pomerania and Poland proper was repeatedly altered in the course of years and that the Polish dukes and kings succeeded in keeping at least the territory between the Noteć and the Warta, when Poland lost Pomerania in the eleventh century. If this reading is admitted, Thietmar's statement becomes more intelligible and the whole incident is lent significance. The territory happened to be a very desirable investment and Thietmar had excellent reasons for stressing the fact.

*   *   *

Interpreted in this way, our sources will also help us to understand the events that took place in Mieszko's country the years following his defeat in 963. In his dealings with the Germans, Mieszko must have noticed the part played by the propagation of the Christian faith in the subjugation of the pagan Slavonic tribes. He certainly must have had some knowledge of the schemes which Otto I was nursing for the benefit of Magdeburg, which the Emperor had planned to turn into an important cultural centre for all lands beyond the Elbe and an advance post for the cultural and political conquest of the Slavonic tribes east of that river.

Otto I laid his plan soon after the foundation of the Danish and Slavonic dioceses. His first intention was to raise the bishopric of Halberstadt to the status of an archbishopric and then to transfer it to Madgeburg, but the opposition of the archbishop of Mainz, his illegitimate son Wilhelm (the offspring of a love affair with a noble Slavonic lady), forced Otto to alter his designs and to make Magdeburg into a new metropolis. The scheme was therefore a carefully laid plan, matured by years of discussion and thought, and Otto was determined to see it through. As already pointed out, it was the same desire which among other reasons drove Otto to canvass for the imperial crown as a necessary step to the control of the Papacy, and the confirmation of the Madgeburg foundation was the first instalment the Pope had to pay Otto for removing the menace of Berengar of Ivrea.

We still possess a document which reveals the grandiose plan as conceived by the Saxon Emperor, the Bull issued by Pope John XII and dated February 12, 962, in which the Pontiff authorised the erection of the Abbey of St. Mauritius, founded by Otto I in Magdeburg in 937, into an archbishopric. Without tracing the limits of the new metropolis, the Pope gave Otto I and his successors the right to establish dioceses in all Slavonic lands, wherever it should be considered suitable, and to subject them to the jurisdiction of Magdeburg(47). In the light of this document, Otto I must have dreamt of a new Empire, universal and Christian, stretching over lands old and new and pivoting round the three centres of Rome, Aix-la-Chapelle and Magdeburg. To inaugurate this noble conception of Magdeburg and its role in the building of the Slavonic world east of the Elbe, Otto I sent, in 961, a missionary bishop to Kiev, Adalbert, a monk of St. Maxim's Abbey in Trier and the future archbishop of Magdeburg. There is still some mystery around this missionary expedition, the whole venture seeming so extravagant to many Russian historians that some of them denied the authenticity of the report such as it is found in only one German source(48).

But there is no doubt that Otto I had designs on Russia and it should surprise no one that a German king of the tenth century should have tried to open contact with that country for the benefit of his own. The distance between Germany and Russia was of course enormous and, considering the limited means of transport of the period, probihitive of anything like regular intercourse. And yet information travelled between the two countries much faster than it would seem. But before discussing Otto's Russian schemes, let us go back to the first origins of the Russian State.

In the political organisation of the so-called Eastern Slavs settled between the Carpathian Mountains and the middle Dnieper, on the banks of the Pripet and in the Upper Dnieper Basin, whither they had moved in successive waves during the first millenary B.C. from the original Slavonic seat between the Elbe, the Vistula and the Bug, the leading part was played by a Germanic nation, the Norsemen from Sweden. It was they who replaced among the Slavonic tribes, later called Russians, the Antes, probably an Iranian offshoot(49), and the Avars, who had overthrown the Empire of the Antes. Avar rule collapsed in its turn, some of the tribes

---

(47) Cf. the easiest available edition of John XIIth's decrees in Migne's *P.L.*, vol. 133, cols. 1027 seq.

(48) In the Continuation of Regino's Chronicle, whose author is either Adalbert himself or one of his closest friends (*M.G.H.S.* I, p. 624, S. in usum scholarum, ed. F. Kurze, p. 170). The author attributes responsibility for the choice of Adalbert for the Russian mission to the archbishop of Mainz and he cannot refrain from one bitter remark which shows what Adalbert himself thought of the expedition : " licet (Adalbertus) meliora in eum (Willihelmum archiepiscopum) confisus fuerit, et nihil unquam in eum deliquerit . . . ." Cf. a short summary of the various theories advanced by Russian scholars on the event in G. Laehr, "Die Anfänge des russischen Reiches," (Berlin 1930), *Historische Studien*, Heft 189, p. 106. This bitterness can be explained by the failure of the mission.

(49) Here I only limit myself to the main facts so as to evoke a clearer picture of the whole process of development. On the Antes, their origin and the complex problems connected with their history see Appendix II.

resumed their previous independent mode of living, while others were subjugated by the Khazars. These belonged to a Turco-Tartar branch. They probably helped the Slavs of later Southern Russia to shake off the yoke of the Avars for good, and stepped straight away into the position which the Avars had vacated. The Khazar Empire had its centre on the lower Volga and on the Don. It extended from the Black Sea to the Aral Sea and, towards the north, as far as the river Oka.

The Bulgars were the next Turkish nation to set up an empire on the Middle Volga and Kama and as they instinctively pressed towards the West, there was serious danger for the frontiers of Europe receding further westward under the pressure of oncoming Asiatic tribes. This danger was averted by the Scandinavians who made their appearance among the eastern Slavonic tribes just in time to forge them into a solid political bloc which proved able to obstruct the westward rush of Asiatic hordes, and even to contribute, at least ultimately, to the expansion of European civilisation towards the East far beyond the Volga and the Ural Mountains.

The advent of the Norsemen amongst the Eastern Slavs is a long and fascinating story(50). As early as the eighth century, explorations on the Baltic brought them to the Balt and Finnish populations on its eastern shores, where they must have heard of the two flourishing empires established on the Volga by the Khazars and the Bulgars. The Khazars at that time carried on a brisk trade with the Arabs of Bagdad, a city that was then at the height of its prosperity and highly appreciated the products from the north, especially furs which were plentiful, and slaves. The Arabs paid well for these commodities and the Khazars rose to be the most influential intermediaries between the interior of future Russia, the Slavonic tribes living there and the Arabs. The Volga was a unique artery of communication.

---

(50) For more ample information on early Russian history, cf. especially two works easily accessible to western scholars : G. Laehr, loc. cit., pp. 12 seq., and G. Vernadsky, *A History of Russia*, vol. I : *Ancient Russia*, where the reader will find a complete bibliography and a detailed discussion of the problems touched upon here. (New Haven, Yale University Press, 1943.) See also S. H. Cross, *The Scandinavian Infiltration into Early Russia*, Speculum (1926), vol. XXI, pp. 504-14. On the Vikings, see F. D. Kendrick, *A History of the Vikings* (London,1930), especially pp. 142-78 (Russia and the East). The whole Russo-Scandinavian problem was gone into by V. A. Moshin " Varyago-Russkoy Vopros " (Varyag-Russian problems), *Slavia* (1931), vol. X, pp. 109-36, 343-79, 501-37, where the history of the controversies on the origin of the Russians is accurately outlined. A full bibliography completes the study. Good information on the history of Kievan Russia will also be found in the recent works of the following Russian scholars : G. E. Kochinym, *Pamiatniki Istorii Kievskogo Gosudarstva IX-XII vv.*, Leningradsky Gosudarstvenny Universitet, Leningrad, 1936 (Documents on the History of Kievan Russia in the IXth-XIIth centuries, published by the University of Leningrad) ; B. D. Grekov, *Kievskaya Rus* (Kievan Russia), Akademiya Nauk SSSR, Institut Istorii, Moscow-Leningrad, 1939, pp. 208 seq. ; M. N. Tikhomirov, *Istochnikovedenie Istorii SSSR s drevneyshikh Vremen do kontsa XVIII v.*, (Introduction to the Sources of the History of SSSR from the early period to the end of the XVIIIth century), Glavnoe Arkhivnoe Upravlenie NKVD, SSSR, Istoriko-Arkhivny Institut, Moscow, 1940). The interest shown these last years in the history of Kievan Russia in USSR is very striking. Cf. also my summary in the *Transactions of the R. Hist. Society* (1947), 4th s., vol. XXIX, pp. 27 seq. (The Kiev State and its Relations with Western Europe). A short summary of the problems related to the early history of the eastern Slavs can also be found in J. Macurek's *History of the Eastern Slavs* (in Czech), (Prague, 1947), vol. I, pp. 1-80, and the bibliographical notes in vol. III, pp. 19-82. The same author published a *Historiography of Eastern Europe* (in Czech), (Prague, 1947), where (pp. 313 seq.), an account is given of the discussions by Russian scholars on the origin of the Russians.

The Jewish elements always numerous on the shores of the Black Sea and the Sea of Azov must have played an important part in those commercial exchanges, since we know that their activities in Khazaria were brisk enough to convert the Khagan of the Khazars and a great portion of the native population to their own faith(51).

But the Norsemen were on the scent and they soon discovered the great natural artery by which all these exchanges were going on—the river Volga; but probably not from the Bay of Riga—rather from the Finnish Bay and from Lake Ladoga(52). Ladoga offered easy access to the Volga via Beloozero ; but there was a third route, via Lake Ilmen, which the Slavs had reached already in the ninth century. On both these routes two important Scandinavian colonies were founded, i.e., in Beloozero and Novgorod(53), by Rurik (probably Roerek) and his brothers.

The native population soon grew familiar with the recurring expeditions of Norsemen warriors and traders. They were coming from Sweden, which must have been known to the Finns, who at that time occupied the sea coast, as Roslagen. This part of Sweden, which still bears that name, was to all appearances the first which the Finns got to know. The Finns transmuted this Scandinavian name into Ruotsi ; the Arabs made them " Rus " and the Byzantines " Rhos." The name of Russia came into the world's map(54). "Varyag" seems to have been a name of later date(55).

(51) I have treated the history of the Khazars and their conversion to Judaism in detail in my book *Les Légendes de Constantin et de Méthode vues de Byzance*, Prague, (1933), pp. 146-211. An abundant bibliography on the subject will also be found there.

(52) G. Vernadsky (*Ancient Russia*, pp. 265 seq.), holds that the Scandinavians started from the Bay of Riga in the direction of the Don river, but produces no conclusive argument in support. The fact that in the area round the Bay and in the provinces of Dvinsk, Vitebsk, Kovno and Pskov Scandinavian remains are so few, prejudices his thesis not a little (Cf. T. J. Arne, " La Suède et l'Orient," *Archives Orientales*, 1914, vol. VIII, p. 44) ; also Laehr, loc. cit. pp. 15, 119). On Swedish antiquities on the route from the Baltic down the Volga towards the Orient, see F. Braun, " Das historische Russland im Nordischen Schrifttum des X-XIV Jht." in *Festschrift E. Mogh* (Halle, 1924), pp. 150 seq.

(53) It is known that some Arab writers (Ibn Rusta and Gardizi) locate the original seat of the " Rus " on an island wooded and marshy, a description that points to the source of the waterways followed by the Scandinavians : Ilmen, the Volkov river and Ladoga, and numerous excavations made in the tableland and at the convergence of the Neva Basin, the Volga, the Dnieper and the Dvina confirm the assumption. The Arab texts in their English translation are open to inspection in C. A. Macartney's book *The Magyars in the Ninth Century* (Cambridge, 1930), pp. 210 seq. Both texts speak of lively trade relations between the Norsemen, the Bulgars and the Khazars, which could only be conveniently carried on along the Volga artery, since the Bulgars were intelligent enough to allow the Viking tradesmen free passage through their territory and make their own profits. That the Arab texts should first mention the Khazars and only then the Bulgars need not imply that the Arab writers had in mind a Russian colony living on the shores of the Sea of Azov and thus in closer proximity to the Khazars than to the Bulgars. The Arabs were of course looking at the land from their own angle and were themselves nearer to the Khazars than to the Bulgars. Nothing then, in my opinion, justifies Vernadsky's theory (loc cit., pp. 283 seq.) that the Arab writers had in view the swamps of the Taman peninsula opposite Kerch in the Crimea.

(54) This explanation has so far been accepted by most philologists and historians. See below, Appendix IV, my own explanation as to how this name came to be so readily adopted by the Byzantines.

(55) The name " Varyag " which the Byzantines gave the Scandinavians (the Arabs made it into Varang) is of Scandinavian origin. Since the publication of V. Thomsen's book (*The Relations between Ancient Russia and Scandinavia and the Origin of the Russian State*, Oxford, 1877), experts have seen in it a derivation from the Nordic word Vaeringjar or confederate, which is similar to the Anglo-Saxon word waereng, which means a stranger or alien. Cf. A. Stender—Peterson's study " Zur Bedeutungsgeschichte des Wortes voeringi, Russ. varag." *Acta Philol. Scandinavica* (1931-2), vol. 6, pp. 26-38.

The Norsemen thus soon got to be known to the Bulgars, the Khazars and also the Arabs, as we owe most of our information about the Norse expeditions to Arab writers(56). The Norsemen went across the Caspian Sea as far as Bagdad. The Khazars must have held them in some respect and it is quite conceivable that the Norsemen, whom the Emperor Theophilus sent to Louis the Pious in 839, as we read in the *Annales Bertiniani* (57), were not simple merchants, but ambassadors from the Khagan who had taken them into his service. At that time, the Norsemen were the only people in Europe to know of the possibility of returning to Khazaria from Constantinople by the Mediterranean and through Germany across the Baltic and via Ladoga over the Volga, when the shorter route by the Black Sea and the Crimea had been cut by new invaders.

Yet the contact established by the Norsemen between the Khazars and the Arabs did not introduce into European history so profound a change as did the discovery by the Norsemen of a route from Novgorod via the Dnieper and the Black Sea, to Constantinople. The Norsemen thus traded with Byzantium from the second half of the ninth century. A third important Scandinavian colony was established east of Smolensk, where the Volga and the Dnieper ran in close proximity. On the way to Constantinople there existed only loosely knit Slavonic tribes, and as the Norsemen always travelled about in strength and fully armed, they found it easy to collect slaves and to supplement their merchandise at little expense. The Slavs soon discovered that it would be cheaper for them to accept any of those marauders as their rulers and protectors, even at the price of a tribute.

The Slavs' geographical advantages were considerable. They were established along the great commercial artery which linked up the north with the Black Sea and the Greek cultural world. They also took over the legacy of the Scythians, the Goths and the Sarmatians who had been in control of that route. Numerous cities had sprung up in the south of modern Russia with a mixed population of Greeks and natives and they

(56) On the Arab sources, find all the necessary details in Vernadsky, loc. cit., pp. 208 seq. The main passages in the Arab writers that concern the Russians have been collected by A. I. Harkavy, *Accounts by Moslem writers on the Slavs and the Russians*, Moscow, 1870 (in Russian), pp. 92, 192, 218. Cf. also A. S. Cook, "Ibn-Fadlan's Account of Scandinav. merchants on the Volga in 922," *Journal of English and Germ. Philol.* (1923), vol. XXII, pp. 51-63.

(57) *M.G.H.S.* I, p. 434 (ad a. 839). G. Vernadsky, loc. cit., pp. 275 seq. quotes this document as main eviddence for the existence of an independent Russian Khaganate, with its centre on the Taman peninsula, and founded by the Ruks Alans and a mixture of Slavs and Scandinavians. But the passage in no way proves the existence of any such political agglomeration ; for if the Russians in question did come from the Taman peninsula and the town called Tmutorakan, the capital of this presumed Khaganate, then why did the Emperor Theophilus not send them back to their destination direct by sea ? There were no hostile populations on that route to threaten the ambassadors on their return home. We have no reason for doubting the authenticity of the statement, but if we assume that the ambassadors came from Khazaria, then all difficulties vanish. As the route from Itil to Sarkel on the Don Delta or to Kherson was the common thoroughfare for Asiatic hordes driving west, it was seldom safe, and in this particular case, the danger seems to have come from the Magyars. The fact that the Emperor Theophilus sent the ambassadors to Louis cannot be dismissed on the ground that he wanted to get rid of them and prevent them reaching home. If such was his intention, there were other ways and means. Why did the Russian ambassadors so meekly walk into the trap ? If the Emperor intended to prevent them reaching home, it would have taken a stronger escort to restrain those determined Scandinavian warriors who certainly knew Europe better than any Greek ambassador.

served as trading centres between the interior of Russia, the north and the east, and the Greek colonies established in the Crimea and the Taman Peninsula(58).

The newcomers to the steppes between the Dniester, the Dnieper and the Don—Scythians, Sarmatians and Goths—were not long in learning the value of this commercial intercourse. They left those centres untouched, contenting themselves with levying tribute and using them for their own profit. The Goths, the last of these " empire makers," were tempted by the Dniester artery to move south and it became the classical line of traffic " from the Varangians to the Greeks." Huns and Avars wrought havoc in Southern Russia, but they were followed by the Khazars who revived the peaceful tradition of the past.

The Slavs who preceded and followed the Goths along the Dnieper took possession of some of the commercial centres and soon learned from the Sarmatians, their new masters, from the Antes and the Croats the secrets of trade. The most important of these centres was Kiev, whence commercial routes radiated north, south and west. The western road was probably opened by the Goths, who used to trade with the Western Roman provinces from their previous seat and continued to trade, once they had settled in southern Russia(59). This probably accounts for the line of communication which ran from Kiev to the cities of Czerwien, Przemysl and Cracow and would explain why Cracow became the capital of White Croatia. From there access was easy through the valleys of the Morava and its affluent to the Danube as well as through the valley of the Vltava and its tributaries to the Elbe. The rise of the Moravians in the ninth century and the commercial growth of Prague in the tenth century must be placed in this setting.

The Khazars, who had held the monopoly of trade with the Islamic East and Asia Minor since the seventh century, saw the value of Kiev and promptly annexed it together with the Slavonic land on the Middle Dnieper. But the Norsemen saw it, too, and since the Khazars were unable to provide the Slavs with adequate protection against marauding nomads, especially the Magyars, who lived at that time in southern Russia, they willingly exchanged the overlordship of the Khazars for that of the Norsemen. It was a smooth and peaceful change-over, the Slavonic cities in many cases settling it with the Scandinavians by the method of protective treaties. Constantine Porphyrogennetos, in his *De Administrando Imperio*(60), states that the Slavs were the confederates (pactiotes) of the Russians.

<hr />

(58) On these cities as enumerated by Ptolemy, see M. Rostovtzeff, *Iranians and Greeks* (Oxford, 1922), pp. 213 seq. On the cities on the Black Sea and in the Crimea, see *ibid.*, pp. 60-82, 146-80. Cf. also Vasiliev, *The Goths in the Crimea*, Monographs of the Medieval Academy of America, no. II (Cambridge, Mass., 1936), pp. 1-87.

(59) See details in M. Rostovtzeff's *Iranians and Greeks*, loc. cit., p. 215.

(60) Bonn, pp. 75, 79 : "The Slavs their confederates." The place Vitichev (Vitetseve) is called "The confederate city of the Rhos." Cf. A. Eck, " En Relisant le Porphyrogénète," *Mélanges Bidez*, vol. I, (Bruxelles, 1934), pp. 342-9. Already Kluchevsky (*History of Russia*, English translation by C. J. Hogarth, London, 1911-31, vol. I, pp. 55 seq.) pictured the Scandinavians as warriors, who offered their services to the rich Slavonic merchant cities. This feature of the Old Slavonic settlement on the Dnieper was rightly pointed out by M. Rostovtzeff, *Iranians and Greeks*, loc. cit., pp. 215.

The tradition which attributes the occupation of Kiev to Askold probably rests on solid ground, but the Varyags must have belonged to a clan other than the Norsemen(61), who settled in Novgorod under Rurik as their chief ; and as the clans were keen on imposing their leadership on as many Slavs as they could, the clans must have been jealous of each other. This would explain the hostilities that later broke out between Novgorod and Kiev. At the outset, Novgorod and Kiev kept strictly to themselves, as the two Norse Slavonic States were independent(62).

The Norsemen of Kiev and their confederates had but one ambition—to capture and plunder the richest city in the world, Constantinople. Their commercial relations with Byzantium had revealed to them how many treasures lay accumulated behind the walls of the " Protected by God," as the Byzantines called it, and to get at those treasures by a surprise attack would have been in the best Scandinavian tradition. Hence their famous attack on Constantinople in 860. The Emperor Michael III was at the time away with his army and his fleet on an expedition against the Arabs in Asia Minor (the Norsemen were well informed of what happened in Constantinople), but the attempt did not succeed. The Emperor got information in time, doubled back and beat off the Russians. Later Byzantine tradition attributed the deliverance of Constantinople to a miracle worked by the Blessed Virgin and the prayers of the saintly patriarch Photius(63), which shows what a deep impression the Russians' daring feat had made on the Byzantines.

The Russians' demonstration on the Bosphorus was pregnant with consequences both for themselves and for Byzantium. First of all, the Byzantines, alarmed by this new threat, sent an embassy to the Khazars to encourage friendly relations against the common danger and to protect their possessions in the Crimea. The two outstanding members of the delegation were the two brothers Constantine-Cyrillus and Methodius, who were destined to become the Patron Saints of all Slavonic nations and by whose religious and literary activities the Russians were to benefit most among the Slavs. Again the Patriarch Photius concentrated all his efforts on the conversion of the dreaded Russians and, as he himself testified in 866, succeeded. Kiev officially became Christian and Askold was baptised

---

(61) N. K. Chadwick, *The Beginnings of Russian History* (Cambridge, 1946), p. 24, thinks that they were of Hálogoland origin.

(62) Much to my regret, I cannot enlarge on this interesting evolution, but for details, see Vernadsky, loc. cit., pp. 278-92, 340 seq. I must, however, confess that his presentation of the settling of the Norsemen in Kiev does not seem satisfactory. There is unfortunately not sufficient evidence for the existence of a strong Varyag colony on the eastern shores of the Sea of Azov and still less for that of a strong Russian Khaganate round Tmutorakan as its capital. The idea is ingenious, no doubt, and would be irresistible, if facts were not facts, but as far as we know them, they do not favour the theory. Especially what Vernadsky has to say on the part which in his opinion that *soi-disant* khaganate played in the establishment of the Scandinavians around the Riga Bay and in Kiev seems to rest on questionable grounds. For this reason, I prefer to keep to the old-fashioned presentation which tallies with the facts as they are known.

(63) For details, consult my books, *Les Légendes*, pp. 148 seq. and *Les Slaves, Byzance*, pp. 137 seq. and A. Vasiliev, *The Russian attack on Constantinople in 860* (Cambridge, Mass., 1946), Mediev. Acad., vol. XII.

with all his followers. A bishopric was created for the Norsemen and the Slavs, and this certainly' in Kiev(64).

The whole history of Russia would probably have shaped differently, had Christianity at this first stage endured in Kiev and spread from there to the other lands in the East. Unfortunately, the first Christianisation of the Russians was of short duration. The *Russian Annals* (65) (*Povest Vremennykh Let, or Tale of Bygone Years*) called the Russian Primary Chronicle *or* the Annals of Nestor, written by an anonymous author about the year 1113, report that Prince Oleg moved from Novgorod with his Varyags, Slavs and Finns towards the south to the Dvina and the Dnieper, by way of the Lovat river, captured the Norse colony near Smolensk and appeared before the gates of Kiev. Unable to resist the onslaught, Askold was killed with many of his warriors—and that was the end of Christianity in Kiev. The new rulers were pagans and Russia was to wait another century for new Christian missionaries. At the same time. the capture of Kiev by the Norsemen of Novgorod united all the Norse settlements in Slavonic lands under one ruler, the founder of the new dynasty. The Russian State was born.

The occupation of Kiev by Oleg occurred about the year 882. The importance of a centre built at the junction of the Desna and the Dnieper was at this time so patent to the new conquerors that they decided to fix their residence there and to leave only a garrison at Novgorod. The next step was the consolidation and extension of their authority over the Slavonic tribes on both sides of the Dnieper and the shifting of the frontiers of the Khazarian Empire more to the east in the direction of the Don. This was done in the years that followed.

A few decades saw the new empire set on its feet. Norsemen and Slavs fused into one people. In 911 the new State obtained international recognition for the first time when Leo VI of Byzantium concluded a commercial treaty with Oleg. The Byzantines, not feeling able to alter the new situation in Kiev, however much they regretted the destruction of the first Russian Christian community by the new rulers, resigned themselves to the slower method of peaceful infiltration, and in spite of the attempt made in 941 by Oleg's son Igor to capture Constantinople, those mutual relations grew into a tradition. Defeated, Igor renewed in 944 the pact of 911(66).

---

(64) Cf. what I have said on this problem in my book, *Les Légendes*, pp. 180 seq.

(65) The chronicle has come down to us in two different versions—the Hypatian and the Laurentian—and was published by the Archeographical Commission appointed in 1843 by the Russian Ministry of Public Instruction, and can be found in the *Polnoe Sobrannie Russkikh Letopisei* : The Hypatian version, vol. II, fasc. I (3rd ed. Petrograd, 1923), the Laurentian version, vol. I, fasc. I (2nd ed., Leningrad, 1926). A modern Russian translation by V. Panov appeared in the Collection *Russkie Memuary, Dnevniki, Pisma i Materialy*, published by the Academy (Drevnorusskie Letopisi, vol. I, Moscow-Leningrad, 1936). There exists an English translation by S. H. Cross (The Russian Primary Chronicle, *Harvard Studies and Notes in Philosophy and Literature*, vol. XII, 1930), with a good and useful introduction. To facilitate research, I quote after the English translation, adding the years of the Byzantine era. The passage on the conquest of Kiev comes under the years 6388-6390 (880-882), S. H. Cross, p. 146. Cfr. also R Foerster, "Die Entstehung der Russischen Reichsjahrbücher," *Jahrbücher für Geschichte Osteuropas* (1936), vol. I, pp. 201 seq., 355 seq.

(66) Cf. on these happenings Nestor's Annals, 6412-6415 (904-907), 6420 (912), 6453 (945). S. H. Cross, loc. cit., pp. 149 seq, 151 seq., 164 seq.

Friendly interocurse between Russia and Byzantium naturally smoothed Christian penetration. The Russian traders had their own quarter in Constantinople near the church of St. Mammas, and we learn from Nestor's Annals(67) that in 944 there existed a church of St. Elias in Kiev where the Russian Christians confirmed by oath their resolve to comply with the stipulations of the commercial pact with Byzantium. The importance of this Christian community in Kiev became apparent when Igor was killed by the Drevlian tribe in revolt and when his wife Olga (Helga) took over the regency.

* * *

This Scandinavian lady was an exceptionally virile woman. She promptly crushed the revolt of the Drevlians, and as their territory formed a valuable link between the southern part of the new Russian State with the North, she joined it to the principality of Kiev and deprived the rebels of the right to their own duke. To enforce the unity of these vast Russian lands, she alternately resided in Kiev and Novgorod with her son Svyatoslav. We also possess valuable information about her financial administration, the collection of taxes and tributes in north and south(68). As a wise administrator, she fully deserves the esteem in which generations of Russians have held her.

Olga was equally quick in realising the importance of Byzantium to Russian life and had the good sense to see that it would be in Russia's best interests to enter into closer relationship with the Empire. Nor was her positive attitude to Christianity dictated only by her feminine instinct, more bent on spiritual things than that of a Norse fighter, but quite as much by genuine statemanship. This alone would explain her receiving baptism in Constantinople.

There still exists a doubt as to whether this baptism took place in Kiev or in Constantinople. Kiev would on the face of it have been the more likely place for it. There lived around the church of St. Elias a large Christian community which had risen on the ruins of the first centre founded by Greek missionaries under Askold and Dir, and it had thrived on commercial contact with Byzantium. Christian influences in Kiev about the year 955 would then have been strong enough to influence Olga and induce her to receive baptism there before leaving for Constantinople. Constantine Porphyrogennetos, who in his Book of Ceremonies gives a detailed account of Olga's reception in Constantinople, has not a word to say about her baptism in that city. There is also a discrepancy between the dates given by the sources. Nestor's chronicle and Jacob, the

---

(67) S. H. Cross, p. 163. Cf. A. A. Vasiliev, *History of the Byzantine Empire* (Madison 1928), University of Wisconsin Studies on the Social Sciences and History, no. 13, 14, vol. I pp. 389 seq.

(68) On the Scandinavian tradition about Olga, see A. Stender-Petersen's *Die Varängersage*, (Acta Iutlandica, 1934), loc. cit., pp. 127-55, and N. K. Chadwick, *The Beginnings of Russian History*, pp. 28 seq. Cf. Nestor's Annals 6453 (945),-6479 (997), S. H. Cross, loc. cit., pp. 164-75.

67

panegyrist of S. Vladimir(69), place Olga's baptism in 955, that is two years before her visit to Constantinople in 957(70).

On the other hand, the old Russian tradition, embodied in the Primary Chronicle and in Jacob's panegyric, and confirmed by the Byzantine chronicler Cedrenus(71), places Olga's baptism in Constantinople. Partisans of the Kiev theory dismiss this tradition and put it down to Greek vanity and prejudice.

These statements are plausible enough ; only, it should be observed that anti-Roman bias was not so strong in Russia in the twelfth century as has been taken for granted ; not strong enough to influence the anonymous author of the Annals. There was even less antagonism between East and West in Kiev in the tenth century. Even the Scandinavians were impressed by the Eastern form of Christianity and by the beauty of its ceremonial. It is a serious matter to discard a national tradition, and in this case, one confirmed by a contemporary Western report found in the Continuation of Regino(72) and coming from the pen of the German envoy to Kiev, Adalbert, or one of his closest friends. It must have been the tradition in the tenth century in Kiev, where Adalbert gathered his information.

As regards Constantine's silence on the event, it should be noted that the imperial writer described only such ceremonies as were likely to be repeated, as for instance, the reception accorded to a Russian ruler and the banquet given in her honour, not exceptional events such as the baptism of a foreign princess. As Russia had joined the Byzantine Christian commonwealth, no Byzantine expected Russian princes to make a habit of being baptised in Constantinople.

We may then conclude that Olga was baptised in 957 in Constantinople. For the latter period, the chronology of the Russian Annals is not reliable. But Constantine witnessed the event and his dating deserves credit(73). At any rate, her journey to Constantinople and her adoption of the name Helen, the reigning Empress's name, indicate that her conversion was the work of the Byzantine missionaries who administered the church of St. Elias in Kiev. The priest who accompanied the princess on her journey was probably a Greek.

The whole incident throws light on Olga's surprising move in sending an embassy to Otto I, after her baptism, in 959. This is vouched for by

---

(69) Published by Sreznewski in the *Zapiski* of the Imperial Academy of Learning, VIIIth series, vol. I (1897), p. 5.

(70) As recorded by Constantine Porphyrogennetos (*De Ceremoniis*, ed. Bonn, pp. 594. 598).

(71) Bonn, p. 329. This report is based on the chronicle of Scylitzes, which stopped at the year 1051.

(72) *M.G.H.S.* in us. schol. (ed. F. Kurz, 1890), p. 170.

(73) For particulars, see Laehr, *Die Anfänge d. Rus. Reich.* pp. 103-6. The foremost exponent of the " Kievan theory " was E. Golubinski, *History of the Russian Church* (in Russian), 2nd ed. (Moscow, 1901), vol. I, part I, pp. 74 seq. Recently G. Ostrogorski, *Geschichte des Byzantinischen Staates* (München, 1940), p. 200, declared himself again in favour of Golubinski's opinion, but without making it clear why he rejected Laehr's arguments. I have not come across his discussion of the subject in *Deutsche Litteraturzeitung* (1931), pp. 173 seq.

the man who headed the German embassy to Constantinople in the Continuation of Regino's Chronicle—Adalbert. Olga's ambassadors were unfortunate in their mission. They first had to wait for the return of Otto, then engaged in one of his expeditions against the Slavs on the Elbe ; and when the German king had met Olga's wishes by choosing a suitable man to be consecrated bishop and to be sent to Kiev in the person of Libutius of Mainz, the would-be apostle of Russia died soon after his consecration. Not until the autumn of 961 could his substitute, bishop Adalbert, set out on his journey to Kiev.

This contact with Germany was evidently designed to meet criticisms that came from Scandinavian pagan elements with regard to Olga's friendship with Byzantium. What gave them point was that the last expedition against Byzantium in 941 was led by Olga's husband. On the other hand, Scandinavians in Russia were pretty well informed about happenings in Germany by their countrymen in Sweden, who were in close touch with the lands under Otto's rule. The fact is that contact between Sweden and the Norsemen in Russia was constant(74). As Olga (Helga) probably came from northern Russia and alternately resided in Kiev and Novgorod, she must have kept in touch with Scandinavia more than any Russian ruler.

Then again, the German King had made a name for himself by his crushing victory over the Magyars at Lechfeld in 955, just the feat that would appeal to Norsemen. Rumours of the exploit must have reached Russia, where the Magyars were notorious and where the older generation still remembered their raids into the southern parts of the new Russian State.

At the same time, Otto may have been equally well-informed on what happened in Russia. We have seen how keenly he followed events on the Baltic Sea and how frequent his contacts were with Denmark. In his desire to keep the Slavs on the Baltic, from the Danish border to the mouth of the Oder, under his control, he must have kept an eye on the other side of the Baltic Sea as well. He was certainly pleased to see the Norsemen of Sweden concentrating on their political and commercial adventures on the Volga and the Dnieper, which left them no time for diversions amongst the Slavonic tribes on whose subjugation Otto was bent. It had been his one desire to extend his empire as far as possible over Slavonic lands and it may be that the Russian initiative had a good deal to do with the final shaping of Otto's schemes. Olga's embassy gave Otto I a feeling that his eastern plans were nearer realisation than it had seemed possible to some of his sceptic counsellors.

But Otto's schemes and Olga's plans came to grief at the very outset. Delay in the despatch of the missionaries wrecked the whole project. Probably before bishop Adalbert had time to reach Kiev, Olga was forced to hand over her powers to her son Svjatoslav and retire to Vishgorod, where she hoped to end her days in peace and prayer. Svyatoslav, the

(74) See instances of intercourse between Sweden and the Varyags of Novgorod and Kiev in F. Braun's well-documented study " Das Historische Russland im Nordischen Schrifttum des X-XIV Jhts," *Festschrift E. Mogk*, Halle, 1924, pp. 150-96.

first Scandinavian prince on the Russian throne to bear a Slavonic name—evidence of the rapid Slavicisation of the Scandinavian element—was a genuine Viking both in character and manner. Proof against his mother's efforts to win him over to Christianity, Svyatoslav, with his bodyguard of Scandinavian warriors (druzhina), only thought of war, plunder and adventure, never paying the slightest heed to her pleading. The German bishop had come too late, and finding no scope for his activities, left Kiev, carrying away no pleasant remembrances and even losing some of his companions on the journey back. But the failure did not daunt the German King, for in 968, as we shall see, he appointed the same Adalbert archbishop of Madgeburg and entrusted him with the task of bringing the Slavonic world under the influence of the German Church.

*   *   *

Otto's designs must have alarmed the Polish Duke, and although Adalbert did not cross the Duke's territory on his way to Russia—he passed through Bohemia(75)—Mieszko learned of Otto's intentions and scented danger for himself and the future independence of his country. Yet he did appreciate the importance of the Christian factor in the German conquest of the Slavs on the Elbe and the Baltic. There was no reason why he should not use the same expedient against the Veletians, thereby depriving the Germans of a dangerous weapon which could be turned against himself and his nation. It occurred to him that it would suit him better to play the part of the Emperor's ally not merely in fighting but in christianising the hostile pagan tribes.

Mieszko's conversion to the Christian faith proved sound statemanship, but he took good care not to ask the Germans, his allies, for priests; for these he applied to his more friendly neighbours, the Czechs, and received in addition the hand of Boleslas I's daughter Dubravka, who became the first Polish Christian Duchess.

The union strengthened Mieszko's position against Germany by a valuable alliance with the Czechs. The friendship was tangible enough, since Boleslas's cavalry helped the Poles in crushing Wichmann and extending their dominion towards the mouth of the Oder. Another result of the union was Mieszko's baptism and the conversion of Poland. Unfortunately, Cosmas, the Czech chronicler, in relating the activities of Dubravka in Poland, is very disappointing. He states in his Chronicle(76), in terms of profound indignation, that Dubravka had the audacity to introduce a new fashion among the better classes of tenth-century feminine society : married as she was, she threw up the ancient custom of wearing a veil and adopted the head gear of unmarried women. The innovation, provoked indignant and severe criticism.

---

(75) We owe this detail to a contemporary source, the *Vita S. Adalberti*, written by Bruno of Querfurt, chapt. 4, *F.R.B.*, vol. I, p. 268.

(76) Chronica, I, ch. 27, *M.G.H.S.* N.S.II (ed. B. Bertholz), p. 49.

However, Cosmas's younger colleague Thietmar, Bishop of Merseburg (975-1018), refused to be shocked by Dubravka's daring innovations in wearing apparel. He has nothing but praise for the Czech Princess's gentleness(77) and for her zeal in converting her husband to the Christian faith. Thietmar's description is certainly true to life and leaves little room for doubt that the princess took a large share in the conversion of Mieszko I and of Poland, as attested by the first Polish twelfth-century chronicler, the anonymous Gallus(78).

Since Bohemia was bi-liturgical at that time, we may assume that, besides Latin priests, there came to Poland priests who used the Slavonic language in the celebration of the sacred mysteries. Recent research has shown that the Czech ruling family was not unfavourable to the Slavonic clergy. There existed in the Castle of Prague, not far from the cathedral church of S. Vitus, a church of Our Lady which became the centre of the Slavonic liturgy of the Roman rite(79). It is because Dubravka must have had something to do with it that Cosmas, who disapproved of the Slavonic liturgy, was so hard on her when he wrote in the twelfth century. Thus, thanks to the Czechs and Dubravka, Poland once again stepped into the sphere of the old Greco-Slavonic culture founded by the brothers Constantine-Cyril and Methodius.

The adoption of Christianity by the Poles through the intermediary of the Czechs could raise no objection on the part of the Germans, since Boleslas I was, like Mieszko, a friend of the Emperor and an ally of the Empire, but his country formed in some way part of the German Federation and as such owed tribute ; and when forced by Otto I in 950 to give up his passive attitude towards the Empire and follow the policy of his brother Wenceslas and his own in the first years of his reign, Boleslas I remained loyal to the Emperor, not, however, without trying to turn the situation to his own profit and to the benefit of his realm. He accompanied Otto I on his expedition against the Magyars and was in command of a thousand of his best warriors at the famous battle of Lechfeld (955). He unexpectedly bore the brunt of the first Magyar onslaught from the rear, where the Czechs, according to Widukind(80), happened to be guarding the army's supplies. After the Magyars' defeat, Boleslas seems to have carried on the war on his own account and he finally drove the Magyars out of Moravia, which they had held ever since the collapse of the great Moravian Empire. Pursuing his success further north-east and south-east, he succeeded in adding to Bohemia's possessions not only a large slice of

---

(77) Chronicon, IV, ch 55, 56, *M.G.H.S.* N.S.I.X, p. 194.

(78) Chronica, I, ch. 5, *S.R.P.*, I, p. 399. Thietmar, whose chronicle is nearest to the events related, dates Mieszko's marriage with the Czech princess from 965 ; so do some Polish Annalists of a later period, but the greater number of them prefer the year 966. Cf. *M.G.H.S.* XIX, pp. 577, 581, 585, 614 seq., 664, 668 (Annales Cracovienses Vetusti, Annales Kamenzenses, Annales Capituli Cracoviensis, Annales Polonorum, Annales Cracovienses Breves, Annales Mechovienses).

(79) Cf. J. Cibulka, " Wenceslas' Rotunda of S. Vitus," *Antholgy of St. Wenceslas* (Praha, 1934), (in Czech), vol. I, pp. 291 seq.

(80) III, ch. 44, *M.G.H.S.* in us. schol., p. 125.

modern Slovakia beyond the Vag river, but also the regions of the upper Vistula including Cracow. Even the Slavonic tribes of Silesia had to acknowledge his overlordship(81). Boleslas thus became the real founder of the Bohemian State, the third Slavonic Empire that rose in the tenth century in Central and Eastern Europe side by side with Poland and the Russia of Kiev.

The Polish acceptance of the Christian faith from Bohemia and not directly from Germany was a master stroke that altered the trend of events in the Slavonic East and proved in the end the death blow to Otto's schemes in that quarter. He who in 967 anticipated his eastern drive to be a walk over and even contemplated bringing Russia into the sphere of Germany's cultural and political influence, was suddenly roused to a sense of sober reality when in the execution of his plans he came upon the unforeseen obstacle erected by the astute Duke of Poland.

Mieszko's alliance with Bohemia, besides reinforcing his own position, reduced Otto's capacity to use that country, which he already held under his protectorate, for trying his fortune beyond the Carpathian Mountains, where Boleslas's Empire was drawing nearer to the frontiers of the new Russian State. Under the protection of this alliance, the Pole could afford to challenge Otto's Magdeburg scheme and slip away from the jurisdiction of Magdeburg. We learn from various sources that he founded a Polish diocese in Poznań (Posen) in 968 and that the first Polish bishop was the priest Jordan.

*   *   *

German and Polish scholars are still at variance regarding the foundation of the Posen bishopric and its subjection to the metropolis of Magdeburg(82). Was it founded by Mieszko, Otto I or the Pope? Was Jordan a suffragan of Magdeburg or did he come directly under the jurisdiction of the Holy See of Rome? As political considerations have somehow clouded the issue, it is no easy matter at the present time to clear up and disentangle the complexities of a controversy as recent as the years preceding the outbreak of the war in 1939.

What we know for certain is that it had been Otto's intention to place the whole of Poland under the jurisdiction of Magdeburg, but Mieszko was too wide awake and upset the programme. German priests

(81) The history of Czech expansion under Boleslas I has been a topic of debate among experts ever since the end of the nineteenth century and more so in recent times. I shall have occasion to discuss some aspects of the problem in greater detail. The debate was lately reviewed by M. Z. Jedlicki, loc. cit., p.54, who also published an important bibliography. The best studies showing conclusively that the regions of Cracow and Silesia were conquered by Boleslas I have been written by R. Holtzmann ("Böhmen und Polen im X.Jahrhundert," *Zeitschrift des Vereines für Geschichte Sehlesiens*, vol. II, 1918, pp.9 seq.), and by J. Widajewicz "The Region of the Vag in the documents of the diocese of Prague, from the year 1086." *Society of the Friends of Science in Poznan, Historical Commission*, tom. XI, No. 4 (1938), (in Polish).

(82) On Jordan see especially W. Abraham, *Organisation of the Church in Poland to the second half of the Xth century* (Lwow, 1893, in Polish). pp. 30 seq.; P. Kehr, "Das Erzbistum Magdeburg und die erste Organization der Christ. Kirche in Polen," *Abhandl. d. Preuss. Akad. d. Wissensch.* (Berlin, 1920), p. 4.

were certainly working with Czech priests in Poland and were doubtless numerous, being the only ones available, but the direction of the mission was not exclusively in German hands.   We have no absolute evidence for the assumption that Jordan, who on Thietmar's showing(83), was exceptionally active in the conversion of the Poles, was a German.   He seems to have come over from Bohemia with Dubravka—which, however, does not prove that he must have been a Czech, as Bohemia at that period had not an exceptionally numerous native clergy of the Latin rite.   In any case, he had not been selected for the bishopric by either Otto I or some German bishop.

Otto's Magdeburg plan went to pieces after the death of Pope John XII (965).   His successor, John XIII, a member of an old Roman aristocratic family, could have but little sympathy with Otto's dreams of a new metropolis ruling over the whole of the Slavonic East.   Not the Emperor, but the Pope fitted into John's ideology as the sole protector of the Church and the champion of its rights.   Nothing but the German bishops' opposition had prevented the Emperor carrying out his scheme under John XII on the strength of his bull of 962 and it was to him a grievous disappointment to see the new Pope disowning his predecessor's decisions.

It should be stated that the Pope's position was more independent than that of John XII.   He had been raised to the papal throne not by the Emperor's choice, but by the votes of the Roman people on Oct. 1, 965, and although he had to appeal to Otto for help, when a year later he was driven out of Rome by a turbulent aristocracy, yet he succeeded in reentering the city before the arrival of the imperial army and saved himself the trouble of having to thank the Emperor for his return.

It thus happened that when the great imperial synod met at Ravenna to discuss among other things Magdeburg's promotion to metropolitan distinction(84), the Emperor saw himself obliged first to confirm the Pope's possession of Ravenna as a little douceur for the Pope's good will in the matter of Magdeburg.   But not even this did induce the Pope to go as far as John XII.   In his foundation bull, issued on October 18, 968(85), the Pope gave the archbishop of Magdeburg the honorary title of Primate of Germany, but seemingly limited his jurisdiction to the dioceses of Havelberg, Brandenburg, Merseburg, Zeitz and Meissen, as only these bishoprics are expressly mentioned in the papal bull.   On the other hand, in the same document we look in vain for a solemn reiteration of the privilege accorded by John XII to Otto I, giving him the right to found dioceses under the jurisdiction of Magdeburg in the Slavonic territory

(83) Chronicon, IV, ch. 56, *M.G.H.S.* N.S. IX., p. 196.

(84) On the happenings at Ravenna consult J. F. Böhmer, *Regesta Imperii* (Innsbruck, 1893) vol. II, pp. 213 seq., with indication of sources.   On Magdeburg and the part it played in the Church history of the tenth century, the most important publications is by P. Kehr, *Das Erzbistum Magdeburg und die erste Organisation der Christlichen Kirche im Polen*, loc. cit. On the foundation bull, cf. *ibid.*, pp. 19 seq. ; also A. Brackmann, *Magdeburg als Haupstadt des Deutschen Ostens* (Leipzig 1937), pp. II seq.   Among the older works on Magdeburg, see especially K. Uhlirz, *Geschichte des Erzbistums Magdeburg unter den Kaisern aus dem Sächsischen Hause* (Magdeburg, 1887).

(85) Ph. Jaffé, *Regesta Pontificum Romanorum* (Leipzig, 1885), vol. I, Nos. 3728-3730.

lying east of the Elbe. It looks as though the Pope intended to reserve to himself the right to deal independently with any situation that might arise in those countries. There is certainly a difference in tone and conception between the document of 962 and the bull of 968, as some scholars have been quick to perceive(86).

But on closer inspection of the 968 bull, it becomes apparent that the difference is not as fundamental as it might seem at first sight. The words— " the same archbishop of Magdeburg and his successors have the right to consecrate bishops in suitable places where, as a result of their preaching, Christianity has progressed, expecially now and in this particular instance (*nominative nunc et presentaliter*) in Merseburg, Zeitz and Meissen "—still allow room for the gradual creation of other bishoprics east of the Elbe. The same policy seems to inspire the Pope in another letter addressed to the archbishop(87). The difference is therefore not so intrinsic after all(88).

What however goes deeper than the general tone of the bull and the theoretical right of founding other dioceses, and has not been sufficiently stressed so far, is this. The name of the Polish bishop as a suffragan of Magdeburg was left out, so that the bull justifies but one possible conclusion, *i.e.* that the Pope refused to meet the Emperor's wishes and that the ecclesiastical organisation of Poland remained independent. Jordan was a missionary bishop directly subject to the See of Rome. Such papal freedom of action would have been impossible but for a certain complicity on the part of the Polish Duke. We have no direct evidence that Mieszko had sent an embassy to Rome, but everything points to the fact that he had done so. It is even possible that his envoy was present at the Ravenna synod. We shall presently have occasion to note that relations between Mieszko and the Papacy were very cordial between the years 973 and 990. This would justify the inference that as a result of the Duke's initiative, prior to the year 973, Rome was growing conscious of the leading part it should play in laying the foundations of Polish Christianity and the Polish hierarchy.

Experts who pretend that Mieszko had to pay tribute for all the lands lying between the Oder and the Warta are of course unable to explain Otto's puzzling attitude in letting the Pope have his own way and the Emperor's inability to obtain, from the Pope and the Duke, Posen's subjection to his beloved Magdeburg. The attitude is indeed inexplicable, if Mieszko was not an ally but a subject of the Empire, whereas it becomes intelligible if we assume that Mieszko was a loyal ally, paying tribute only for the lands between the Baltic and the lower Warta which at the time of the foundation of Posen he was busy conquering.

Had Otto I actually been overlord of all the territories between the Oder and the Warta, he would then have acted not only as Protector of the Faith, but also as the supreme ruler of the country, in which case the Pope would have found it hard not to place dioceses, founded by the Emperor in

(86) Such is especially the interpretation by A. Brackmann, " Die Ost-Politik Ottos des Grossen," *Hist. Zeitschr.* (1926), vol. cxxxiv, p. 248.

(87) Jaffé, loc. cit., vol. I, No. 3731 ; cf. P. Kehr, *Erzbistum Magdeburg*, loc. cit., p. 23.

(88) J. Kirchberg, *Kaiseridee und Mission*, loc. cit., pp. 38 seq., rightly points this out.

his own tributary States, under the jurisdiction of Magdeburg. But the Emperor was a determined man and he was still clinging to his pet scheme when he wrote (18th October, 968)(89) to the German bishops and counts announcing the foundation of the Magdeburg metropolis and declaring that Magdeburg would exercise jurisdiction over all lands beyond the Elbe, whether Christian already or destined to be converted to Christianity in the future: just a characteristic piece of strategy designed to cover his retreat and prepare the ground for future attempts. A similar manoeuvre is discernible in a document drawn up by Hatto, archbishop of Mainz(90), to give his support to the foundation. It all points to the inference that the Pope must have had some good reason for refusing to subject the Polish bishops to the German metropolis in deference to the Emperor's wishes; and that special reason was not only the Pope's idea of Rome's task in the foundation of bishoprics, but also the more earthly motive of Mieszko's independence and the desires he had expressed through his special embassy to the Holy See.

When discussing the pros and cons of Mieszko's embassy, German and Polish experts have characteristically omitted a detail which has its importance in the solution of this problem. The first Czech chronicler Cosmas(91) wrote a detailed account of the pilgrimage which Mlada, daughter of Boleslas I, made to Rome. Wishing to introduce the religious order of St. Benedict into Bohemia, the Princess joined a Benedictine Abbey in Rome and after a good grounding in monastic discipline, was consecrated by the Pope first abbess of her future foundation in Prague. According to the same chronicler, she brought a letter from John XIII, in which the Pope not only gave his consent to the foundation of a Czech Benedictine convent for ladies, but also approved the creation of a new bishopric in Prague.

Cosmas naturally attributes the initiative of this request and of Mlada's pilgrimage to Boleslas II, her brother, but this, Cosmas' own narrative shows to be innacurate. We know that the pious canon harboured an intense dislike for Boleslas I, the presumed murderer of his brother, S. Wenceslas, and consequently fathered many of his good deeds on his son, Boleslas II. Fortunately, though his quotation from the Pope's letter be far from absolutely reliable(92), he has left in the text as he arranged it the Pope's

---

(89) *M.G.H.* Dipl. I, no. 366, pp. 502 seq.

(90) Published by P. Kehr, " Urkundenbuch des, Hochstiftes Merseburg, *"Geschichts-quellen der Provinz Sachsen* (1899), Bd. xxxvi, p. I, seq. no. 3.

(91) Chronica, I, ch. 22, *M.G.H.S.* N.S., II, pp. 42 seq.

(92) As the text is important, I quote it here in full in order to help the reader in verifying my interpretation. Cosmas, I, ch. 21, loc. cit., p. 43 : " Johannes, servus servorum Dei, Bolezlao catholice fidei alumno apostolicam benedictionem. Iustum est benivolas aures iustis accommodare peticionibus ; quia Deus est iusticia et, qui diligunt eum, iustificabuntur et omnia diligentibus Dei iusticiam cooperantur in bonum. Filia nostra, tua relativa, nomine Mlada, que et Maria, inter ceteras haud abnegandas peticiones cordi nostro dulces intulit ex parte tui preces, scilicet ut nostro assensu in tuo principatu ad laudem et gloriam Dei ecclesiae liceret fieri episcopatum. Quod nos utique leto animo suscipientes, Deo grates retulimus, qui suam ecclesiam semper et ubique dilatat et magnificat in omnibus nationibus. Unde apostolica auctoritate et sancti Petri principis apostolorum potestate, cuius, licet indigni, tamen sumus vicarii, annuimus et collaudamus atque incanonizamus, quo ad ecclesiam sancti Viti et sancti Wencezlai maitirum fiat sedes episcopalis, ad ecclesiam vero sancti Georgii martiris, sub regula sancti Benedicti et obedientia filie nostre, abbatisse Marie, constituatur congregatio sanctimonalium. Verumtamen non secundum ritus aut sectam Bulgarie gentis vel Ruzie, aut Slavonice lingue, sed magis sequens instituta et decreta apostolica unum pociorem tocius ecclesie ad

designation of Mlada as " filia nostra, tua relativa,"—our daughter and yours—which leaves little doubt as to which of the two Boleslas' the letter was addressed to.   What is probably true is that Mlada, henceforth called Mary by her religious name, on her return from Rome, was greeted by her brother, since, according to the chronicler, Boleslas I had died that same year (15th July, 967)(93).   We shall probably have to abide by this date, although it is recorded by none but Cosmas and though some historians recently proposed the year 972 as more likely(94).

If the date 967 is exact, Mlada could not have been sent by her brother, and on Cosmas's own showing, Mlada had first to learn the practice of religious life in Rome.   Her sojourn there must have lasted at least a year, the minimum probationary period required for abbatial consecration by the Pope.   If the date of her return as suggested by Cosmas is correct, she must have left for Rome in 966 at the latest, and probably before.   It is also admitted that the letter of Pope John XIII (965-972) regarding the foundation of the abbey and of the bishopric, as preserved by Cosmas, cannot be genuine(95) for it has certainly been doctored in the second half of the eleventh century either by Cosmas or some other writer, but there is no reason for questioning the fact that Boleslas I had endeavoured to secure for his lands an independent ecclesiastical organisation and that he had sent his daughter Mlada to Rome with this request.

Concomitant with this diplomatic proceeding from the Czechs, a similar move from the Poles may be taken for granted, if it be remembered that Mieszko's wife was Mlada's sister and that Polish-Czech military co-operation in 967 on the lower Oder (the main military operation took place probably after the death of Boleslas I, though Czech participation may have been engineered by him) points to the cordiality and frequency of relations

placitum eligas in hoc opus clericum Latinis adprime literis eruditum, qui verbi vomere novalia cordis gentilium scindere et triticum bone operationis serere atque manipulos frugum vestre fidei Christo reportare sufficiat.   Vale."

(93) Cosmas, Chronica, ch. I, 21, *M.G.H.S.* N.S. II, p. 4.

(94) V. Hrubý, " Original Boundaries of the Diocese of Prague and the Boundaries of the Czech Empire in the Xth century " *Časopis Matice Moravské* (1926), vol. L, pp. 85-154. I have gathered the outline of this study only from the review made of it by V. Chaloupecký in *Czech Hist. Rev.* (1927), vol. xxxiii, pp. 352-9. Chaloupecky also seems inclined to accept Hrubý's suggestion about the date of Boleslas I's death.   It looks as though both historians had been influenced by Cosmas who dates the foundation of Prague from 967, though the date 973 should be considered the true one.   But this is not convincing.   If the Pope's letter is genuine, at least in its main drift, as we have tried to show, then Cosmas's statement that the bishopric of Prague was founded in 967 has some truth in it, as the Pope's consent to the foundation was obtained in that year.   I explain in the following pages how the foundation, which was decided on in 967, happened to be carried out only in 973.   Cosmas confuses many things, for instance the death of Thietmar, first bishop of Prague, which occurred in 982, and which he places in 969, but there is no serious reason why we should be sceptical in this particular case, since the date of a reigning prince's death must have been known in Prague, even in Cosmas's days.

(95) Cf. V. Novotný, loc. cit., vol. I, p, 585.   The last portion of the text as given by Cosmas is certainly interpolated.   It belongs to the mentality of the twelfth century, when Cosmas was writing and when opposition to the Slavonic liturgy was general.   Cosmas was one of its fiereist opponents, so that the words " not in accordance with the rite or sect of the Bulgarian people or of the Russians or of the Slavonic language "—could not have been written in a tenth century document, and certainly not in 967, or in 972, since the Russians had not yet been converted at that time and the Slavonic rite could hardly have been widespread in Russia of Kiev at that period.   Contact between the Slavonic clergy and Russia was exceptionally frequent in the eleventh century and Cosmas must have known of this.

between the two countries.   A common intervention in Rome by Mieszko and Boleslas I to obtain ecclesiastical independence is therefore, if not certain, at least very likely.

It is not implied that in presenting their request, the Dukes acted without previously informing the Emperor; if Mieszko I could perhaps have dispensed with the formality, Boleslas I certainly could not.   And Otto I happened to be in Italy in 967.   Nor is there any reason for rejecting altogether the possibility of the Pope's willingness to oblige Boleslas I, whose petition could only be acceptable to the Pope if it fitted in with his own ideas.   Even if we must disallow the authenticity of the Pope's letter in the wording as published by Cosmas, there is no reason to doubt that Mlada did bring back a letter from the Pope addressed to her father, but actually received by her brother, mainly referring to the same topics as mentioned in Cosmas's version.   But the Czech case differed from the Polish, as the foundation of a diocese at Prague depended far more on the Emperor's goodwill than the foundation of a Polish diocese.   Bohemia was considered to be part of the Empire and ecclesiastically belonged to the diocese of Regensburg.   As a Christian duke, the Pole had to defer to the generally accepted ideology which gave the Emperor, Protector of the Church, a say in all matters that concerned her interests; it must therefore be assumed that he somehow informed the Emperor, whether directly or by way of the Pope, of his intention.   Yet the fact that both Slavonic princes had summoned the courage to apply to Rome for independent ecclesiastical régimes in their respective States testified to the strength they had drawn from their mutual alliance under the very eyes of the German King and Roman Emperor. That Otto I was unable to wreck Mieszko's plan and saw himself forced to give his consent to the creation of an independent Polish bishopric was the acid test of Mieszko's strength and revealed the obstruction which Otto's eastern expansion schemes would have to face.   Be it said again, it was the alliance with the Czech that was responsible for the stalemate.

*   *   *

Concerning the foundation of the bishopric of Prague, the main particulars have come to us from S. Wolfgang's biographer, Othlon, who wrote his work probably about the years 1060-63(96), and from Cosmas. In the latter's chronicle(97) we read that the bishop of Prague, Gebhard, the brother of the Czech Duke Vratislav, was granted at a Reichstag in Mainz (it could be none but the Easter meeting of 1085) a special privilege by the Emperor Henry IV, in virtue of which the diocese of Moravia, erected in 1063, was abolished and its territory incorporated once more into the diocese of Prague.   In order to substantiate his claim, the bishop, says Cosmas, who attended the proceedings in the capacity of episcopal secretary, produced a document that had been issued to Adalbert and confirmed the decision of the Emperor Otto I and Pope Benedict VI.   This decision was the

---

(96) Vita S.   Wolfkangi auctore Othlone, *Acta Sanctorum*, Novembrer, vol. II, pars. I, pp. 565-82.   Cf. H. Delehaye's introduction and commentary, *ibid.*, pp. 527-65.
(97) Chronica, II, ch. 37, *M.G.H.S.* N.S., II, pp. 134-40.

original foundation charter of the bishopric of Prague. By its terms the new diocese of Prague included not only the whole of Bohemia, but also Moravia, with the territory of the river Vag in modern Slovakia as far as the Tatra Mountains, Silesia, the region of Cracow and the rest of the territory reaching eastward as far as the rivers Bug and Styr(98).

The prelates and nobles who attended the meeting were all favourably impressed by the argument and considered Gebhard's plea to be well founded, with the result that the Emperor confirmed the original decision by a special charter issued in Regensburg on April 29th, 1086. Cosmas gives us the text of the charter and his transcription was corroborated as generally reliable by the discovery of a twelfth century copy of the document in the Imperial Archives of Munich. There are not many documents relating to the history of Central Europe that have been as constantly and passionately discussed by German, Czech, Polish and Russian scholars as this foundation charter of the Prague bishopric. Many have regarded it as a fabrication by the impetuous bishop Gebhard, or perhaps his secretary, while others, though doubtful of some of its details, defend its genuineness. The bibliography bearing on the subject is enormous(99).

What looked suspicious to many was its geographical information on the frontiers of the new foundation. Were they copied from a document that traced the frontiers of Great Moravia ? Are we to take them for the

---

(98) According to Cosmas, Chronica, II, ch. 37, loc. cit., pp. 137 seq., the frontiers of the diocese were as follows : Tugast (probably the region of Taus-Domažlice in western Bohemia) que tendit ad medium fluminis Chub (the river called Chambfluss by the Bavarians), Zelza (probably the territory of the tribe of Zetlici, settled in the districts of Schlackenwerth and Karlsbad) et Liusena (Saaz) et Dasena (regions of Tetschen, Děčín and Bilina), Lutomerici (a tribe whose name survived in the town of Litoměřice or Leitmeritz), Lemuzi (on the river Bilina) usque ad mediam silvam, qua Boemia limitatur.   Deinde ad aquilonem hii sunt termini: Psouane (a tribe living between Mělník and Stará Boleslav, or Alt Bunzlau), Chrowati (Croats living in eastern Bohemia) et altera Chrowati (the Croats living outside Bohemia, probably on the territory of the former White Croatia), Zlasane (tribe settled on the river Sleza or Lohe), Trebowane (tribe in Silesia, probably on the left bank of the Oder), Bobrane (tribe on the Bober river), Dedosesi (probably on the upper Bober and the Oder) usque ad mediam silvam, qua Milcianorum (in Upper Lausitz) occurrunt termini.   Inde ad orientem hos fluvios habet terminos : Bug scilicet et Ztir (the rivers Bug and Styr) cum Krakowa civitate provinciaque, cui Vag nomen est, cum omnibus regionibus ad predictam urbem pertinentibus que Krakova est.   Unde Ungarorum limitibus additis usque ad montes, quibus nomen est Tritri (Tatra Mountains), dilatata procedit.   Deinde in ea parte,· que meridiem respicit, addita regione Moravia usque ad fluvium cui nomen est Vag, et ad mediam silvam, cui nomen est More (probably Mailberg), et eiusdem montis eadem parochia tendit qua Bavaria limitatur. . . .
The most important study dealing with the identification of these geographical indications contained in the document was written by J. Kalousek, " Über den Umfang des Böhmischen Reiches unter Boleslas II," (Sitzungsber. d. k. Böhm. Gesellschaft der Wiss. 1883, vol. XXXII.). Cf. V. Novotný, loc. cit. vol. I, pp. 567 seq.

(99) The works relating to this problem and published down to the year 1904 were reviewed in a study by J. Pekař, " Contribution to the controversy on the foundation charter of the bishopric of Prague," Czech. Hist. Rev. (in Czech), vol. X (1904), pp. 45-58.   A more recent bibliography is found in B. Stasiewski's Untersuchungen über die Quellen für die älteste Geschichte und Kirchengeschichte Polens (Breslau, 1933).   But none of the studies offers an adequate answer to all the questions raised by this complicated problem, though many have contributed to its final solution.   The best contributions in my opinion come from two German scholars : W. Schulte, " Die Gründung des Bistums Prag," Historisches Jahrbuch (1901), and R. Holtzmann, " Die Urkunde Heinrichs IV für Prag vom Jahre 1086," Archiv für Urkundenforschung (Berlin, 1918), Bd. VI, (Festschrift für H. Breslau).   The more recent study by S. Stasiewski is misleading and lacks the historical flair of the two other works.   Cf. also the commentary on the charter by the Bollandist H. Delehaye in the A.S., November, II, pars. I, pp. 542 seq. (Brussels, 1894).   It is well balanced and points to the best solution which, however, the author just misses.   The best edition of the charter is found in G. Friedrich's Codex Diplomaticus et Epistolaris Regni Bohemiae (Pragae, 1904-1907), vol. I, pp. 92 seq.

boundary line of the Przemyslide State ? Or were they the landmarks of the new bishopric's missionary territories ? As we shall have occasion to return in detail to some of the problems raised by this document, it will be enough for the present to consider some of its implications as regards the creation of this new ecclesiastical province.

Despite all the difficulties raised, it must be admitted that if we analyse this charter in close association with its contemporary background and all other contemporary sources, the problem is considerably simplified. It is first of all established that the diocese of Prague was founded, not by Otto II, as some scholars would have it, but by Otto I, as is proved by the version we owe to Cosmas. True enough, our second source, Othlon(100), attributes the foundation to Otto II, but he obviously refers to the Emperor who confirmed the election of S. Wolfgang in 972 and that Emperor was not Otto II, but Otto I. The negotiations, however, were started, as has been stated, by Boleslas I under the pontificate of John XIII who died in 972. If Boleslas I died probably in 967, then Otto I's hesitations in confirming and implementing the decision admit of only one explanation, the unwillingness of the bishop of Regensburg Michael (942-972) to give his consent. We have no direct evidence of the bishop's obstructive attitude, but there are serious indications that he had set his face against the scheme(101). S. Wolfgang's biographer, Othlon, in recording his hero's consent to the foundation of a special bishopric for the Bohemian nation, insists that the Saint had to disregard the unanimous opposition of his counsellors. Due allowance being made for the biographer's tendency to panegyrise, his account leaves the impression that Wolfgang's sweet reasonableness did help the Emperor in getting round some serious difficulties that beset the realisation of his old scheme.

Should the reader wonder why the Emperor did not break the opposition by less sophisticated means, he must remember that, to be true to his own Church policy, Otto could not consistently disregard a bishop's wishes. He had founded his royal power on the support of the bishops against the nobles and could not afford to create new entanglements, especially as the concession he was asking for was of no vital importance to the Empire: whether Bohemia had its own bishop or was subject to Regensburg mattered little imperially. We have only to remember the complications created by the archbishop of Mainz, Otto's own son Wilhelm, when he refused to consent to the raising of Halberstadt to archiepiscopal rank and its translation to Magdeburg; and when in 961 Wilhelm met his father half way by consenting to part with a small portion of Halberstadt's diocese to which Magdeburg belonged, then trouble started all over again with Bernhard, the bishop of Halberstadt, who of course did his best to wreck the King's

---

(100) Vita S. Wolfkangi, chapter III, 29, A.S., Nov. II, pars. I, pp. 578 seq.

(101) The bishops were, in accordance with canon law, perfectly entitled to withhold their consent from the division of their dioceses, as is evident from the canons that concern the bishops in Burchard's Collection (Burchardi Wormacensis Episcopi Decretorum libri XX, lib. I, especially ch. 66, lib. III, ch. 148, P.L., vol. CXL, cols. 565 seq, 702). Burchard (d. 1025) collected all the canons that were in ecclesiastical practice during the tenth and at the beginning of the eleventh century, and canonical prescriptions bound kings and emperors as well. Cf. Burchardi Decretum, loc. cit., lib. XV, chs. 7, 8, 9, 10, ibid., col. 896.

scheme.   Otto I possessed his soul in patience till the bishop died in 967 and only then did he apply to the new Pope, John XIII, for implementing his predecessor's confirmation.

The bishop's refusal, which contributed most to Otto's failure, was a bitter disappointment; and with circumstances so completely altered in Rome in 968, thanks to Poland's intervention, the time for execution slipped by.   He learned then by experience how difficult it is to trespass on a bishop's privileges and emoluments.   And as history repeats itself, Otto had a similar experience with Michael, bishop of Regensburg.   Here again, being away in Italy and too busy, or too shrewd to quarrel with his prelates, who after all were his best champions, the Emperor preferred to wait till Michael died (972) and made room for a more pliable prelate. Otto's selection for Michael's succession of the saintly Wolfgang who was not a Bavarian, but a Suabian, may point to a fear of trouble with Regensburg, as though the Bavarians were not in a mood to put up with any further curtailments of their rights over Bohemia.   It was a sufficient reason for choosing as the next occupant of the See a non-Bavarian, who would not be so sensitive to Bohemia's loss to his jurisdiction.   As a new Czech diocese meant a further inroad on Bavarian influence in that country and a slight on Bavarian prestige in the Kingdom, a process of decline started by Henry I when he won for himself the allegiance of Wenceslas of Bohemia, there was some reason to justify the native Bavarian clergy's reluctance in the matter.   We may also assume that considerations such as these decided Otto I to consider with favour Boleslas' demand for the creation of a Czech bishopric.

That is how the foundation could not be made good till the year 973, very probably at the imperial Diet in Quedlinburg at Easter, the last Reichstag to be presided over by Otto I, and was confirmed by the successor of John XIII, Benedict VI (972-974), as mentioned in Cosmas' charter of 1068.   By its terms, the lands of the Przemyslides were to be subject to the jurisdiction of only one bishopric, that of Prague, whose frontiers were strictly delimited as laid down in the charter.   They were not merely the boundary lines of the missionary field of the bishop of Prague.   All the regions enumerated in the charter could be considered to be at least nominally Christian and as such be made part of a regularly constituted diocese.

It will be remembered that Ibrahim ibn Jacub has given us valuable information about Mieszko's state and what he says about the country of Boleslas I corroborates the fact that the Czech Duke was in possession of Cracow.   This is what he writes(102): "At present (the Slavs) have four kings: the king of the Bulgarians, Bûîslâw (Boleslas), the king of Prague, Bohemia and Cracow, Mesheqqod (Mieszko), the king of the north and Náqûn (Naccon, Duke of the Obodrites) . . . As regards the country of Bûîslâw (Boleslas) it stretched from the town of Prague to the town of Cracow, the length of a three weeks' journey and it is bounded along its full length by the land of the Turks.   The town of Prague is built of stone and

(102) G. Jacob's translation in Hirsch, *Widukinds Sächsische Geschichten*, pp. 182, 184. The opinion that Ibn Jacub was thinking of Cracow found confirmation in B. Spuler's " Ibrahim ibn Ja'Qub-Orientalische Bemerkungen," *Jahrbücher für Geschichte Osteuropas* (1938), vol. III, pp. 1-10.

mortar and is the greatest commercial centre of those parts. From the town of Cracow there come Russians and Slavs with their articles for sale and their ranks are swelled by Mohammedans, Jews and Turks from Turkish territory, also offering their wares and currency in return for slaves, tin and various furs.'' We may infer from this that Boleslas' hold on this region would have been practically impossible if he had not at the same time exercised political control over Moravia, which at that period included a substantial portion of modern Slovakia. The indications of the charter therefore rest on solid foundations.

There is one statement in the charter which may be taken for Boleslas' wishful thinking, when it fixes the rivers Bug and Styr as the eastern boundaries of the diocese. Now, in 973 this region was already, as we shall see presently(103), in Polish hands. Its inclusion by the charter in the diocese of Prague may mean that at that time Boleslas had not quite renounced the notion of getting those lands under his own control. Both rivers had probably formed the eastern frontiers of White Croatia in the distant past, before it was disrupted by Svatopluk of Moravia, to be included in his Empire.

One can understand why the Emperor included this region as though it belonged to the Bohemian State, for it was Germany's interest to encourage Czech extension eastward as far as possible. Bohemia's eastern extension meant neither more nor less than the Empire's eastern extension; the nearer it would creep to Russia of Kiev the better for Germany. Otto I had failed in his first endeavour to extend his influence so far, but the future held possiblities and it was sound political wisdom to prepare opportunities to that effect.

But the birth of the new ecclesiastical formation was not to be an easy one. Though the charter of the new diocese had received approval in 973, we learn that Prague did not get its first bishop till three years later—Thietmar, the Saxon—and he was consecrated by the archbishop, not of Salzburg, but of Mainz, Willigis(104). It was also disappointing to see that in spite of the previous decision to the contrary, the diocese of Prague did not, on starting to function, include the whole of the Przemyslide State. A charter emanating from the chancellery of Willigis mentions on April 28, A.D. 976, besides the bishop of Prague, an *episcopus Moravorum*(105), a bishop of the Moravians. Late tradition, recorded by Cosmas(106), knows of a Moravian bishop Vracen, who may be identical to the bishop of the charter mentioned above. But the enigma remains and has so far eluded solution.

The clue may be found in Germany's political conditions at the time. It is known that Otto II found a competitor in the person of his cousin Henry II, Duke of Bavaria, whose revolt occurred in 974 and was crushed the very same year. Henry was four years old in 955 when his father

---

(103) See below, pp. 88–89.

(104) Cosmas, Chronica, I, ch. 23, *M.G.H.S.* N.S. II, p. 45.

(105) Cf. J. F. Böhmer-C. Will, *Regesten zu Geschichte der Mainzer Erzbischöfe* (Innsbruck, 1877), vol. I, p. 119, No. 13.

(106) Chronica II, ch. 21, *M.G.H.S.* N.S., II, p. 113.

Henry I, Otto's brother, died.   For years the regency was carried on by his mother, the late Duke Arnulf's daughter, but when the young Duke reached his majority, he began dreaming of higher prospects and looking about for friends to help him in the performance.   There is justification for putting down some clashes between Otto II and Boleslas II, as reported by some Annals in 975(107) to Boleslas' participation in the Bavarian revolt.   As we shall see later, the same Bavarian Duke will, after the death of Otto II, try his luck again to secure the throne for himself, supported by the Dukes of the Obodrites, of the Poles and the Czechs.   Bearing all this in mind, we must agree that the lively interest which this same Duke Henry II was taking in the foundation of the bishopric of Prague, as evidenced in the Life of S. Wolfgang(108), must have looked suspicious, to say the least.   The reverse should have been expected since it seemed to be in Bavaria's interest to keep Bohemia as long as possible under the influence of Bavaria's ecclesiastical authority; but to our surprise, Othlon states that the Bavarian Duke Henry II repeatedly pleaded with the Emperor on behalf of the foundation, urging him to " use his royal power, for God's love, to put into execution what had been begun for the benefit of his people."   We have seen that the Bavarian clergy opposed the erection of Prague into a separate bishopric.   In that case the Bavarian Duke's attitude must have been prompted by the desire to enlist Boleslas in his political schemes.

It is no wonder then that Otto II decided to make some alterations in his original plan and take his precautions.   It was only in 975, after he had crushed Henry II's revolt and made sure of the submission of Boleslas II, that he proceeded with the foundation of the bishopric.   For the obvious purpose of keeping Bavaria and Bohemia apart, the new diocese was not placed under a Bavarian metropolitan, but under Mainz, although Salzburg should have been its normal metropolitan, since Regensburg, out of whose territory the new foundation was carved, belonged to it.   Nor was this all.   In order to make sure of a strong Saxon influence in Prague, a Saxon, Thietmar, and a monk from Magdeburg, who had worked in Bohemia for several years and knew the Czech tongue, was chosen as the first bishop; and to prevent the power of the bishop of Prague from becoming a political menace, a new bishopric of Moravia was set up as a counterpoise and also subjected to Mainz.   It was evidently considered easier to control a territory if it was ruled by two rival bishops whose investiture was ultimately in the emperor's hands than one ruled by a single prelate.   This was the real reason why the short-lived diocese of Moravia was created, and the fact that Moravia had once in the past possessed an independent ecclesiastical organisation of its own could be shrewdly pleaded to silence opposition.

That is how all the difficulties which the problem of this famous foundation charter presents can be straightened out.   The reason why so many scholars failed to find their bearings in the thick undergrowth of theories and hypotheses was their neglect to consider the problem within the frame of Germany's contemporary political conditions.   The struggle

(107) For details, cf. V. Novotný, loc. cit., vol. I, pp. 593 seq.
(108) III, ch. 29, A.S., loc. cit., p. 578.

between Saxony and Bavaria for political leadership in Germany, which had grown to such proportions under Henry I, and after its forceful settlement by Otto I, flared up again in another form on the accession of Otto II, holds the key to the right solution of this puzzle in Czech and German history.

*   *   *

The Easter Reichstag of 973 in Quedlinburg, to whose decisions this charter probably owes its existence, was an event in contemporary history and the Annalist of Quedlinburg(109) remembered with a regretful pang the splendid array, the gorgeous setting of an assembly attended by what was bravest and noblest in those parts: Mieszko I, Boleslas II of Bohemia, twelve envoys from Hungary, two from Bulgaria and, as stated in the Annals of Hildesheim(110) some from Russia and Denmark, and even from Byzantium. It was a last survey of the great Emperor's life work.   Probably many plans for the immediate future were conceived there, but we do not know them, for the unexpected death of Otto I on the 7th May of that same year doomed them to oblivion.   We can only guess that things took their own course, so different from what the Emperor imagined—when for the last time he swept his eyes over the brilliant galaxy of warriors, nobles and friendly princes.

Mieszko's attendance at the Reichstag of Quedlinburg has been seized upon by some historians as evidence that Mieszko was a tributary to the Emperor for a large portion of his lands and attended the Reichstag by Otto's orders as his vassal.   Such was not the case.   Thietmar of Merseburg(111), who volunteers the information, also mentions in a previous chapter that on learning of a clash between Mieszko and Count Hodo, the Emperor sent a special message to both of them ordering them to keep the peace if they wished to remain the Emperor's friends.   The incident was evidently one of the subjects discussed at Quedlinburg, and as Mieszko, who was busy consolidating his conquest of Western Pomerania, was anxious to be on good terms with the Emperor, it is small wonder that he should be present at the Reichstag where the Emperor was to arbitrate in his quarrel with Hodo.

We may even accept the assertion in the Annals of Altheim(112) that Mieszko had offered to the Emperor his own son as hostage.   Not that he was afraid of the Emperor; but anxious as he was for the permanence of his conquest, he felt it imperative under the circumstances to remain on good terms with Otto I.   Besides, his conscience was clear, as all the reports on the incident in our possession assume the fiery Count and not the Polish Duke to have been responsible for the clash.   The defeat Hodo had suffered was serious and the surrender of Mieszko's son as hostage was meant to demonstrate to the Emperor that the Duke was bent not on war

---

(109) *M.G.H.S.* III, p. 63.
(110) *Ibid.*, p. 62.
(111) Chronicon, II, ch. 31, *M.G.H.S.* N.S. IX, p. 76.
(112) *M.G.H.S.* XX, p. 787.

83

but on the defence of rights acknowledged by Hodo's predecessor Gero and by the Emperor.

It is even possible that the hostage in question was the Duke's own heir apparent Boleslas, son of his Czech wife, Dubravka. He must have been seven at the time. His tombstone(113) in the cathedral of Poznan bore an inscription saying that when he was seven years old his hair was cut and sent to Rome. Though the epitaph is comparatively recent, dating from the fourteenth century, it may yet embody an old tradition. Cutting a boy's hair on his reaching the age of seven was an ancient Slavonic custom, observed with great solemnity from pagan days, but which the Church christianised by giving it the form of a ritual. We can read in the Slavonic Life of S. Wenceslas(114), written soon after 929, a short description of the religious ceremony as performed in the saint's childhood. Mieszko's son was seven years old about 973. The gift of the boy's hair to Rome was a token of Mieszko's and Dubravka's piety, showing that cordial relations between Poland and the Holy See, so effectively inaugurated about 966 by Mieszko's sister-in-law Mlada, were developing favourably. At the same time Mieszko's display of friendly relations with the Holy See served as a shrewd hint addressed to the Emperor that it would be wise to be careful about the treatment of a child that was under the special protection of S. Peter(115).

Similarly, when in 974, after the death of Otto I, Mieszko joined Henry II, Duke of Bavaria, in his revolt against Otto II, it would be wrong to assume that the Pole resented the surrender of his son and took this opportunity to sever his relations with the Empire. Henry II of Bavaria was the second Otto's cousin and many were convinced that he would be a better king than the youthful Otto II. Mieszko's support of the pretender rather showed that he had no intention of cutting himself adrift, though it may very well be that Henry had promised Mieszko, in return for his services, to release him from the tribute for Western Pomerania, which was then safely in Polish hands.

Again on this occasion and in 976, in the course of the Bavarian Duke's second revolt, the Poles acted in concert with the Czechs, Boleslas II being also a warm supporter of the Bavarian Duke. However, it all came to nothing and Otto II, after defeating his cousin, soon proceeded to deal with his allies. But his two expeditions into Bohemia proved a failure and Otto II was only too pleased, when in 977 Boleslas II, proving the better fighter, made him offers of peace and undertook to acknowledge him as the legitimate emperor (116). There is no sign of any such expedition against

---

(113) Epitaphium Chrabri Boleslai, ed. A. Bielowski, *Monumenta Poloniae Historica*, vol. I, pp. 320-2.

(114) Cf. its new edition in *Anthology of St. Wenceslas*, loc. cit. The origins and expansion of this custom was studied at length by K. Potkanski in " The cutting of a boy's hair amongst the Slavs and Germans " in the *Proceedings of the Polish Academy, Hist. Philos. Section*, series II (1895), tome VII, pp. 331-422 (in Polish).

(115) Cf. M. Z. Jedlicki, loc. cit., p. 136.

(116) The main sources for this conflict are the Annals of Thietmar (Chronicon, III, ch. 7 *M.G.H.S.* N.S. IX, pp. 104 seq.) and of Altheim (*M.G.H.S.* XX, p. 788).

Mieszko; but at the time (979 or 980) Mieszko, after losing his wife in 977, married Oda, daughter of Theodoric, Count of the Northern Marches, his relations with Otto II and the Empire were again on the old footing of an alliance and the tributary obligations for Western Pomerania. Thietmar of Merseburg(117) was very shocked by this union, Oda being a nun; but the pious German bishops had to overlook the impropriety for the sake of peace. Mieszko's son, Boleslas the Great, married, according to Thietmar, probably in 984, the daughter of margrave Ridgag of Meissen(118).

*   *   *

Dubravka's death in 977 was a sore blow to the Polish-Czech alliance. The bond that united the two nations was severed and soon the policies of Mieszko and his nephew Boleslas II drifted apart as a result of recent developments among the Polabians, the Baltic Slavs and in Russia. German rule in the Slavonic lands on the Baltic and between the Elbe and the Oder was ruthless; nor were the methods of christianisation adopted by the Germans such as would appeal to the Slavs. Military occupation and the margraves' unceasing vigilance alone could maintain peace in these occupied areas. The Slavs were champing their bits and constantly but vainly looking for opportunities to shake off the yoke of the Germans and their God, when Otto II gave them a chance by relaxing his grip on the Elbe and seeking adventures in Italy. Anxious to play his part as emperor and defender of Rome and Christianity, he had in 982 planned an expedition against the Arabs who had invaded South Italy from Sicily. But the disastrous battle of Calabria brought his dreams to an abrupt conclusion. He died the next year(119).

These events raised new hopes in the hearts of the Slavs, and all the conquered tribes from the mouth of the Elbe and the Danish border to the Oder, combined in a revolt, which swept all before it(120). 983 is still a black year in the German annals and one of the most disastrous years in the history of Germany. The infuriated Slavs plundered Hamburg, captured by the Christian Duke of the Odobrites, destroyed Havelberg, razed Zeitz to the ground and sacked Brandenburg, where they disinterred the body of the late bishop Dodlo, whose ingenuity in extorting tithes from the pagan and semi-Christian Slavs under his rule had left evil memories. After several bloody battles, the margraves' armies routed the rebels without being able completely to subdue them, with the result that the rebels succeeded in preserving their regained freedom, though under German supremacy. In 996 Otto III, after a protracted struggle, was compelled to accept the position as it stood(121).

---

(117) Chronicon, IV, ch. 57, *M.G.H.S.* N.S. IX, p. 197.

(118) Chronicon, IV, ch. 58, *M.G.H.S.* N.S. IX, p. 198.

(119) On Otto II's intervention in Italy, see futher details in J. Gay, "L'Italie Meridionale et l'Empire Byzantin," *Biblioth. des Ecoles Françaises d' Athènes et de Rome* (Paris 1940), vol. XC, pp. 329-42.

(120) The main source for the history of this insurrection is Thietmar, Chronicon, III chs. 17-19, *M.G.H.S.* N.S. IX, pp. 118-121. Cf. also Helmold, loc. cit., transl. by Tchan, p. 72.

(121) Cf. L. Giesebrecht, loc. cit., vol. I, pp. 280-3 W. Thompson, *Feudal Germany*, pp. 790 seq. More details in W. Bogustawski, *History of Western Slavdom*, vol. III, pp. 322-42.

The work of Henry I and Otto I in the territory between the Elbe and the Oder was all but completely destroyed, leaving the Germans with a precarious hold on Holstein, near the Danish border, and on the land of the Serbs, where the iron discipline set up by Otto I had stood the strain of the insurrection. Thus ended the first phase of the German *Drang nach Osten*. The second phase did not start till the second half of the eleventh century, when once again the German armies were able to cross the Elbe and secure a foothold on the right bank of the river. Then it was that the new German colonists beheld in dismay, as the chronicler Helmold has it, the ruins of the first colonising and Germanising attempts, the destroyed cities overgrown by forests, the wild undergrowth covering the last traces of furrows made by their forerunners; they had paid heavily for a soil wrenched from the native Slavonic population.

Upheavals such as these necessarily influenced the Polish-Czech relations with the Reich, and those of Poland with Bohemia. As Christian nations, Poles and Czechs used to look upon their Slavonic neighbours with something like contempt for being only heathens; and the Poles in addition treated them as dangerous enemies who blocked their drive towards the West and to the mouth of the Oder. It was therefore only natural that the Slavonic uprising should have alarmed even Mieszko, who remembered what they had meant to him in the past and could hardly expect anything better for the future. Had the Veletians succeeded in crushing the imperial troops, it was evident that his own turn would come next.

*   *   *

And yet, at the first sign of revolt, Mieszko failed to realise the danger, for we read in Thietmar's chronicle(122) that in 984 the erstwhile Duke of Bavaria, Henry II called the Quarrelsome, was approached by Mieszko I of Poland, Boleslas II of Bohemia and Mistivoi, Duke of the Obodrites and victor of Hamburg, and proclaimed rightful emperor. This toying on the part of the Slavonic dukes with dangerous adventures for the benefit of one, who after barely recovering his freedom on Otto It's death, was again hankering after the throne, throws an interesting sidelight on the restlessness of the period. Once more the Czech Duke's support of the pretender was more whole-hearted than the Pole's and by the same token, Boleslas II was also prompter in seizing the reward for his services by occupying the town of Meissen in the land of the Serbs, in the hope of making it a jumping-off ground for Czech expansion towards the north. However, Henry's candidature came to grief again and the boy-king Otto III, with the help of his mother Theophano and the majority of the German princes, maintained his right of succession. Henry made peace with the regency and recovered his Bavarian Duchy. This put an end to Czech hopes of expansion and Boleslas II had to evacuate Meissen(123).

---

(122) Chronicon, IV, ch. 2, *M.G.H.S.* N.S. IX, p. 132.
(123) Thietmar, Chronicon, IV, chs. 5, 6, *M.G.H.S.* N.S. IX. pp. 136, 138.

Mieszko was nimbler than Boleslas II in changing his mind and his policy. We read in the Quedlinburg Annals that Mieszko already in 985(124) helped the Saxons to subdue the Slavs in revolt; that the year following, both Dukes presented themselves at the Easter Reichstag in Quedlinburg(125) and that Mieszko had brought numerous presents to the young King, including a camel, which at the time was a most uncommon sight in the West. But the hump-backed beast did not end its glorious career at Otto III's court ; it made its solemn appearance not only in contemporary annals and chronicles, but it is found proudly sauntering through all the books that deal with the early relations between Poland and Germany. It is the general interpretation that Mieszko, in addition to the camel, made a present to the young King of his country's independence. This seems to be borne out by the Annals when they state that Mieszko submitted to the King's authority, and by Thietmar(126) who affirms that Mieszko offered himself to the King.

Experts who have had to deal with this incident have omitted to place the problem in the setting of previous happenings. At the Reichstag of Quedlinburg the flirting incident between Henry of Bavaria and the Slav dukes was definitely settled. Mieszko, by lending his support to Henry of Bavaria, had severed his relations not only with the King but with the Empire. We may assume that the unsuccessful pretender rewarded Mieszko for his pains by remitting the tribute for West Pomerania; but when the adventure failed, the necessity remained for the Polish Duke to patch up his alliance with the Emperor and to renew his promise to pay the tribute. Again, the initiative came from Mieszko who by this time must have realised that the danger coming from the rebellious Slavs was greater than at first supposed and chiefly that his conquest of Pomerania was seriously imperilled by the Veletian menace. There could be no question of Poland's submission to Germany or of any feudal ties between the King and the Duke, and there was absolutely no reason for Mieszko to go further in 986 than he had gone in 963, since the imperial regency was as anxious to secure his assistance as he was to get the support of his German neighbours and his allies against the common enemy. Both were actually combining action against the Slav rebels in 987 and in 991(127).

Another danger coming from the Danish border hastened Mieszko's decision. Some sources mention a landing on the Pomeranian coast in Wollin by a Danish force led by the dethroned King Harald Blue Tooth, with whose help the Swedish pretender Styrblörn hoped to ascend the Swedish throne—so many new complications that probably arose between 984 and 986. The occupation of Wollin by the fugitive Danes certainly spelled danger, forcing Mieszko not only hurriedly to renew his alliance with the Empire and the young Otto III, but also to start negotiations with the King of Sweden, Eric the Victorious, who also felt threatened by the coalition of the

---

(124) *M.G.H.S.* III, p. 66.
(125) Ibid., p. 67.
(126) Chronicon, IV, ch. 9, *M.G.H.S.* N.S. IX, p. 141.
(127) Annales Hildesheimenses, *M.G.H.S.* III, pp. 67 seq.

allied Danish and Swedish fugitives then firmly established on the Baltic coast(128). In order to lubricate this Polish-Swedish alliance with a marriage, Mieszko I gave to Eric his daughter, called in Scandinavian sources Sigrid Storrada and whose Slavonic name may have been Swientoslawa. The new alliance enabled Mieszko I to give the Danish menace very short shrift. According to some Scandinavian sources, Iomsborg, the Scandinavian name for Wollin, was reduced to subjection by Mieszko and the Scandinavian garrison forced to accept his overlordship. His alliance with the German Empire benefited him in another way: carrying on the war with the Ratarians of the Veletian confederation, the Pole crossed the lower Oder and captured the important fortress of Stettin(129), a prize that insured the Polish hold on Western Pomerania against attacks from west and north.

The conquest of Pomerania was a remarkable feat. It was made permanent by the occupation of Stettin, but it also put an end to all further Polish expansion to the north-west, for it would have been difficult for the Poles to cross the Oder to any profitable extent, guarded as it was by the warlike Veletians. Their territory came anyhow within the sphere of German interests, which Mieszko felt in honour bound to respect. The Polish State had therefore to alter its line of expansion. Good prospects seemed to open to the south-east where the Russian State founded by the Varyags of Kiev and Novgorod was gradually breaking the ground in Europe's history.

We have already seen that the Poles had crept within measurable distance of the region which the Russians could consider to be within the sphere of their own interests. They must have done so at an early period, though it is difficult to say when exactly it did happen. Was it after the collapse of the Moravian Empire at the beginning of the tenth century or after the defeat of the Magyars by Otto I in 955 ? Both dates can be defended, but since the Czechs started expanding towards the East probably only after the Magyar defeat, it seems more likely that Polish expansion in the same direction started about the same time. We may then assume that after the destruction of the capital of Svatopluk's empire in Moravia, the Vistulanians, released from their bonds, carried on their quasi-independent existence, with probably some sort of recognition of Magyar supremacy. When Magyar power broke in its turn, Czechs and Poles made for what remained of the spoils of the Moravian Empire as they fell from Magyar grip. The Czechs succeeded in occupying Moravia, Silesia and the region of Cracow, but had to leave the rest of the former White Croatia to the Poles. Either Mieszko or his father Ziemomysl annexed the greater part of this territory which centred on Sandomierz and from there forged ahead towards the south in the

---

(128) Poland's relations with Scandinavia in the days of the early Piasts have been studied specially by L. Koczy (*Polska a Skandynawia za pierwszych Piastow*, Poznan, 1934, pp. 1-11). I have been unable to find this publication in Great Britain. Prof. Z. Wojciechowski, in his book *Miesko I and the Rise of the Polish State*, loc. cit., pp. 89 seq., gives in English extracts from Koczy's book with some original comments. Cf. also L. Koczy's study, "Jomsborg," (in Polish), in *Kwart. Hist.* (1932), vol. XLVI, pp. 211-320. Cf. also L. Giesebrecht, *Wendische Geschichten*, vol. I, pp. 205-50.

(129) Cf. Z. Wojciechowski, loc. cit., pp. 98 seq. We shall return to this problem later.

direction of the Carpathian Mountains as far as the upper Styr and the Bug, once the frontiers of the Moravian Empire. Boleslas I, who fancied himself as the heir of Svatopluk's realm, resented the loss of those Moravian possessions and neither he nor his son Boleslas II ever gave up hopes for their recovery. This much is suggested by the foundation charter of the bishopric of Prague, since, evidently at the suggestion of Boleslas II, Otto I traced the Styr and the Bug as the eastern limits of the Prague diocese.

We find then at this period two Slavonic political units, Bohemia and Poland, competing for the same territory, when a third competitor appeared on the scene—the Russian State. How it arose, developed and began to feel an interest in the contested territory will be the subject of our next inquiry.

The Russian State of Kiev had by this time successfully outgrown its critical age under the rule of the Duke Svyatoslav, the last Varyag adventurer on Kiev's throne. This stage might have ended disastrously for Europe had Svyatoslav carried out his scheme of transferring his residence to Bolgar on the Middle Volga (130) where he would in all likelihood have fallen under the spell of Arab civilisation and Mahomed's religion, when a chance occurrence saved Russia and Europe from the danger. Whilst Svyatoslav was busy celebrating his victory with his druzhina in sight of the sluggish waters of the Volga, an embassy arrived from Byzantium, sent by the Emperor Nicephorus Phocas, who after his defeat of the Arabs was contemplating the liquidation of the Bulgarian State in the Balkans and asked the Grand Duke of Kiev for auxiliary troops by the terms of the treaty of 944. The imperial ambassador Kalokyres had, besides, a plan of his own which he secretly explained to the Duke, suggesting that once the Bulgarians were defeated the Byzantine Emperor should be deposed and replaced by himself.

Here was something to fire the adventurous imagination of the Russians. The Volga was promptly forgotten and instead of quietly settling down among the defeated Bulgarians on the Volga, the Varyags moved southwards to make an end of the Bulgarian State on the Danube. Thus started a curious episode in Russian history, an experiment which looks out of place in Russia's later growth but was in fact a last flicker of the old Viking spirit. The story of this Russian adventure reads like a novel. But Svyatoslav, though he did defeat the Bulgars on the Danube failed, for all his valour and cunning, to hoodwink the Greek Emperor. Having learned of Kalokyres' secret plot, the Greeks induced the Pechenegs to attack Kiev and whilst Svyatoslav was busy plundering the Bulgarian cities, Kiev stood in imminent danger of being sacked and plundered. Only an accident saved Kiev, which was gallantly defended by Olga and her grandsons. Svyatoslav hastened back, and once the danger had passed returned to Bulgaria. There he rallied a great number of boyars to his cause in opposition to the Greeks. Another war with Byzantium followed the murder of Nicephorus Phocas in 970 and the Russians were able to hold Bulgaria as long as the usurper John Tzimisces was

---

(130) On the Volga Bulgars cf. a recent study published by the well-known Russian archeologist A. P. Smirnov, *Essays on the History of the Ancient Bulgars* in Trudy Gosud. Istor. Muzeya, vyp. XI, Sbornik statey po Arkheologii S.S.S.R. (Moscow, 1940), pp. 55-136, (in Russian).

busy with the insurgents.   Once more the fate of this part of Europe and of Russia hung in the balance, for Svyatoslav took such a fancy to Bulgaria that he decided to transfer the centre of Russian power to Pereyaslav on the Danube.

One might again speculate as to what would have happened if this adventurous, half-Slavicised Viking had carried out his plan and placed his dynasty on the throne of the Tzars in Bulgaria.   But the Byzantines took good care to keep this dangerous rival at a safe distance, and in 971, after crushing the rebels, John Tzimisces launched his campaign against Svyatoslav, penetrated with his " immortals " (the Byzantine version for the suicide squad) through the passes into Bulgaria, surprised the Russians and encircled them in Silistria.   It was a memorable siege in which the Varyags and the Slavs did wonders, but had to give in in the end and yield to the superior strength of Byzantium.   A new treaty was signed, which was but another version of the pact of 944, and eventually the two opponents met on the banks of the Danube, Svyatoslav, a simple and sinister barbarian, sitting in his barge, and the Emperor, riding on horse-back in golden armour, and with a splendid retinue.   The Bulgarian episode ended tragically(131), for Svyatoslav was killed by the Pechenegs on his way home and his skull was used as a wine cup at the great festivals of the nomadic barbarian princes(132).

It was also the end of the policy of fluctuation and hazardous enterprise in Russian history.   The new Russian State stopped drifting towards the Asiatic East and Islamic culture to return to Olga's programme of steady development, as it was carried out by the greatest figure in the Russian Annals, Vladimir.

He was Svyatoslav's illegitimate son and when his father divided his lands between his sons, prior to his Bulgarian venture, Vladimir received Novgorod which neither Yaropolk nor Oleg wanted as a gift.   But when Oleg lost his life in a battle with his brother Yaropolk, Vladimir, fearing a similar fate, fled to Scandinavia, later to return with an army of adventurers, captured Kiev and after Yaropolk's death in the field made himself sole master of Russia.   The new Duke finally abandoned the idea of transferring his capital to the east and contented himself with levying a tribute from the defeated Bulgarians of the Middle Volga.   One of his first military under-takings was directed against the West, for Nestor reports that in 981 Vladimir marched against the Lyakhs (the Russian name for the Poles, also used by other Polish neighbours such as the Czechs and the Magyars) and took their cities, Przemyśl and Cherven (Czerwień) among them(133).

(131) This exciting episode in Byzantine history was described with masterly verve by the French Byzantinist E. Schlumberger, *L'Epopée Byzantine à la Fin du Xe s. Jean Tzimisces*, vol. I (Paris, 1896), pp. 1-174.   Cf. also V. V. Vasiliev, " History of the Byzantine Empire," *Univ. of Wisconsin Studies in the Soc. Sc. and Hist.*, Nos. 13, 14 (Madison, 1928), vol. I, pp. 389 seq.

(132) Cf. on this episode the short study by F.I., Uspensky, " Znachenie pokhodov Sovyato-s'ava v Bolgariu " (The meaning of Svyatoslav's expeditions against Bulgaria), *Vestnik Drevney Istori*, vol. 4 (1939), pp. 91-6.   For details, cf. G. Laehr, loc. cit., pp. 58-73, with main sources and bibliography.

(133) Nestor's Annals, 6489 (981), S. H. Cross, loc. cit., p. 182, (ad a. 6489-981). See R. Jakobson's study, " Die Reimwörter Čech-Lech," published in 1938 in *Slavische Rundschau* (vol. X, pp. 10-5).

This short reference casts a flood of light on the political conditions in that part of Europe. As this is the first mention in the Russian Annals of the Red Cities and as we have no other information about that country, it may be inferred that the cities originally belonged to the Poles, which would substantiate the assumption that the Poles had occupied them after the Magyar defeat. How then did the Russians come to step in? A Polish drive towards Russia was a possibility at this period, as Polish expansion was then in full swing, but the chronicler's silence about any such move on the part of the Poles seems to suggest that this time the initiative came from Vladimir, and it was the first symptom of Russia's renewed interest in the West.

As the future was to show, Vladimir's drive and the occupation of the Red Cities or the country later known as Eastern Galicia were the start of the long struggle between the Poles and the Russians of Kiev, or the Ukrainians of the present day, which for centuries has defeated various efforts at friendly relations between the two Slavonic nations. To judge the nature of this conflict aright it may be as well to consider its origin. It really began as a contest between Poland and Bohemia for the last remnants of the Moravian Empire, both having a certain claim over this territory—Bohemia as the normal heir of the Moravian Empire, and Poland, because the old Vistulanian State, a remnant of the dismantled state of White Croatia, consisted of tribes belonging mostly, if not exclusively, to the Polish linguistic branch of the Slavonic race. It is probable that Kievan Russia's interest in this territory was due to the fact that she was already in possession of part of the old White Croatia. It is also likely that some tribes belonging to the eastern Slavonic branch entered into the political partnership set up in the north of the Carpathian Mountains by the Sarmatian Croats.

The moment the Kievan dukes turned their eyes to the West and made their pressure to be felt in that direction, it was but natural that they should annex what lay within their reach, *i.e.* the territory that formed a link between the tribes of the Polish branch and the Eastern Slavs. Any differentiation between Slavonic tribes being hopeless at that time, the final inclusion of the Slavs of that territory in either the western or eastern Slavonic group would have to be decided by the group that could hold power longest and best.

This incident had its importance in Russia's own future growth, for it brought the duchy of Kief into direct contact with two Slavonic States that were already Christain—Poland and Bohemia; and since Bohemia was regarded as being part of the Empire, Russia came, through Czech intermediary, into touch with the Ottonian Empire. Since we learn from the Annals of Lambertus (134) that in 973 a Russian embassy attended the last Reichstag held in Quedlinburg, Vladimir's predecessor Yaropolk must have opened negotiations with the Emperor Otto I, and thereby justified Olga's foresight. Russia's occupation of the Red Cities and her further advance towards the Carpathian Mountains could only accentuate her tendency to some sort of westernisation. The gate to the West was thus thrown open to

(134) *M.G.H.S.* III, p. 63.

Vladimir and his Russians by a combination of circumstances often overlooked by historians who happen to be interested in this period.

Be it observed meanwhile that Vladimir's drive beyond the Styr and the Bug made an end of Polish hopes of expansion in a south-easterly direction. The Russian State rose to be a solid and powerful political structure which Mieszko was too shrewed to challenge, and its renewed interest in the West gave him to understand that Vladimir was not going to relax his hold on his latest acquisition. Mieszko then decided to turn his attention to the tribes of the Polish group, whose lands lay within the boundaries of another State, to wit the remnants of White Croatia, including Cracow and Silesia which had been annexed by Boleslas I, probably after the Magyar disaster. True to his policy to gather all the tribes of the Polish group under his authority he concentrated on Bohemian affairs.

Here the prospects seemed alluring. Mieszko must have known his brother-in-law fairly well to realise that Boleslas II was not the equal of his father as either a soldier or a statesman. As the Czechs' unsuccessful pressure towards the north, their attack on Meissen and their secret sympathies for the Veletians had aroused suspicions in Germany, Mieszko ielt he had little to fear from that quarter, were he ever to try his luck on territory that included the State of the Przemyslides.

He also knew that the position of the Przemyslide dynasty had nothing like the solidity of the Piast dynasty in Poland. The subjugation of the various Slavonic tribes settled in Bohemia, though progressing, had not yet been completed when Boleslas II ascended the throne ; and there was still one dangerous partner to deal with, the Slavniks, whose territory extended, according to Cosmas(135), over the whole east and south-east of Bohemia as far as the frontiers of Ostmark—the future Austria—and of Moravia; at comprised also part of Silesia, especially the upper Neisse, the territory later to go by the name of the County of Glatz (Kladsko).

There still runs a lively controversy among experts on the formation, the composition and the political character of the Slavnik dukedom; but the foundation charter of the bishopric of Prague, which locates the Croats on the territory described by Cosmas as belonging to the Slavnik dukedom, gives us the best clue to the solution(136).

The Slavniks were originally Croats who imposed their leadership on Slavonic tribes settled in the eastern part of Bohemia. A similar process went on in Western Bohemia, where the Czechs, coming from the north, the land of the Serbs, gradually imposed their authority on the local Slavonic tribes. Cosmas(137) gives an idea of the method, when he refers to the fusion of the Czechs with the Lemuzians of Northern Bohemia.

---

(135) Chronica, I, ch. 27, *M.G.H.S.* N.S. II, pp. 49 seq.

(136) See for the detailed discussion of this problem Appendix II, pp. 292. I am giving here the results of the investigation.

(137) Chronica, I, chs. 10-13, *M.G.H.S.* N.S. II, pp. 22-32. It is not without interest to note that the defeated prince of the Luchanians had in his service a Serb called During, who was charged with the education of his son. It is also possible that the Przemyslide Borzivoj's friendship with the chief of the Pshovanians (his wife S. Ludmila was a daughter of Slavobor, the prince of the tribe), helped to consolidate the Przemyslide dynasty.

And this is all we know about the growing power of those Czechs under the ducal family founded by Przemysl. As to how the Slavniks came to dictate to the other local tribes in Eastern and South-eastern Bohemia, we are left in the dark. The names of some of the tribes of Western and Northern Bohemia owe their survival to the Foundation Charter of the Prague diocese, but we know next to nothing about those of Eastern and Southern Bohemia.

Thus, when Bohemia began to assert itself in Central Europe, the country was divided into two independent dukedoms, governed by two ducal families, the Przemyslides and the Slavniks. The two dynasties were first drawn together at the time of the Frankish attacks on the Slavonic tribes settled on the territory formerly occupied by the Boii, and later during the Moravian period, when both dukedoms had a Moravian prince as their common master. Their common action became manifest to the outside world in 895, when the whole of Bohemia drifted away from Moravia to enter into political relationship with East Francia, as represented by Bavaria(138). They also fought side by side against the Zlichanians. Their subjugation was the combined work of the Croats and the Czechs at the beginning of the tenth century. We read in the Legend of S. Wenceslas written by a Slavnik, Christian by name(139), that Wenceslas, a Przemyslide prince, went to war with the prince of Kurzim, which lay within the territory of the Zlichanians, and that this territory was ruled by the Slavniks.

After the defeat of the Magyars at Lechfeld, the Przemyslides and the Slavniks invaded Moravia and White Croatia. As the Slavniks were of Croat origin there must have been some understanding between the Croats of Bohemia and those of the Cracow region and this helped Boleslas I in setting up his federal state. All known sources speak almost exclusively of the Przemyslides, and this has misled most historians who have dealt with this period into the general belief that the Slavniks played only a minor part in the organisation of Bohemia(140). However, the writers of those sources should not be taken too literally, since they wrote many decades after the extermination of the Slavniks by the Przemyslides and could scarcely be unbiassed.

The two dukedoms were comparable in size and the Slavniks were independent, though they freely acknowledged the political leadership of the Przemyslides. As the territory of the Slavniks bordered on Ostmark (later Austria), Moravia and what was White Croatia, Slavnik co-operation was essential to the stability of the so-called Przemyslide State. It is also possible that the territory of the Slavniks came more under Christian influence than the rest of Bohemia, owing to the many Christian refugees who, after the collapse of Great Moravia, crossed the border in search of new opportunities.

(138) See *supra* p. 21. For more details, see *infra* p. 295.

(139) Vita Wenseslai, *F.R.B.I.*, p. 227; ed. by J. Pekař. *Czech Hist. Rev.*, 1905, pp. 125 seq. The incident is recorded in greater detail by the chronicler Dalimil (*F.R.B.* III, p. 56). Cf. Marquart, *Osteuropäische und Ostasiatische Streizüge* (Leipzig, 1905), p. 124; V. Hrubý, "The Original Boundary" (in Czech), loc. cit., pp. 85 seq.; V. Novotný, *Czech History* (in Czech), vol. I, p. 462.

(140) There has been so far only one monograph on the Slavniks, one written by J. Loserth "Der Sturtz des Hauses Slavnik," *Abhandlungen für Osterreichische Geschichte*, Bd. LXV (1895),

This would suggest that the Slavniks were better prepared to join the comity of a Christian empire than the Przemyslides. The position of the Slavnik dukedom must have been appreciated by the Bavarian Duke, since he gave away his daughter in marriage to the reigning Slavnik Duke, S. Adalbert's grandfather. It is also possible, though there is no evidence for it, that the peace concluded between Boleslas I and Otto I was expedited at the instance of the Slavniks.

This situation was fraught with danger, but the statesmanship of Boleslas I, one of the ablest rulers of the Przemyslide dynasty, had so far succeeded in eluding it and in preserving the unity of Bohemia. There were other ways and means for maintaining the good understanding between the two leading families, such as ties of parentage and marital relationship, and it is even reasonable to presume that Strzezislava(141), wife of the Duke Slavnik, a contemporary of Boleslas I, was a sister of the great Przemyslide Duke.

Though it is unlikely, as historians have generally assumed, that the Slavniks were related to the Saxon royal family (we have shown that relationship with the Bavarian Dukes was more likely), they must have been loyal to the new rulers of the German Empire. Intercourse with Saxony was frequent and increased the danger of a possible split between the two families. We remember what gigantic plans Otto I had prepared concerning the Slavonic East and it is only reasonable to postulate that the Slavniks' sympathy with the Saxon dynasty received special consideration in Otto's designs. All these circumstances should be present to our mind in following up the subsequent growth of Central Europe and in trying to disentangle the triangular contest between the three Slavonic dynasties—the Piasts, the Przemyslides and the Slavniks.

---

(141) The name of Adalbert's mother has been preserved by Cosmas (Chronica, I, ch. 28 *M.G.H.S.* N.S. II, p. 51) and by the Annals of Prague (*F.R.B.* II, p. 377). The German author of the Passio S. Adalberti (*F.R.B.*, I, p. 331) calls her Adilburc ; but since he states that both parents were of Slavonic origin, we may assume that the name is the German translation of Strzezislava, which is quite admissible. All the sources extol the piety and character of Adalbert's mother. That she was a sister of Boleslas I has been suggested by Loserth, *Der Sturtz des Hauses Slavnik*, pp. 34 seq., but this is not certain. Dalimil (*F.R.B.* III, p. 65) states that Adalbert's father was a brother-in-law of the Duke of the Zlichanians, which, if true, would throw a dfferent light on the relations between the Przemyslides and the Slavniks, such as they were believed to be, and would confirm the suggestion we put forward that the Zlichanians were brought to submission by the Slavniks with the help of the Przemyslides. The matrimonial union between the Slavnik and the Duke of the Zlichanians was, in this case, intended to strengthen the power of the Slavniks in the subjugated territory.

CHAPTER III

THE CONTEST BETWEEN THREE DYNASTIES ; PIASTS, PRZEMYSLIDES, SLAVNIKS.

THE SLAVNIKS AND MAGDEBURG—A COMPROMISE BETWEEN THE PRZE-MYSLIDES AND THE SLAVNIKS : THE SLAVNIK ADALBERT IS MADE BISHOP OF PRAGUE—ADALBERT AND THE CLUNY REFORM—WHY ADALBERT LEFT BOHEMIA—FIRST POLISH-CZECH CLASH—POLISH EXPANSION AND A PAPAL DOCUMENT—A CZECH EMBASSY TO ROME—REASONS FOR THE FATAL CONFLICT—THE END OF THE SLAVNIKS AND OF A DREAM—CZECH BISHOP AND GERMAN EMPEROR—S. ADALBERT AND GRECO-SLAVONIC CULTURE —PRUSSIANS AND POLES—S. ADALBERT'S MARTYRDOM IN PRUSSIA—HIS POSTHUMOUS FAME.

Confirmation of the Slavniks' sympathy with the Saxon dynasty is found in what S. Adalbert's biographers say about the Slavniks' ties with Magdeburg. From them we learn first of all that in A.D. 961 the missionary bishop Adalbert(1), who had been sent to Kiev by Otto I, made a prolonged stay at the Slavnik residence at Libice and performed there some episcopal functions, the writers stating as the reason for his tarrying there that young Vojtiekh, youngest son of the Duke Slavnik, born about the year 956, was one of a number of children to be confirmed by the future archbishop of Magdeburg. This simple incident would not give us the right to conclude that Adalbert, once archbishop of Magdeburg, thought of extending his jurisdiction to the Slavniks' territory, for he must have completely forgotten about the incident, as some time later he confirmed the youth a second time by mistake.

We further learn that in 972 Slavnik's son again saw the archbishop on the above occasion in Magdeburg, where his parents had sent him for his education. The incident is significant; for encouraged by Otto's plans concerning Magdeburg and its role in the East, the city had grown to be a cultural centre in the West, boasting not only a school founded by the Benedictine abbey and a convent school for girls of the better classes, but also an episcopal school, so planned as to attract the sons of Slavonic nobles living on the right side of the Elbe. The Rector of this establishment, one Otrik, was a celebrated scholar who, together with Gerbert of Aurillac, later Pope Sylvester II, was counted among the outstanding figures of the intellectual world of the West in the second half of the tenth century.

The Archbishop of Magdeburg greatly appreciated the compliment paid by the second ducal family in Bohemia in sending its son to his school.

---

(1) Bruno of Querfurt, Passio S. Adalberti, ch. 4, *F.R.B.* I, p. 268. There exists only one good biography of S. Adalbert, written by the German Church historian H. G. Voigt (*Adalbert von Prag*, Berlin, 1898), where also (pp. 221 seq.) a detailed list of the sources for the life of S. Adalbert is to be found. We also possess two biographies by contemporary writers, S. Bruno of Querfurt and the monk John Canaparius, of Monte Cassino. See detailed bibliography on S. Adalbert in Zibrt, *Bibliography of Czech History* (in Czech), (Prague , 1902), vol. II, pp. 960 seq. Cf. Novotný, loc. cit., vol. I, 1, pp. 261 seq.

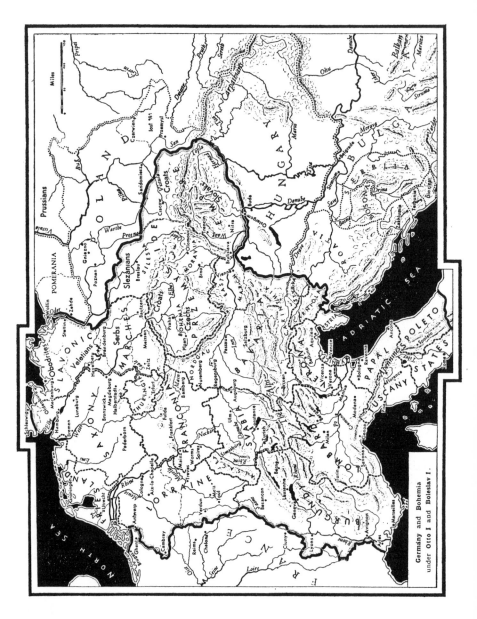

Germany and Bohemia under Otto I and Boleslav I.

From the first he intended to prepare the boy to be a future bishop of the Czechs and for this reason conferred on him at his second confirmation his own name Adalbert. Since then Vojtiekh has been better known in all Western countries by his second Latin name than by his own Slavonic one. It is of some interest that the Przemyslides did not favour the Slavniks' choice in their own case, for Boleslas I sent his son Christian Strakhkvas, as Cosmas calls him, not to Magdeburg but to Regensburg(2), the old Bavarian seat of learning that had been patronised by his ancestors.

(2) Cosmas, Chronica, I, çh. 18, *M.G.H.S.* N.S. II, p. 36.

96

Now the fact that the two most prominent families of Bohemia sent their sons to Germany to finish their education is significant and proves that in the second half of the tenth century the orientation of Bohemia towards Western culture as represented in these parts by Germany, was defiinite. But this does not mean that the Greco-Slavonic culture imported into Central Europe by Constantine-Cyril and Methodius had ceased to produce any literary achievements or had no followers in Bohemia. It is certain that both Adalbert and Christian were acquainted with the fundamentals of this culture and we shall see later that Adalbert was in no way unfriendly towards the Slavonic liturgy. Both clergies, Latin and Slavonic, were still working side by side in Bohemia, although political interests worked more in favour of Latin culture.

Adalbert spent nine years in Magdeburg. His companion there was one Radla, son of a subject of the Slavnik family. He was just a little older than Adalbert and had been his companion at Libice where they had both received their elementary education. Legends have preserved some interesting details illustrating the educational system of Western Europe in the tenth century. It appears that the Rector was satisfied in every respect with his pupil. Not only was Adalbert diligent and quick at his studies, but his parents were very lavish in their payment of the master's services, a consideration which the " new Cicero," as Otrik came to be called by his contemporaries, appreciated. The educational methods in that city, so we learn, were somewhat " old-fashioned." When the time-honoured and customary practice of reminding the student of his duties was applied to Adalbert, the boy duly promised in Slav, German and Latin that he would behave in future and strictly attend to his lessons(3).

Such contact of the Slavniks with Magdeburg had its drawbacks and must have attracted attention in the leading circles of Prague; but Boleslas II took a decision which not only removed all possible danger for the future but turned the incident to the profit of Bohemian unity.

After the archbishop's death in 981 and Otrik's departure from Magdeburg to take up an important post at the royal court, Adalbert returned home. His father Slavnik died that same year and his eldest brother Sobieslav, also called Sobiebor, rose to be the head of the Slavnik family.

*　　*　　*

We learn from Cosmas (4) that Adalbert became a member of the clergy at the cathedral church of Prague, having been ordained sub-deacon by Bishop Thietmar. It is said that his appointment had a political purpose. Apparently the two leading families of Bohemia had come to an agreement to assure the pacific development of the Slavonic tribes in the country. It must be remembered that the Przemyslides had also destined a member of their family—Christian-Strakhkvas—to an ecclesiastical career. Neverthe-

---

(3) Canaparius, chs. 3-6, *F.R.B.* I, pp. 236-9 ; Bruno, chs. 3-6, *Ibid.*, pp. 267-9.

(4) Chronica, I, ch. 25, *M.G.H.S.*N.S. II, p. 46. Otrik is also mentioned several times by Thietmar (Chronicon, III, chs. 12, 13, 15 ; IV, ch. 28 ; VI, ch. 36, *M.G.H.S.* N.S. IX, pp. 110, 112, 114, 115, 165, 318).

less, Boleslas II renounced every intention of raising his brother to the highest ecclesiastical dignity in Bohemia and signified his willingness to let it be reserved to a member of the Slavnik family, agreeing that Adalbert should succeed Thietmar as bishop of Prague.

This was an important concession on the part of the Przemyslides, for it must be noted that the bishop of Prague held a strong and influential position in the country.   It is true that the bishop had to be elected by a " national " assembly presided over by the ruling prince(5) ; but it was the emperor who actually made the investiture.   Thus the position of the bishop of Prague was made independent and only the gravest reasons could have prompted the Przemyslides to cede this influential post to the Slavniks. It meant that the position of the Slavniks in Bohemia was secure and that the Prezmyslides could not claim exclusive control of affairs in the land.

On the other hand, the Przemyslides knew how to turn the agreement to their own advantage.   The first result of the arrangement was the consolidation of their power in Bohemia.   All possible attempts on the part of Magdeburg to split Bohemian unity in ecclesiastical matters were checkmated, a thing in itself worth a great deal.   Furthermore, it seems that with the help of the Slavniks the Przemyslides hoped to gain ascendancy over Moravia and those regions which had fallen to the sword of Boleslas I and of the Slavniks.

It will be remembered that these eastern parts had been ecclesiastically placed under the jurisdiction not of Prague, but of a bishop of Moravia, an arrangement that was certainly not in the Przemyslides' interest and we understand that they were ready to move heaven and earth to wipe the diocese of Moravia off the map; they had not asked for it and its creation was contrary to the original intentions of Otto I and the Czech rulers.   They preferred having the whole of their dominion under the one bishop of Prague who could be controlled more easily.   But in order to achieve this, they needed the backing of the Slavniks and, considering the importance of their object, the Przemyslides thought the concession they were offering to be well worth it.

The arrangement between the two families was implemented much earlier than anticipated. Bishop Thietmar fell ill and died on the 2nd January, 982.   The formal election of the new bishop took place on the 19th February of the same year, the meeting being held at Levý Hradec, the place where the Czech prince Borzivoj had built the first Christian church in Bohemia.   The " national " assembly elected Adalbert to the vacancy.

At this time the new bishop of Prague was probably 27 years of age and therefore had not actually attained the canonical age for the dignity as laid down by the Church.   This circumstance may bear out the view that so important were the stakes that this slip in ecclesiastical routine had to be overlooked.

---

(5) Such at any rate is the view of the two biographers who record the " election " of Adalbert (Canaparius, ch. 7 ; Bruno, ch. 8, *F.R.B.* I, pp. 240, 270). Cf. Cosmas' account of the " elections " of the first three bishops of Prague : Thietmar, Adalbert and Thegdadus (Chronica, I, chs. 23, 25, 31, *M.G.H.S.* N.S. II, pp. 44, 46, 56).

Events proved that Boleslas II, in concluding the compromise with the Slavniks, had been right in his calculation. Adalbert actually succeeded in liquidating the Moravian diocese and in gathering the whole territory of the new dominion under his jurisdiction. Cosmas(6), in relating how bishop Gebhard had prevailed upon the Emperor Herny IV to wind up the Moravian diocese, mentions in this connection the name of Adalbert and states that Gebhard's main argument for the request rested on his production of a privilege granted to S. Adalbert and confirmed by Pope Benedict and the Emperor Otto I. Cosmas could only mean a privilege granted to bishop Adalbert which duplicated a decision previously taken by the Emperor Otto I and Benedict VI. By its terms the bishop of Prague was empowered to place the territory of Moravia under his own jurisdiction. The original imperial and papal rescript was then transferred from the text of Adalbert's privilege and included in the imperial charter of 1086.

A later document, a catalogue listing the bishops of Moravia, called *Granum Catalogi praesulum Moraviae* and composed about A.D. 1421(7), provides further details on the event, for we read there that the transaction had been carried out in the third year of Adalbert's episcopal tenure and was sanctioned by Otto II, Pope Benedict VII and Boleslas II. It is true that the catalogue is of comparatively recent date, and that the author's knowledge of the beginnings of ninth century Moravian Christianity is of the scantiest and based only on contemporary legend. Such ignorance was general and widespread in his days, but this is no reason for assuming that he was similarly ignorant of developments in the tenth century. The accuracy with which he endeavours to record the fusion of the two dioceses under Adalbert, supplying details which even Cosmas omits, shows that there is a good deal behind his information. The very fact that Cosmas mentions Pope Benedict VII and Otto II, though he confuses the names, shows that the author of the Catalogue drew his information from a local tradition.

If we accept the above account, then Adalbert, having been elected bishop in 982, received his privilege in 985, a date that fits into the general frame of the period. That year, Henry II of Bavaria, after his rebellion against the young Otto III, was quietly put back into his place to rest con-tented with his dukedom and Boleslas II, after evacuating Meissen, was only too glad to come to an agreement with the young Emperor. This was the right moment for the Regency to evidence its good will and enlist the Czech Duke into the service of the new régime by a harmless concession. Adalbert's character was an excellent guarantee for future good under-standing; his Magdeburg education pleased and flattered the Saxon royal

(6) Chronica, II, ch. 37, *M.G.H.S.* N.S. II, p. 135 : Replicat coram omnibus privilegium . . . .(prolatum ?) olim a Sancto Adalberto episcopo, suo antecessore, confirmatum tam a papa Benedicto quam a primo Ottone imperatore. . . . (He produces before the assembly the privilege once obtained by bishop S. Adalbert, his predecessor, confirmed by Pope Benedict as well as by the Emperor Otto I. . . .). on the Foundation Charter cf. pp. 77, seq.

(7) Published by J. Loserth, "Das Granum Catalogi Praesulum Moraviae," *Archiv für Oester. Geschichte* (1892), vol. LXXVIII, p. 66 : in the days of S. Adalbert, second bishop of Prague, in the third year of his incumbency, the diocese of Moravia was joined to the diocese of Prague with the authorisation of Pope Benedict VII and the Emperor Otto II and with the consent of the pious Boleslas, Duke of Bohemia, and it was still in force at the time of Severus, sixth bishop of Prague, and the Duke Vratislas. . . .(A.D.1063). Cf. R. Holtzmann, *Die Urkunde Heinrichs IV*, loc. cit., pp. 189 seq.

House and set the German Church's mind at rest, neither of them feeling that there was anything to fear from a product of that famous German intellectual centre. Thus did the young Slavnik prince and bishop fulfil the Przemyslides' oldest wish and highest expectation.

*   *   *

In the meantime, as Adalbert was about to start on his episcopal career, his character had undergone a remarkable change. When he returned from Magdeburg, his biographers, the monk Canaparius and Bruno of Querfurt, testify that Adalbert was a young man of pleasing appearance and correspondingly light-hearted inclinations. It seems that all Prague was very favourably disposed towards this young cleric who promised to become an amiable and worldly ecclesiastical prince(8).

Adalbert's biographers, however, do not omit to point out that from time to time he did go through serious moments when he wrestled with the spiritual problems that beset him. They both describe how Adalbert assisted at the last moments of bishop Thietmar who on his death-bed blamed himself bitterly for not having practised asceticism, for having preferred the easy to the thorny path and thus endangered his salvation. So profoundly was the young sub-deacon moved by the confession of the dying bishop that from that day he abandoned his manner of life and turned to asceticism and works of piety.

This account of Adalbert's " conversion " doubtless has a solid basis of truth, although his biographers are probably exaggerating Adalbert's worldliness previous to his conversion in order to insist upon the change for the better. Bishop Thietmar had been a Benedictine of the Abbey of Magdeburg and it does not seem that the life he had lived was unworthy of a monk and a bishop. On the contrary, he appears to have been affected by the celebrated movement for the reform of monastic life which in his day swept over the whole Christian world. This reformation originated in France at the beginning of the tenth century and reached its zenith at Cluny(9). From there it spread as far as the Rhineland. As the monks of Magdeburg came from Triburg, it is very likely that echoes of this idealistic movement had reached their cloister.

Its followers proclaimed monastic life to be the ideal of Christianity. They advocated asceticism as the best assurance of eternal salvation. As all the great minds of the tenth century were touched in some degree by the influence of this movement, it is not surprising that Thietmar on his death-bed came to regret his lukewarm attitude towards those ascetic practices and meditations which, according to these teachings, came nearer to the true Christian ideal than a bishop's office. Naturally, there was some exaggeration of the monastic ideal, since no movement is free from a tendency to over-estimate the ideals for which it strives.

(8) Canaparius, chs. 6-12 ; Bruno, chs. 7, 8, 9, 11, *F.R.B.* I, pp. 239-45, 269-75.
(9) On Cluny, see J. Evans, *Monastic Life at Cluny*, 910-1157 (Oxford, 1931), with its abundant bibliography.

Adalbert may have been influenced by this emotional wave already at Magdeburg where he was in frequent contact with the local Benedictines. A stay in Italy proved even more decisive in bringing about his complete conversion. He went there to receive the investiture from the Emperor. After confirming Adalbert's election, Otto II performed the ceremony at Verona on June 3, 983. In the same month, on the feast of St. Peter and S. Paul, the archbishop of Mainz consecrated Adalbert bishop of Prague. Adalbert went from Verona to Pavia where he met Mayolus, the abbot of Cluny, and Gerard, the bishop of Toul. The conversations which the young bishop had with the abbot, a prominent representative of the movement, could only intensify the longings which had seized him at Thietmar's death-bed. He returned to Prague where, barefooted, in true monastic style, though in his bishop's attire, he entered his cathedral indifferent and deaf to the joyful acclamations of the multitude.

We know very little about Adalbert's administration of his extensive diocese. This need cause no surprise, since both his biographers were monks soaked in the ideals of monastic reform who for this very reason set little store by his pastoral work(10). That explains why we hear so little about events in Bohemia during Adalbert's five years' residence in his diocese. His biographers only harp on the difficulties and the ill-will of a powerful aristocracy that frustrated all the bishop's efforts to eradicate some abuses among clergy and laity, and they refuse to see anything outside this uninspiring theme. Harassed on all sides and conscious of the futility of his endeavours, the young bishop decided to abandon his diocese and take refuge in a monastery where he would be free to live up to his monastic ideals. Accordingly, he left Prague in 990 and, accompanied by a few servants and his step-brother Radim-Gaudentius, went to Rome.

*   *   *

But Adalbert's work and departure as set forth by his biographers fail to carry conviction; there must have been some reasons other than those advanced by them to account for such a step. At the outset, Adalbert's activities augured well, the truce between the Slavniks and the Przemyslides held promise of all the support he needed and the first results of his administration were exceptionally promising. Whence, then, came this sudden opposition of the aristocracy to Adalbert's pastoral work and why did the bishop so quickly lose heart and leave his see ?

Adalbert's departure from Prague has generally been explained as the result of a misunderstanding between an idealistic bishop and his semi-barbarian followers who lacked all comprehension of their holy shepherd's pious ideals. Such an explanation, however, raises a serious difficulty. How can a gesture such as resignation be reconciled with the obligations

(10) Both biographers agree on the bishop's great spirit of charity. Canaparius (ch. 12, F.R.B. I, p. 244) particularly praises the fervour of his preaching. We possess one homily ascribed to S. Adalbert, which he preached in Rome at the convent where he took refuge after his flight from Prague. Delivered in honour of S. Alexius, it follows almost word for word a homily by S. Bede, though one passage shows that the bishop did have original ideas of his own. The homily has been published by H. G. Voigt, loc. cit., pp. 358-65, from a Ms. of Monte Cassino.

of a bishop who is not allowed to leave his diocese except for serious reasons or without leave from his superiors, the metropolitan and the pope ? His biographers must have been aware of the difficulty, for Canaparius turns it by stating(11) that Adalbert left Prague with the pope's permission. But this is not correct and is contradicted by Bruno(12) and by Canaparius himself elsewhere(13). One is led to infer from the account that Adalbert informed the pope of his decision only after his arrival in Rome, when he asked him to sanction it and handed to him, so it seems, his episcopal ring and cross as a sign of formal resignation. If he did, the fact is that neither the metropolitan of Mainz nor Pope John XV made any move to provide for his successor and the diocese was administered by provost Viliko, one of Adalbert's faithful friends and followers.

Historians who favoured the above explanation also knew how serious the difficulty was, and to overcome it they chose to paint religious and moral conditions in Bohemia at that time in the darkest colours, taking pains to point out that Christianity was but in its early stages in that country and that many pagan abuses were still practised by the people. Adalbert, on such a dark background, stood out in vivid contrast, a lonely figure bursting with ideals ; his holy life was such as constantly pricked the conscience of the other clergy living their unhallowed lives; his admonitions provoked the hatred of a vicious aristocracy. Feeling completely under the attraction of the ideals of the monastic reformers, Adalbert longed ardently to live the life of a monk and the difficulties obstructing his path offered him the best opportunity for realising his ideals.

Such an explanation of the facts cannot be accepted. In the first place, the moral situation in Bohemia in the second half of the tenth century does not justify the dark picture drawn to represent it. It was certainly not so bad as to induce a bishop to break his staff over the heads of his own people and to quit his post for a monastery with the object of trying to save his own soul when he had not been able to save the souls of his spiritual children. After all, what were the abuses which in the biographers' opinion mainly forced the bishop to leave his diocese ? Bruno(14) mentions such things as the growing habit of marriage between near relations, polygamy among the upper classes, the sale of Christian prisoners to Jewish slave traders, breaking the rules of fasting, working on Sundays and marriage of the clergy. He also records that the aristrocacy protested and took sides with the clergy against a bishop who was only trying to induce them to lead better lives.

It was all very regrettable, but by no means unusual, and the same, if not worse, was found among other nations of the period. Before Adalbert's day, S. Constantine-Cyril and S. Methodius had had to fight in Moravia of the ninth century the abuse of marriage between relations, and polygamy in certain disguised forms was prevalent among the aristocracy of all nations. Curiously enough Adalbert had a case of secret polygamy in his

(11) Ch. 13, *F.R.B.* I, p. 245.
(12) Ch. 12, *ibid,.* p. 276.
(13) Ch. 18, *ibid.*, p. 251.
(14) Ch. XI, *ibid.*, p. 275. Cf. Canaparius, ch. 12, *ibid.* p. 244,

own family, as his father had a second " wife," the mother of Radim-Gaudentius who nevertheless became his half-brother's best friend and most faithful adherent(15).

Nor should we forget that not only in Bohemia but also in Germany and in other countries at that time very many priests were married. It was not until the eleventh century that the great reformer, Gregory VII, succeeded in re-introducing the ancient practice into the life of the Church. It is possible that S. Adalbert had taken some steps to restore clerical celibacy, but the difficulties which he encountered in this and in all his other efforts aimed at reform would scarcely have provided him with sufficient justification for throwing up his work and seeking refuge behind the walls of a monastery.

Historians who insist on the debased condition of moral and cultural life in Bohemia at this time are, moreover, contradicted by historical facts. The most recent discoveries have demonstrated that the cultural life of Bohemia in the first half of the tenth century had reached a very high level indeed. The country had offered asylum to numerous disciples of S. Methodius and S. Constantine-Cyril after the destruction of the Moravian Empire, and they brought with them, as previously noted, the Greco-Slavonic culture as inspired by Byzantium. It is true that the level of that culture had been lowered in the second half of the century by the severance from its sources. It is impossible, however, to accept the view that decadence had set in to such an extent as to justify the biographers' rhetorical strictures.

If we hold that Adalbert grasped the first opportunity for quitting his diocese, the first, that is, to give it an appearance of legality, we are placing him in a curious light ; but if we insist that his behaviour was not only correct but holy and exemplary, then we endorse the opinions concerning monasticism that have been held by some of the reformers of the tenth century. Such exaggerations, however, are not in line with the ideas of the Church in regard to the episcopal dignity.

Moreover, to defend Adalbert's attitude in this way is to do the holy man a real injustice. He was always devoted to his duties as a bishop and attentive in his observance of the rules of the Church. We have noted that he presented his case to the highest authority in Rome and we shall likewise see that he obeyed and resumed his episcopal duties when circumstances altered. Besides, it should be remembered that when Adalbert went to Rome, he had no intention of entering a monastery, but was rather planning to go on a pilgrimage to Jerusalem and to settle down somewhere in a foreign land. To verify our reading of the facts, we shall now examine the circumstances of Adalbert's stay in Italy.

(15) Bruno (Ch. 28, *F.R.B.* I, p. 296) expressly states that Radim, called Gaudentius after his religious profession, was Adalbert's brother only on his father's side (Gaudentius, ex parte patris caro et frater suus). In referring to Adalbert's father, Bruno (ch. I, loc. cit., p. 266) underlines the fact that Slavnik did not take some of the Lord's precepts too literally : A lord of the country, yet a very average man ; slack at his prayers, yet open to kindness and mercy ; lax in morals, yet generous to the poor.

When the widow of Otto II, Theophano, who was living in Rome at the time, heard of Adalbert's intention to visit the Holy Land, she asked him to call on her and gave him a sum of money so large that Gaudentius who accompanied him could scarcely carry the weight of silver and gold coins. Evidently, the Byzantine Emperor's daughter found her delight in assisting pilgrims in crossing Greece, her native land, on their way to Jerusalem. But Adalbert secretly gave all the money to the poor and started on his journey to the East as a penniless pilgrim with but three companions.

He failed to reach Jerusalem. He broke his journey at the celebrated Benedictine Abbey of Monte Cassino where he received hospitality as a pilgrim together with sound advice from the abbot and some of the older brethren who endeavoured to dissuade him from his project. What we learn about the Abbey from Adalbert's biographers does not suggest a Monte Cassino quite as zealous at that moment as it had been known to be in the past ; the wave of reform had evidently not yet reached the " Holy Mountain." However, the abbot seemed to be a man of wisdom and judgment. He pointed out to Adalbert that there is much more merit in our Lord's eyes in calmly and patiently enduring the trials of life than in wandering leisurely from place to place.

Adalbert took the abbot's advice and stayed at the Abbey, probably intending to join the monks of Monte Cassino. We still possess a document testifying to the close relations which Adalbert kept with some of the brethren of the Abbey—it is the Life of S. Wenceslas, written by Laurentius, a monk of Monte Cassino, at the suggestion of St. Adalbert. But when it dawned on him that the monks were inclined, perhaps even anxious, to take advantage of his episcopal dignity to improve the material interests of the Abbey and help its reputation, he felt indignant and left without a moment's delay for Valleluce, near Monte Cassino, where the Greek abbot, S. Nilus, renowned for his pious and ascetic life, was then living. Nilus was born at Rossano in Calabria in the year 910 and he died in 1005. His activities in Italy provide evidence of the importance of the Greek element in the religious life of Southern Italy and the close contact that existed between Greek and Latin monasticism in the tenth century. S. Adalbert was greatly impressed by Nilus and according to Canaparius, the Greek abbot declared that he had never met a young man so deeply imbued with zeal and " love for our Saviour ".(16).

Not afraid of its grim discipline and apparently not troubled by the differencies of rite and rule, Adalbert would have liked to stay on in the Greek monastery. Nilus, however, could not keep him, as his monastery stood on land that was the property of Monte Cassino ; but he gave Adalbert an introduction to Abbot Leo, of the monastery of S. Boniface and S. Alexius in Rome.

At this period, Italy also was in the grip of a movement for the reform of monastic life, one that had nothing to do with the Cluny reform, but

---

(16) Ch. 15, *ibid.*, p. 248. For further particulars on S. Nilus' activity, see his Life (*P.G.* vol. CXX, cols. 16-165) and that of his disciple S. Bartholomew of Grottaferrata (*P.G.* vol. 127, 476-97). Cf. also G. S. Minassi, *S. Nilo di Calabria* (Naples, 1892).

was due to the influence of Greek monasticism as prevailing in Southern Italy and represented by Nilus. Abbot Leo was another champion of the movement, besides being a favourite with the pope who had charged him with an important mission to the French court. Abbot Leo received Adalbert with great affection and admitted him and his step-brother Radim-Gaudentius to the noviciate for a year. The saint took his solemn vows on April 17, 990.

Due allowance being made for Adalbert's biographers being monks and making the most of their hero's monastic inclinations, they yet entirely fail to convince the reader that such was the principal motive of Adalbert's resignation. It must be sought elsewhere. A hint to this effect is found in Cosmas(17). From him we learn that when Adalbert realised the difficulties to be too much for him, he asked Strakhkvas (Christian), brother of the ruling Duke of Prague, to take over his episcopal see. Strakhkvas was at that time a monk of the monastery of S. Emeram at Regensburg and in trying to persuade him to accept, Adalbert expressed confidence that he (Christian) would be better able to exercise these episcopal functions since he would have the full support of the reigning Duke. From this statement we must conclude that at that time Adalbert did not have such support from Boleslas II; therefore, something must have happened to rob him of ducal favour. Whatever it was, something came between the bishop, a Slavnik, and the duke, a Przemy-slide. What was it ?

Both Adalbert's biographers, Canaparius especially, speak about the sale of Christian prisoners to slave traders. Even before their time, the Legends of S. Wenceslas and the records of the Arab traveller Ibrahim ibn Ja'cub(18) repeatedly mentioned that in the tenth century Prague was an important centre of the slave trade. Trading in this human commodity was a well-known feature of tenth century Prague and Jewish slave dealers used to provide the Arab courts of the Spanish Caliphs with slaves from this emporium.

*   *   *

Adalbert complained not so much about the trade itself as about the fact that he was forcibly prevented, his means being limited, from redeeming many Christian prisoners who had been sold to the Jewish traders(19). Where did these Christian prisoners come from ? They could have been natives, it is true, as slavery was a regular feature of tenth-century life in Bohemia. But as the sources insist on the great number of these prisoners, it is more likely that the Czechs took them in a war with a Christian country—but which country ? Not Germany, as we have no record of

---

(17) Chronica, I, ch. 29, *M.G.H.S.* N.S. II, pp. 52 seq.

(18) Cf. Ja'cub's translation in P. Hirsch, *Widukind*, loc. cit., p. 184. Details on this commercial activity in Xth-century Prague can be read in J. Schránil, *Die Vorgeschichte Böhmens und Mährens* (Leipzig, 1928), pp. 31 seq.

(19) The point is made by the two biographers : Canaparius (ch. 12, loc. cit., p. 244) : "Owing to the Christian captives and prisoners whom the Jewish trader had bought with his ill spent gold and whom the bishop could not redeem." Bruno (ch. II, loc. cit., p. 275) : "they even sold Christian prisoners to the wicked Jews." Cf. Voigt, loc cit., p. 53.

any war between Germany and the Czechs at this period. Not Hungary, as the Maygars could scarcely be called Christians at this time. Nor was there any fighting between them and the Czechs. Which country then were the Czechs fighting some time between the years 987 and 990 ?

From Thietmar of Merseburg(20) we learn that in 990 Boleslas II addressed a request to the Polish Duke petitioning the return of territory (the source speaks of a kingdom—*regnum*) which had been taken from him. So there may have been a military conflict between the Poles and the Czechs before 990 and this conflict was started by Mieszko I, Duke of Poland. It should also be noted that in 990 Boleslas II concluded, according to Thietmar(21), an alliance with the pagan tribe of the Veletians (Liutici) and this pact was aimed at the Poles. The Czech Duke was evidently planning war with his neighbours.

From all this it must be concluded that the Christian prisoners referred to by Adalbert's biographers were Poles captured by the Czechs in a campaign fought some time before 990, probably in 987 or 988. It appears that the Czech Duke was greatly incensed over his ill fortune in that campaign and failed to observe the customary rule among Christian princes by ordering that the Polish prisoners should be sold to the Jewish slave traders. The bishop apparently reproved the Duke and endeavoured to save the Christian Polish prisoners from their terrible fate. We may also presume that he declined to approve of war between two Christian countries.

In so doing, Adalbert was only fulfilling the duties of a bishop whose business it is to enforce Christian principles even in the political life of his people and Boleslas II had no reason for disliking or persecuting his bishop for being asked to act up to his Christian principles. The duke was neither a pagan nor a particularly bad Christian ; so there must have been something operating behind the scenes to deepen the antagonism between the duke and the bishop ; some political issue that complicated matters and rendered Adalbert's position somewhat delicate. As he was a Slavnik, there may have been a clash of interests between the two Bohemian dynasties.

There will be no satisfactory answer until we discover the true motives behind the Polish-Czech war prior to the crisis between the bishop and the duke. We must find out which country it was that Mieszko I took from Boleslas II and how the incident influenced the relations between the Przemyslides and the Slavniks. Expert opinion is still divided on all three problems and despite the number of hypotheses tried by Polish, Czech and German scholars, a solution has so far not been discovered.

By a stroke of good fortune we are to-day in possession of a valuable document which was made public only a few decades ago and was found in the Collection of Canon Law edited by Cardinal Deusdedit about the year 1080 in Rome(22). There we find a document starting with the

---

(20) Chronicon, IV, ch. 12, *M.G.H.S.* N.S. IX, p. 146 : Si regnum sibi ablatum redderet.
(21) *Ibid.*, IV, ch. II, p. 144.
(22) On this Collection and the document it contains, see Appendix V, pp. 315.

words " *Dagome* (Dagomae in the best M.S.) *iudex.*" It records the solemn donation of the whole of Poland to the Holy See made by Dagome, the judge, and the senatrix Ote. German and Polish specialists still discuss its meaning, but an impartial examination shows that the Polish Duke Mieszko (the only possible meaning of Dagome) and his wife Ote made a donation before the year 992 (the year of Mieszko's death) of their country to the Holy See. From the description of Poland's frontiers, we learn that Mieszko was in possession of the whole of Pomerania, including the city of Stettin, called Schinesne in the document and mentioned twice : and also, that he must have been master of the whole of Silesia and of the region of Cracow (Cracoa).

Thus, the two territories which were part of the Przemyslide dominion, must have been lost to Boleslas II between the years 987 and 990. This would establish the nature and the extent of the conflict between the Poles and the Czechs and the way it affected S. Adalbert's position.

The reader will remember that according to the sources quoted we must assume two armed conflicts, of which the minor one led to open hostilities. What was the cause of the first prelude ? Historians have generally taken it for granted that the first clash occurred somewhere on the Silesian borders where Mieszko was perhaps trying to readjust his frontiers, but their conjecture does not fit some of the facts(23). First of all, we know from Thietmar that the Czech had asked the Pole for the return of his province (kingdom), which suggests that previous to the major conflict Boleslas II had lost substantial territory, something much more than a small border district.

On the other hand, we know that Boleslas II was making preparations for his campaign and as Thietmar has it, approached the Veletians, Poland's worst foe, for help in his venture. The indications are that there must have occurred something more provocative than a mere incident on the Silesian frontier. Now that we know the nature and the composition of the Przemyslide dominion better, we are entitled to think that the true reason for the major conflict was the transfer of the lands which had recently belonged to White Croatia, from the Przemyslides to the Piasts.

There is nothing extravagant about this suggestion. The loss was only the natural consequence of the steady and all-round growth of Poland's power under the capable Piast prince. Indeed, it was Mieszko's settled purpose to unite all the Polish tribes under his leadership. As the Croats had long been assimilated, the lands of White Croatia were exclusively occupied by Polish tribes. They naturally became the first object of Poland's ambition. The Vistulanians round Sandomierz on the confluent of the San and the Vistula had joined the Piasts after the Magyar defeat in 955 or soon after the Moravian collapse, but Boleslas I prevented

(23) Cf. V. Novotný, *Czech History* (in Czech), vol. I, 1, p. 620, who discards the suggestion made by K. Potkański " Cracow before the Piasts," *Proceedings of the Cracow Academy. Phil. Hist. Class* (Cracow, 1897), vol. IX, pp. 244 seq. (in Polish) to the effect that it may have been the territory of Cracow.

the Poles from taking over the bulk of White Croatia. However, time failed him for consolidation. We may at any rate assume that what was left of Croatia belonged to the Czech State exactly like the territory of the Slavniks and must have had its own princes or a duke. For this very reason, Mieszko must have found little difficulty in substituting Polish authority for that of the Czechs. It was by and large a struggle between dynasties, whose success would depend on their respective means for enforcing their claims. As the ever-growing might of the Polish State under Mieszko must have impressed the border tribes, it is small wonder that the Polish tribes of erstwhile White Croatia should have fallen to its ascendancy so easily. Those territories could with some show of reason be called a kingdom, since before they were disrupted and conquered by Svatopluk of Moravia they formed an imposing part of White Croatia.

If the defection of the White Croatian Polish tribes from Przemyslide allegiance to the benefit of the Piasts be the true reason of the first conflict between the two Slavonic dukes, subsequent developments are rendered more intelligible, for they revealed the growing strength of the Piasts. They ceased to be allies and became dangerous rivals of the Przemyslides. It was only to be expected that such a change should produce profound reactions in the Slavnik dukedom. The possession of Moravia, which at that time still comprised territories as far as the Danube and beyond the Vag, was in danger. No wonder then that Boleslas II, alarmed by the Polish Duke's expanding influence, should have considered it necessary to put a stop to any further encroachments on his lands and to redeem his lost prestige by a successful war. By the same token, we are made to understand why he tried to enlist Veletian assistance : there was a major issue at stake. The position had been completely altered to his disadvantage. By finding themselves Poland's next-door neighbours, the Slavniks had risen to prominence ; and the memories of the old tribal commonwealth of Bohemian and Polish Croats, of the glorious past of White Croatia which had included the Slavniks' East Bohemian possessions, gave the Przemyslides food for anxious thought.

It also throws light on the estrangement between the Przemyslides and the Slavniks, which proved so detrimental to Adalbert's diocesan activities. For Adalbert's brother Sobiebor, the head of the Slavnik House, must have refused this time to endorse Boleslas II's foreign policy and vetoed hostilities with Poland, as may be inferred from the fact that Boleslas attacked the Poles not from south-eastern Bohemia or from Moravia, which would have given him direct access to Cracow, the "rebels" headquarters, but from north-eastern Bohemia which was part of his own dukedom, obviously because, besides being nearer to his new allies, the Veletians, he could not risk an attack from Moravia without the Slavniks' support. On the other hand, any increase of power in Silesia or the reconquest of this country would have served his interests by giving him a hold on the borders of the Slavnik dukedom, which included Kladsko in Silesia.

But the war turned out to be a costly business for the Czechs. Thietmar (24) is once more our best informant. Boleslas' alliance with the Veletians did more to help than to injure the Poles. In German eyes the alliance of a Christian duke with the pagan Veletians was not only an abomination but an insult to Germany, since the Veletians were Germany's most dangerous foes, rebellious to all her attempts at " pacification." This was a case where the Germano-Polish alliance against pagan tribes, the common enemies of both countries, had automatically to come into operation, and when Mieszko asked for help, the Regency, without a moment's hesitation, sent him an auxiliary corps. This rather complicated matters for Boleslas II who could not afford to tackle Poland and Germany at the same time. In vain did he try and appeal to the German generals, who by sheer ill luck had fallen into his hands, to help him in arranging an amicable settlement, and threaten them with death if Mieszko refused to return the territory he had seized : the Pole knew he was getting the best of the bargain and pointed out that it was not his business but the Emperor's to protect and avenge his Germans. According to Thietmar, Boleslas II only succeeded in capturing one place on the Oder, the only trophy he got, and this apparently not for very long(25). He not only failed to recover Cracow, and Silesia, but lost his prestige into the bargain. Evidence of the territorial losses sustained by Boleslas II is to be found in the document " Dagome Iudex."

The Act of Donation of Poland to the Holy See of Rome was to be Mieszko's last political act, for the Duke died in 992, to be succeeded by Boleslas the Great, also called the Brave, his son by his first marriage with the Czech princess Dubravka. The donation, the first of its kind in history, was carried out by a special Polish delegation sent to Rome between the years 990 and 992. By placing Poland under the special protection of the See of S. Peter, Mieszko consolidated his power over the newly conquered countries and at the same time strengthened his position in relation to Germany, his ally. There exists no reason for construing the act into a hostile move against the Emperor Otto III, for the young Emperor must have been previously informed of Mieszko's intention, and such a donation was in perfect keeping with Otto's ideas about the pope's and the emperor's office, as will be made clearer presently. To his way of thinking, pope and emperor needed to be united by the closest bonds, the emperor being the supreme secular head of Christendom and the pope its supreme spiritual head. The Emperor could therefore not look upon a reinforced papal power in Poland as prejudicial to his own position. On the other hand, in placing his country together with all his new acquisitions under the protection of the supreme spiritual head of Western Christendom, Mieszko safeguarded his own

---

(24) Chronicon, IV, chs. 11-13, *M.G.H.S.* N.S. IX, pp. 144-8.

(25) It has been generally assumed that the name of the locality which Thietmar could not identify was Niemcza (modern Nimptsch) in Silesia on the strength of a remark in the Annals of Sázava where we read that in 990 the town of Niemcza was lost (*F.R.B.* II, p. 240). Novotný, loc. cit., p. 624, rejects this identification, but it may be accepted, if we take the Annalist's remark to mean that the place, recently recaptured, was lost to the Poles that same year.

position within the ambit of his partnership with the emperor ; and as the initiative had come from the Polish Duke, Poland's independent position with regard to Germany and the Empire was once for all made clear to the whole of Europe. It was shrewd of Mieszko to be able to assert his independence without damage to his good relations with the German Empire.

It thus fell to a Polish Duke to inaugurate the policy that was to be imitated by other nations in the eleventh, twelfth and thirteenth centuries, when the Papacy was at the height of its prestige and power. This explains why the Polish Act of Donation was included in a collection of canon law designed to illustrate the authority of the Papacy and enforce its medieval claims. It is useful to observe that in following Mieszko's example, princes were actuated not so much by their piety as by their desire to protect themselves against imperial encroachments. They felt that the make-believe gift of their nation to a spiritual institution such as the Holy See, was the best and cheapest insurance for the preservation of their national independence.

*   *   *

Such were the events prior to Adalbert's departure from Prague and they account for much of it. Their repercussion was soon felt in Rome. In the year 992 a delegation arrived there to request the Pope to send Adalbert back to Prague. Both biographers(26) of the saint state that it was Adalbert's wish to remain in Rome and that his brother monks exerted all possible pressure to make him refuse the Czech invitation and stay with them in the monastery.

The Pope summoned a special local synod to discuss the case. This convocation is noteworthy for the light it throws on Church conditions in the tenth century and as evidence of the state of affairs existing between the champions of two different schools of thought. There were the reformists who maintainted that because monasticism was the highest degree of the Christian ideal, a bishop who had become a monk could not be compelled to return to his episcopal duties. Ranged on the other side were the canonists and the defenders of the old Church practice which insisted that the bishop's first and most sacred duty was to look after his flock (27).

The synod decided that the old practice was to be observed. John XV sanctioned the decision that Adalbert should return to his see, since the circumstance that had hampered his episcopal functions had

---

(26) Canaparius, ch. 18 ; Bruno, ch. 15, *F.R.B.* I, pp. 251, 280 seq.

(27) It is interesting to note that a similar problem exercised the minds of the Eastern Church in the ninth century. The Council of 879-80, which rehabilitated the Patriarch Photius, issued a special canon forbidding bishops who had become monks, to leave their monasteries and to re-occupy their seats. This canon could not have been quoted at the Roman synod of 992, since it was not introduced into Western canonical legislation till the eleventh century. This fascinating problem is discussed at length in my book on *The Photian Schism, History and Legend,* (Cambridge, 1948, p. 331 seq.). There I endeavour to trace this canon throughout the main Western canonical collections—some of them not yet published—anterior to the Collection of Gratian.

ceased to exist. Adalbert submitted to the decision, but asked first, say the Legends, for the delegation's solemn assurance that the Duke would always support his attempts to root out the abuses against which he had striven. The promise was given.

The Legends make it clear that the bishop laid down his conditions and that a formal compromise was reached between Adalbert and Boleslas II, represented by his brother Christian Strakhkvas. Confirmation of this is found in a tenth century copy of the text of a solemn declaration made by Boleslas II to Adalbert. These are the words(28) : " In the year of the Incarnation 992, when Pope John XV was sitting on the most holy throne of the Blessed Apostle Peter, in the reign of Otto III, most august King, at the Lord-inspired request of the second bishop of the Holy Church of Prague, Adalbert, the monk, the Duke Boleslas, in the presence of all his nobles, has given to the above named bishop leave to dissolve, according to canonical prescriptions, marriages found to have been contracted between relations, and also to build churches in suitable places and to collect tithes." Another favour granted to Adalbert was, so it appears, permission to erect within the diocese of Prague an abbey of the Reformed Benedictine monks(29).

All this makes one suspect that something must have happened, too serious to be recorded in the Legends. What was the real reason for this sudden volte-face in Bohemia ? Why did Boleslas II, who was on such bad terms with his bishop in 988, suddenly petition the Pope to send Adalbert back to Prague ?

The answer is to be found in the political change that had come over Bohemia. The loss of a war could not be expected to enhance the prestige of Boleslas II. Then, the influence of the Slavniks who had opposed the Polish war was growing and they could hardly fail to come under the influence of the Piasts. The Polish Duke enjoyed the favour of the Emperor, his ally, and of the Papacy, under whose protection he had recently placed his country. Boleslas II must have discerned looming in the distance the possibilities of a Polish-Czech State under the Piasts, from which the Przemyslides would be completely eliminated, should they refuse to submit to the Piasts and to be content with the position they would have occupied as local princes.

He saw but one way to avert the threat and that was a whole-hearted reconciliation with the Slavniks : but this was unthinkable as long as the Bishop of Prague remained in exile in Rome, and the first step towards

(28) Friedrich, *Codex Diplomaticus*, vol. I, No. 37, p. 43. Cf. Voigt, *Adalbert von Prag*, p. 268.

(29) The chronicler Pulkava of the fourteenth century (*F.R.B.* V, p. 27) dates the foundation of the Brzevnov Abbey from 992 and its consecration from 993. His statement must reflect an old tradition. The Foundation Charter (Friedrich, *Codex Dipl.*, vol. I, No. 375, p. 347) is not genuine and was written in the fourteenth century, but as we have the text of a papal bull of 993 by which Pope John XV took the Abbey under his special protection and as this document seems to be genuine, at least in its main contents, the foundation of the Abbey by Boleslas II in 992 must be taken for granted. Cf. G. Friedrich—" On the privilege of Pope John XV " (in Czech), *Czech Hist. Rev.*, vol. XI, pp. 12 seq., and Novotný, loc. cit., pp. 635 seq. According to Pulkava, Adalbert brought twelve monks from his Roman Abbey to Prague, an indication that the founding of a Czech Abbey had by then been decided in Rome and that the Duke must have given his consent through his brother, his representative in Rome.

peace with the Slavniks would be to offer Adalbert full satisfaction. This he was quick in doing and he readily submitted to Adalbert's conditions. Thus again, as in 981, Adalbert healed the cleavage between the two leading families in Bohemia and restored the unity of the land under Czech supremacy. Mieszko's death in 992 gave Boleslas II of Bohemia the chance he had been looking for, and as Boleslas the Great's policy was still in the making, the Czech Duke was given the opportunity to retrieve his dynasty's prestige.

Our conjecture seems to be borne out by Adalbert's biographers Canaparius and Bruno, who both assert that the Czech embassy to Rome was headed by the reigning Duke's brother. Bruno even gives his name and that of his companion : " were chosen for this mission the saintly man's preceptor, Radla the Wise and, because he was the natural brother of his country's ruler, Christianus, a monk and well-spoken man." Christian can only be identified with the brother of Boleslas II, the same as was offered the bishopric of Prague by Adalbert before he left for Rome. As Radla was attached to the Slavnik's court at Libice, it is obvious that he was to represent the interests of the Slavniks in Rome. Therefore, the composition of the embassy as detailed by the biographers, suggested that the whole of Bohemia was demanding Adalbert's return and that once again the reinstatement of a Slavnik on the episcopal throne of Prague was to be the basis of the compromise.

There is, however, one difficulty : we know of yet another Christian, also a monk, a very wise man and a relative of Adalbert's ; and as this Christian claimed to be the bishop's uncle, he may have been a brother of the reigning Slavnik Duke. He wrote a Life of S. Wenceslas in Latin and in the preface dedicated his work to his nephew Adalbert. On the face of it, it would not seem impossible to identify him with the head of the Roman embassy, as the biographers do not expressly give the name of the reigning duke, whether Przemyslide or Slavnik ; but were it true, we would have to postulate the embassy and Adalbert's recall to have been a purely Slavnik concern and not the result of a compromise between the Przemyslides and the Slavniks—only another humiliation inflicted on Bolelas II by his rivals.

This view would perhaps make the outbreak of hostilities which soon followed between the two families more understandable, but it is mistaken. The identification of Adalbert's uncle with the head of the Roman mission does violence to the texts which expressly state that the head of the embassy was a brother of the reigning duke of the country where Adalbert's see was situated; this can only be Boleslas II, since Prague stood on the territory of the Przemyslides. But who was the reigning prince of the Slavniks ? If Christian was his brother, then Sobieslav could not be Adalbert's brother, but his uncle, which would contradict both Bruno (30) and Cosmas (31). The account by Adalbert's biographers makes it clear that Boleslas II freely and willingly co-operated for a time with

---

(30) Ch. 21, *F.R.B.* I, p. 288.
31) Chronica, I, ch. 29, *M.G.H.S.* N.S. IX, p. 53.

Adalbert after his return; nor could the foundation of a Benedictine abbey near Prague have been realised without Boleslas' active co-operation. In any case, although the Slavniks' position had benefited by Boleslas' loss of prestige, they were by no means able to dictate to the Czech Duke, plant their own bishop on his premises without Boleslas' consent and obtain for behaviour so insulting to the reigning Duke the approval of the metropolitan of Mainz and of the Holy See of Rome. Not for a moment could such an assumption be entertained. So we are forced back to the interpretation given above and see in the reinstatement of Adalbert in Prague a new and hopeful compromise between the Przemyslides and the Slavniks.

* * *

This would be borne out by the hearty reception Adalbert was given on his return to Bohemia, though one of his biographers (32) is at pains to describe his disappointment when, on arriving with his fellow-travellers at a town near the border—presumably Pilsen—on a Sunday, he found himself witnessing a rowdy and holiday-spirited market day. Adalbert, they say, took this to be a bad omen for the future because one of the main objects he hoped to achieve with the aid of the Duke was the enforcement of the holiness of the Sabbath.

Adalbert seems for all that to have been cordially greeted in Prague by both the populace and the Duke. Boleslas even hastened to fulfil one of the conditions which the bishop had laid down for his return—the foundation of the Benedictine abbey; for on January 14, 993, Adalbert had the great joy of consecrating the church of the abbey in Brzevnov, near Prague. Its first abbot was the monk Anastasius, but of him we shall have more to say anon. The abbey was dedicated to Our Lady, S. Benedict, S. Boniface and S. Alexius, a selection designed to mark the intimate association of the new Abbey of Brzevnov with its Mother House in Rome and with Monte Cassino.

Adalbert used to spend a great deal of his time with his brethren. It is said that right down to the fourteenth century the monks of Brzevnov used to display to their distinguished visitors a pair of gloves made by the saintly bishop (33), a tradition which confirms that Adalbert used to stay at the abbey and that he insisted on the strict observance of S. Benedict's rule making manual work obligatory on all the members of the monastery.

Our principal sources are very reticent about Adalbert's diocesan work and say little about the way the Przemyslides and the Slavniks fared in their mutual relations. They confine themselves to the bare statement that the Duke never seriously meant to co-operate with the bishop and that aristocratic circles continued to be frankly hostile. But both of these contemporary writers describe at great length a remarkable incident which was to prove fatal to Adalbert and his family (34).

The wife of one of the members of the influential Vrshovci family,

---

(32) Bruno, ch. 15, loc. cit., p. 281.

(33) Cf. Voigt, *Adalbert von Prag*, pp. 85, 282.

(34) Canaparius, ch. 19; Bruno, ch. 16, *F.R.B.* I, pp. 253 seq., 281 seq.

fervent supporters of the Przemyslides, was accused of adultery—it was even suggested that her guilty partner was a man of the Church—and in accordance with the barbarian custom that survived from pagan times, she had incurred the penalty of death. The unfortunate woman took refuge in the bishop's house and Adalbert, moved by Christian charity, decided to save her. He hid her in the church of the Benedictine Sisters adjoining his residence.

Both Canaparius and Bruno of Querfurt vividly relate the event in great detail, for they saw in it the climax of the whole drama. A crowd of people led by the Vrshovci went in search of the woman and forced their way to the very doors of the bishop's house which stood in the grounds of the Castle of Prague. Adalbert showed himself to the mob and stood ready to sacrifice his own life to save the life of a penitent sinner and to defend the sacred right of asylum claimed at that time by the Church, when every malefactor who took refuge in the sacred precincts and in doing so asked for mercy, had to be spared for as long as he remained under the Church's protection. So anxious was Adalbert to stand by the victim of the fury of the populace that he was even prepared to take the responsibility for her downfall.

Details preserved by the biographers would seem to suggest that the whole episode had been engineered by the Vrshovci against Adalbert, not so much because he was a bishop as because he was a Slavnik. The ringleaders merely smiled at the bishop's attempt to turn the anger of the mob against himself. It was far from their intention, they said, to crown him with the laurels of martyrdom; but they openly threatened to take revenge on the wives and children of his brothers. This crude display of animosity was enough to show that the tension between the supporters of Boleslas and the Slavniks had not relaxed; it had grown more menacing than ever.

In the end, the Vrshovci forced the doorkeeper of the convent to tell them where the woman was hiding and to hand over to them the keys of the church. The unhappy adultress was dragged away from the altar to which she clung in her desperation and was put to death on the very steps of the holy place where she had sought sanctuary.

The incident constituted a very serious breach of the Church's prescriptions regarding the rights of refuge in holy places. It was, moreover, a heavy blow to the prestige of the bishop. According to Thietmar(35), Adalbert had no option but to excommunicate the ringleaders of the outrage, which of course exasperated his opponents who promptly retorted by intensifying their campaign. Eventually, Adalbert saw that any further stay in his diocese would be useless and once again, with regret and sorrow, he left his See of Prague(36).

---

(35) Chronicon, IV, ch. 28, M.G.H.S. N.S. IX, p. 165.

(36) Novotný, *Czech History* (in Czech), vol. I, 1, p. 639, places the interviews between Adalbert and Christian-Strakhkvas this year against the general opinion which made Adalbert offer his see to Christian prior to his first departure for Rome. I do not think that the general belief should be abandoned. This time there was no need for Adalbert to observe any formalities before leaving Prague, since he had returned on the understanding that his conditions should be fulfilled.

The biographers, our only source in this matter, only stress the moral and religious side of Adalbert's difficulties in Prague and of the last incident, but take no notice of the political complications that gave rise to and followed it; yet it does look as though the Duke's efforts had miscarried and that the friendly understanding between the two families which he had hoped for, came to nothing.

What happened afterwards made it evident that the incident of the adultress was merely a symptom, and it is likely that the Vrshovci who had taken a hand in the estrangement were in a position to make their influence felt in the administration of justice throughout Boleslas' dukedom. They were his keenest supporters and together with other adherents urged the Duke to make an end of all the unpleasantness for which the Slavniks were responsible. It was their policy to conclude the matter even by the use of force in the hope of taking the Slavniks' place in Bohemia.

The Slavniks must have been alive to the danger and they realised that it could only too easily end in disaster. Shortly after the incident which caused Adalbert to leave Prague for the second time and regain his refuge in Rome, his brother Sobieslav, the head of the family, was taking, according to Bruno (37), a body of his serfs to the court of the Emperor. As attested by the Annals of Hildesheim (38), Boleslas was also sending a detachment of his followers, headed by his son, to help in an expedition against the Polabian Slavs; whilst the Polish Duke, Boleslas the Great, was in the capacity of Otto III's ally contributing his contingent under his own command to the Emperor's army. All this time Otto III was making preparations for a campaign in September 995.

On Bruno's testimony, it had been Sobieslav's intention to call the Emperor's attention to the difficulties constantly cropping up between his family and the Przemyslides and their adherents; and he meant to express his fear that the Duke of Prague was planning a massacre of the entire Slavnik family. At the same time, it was part of his plan to approach the Polish Duke with a request for help, should things come to the worst.

One point needs noting—the fact that Sobieslav was taking a contingent to help the Emperor and that his men were not part of the army of Boleslas II, not only proved the independent position which the Slavniks held relatively to the Przemyslides, but also the strain in their relations. Old antagonisms were revived, and again Poland's fascination cast its spell on the Slavniks.

Another point that warrants this conclusion. Czech and Polish numismatists were puzzled by some recently discovered coins of apparently Bohemian origin. They evidently dated from the tenth century, but they could not have come from the Przemyslides' mint. The obverse of the coin had the Latin inscription—*Hic denarius est episcopi* (This is the bishop's denarius); but on the reverse the inscription is not clear. Some experts thought that they could decipher the names of Adalbert and Boleslas II; hence, they concluded, those coins came from a common mint

---

(37) Ch. 21, loc. cit., p. 288.
(38) *M.G.H.S.* III, p. 91.

shared by the duke and the bishop. Later discoveries, however, have revealed that the inscription includes the names of Sobieslav (not Boleslas) and Libice, the seat of the Slavniks; hence, one is obliged to conclude that the money must have issued from the mint of the Slavniks(39).

This discovery throws a new light on the position of the Bishop of Prague and his relations with the ruling Duke of Bohemia in the first years of the existence of the see. It must be remembered that the investiture of the bishop had to be performed not by the duke, but by the emperor, which further corroborates the contention that the bishop held a position of independence.

Furthermore, this discovery confirms what has been stated about the political standing of the Slavniks, chiefly in relation to the Przemyslides. The fact that Bishop Adalbert was at pains to assert his connection with the Slavniks on his coinage and to refer in the inscription not to Prague, but to Libice, that is to say, not to his see, but to his ancestral home, proves that the Slavniks regarded themselves as an independent dynasty which was bound to the dukedom of the Przemyslides only by free and reciprocal agreement. At the time when these coins issued from the mint, the Slavniks were insisting on their independence more than ever, an indication that the money was minted some time between the years 992 and 995, prior to the conflict which broke out between the rival parties.

In the light of these facts it is possible to get a clearer view of both the general political structure of Bohemia at that time and of the magnitude of the danger which again loomed before the eyes of the sanguine and inconsistent Boleslas II. He failed to follow his father's policy of friendship with Poland, the only policy able to check the dangerous attraction exercised by the growing power of the Piasts over the Bohemian tribes. The consequence of this policy was not only military defeat, but loss of political prestige liable to end in disaster for his dynasty. His attempts at reconciliation with the Slavniks had miscarried, because the Vrshovci were sabotaging it for selfish purposes and because the new ruler of Poland, Boleslas the Great, proved to be as valiant as his father and most unlikely to rest content with the territories which his father had forged into a single State. Poland's credit was again in the ascendant and Boleslas II, who had not inherited his father's soldierly genius, found himself unable to check it. We must keep these things in mind in order to understand the position in Bohemia and realise the feelings of the unfortunate Boleslas II in this hopeless quandary.

*   *   *

The fanatical wing of the Przemyslides' followers, especially the unscrupulous Vrshovci, advocated drastic action against the Slavniks whilst there was yet time, and accepting their view that delay was dangerous, Boleslas started military operations against the Slavniks in the autumn of 995.

---

(39) The detailed bibliography of works dealing with this topic was recently reviewed by the Czech expert G. Skalsky in a study published in the *Czech Historical Review* (1939), vol. XLV, pp. 104, 371. I have not been able to see his study on The Denarius of Adalbert, bishop of Prague, published in the *Czech Numismatic Review* (1929), vol. V.

At that moment, however, it looked as though the Slavniks were ready for him, for to everybody's surprise the Duke of Prague suddenly agreed to call a halt and postpone a settlement of the quarrel until a time when Sobieslav should return from the imperial expedition (40).

But Boleslas' die-hards insisted on forcing a decision, even if it meant a breach of promise. At length Boleslas, thoroughly alarmed, yielded to pressure, and on the eve of the feast of S. Wenceslas, September 28, Bohemia's national day, his armed forces appeared before Libice.

The Slavniks, who had trusted the Duke's word, had demobilised their troops and the men who a few weeks earlier had rallied against Boleslas were now engaged in gathering the harvest, a task which the first operations had delayed. It was with the utmost difficulty that a handful of serfs were mustered to the defence of Libice. They fought like lions, though the position was hopeless from the start. Boleslas' soldiers refused to observe the customary armistice of the feast day of S. Wenceslas. For three days the battle raged furiously and the dwindling body of Slavnik serfs made the attackers pay dearly for every yard they advanced. After the loss of the castle the Slavniks took refuge in the church, but left their asylum on a pledge of the honours of war. Every one of them was slain. The Przemyslides' vengeance was grim. All the members of the Slavnik family, with their wives and children, were put to the sword; only the absentees, Sobieslav, Adalbert and Radim-Gaudentius escaped with their lives.

Boleslas II hastened to occupy all the positions of strategic importance in the territory of the Slavniks, and in the space of a few days the problem of this family feud was liquidated for ever. But Boleslas gathered no glory from his crime. His treachery and cruelty are a blot on the history, otherwise glorious, of the Przemyslide dynasty, though it may be said in extenuation that his was not the only example of brutality displayed during the early Middle Ages in the removal of undesirable political rivals.

The Czech chronicler Cosmas (41), who was partial to Boleslas II, tries to exonerate the Prince, and to shift the responsibility for the crime on to high officials, the Vrshovci among them. In stating that Boleslas " was not completely his own master," Cosmas had undoubtedly in mind that the prince was paralysed and that the Vrshovci were the real villains of the piece whose interest it was to get hold of the Slavnik's possessions. Thietmar (42) confirms Boleslas' physical affliction in the last years of his reign, but adds that he was stricken for his " disobedience to Christ," which would make his paralysis a punishment, not an excuse. Bruno, who gives the best account of the massacre which he quotes from an eye-witness, Adalbert's former preceptor Radla, roundly accuses Boleslas of the misdeed, which makes it difficult to accept the Duke's exculpation by Cosmas. Generally speaking, Cosmas paints Boleslas II in colours far too bright and discovers in him the ideal of the Christian prince. The

---

(40) This is my interpretation of Bruno's account of the conflict, ch. 21, *F.R.B.* I, p. 288.
(41) Chronica, I, ch. 29, *M.G.H.S.* N.S. II, p. 53.
(42) Chronicon, VII, ch. 56, *ibid.*, IX, p. 468.

picture is thoroughly misleading. In forming his opinion Cosmas was influenced by Boleslas' largesse to the Church, a performance which, as a canon, he was only too ready to appreciate. In addition he was also guilty of misrepresenting the reign of the Duke's predecessor Boleslas I, the brother of S. Wenceslas (43).

At the time Cosmas was writing—he died in 1125—the Legend of S. Wenceslas had attained considerable fame, which cast a shadow over the memory of his brother and successor, an obvious thing to happen; if Wenceslas had to be exalted as one of the greatest martyrs for Christ, then the man responsible for his death had to be lowered to the level of a cruel pagan. Accepting this current opinion, Cosmas improved on the tale and took pains to embroider it.

It should also be noted that the first biography of Wenceslas, the old *Slavonic Legend* written soon after the saint's death (44), without glossing over Boleslas' participation in the plot against his saintly brother's life, presents Boleslas I in quite a different and more sympathetic light. Its author attributes the actual deed not to Boleslas I, but to the men responsible for the plot who had inveigled the young and inexperienced prince into their schemes. Later, Boleslas bitterly regretted the deed and paid due honour to his brother's remains by transferring them from Stará Boleslav to the cathedral church of his residential city, Prague.

What is certain is that the reign of Boleslas I was in many ways a blessing for Bohemia, and many achievements for which Cosmas gave the credit to the son, Boleslas II, were actually the acts of his father.

Finally, it should be observed that all the prominent followers of the Slavniks who escaped the slaughter, fled to Poland. Only Radla, Adalbert's associate at Magdeburg, seemingly took refuge in Hungary where he may have been working before at Adalbert's behest. Even Anastasius, the abbot of Brzevnov, left Prague for Poland; and when Sobieslav heard of the terrible fate that had overtaken his family at Libice, he headed for Poland with all his followers. No help was forthcoming from either the Emperor or the Duke of Poland and the leader of all that remained of the Slavniks had no option but to wait at the Polish court until such time as an opportunity for revenge would offer.

Such was the end of the first attempt to build a Central European State uniting all Polish and Czech tribes under the sceptre of the Polish Piast dynasty and able to deal with Germany on equal terms. This idea runs like a strand through the design of all the happenings in Poland and Bohemia in the last quarter of the tenth century. It is the struggle for the political integration of all the Slavs living in the Vistula, Oder, Elbe, Morava and Vag valleys, from the Danube to the Baltic Sea, that makes up

---

(43) As has already been shown by J. Loserth ("Studien zu Cosmas von Prag," *Archiv für Österr. Geschichte*, 1894, vol. 61, pp. 1 seq.), Cosmas simply applies to Boleslas I the words with which Regino of Prüm, one of Cosmas' sources, extols the deeds of Louis the German. This explains many things and suggests that Cosmas must have lacked first-hand documents on the reigns of Boleslas I and his son. Cf. also B. Bretholz, " Mähren und das Reich Herzog Boleslavs II von Böhmen," *Archiv für Österr. Geschichte* (1895), vol. 82, pp. 141 seq.

(44) Last edition by M. Weingart in *Anthology of St. Wencelas* (in Czech), vol. I, pp. 976-83.

the background of the lively drama of Adalbert's life. It is because historians have failed to grasp the inner meaning of this struggle that Adalbert's activities and especially his resignation from the see of Prague have been misjudged.

But it was difficult for the Czechs to appreciate the implications of the feud between the Slavniks and the Przemyslides. They could scarcely be expected to look back regretfully on the events of 995, since fate decided in favour of the Przemyslides, whose dynasty became the symbol of Czech mediaeval glory. For them the massacre of the Slavniks marked a last phase in the unification of Bohemia and only very few could view the facts from a different angle and realise that the same unification could have been achieved under the Slavniks as well. But at that period national sentiment was in its first stage and the amalgamation of the different tribes had to proceed on the lines of suppression or subjection of the ruling families. A similar process went on in Bohemia. The Czechs and their ruling dynasty had the advantage of first occupancy and the geographical configuration of Bohemia must have given its inhabitants, as far back as its occupation by the Celtic Boii, a presentiment that they would eventually fuse into some form of political unity. The disappearance of the Slavniks did seal Bohemian unity; but a Slavnik victory, though it would have meant the doom of the Przemyslides, would have been no bar to Bohemian unification. On the contrary, it would have powerfully contributed to the formation of a *Sclavinia* from the Danube and the Elbe along the Baltic Sea to the frontiers of Russia, which was then coming into its own, to take its place side by side with *Germania* and *Gallia* and steer the course of European history.

There was only one Slavonic dynasty left at that time able to carry out such a design, that of the Piasts. Mieszko's policy was inspired by the desire to unite first all the Polish tribes, their unification to be followed by the rounding up of all the tribes that were akin to the Poles, beginning with those that occupied Bohemia, Moravia and modern Slovakia and ending with the Slavs living on the right bank of the Elbe. The scheme was not so fantastic as historians have generally taken it to be; for they have so far not taken into account the existence of the three Slavonic States of White Croatia, White Serbia and Moravia. The Przemyslides came under the spell of the same tradition, gone yet not forgotten, but they had neither the strength nor the breadth of vision for such a task. Only the Piasts possessed the necessary stability for it and Mieszko I did unite Poland and the lands of former White Croatia. There still remained the old Moravian Empire and White Serbia to gather in, but with the help of the Slavniks, such an undertaking would not have been beyond the strength of Mieszko's son, Boleslas the Great(45).

*   *   *

Whilst his relatives were being massacred at Libice, Adalbert had already reached the monastery in Rome where he was received with

---

(45) In Polish History he is more frequently alluded to as : *Chrobry*, the Brave.

cordiality and appointed prior of the abbey. In this capacity he found opportunities to keep in touch with the outer world; for the abbey, as his biographers point out, had become a reform centre where the spiritual élite of Rome used to meet. Thanks to Adalbert, the reformatory ideals of the Greek monk Nilus found their way to Rome and spread to Bohemia, Hungary and Poland. It was in the spring of 996 that the Emperor Otto III paid a visit to Rome. If Adalbert had not already learned of the catastrophe that had overtaken his family, he certainly heard of it this time. His only consolation was the hope that now he would be left in peace to devote himself to the ascetic and contemplative life.

Canaparius(46) says that while on this visit to Rome, the Emperor Otto III saw a great deal of Adalbert, that he enjoyed talking to the bishop and paid much attention to his counsels. But the friendship between the German Emperor and the Bishop of Prague must have been of older date. Cosmas(47) states that Adalbert had previously paid a visit to Otto II at Aix-la-Chapelle, and that the Emperor held the bishop in such high esteem that he asked him to sing High Mass on Easter Day in the presence of the court and a great number of bishops. On this occasion Adalbert was allowed to place the imperial crown on the Emperor's head, a privilege that belonged to the archbishop. Then the Emperor asked him to hear his confession and presented him with the liturgical vestments which he had worn at the High Mass. These vestments were still treasured in Prague cathedral in Cosmas' days.

Here the good canon makes another mistake : Adalbert could not have met Otto II at Easter time at Aix-la-Chapelle, because the Emperor was in Italy in 982 and died there the following year. Adalbert had seen him at Verona, when he received his investiture from the Emperor. On the other hand, we cannot discount Cosmas' statement altogether, because some of the details he gives inspire confidence, and it may have been Otto III whom Adalbert visited at Aix-la-Chapelle, only it must have been either in 992 or 995, as Otto III spent his Easter in that city only in those years. In the spring of 995 Adalbert was on his way from Prague to Rome, but Cosmas states that he returned to Prague after meeting the Emperor. The year 992 would fit in with Adalbert's visit, as he was on his way from Rome to Prague after his family's second reconciliation with Boleslas II. In March of the same year a synod was held at Aix-la-Chapelle, when German and French bishops, under the papal legate, took important decisions against the French King Hugh Capet and his bishops, who had, without the Pope's consent, deposed the archbishop of Rheims, Arnulf, at a synod held the previous year at Saint-Basle near Rheims. This synod was part of the struggle for the possession of Rheims between Arnulf and the famous Gerbert, the future Pope Sylvester II. It is likely that Adalbert, who, when in Rome, must have known of the convocation of the Aix-la-Chapelle synod, attended it on his return as a bishop of the " *Reichskirche* "

(46) Ch. 22, *F.R.B.* I, p. 255.
(47) Chronica, I, ch. 28, *M.G.H.S.* N.S. II, pp. 50 seq.

and there met the young Emperor(48). This way it would seem natural that the Emperor wished to honour the young bishop in order to improve his own position in Bohemia. That same year (992) the Czech bishop and the German Emperor became friends.

Unfortunately for Adalbert, there was among the Emperor's entourage in Rome the Archbishop of Mainz, Willigis, and his presence there frustrated Adalbert's hopes ever to be able to spend the rest of his life in the seclusion of his beloved monastery. It is admitted that Adalbert had made his second departure from Prague without the knowledge of his metropolitan, for Willigis, on learning what had happened, insisted on the absentee bishop returning once more to his see of Prague. It is hard to say why the archbishop was so emphatic, as he certainly knew what had happened at Libice ; but perhaps it was his view that the return of Adalbert and his reconciliation with the Duke would prevent further complications.

The Emperor could not oppose such a request ; neither could the new Pope, Gregory V, since the metropolitan was only enforcing a prescription of the Church and, as Canaparius seems to suggest, had had a hand in the elevation of the youthful Bruno, son of the Duke of Carinthia and Otto III's relative, to the papal throne. Another synod was called. Its decision was that the archbishop's orders had to be obeyed. Willigis left Rome immediately after the meeting of the synod but he repeatedly insisted by letter on the strict execution of the synodal decisions.

Adalbert however seemed to know the position better. He could see that the archbishop's hopes for reconciliation were illusory and that Boleslas was far from desiring the presence of any of the Slavniks in Bohemia where he was the sole master. Nevertheless, he declared his willingness to submit to the decision. But after the departure of Willigis, according to Bruno(49), he requested the Pope to receive him and from him obtained permission to go wherever he wished to preach the Gospel to the pagans as a missionary, if the Czechs refused to countenance his return.

In the latter half of July, 996, Adalbert left Rome accompanied by Notkerius of Liège, the celebrated scholar, known in the history of education for his endeavours to reform the educational system of the tenth century. In September Adalbert was in Mainz and once more in the presence of his metropolitan. Here he also met Otto III who had in the meantime left Rome.(50)

---

(48) Cf. what H. Leclercq says on this synod in his translation of Hefele's Konziliengeschichte (*Histoire des Conciles*, vol. IV, 2, Paris, 1911, pp. 873 seq.). On the Gerbert incident, see F. Lot, *Etude sur le Règne de Hugues Capet* (Paris, 1903, Biblioth. de l'Ecole des Hautes Etudes, vol. CXLVII), pp. 83 seq. Already in 1898 M. Dvořák called experts' attention to this synod in explanation of Cosmas' statement " A Contribution to S. Adalbert's Biography," *Czech Historical Review* (1898), vol. IV, pp. 62 seq. (in Czech).

(49) Ch. 18, *F.R.B.* I, p. 286.

(50) Canaparius, chs. 22, 23, *ibid.*, pp. 256 seq. There still exists at Rome a monument recalling the saint's stay in the Holy City, the baptismal font in the church of S. Bartholomew on the Tiberian Island. It represents Adalbert and Otto III and is, according to recent research, of the Ottonian period. Cf. O. Homburg, "Ein Denkmal Ottonischer Plastik in Rome," *Jahrbücher der Preuss. Kunstsammlungen* (1936), vol. LVII, 3, pp. 130-40 ; Geza de Franchovichova " Contributi alla scultura Ottoniana in Italia. Il puteale di S. Bartolomeo all'Isola in Roma," *Bolletino d'Arte del Ministerio dell' Educazione Nazionale.* (1936), vol. V, pp. 207-24.

M.   E

Adalbert's biographers and some German historians agree that the relations between the Czech bishop and the German Emperor became extremely friendly and intimate during their stay in Mainz. Night and day the Emperor loved to talk to the bishop who had to sleep near the Emperor's apartments so as to be always at hand. The biographers stress the point that it was Adalbert's hope to fill the heart and the soul of the Emperor with sentiments of real Christian humility and a longing for the things of the spirit.

This friendship between a Czech bishop and a German Emperor was something unique in history. By his character and his work, Otto III represented the cultural current and the spirit of the tenth century. He was of German stock, a chief of a German tribe which had been christianised for not quite two centuries and which had by its inherent qualities and boundless energies won for itself the first place in the German Empire. The Saxons were the true representatives of the young, half-barbaric element which at this time was pushing forwards in all directions in its desire to secure a place in the sun of might, culture and glory.

On the other hand, Otto III was saturated with the notion of his own imperial dignity, and believed himself to be the successor and heir of the Roman emperors and of Charlemagne. Faithful to their mission, he planned to realise their dream and to become the ruler of an immense Empire which would cover the whole known world. The ideas of the classics —if it is permissible to speak of a classical tradition in the West in the tenth century—had subjugated his young mind just as they had mastered so many representatives of the so-called Ottonian Renaissance. Moreover, Otto III was extremely proud of his mother's Greco-Byzantine origin. Sometimes he could not disguise his contempt for his uncouth Saxon warriors and their simple, half-barbarian, straightforward manners, although even in Italy they proved his sole support. Otto's passionate and dreamy nature was attracted by the mystical flame which burned in the souls of many religious enthusiasts in monasteries, convents and other pious establishments. There were moments when the Emperor was almost overcome by a longing to doff his crown and kingly robes and to sit at the feet of some humble friar to learn his secrets of mortification and spiritual life.

Some German historians consider that the intimacy with the humble Czech bishop was unfortunate for Otto III's spiritual growth. Such opinions originated from the mistaken ideas on Adalbert. Many historians for example, look upon him as a fanatical mystic, a dreaming monk who had been swept off his feet by the notion that there was nothing in the whole world more precious than the retired and contemplative existence in a monastic cell. We have seen what these opinions are worth. The fact is that few historical writers paid sufficient attention to the political background on which the drama of Adalbert's whole life unfolded(51).

(51) A. Cartellieri "Otto III, Kaiser der Römer," *Judeich-Festschrift*, Weimar, 1929, pp. 174-205, rather stresses the influence of Sylvester II, of Bishop Leo of Vercelli and of the Chancellor Heribert on the growth of the young emperor's political thought.

At the same time, Otto III was not, as he has often been pictured, an eccentric dreamer, who had lost his foothold on the solid ground of his German country and within the tradition of Charlemagne and Otto I, his ancestor, and who abandoned himself to Roman and imperial vagaries ; nor was his an unbalanced mind with a morbid passion for ascetic extravagances. We shall have an opportunity in the next chapter to show how misleading this presentation of the young Emperor really is. The pity is that Adalbert's biographers were so engrossed in the religious aspect of this contact that they had no room for information on the Emperor's conversations with Adalbert, when there is excellent reason for assuming that asceticism and piety were not the only topics of their talks. Many of Otto III's plans for the future, especially for the christianisation of the East and of Hungary, must have been ventilated between them, so that not only Gerbert of Aurillac, the future Sylvester II, but also Adalbert, the Bishop of Prague, must have been to an appreciable extent responsible for the plan of the *Renovatio Imperii* as conceived and put into execution by Otto III.

The various items of information supplied by Adalbert's biographers concerning his stay at Mainz, his pilgrimage to a number of sacred shrines in France and his journey to Poland are confused and contradictory. Hence it is difficult to determine exactly the sequence of these various events. For instance, Canaparius(52) affirms that Adalbert left Mainz directly for Bohemia and that it was only on his arrival in that country that he learned what had happened at Libice. Then he went to Poland. But we already know that it was impossible for things to have happened in this way.

What most nearly approximates to the truth would be the following. Adalbert went to Mainz in order to inform his metropolitan, Archbishop Willigis, of the latest papal decision concerning his future in the event of the Czechs' refusing to receive him. Willigis, of course, could not know of this decision which was taken only after his departure from Rome. It seems that Adalbert sent a messenger from Mainz to Bohemia, with the consent of both the Emperor and the Archbishop, in order to learn the opinion of the Duke of Prague concerning his return. In the meantime, before the messenger returned, Adalbert decided to make a pilgrimage to some holy shrines in France. Either on foot or on horseback, he visited the graves of S. Martin of Tours, of S. Denis at St. Denis, near Paris, of S. Benedict at Fleury and of S. Maurus at St. Maure.

He then returned to Mainz ; but no reply had yet come from Bohemia. Moreover, the Emperor wished to retain Adalbert's company for as long as possible. It is not known whether the Duke's reply reached Adalbert while he was still in Mainz or when he had gone thence to Poland. It was, of course, in the negative just as Adalbert had expected. Thus, he was now free and, in accordance with the Pope's decision, could start upon his missionary work as an *episcopus regionarius*.

It appears that after the refusal of Boleslas II to receive Adalbert once more, Willigis regarded the see of Prague as definitely vacant. Cosmas

---

(52) Ch. 25, loc. cit., p. 258.

states(53) that he intended to consecrate a new bishop of Prague, the one elected by the Czechs. This was the duke's brother, Strakhkvas-Christian, to whom Adalbert had once offered the vacancy. But this plan came to nothing as, according to Cosmas, Christian had a stroke during the consecration ceremony.

*   *   *

Adalbert was received with great cordiality by the Polish Duke, Boleslas the Great, who expressed the desire to keep him in his dominions. But Adalbert meant to stay in Poland only until he could make up his mind as to where he was going to preach the Gospel. Meanwhile, he did good work in Poland. Many Polish districts cherish traditions claiming that he visited them, but only one of these has stood the test of history. Bruno of Querfurt(54) confirms the claim that Adalbert stayed for a time in Gnesen (Gniezno). Little did he dream at the time that this name was to become famous throughout the West for its association with his last resting place.

There is some historical evidence, however, for the fact that Adalbert founded a Benedictine monastery in Poland, either at Meseritz (Miedzyrzecz) or at Tremessen (Trzemeszno), as the anonymous author of his *Passio*(55) suggests. The abbot of this new foundation was probably that same Anastasius who had been abbot of Brzevnov and who fled to Poland after the massacre at Libice.

There exists a tradition in Poland that Adalbert introduced a more rigorous fasting practice during Lent. All we know is that as early as the year 1248 the Lent period in Poland started not on Ash Wednesday, but on the third Sunday before that date, Septuagesima(56).

Another old tradition ascribes to Adalbert the authorship of the oldest Polish hymn in honour of the Virgin, called *Bogurodzica*, or the Mother of God. There is abundant literature in existence dealing with this composition. The oldest manuscript of the hymn dates from the fifteenth century. The hymn itself, however, contains elements of an ancient character, and it has been generally agreed that in its present form it dates at least from the twelfth or thirteenth century.

According to the latest findings by a Polish expert(57), the first stanzas of the hymn were written in the second half of the tenth century, certainly not later than the eleventh. Their metre and construction recall the Byzantine forms of the ninth and tenth centuries. S. Adalbert must have

---

(53) Chronica, I, ch. 30, *M.G.H.S.* N.S. II, p. 54.

(54) Ch. 24, *F.R.B.* I, p. 292.

(55) Ch. I, *ibid.*, p. 231.

(56) Cf. Voigt, *Adalbert von Prag*, pp. 295 seq.

(57) J. Birkenmayer, *The Authorship of the Hymn Bogurodzica* (in Polish), (Gniezno, 1935) ; *idem, Bogurodzica Dziewica* (in Polish), Lwów, 1937. I have not been able to trace these two publications in G. B. See history of the problem in J. Loś, *The Beginning of Polish Literature* (in Polish), (Lwów, 1922), pp. 348-80. Another specialist in Old Slavonic hymnology, R. Jakobson, discovered in the hymn three linguistic shifts, the Old Slavonic as a basis, the Greek and the later Polish. According to him, the hymn in its oldest form belongs to Old Slavonic literature of Czech origin. This study, published in *Slovo a Slovesnost* (1935), vol. I, was not to be found in any British library.

learned Greek religious compositions in the Greek Abbey of S. Nilus, where Byzantine art was at its best in the tenth century(58). No historian can pronounce judgment on a matter that is mainly philological, but historical evidence favours the attribution. This may yield the observation that Adalbert made it a practice to bring his religious teachings home to the people by encouraging the use of the national language in worship.

A Czech tradition also attributes to Adalbert the authorship of the oldest Czech hymn, the *Hospodine Pomiluy Ny* (Lord, have mercy on us), which is the Czech equivalent and enlarged version of the *Kyrie eleison*. This tradition has been questioned even more than that of the Polish hymn. All that is known is that in tenth-century Bohemia, according to Cosmas (59), the upper classes used a well known German chant—Christus Keinado —whereas the people sang their own Czech Krlesh (Kyrie). More recent researches by Czech experts have, however, shown that the origin of the Czech hymn goes as far back as the period between the second half of the tenth century and the end of the eleventh(60). This would allow S. Adalbert to have been in some way associated with it.

The scepticism with which this tradition has so often been treated by Czech, Polish and German specialists was generally due to a widespread belief that Adalbert, a rigid Roman monk, must, as a matter of course, have been averse to the use of the Slavonic liturgy in divine worship ; and this prejudice has in its turn spread owing to the neglect of the historical background of Adalbert and his life.

Far from there being any evidence for Adalbert's hostility to the Slavonic liturgy as still practised in his day in parts of his vast diocese by the last of the Slavonic priests, there are many instances, some of them confirmed by recent discoveries, that prompt us to revise the general notion, which had many followers even among Czech historians, about the existence and expansion of the Slavonic liturgy and Slavonic literature in Bohemia in the tenth and eleventh centuries. It has been shown that even Wenceslas, responsible though he was for Bohemia's orientation towards the West, had no quarrel with Slavonic liturgy and literature ; he must have been rather popular among the Slavonic clergy, since the earliest and most reliable account of his life and martyrdom was written by one of them in the so-called first Old Slavonic Legend. The Slavonic school had its centre in Prague near the duke's residence, whereas the Latin school was established at Budech, out in the country. Wenceslas'

---

(58) Historians overlook the fact that at that period there existed in Rome several Greek monasteries. Cf. my book *Les Légendes de Constantin et de Méthode*, pp. 284 seq.

(59) Chronica, I, ch. 23, *M.G.H.S.* N.S. p. 45. On this Old German chant and the first Czech hymn, cf. A. Kraus, " Christe ginâdô a Hospodine pomiluj ny," *Proceedings of the Royal Scientific Association of Bohemia* (Prague, 1898), vol. XIII.

(60) Cf. what the foremost Czech modern specialist in Old Slavonic, the late M. Weingart, has to say on the origin of this first Czech hymn in *Byzantinoslavia* (1930), vol. II, pp. 447-53 in the course of his review of R. Jakobson's booklet on the Old Czech hymns (Prague, 1929). I have not seen R. Jakobson's answer to Weingart's criticism, published in *Slovo a Slovesnost*, vol. I, 1935, and reiterating the Old Slavonic origin of the hymn. On the history of the music of this hymn, cf. D. Orel, "Musical Data in Connection with S. Wenceslas" in *Anthology of S. Wenceslas* (Prague, 1937), vol. II, pp. 28 seq. (in Czech).

brother, Boleslas I, also kept an even balance between the Latin and the Greco-Slavonic forms of Christianity in Bohemia.

The Slavniks undoubtedly upheld the same tradition, for we find Adalbert's uncle, Christian, the author of the best Latin biography of S. Wenceslas, well acquainted with Greco-Slavonic literature and producing a work of literary and historical value, the first history of Christianity in Moravia and Bohemia. For the composition of his work Christian drew inspiration from all the Old Slavonic literature in existence. He knew the first Old Slavonic Legend of S. Wenceslas, the Slavonic biographies of SS. Constantine-Cyril and Methodius, written in Moravia at the end of the ninth century, and perhaps even the Slavonic Life of Methodius' disciple, S. Naum. That he wrote in Latin is of itself no proof that he belonged to the Latin and Western cultural movement. There was nothing to prevent champions of the Slavonic cultural movement choosing the language that suited their propaganda best.

Adalbert must have shared his uncle's convictions; otherwise Christian would hardly have dedicated to his nephew a work so sympathetic to Greco-Slavonic culture and liturgy. And what confirms our surmise is that almost at the same time as Christian was writing his work, another Slavonic Legend on S. Wenceslas was being written in Bohemia in Adalbert's own diocese, perhaps even in Prague. It was the Slavonic translation of the Latin Legend written in the second half of the tenth century by Gumpold, bishop of Mantua, at the special request of the Emperor Otto II. The translation is in reality a revised and substantially enlarged Slavonic edition of Gumpold's Legend.

This Slavonic version was known and widely read in Bohemia in the second half of the tenth century and in the following years. Then it found its way to Russia where it was used in the liturgical books of the Russian Church in commemoration of the saint. At the same period, the First Slavonic Legend also penetrated into Russia, Croatia and Dalmatia, where some remnants of the Slavonic liturgy are still extant to-day(61). The Slavonic Life of S. Vitus may also have been written in the tenth century, probably after the erection of S. Vitus' Church by S. Wenceslas. We can also trace to this period the existence and expansion of Slavonic literature throughout the eleventh century as well as the so called Fragments of Prague.

Not until the end of the eleventh century(62) did hostility to the Slavonic liturgy grow under the impulse of the new reformist movement which Gregory VII stimulated so energetically. Canon Cosmas for instance, Czech patriot though he was and a married man to boot, was a

---

(61) See latest edition of these versions by J, Vajs and J. Vašica in *Collection of Old Slavonic Literary Records on S. Wenceslas and S. Ludmila* (in Czech). Precise indications on this difficult subject will be found in M. Weingart's review of this book in *Byzantinoslavica* (1930), vol. II, pp. 453-7. Cf. what I say on the penetration of Slavonic literature from Bohemia into Kievan Russia in ch. VI.

(62) The expulsion of the Slavonic monks from the Abbey of Sazava by Spytihniev II (1055-1056) may have been prompted by motives other than hostility to the Slavonic liturgy See Novotný, loc. cit., p. 96.

sworn enemy of the Slavonic liturgy. Because he happened to be the first Czech chronicler, his views on his pet aversion were widely propagated, inducing many a modern historian to minimise the importance and the expansion of Slavonic liturgy in Bohemia(63). To-day, in the light of modern research, this view has to be revised and credit must be given to S. Adalbert for having contributed by his friendly attitude to the survival of Slavonic literature and liturgy in Bohemia.

One point may elucidate Adalbert's association with Greco-Slavonic culture as introduced into Bohemia by SS. Cyril and Methodius. It will be remembered that Boleslas II, as attested by the document previously mentioned, gave Adalbert leave to build churches wherever he should consider it advisable, and this clause was generally understood to have had something to do with the opposition of the nobles which Adalbert's two biographers so deprecate. It was suggested that as a keen believer in the Cluniac reform, Adalbert fought the custom that made the nobles owners of the churches they built on their land, to the prejudice of episcopal rights and privileges(64).

But this opinion, however general it is, cannot be defended, for it is impossible to make the Cluniac reformers of the tenth century responsible for any opposition to this practice. Their reform was strictly monastic and the foremost champions of the movement were mainly interested in the reform of abbeys and monks, and in their abstention from unsolicited interference in public life. They were not interested in ecclesiastical administration, however much they deplored the evils of secular intrusion into Church matters. Opposition to this and to the system of church administration originated much later, in the first half of the eleventh century, and not in Cluny, but in Lorraine, whence it spread to Rome under the Lorrainer Leo IX and his successors. The fact is that Cluny had very little in common with the reformists of the eleventh century(65). It would be preposterous to throw back to Adalbert's days a movement that started only half a century later. Nor can it be said that Adalbert was a prominent forerunner of the reformists. The practice of proprietary churches was general in Germany and Adalbert must have been brought up to this environment in Magdeburg, while his short contact with the Abbot of Cluny and with Gerardus, the Bishop of Toul, could scarcely be appealed to as the only source from which he borrowed his ideas.

But there is another contingency which, as it seems to me, may well have influenced Adalbert. We should bear in mind that the system of proprietary churches against which Adalbert is stated to have been battling was a Germanic institution which amounted in a sense to a germanisation of the old ecclesiastical system as it had grown up in Roman and Greek

(63) These problems are discussed more in detail by the late professor M. Weingart in the introduction of his critical edition of the first Slavonic Legend of S. Wenceslas, published in 1934 in *Anthology of S. Wenceslas* (in Czech), vol. I, pp. 862-1088.

(64) Cf. chiefly Novotný, loc. cit., vol. I, 1, p. 628.

(65) The role of Cluny in Church reform was specified only quite recently. For a comprehensive survey of this problem, see Z. N. Brook's handbook *A History of Europe from 911 to 1198* (London, 1938), pp. 115-24.

Christianity(66). The Greeks never had any knowledge of such lay interference in their ecclesiastical life and we are apt to forget that Christianity
was introduced into Bohemia by the two Greek missionaries SS. Cyril
and Methodius. We must of course assume that they also introduced
into Moravia the old ecclesiastical practice as it had prevailed in Byzantium
and in Rome and we are given to understand that S. Methodius, Archbishop
of Sirmium and Moravia, strongly objected to certain Germanic practices,
since his biographer makes him stand up for his rights in the presence of
the Frankish bishops with exceptional spirit(67).

Now it may be that what he found fault with was the Frankish system
of proprietary churches which had spread over the whole sphere of the
Frankish Church's influence. There is in the life of Methodius a riddle
which historians have failed so far to clear up—the estrangement between
the saint and Svatopluk. Why did he favour the Latin priests and why
did he apply to the Pope for the appointment of the Frankish Bishop
Wiching in Nitra under Methodius' metropolitan jurisdiction, when it
should have been in his interest to support his own archbishop and his
Slavonic priests, since he was fighting the Franks militarily as well
as politically ? It seems that the answer is to be found in the in-
compatibility between the Frankish and Greek methods of Church
administration. Svatopluk possibly preferred the Frankish to the Greek
system for the control it gave him over his Church and over its funds.
The founder of a church building had a right to its income ; and it was
on this principle that the Franks were colonising ancient Pannonia in
Svatopluk's day. That he should favour it was understandable, but the
Greeks considered it to be alien to Church tradition.

If this be admitted, it would follow that Methodius' disciples, as
Slavs trained in his Greek discipline, stood for the old Roman and Greek
practices. This would also explain why the Slavonic liturgy, for all its
popularity, survived no longer than it did ; for it was severely handicapped by the fact that Methodius' disciples disapproved the Frankish
practice and that this opposition became a tradition in the Slavonic
Church in tenth century Bohemia, whereas the nobles, for their own
private purposes, were rather in favour of the Latin missionaries, whose
system gave them a lucrative share in the administration and emoluments
of the Church. It was an uneven struggle and its outcome a foregone
conclusion.

This lends the problem a new aspect and even if there is no conclusive
evidence to produce, it deserves the experts' consideration. It would
make it possible that S. Adalbert was acting under the influence of the old
Greco-Roman tradition brought to Bohemia by the Greek and Slavonic
missionaries when he asked the duke for permission to erect churches

---

(66) See what I said on this evolution in my booklet *National Churches and the Church
Universal* (London, 1944), pp. 33 seq.

(67) Vita Methodii, ch. IX, Cf. my French translation in *Les Légendes de Constantin et de
Méthode*, p. 388.

wherever he would consider it necessary, in disregard of the interests of the local aristocracy(68).

* * *

It had been Adalbert's first intention to preach the Gospel to the Veletians, also called Liutici, who had often been the Czechs' military allies. It was a pity that he found himself unable to realise the project, as his activity among the Polabian Slavs would have been of first-rate importance. The main reason why these tribes had refused to accept Christianity was that German priests were trying to convert them not only to the Christian faith, but to German political supremacy as well. This meant that they would have embraced Christianity at the cost of their liberty. The reader will remember the fierce determination with which the Slavs on the Baltic coast and beyond the river Elbe defended their territory against German penetration. In their estimation, the Christian God was no other than the German God, and they refused His Gospel as obstinately as they refused the German yoke. Many are the accounts by contemporary chroniclers, such as Widukind, Thietmar and Helmhold, to mention only the best, disclosing the ruthlessness of German missionary methods(69).

This is more than enough to explain why German missionary activity remained fruitless so long, and why the bishoprics founded by Otto I in conquered Slavonic territories remained for many decades nothing better than a sort of *Burgwarde*, ministering only to the garrisons of occupation and a few German colonists. The history of the " conversion " of these Slavonic tribes has no place in our ecclesiastical annals which Christianity can be proud of. Adalbert, as a member of the famous Slavonic family, would certainly have been successful. His friendship with the emperor was a sure guarantee that there would have been no objection from the German side to his working among them.

It is probable that Boleslas the Great was the one responsible for Adalbert's change of plans. It was just at this time that the Polish Duke started attempts to extend Polish influence in a north-eastern direction over lands inhabited by the Prussians—Pomerania, which his great father had conquered, serving as an excellent base for further expansion. Gdansk (Danzig), on the mouth of the Vistula, had long been in Poland's grip. It stood on the territory inhabited by a tribe of Slavonic Pomeranians, kinfolk to the Poles, and together with Stettin and Wollin, proved a valuable asset among the Polish possessions on the Baltic.

The Prussians who belonged to the Baltic racial group, which in pre-historic days had shared a common language with the primitive Slavs, lost a march in their race for the shores of what is still known as the Baltic Sea where the Slavs arrived first and peacefully settled down as their neighbours. The Prussians were thus closely related to the Lithuanian and Latvian tribes,

(68) On the introduction of the system of proprietary churches in Bohemia, cf. K. Krofta, " The Papal Curia and the Ecclesiastical Administration in Czech lands before the Hussite period," *Czech Hist. Rev.* (1904), vol. X, pp. 15 seq. (in Czech).

(69) Cf. J. W. Thompson, *Feudal Germany* (Chicago, 1928), pp. 387-451.

two nations still extant in those parts.   As the Estonians, a tribe of Finnish stock, were slowly pressed back towards the sea shore, where some of their settlements are still found barring the way to the Lithuanians, the Latvians succeeded in penetrating to the much coveted Baltic shores(70).

Historical records on the Prussians and on the Balts are scarce ; but we know that some of the tribes, together with some Slavs, must have been for a short spell under the domination of the Goths, an East-Germanic nation, which halted on the lower Vistula at the beginning of the Christian era in their migration from Scandinavia, the home of all Germanic nations, towards the warmer shores of the Black Sea.   Tacitus, who was writing at this period, was interested in the amber-producing coast of the Baltic and in one of the last chapters of his *Germania*(71) supplies some information on the people settled there ; he calls them Aestii in a passage that has puzzled both philologists and historians.   Does the name stand for the Finnish Estonians, the Prussians, or for the whole amber-producing country ?   It is impossible to tell.   It seems, however, established, as confirmed by the first Russian chronicle(72), that the Prussians reached the shore before the Latvians and that by the tenth century they were firmly settled between the mouths of the Vistula and the Niemen.   They were, however, unable to make the best of their advantageous position on the coast, for the Vikings had preceded them. Their fleet controlled the whole of the Baltic and jealously excluded all other populations on the Baltic coast—Finns, Prussians and Slavs—from any maritime activity.

But from the second half of the tenth century the Poles developed into dangerous neighbours.   Their power hampered Prussian expansion towards the interior, with the result that the Prussian habitat remained locked in between the lower Vistula, the Baltic, the Niemen river to the east and the Mazurian Lakes to the south.   The Prussians had to thank their contact with the Roman Empire, and after its destruction, with the Scandinavians and their trading centres in Novgorod and Kiev, where they met travelling Arab merchants, for the small amount of culture they did possess.   Ibrahim-ibn-Jacub(73), the famous Arabian traveller of the tenth century, knew the Prussians well and was favourably impressed by their manners and their customs.   As Christianity could only penetrate into their territory from the Polish side in the tenth century, the Prussians learned at the same time to fear and to distrust the Poles' growing influence over the Baltic and Eastern Europe; and as their tribal organisation rather favoured pillage and conquest,

(70) Summary indications on the origin of the Finns and the Balts in general will be found in F. Lot, *Les Invasions Barbares* (Paris, 1937), vol. I, pp. 332 seq. and vol. II, pp. 48 seq.   More detailed information on the ancient Prussians with the principal bibliographical data of Prussian history is given by H. Łowmianski, *The Ancient Prussians*, The Baltic Pocket Library (Torun-London, 1936).   Cf. also Voigt, *Adalbert von Prag*, pp. 119 seq., 298 seq.

(71) Ch. 45, ed. E. Koestermann, p. 246 : On the right shore of the Suevic sea live the nations of the Aestii, whose rites and customs belong to the Suevi, but whose language is akin to British.   The reader will note that Tacitus believes the ancient Prussians and the old Britons to use a similar language.

(72) S. H. Cross, loc. cit., p. 137 : The Lyakhs (Poles *i.e.* Pomeranians), the Russians and Chud (Finns) border on the Varangian Sea.

(73) F. Westberg, "Ibrahim's-ibn-Ja'kub's Reisebericht über die Slavenlande," *Memoires de l'Academie Imper. des Sciences de S. Pétersbourg* (1899), Cl. Hist.-Phil., VIIIe Serie, t. III, No. 4, p. 56.

clashes between Prussians and Poles must have been frequent after the Piasts had consolidated their hold on Pomerania and thereby completed the encirclement of the Prussians from the West. To deal with these restless and dangerous neighbours a well-equipped and well organised army, the work of Mieszko I and his son, Boleslas the Great, kept a vigilant eye on them and checked their predatory incursions. It must have occurred to Boleslas the Great how much preferable it would be to incorporate Prussia into the Polish State, or at least to place it under Poland's preventive protection, because two early chroniclers—Adam of Bremen(74) and the anonymous Gallus(75)—attribute the conquest of Prussia to that monarch. But the first step in any such scheme had to be the conversion of the Prussians; and Boleslas the Great conceived the idea of using for this purpose his famous guest, Vojtiekh, or Adalbert, the former bishop of Prague. The pious missionary bishop agreed to the Duke's suggestion, since the possibilities of his missionary activity, at least at the start, depended on the support of the Polish Duke in any case. Even if Adalbert had been able to realise his first plan to preach the Gospel to the Veletians, he would have needed the Polish Duke's protection at the opening stage of his mission, since no encouragement was to be expected from Boleslas II of Bohemia, the murderer of his relatives. By agreeing to carry the Gospel to the Prussians Adalbert received the fullest support of Boleslas, as his plan fitted in perfectly with the Duke's political intentions.

* * *

In the early spring of 997, Adalbert went with a few companions to Danzig. From Danzig, accompanied by a bodyguard of Polish soldiers, he proceeded by water into the interior of the country. The general opinion is that his objective was the part of Prussia known as Samland. As soon as he arrived there to commence his missionary work he fell into the hands of a band of Prussians and was murdered. Not far from Königsberg, near the place formerly called Romove, to-day Fischhausen, one can still see the spot where he is said to have been martyred on April 23rd, A.D. 997.

That tradition, however, does not seem to tally with the facts as they are known. Apart from the two contemporary biographies, the oldest document giving details of Adalbert's death is a manuscript entitled *Passio S. Adalberti Martyris*(76). This account was written some time between the years 1006 and 1025, when Adalbert's remains were still at Gnesen whence they were transported to Prague in 1039. The author of the manuscript was, if not a Slav, at least a German who had lived in Poland and who had had the opportunity of collecting many details concerning Adalbert's end at a time when such details were fresh in the memory of the martyr's contemporaries. The author does not say much about the actual route which Adalbert followed into the interior. He merely states that the bishop went by water

---

(74) Gesta Hamburg. Ecclesiae, II, ch. 77, Schol. 25, *M.G.H.S.* VII, p. 318, *Scriptores Rerum Prussicarum*, I, p. 238.

(75) Chronica Polonorum I, ch. 6, *M.G.H.* I, p. 400.

(76) *F.R.B.* I, pp. 231-4. Cf. Voigt, loc. cit., pp. 226 seq.

to his destination, a large city of Prussia. This reference gave rise to the view that Adalbert went from Danzig by sea to Samland, the centre of the country where Königsberg stands to-day.

At that time, however, the delta of the Vistula had many mouths and a number of lagoons known as Haff were also referred to as " the sea." Slavs and Prussians, not being sea-faring, must have failed to make the distinction. Moreover, there is no reason why Adalbert should have wanted to start his preaching campaign in the centre of the country. It was usual for missionaries to start their work at the frontiers of the country they visited and to work their way inland. The *Passio S. Adalberti* refers to a " large city of Prussia " as the place where Adalbert intended to commence his missionary campaign. It appears that he began by addressing his Prussian audience in Polish. It was a language he knew, which was then akin to Czech, the difference being not greater than that between American and English speech ; but he could hardly be expected to have learnt Prussian. Nevertheless, his listeners appear to have understood him. While it was possible to suppose that Prussians living on the border would understand Polish, it was not to be expected that a similar knowledge of a neighbour's language should exist in the interior. Experts seem to have forgotten that an important Prussian commercial and cultural centre, Truso, stood not very far from Danzig(77). On all counts, therefore, this was the place where Adalbert proposed to open his campaign. This conforms to what the author of the *Passio* says. The easiest access to Truso was made by boat from Danzig through the Delta of the Vistula, by the Elbing canal into the Haff and thence to the mouth of the river Elbing. In all probability this was the route which Adalbert followed. The Polish bodyguard accompanied him and his companions as far as the mouth of the Elbing. From there Adalbert set out for Truso on foot.

Events can be recapitulated according to the sources as follows : When Adalbert and his companions reached the city, the first thing he was asked was from where he had come. His reply was that he had come from Poland, from the court of Duke Boleslas. This answer aroused the suspicion that he might be a spy in the service of Poland. After so many frontier incidents it was not to be wondered at that the Prussians felt distrustful of any who came over the Polish border. And the nearer to the Polish frontier the Prussians lived the deeper was the distrust. The Prussian authorities refused Adalbert and his companions permission to stay in the country. They were conducted to the sea shore, put in a boat, and instructed not to return on pain of death.

Adalbert was chagrined by this initial reversal. He hoped, however, that he could still realise his object and find an opportunity to explain his peaceful intentions and gain the necessary permission to proceed with his

---

(77) Cf. the most recent and penetrating study on Adalbert's mission in Prussia published by R. Hennig, " Die Missionsfahrt des Hl. Adalbert ins Preussenland," *Forschungen zur Preussischen und Brandenburgischen Geschichte* (1935), t. 47, pp. 139-48. Cf. also what F. Duda says on the place of S. Adalbert's martyrdom in his book, which incidentally gives an excellent history of Eastern Pomerania *Territorial evolution of Polish Pomerania* (Cracow, 1909), pp. 47 seq. (in Polish).

mission. So instead of pushing out to sea he remained on the coast for some days to devote himself to prayer. It was there he was surprised by a band of Prussian soldiers, probably a coastal patrol. The Prussians pointed out to him that he was disobeying the orders of the authorities by not leaving the country and one of them, a certain Sikko, whose brother had been killed in the war with Poland, stepped up to the bishop while he was in the act of praying and slew him. Adalbert's companions were not molested; but the bishop was beheaded and his corpse thrown into the water. In the light of this reconstruction of the events, it may be assumed that the martyrdom of Adalbert took place at a spot between the Nogat and the Elbing canal of the Vistula.

The body of the bishop was carried across the estuary by the current and washed up on the Polish shore, which explains why his remains came so promptly into Christian hands and why Boleslas so speedily got the news of Adalbert's death. Soon after, those of Adalbert's companions who had been able to flee from Prussian soil, brought confirmation of the tragedy. Boleslas the Great buried Adalbert's remains in Gnesen with all the solemnity due to the relics of a saint and a martyr. He was also able to recover the head which had been found by a traveller.

* * *

Adalbert can rightly be called a martyr because he gave his life for Christianity, and his intentions were absolutely pure. The news of his glorious end spread like wildfire through all Western Christendom. The Christian of the tenth century most valued two great ideals : a life of mortification and meditation in the monastery and death for Christ. It was a period of mysticism and romanticism and the Bishop of Prague became an example to the whole of Western Christendom because he realised its two most sacred ideals, monasticism and martyrdom.

When Otto III learned of the tragic end of his friend his first reaction was to rejoice and give thanks to God that he had found one who could and would intercede for him in heaven. A similar view was taken in Rome and in other centres of the reformed monasticism where Adalbert's example had been known and admired. His glorious end also inspired Canaparius, a monk in the convent of S. Alexius in Rome, to tell the story of his life. His biography of S. Adalbert, written in the year 999, is quite one of the best concerning Adalbert's life and period.

Adalbert's example attracted great numbers of his contemporaries. One of his most devoted followers was Bruno of Querfurt, the son of a Saxon Count educated at the same school in Magdeburg as Adalbert, and from 996, a monk in the same convent in Rome. This austere German was so devoted to the memory of the Slavonic bishop that he followed in Adalbert's footsteps. Inspired by Adalbert's example, Bruno strengthened the hold of Christianity in Hungary and Poland where he mad the acquaintance of Adalbert's friend, Boleslas the Great. Bruno's letters to the Polish King have only recently become known to scholars, and provide one of our best sources for the history of Boleslas the Great and of his relations with Germany.

Like Adalbert, Bruno also gained a martyr's crown in Prussia in 1009. He is the author of a second biography of the Czech bishop, a work surviving in two versions, one long and one short. Both of these versions seem to have been written after 1004, when Bruno met Adalbert's former companion, Radla, in Hungary and received from him certain important details on Adalbert's life. The two biographies written by Canaparius and by Bruno are supported by numerous legends which came into being in the twelfth, thirteenth, fourteenth and fifteenth centuries(78). They all agree in testifying to the way in which the martyred bishop of Prague was esteemed and worshipped in Poland, Germany, Bohemia, Moravia and Silesia, Hungary and Italy.

Of all those who deserved the honours of worship sanctioned by the Church, few men met with so tragic a destiny as this Slavnik. As the scion of a ducal family he found himself forcibly entangled in affairs of State. His elevation to episcopal dignity was prompted by political considerations and embodied a compromise designed to consolidate the unity of Bohemia. Change in the political situation in Bohemia and war with Poland drove Adalbert from Prague to Rome, to Monte Cassino, to S. Nilus in Valleluce and finally to the convent of S. Alexius. Another political change was responsible for bringing him back to his Bohemian see. Twice did he leave the secluded life of his beloved convent to plunge back again into active life.

It was the idealisation of Adalbert and of his life and death which for centuries obscured other elements in his story. These may have been less idealistic ; but they were certainly more human, and they enable us to see more deeply into the soul of the Saint. It is difficult to suppress a feeling of pity as disaster overtook Adalbert's family, when the glory of the Slavnik Dukes perished in scenes of carnage and blood. Not even a Bishop and a monk, trained in subduing his feelings, could stifle the cry of horror that burst from his soul. And yet Adalbert was ready to forgive and to resume his sacred office for the benefit of his countrymen. No ·deep thought is needed for one to realise the misrepresentations that have distorted the biography and the injustice that has marred the memory of a great man, so often pictured as a coward fleeing from the trials of his episcopal duty to seek relief in monastic seclusion.

But it was Adalbert's destiny to be forced into an active part in the political development of his contemporary world till the end of his days. Religious enthusiasm alone inspired his missionary activities in Prussia ; and yet, all unconsciously, his spiritual attainment served Boleslas the Great's political plans. Again, it was political interest—the rivalry between Prussians and Poles—that accounted for Adalbert's martyrdom and brought to an untimely end a spiritual work that had barely begun.

---

(78) Cf. Voigt, *Adalbert von Prag*, pp. 230 seq.

134

The tragedy and the impressive importance of this ascetic's life did not escape Adalbert's contemporaries, who forthwith wreathed his name in a halo of saintly popularity that was never to be dimmed. The end of his life did not spell the end of his action, for Adalbert continued to play his part in the political projects of his friend, Emperor Otto III, as well as in the destinies of countries other than his own—Poland and Hungary.

CHAPTER IV

OTTO'S "RENOVATIO IMPERII," POLAND, BOHEMIA, HUNGARY AND RUSSIA

POLITICAL IDEALS OF OTTO III AND SYLVESTER II—POLAND AND THE NEW
ROMAN EMPIRE—WESTERN AND EASTERN CHRISTIANITY IN HUNGARY—
CHRISTIANISATION OF HUNGARY AND THE CZECHS—HUNGARY AND THE NEW
ROMAN EMPIRE—THE FIRST HUNGARIAN ARCHBISHOP A CZECH ?—OTTO II
AND RUSSIA—GERMAN OR GREEK CHRISTIANITY IN KIEV ?—THEOPHANO
AND THE ROMAN EMBASSY TO KIEV—OTTO III, ROME AND RUSSIA OF KIEV—
AN INDEPENDENT ARCHBISHOP OF KIEV ?—OTTO III's IMPERIAL IDEOLOGY
AND THE GERMANS—THE EMPEROR'S ACHIEVEMENT.

The moment has come to examine how recent events on the Baltic Sea
and on the Elbe, and developments in the new States of Central Europe
contributed to the shaping of the German Empire's policy. We have seen
how the Carolingian Empire had died a not very glorious death while the
memory of Charlemagne, far from perishing with it, had survived to be
the guiding inspiration of the first Otto's life work. Although Otto I never
came anywhere near the ideal of Charlemagne or the success of the first
renovator of a Christian and Roman Empire, he endeavoured to carry it
into effect and bequeathed it to his son and successor.

Under Otto II, the Carolingian idea followed its normal course
unaltered. His marriage with the Byzantine princess Theophano averted a
dangerous conflict between the West and Byzantium. Their interests had
clashed under his father in South Italy where Otto I realised in the light of
the Italian campaign that he would never be able to incorporate the whole
Christian world into his Empire and learned to confine his imperial ambition
to the West. The union of the Saxon House with the Byzantine Basileus was
the only way out of the impasse. It appeared however that the Ottos did not
view the union from the same angle as the Byzantines. The latter took the
marriage for a mild surrender to the Byzantine Emperor, which turned the
so-called Western Emperor from a rival into an ally and saved the unity of the
Roman Empire of which Byzantium considered itself to be the only lawful
heir; but the Ottos rather took it for a guarantee of their imperial claims and
a proof that they were at least as good as the Byzantine Emperor. Otto II
also fancied himself as the protector of the Church of Rome, in which
capacity he made the ill-fated expedition into Calabria the year before
his death to put a stop to the Arab incursions which infested the whole of
Central and Southern Italy.

But after Otto II's death things began to happen in Germany. The
insurrection of the Slavs on the Elbe and on the Baltic in 983 shattered many
a Saxon dream; and as the long Regency was bound to check the development
of a strong imperial rule, the great traditions of Charlemagne and Otto I
began to decline. The question then arose—how was the Empire to carry

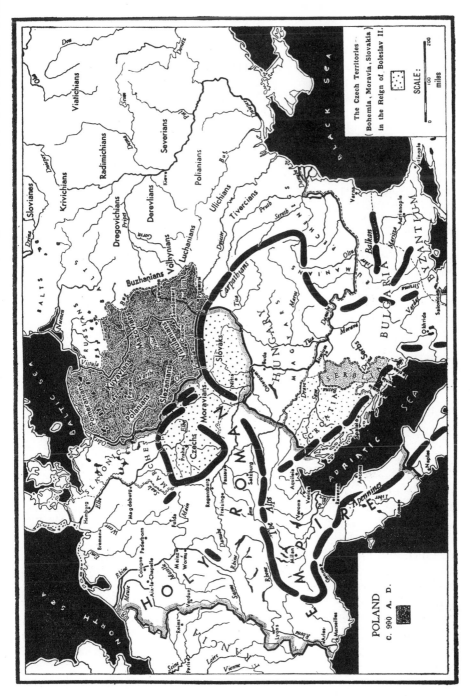

The Czech Territories
(Bohemia, Moravia, Slovakia)
in the Reign of Boleslav II.

SCALE:

POLAND
c. 990 A.D.

out the duty, considered sacred, however selfish at times, of converting the pagan nations and gathering them into the Christian and Roman Empire ? Bohemia had long been Christian and turned its faith to good account by the conversion of Poland. The Poles were Christians; they had their own bishop and were strong enough not only to maintain their own independence, but to expand their dominion as well. But the whole work of Henry I and Otto I among the Polabian Slavs had been undone by the revolution before it was crushed. Most of the bishops whom Otto I had detailed to the recently founded sees among the Slavs had to run for their lives leaving their dioceses, never flourishing in the things of the spirit, to fall back to a state of mission territories. Unable to tackle the new menace by its own strength the Empire was only too glad to see young Poland step in and offer, as a new Christian Power, its help to the Protector of the Church in crushing the common enemy of the faith. Simultaneously a new State was rising to prominence in the Danubian Basin. The heavy blows dealt by Otto I to the Magyars soon forced them to toe the line with their Christian neighbours in Central Europe. Nor was Germany, as will presently be seen, the only agency for introducing the true faith into Hungary.

The privileged position of the German Church in Central and Eastern Europe as established by Otto I, was passing into other hands. In Bohemia, the Germans were forced to make important concessions to the Czechs, and we have seen that the second bishop of Prague was not a German, but a son of the soil. Evidently, a new spirit was sweeping over Central and Eastern Europe to displace the old imperial ideal.

At the same time the heir to this ideal, the young Otto III, knew far more about the old Roman tradition than his two great predecessors. The influence of his mother, the Greek princess Theophano, to whose exclusive care the child had been left after the tragic death of Otto II, reared his mind to a classical outlook. With the Byzantines the Roman Empire had always been much more than a historical memory or an inspiring ideal: it was an actual reality, for they were in every respect the only true heirs to ancient Rome. This early training and the knowledge of the Greek language which Otto received from his mother paved the way to the intellectual ascendancy which the greatest contemporary scholar in the West, Gerbert of Aurillac, was to gain over Otto after Theophano's death in 997(1). Classical reminiscences were sprinkled all over Gerbert's correspondence(2), and the spirit of Cicero and other classical writers had made him an enthusiastic admirer of the old Roman Republic and Empire. Gerbert owed knowledge and position to his early education in Catalonia where classical studies had largely benefited by the enriching influence of Arabian culture. The Carolingian tradition throbbed in the heart of this sensitive Frenchman, but it was the ideals of imperial Rome that fired his imagination. He scorned Byzantine claims to universal domination and championed the Western

---

(1) On Gerbert-Sylvester II cf. chiefly Duc de La Salle de Rochemaure, *Gerbert (Sylvestre II), le Savant, le Faiseur de Rois, le Pontife* (Paris-Rome, 1921) ; F. Eichengrün, " Gerbert (Sylvester II) als Personlichkeit " (Leipzig, 1928), *Beiträge zur Kulturgesch. des Mittelalters und Renaissance*, vol. 35. Full bibliographical indications on his literary activities in M. Manitius, *Geschichte der Lateinischen Literatur des Mittelalters* (München, 1924), vol. II, pp. 729 seq. On his relations with Otto cf. P. Schramm, " Kaiser, Rom und Renovatio," *Studien der Bibl. Warburg* (Berlin, 1929), vol. XVII, part 1, pp. 96 seq., and A. Cartellieri, *Otto III, Kaiser der Römer*, quoted supra.

(2) Gerbert's letters have been published by J. Havet, " Lettres de Gerbert," *Collection de Textes pour servir à l'étude et à l'enseignement de l'Histoire* (Paris, 1889).

Emperor's claims not only to Italy, but to Gaul and the lands " of the valiant Scyths," *i.e.* the Slavs(3). He thus acted as a link between the Western imperial idea and that of the 'Western Roman Empire of which Charlemagne knew nothing.

This scholar, who had gained complete mastery over the young Emperor, was the prime mover of the *Renovatio* of the Roman Empire proclaimed by his faithful disciple, whom the master proudly surnamed *Imperator Romanorum* and *Augustus*. Under his tuition Otto elaborated his own conception of a Roman Empire by adapting the heritage of Charlemagne and Otto I to the new conditions, raising the old Roman ideal from the oblivion where it had been relegated by those two emperors, and setting it up at the very heart of the new Empire, with Rome once again as its world centre.

It was in 998 that Otto III made a start with his plan when in the course of his second Italian campaign he succeeded in crushing the powerful Roman family of the Crescentii; after which, to end once for all their attempts to monopolise control over the Papacy, he set on the papal throne his own teacher and inspirer, Gerbert, thenceforth known as Sylvester II. The fall of the Crescentii(4) accelerated the realisation of the *Renovatio Imperii*, as this Byzantinophil clan had always thwarted German penetration into Rome. Otto III had evidently to rely for support on their rivals, the Counts of Tusculum, the other leading family of the Roman aristocracy, admirers of Roman antiquities and keen on reviving the past glories of Rome and its political institutions. In their eyes, Otto was of course the very Emperor elected by Providence to realise their lofty dreams.

Otto III accepted their invitation with all the eagerness of a sensitive youth who wants to see his plans take shape directly they have been laid—though it should be added that, when he introduced the old Roman and Byzantine titles and functions into his administration(5), he proved himself not to be the Utopian he was taken for. The titles meant more to him than forgotten words buried in a dictionary of Roman and Byzantine antiquities. The Counts of Tusculum and their friends saw in them the symbols of Rome's ancient glory and a guarantee that it was being furbished up by this Saxon-Greek cross-breed hailing from the cold and stern land of Germany which they had learned to fear and dislike. The titles of *patricius*, *praefectus*, *magister*, etc. were to convince the Romans that they had nothing to fear from the North, now that the new emperors were "converts" to the

---

(3) J. Havet, loc. cit., p. 237 : Nostrum, nostrum est Romanum imperium. Dant vires ferax frugum Italia, ferax militum Gallia et Germania, nec Scithiae desunt nobis fortissima regna.

(4) On the Crescentii, cf. F. Gregorovius, *Geschichte der Stadt Rome im Mittelalter* (Stuttgart, Berlin, 5th ed., 1904), vol. III, pp. 401 seq., or English translation by G. H. Hamilton, *History of the City of Rome in the Middle Ages* (London, 1903), vol. III, pp. 417 seq. For rapid information on Italian history at this period, see L. M. Hartmann, *Geschichte Italiens im Mittelalter* (Gotha, 1915), vol. IV, I, pp. 95 seq. Cf. also W. Kölmel, " Rome und der Kirchenstaat im 10. und 11. Jh. bis in die Anfänge der Reform," *Abhandl. für Mittelalter. u. neure Geschichte* (Berlin, 1935), 78 H.

(5) Cf. L. Halphen, "La Cour d'Otton III à Rome," *Mélanges d'Archéologie et d'Histoire* Paris-Rome, 1905), vol. XXV, pp. 349-63 ; P. E. Schramm, *Kaiser, Rom und Renovatio*, part II, pp. 16-33, (Der " Byzantinische Hofstaat " Ottos III, sein historischer Kern und dessen Bedeutung).

Roman imperial ideals and the trustees of Rome's splendours. Even the Byzantine titles which Otto III adopted for his various services in court and palace were taken seriously. The Romans were familiar with them and held them in such esteem just because. Byzantium still occupied the world's cultural and political centre, the influence of which, paramount as it was in South Italy, could be felt in Rome.

It will help our inquiry into Otto's plans as they affected Poland and Hungary to consider how the young Emperor meant to define relations between Emperor and Pope. In this respect he harked back to the old conceptions of Constantine the Great, Charlemagne and Otto I, though there remained a difference between what he tried to do and what Charlemagne and Otto I had contrived. Whilst Charlemagne acted as the supreme head of the Western Christian commonwealth, he allowed the spiritual power represented by Pope and bishops, if not in theory, at least in practice, only a very secondary place in his political scheme. Otto I also acted much like a supreme master, at any rate, of his own *Reichskirche*, and he was liable to be intensely annoyed whenever any bishops shielded themselves behind canonical prescriptions, which he could not alter, to oppose his personal wishes.

In one respect only did Otto III's notion of imperial power recall that of Charlemagne and Otto I; he was equally determined not to allow the spiritual power any superiority over temporal and imperial rights. Such a tendency of course had existed at the papal Curia before Charlemagne rose to power and was embodied in the famous *Donatio Constantini*. How little Otto III and his collaborators thought of the Roman Curia's efforts to impress the Frankish emperors with this forgery and bring them under papal control was soon made evident by the way Otto III treated this document.

When in January, 1001, he announced his gift of the counties of the Pentapolis to his former preceptor Sylvester II(6), he bluntly declared that whatever was said in the *Donatio Constantini* and in writings of the same class about the Pope's rights over some Italian territories, lacked any foundation. As regards the *Donatio Constantini*, Otto III, or rather the writer of his charter, Bishop Leo of Vercelli, roundly accused the papal cleric, John of the Mangled Fingers, of having copied the forgery in gold letters and put it into the shape of a genuine decree, a statement which was not verified till the fifteenth century, when the spuriousness of the *Donatio Constantini* was finally exposed. That was how Otto III disposed of a deed which in the hands of the Curia might have proved a dangerous weapon against his new order. Henceforward he was left free to select Rome for his residence and to remain the supreme master even of the papal *patrimonium*, his new donation having been made, not to the Pope, but to St. Peter.

This does not mean that Otto III intended to go further than Charlemagne or that the imperial document of 1001 implied any derogation from the rights of the Pope, an assumption which rests on the false supposition that Sylvester II was a believer in the authenticity of the *Donatio*. It is true

---

(6) *M.G.H. Dipl.* II, No. 389, pp. 818-20. Cf. G. Laehr, *Die Konst. Schenkung*, pp. 22, 183 seq., and especially P. Schramm, loc. cit., vol. I, pp. 71 seq., 163 seq.

that the Curia had often disclosed pretensions similar to those contained in the *Donatio*, but that does not prove that Sylvester was in any way a party to them.

It appears that since the days of Otto I there had been serious misgivings at the German kings chancellery about the authenticity of the deed; and Gerbert must have been aware of it, since he was in Otto's service before he became a pope. It would be too much to assume the absolute immunity of his critical spirit against certain arguments which were based on strong traditions, especially the account by John of the Mangled Fingers ; but there is little to authorise one to suppose that on becoming pope, he veered round and considered it his duty to repeat his predecessors' extravagant claims.

On the other hand, we must own that Otto's *Donatio* did justice to the Gelasian theory of the divine origin of both powers on which their respective claims were based(7). What Pope Gelasius had said in the fifth century on the divine origin of the secular and the spiritual powers and on their mutual friendly relations had by the ninth and tenth centuries become a commonplace in Western Christendom, sanctified moreover by S. Augustine whose writings on the City of God were then and remained throughout the Middle Ages a favourite with the few intellectuals of the new nations.

To this generally accepted thesis Otto III does justice when he makes it clear in his *Donatio* that " Rome is the head of the world and the Roman Church has been set up as the Mother of all Churches." Sylvester II must besides have profited by his personal experience during his struggle for the archbishopric of Rheims, realising that both powers—the spiritual and the temporal—were of equal moment and that only perfect co-ordination between the two could benefit the Church in general and every Christian in particular. He must have been partial to Gelasius, since he loved to quote his decisions in support of his own claims(8), and his letters(9) make it clear that before he became pope he was no partisan of the theories that had produced the *Donatio Constantini*. He must have imparted his conviction to his pupil and made up his mind before ascending the papal throne to carry out his own and Gelasius' ideas on the collaboration of both powers.

It was therefore not without design that Gerbert chose, after his election to the papacy, the name of Sylvester after Sylvester I, who in association with Constantine the Great elaborated, at least in legendary tradition, the ideal of a complete understanding and collaboration between the representatives of the two powers. Such was in Gerbert's mind the papal view of the *Renovatio*. Naturally, the positions of the two forces in Rome and in Italy had to be re-considered, defined and set on an acceptable

---

(7) On the Gelasian theory and its importance in the development of political thought in the Middle Ages see R. W. and A. J. Carlyle, *A History of Medieval Political Theory in the West* (Edinburgh-London, 1903-1936), vol. I, pp. 190 seq. Cf. also W. Kissling, " Das Verhältnnis zwischen Sacerdotium und Imperium nach den Anschauungen der Päpste von Leo dem Grossen bis Gelasius I (440-496)," *Görres-Gesellschaft, Veröf. d. Sekt. f. Rechts-u. Sozialwissenschaften* (1921), 38 Heft ; L. Knabe, " Die Gelasianische Zweigewaltenlehre bis zum Ende des Investiturstreites," *Hist. Studien* (Berlin, 1936), Heft 292.

(8) J. Havet, *Lettres de Gerbert*, pp. 208-11, 213-5.

(9) Ibid., for instance, pp. 18, 176 seq., 220 seq., 230.

basis. The new *Donatio* of Otto III supplied this foundation. Leo of Vercelli, who wrote the document, displayed exceptional diplomatic skill in its composition, where he reached a compromise between old-fashioned ideas still nursed by many curialists and those of the imperial advisers, supported by the new Pope. This is a matter that has often been overlooked by historians. In drawing their analogy between the partnership of Constantine-the-Great with Sylvester I and that of Otto III with Sylvester II, some of them overstressed the importance of the emperor at the expense of the pope and loved to picture Otto III as a new Constantine, imposing his will and decisions on the Church (just what the real, and not the legendary, Constantine is supposed to have done), and handling Gerbert as a tool. But this view of Constantine was ûnknown to Otto III and Gerbert, the ideal of the Western Christian commonwealth being then the perfect collaboration between the *Sacerdotium* and the *Imperium*. It was the ideal Gerbert had inculcated into his disciple, the goal for which both master and pupil were striving. Neglect of this consideration would expose one to misread some events of Otto's reign.

*   *   *

The above reflections applied to the relations between Otto III, the Pope and Boleslas the Great may provide us with the key to Otto's performance in Poland. We learn, chiefly from Thietmar(10), from the Annals of Quedlinburg(11) (*ad ann.* 1000) and from the *Anonymus Gallus*(12) that Otto III went with lavish display to Poland, on a visit to the grave of his friend, S. Vojtiekh (Adalbert) in Gnesen, and that to honour the memory of this great saint the Emperor raised Gnesen, where the martyr's body had been laid to rest, to the rank of an archbishopric, with the three bishops of Cracow, Kolberg (Kolobrzeg) on the Baltic shore, and Vratislava (Breslau) as suffragans. The Duke Boleslas the Great, who received the Emperor with due reverence, was made *Patricius* and friend of the Empire, and to him Otto surrendered all rights over the Church in Poland such as he himself exercised in the Empire. He even refused to accept the tribute offered by Boleslas in good cash, and greatly pleased with the gift of a precious relic of S. Adalbert, he returned to Aix-la-Chapelle escorted by three hundred well armed men of Boleslas's crack troops.

Though details of these events have been differently explained, the importance of the imperial gesture has never been questioned. But new light was recently shed on the Gnesen incident by some German and Polish scholars(13). As there remain some details to be cleared up, we must try and reconstruct the events as far as our sources permit.

---

(10) Chronicon IV, chs. 45-7, *M.G.H.S.* N.S. IX, pp. 183-6.
(11) *M.G.H.S.* III, p. 77.
(12) I, ch. 6, *M.P.H.* I, pp. 399 seq.
(13) Especially P. Schramm, loc. cit., pp. 135-46 ; A. Brackmann, " Der Römische Erneuerungsgedanke und seine Bedeutung für die Reichspolitik der Deutschen Kaiserzeit," *Sitzungsberichte der Preuss. Akad. Hist. Phil. Kl.* (1932), pp. 346-74 ; Idem, " Die Anfänge des

142

It should first of all be noted that whatever the young Emperor intended to do in Poland was planned in agreement with the Pope, Sylvester II. The " Act of Gnesen," rightly explained, sheds a flood of light on the place Otto III meant to assign to the Pope in his *Renovatio Imperii.*" It is a notable fact that the future archbishop of Gnesen, Gaudentius, S. Adalbert's half-brother, had been consecrated in Rome before the Emperor started on his pilgrimage and an imperial document issued in Rome on Dec. 2, 999, actually mentions the name of Gaudentius, Archbishop of S. Adalbert the Martyr(14). This points to the fact that all the details of the expedition had been fully discussed and settled in Rome and that on this special occasion the Pope had gladly co-operated with the Emperor.

We should not be misled, as so many have been, by the fact that the Emperor acted in Gnesen alone and that the Pope's share in the move was minimised by all contemporary and later accounts, for he acted as the Protector of the Church in the execution of a common decision. Such a notion of the imperial role in the Christian Commonwealth must have been acceptable to Sylvester II, if it was not actually suggested by him : it supposed a common accord between the two powers—the spiritual and the secular—on the lines of the so-called Gelasian definition and S. Augustine's writings, as has been explained.

This is the true reason why Otto, on his way to Poland to carry out the decision taken by the two heads of Christendom for the promotion of Christianity in the East, assumed the title of " Servant of Jesus Christ," to stress the function he had undertaken to perform in the Christian Church ; he was as much the servant of Jesus Christ as was the Pope and was, by common agreement, to act accordingly.

But how did Gaudentius find himself in Rome in 999 ? We know that he was in Poland in 997, the year his brother met his glorious death, and it is not any pious pilgrimage or any desire to end his days in the monastery where he had lived with his saintly brother that would account for his presence in the centre of Christendom at that time, when he could

Polnischen Staates," ibid. (1934), pp. 984-1115 ; Idem, Reichspolitik nnd Ostpolitik im frühen Mittelalter, ibid. (1935), pp. 946-66 ; Idem, " Kaiser Otto III und die staatlichen Umgestaltungen Polens und Ungarns," *Abhandlungen der Preuss. Akad. Hist. Phil. Kl.* (1939) ; F. Baethgen, " Zur Geschichte der ältesten deutsch-polnischen Beziehungen," *Altpreussische Forschungen* (1936), 13 Jahrg., pp. 1-16 ; G. Sappok, " Die Anfänge des Bistums Posen und die Reihe seiner Bischöfe von 968-1498." *Deutschland und der Osten. Quellen und Forschungen zur Geschichte ihrer Beziehungen* (Leipzig, 1937), Bd. 6 ; Idem, "Polen, Reich und Pommern im 10. Jhdt.," *Jahrbücher zur Geschichte Osteuropas*, (1937), vol. II, pp. 201-23. Some opinions defended by A. Brackmann in his short but vigorous studies caused a stir in Polish scientific circles, but were refuted among others by M. Z. Jedlicki in his article on " La Création du Premier Archevêché Polonais à Gniezno et ses conséquences au point de vue des rapports entre la Pologne et l'Empire Germanique," *Revue Historique de Droit Francais et Etranger* (1933), pp. 645-95 ; " Die Antänge des Polnischen Staates," Reply to A. Brackmann in *Historische Zeitschrift*, (1935), vol. 152, pp. 519-29, and in his book *Poland's Legal Relations* quoted previously and published in Poznan, 1939. The book by Z. Wojciechowski, *Mieszko I and the Rise of the Polish State* (The Baltic Pocket Library, Torun-London, 1936) marks substantial progress on studies of older date on the same subject and successfully refutes some exaggerations or false statements by German specialists. Cf. also the remarkable work by S. Zakrzewski, *Boleslas the Brave the Great* (in Polish) (Lwów-Kraków, 1925).

(14) *M.G.H. Dipl.* II, No. 339, p. 769 : Gaudentius archiepiscopus sancti Adalberti martyris interfui et subscripsi. . . .

have honoured his brother's memory just as well by staying in Poland near his grave and carrying on his work. He would have found there a monastery founded by Adalbert that certainly needed his patronage more than S. Alexius. The fact is that Gaudentius was sent to Rome on a special mission by Boleslas the Great to negotiate, on the Polish Duke's suggestion, an independent ecclesiastical organisation for Poland. The request had its precedent ; just as the foundation of the first Polish bishopric in Poznan (Posen) had been negotiated on Mieszko's initiative by his special embassy to Rome, so the archbishopric of Gniezno (Gnesen) owed its origin to Boleslas the Great(15).

The Polish move in Rome was the logical sequel to the position Poland held vis-a-vis the Papacy and the Empire. Poland stood completely outside the Roman Empire created by Otto I and its duke was no more than an ally of the king and emperor. The *Donatio* of Mieszko I had only accentuated this situation, besides drawing closer the ties that bound Poland to the Papacy. Against that *Donatio* the Regency was powerless, though it must have been evident at Theophano's court that Mieszko's action was indirectly a slight on the emperor's prestige in the Slavonic East. Mieszko had at the same time prepared the ground for the step to be taken by his son and aimed at the creation of an independent ecclesiastical organisation for Poland. For this the pope's consent was essential in virtue of a canon law which the emperor was in duty bound to respect.

These facts are sometimes overlooked by scholars who happen to deal with the problem. It is therefore irrelevant to stress Otto's independent action in Gnesen and conclude that the Emperor had not consulted the Pope. On the contrary the new regime made the Pope's collaboration absolutely necessary if the Emperor was to rally the Polish Duke to his Renovation of the Roman Empire on terms compatible with Polish independence ; and those terms implied a sort of federation of Christian rulers under the leadership of the emperor, head of Christendom, without prejudice to the full independence of the heads of the federated States.

The arrival of the Polish embassy in Rome with the request for an independent Polish hierarchy gave the first impulse to negotiations between the Pope, the Emperor and the Duke, under conditions that assured their smooth working. First of all, the Pole's request was made in the name of S. Adalbert, martyr and Patron Saint of Poland, and presented by his own brother, who had been singled out by the Duke to become the head of the Polish Church. We know how sincerely Otto III loved his friar Adalbert ; the saint's memory was held in equal veneration by the Romans and the Pope professed the deepest and tenderest respect for the martyr(16).

---

(15) It is possible that Boleslas had planned two Metropolitan Sees for his country, one for Gnesen and the other for Sandomierz. Gnesen was founded in 1,000, the other foundation, realised later, was short-lived. For more details, see *infra*, p. 188 seq.

(16) It should be noted that the name of SylvesterII has often been associated with S. Adalbert. Some scholars have tried to prove that Adalbert's first biography, which was published in Rome, had been written by the Pope himself. The work was actually sponsored by the Emperor, who possibly also inspired its composition ; but the real author was not Sylvester II, but John Canaparius, a monk, and later Abbot of S. Alexius. The work faithfully

Secondly, the renewal of the Duke's alliance with the Emperor on the basis of the new imperial conception made more active the Pole's partnership in the christianisation of the Polabian Slavs, who, as long as they clung to their paganism constituted a menace to both the Duke and the Emperor.

That was how Boleslas the Great was led eagerly to adopt the new scheme sponsored by the Pope and the Emperor and decided to join the Roman Empire renovated as a federation of Christian princes under those two leaders. It thus happened that the imperial expedition to Gnesen was a premeditated and well-planned performance in which the three interested parties—the Emperor, the Pope and the Duke—co-operated for a common purpose. We may even go so far as to suggest that this Polish embassy, as an indication of the Pole's evident desire to make a bid for complete independence within limits, precipitated Otto III's change of outlook, as he found himself faced with the new and glaring evidence that the position of the East had radically altered and that the methods used by Charlemagne and Otto I were in 999 completely out of date. We may take it for granted that Boleslas the Great had previous knowledge of the *Renovatio* and had expressed his consent. When the young Emperor, escorted by some high officials of his regenerated Roman Empire and by the representatives of the Pope, reached the Polish borders in the early spring of 1000 after a rapid and exciting journey in trying winter conditions, he was received by the Duke with joy and reverence.

Otto III was of course fully conscious of acting the part of the new Roman Emperor—*Romanus, Saxonicus et Italicus*—as he was proud to call himself(17). When he addressed his rebellious Romans in 1001(18), he took care to point out that he had extended Rome's renown further east than his Roman predecessors had ever penetrated ; and Poland's accession to the Empire was held up to the Romans as Rome's achievement and as one more proof that its old splendours owed their revival to the new Emperor, the successor of Augustus.

The position held by the Polish Duke in the renovated Roman Empire had also to be invested with a new dignity in the eyes of the world by the title which the Emperor conferred on Boleslas the Great. At a special ceremony organised for the solemn proclamation of the new archbishopric, Otto III conferred on the Duke the title of *Patricius*(19),

reflects the opinions of the Emperor and the Pope on Rome as the only centre of imperial and sacerdotal power in the Christian Commonwealth. Cf. A. Kolberg, " Die von Papst Silvester II edierte Passio S. Adalberti," *Zeitschrift für die Geschichte und Altertumskunde Ermelands*, t. XVI, pp. 557-648 ; W. Kętrzynski, " The Oldest Biographies of S. Adalbert and their authors" (in Polish), *Proceedings of the Acad. of Cracow*, t. 43, seria II, 18, pp. 252-95 ; H. Voigt, " Der Verfasser der Römischen Vita S. Adalberti," *Sitzungsber. d. Böhm. Gesellsch. d. Wissenschaften* (1903).

(17) *M.G.H. Dipl.* II, No. 390, p. 821 (a charter for Hildesheim).

(18) The main source for the happenings in Rome that year is the *Vita Bernardi Ep.*, written by Thangmar ; it also gives the text of the Emperor's speech (*M.G.H.S.* IV, ch. 25, p. 770). Cf. Gregorovius, *Geschichte der Stadt Rom*, vol. III, p. 471 ; Hartmann, *Geschichte Italiens*, vol. IV, I, pp. 143, 159.

(19) Cf. A. Brackmann, *Kaiser Otto III*, loc. cit., pp. 19 seq. Zeissberg in his study, " Otto III und Boleslaw I von Polen," *Zeitschrift für die Öster. Gymnasien* (1867), Jhg. 18, pp. 341 seq. already called attention to the significance of the fact that Boleslas the Great was made a Patricius of the Roman Empire.

crowned him with a diadem and handed him a replica of the spear once used by S. Mauritius(20), whom legend had transformed into a Western S. George, as the insignia of his dignity.

The title, the meaning of which is still controverted, was an old Roman distinction that had never been forgotten, though its meaning and usage had undergone some changes in the course of centuries. The title *Patricius Romanorum*, revived in 754 by Stephen II, gave its holders, Pippin II and his sons, special rights in Rome and the function of Protector and Defender of the Church. This new application of an old title was after 800 made part of the imperial attributions, but in its subsequent use it was conferred on the Governors of Rome as the emperor's representatives ; and under the regime of the Crescentii, it designated the real master of Rome. Otto III then revived it. It is known that he used to appoint deputies in Rome and Germany to act for him in his absence and to them he gave the title of patricius(21), the spear of S. Mauritius remaining the symbol of imperial power and being carried in solemn procession before either the emperor in person or the patricius.

The patrician title was meant to make Boleslas the Great rally to the revived Roman Empire, but what difference it made to Poland's status it would not be easy to define. It certainly did not affect Poland's independence in the slightest. When Otto conferred the honour on Boleslas, it could not occur to the Emperor to make him an independent duke, since Poland had never been anything else relatively to Germany. The tribute the duke paid for holding Pomerania had nothing to do with Poland's sovereignity. A remark by the Annalist of Quedlinburg(22) would seem to suggest that on this occasion the Emperor cancelled the tribute and the passage has recently been interpreted in this sense(23). By itself, however, it is not conclusive and I am not surprised that the interpretation has been questioned(24). I would adopt this view on the ground that the Emperor's refusal for once to take the tribute as a gesture of courtesy between guest and host did not imply its suppression for good, were it not for a passage in Thietmar's Chronicle which rather favours the first interpretation.

Thietmar, in recording the havoc wrought on German territory by Boleslas the Great in his campaign against Otto's successor Henry II, bitterly complains of Otto's Polish policy(25) : " God forgive the emperor

---

(20) For details, see A. Brackmann, " Die politische Bedeutung der Mauritius-Verehrung im frühen Mittelalter," *Sitzungsberichte Preuss. Akad., Hist. Phil. Kl.* (1937), vol. XXX. Cf. also A. Hofmeister, " Die Heilige Lanze ein Anzeichen des alten Reichs " (Breslau, 1908), *Untersuchungen für Staats und Rechtsgeschichte* (Ed. Gierke), No. 96.

(21) More details will be found in A. Brackmann's *Kaiser Otto III*, pp. 13-9 ; and especially in S. M. Jedlicki's study *La Création du premier de l'Archeveché*, pp. 685-90.

(22) Ad a. 1000, *M.G.H.S.* III, p. 77 : there, after a hearty welcome from the Slav Duke Boleslas, he was graciously offered rich gifts of all sorts thoughtfully gathered from every corner of the world (Xeniis omnigeni census ubique terrarum studiosissime quaesiti) ; but he accepted none of these at that time, as he had not come to take or to receive, but to give and to pray.

(23) M. Z. Jedlicki, *La Création du premier Archeveché*, p. 688 ; Idem, *Poland's Legal Relations*, p. 163.

(24) A. Brackmann, *Reichspolitik und Ostpolitik*, p. 961.

(25) Chronicon, V, ch. 10. *M.G.H.S.* N.S. IX, p. 232.

146

for making a lord of a tributary and raising him to such heights. . . . '' On the face of it, the words convey the meaning that some radical change must have taken place in Boleslas's tributary relations to Otto's Empire and that Otto remitted Poland's tribute for its tenure of Western Pomerania. The unwillingness of some historians to admit so much is due to their tendency to overrate Germany's strength under Otto III. But the insurrection of the Polabian Slavs after the death of Otto II and the long Regency that tided over his successor's minority had so radically altered the position that Poland's collaboration in subjugating the pagan Slavs could not be dispensed with. By adopting Otto's imperial plans Boleslas the Great rendered the young Emperor a signal service which made a small sacrifice on his part well worth it. The remission of a tribute was a moderate price to pay, considering the stake.

By accepting the title of Patricius, Boleslas the Great implied that his country would henceforth join the Roman Empire and that he acknowledged the Emperor as head of the Christian Commonwealth, whereas the Emperor, in conferring the title on the Duke, surrendered all the rights which in his capacity as Head of the Christian Commonwealth he had over the Duke's lands. The head of that Christian Commonwealth was in virtue of his office the protector of the Church, possessing the right of appointing bishops and of submitting to the pope plans for new episcopal foundations. This was something palpable ; an integral part of the ideology of Charlemagne and Otto to which the Papacy had given its blessing. The system prevailed in Rome and in the Empire in the tenth century and was certainly acquiesced in by SylvesterII(26). Otto, in making his Polish Patricius, relinquished those rights over Polish lands at a ceremony which in some respects recalled the Byzantine practice. For the purpose of lending substance to the idea of a single emperor, representative of Christ and ruler of the whole Christian world, Byzantine emperors also conferred imperial titles on barbarian princes settled on lands that once belonged to the Roman Empire.

There remains one minor point which has puzzled many German and Polish scholars: why was the diocese of Poznan (Posen) not placed under the jurisdiction of the metropolis of Gniezno (Gnesen) ? Would the omission prove that Posen always was and remained subject to Magdeburg ? Or did bishop Unger protest against a redistribution and refuse his consent to the contraction of his vast diocese, which up till then extended over the whole of Poland, thereby forcing the Emperor to leave the diocese of Posen outside the organisation ?

A protest at this time, and an energetic one at that, from a German bishop against the infringement of his rights and the clipping of his revenues should cause no surprise ; and because it would not have been an isolated instance, this explanation has so far found wide acceptance(27). It is also

---

(26) For further details, cf. M. Z. Jedlicki, *Poland's Legal Relations*, pp. 139-69, as well as for all the bibliographical references to the many problems connected with the "Act of Gnesen."

(27) Cf. G. Sappok—*Die Anfänge des Bistum Posen*, pp. 42 seq., who enlarged on the ideas of his master A. Brackmann. *Die Ostpolitik Ottos des Grossen*, pp. 245 seq.

borne out by Thietmar who in his Chronicle(28) complains that the Emperor had acted without the consent of the local bishop and therefore questions the legitimacy of the new foundation. The explanation, however, though correct, does not tally completely with another statement by the same writer who asserts in the same chapter that Unger was on that occasion present at Gnesen, that he received the Emperor with honour (venerabiliter) and conducted him into the church where the relics of S. Adalbert were venerated.

It should be remembered that on this and on other occasions Thietmar passionately championed the archbishop of Magdeburg, neither of them feeling able to put up with the idea of a separate ecclesiastical organisation for Gnesen ; still less did they relish the Emperor's attitude of brushing them and their point of view aside to take the unprecedented step of creating a new metropolis in the East. All the opposition to the project came from the German side and found in Thietmar a faithful and persevering spokesman.

Unable to quash the opposition, the Emperor could simply ignore it : so he decided—and this is my way out of the difficulty—to leave the diocese of Posen outside the new scheme and Boleslas the Great agreed to the compromise. It did not suit his policy to have Posen ecclesiastically subjected to Magdeburg and he was strong enough to prevent it ; so, the only alternative was for the Emperor to let Posen carry on its own independent existence as a missionary bishopric, at any rate for the time being. The solution pleased bishop Unger, who was glad to keep his independence and Posen was never affiliated to Magdeburg despite the many efforts from that quarter, as P. Kehr(29) found out long ago.

*   *   *

Poland was not the only country Otto III intended to incorporate into his resurrected Roman Empire, and similar to his intervention in Poland were his overtures to Hungary, which at the time was coming to the fore as a new State and pleading for recognition by contemporary Europe and its representative leaders, the Emperor and the Pope. But her conditions and her ties with Germany were all her own and very unlike those of Poland. Until 955 the Magyars had been the most dreaded enemies of Western Europe. Even Byzantium had learned to fear their depredations, though be it said that at the beginning of the tenth century the eastern capital had made use of them against the first Bulgarian

---

(28) Chronicon, IV, ch. 45, *M.G.H.S.* IX, p. 184.

(29) " Das Erzbistum Magdeburg und die erste Organisation der Christlichen Kirche in Polen," *Abhandlungen Preuss. Akad., Hist. Phil. Cl.* (1920). The history of the controversy and all the biographical indications are to be found in a recent publication by K. Buczek " First Polish Bishoprics " (in Polish), *Kwart. Hist.* (1938), vol. LIII, pp. 169-209. I have not been able to consult the study by G. Labuda, " Magdeburg i Poznań," the Review *Roczniki Histor.*, in which it was published (vol. XIV, 1938) not being available ; nor the other study by W. Abraham, *Gniezno, Magdeburg* (Cracow, 1921), in which the writer abandoned his opinion (expressed in his book, written in Polish, *The Organisation of the Polish Church up to the second half of the twelfth c.*, Lwów, 1893, p. 37), and rallied to Kehr's lucid conclusions.

Tsar(30), just as the German King Arnulf had used their alliance to check the dangerous growth of the Moravian Empire.

Civilised Europe heaved a sigh of relief at the news of the crushing defeat Otto I inflicted on them in 955 at the memorable battle of Lechfeld. Cut off from the Asiatic steppes whence they hailed and from their kinsmen the Ostyaks and the Voguls(31)—two tribes that never broke away from their primitive conditions, and irrevocably driven back from the west, the Magyars were forced to submit to the inevitable, to abandon the profitable occupation in which they had excelled as the scourge of the West, and settle down for good in the Danubian basin. There they were able to maintain at least their independence, though their territory was to lose some valuable portions, including part of the land conquered from the Moravians. Contenting himself with his victory, Otto left them Pannonia, which in the ninth century had belonged to the Carolingian Empire. Having found their home, the Magyars eventually came under the cultural influence of their civilised neighbours.

There are indications that the Magyars became acquainted with Christianity to some extent in the course of their migrations. As shown by the list of bishoprics established by the Byzantine Church around the Crimea(32), there was after the sixth century intense missionary activity among the Turkish tribes and the remnants of the Huns who lived near the Bosphorus. It is suspected that a Magyar tribe lived among them and was contacted by missionaries who worked among the Onogurs. These Onogurs, like the Magyars, belonged to the Bulgarian State near the Sea of Azov, and they had their Byzantine bishop in the eighth century. It is also possible that the Magyars came into touch with ninth century Slavonic Christianity in Danubian Bulgaria and in Moravia before their invasion of the Danubian basin(33).

In the same way, the Magyars may have come to the knowledge of Islam through the Khazars. But the point is that the first contacts with Byzantine Christianity in southern Russia would best explain the subsequent influence of eastern Christianity on early Magyar history in Europe. For centuries Magyars moved in lands that lay under the spell of Byzantine civilisation, so that once they reached their final settlement, they welcomed Byzantine missionaries without much difficulty. Hence the oldest feature of Hungarian Christianity was Byzantine, under the Duke Geiza, the father of S. Stephen. We learn that the Emperor Constantine Porphyrogennetos,

---

(30) Cf. S. Runciman, *A History of the First Bulgarian Empire* (London, 1930), pp. 145 seq.

(31) Cf. F. Lot, *Les Invasions Barbares*, vol. II, pp. 76 seq., for a rapid survey of the main problems connected with the origin of the Magyars. For deeper study, see C. A. Macartney, *The Magyars in the Ninth Century* (Cambridge, 1939). I call the reader's attention to the studies by the same English scholar on the sources of early Hungarian history : " Studies on the Early Hungarian Sources," *Ostmitteleuropäische Bibliothek*, Nos. 18, 21 (Budapest, 1938, 1940). Cf. also F. Eckhart, *Introduction à l'Histoire Hongroise* (Paris, 1923), for bibliographical indications ; and H. Grégoire, "L' Habitat Primitif des Magyars," *Byzantion* (1938), vol. XIII, pp. 267-86.

(32) Cf. my book *Les Légendes de Constantin et de Méthode*, pp. 157-68.

(33) Available data on the Magyars' first approach to Christianity are summarised by G. Moravcsik in his study " Byzantine Christianity and the Magyars in the First Period of their Migrations," *The American Slavic and East European Review* (1946), vol. V, pp. 29-45.

after the Magyars' defeat by the Byzantines, received two of their dignitaries—Butzu and Gylas—in Constantinople(34) and had them baptised about the year 950. Gylas, who had ruled over the eastern part of Hungary, became a fervent Christian. As Geiza married his daughter (Thietmar(35) at any rate calls him the uncle of Stephen I), Greek Christianity penetrated into western Hungary.

It was there that Eastern Christianity came into touch with the German representatives of Western Christendom. We hear that about 971 Wolfgang of Einsiedeln, who in 972 became bishop of Regensburg was, according to his biographer Othloh(36), working on the borders. But the most zealous among the German missionaries active among the Magyars was the famous bishop of Passau, Pilgrim. We still possess a letter sent by him to Pope Benedict VII(37), in which he boasts of his success with the Hungarians and takes credit for applying in his missionary work the method followed by the Holy See in the conversion of England (*quemadmodum in gestis Anglorum didici*), a pardonable exaggeration, as his main apostolic merit consisted in claiming to have his see raised to metropolitan rank. We know that this was ever his heart's desire and that he spent his life in trying to extend his diocese as far east and south-east as possible by mixing his missionary zeal with shrewd diplomacy, and also by forging a few bulls. But not even his spurious bulls convinced the suspicious Romans(38).

Already in 901 the German clergy had shown a somewhat overbearing interest in territories north and south of the central Danube, when the Bavarian bishops hotly protested(39) against Pope John IX's attempt to reorganise the Moravian Church, then stricken by Methodius's death and the departure of his suffragan Wiching from Nitra. But what happened to the legates sent that same year to Moravia, whether they had time to carry out their mission, or whether any of the new bishops survived the turmoil of the Magyar invasion, has never been known.

The German bishops' complaint supplies at any rate a shrewd hint as to what happened, when Henry the Fowler and Otto I checked the Magyar invasion and when the Pope tried to convert these Asiatic hordes. The

(34) Georgii Cedreni *Historiarum Compendium* (Bonn, vol. II, p. 328). Cf. K. Schünemann " Die Deutschen in Ungarn bis zum 12. Jahrhundert," *Ungarische Bibliothek* (Berlin-Leipzig 1923), vol. VIII, pp. 32 seq.

(35) Chronicon, VIII, ch. 4, *M.G.H.S.* N.S. IX, p. 496.

(36) Ch. 13, *M.G.H.S.*, IV, p. 530.

(37) S. F. L. Endlicher, *Rerum Hungaricarum Monumenta Arpadiana* (St. Gallen, 1849), pp. 131-3.

(38) On Pilgrim, cf. E. Dümmler, *Pilgrim von Passau und das Erzbistum Lorch* (Leipzig, 1854) ; A. Hauck, *Kirchengeschichte Deutschlands* (Leipzig, 1906), vol. III, pp. 163-82. Cf. also the observations by A. Brackmann in *Der Röm. Erneuerungsgedanke*, pp. 363 seq. It is not, however, meant that Pilgrim's activities in Hungary yielded no results. We find in the Necrologium of St. Gallus Abbey a notice to the effect that Bishop Prunwart baptised a great number of Hungarians together with their king (*M.G.H. Necrologia* I, pp. 466, February 2). This bishop may have been one of the missionaries sent to Hungary by Pilgrim and Geiza's baptism might thus be credited to a priest on the same mission. It appears that in spite of his hobby of forging bulls, Pilgrim was actuated by a sincere desire to promote the interests of the Church.

(39) " Epistola Theatmari Juvavensis eclesiae earchiepiscopi et aliorum Episcoporum Bavariensium ad Johannem P. IX scripta a. 900," *P.L.*, vol. 131, cols. 34-8.

German episcopate's main preoccupation was to get those new countries under their jurisdiction and the two suffragans of Salzburg-Regensburg and Passau made a private deal of their own by which the region east of Danube, *i.e.* Bohemia with all the lands belonging to it, would be marked down as the sphere of Regensburg, while Passau would get the lands south of the Danube with old Pannonia and as much of the rest of the Danubian basin as was occupied by the new " candidates to the Christian faith."

By the terms of this arrangement even the region between the Danube and the Tatras (later Slovakia), where the last remnants of Moravian Christianity were still surviving, was earmarked for Regensburg. Evidence of this is found in the existence at Nitra of a very old church which was consecrated to S. Emmeran, the Patron Saint of Regensburg, and is borne out by the old Legend of SS. Andreas and Benedict(40), written about 1070 by the old bishop Maurus of Pecz. Churches dedicated to S. Emmeran can be traced also in Bohemia.

We have seen(41) that after the erection of Prague's bishopric the territory of the Przemyslide State was exempted from the jurisdiction of Regensburg to become independent under the metropolis of Mainz, and we remember how the Moravian diocese was founded. It is therefore not exact to say, as many scholars have done, that the Moravian diocese was created at the suggestion of bishop Pilgrim of Passau, an assumption which is contradicted by the famous bishop's own letter on his Hungarian missionary achievements. Though he makes a statement that cannot be verified by other documents, *i.e.* that four of the bishops operating over the territory invaded by the Magyars had survived in Moravia, his main interest centres on the region south of the Danube, when he speaks of the seven bishops of eastern Pannonia and Mesia, whose territory he claims as part of his diocese. But Moravia never belonged to Pannonia.

This explains why Pilgrim was so keen on his mission in Hungary. But for all the work the German missionaries had done, it remained for long an open question whether East or West would eventually prevail in that country. This makes it of special interest that the Czechs, led by their saintly bishop Adalbert, should have come forward to help in finally winning over Hungary to Western civilisation. Though Adalbert's share in the christianisation of the Magyars has never been questioned, there still prevails some hesitation among experts in defining the part he played in the conversion of that country. Later medieval Hungarian and Polish tradition makes much of Adalbert's work among the Magyars, but modern, especially German and Magyar critics are more inclined to minimise his activity in Hungary(42). Are these modern critics right, or does early

---

(40) Maurus ep., " Legenda SS. Zoerardi et Benedicti," *Scriptores Rerum Hungaricarum* (Budapest, 1938), vol. II (ed. E. Madzar), p. 359 (ch. 2). *Ibid.*, p. 356, a complete bibliography of the Legend and its two heroes. Cf. also R. Holinka, *SS. Svorad and Benedikt* (Bratislava, 1934), in Slovak.

(41) *Supra*, ch. II, pp. 77 seq.

(42) Cf. K. Schünemann especially, loc. cit., pp. 35 seq., who, misled by the prevailing ideas, has a poor opinion of S. Adalbert. Judging from the reviews of his work written in Magyar only (*Magyar History*, Budapest, 1928-34, I, pp. 171 seq., 641), B. Hóman, the modern historian of Hungary, seems willing to do better justice to the old Magyar tradition

medieval Magyar and Polish tradition rest on firmer ground than they are inclined to admit ?

*　　*　　*

For want of contemporary sources the question is not easy to answer. There exists only one authoritative account, however short, of Adalbert's doings in Hungary. His biographer Bruno of Querfurt says briefly in chapter sixteen of his work(43) : "We should not omit to mention that besides sending his missionaries to the neighbouring Hungarians, Adalbert also visited them personally ; and when they had forsaken some of their errors he raised over them the shadow of the Christian symbol." This account by Bruno is capped by a reference in Canon Cosmas's chronicle(44), where it is stated that "Adalbert gathered into the nets of the Faith Pannonia (Hungary) and Poland." A third statement representing a Hungarian tradition of the second half of the eleventh century is found in the biography of King Stephen I(45), the author of which asserts that Geyza, Stephen's father, was informed in a vision of S. Adalbert's arrival into his kingdom and gave the appropriate orders. On learning that "the bishop of the Bohemian Church was entering his territory, the Duke with all his followers went out to meet Christ's paladin, received him with honour and in obedience to the vision gave every sign of good will to become, for the love and fear of God, his obedient son in every way. Then, by the Duke's orders, those unruly people held meetings everywhere, the saintly bishop prayed incessantly, native disciples were converted and baptised and churches were built in many places. The light which shines on every man thus began to shed its lustre upon Hungary ". . . . In the next chapter the author of the Legend goes so far as to assert that Stephen was baptised by Adalbert. Thus far our main sources on Adalbert's work in Hungary; but what is one to make of these statements ?

Bruno's brief account is straightforward and puts Adalbert's work among the Hungarians beyond dispute, though the question is left open as to how extensive Adalbert's Hungarian activities were and what share in the christianisation of the Magyars falls to the credit of the bishop of Prague. But even Bruno's short account conveys Adalbert's rather prolonged and repeated action in Hungary, as suggested by the Latin construction—nunc . . . nunc.

The sceptical view taken by so many of Adalbert's and his missionaries' achievements in Hungary was apparently founded on the difficulty of imagining how the bishop of Prague could possibly have reached

concerning Adalbert. Cf. also his short study written in English and published in *Archivium Europae Centro-Orientalis* (1938), vol. IV ("King Stephen the Saint," pp. 15-50, especially p. 22).

(43) *F.R.B.* I, p. 282 : Non tacendum, quod iuxta positis Ungris nunc nuntios suos misit, nunc se ipsum obtulit, quibus ab errore parum mutatis umbram christianitatis impressit.

(44) Chronica, I, 31. *M.G.H.S.* N.S. II, p. 56 : Adalbertus retibus fidei cepit Pannoniam simul et Poloniam. . . .

(45) "Vita S. Stephani Regis (Legenda Major)" chs. 4, 5; latest edition by E. Bartoniek in *S.R.H.*, 1938, vol. II, p. 380. The Legend was written between 1077 and 1083.

Hungary. For one thing, there were the controverted problems of Moravia and of the boundaries of his diocese. But as shown above, these difficulties were not insuperable. Moravia was not a *terra nullius*, *i.e.* a no man's land or territory over which the Magyars of the second half of the tenth century still exercised some sort of control. It belonged, together with the major part, if not the whole of modern Slovakia, to the Przemyslide State and to the diocese of Prague. In the circumstances it was only to be expected that Adalbert should organise religious life in the eastern part of his vast diocese, whence it was not such an arduous task to cross the Danube and step into Hungary. Adalbert must have been interested in this side of his diocese, were it only because he was anxious to recover this territory for his diocese and meet the wishes of Boleslas II and of the ecclesiastical authorities who had consented to the transaction in the face of serious opposition. Hence his prolonged and frequent sojourns in those regions were after all not unlikely.

Adalbert's efforts in those parts of his diocese as well as in Hungary were facilitated by the remnants of Moravian Christianity still surviving there. It is true that the most important centre of the Moravian Empire had been destroyed by the invaders and that the country had been robbed of most of its clergy, but this does not mean that every vestige of Christianity had disappeared. It was, as already stated, the centre of Moravia which suffered most from the onslaught. But once they had mopped up all likely centres of resistance and ravaged the country, the Magyars seem to have lost interest in the region north of the middle Danube and contented themselves with a tribute and occasional predatory raids over the borders. As the flat terrain of Pannonia and the steppes between the Danube and the Tisza suited their nomadic ways of life best, Boleslas I had no difficulty in annexing Moravia and the greater part of modern Slovakia, probably after the Magyar disaster in 955. Religion then apparently took a new lease of life and the record of a church dedicated to S. Emmeran in Nitra is a sign that Latin priests had started operating in the valley of the Vag. The foundation of a Moravian diocese in 975 meant at any rate that religious life had not completely disappeared in Moravia, whilst the religious position in modern Slovakia must have been even better.

We have no information as to what happened in the region north of the middle Danube throughout the tenth century, so that even the fact of this region being part of the Przemyslide State has been denied. Magyar historians reject(46) such evidence as the Prague Charter and the papal document *Dagome Iudex*, and base their conviction only on the first Hungarian chronicle called the " *Anonymus*"(47), by which the occupation of this country is attributed to Arpad, the conqueror of Moravia and Pannonia. But evidence from the " *Anonymus* " is hardly conclusive,

---

(46) As an illustration, cf.what E. Kniezsa says on this problem in his review of J. Macúrek's Czech "History of the Magyars and the Hungarian State" (*Praha*, 1934), published in *Archivum Europae Centro-Orientalis* (1937), vol. III, p. 360.

(47) "*Anonymi Gesta Hungarorum*," ed. A. Jakubovich, *F.R.H.*, I (1937), especially pp. 74 seq. (chs. 33-37). Cf. C. A. Macartney, *Studies*, vol. II, pp. 115 seq., 136 seq., 147 seq., 220 seq.

M.   F

for we know that this chronicle is a thirteenth-century compilation(48), the untrustworthiness, of which in regard to the first period of Hungarian history, should deceive no one; a mixture of fact and legend, of repetitions and contraditions. But in reporting on the occupation of modern Slovakia, the author unwittingly bears out the fact that this country did belong to the duke of Bohemia, for he states(49) that the whole territory between the Vag and the Hron, from the Danube to the river Moravá, had been occupied after Attila's death (sic) by the duke of Bohemia, who in turn placed the province under the duke Zubur. Magyar tradition knew of a Czech dominion over Slovakia even before its occupation by the Magyars. This only materialised in the beginning of the eleventh century, as we shall see later; but true to his method, the *Anonymus* attributes the occupation to Arpad. As a matter of fact it was not Arpad but S. Stephen who imposed Magyar domination on the lands between the middle Danube and the Tatras.

Warrant for this tradition is provided by the Arab geographer Idrisi(50) who calls the territory of Slovakia and Moravia by the name of Bohemia and gives Esztergom as the capital of the country. He flourished in the twelfth century, but the material he uses in his description is much older, probably dating from the tenth and twelfth centuries.

If Czech rule extended even as far as Esztergom then this region belonged also to Adalbert's diocese. This would make it more intelligible why about the year 1010 Stephen founded the Hungarian diocese of Esztergom, why it included the whole of Slovakia and why it became the see of

(48) A. Jakubovich, in the introduction to his edition (loc. cit., pp. 15 seq.) goes over the whole literature connected with the origin and date of the Anonymus. He dates it from the twelfth century or the beginning of the thirteenth.

(49) Ch. 35, loc. cit., p. 77 : "The inhabitants of that province found themselves facing the combination of Slavs and Bohemians supported by the duke of the Bohemians, since after the death of Attila the duke had annexed the territory which lies between the Vag and the Hron from the Danube to the Morava river and made it into a single duchy. At the same time Zubur was, by permission of the duke of the Bohemians, made duke of Nitra." A short commentary added by D. Pais to this extract in Jakubovich's edition gives the opinion that generally prevails among Hungarian specialists on this problem.

(50) P. A. Jaubert, " Géographie d'Idrisi," *Receuil de Voyages et de Mémoires publié par la Société de Geographie* (Paris, 1940), vol, II, p. 371 (Sixième Climat, deuxième section) : " La plus célèbre, la plus vaste et la plus populeuse d'entre les cités de la Bohême est Ostrikouna ou Ostrighouna (Esztergom), qui est la capitale et le chef-lieu du gouvernement. . ." The description of this part of Europe by Idrisi is hopelessly confused. In the preceding passage the Arab makes Vienna " dépendre de la Noamia, qu'on écrit aussi par un B (Bohême), province très vaste, très peuplée et très fertile qui compte au nombre de ses principales villes : Djikelburk, Chebrouna (Soprony ?), Vienne, Massau ou Dassau, Machla, Agrakta et Ostrikouma." Here again Esztergom figures amongst the Bohemian towns. This part of the famous Arab geography needs re-editing : but the pity is that only the portion concerning Finland and Northern Europe has found a modern editor and commentator—O. J. Tallgren Tuulo and A. M. Tallgen, " Idrisi, la Finlande et les autres pays Baltiques orientaux " ; *Studia Orientalia* (Helsingfors, 1930), vol. III ; O. J. Tuulo (Tallgren), "Du Nouveau sur Idrisi," *Ibid.* (1936), vol. VI. Cf. V. Chaloupecký's review of V. Hrubý's *Original boundary,* quoted above, *Czech Hist. Rev.* (1927), vol. XXXIII, p. 357. Idrisi obviously means in this passage to speak only of Moravia and Slovakia, since he describes the rest of Bohemia in the sixth Climate, 3rd Section (loc. cit., p. 375) : " La présente section comprend le restant de la Bohême, la Pologne, la Saxe et la Germanie. Les villes de la Bohême sont : Bassau, Agra, Abiah, Biths, Sinolaws, ville de Carinthie ; Bedhrawa (Peterwaradin), Belgraba (Belgrad), Ostrigouna (Esztergom), Chebrouna (Soprony ?), Gharmasia, Titlous (Titul), Neitherm (Nitra)." Here the confusion is considerable, though it should be noted that Idrisi insists on Ostergom belonging to Bohemia : a simple error ? or the remnant of some old tradition ?

the Hungarian archbishop, though the old royal residence was at Visegrad—for the simple reason that it was an old Christian centre from which Adalbert's missionaries radiated into the interior of Hungary. In addition, Adalbert found in Esztergom an excellent training centre where he could prepare his plans in peace.

Without forgetting that we started on this line of argument from very slender premises, we may yet conclude that the information we possess about Adalbert's work in Hungary is made consistent ; even the statement in S. Stephen's Legend crediting S. Adalbert with the baptism of the first Hungarian king will sound less extravagant ; if the future King was not actually baptised by Adalbert, he was certainly confirmed by him(51).

We must remember that Adalbert was in all probability related to the duke of Bavaria and that it was to the Bavarian court that young Stephen applied for a bride. This might be more than mere coincidence ; for however friendly with the Germans and especially the Bavarians, Geiza may have been, he must have been anxious to effect the entry of Christianity into his land through a safer channel and one less liable to assist a dangerous neighbour in furthering his political interests under the pretext of cultural intercourse. This was no other than the channel connecting Hungary with Czech Christianity. The Slavniks' friendly relations with the dukes of Bavaria, Hungary's next door neighbours on her western frontier, and the cordial friendship that was later to bind Adalbert to Otto removed the apprehension a Czech cultural penetration into Hungary might have provoked in Germany.

The beginnings of Christianity in Hungary were of course slow and Bruno is right in confessing that in Adalbert's time the Magyars abandoned their errors only in part and that he could raise over them no more than " a shadow of the Christian symbol." Geiza himself is stated to have boasted that he was rich enough to afford sacrifices to all the gods, Christian as well as pagan, as Thietmar indignantly notes in his chronicle(52). But it appears that the real moving spirit of Geiza's Christian zeal was his wife, and Bruno asserts(53) that she was responsible for the introduction of Christianity into Hungary.

She must have been an exceptionally vigorous lady, a genuine *mulier fortis*, though not exactly the type of woman as pictured by Holy Writ. Bruno does not attempt to disguise the fact that she wielded a very comprehensive authority over her husband, who for all his airs of independence had frequently to give in to her views on how to govern a country, and to do as he was told. Thietmar(54) pays tribute to her beauty, though it is curious that he should only know her by the Slavonic name of " Beleknegini," or the White Lady. Rumours that reached him in Merseburg had it that the White Lady was a heavy drinker and used to ride like a

---

(51) Such is also the conclusion arrived at by B. Hóman, loc. cit., p. 177.
(52) Chronicon, VIII, ch. 4, *M.G.H.S.* N.S. IX, p. 496.
(53) Ch. 23, *F.R.B.* I, p. 291 : "In those days he had sent to the great ruler of the Hungarians, or rather to his wife, who held the whole kingdom in the hollow of her hand..."
(54) Chronicon, VIII, ch. 4, loc. cit., p. 498.

seasoned cavalry man. Once, on being provoked and angered by a man, she killed him outright with her own hands. Even Thietmar is not unduly prudish in referring to her exploits, though he could not, in deference to his priestly character, suppress the remark that she ought to have clung to her spindle and given more thought to the Christian virtue of patience. But how was one to be hard on a Duchess who had deserved so well of Hungarian Christianity and who after the murder of Adalbert's relations gave hospitality to the Czech refugees who had helped the bishop in his Hungarian activities ?

However that may be, the bishop of Prague and his disciples, together with Pilgrim of Passau and the German missionaries, deserve credit for their turning the Magyars in the direction of western civilisation. The Magyars of medieval days proudly cherished his memory and in the fourteenth century the Magyar students at the University of Paris completed the calendar of the " German nation," to which they belonged together with the Czechs and the Poles, by adding April 24 as the feast of S. Adalbert, *Apostoli Hungarorum*(55).

The final christianisation of the Magyars should go to the credit of Stephen I (1000-1038). When Stephen began his reign, German influence must have been widespread throughout Hungary, as evidenced by Stephen's marriage to the Bavarian duke's daughter; but it was not so potent as to make Stephen gravitate towards the German Empire in politics as he had done in love. Shrewder than his father, he showed for instance no inclination to meet the Germans' wishes, expressed by Pilgrim of Passau, to submit his new Christian Church to theirs, and preferred to apply to Rome for its needs rather than to Germany. We are not so well informed about the Magyar as about the Polish Church ; but a letter from Gregory VII addressed on the 28th October, 1074, to the Hungarian King Solomon(56), contains the claim " the kingdom of Hungary belongs to the Church of Rome, since it was offered and devoutly presented years ago to S. Peter by King Stephen."

If this claim is examined in the light of events in tenth-century Europe, not in that of Pope Gregory's political ambitions or under the influence of modern prejudice, its genuine character will be estimated aright. In its literal sense it only states that Stephen I had offered his kingdom to S. Peter, and though the award might make some modern historians shake their heads, it certainly did not work any dismal effects on contemporary Europe. We must see in Stephen's cession an act similar to the *Donatio* effected some years before by Hungary's neighbour, Mieszko I of Poland. In Stephen's days the Pole's donation was certainly not as unknown to his contemporaries as it was to modern Europe before the publication of the famous document *Dagome Iudex*. We can just imagine

---

(55) For particulars, see P. Perdrizet, *Le Calendrier de la Nation d'Allemagne de l'Ancienne Université de Paris* (Paris, 1937).

(56) Registrum Gregorii VII, lib. II, No. 13 (ed. E. Caspar, " Das Register Gregors VII," *M.G.H. Ep. Selectae*, vol. I, 1920, p. 144) : Regnum Ungaricum S. Romanae ecclesiae proprium est, a rege Stephano olim beato Petro cum omni iure et potestate sua oblatum et devote traditum.

how the news of it spread among the neighbours of Germany and Poland and how it was discussed at the courts of Eastern and Central Europe. Everybody must have felt that there was something new and unusual astir and it is interesting to watch the newly-converted nations which bordered on Germany trying to slip away from the grasp of the German Church and of the Roman Empire. In this case the Polish precedent must have been an inspiration to Hungary. We shall presently see that contact between Christian Poland and Christian Hungary was frequent thanks mainly to the Czechs whose presence seems to have been, at that period at any rate, an indispensable link between the countries of Eastern and Central Europe.

The Hungarian *Donatio* was also a step in the development of the Ottonian scheme and bears out our contention that Otto III could not adopt the pose of an omnipotent Emperor. He had to respect the *Sacerdotium*. At that time the Papacy held a high place in the religious reverence so characteristic of the newly converted Slavs and Hungarians.

Gregory VII, whom we have to thank for this piece of information, did of course strain the sense of Stephen's Donation by pretending that Hungary had become a fief of the Papacy. That could never have occurred to anyone in the tenth century. The Pope's words only illustrate how the papal ideology had developed in the seventy years that intervened between Stephen's presentation and Gregory's letter. The fact remains that no serious doubts could be cast on the historicity of Hungary's *Donatio* by Stephen I.

Its accurate date is, however, difficult to ascertain. Thietmar has favoured us with only a very short statement(57) : " By the grace and favour of the above-mentioned Emperor, Waic (Magyar name for Stephen I), brother-in-law of Henry Duke of Bavaria, received the crown and the blessing, and erected episcopal cathedrals in his realm." No hint of any special date is given ; but since Henry of Bavaria was in Rome at the beginning of 1001(58), we may reasonably assume that he was there on business on behalf of his brother-in-law, the duke and the future king of Hungary. In that case the *Donatio* of Hungary to S. Peter would have been implemented at the beginning of 1001 at the latest, if not earlier.

Thietmar's short statement shows to what extent Otto III had taken a hand in the organisation of Christian Hungary ; and judging from what Ademar of Chabannes(59) and the Annals of Verdun(60) have to say about the conversion of Hungary by Otto III, it looks as though his contribution to Hungarian affairs had impressed some contemporary writers. But again, we cannot exclude the Pope's action from the negotiations ; Pope and Emperor concerted measures, the latter only seizing his chance

(57) Chronicon, IV, ch. 59, *M.G.H.S.* N.S. IX, p. 198.
(58) He was present at the Roman synod, as we learn from " Vita Bernwaldi " (ch. 22, *M.G.H.S.* IV, p. 7687, and from the Annales Ratisbonenses, Supplementum (*M.G.H.S.* XXXi, p. 746).
(59) *M.G.H.S.* IV, pp. 129 seq. The Annalist attributes the baptism of Stephen I to S. Bruno. Otto III was his godfather and presented him with the Holy Spear.
(60) Annales Virdunenses, ad a. 988 (1010), *M.G.H.S.* IV, p. 8 : Hungari christiani fact ab Ottone coacti.

to extend his revived Roman Empire over the new Hungarian State. The procedure recalled that followed in the case of Poland, except that this time the Emperor did not go to Hungary. A solemn embassy brought an imperial letter to Stephen I and presented him with a royal crown and the Holy Spear.

Confirmation of this is again found in the letter from Gregory VII to Solomon(61), in which the Pope writes that the Emperor Henry III, after defeating Solomon's predecessor in battle on the Raab river in 1044, sent to S. Peter in Rome the imperial insignia, the spear and the crown, knowing well that the dignity thereby symbolised originated from Rome. This statement, in combination with Thietmar's evidence, means that Otto III conferred on Stephen I the rights that belonged likewise to the Emperor as the Defender of the Church. Stephen I was even made a Patricius of some sort, invested like Boleslas the Great with the Emperor's rights over the Church in his realm ; but instead of a diadem, Stephen was presented with a crown, a concession to a sovereign whose position was even more independent than that of Boleslas the Great. Papal collaboration in the transaction again needs stressing for, though particulars and authentic documents be lacking (the famous Bull of Sylvester II so often appealed to by modern Hungarians is a forgery, probably of as recent a date as the seventeenth century), the Pope's consent and collaboration is only a logical inference from the fact that Hungary belonged to S. Peter on the strength of the *Donatio*.

After all we have said it will be seen that Hungary's case was not on all fours with that of Poland. For one thing Stephen I was an independent ruler, a fact it was not in Otto's power to alter. It is somewhat puzzling that Otto I never thought of imitating Charlemagne who defeated the foreign invaders, the Avars, in Hungary and completely rid Europe of the scourge. It would not have been so difficult for Otto I to do the same with the Magyars, since he could count on the assistance of the Bohemian duke who reconquered Moravia and Slovakia, and every German, especially the Saxons and the Bavarians, would have rallied to him with enthusiasm had he decided to make an end of the Magyars and to join Pannonia to his empire. Had he done so there would never have been any Hungary, and German expansion would have followed its line of least resistance in the direction of ancient Pannonia, Dacia and the Carpathians as it had done in the Frankish period. But this time not the Saxons but the Bavarians would have taken the lead, probably the reason why the Saxon Otto I left Charlemagne and the Danubian Basin severely alone. The result was that the Magyars were given enough breathing space to reorganise their possessions on the Danubian Plain and the forty years that followed their defeat were sufficient for the work to be done well.

(61) *Registrum Gregorii VII*, loc. cit., p. 145. The same tradition is traced in the letter sent by Urban II in 1096 to King Koloman, the Pope stating that Stephen I received from the Church of Rome not only the grace of the faith, but also the rights of royal dignity (Urbani II Litterae, *P.L.*, vol. 151, col. 481). Cf. P. von Vaczy, *Die erste Epoche des Ungarischen Königstums* (Pécz-Fünfkirchen, 1935), a book which I have not had the good luck to come across in Great Britain.

Otto III had to take the consequences of his grandfather's policy. Stephen was independent and quite able to set his realm on its own feet without Germany's interference ; there were no common neighbours in whose conversion and subjugation he had to share interest with Germany, as was the case with Poland. Only one factor he had to respect and that was the Papacy. The Emperor's luck would have it that the Pope was one who had been associated with him in launching the scheme of the renovated Roman Empire and who was therefore interested in Hungary's entry into the Roman and Christian Commonwealth, their common creation.

We find here an illustration of the Pope's procedure in reconciling the two doctrines current in the political life of his time, those of the co-existing royal and imperial powers. Stephen I must have been aware of the fact that on the strength of the old Rex-Sacerdos theory kings also were leaders of the faithful in their respective realms and because it was his desire to exercise such powers, he addressed himself to Rome(62). It was this principle which the Pope brought into harmony with the conception of a Roman and Christian commonwealth. Stephen, as a Christian ruler, had to become a member of this commonwealth in order to receive in return the royal dignity with all its prerogatives from the two supreme powers that jointly ruled over all Christians. The Hungarian incident is a case in point showing the necessity of collaboration between those powers in the new " order " as established by Pope and Emperor(63).

Invested with new dignity and armed by Pope and Emperor with his new powers, the first Hungarian king could proceed with the ecclesiastical organisation of his country. It is generally believed, as we find it stated in the Legend of S. Stephen(64), that Stephen lost no time in creating a Hungarian archbishopric at Esztergom (Gran) and ten other bishoprics. But the statement needs qualifying, for the fact is that Stephen proceeded very slowly. The first ecclesiastical institution in Hungary appears to have been the Abbey of S. Martin, first founded by Geiza, but erected and completed only in 1002. Its first abbot was Astrik, or Anastasius(65).

It would be impossible to follow later developments with anything approaching accuracy. The first bishopric the existence of which can be

(62) Cf. what J. Deér says in his *Heidnisches und Christliches*, pp. 77 seq. of the "Gottes-gnadentum " or the divine rights of rulers amongst Turkish nations.

(63) P. von Vaczy, in his review of A. Brackmann's *Kaiser Otto III* quoted above, rightly calls attention to the difference in character between imperial interventions in Hungary and Poland, as also to Stephen's desire to be the Rex-Sacerdos of Hungary ; but he never got to the bottom of the problem. *Archivum Europae Centro-Orientalis* (1939), vol. V, pp. 328-32. Cf. also B. Hóman's *King Stephen the Saint*, pp. 23 seq.

(64) Vita Maior, ch. 8, *S.R.H.* II, p. 383 : "Provincias in decem partitus est episcopatus, Strigoniensem ecclesiam metropolim et magistram per consensum et subscriptionem Romanae sedis apostolicae ceterarum fore constituens."

(65) This may be inferred from Stephen's charter issued in favour of S. Martin's Abbey and published by J. Karacsonyi : *Szent-István Király Oklevelei ès a Szilveszter-Bulla* (Budapest, 1891), p. 147 : . . . . ."At the instance, on the advice and with the consent of the lord Anastasius, Abbot of the monastery of S. Martin, situated on the mountain that dominates Pannonia, which was founded by our father and which with the help of God we have completed for the salvation of our soul and the stabilisation of our kingdom, we confer (on this monastery) the same freedom as is possessed by the monastery of S. Benedict on Monte Cassino." On this charter cf. H. Bresslau, " Zu den Urkunden König Stephans von Ungarn," *Archiv f. Urkundenforschung*, (1918), vol. VI, pp. 65-76.

proved by charters dated about 1009, was Vesprim, that foundation possibly dating from 1006(66). According to Alberich's chronicle, the cathedral church of Esztergom was founded in 1010(67), though a Hungarian archbishop was present in Bamberg in 1007(68). His name was Astrik, evidently the same as Anastasius, the first Hungarian abbot. In 1012 we find him active in Germany where he is again called Archbishop of Hungary not of Gran(69), and the Legends of S. Stephen(70) praise his merits in connection with Hungary.

It should be pointed out here that the slow but steady progress of Hungary's ecclesiastical status only proves Stephen's practical sense. Though in 1001 there could scarcely be priests enough in Hungary to fill every important post in the ten dioceses, Stephen was too keen on the independence of his country to rush events and he preferred to rear a native clergy gradually rather than throw open the gates of Hungary to priests from Germany, who could be had for the asking, but were interested in Hungary in more ways than one. We may presume that S. Martin's Abbey was something of a training centre, so that Abbot Anastasius' share in the formation of Hungary's Christianity could hardly be exaggerated.

* * *

There remains the important problem : who was the first archbishop of Hungary before his archiepiscopal seat was fixed at Gran ? All the sources call him Astrik, but who exactly was he ? There are three candidates for the honour : Anastasius, the first abbot of Brzevnov, near Prague, founded by S. Adalbert ; Aschericus, a priest of S. Adalbert mentioned in Bruno's biography of the saint(71), and Radla, who was the saint's companion in Magdeburg and remained loyal to the House of Slavnik to the very last. As eye witness (72) of the massacre of the ducal family he reported it to Bruno. All three were intimately associated with the name and life of S. Adalbert.

The question as to which of them occupied the See of Gran has not yet been answered, though several theories have been advanced by Hungarian, German, Czech and Polish historians. Astrik (Asterichus), archbishop of Hungary, has often been identified with Anastasius the Abbot of Brzevnov who left Bohemia after the massacre of the Slavniks—a very likely guess, as all the supporters of the Slavniks seem to have fled the country in fear of further unpleasantness. After reaching Poland, Anastasius was made abbot of the first Polish monastery, *ad mestri locum*, founded

---

(66) Vita Maior, ch. 9, *S.R.H.* I, p. 385. Cf. V. Chaloupecký, Radla-Anastasius, *Bratislava* (1927), vol. I, pp. 266 seq. (in Czech).

(67) Alberici Monachi Trium Fontium Chronica, *M.G.H.S.* XXIII, p. 779.

(68) *M.G.H.S.* IV, p. 796.

(69) Jaffé, *Bibliotheca Rerum Germanicarum*, vol. V, p. 481.

(70) Vita Maior, ch. 7, 8, *S.R.H.* II, pp. 38 seq. ; Legenda S. Stephani Regis ab Hortvigo episcopo conscripta, ch. 9, *S.R.H.* II, p. 412.

(71) Ch. 17, *F.R.B.* I, p. 284.

(72) Ch. 21, *F.R.B.* I, pp. 288 seq.

by Adalbert. It is generally identified with Trzemeszno, but may well have been Międzyrzecz(73).

Some historians, however, are of opinion that the above cryptogram conceals the name of the Hungarian monastery of S. Martin on the Pannonian Mountain, in which case, according to the same historians, Anastasius of Brzevnov would have been made not the first Polish abbot but the first Hungarian abbot and the first Hungarian archbishop as well(74). Then, who is this Anastasius of Brzevnov ? His nationality, as we have said, is not known ; but might he not be the priest Aschericus who, according to Bruno, was with Adalbert in Rome, where he left him after a quarrel, later to repent and return ? If this is the same man then Anastasius probably came from Adalbert's diocese, since he is designated as Adalbert's priest, possibly a Czech or a Croat from Bohemia, a guess that may come very near the truth. But others have suggested that this Aschericus came to Hungary straight from Rome, being sent by Adalbert.

The third "candidate" for the see of Gran, Radla, is the least popular of the three, though he deserved better treatment. It is certain that Radla was in Hungary, because the second edition of Bruno's *Vita*(75) has preserved fragments of two letters which Adalbert sent from Poland to Hungary on the subject of Radla. The first was addressed to the wife of the Duke Geiza, Adalbert requesting the duchess to send his *papas*, i.e. preceptor, if she could spare him, back to him ; and the identity of the *papas* with Radla can be established on the evidence of another statement by Bruno(76).

The second letter was addressed to Radla himself, Adalbert asking him to join him at any cost ; and if he could not obtain the duchess's permission to leave her service, to flee from Hungary in secret and rejoin "his Adalbert." The bishop wanted to persuade his former preceptor and friend to join him in his missionary work among the Prussians whom he was planning to visit. But Radla did not accede to his friend's wishes probably explaining to the messenger that he had a sufficiently promising field for his missionary activities in Hungary. Adalbert's second biographer, Bruno of Querfurt, visited Radla during his stay in Hungary between 1004 and 1007, as he says in chapter 23, when he gathered fresh information from him and conceived the idea of publishing another account of his hero's life.

Bruno states that at the time of his correspondence with Adalbert (997 A.D.) Radla was already a monk. This would justify the conjecture

---

(73) T. Wojciechowski, *Szkice Historyczne XI. w.* (Warszawa, 1925) (ed. St. Zakrzewski) ; R. F. Kaindl, *Beiträge zur älteren Ungarischen Geschichte* (Wien, 1893), pp. 21 seq. Cf. Passio Adalberti, ch. I, *F.R.B.* I, p. 231. A Benedictine Abbey at Mezerici, between the Obra and the Warta rivers, is mentioned in 1005 by Thietmar (Chronicon, VI, ch. 27, *M.G.H.S.* IX, p. 306). Trzemeszno seems to have been founded later and is known as an Augustinian Abbey. Cf. R. F. Kaindl, "Zur Geschichte des hl. Adalbert," *Mitteilungen des Instituts für Oester. Geschichtsforschung* (1898), vol. XIX, pp. 545.

(74) F. Hýbl, "Bruno of Querfurt," *Czech Hist. Rev.* (in Czech, 1898), vol. IV, pp. 174 seq. Cf. especially V. Chaloupecký, *Radla-Anastasius*, pp. 210-28, who reviews the problem historically ; his study is the best contribution to the Anastasian problem so far.

(75) Ch. 23, *F.R.B.* I, p. 291.

(76) Ch. 15, *F.R.B.* I, p. 280.

that on entering the monastery Radla changed his name into Anastasius in obedience to a rule of the eastern monasteries, which was not unknown in Bohemia and Hungary, where both churches, Eastern and Western, were vying for supremacy in the ninth and at the end of the tenth century. The name Astrik (Aschrik) could very well be a Hungarian, or more probably a Slavonic equivalent for the Latin Anastasius(77). Thus, Radla-Astrik, or Anastasius, who in 979 was at the Hungarian court in the service of the duchess, and who became abbot of a Hungarian monastery, would have become later the first Hungarian archbishop of Gran.

But how can we explain that this Radla-Astrik-Anastasius, who is spoken of by Bruno (ch. 23) as a monk, is mentioned by the same author as a cleric staying with the Slavnik family at Libice and was a witness of the massacre? Did he then become a monk in Hungary? This would not be impossible, as we know that by then the Duke Geiza had founded a monastery of S. Martin's Hill near Gran in commemoration of a saint whose memory was associated with Old Roman Pannonia. It would not be such a piece of wild speculation should somebody suppose the existence near Gran or Esztergom, even before the country's official conversion, of a monastery of Slavonic rite, a last battered stronghold of Moravian and Graeco-Slavonic Christianity that became the basis of Geiza's foundation. Even after the destruction of the Moravian Empire religious life went on in the eastern parts of what was soon to be called Hungary. This remnant formed a solid nucleus for the conversion of the Magyars, and Adalbert made good use of it as part of his diocese.

It is equally possible, if not more probable, that Radla became a monk in Bohemia, where the first abbey had been founded by Adalbert in Brzevnov. When Adalbert left Prague for the second time, Radla, his faithful supporter, must also have left Brzevnov to take refuge with the Slavniks at Libice for better protection against Adalbert's enemies and to wait for better days. It was there he witnessed the eclipse of Slavnik glory. Unable to stay any longer in Bohemia he left, probably not alone, for the easternmost part of Adalbert's diocese on his way to Hungary. The warm reception which awaited him at the Hungarian court and the interest which the Duchess, Geiza's widow, took in his fate, show that he was not unknown in the country and would entitle us to suggest that he used to accompany his bishop on his missionary tours in Hungary. This would best explain his influential position at court. Radla-Anastasius-Astrik then informed Adalbert, who was then staying in Rome or at the emperor's court in Mainz, where he was and how well his work was proceeding in Hungary.

This makes it unnecessary to assume that Adalbert, when in Rome for the second time, sent the priest, called Aschericus by Bruno, presumably a member of Adalbert's clergy, to Hungary on a mission which recent events in Bohemia had cut short. What really happened was that

---

(77) Voigt, *Der Verfasser der Röm. " Vita,"* pp. 89, 117, 164. Cf. idem, *Brun von Querfurt* (1907), p. 262.

Radla carried on Adalbert's work and that the latter knew all about it since he addressed him a letter from Poland.

What also enfeebles the hypothesis of Adalbert sending Aschericus-Anastasius from Rome to Hungary is that Bruno met Radla in Hungary in 1004 and was glad to gather from him such details of Adalbert's life as he did not know. Had Adalbert sent Aschericus-Anastasius from Rome to Hungary Bruno would have met him there also. In this case we would expect Bruno to mention him as well as Radla. The same line of argument applies to that other Anastasius, who is supposed to have come to Hungary from Poland after first leaving the Abbey of Brzevnov and then the Polish Abbey, both founded by Adalbert. But such mobility would be deemed excessive for an abbot. We could understand that this Anastasius had to leave Brzevnov because his association with the Slavnik Adalbert made his residence in Bohemia undesirable, whilst his presence at Brzevnov would only have exposed the abbey to the reigning duke's retaliation ; but to leave the newly founded Polish abbey, Anastasius could only be prompted by a feeling of disappointment at having been ousted from the leadership of the new Polish Church by Gaudentius, Adalbert's half-brother, and by the hope of finding better scope for his ambition in Hungary. Such motives are, of course, human, but it does seem daring or even unfair to father such feelings on Anastasius, who had spent years in the best reformed and reformist monastery of Rome. And what hopes could Anastasius have of ejecting from Hungary a man like Radla, knowing that he was a favourite at the Hungarian court ?

This makes it unnecessary to assume, in order to lend colour to such theories, that Adalbert, after leaving the Emperor in Mainz, first went to Hungary, where he left Radla in charge, and reached Poland after only a short stay in Hungary(78). We are asked to do violence to the text of the *Passio Adalberti* and to read there that Adalbert went *in Pannoniam* instead of *in Polianiam*, and to read into the ambiguous designation of the locality where stood the new abbey founded by Adalbert *ad Martini locum* instead of *ad mestri locum*, which would make it the abbey of S. Martin in Hungary instead of the abbey at Mezerici. It does not seem scholarly to take such liberties with texts.

Now that we have embarked on suppositions, let us venture a little further. We find in the diploma issued on April 4, 1001(79), in Rome by Otto III for the monastery of Farfa, among the list of witnesses to the deed, the name of Anastasius, Abbot of S. Mary's Monastery, of the Slavonic Province. Professor Schramm in his great work on *Renovatio* speculates that this ecclesiastic had been working in Hungary and had been sent to Rome as ambassador by the duke with the request for a Catholic Hierarchy to be founded in his country(80).

---

(78) As proposed by Chaloupecký, *Radla-Anastasius*, pp. 214 seq.

(79) *M.G.H. Dipl.* III, No. 396, p. 828 : Anastasius Abbas monasterii sancte Marie Sclavanensis provincie.

(80) *Kaiser, Rom und Renovatio,* vol. I, p. 153.

The interpretation sounds plausible but for one difficulty : in the document, Anastasius is designated as abbot of S. Mary's Monastery of the Slavonic Province and this designation seems at first sight to apply best to the Anastasius who was once abbot of Brzevnov and of Trzemeszno. The attribution of the monastery to a Slavonic Province would in this case be more comprehensible. We would then have to suppose that this Anastasius left Poland for Hungary, as said before, prior to A.D. 1000. He may have been sent to Rome by the Duke Stephen on a special mission, in which case the designation as used in the charter for Farfa, of Anastasius, Abbot of S. Mary's Monastery of the Slavonic, i.e. the Polish, Province, would fit him better.

It has, however, been stated already that such an interpretation presents other difficulties. One thing is certain in all these conjectures : Radla was working in Hungary and was a great favourite at court. Then why was he superseded by a newcomer from Poland ? Radla also knew Rome, having stayed there as ambassador as early as 992 ; and he also could take advantage of Adalbert's popularity in Rome to the great benefit of his mission better than anybody else, having been the Saint's preceptor and companion.

The designation in the Farfa document also fits Radla-Anastasius, since we may assume that in 1001 he was abbot of the abbey which Duke Geiza had founded and which remained to be built and was formally opened the following year. It is true that Stephen's Legend(81) gives the abbey the title of S. Martin ; but in another chapter(82) the same source states that the monastery was dedicated to S. Benedict. In the sixth chapter the author, in recording a victory won by Stephen over some pagan re-actionaries, attributes his success in the first place to Our Lady, and then to S. Martin and S. George. As in other instances he commends Stephen's special devotion to Our Lady, whom he had chosen as Hungary's Patroness, it is only reasonable to admit that the first Hungarian monastery was dedicated not only to S. Martin, but also, and in the first place, to Our Lady. Brzevnov had also several titular patrons.

The designation of the monastery as belonging to the Slavonic province can also be explained. It must be borne in mind that in 1001 the hierarchy was not yet established in Hungary and that this establishment was the very object of Anastasius' embassy. The monastery could therefore not be stated to belong to the Hungarian province since there was no Hungarian province to belong to. But as it had to belong to some ecclesiastical organisation, there was only one diocese that could lay claim to a certain right over northern Hungary and that was the diocese of Prague. It will be remembered that this diocese in Adalbert's days included almost the whole of modern Slovakia as far as it was inhabited at the time ; that the bishop of Prague had worked in those parts and that he was the only ecclesiastical superior to organise any sort of monastery in those regions. As long as a religious hierarchy was lacking in Hungary the bishop of

---

(81) Vita Maior, ch. 5, *S.R.H.* I, p. 381.
(82) *Ibid.*, ch. 7, p. 383.

Prague had to administer religious life there, the more so as his priests were working in Hungary and had authority over the first monastery. But if Esztergom at that time still belonged to Bohemia—not an impossible supposition—then the problem is more soluble still, for even Radla-Anastasius could in 1001 be called of S. Mary's Monastery of the Slavonic, i.e. Bohemian-Moravian province.

We may now sum up what has been said about the first Hungarian archbishop. He was very probably the preceptor of S. Adalbert, Radla, a Czech or Croat from Bohemia, who figured in Hungarian history under his religious name of Anastasius-Astrik. As regards the other candidates for the same dignity, it would seem that we must identify the abbot of Brzevnov, Anastasius, with Astericus, the priest of Adalbert's diocese, who stayed with him in Rome and is mentioned by Bruno of Querfurt. This Anastasius became abbot of the first Polish monastery and was likewise a Czech or Croat from Bohemia.

Granted that Bruno speaks of the priest Astericus only in connection with Adalbert's second stay in Rome : but in this chapter he also harks back to what happened in the course of Adalbert's first stay. Although Canaparius(83) states that two of Adalbert's companions left him on learning that the bishop intended to be a monk, one of them could be Astericus, the possibility being left open for him to change his mind and return to his master, since Bruno duly reports his repentance.

One point still deserves to be stressed ; the identification of the Anastasius of the Farfa document with Stephen's ambassador allows us to draw a closer analogy between the Hungarian embassy and the Polish embassy sent to Rome by Boleslas the Great. In other words, just as the Pole sent his candidate for the archbishopric of Gnesen to Rome, so did Stephen send to Rome his candidate for the archbishopric of Hungary, with this difference, that the candidate for the Hungarian archbishopric was not consecrated in Rome as was the candidate for the Polish archbishopric, since the Roman Curia puzzled more over the Hungarian than over the Polish case. Polish Christianity was more mature and a bishop had been administering the country for years ; Boleslas the Great was more businesslike, and all his plans were ready to the smallest detail for the ecclesiastical reorganisation of the country, whereas Hungarian Christianity was only in its teens and could afford to abide its time. It is likely that the Roman Curia meanwhile sent bishops as legates, together with Anastasius, to Hungary to perform the necessary consecrations in accordance with King Stephen's wishes.

The establishment of the hierarchy was a gradual process, apparently not round Esztergom as its centre, for we find Anastasius, styled archbishop not of Gran but of Hungary, attending a synod in Frankfurt in 1006, at the consecration of the church in Bamberg in 1012 and he is again mentioned in 1036 by the biographer of S. Emmeran, Arnold(84), who met him after

(83) Ch. 16, F.R.B. I, p. 249.

(84) Arnoldus de S. Emmerano, M.G.H.S. IV, pp. 547, 563. Arnold, who had been sent by his abbot from Regensburg to Hungary on an unknown errand, spent six weeks with Anas-

his accident in Hungary. It is quite possible that his see was at first at Calocza(85) and that Esztergom became the centre of Hungarian Christianity only after the conquest of the territory between the Danube and the Tatras, about 1010, this country being riper in the faith.

We may hold that the Polish example somehow inspired Stephen of Hungary, as intercourse between Hungary and Poland was at this early period fairly frequent, thanks to the Czech missionaries and S. Adalbert's disciples who were working in both countries. No wonder then that Stephen charged his Astrik (now, I hope, satisfactorily identified with Radla) with peace negotiations between Poland and Hungary in 1000. On this occasion, Radla may very well have yielded to his aversion to the Przemyslides, who were then busy trying to negotiate an alliance with the Hungarians against Boleslas the Great.

One thing is certain, the first archbishop of Hungary was not only a priest on intimate terms with S. Adalbert, he was a native of Bohemia, very probably a Czech or a Croat from the Slavnik country. But whatever we have said on this problem should set out in relief the share which the bishop of Prague had in the christianisation of Hungary. Adalbert and his Czech or Croat priests were instrumental in Hungary's final orientation towards Western civilisation. His work in Hungary gave the necessary stimulus to the development of that country and helped to mark the boundary between Western and Eastern civilisation on the lower Danube and in Transylvania.

Bohemia's contribution to the spiritual growth of Poland and Hungary in these vital years has been a surprise to many. The Czechs and the Slavicised Croats were at that time far more civilised than the Poles and the Magyars and well did they fulfil their Christian duty towards their less fortunate neighbours. For we find them everywhere, ever ready to hand on to their neighbours and their erstwhile enemies the common Christian inheritance. It was a great task and their loyalty to it saved the Poles and the Magyars many a disappointment that would have been theirs had their Christianity come direct from Germany.

The Czechs owed their privileged position to their acceptance of Christianity, not at the hands of Germany, but mainly of Byzantium, and to their inheritance of Graeco-Slavonic culture founded by SS. Constantine-Cyril and Methodius in Moravia. It only shows what Europe lost when this civilisation perished for lack of priests and for lack of contact with its fountain head, Byzantium. The successes scored by that civilisation give us an idea of what might have happened in Eastern and Central Europe

tasius as the bishop's guest. Unfortunately, instead of initiating us into the life of his generous host, the monk branches out into a lengthy description of a marvellous vision he had in whch he had a good look at the Devil for three consecutive hours. All we learn is that during ihis stay in Hungary he composed some liturgical invocations to S. Emmeran which Anastasius later sang with his clerics in honour of that saint.

(85) The Legend of S. Stephen written by bishop Hartwig probably between 1112 and 1116 designates Anastasius as bishop of Calocza (ch. 8, *S.R.H.* II, p. 412) ; but this may be a later interpolation. However that be, he often seems to have stayed near the King's residence which was not situated at Esztergom, but at Alba Regia. A charter of the year 1015 (Karác-sonyi, loc. cit., p. 84) calls Anastasius archbishop of Calocza, but the document is to all appearances not genuine. Cf. K. Schünemann, *Die Deutschen in Ungarn*, pp. 47 seq.

had this culture but found more favourable conditions for its expansion and growth.

* * *

Europe's loss is made all the more evident by contrast with the cultural and political progress of the more eastern countries under the Russian rule of Kiev and inhabited then by Slavonic tribes later to be known as Russians and Ukrainians. We noted once that the ambitions of Otto I stretched beyond the Carpathian Mountains and aimed at planting the German cross on the fertile plains of the Ukraine, only to be foiled by the pagan reaction under Svyatoslav, when Otto's missionary bishop barely escaped from Kiev with his life. It will likewise be remembered that Svyatoslav's successor Yaropolk reopened contact with Otto I, and that Russian ambassadors were present at the emperor's last Reichstag at Quedlinburg in 973. This was significant as an indication that Svyatoslav's reign did not bring about a complete severance from the West. After that date the change on the German throne must have hampered Russo-German relations to some extent and explains the dearth of first-hand information on this subject from either side.

One interesting event is recorded by the Chronicle of Nikon, a local chronicle posterior to Nestor's Annals and dependent on them ; it states that in 979 envoys from the Pope appeared at the court of Yaropolk(86). The statement stands alone in contemporary Russian and western Annals. Moreover it looks inaccurate, as Yaropolk must have been dead by 979 ; not a serious difficulty, it is true, as the dating of this event and of Vladimir's capture of Kiev is uncertain(87). Much more inexplicable is the information volunteered by the chronicler that the Pope of Rome should have taken this sudden interest in Russian affairs. At any other period, say in the ninth or the eleventh century, such courtesy visits by special ambassadors from the pope bearing invitations to accept the Christian faith were normal enough ; but that such a move should be attributed to Pope Benedict VII (974-983), whose reign was still clouded by the struggles between the aristocratic parties in Rome and the supporters of the Emperor Otto II, needs explaining. His predecessor, the impetuous Boniface VI, had been driven from his See and taken refuge in Constantinople, fully determined to return to Rome, which he did in 984(88). It was no time for sensational undertakings on the part of the pope and it was as much as Benedict VII could do to cling to his position for a few years without any direct interference from Otto II until, to his great relief, the Emperor yielded to his entreaties and entered Italy in 980.

Under the circumstances, it is impossible to give credit to the story that Benedict VII should ever have dreamt of such a step as sending a

---

(86) Nikonovskaya Letopis, *Polnoe Sobranye Ruskikh Letopisei*, vol. IX, ad a. 6487, p.39 : That same year ambassadors from the Pope came from Rome to Yaropolk.

(87) Cf. *infra* p. 172, seq,. and G. Laehr, *Die Anfänge des Russ. Reiches*, p. 142.

(88) Cf. L. Duchesne, *Liber Pontificalis* (Paris, 1892), vol. II, pp. 257 seq.

special embassy to Russia with greetings to the pagan Duke Yaropolk ; and if it ever did occur to him to do so, he could scarcely have made the move without consulting the Emperor, dependent as he was on his support and good will.

Taking all this into consideration, one can hardly admit the Russian chronicler's report to be accurate. And yet, if it did contain a grain of truth, it might be open to a different interpretation, for the embassy was possibly sent, not by the Pope, but by the Emperor Otto II. A German embassy to Russia in 979 would not be any more abnormal than the Russian embassy to Germany had been in 973. In that case, Otto II would have sent to Kiev the answer to the Russian deputation received by his father, and returned the compliment. Even if the chronicler's date is open to criticism, the fact of the embassy need not be ruled out, as any date between 973 and 979, the length of Yaropolk's reign, would meet the case.

To this reading it may be objected that the chronicler asserts that the embassy came from Rome and from the Pope ; but we must remember that at that time, even more so than at the period when the Russian chronicles were written, the Russians looked upon Germany as the representative of Rome. In their eyes German Christianity was neither more nor less than Western Roman Christianity. This is how the author of the first Russian Annals introduces the Germans who according to his story came to Kiev to explain their religion to Vladimir(89) :—" Then came the Germans, stating that they had come as the emissaries of the Pope. They added : ' Thus says the Pope : Your country is like our country, but your faith is not like ours '." And the Greek scholar who in the chronicler's account came to explain the principles of the Greek faith is made by the annalist to say : " We have also heard how men came from Rome to convert you to the Roman faith." This sufficiently illustrates the Russian chronicler's habit of identifying Germany with Rome and makes allowance for a similar confusion by the writer of the chronicle of Nikon. In the minds of the pious annalists, Rome was much more real than Germany and they venerated her as one of the holiest places in all Christendom(90). As the Germans could only select an ecclesiastic to head their embassy, the mistake was only too easy.

Should this reading prove right, we would find here additional confirmation of the interest Germany and the new Roman Empire were taking in the nascent State of Kievan Russia. But in one matter the German Church as representing Roman Christianity completely failed : Russia's Christianisation was the work, not of Germany, but of Byzantium. As this turning point in Russian history has its bearing on the relations of the

---

(89) Ad a. 6694 (986), S. H. Cross, loc. cit., pp. 184, 185.

(90) The Russians as a matter of course inherited from Byzantium the respect which Eastern Christianity professed for Rome ; in fact, the animosity of the East against Rome started only much later and affected Russia not earlier than the twelfth century. Cf. what I say on the esteem in which Rome was held in the East until the ninth century in my book—*Les Légendes*, pp. 291-5. In this respect Russian mentality is well illustrated in the *Book of Degrees*, where the author makes Vladimir, after his conversion, despatch envoys to all the famous places in Christendom, including Rome.—*Poln. Sobranie Russk. Lietop.*, vol. XXI (1908), p. 103.

Eastern Slavs with the Roman Empire as designed by Otto III, it claims a more detailed study.

*   *   *

In the Annals of Nestor(91) we are given this pretty story of Vladimir's conversion : the Khazar envoys exalted Judaism, the Bulgars recommended Mohamedanism, whilst the Germans and the representatives of Byzantium refuted both these creeds and detailed the beauties of Christianity. Having listened to all of them and to the reports from the envoys he had sent to various countries to inquire into their religions, Vladimir decided to embrace the creed of the Greeks. These disputations are of course discredited by all historians and relegated to the lumber-room of legendary fabrications, though it may be observed that they are in the best manner of the period. We have for instance the account of a lengthy controversy between Constantine-Cyril and the Jews, Moslems and pagans at the court of the Khazar Khagan, found in his Slavonic biography written in the ninth century(92) ; and what Nestor wrote on the delegates' endeavours to convert Vladimir to their respective faiths, at least reflects the spirit of Russia at the beginning of his reign. The Volga Bulgars were gradually recovering from the blow Svyatoslav had dealt them and to complete the Vyatichians' subjection, Vladimir is reported to have launched an expedition against their neighbours, the Bulgars. Now from what Nestor writes about these(93), we can gather that the Bulgars with their Mohamedanism and their Arab culture still fascinated the Russians of the period.

Contact between Vladimir's Russia and the Khazars was frequent and it need not surprise anybody that the Jews who occupied an influential position in Khazaria should have attempted to gain a hold on Russia, a country they had learned to respect after the destruction wrought on the Khazarian empire by Svyatoslav.

That the author of the Annals of Nestor should introduce the Germans as the Pope's emissaries to take part in the discussion, is interesting quite apart from the fact that the discussion reflects the controversial atmosphere between Rome and Constantinople in the eleventh and twelfth centuries, and that the author takes the opportunity to blame the Germans for their habits of fasting and for the use of the wafer at Mass. It forcibly recalls other German efforts, of which the Russian tradition must have kept some remembrance, to secure a foothold in Kievan Russia.

Equally interesting is the way Vladimir's envoys described the impressions they had gathered in Germany : " Then we went among the Germans and saw them performing many ceremonies in their temples, but we beheld no glory there. Then we went on to Greece where the Greeks took us to the edifices where they worship their God, and we knew

---

(91) Ad a. 9493 (985), S. H. Cross, loc. cit., pp. 183-99.
(92) Cf. F. Dvornik, Les Légendes, pp. 198 seq. Ibid., the French translation of the Vita Constantini, chs. IX-XII, pp. 360-70. Ibid., pp. 168 seq., cf. what I say about a similar discussion at the court of the Khagan of the Khazars before their acceptance of Judaism.
(93) Ad a. 9493 (985), S. H. Cross, loc. cit., p. 183.

not whether we were in heaven or on earth. For on earth there is no such splendour or such beauty and we are at a loss how to describe it.'' The contrast points to a preference for Byzantine civilisation with which Germany found it difficult to compete. And yet, though the Greeks won the battle in the end and transmitted their religion and their civilisation to Russia, the question as to whether the first introduction of Christianity into Russia came from the West or from the East still remains a subject of debate among specialists. Nestor's version of the conversion of Russia has again been questioned of late, and since it would be rash to pretend that the credit for sowing the first Christian seed in Russia should go to Germany, that country's conversion is being credited to Scandinavian priests(94). Another debated topic is the establishment of the first hierarchy in Russia. Was it due to Byzantium, to Rome, or to the Bulgarian Patriarchate of Ochrida(95) ? Other problems gather round the introduction of the Slavonic letters and liturgy into the young Russian Church. This is not the place to discuss them at length, but as their solution may contribute to the understanding of the problems under discussion, let us try and throw some fresh light on at least some of them.

As regards the Scandinavian theory, there is the damaging fact to be taken into account that the introduction of new Scandinavian elements by Vladimir would have coincided with a pagan reaction in Kiev(96). This alone would invalidate every argument produced in support of the theory. There is no evidence whatever for any unprecedented display of missionary activity among the Scandinavian clergy at this period. Nor do we understand why Vladimir should have had to be instructed in the Christian religion by Scandinavian missionaries during his stay at Novgorod(97), which was probably more infected with paganism than Kiev, since, unlike Kiev which could draw its Christian inspiration from Byzantium, Novgorod had only the *hinterland* of half-Christian Scandinavia to look to. Novgorod was besides swept by the pagan revival engineered by Vladmir's uncle Dobrynya(98), and by the accounts of some later chronicles(99), its Christianisation proved to be a very hard task indeed.

---

(94) The Scandinavian theory was developed by N. de Baumgarten in his " St. Vladimir et la Conversion de la Russie," *Orientalia Christiana* (1932), vol. XXVII. Cf. M. Jugie, " Les Origines Romaines de l'Eglise Russe," *Echos d'Orient* (1937), vol. XXXVI. A refutation of all the theories that underestimate the importance of the Byzantine element in the christianisation of Russia was attempted by V. Laurent, "Aux Origines de l'Eglise Russe. L'établissement de la Hiérarchie Byzantine," *Echos d'Orient* (1939), vol. XXXVIII, pp. 279-95. Cf. also the article "Russie" in the *Dictionnaire de Théologie Catholique* (first part written by J. Ledit, cols. 207-16), vol. XIV (Paris, 1939).

(95) The foremost champion of the Bulgarian theory is M. D. Priselkov, " Studies on the religious and political history of Kievan Russia in the X-XII centuries" (Saint Petersbourg, 1913), in the *Zapiski of the Historico-Philolog. Faculty of St. Petersburg University*, vol. CXVI. This theory was recently revived by H. Koch in a useful study " Byzanz, Ochrid und Kiev 987-1037 " *Kyrios* (Berlin, 1938), vol. III, pp. 254-92. Its bibliography on all problems bearing on the Christianisation of Russia is valuable.

(96) Nestor's Annals ad a. 6686-6688 (978-980), 6491 (983), S. H. Cross, loc. cit., pp. 180-182.

(97) N. de Baumgarten, loc. cit., p. 62.

(98) Nestor's Annals aa a. 6686-6688, loc. cit., p. 181.

(99) All these accounts are mentioned in detail by N. de Baumgarten on pp. 91 seq., and yet he maintains in the face of them that Vladimir made his first acquaintance with Christian doctrine in that city.

The part which Olaf Tryggvason played in Vladimir's conversion, to judge by its poetical treatment in the Scandinavian "sagas," mostly of much later origin(100), has been overrated. Before he recovered his throne in Norway, this Scandinavian hero was far more interested in plundering the British Isles than in preaching the Christian faith. True enough, the account of Russia's conversion in Nestor's Annals was written by a cleric imbued with the Greek tradition and anxious to advertise Byzantium's contribution to the achievement ; he even introduces into his narrative snatches of anti-Latin polemics that belonged to the eleventh century—but that would not imply that he studiously eliminated every detail that might have favoured the share of the West in Russia's conversion. Even admitting that some of Nestor's statements must be taken with caution, as his chronicle may have been recast after the Mongolian invasion which destroyed the original copies of so many Russian literary documents—a supposition that remains to be proved—we may not for that reason throw overboard every tradition and draw conclusions from materials that are still less reliable than even Nestor's so-called second version.

We must then take Nestor's account of events as a basis, legendary in many parts, that is understood, but sufficiently reliable in its historical outline, for the re-construction of Vladimir's conversion, with the assistance of Arab(101), Byzantine and other Russian sources. To explain the part which Byzantine political commitments played in the event, let us recall the Russo-Byzantine treaties of 944 and 971 by the terms of which the Russian duke undertook to help the emperor with auxiliary troops whenever requested to do so ; and it was this clause which prompted the Emperor Basil II to apply to Vladimir for military aid to help him in dealing with the revolt of Bardas Phocas. To get rid of his Scandinavians who were clamouring for arrears of pay and were beginning to be troublesome, Vladimir was only too ready to oblige, but on condition that the Emperor should give him his sister in marriage. There is also historical truth in the report that after crushing the rebels, when the Emperor showed reluctance in meeting the barbarian's demand, which in the eyes of the Byzantines was too shocking to deserve consideration, Vladimir attacked and captured Kherson in the Crimea and did not break off hostilities until the Emperor sent him the coveted lady. Vladimir was baptised in Kherson(102) and there he married the trembling princess who had at least the comfort to know that for her sake her husband had dismissed his five wives and 800 concubines(103). Eight hundred concubines sounds ex-

(100) N. de Baumgarten, loc. cit., pp. 66 seq., admits that nine-tenths of the accounts in the sagas are the product of " political exaggeration." The main saga on Olaf Tryggvason is Snorre Sturlason's (1178-1241) *Heimskringla*, ed. E. Monsen, A. H. Smith (Cambridge, 1932). On Olaf's stay in Russia, see pp. 118 seq., 129 seq.

(101) The main Arab source is the Chronicle written by Yahya of Antioch and first translated by Baron W. R. Rosen in his book : *Emperor Basil, the Slayer of Bulgarians* (in Russian) (St. Petersburg, 1883), pp. 23 seq. A complete edition with a French translation was published by J. Krachkovsky and A. Vasiliev " Histoire de Yahya-Ibn-Sa'id d'Antioche," *Patrologia Orientalis* (Paris, 1932), vol. XXIII, pp. 423 seq.

(102) Loc. cit., ad a. 6496 (988), S. H. Cross, loc. cit., pp. 199-205. A complete list of sources bearing on Vladimir's conversion is found in H. Koch's study : *Byzanz, Ochrid und Kiev*, pp. 290-2.

(103) Loc. cit., ad a. 6486-6688 (978-980), S. H. Cross, loc. cit., p. 181.

travagant, even for a Viking, but the pious monk must have made additions to the number, only to show how baptism had transformed this pagan soul and how thoroughly this new Christian had conquered himself.

However, it appears that the principal wives can be identified and belong to history. Two of them were Czechs, one Bulgarian and one Greek, a former nun who had been driven from her convent by Svyatoslav, was offered to Vladimir's brother Yaropolk and eventually married the man responsible for his death. These ladies were certainly Christians but the fifth of the wives was a Scandinavian called Rogned, and a pagan. Incidentally, this also explains where Vladimir happened to learn the principles of Christianity. It was not in Novgorod, but in Kiev that he got to know them from his wives and from the Christian colony of the city.

It has been suggested that Vladimir had decided to be a Christian well before the Greek intervention and that he was actually a Christian when he addressed his request to the emperor, his " private " conversion having taken place in 987(104). The date is suggested by the panegyric of Vladimir attributed to the monk Jacob(105) who also pretends that Vladimir captured Kherson three years after his baptism ; but he is not consistent in his statements. As according to him Vladimir took Kiev eight years after Svyatoslav's death, and as this occurred in 972, the capture of Kiev must have happened in 980 and not, as the monk states, in 978 (6486), which rather shakes one's confidence ; and as, according to the panegyrist, Vladimir's baptism took place ten years after Yaropolk's death, the event should be placed in 990, which would not suit the theorists who are all for a private conversion before the Greeks officially stepped in(106).

We had therefore better keep to the tradition as recorded by the oldest Russian chronicle which for all its legendary embellishments is still able to stand up to criticism. There was no private conversion, and the Greeks' contribution to the public conversion was what it was stated to be ; the baptism took place in Kherson and was followed by the convert's marriage with the princess " born in the purple." One realises how, by thus feeling associated with the Emperor whom he admired for his wealth and magnificance, if for nothing else, the proud Varyag's prestige rose in his own estimation. After all, Vladimir tried the same thing as Olga who was baptised in Constantinople, only with better results. As to the year of Vladimir's baptism, the most likely date is 989, since it is all

(104) Even the classical Russian Church historian E. Golubinsky, *History of the Russian Church* (in Russian), Moscow, 1901), vol. I, 1, pp. 130 seq., admits the " private " baptism in Vladimir's case.

(105) V. J. Sreznevsky, "In Praise of Vladimir" (in Russian), *Zapiski Imp. Akademii Nauk*, S VIII, vol. I (1897), No. 6, pp. 7, 8. Cf. N. de Baumgarten, loc. cit., pp. 63 seq. The Arab and Greek sources quoted by Baumgarten in support of his theories do not disclose anything serious enough to make me abandon the old tradition, whereas a careful reading reveals facts that contradict his statements. The handling of sources seems to be the weak spot of this protagonist of the Scandinavian theory.

(106) M. Hrushevsky, in *Geschichte des Ukrainischen Volkes* (Leipzig, 1906), vol. I, pp. 623 seq., studied this problem in detail and proposed the year 979 for Yaropolk's death : in this case the conquest of Kherson and Vladimir's baptism should be dated 989.

but certain that Vladimir captured Kherson in 989. Here the date proposed by Nestor needs correction(107).

Nestor further tells us how the new Christian Duke amused his wife by ordering the statue of Perun, chief god of the Slavs, to be beaten by twelve strong men, and giving her the display of his people's mass baptism in the waters of the Dnieper. There may be some exageration in the tale, given the chronicler's obvious pains to make the story of the end of Russian paganism as edifying as possible and raise a smile among his readers over the fate of the statue their fathers once had adored.

*   *   *

There remains the problem, still debated by experts, of the introduction of the Slavonic language into the Russian Church. For the right solution we should remember how Svyatoslav stood with Bulgaria. That the Russian Christians in Kiev should be interested in the Slavonic books and liturgy which were discovered on the Duke's expedition to Bulgaria, was only to be expected. It is also possible that some Bulgarian priests entered Kievan Russia and that the Bulgarians deserve more credit for the conversion of Russia than they ever received. Their contribution to the slavicisation of the Russian Church is undeniable. After the final subjugation of Bulgaria to Byzantium by Basil II(108), called " the Slayer of Bulgarians," a number of Bulgarian refugees sought shelter in Kievan Russia which they knew to be Christian at the time. This would be enough to explain the penetration into Kievan Russia of Slavonic letters and liturgy and the hold they took on the Russian Church.

In dealing with the establishment of the hierarchy in Kievan Russia we again come up against the problem of Russia's relations with the West. On these the chronicle of Nikon offers information which is interesting but as puzzling as ever. It states(109) that in Kherson "ambassadors from Rome came to Vladimir and brought him relics of saints ;" and the Book of Degrees(110) endorses the statement, which has served many scholars as material for a number of theories on Russia's contact with the West. Some pretend that in his anxiety to keep his young Church independent of

---

(107) The date of the capture of Kherson has been fixed by Vasilievsky, "A propos the history of the years 976-986 " (in Russian), *Trudy*, vol. VI, 1909, pp. 56-124. Cf. the discussion of this detail in Laehr, loc. cit., pp. 110-5 : Exkurs U, Die Quellen über die Taufe Vladimirs. Hrushevsky's research seemingly points to the same conclusion, as stated in the previous footnote. The date can be reconciled with what Jacob says in his *In Praise of Vladimir*, p. 7 ; if we do not insist on taking his statement about Vladimir's baptism, which he places in 987, too literally and read it only as a promise to accept Christianity, the capture of Kherson may then have taken place three years after this promise, *i.e.* in 989. It should, however, be added that Vladimir did not accompany his troops to Byzantium, there being no evidence for it in either Byzantine or other sources. Cf. also G. Ostrogorsky, " Vladimir and Byzantium " (in Russian), *Anthology of S. Vladimir* (Beograd, 1938), pp. 31-40. Ostrogorsky favours the year 988 for Vladimir's baptism, not unreasonably, but the year 989, after the capture of Kherson, seems preferable to me.

(108) On this, see v. G. Schlumberger, *L'Epopée Byzantine à la fin du Dixiéme Siècle* (Paris, 1900), vol. II, pp. 333-432. Cf. *ibid.*, vol. I (1896), pp. 715-77 ; vol. II, pp. 1-42, on Basil II's relations with Vladimir and on the latter's baptism and marriage.

(109) *Poln. Sobr. Rus. Liet.*, vol. IX, p. 57.

(110) *Ibid.*, vol. XXI, p. 103 (ch. 35).

Constantinople, Vladimir asked the Byzantines to set up in Kiev an auto-cephalous metropolitan, but on their refusal turned to Rome and had his hierarchy consecrated by the papal legates(111). Others, loath to credit Rome with such a preponderant share in Russia's christianisation, pretend that Vladimir addressed himself to Ochrida and obtained his autocephalous archbishop from the Bulgarian Patriarchate.

As regards the despatch of a papal embassy to Vladimir, we find no corroboration of it in any Western document. This is embarrassing; but on the other hand, the Russian chronicle states that Vladimir's contacts with Rome were frequent, whilst another report has it that in 994 the Russian ambassadors sent by Vladimir returned from Rome(112). We shall see presently what our sources have to say about other embassies.

The Pope who took the initiative could be none but John XV (985-96), who succeeded to the throne after a period of ecclesiastical disturbance that marred the ephemeral reigns of John XIV (983-4) and Boniface (984-5). The latter returned from exile, but there are serious doubts about the natural death of both Popes, and in any case it is well known how the hatred of Boniface's former friends hounded him to the very grave. John XV himself was under the control of the Crescentius clan and married his brother to the daughter of the Patricius; but when he eventually lost the Patricius' favour and support, the Pope was forced to apply to the young Emperor Otto III for assistance and died before meeting his rescuer. Though action such as is mentioned by the Russian chronicle, is not absolutely incompatible with John XVth's reign, we are not sufficiently informed about the doings of the popes of this period to explain his sudden interest in Russia. Perhaps the Pope's relations with Germany might solve the enigma.

We learn from S. Adalbert's biographers that the Empress Theophano, widow of Otto II, was in Rome in 989 and 990. It may be that John XVth's call for help after the first breach with the Patricius decided her to pay closer attention to Italian affairs and to German interests in Italy. How-ever, as the Patricius had thought better of it and made peace with the Pope, her services in that particular line were not required. She arrived before Christmas in 988. Theophano was intelligent and resolute, and is generally acknowledged to have handled State affairs during her son's minority with such remarkable skill that her contemporaries respected her, as we gather from Thietmar's opinion of her administration(113). In Rome, she acted as Regent in the exercise of her imperial prerogatives and her stay there, which must have lasted till the first months of 990(114), was devoted to some purpose, as the Annalist of Hildesheim(115) notes that she brought the whole country under her son's authority.

---

(111) Cf. N. de Baumgarten loc. cit., pp. 100 seq.
(112) Chronicle of Nikon, loc. cit., vol. IX, p. 65 (ad a. 6502).
(113) Chronicon, IV, ch. 10, *M.G.H.S.* N.S. IX, p. 42 : Regnum filii eius custodia servabat virili (She governed her son's kingdom with manly watchfulness).
(114) For details, see R. Wilmans, *Jahrbücher des Deutschen Reiches unter der Herrschaft Otto's III* (Berlin, 1840), vol. II, 2, pp. 63-6. Cf. J. Haller, *Das Papsttum, Idee und Wirklichkeit* (Stuttgart, 1937), vol. II, I, pp. 204 seq., on the situation in Rome at this period.
(115) Ad a. 989, *M.G.H.S.* III, p. 68.

It follows then that the papal embassy recorded by the Annals of Nikon must have left Rome about the time Theophano was there, and if it did go at all, it must have done so with the knowledge and at the suggestion of the Empress. What justifies my surmise is that Theophano was a Byzantine princess and that Princess Anne who married Vladimir in 989 was her relative(116). It was only natural then that Theophano, who kept herself informed of happenings in Constantinople, should do the feminine thing and send her cousin a wedding present from Rome—some relics of saints, which at that time were considered to be the most valued gift. At the same time the Empress, who had the interests of her son at heart, could not forget the eastern borders of his Empire and carried out the policy of her late husband who, as stated before, had kept in touch with Russia of Kiev. No doubt the Pope's co-operation was asked for and used, and this would be enough to justify the chronicler's statement. Such must have been the most likely preliminaries to the despatch of ambassadors to Kherson and Kiev, whereas it would be difficult to imagine John XV acting on his exclusive initiative.

In any case, there is nothing to show that John XV had anything to do with the establishment of the hierarchy in Kiev. He would never have dreamt of such a thing, and the Patricius, who controlled the Pope's relations with foreign States, would never have felt interested, unless the Russian had sent him a handsome present, a weakness for which he was notorious. It appears that Vladimir did send envoys to Rome, perhaps with some presents, but only much later, in 1001, when the Patricius had lost his position and Otto III took matters under his personal control. But this is another story that will be dealt with presently.

As to Vladimir's share in this exchange of compliments, since, according to the Chronicle of Nikon and the Book of Degrees(117), he sent similar embassies to all the famous Christian centres and shrines—to Jerusalem, Egypt (probably Alexandria) and Babylon, which may mean Antioch—the embassy to Rome loses much of its political significance. It was a normal act of courtesy by which the newly baptised Duke informed Christendom of his country's entry into the Christian commonwealth. There may have been other things at stake in the case of Rome, as will be seen later, but they had nothing to do with Rome's consent to the foundation of a Russian hierarchy.

*   *   *

The alternative theory which credits the Bulgarian Patriarchate of Ochrida with the creation of the Kiev hierarchy as the logical sequel to Bulgaria's share in Russia's conversion, may deserve attention, only the

---

(116) For details see P. E. Schramm, " Kaiser, Basileus und Papst in der Zeit der Ottonen,' *Historische Zeitschrift* (1924), vol. CXXIX, p. 428. It was Anne, daughter of the Emperor Romanos II, who was at first destined to become Otto II's bride, which makes one understand better the interest which the widow of Otto II took in the fate of the princess.

(117) *Poln. Sobr. Rus. Letop.*, vol. IX, p. 68 (ad a. 6509) and vol. XXI, p. 127 (ch. 67)

evidence for the existence of an autocephalous archbishop in Kiev between 987 and 1037 is not convincing.

It is known that in the Byzantine Church the title of archbishop used to be conferred on prelates who were exempt from the jurisdiction of other metropolitans and enjoyed some independence by being directly subject to the Patriarch. They were therefore called autocephalous. The archbishops of Cyprus, and later of Bulgaria, were more autocephalous still and were almost equal to the Patriarch. Now, there are two Russian sources which mention an archbishop in Kiev in the first quarter of the eleventh century : the *Chtenie*, on the Life and Martyrdom of SS. Boris and Gleb, Vladimir's sons who were done to death by their jealous brother Svyatopluk, written by Nestor, monk of Pechersky Monastir, probably after 1081 ; and the *Skazanie*, about the same saints, written by the monk Jacob at the end of the eleventh or the beginning of the twelfth century(118). Both biographies mention two ecclesiastical dignitaries of Kiev—John and George. John is mentioned in the reign of Yaroslav who dethroned his brother and is given a leading part in the translation of the relics of the two brothers venerated as saints. The ceremony may have taken place either in 1020 or in 1026, as in both years the 24th July, the day of the translation, fell on a Sunday. Both biographers(119) make John an archbishop and Nestor calls him a metropolitan.

George is mentioned in connection with the consecration of the new church built by order of Yaroslav's successor Izyaslav (1054-1073) for the relics of the two saints, Nestor calling him both archbishop and metropolitan, and Jacob, only metropolitan of Kiev(120). These two documents are the most relevant to the matter under discussion. Various chronicles of later date mention an archbishop(121), but they cannot be taken as evidence, since they record the history of the establishment of the Russian hierarchy in legendary form and attribute it to the Patriarch Photius who had died a century earlier.

In corroboration of these texts from Russian documents, a passage is quoted from Thietmar's(122) Annals stating that in 1018 Svyatopolk, on entering Kiev with his victorious troops and their Polish auxiliaries, was greeted by the archbishop of the city. The reference, though regarded as the most conclusive, cannot be taken as evidence for Kiev's possession of an autocephalous archbishop, since Thietmar could not know the difference between the archiepiscopal functions in the Greek and Latin Churches, and as a Latin, he only meant the bishop of Kiev whom he took for a metropolitan, not an autocephalous archbishop.

---

(118) The most recent and best edition of all documents that concern the two Russian saints is by D. J. Abramovich, "The Lives of the Saintly Martyrs Boris and Gleb" (in Russian), in *Pamyatniki Drevnerusskoy Literatury*, vol. II (St. Petersburg, 1916). On the historical value of the documents, cf. A. H. Shakhmatov, *On the Oldest Collections of Russian Chronicles* (in Russian), (St. Petersburg, 1906), pp. 29-97.

(119) Abramovich, loc. cit., pp. 17-19, 53-55.

(120) Loc. cit., pp. 21, 55, 56.

(121) Cf. N. de Baumgarten, *St. Vladimir et sa Conversion*, pp. 98 seq.

(122) Chronicon, VIII, ch. 16, *M.G.H.S.* N.S. IX, pp. 530 seq.

Then again, archbishop John who presided at the translation of the relics very probably did not reside in Kiev, as the way the two biographers of SS. Boris and Gleb refer to him suggests that he had come to Kiev for that special purpose(123). This fact gave the champions of the Bulgarian theory the idea that this John was archbishop of Ochrida and served them as evidence to prove that Vladimir obtained his archbishop from the Bulgarian Church.

But why ?(124) Is it not more logical to assume that this archbishop was the incumbent of Kherson who'had the young Christian Church of Russia under his care and supervision ? Barring this indication, there exists no evidence of any official approach by Vladimir to the Bulgarians, while nothing in the sources that deal with Vladimir's conversion suggests any breach between him and the Greeks, or that the Greeks turned down his request for an autocephalous Church. On the contrary ; there is good evidence of the cordial collaboration between the Church of Kherson and Vladimir in the conversion of his people, and the first priests to be placed in charge of the church of Our Lady in Kiev came from Kherson(125).

Besides, there was no need for Vladimir to ask the Greeks for an autocephalous establishment in Kiev : not being in the same position as the Bulgarians, next-door neighbours to Byzantium, who had their own reasons for distrusting the Byzantine Church, and having little to fear for the independence of an empire as vast as his, Vladimir knew he could safely leave the door ajar to Greek influences. He could not then foresee the complications that were to arise in the eleventh century between the native clergy and the Greek hierarchy.

Neither could he expect to obtain autonomy for his Church as was the case with Cyprus and Bulgaria, for it was not a usual practice for Byzantium to grant it, except as a result of normal development. If he really wanted a certain amount of independence for his Church, he actually had it when he accepted the services and supervision of the incumbent of Kherson, who was an archbishop(126). This, as matters stood and developed, proved a distinct advantage, since Kherson, after its capture, was at his mercy, and even after its cession to Byzantium, the archbishop and the Church of the city remained as useful agents who would see to his local interests. Kherson was a rich trading centre and commercial intercourse between this city and Kiev was to Russia's profit. These considerations were overlooked when scholars indulged in theories at variance with the hard facts of history.

---

(123) Cf. Priselkov, *Studies on. . .Kievan Russia,* pp. 50 seq. ; H. Koch, *Byzanz, Ochrid und Kiev,* p. 275.

(124) If the lives of the two saints offer features that are distinctly Bulgarian in character, it should be remembered that their mother was probably the Bulgarian lady referred to as one of Vladimir's five wives.

(125) Nestor's Annals, ad a. 6497 (989), S. H. Cross, loc. cit., p. 207.

(126) Cf. the *Notitia Episcopatuum* (List of bishoprics) drawn up in the reign of Leo the Wise (886-911) and published by H. Gelzer, " Ungedruckte und ungenügend veröffentlichte Texte des Notitiae Episcopatuum," *Abhandl. d. Phil. Philol. Kl. d. Bayer. Akad.,* vol. 21 (München, 1906), p. 550.

It is regretable that we do not know the names of the archbishops of Kherson who flourished at that period. Previous to it, the last incumbent known to us was Paul who attended the Council of Photius in 879-880 ; then follows a gap in the succession down to the reign of Alexios Comnenos in the eleventh century when we identify archbishop Theodore(127). It is therefore not impossible that archbishop John mentioned by the biographer Nestor should have been archbishop of Kherson.

We may then conclude that Vladimir contented himself with an archbishop in Kherson in the capacity of a supervisor who did the necessary consecrations of bishops and priests for the new Church, as an arrangement that suited him best ; and that the Russian Church had no metropolitan or archbishop of its own, contrary to the opinion of almost all the Church historians, for a period of about fifty years, until the reign of Yaroslav who founded the metropolis of Kiev and placed all the Russian bishops under the metropolitan's jurisdiction(128). We read in the first Russian Annals : '' Yaroslav built the great citadel in Kiev, near which stand the Golden Gates. He also founded there the metropolitan church of S. Sophia, the Church of the Annunciation by the Golden Gates and the monastery of SS. George and Irene.'' The first metropolitan after the re-organisation was the Greek Theopemptos, as we learn from the Russian Primary Chronicle(129).

This change in no way meant the degradation of the Kievan see, as alleged by the champions of the autocephalous theory. On the contrary, Yaroslav stabilised the ecclesiastical organisation of Kievan Russia and as Russian Christianity found its own feet, Kherson fell into the background. Thus much is endorsed by the biographies of SS. Boris and Gleb. The way the biographers describe the translation of their relics gives the impression that all available Russian bishops gathered round their metropolitan to render the occasion more solemn. Only Nestor gives the metropolitan the title of archbishop—no doubt, a slip of the pen, as everybody agrees that at that period there was no archbishop in Kiev, but a metropolitan. The monk Jacob is more accurate. He calls George a metropolitan and gives the names of all the bishops present at the ceremony : Neophyt of Chernigov, Peter of Pereyaslav, Nicetas of Belogorod, Michael of Gurgen and the abbots Theodosij of Pechersky, Sofronius of S. Michael

---

(127) Cf. Le Quien, *Oriens Christianus* (Paris, 1740), voll. I, col. 1331 ; also H. Koch, loc. cit., pp. 273 seq., on the untrustworthiness of Russian tradition concerning the names of the first metropolitans of Kiev.

(128) Ad a. 6545 (1037), S. H. Cross, loc. cit., p. 226.

(129) Ad a. 6547 (1039), loc. cit., p. 227. It was gratifying to see that G. Vernadsky gave up the Bulgarian theory in his study " The Status of the Russian Church during the first half-century following Vladimir's conversion " in *The Slavonic and East European Review* (1941), vol. XX (The Slavonic Year Book), pp. 295-314. His " Tmutorakan theory," holding that the archbishop in charge of the young Russian Church was the titulary of Tmutorakan, is, however, unacceptable. There is nothing to warrant the importance which Vernadsky attributes to Tmutorakan in Russia's early religious history and no evidence for stating that " the archbishop of Tmutorakan received the position of an autocephalous prelate " as a result of Vladimir's campaign and lost it again under Yaroslav. Such manipulations of sees are unthinkable in Eastern canon law.

and Germanicus of S. Spas(130). The metropolitan George may have been the successor of Theopemptus(131).

*   *   *

Examination of the conditions under which Kievan Russia joined the Christian commonwealth has yielded some interesting results. Though many a theory purporting to link Russia of Kiev with Western Europe has to be jettisoned, there remains the satisfaction to find that contact with Central Europe and with Germany, which represented the West in Russian estimation, remained unbroken and can be traced back to Otto I and to Otto II and the Regency under the Empress Theophano during the minority of Otto III(132). The first Otto's obsession to move the frontiers of his reorganised Empire as far as Kiev was after all not the figment of a morbid brain, since it somehow survived in the short reign of his son Otto II and was given a new lease of life by his daughter-in-law, the Greek Theophano.

It was consequently more than a characteristic instance of heredity that the idea which had inspired Otto I should have been restored to a programme of practical politics when his grandson ascended the throne and proclaimed his Renovation of the Roman Empire. Meagre as our information is about the third Otto's intentions towards Kiev, we may reasonably suppose that this new country was included in the imperial scheme, for we learn from the Chronicle of Nikon(133) that Otto III, before starting on

---

(130) Cf. *ibid.*, pp. 104, 105, 107, 112 the references to George in the various lessons of that saint's hours.

(131) We can trace one other Greek prelate who was transferred from a Greek see to Russia— the bishop of Sebaste, Theophylactus, as we learn from a Greek list of episcopal changes (*P.G.*, vol. 119, col. 905) reedited with additions by the Byzantine theologian Nicephorus Callistus (*P.G.*, vol. 146, col. 1196). The transfer must have taken place between 1016 and 1025, but we cannot tell whether this bishop became the titular of Kiev or of some other Russian diocese. Le Quien in his *Oriens Christianus*, vol. I, col. 1261, wrongly identifies this bishop with Theopemptus who is only heard of in 1037. There is a reference to a Bulgarian bishop of Kiev, Alexius by name (Frisius, *De Episcopatu Kiovensi eiusque Praesulibus Brevis Commemoratio*, Warsaw, 1763, pp. 7, 27, 28), but it is too vague and the evidence produced by the author cannot be traced ; otherwise, it would be excellent warranty for the Bulgarians' share in the conversion of Russia. Theophylactus is made the first metropolitan of Russia by E. Honigmann ("Studies in Slavic Church History," *Byzantion*, 1944-5, American series, vol. III, pp. 128-62) on the assumption that before his transfer to Russia, he was metropolitan of Sebasteia of Armenia Minor. This is produced as evidence that Kiev was a metropolitan see as early as the reign of Basil II, before Yaroslav's alleged creation of the Kievan metropolis. A good solution, if it could be proved. But there is no question of bringing in the Armenian Sebasteia : the Sebasteia under the metropolis of Laodicea is more pertinent. The last bishop of this city on the list of Le Quien (*Oriens Christianus*, vol. I, col. 808) was the Church historian Theodore, who must have written on the reign of Basil II, as we learn from casual remarks in the list of episcopal changes mentioned above (*P.G.*, vol. 119, cols. 905, 906). Le Quien knows of another bishop of the same city, Constantine, who was present at the Photian Council of 879-880 (Mansi, *Conciliorum Amplis. Collectio*, vol. XVII, col. 377). Theophylactus should therefore be placed between these two names, for he must have preceded Theodore. The transfer of a metropolitan was a more serious affair than the transfer of a bishop. As there were several Greek bishops in Russia, the obvious thing was to appoint one of them metropolitan of Kiev, if there was a metropolis at Kiev at the time, rather than to send one from Byzantium. E. Honigmann does not prove this.

(132) There exists a study by Th. Ediger on the relations of Russia with Germany and Rome (*Ruslands älteste Bezichungen zu Deutschland, Frankreich und der Röm. Kirche*, Halle—Dissertation, 1911), but I have been unable to see it.

(133) Loc. cit., vol. IX, p. 68 (ad a. 6508-1000) : The same year there came ambassadors from the Roman Pope and from the Czech and Hungarian kings.

179

his journey to Poland, sent an embassy to Vladimir. The writer there points out that the embassy was sent from Rome, as though the Emperor were trying the same manoeuvre in Russia as in Poland, again with the Pope's co-operation.

A Russian embassy to Rome is mentioned in 1001(134), the same as reported above and sent also to other patriarchial sees, but carrying at the same time the reply to the imperial letter of the previous year. What that reply was has remained a secret. Otto's overtures to Russia of Kiev must have been allowed to lapse since nothing more is heard of any other embassy ; which does not mean that Otto III had thrown up his plans for extending his Empire as far eastward as possible. More would have been heard of it, had it not been for the Emperor's premature death which brought all his earthly plans to an abrupt end.

The endeavour to rally Russia to the new Roman Empire need not be interpreted as a move against Byzantium or as one of Otto's wiles to outwit the Eastern Emperor. We know that there was an anti-Byzantine feeling at the court of Otto III and that a clash between the two imperial views seemed inevitable after the proclamation of the *Renovatio*, when suddenly Otto III turned to Byzantium with the domestic request for a Greek bride. Under the circumstances, anti-Byzantine feelings could scarcely affect his political outlook.

What seems more likely is that Otto III and his adviser, Gerbert-Sylvester II, looked upon the Slavonic world, which by the end of the tenth century rose to be a new factor in the world's history, as part of the new empire, as witnesses Gerbert's outburst, boldly proclaiming that not only Italy and Germany, but also Scythia (Slavonic lands) owed obedience to the Roman emperor. The same pretension was illustrated in " Otto's Gospel," where he is painted in full imperial regalia, receiving the homage of Italy, Gaul, Germany and Slavonia.

One more indication marking the scale on which the Emperor and the Pope erected their designs. In 1000 A.D., when the Doge of Venice had conquered Dalmatia, the Pope immediately sent his legates to the " Duke of the Venetians and the Dalmatians," asking him for detailed news of his campaign. The Pope on this occasion certainly did not act on his own, but in virtue of his partnership in the *Renovatio,* the union of all Christendom under one emperor and one pope by the concerted action of the *Imperium* and the *Sacerdotium*. That is why, at the synods held in the presence of the Pope and the Emperor, both ecclesiastical and imperial matters came up for discussion and were decided upon without any distinction between them. Now that the activities of Sylvester II are being brought to the surface by modern research the masterly conceptions of this great Frenchman are beginning to be better understood.

* * *

As regards Central and Eastern Europe, the way Otto III and Sylvester II conceived the *Renovatio Imperii* was after all best calculated to assure the

(134) *Chronicle of Nikon,* loc. cit., vol. IX, p. 68 (ad a. 6509-1001), *Book of Degrees,* loc. cit., vol. XXI, p. 127.

independence of the rising States and to bridge the gap between the Roman and post-Roman periods and the new era in which the new nations were destined to play their parts. Moreover, Otto's conception offered the only possible policy for Germany to secure supremacy in Central and Eastern Europe without prejudicing the national growth of the younger nations; and to secure their adhesion, the young Emperor made a substantial concession by sacrificing the supremacy of the German Church. Such has been so far the common estimate of Otto's work. Most German historians have deplored Otto's concession as putting an end to German missionary expansion towards the East(135). This view has to a great extent prevented modern history from appreciating Otto III at his full value and caused him to be treated either as an unbalanced youth, or as a despot who considered it his function to control the pope as he controlled his own German subjects.

It has been commonly believed that contemporary Germans did see the danger for the future of Germany of Otto's theories, which would explain how the best German minds, such as Thietmar and the bishop of Posen, Unger, challenged this semi-Greek ruler's new-fangled imperial concepts, advocating instead the old Germanic tradition of Charlemagne and Otto I. But these views are open to revision now that research has thrown a new light on the events of that period and revealed aspects that call for reconsideration.

In the first place, Otto's sacrifice of the German Church's missionary role was not as heavy as some historians have imagined it to be; as a matter of fact, there was hardly anything left of it in Otto III's days. The insurrection of the Polabian and Baltic Slavs in 983 had shattered this German dream for at least two generations; and the long Regency weakened imperial prestige at the critical moment when Poland was rising to a position of sufficient importance to claim its share in the christianisation and subjugation of the Polabian and Baltic Slavs. Far from Germany trying to thwart these pretensions, she was only too glad to accept Poland's offer. Nor were the German missionaries even in a position to oust the Czechs from Poland and Hungary, at least in deference to the saintly memory of Vojtiekh-Adalbert, Bishop of Prague, under whose auspices the Czech missionaries were working. All this happened without any fault of Otto's and beyond the range of his responsibility. Nor could anyone have foreseen then that a new drive in the eleventh and twelfth centuries would take the Germans across the Elbe and open up unexplored fields for the Church. Henry the Lion of Saxony and the heroes of the second wave of the Drang nach Osten were not yet born and Poland showed no signs of the paralysis that came over her under Boleslas the Great's successors. Otto III did then all he could for German prestige within the limits of reason.

It is not even true to say that Otto's contemporaries looked upon his

(135) This appreciation of Otto III can be found even in the famous *History of the German Church*, by Hauck, vol. III, p. 272 : " Otto sacrificed the missionary possibilities of the German Church to the ideal of a Christian universal Reich, composed of independent States. This has often been deplored. . . . The fact is that Otto thereby only prevented the further expansion of the German people towards the East and deprived the German Church of a mission which she had so far fulfilled with signal success."

dreams as something alien to German interests. Otto III was not building his visions only on the classical traditions of Rome and its Caesars, but feeling more conscious of his Saxon stock than he ever got credit for. For him, too, Charlemagne remained the lodestar and Otto I, the inspiration. Nor was Rome to be the only centre of his Empire. He threw up his grandfather's designs meant for the benefit of Magdeburg, but Aix-la-Chapelle saw some of her best days under his reign. It was between Rome and Aix-la-Chapelle that Otto III shared his most valued treasure, the relic of S. Adalbert presented to him by Boleslas. When he opened Charlemagne's grave and contemplated with reverence the human remains of the great Emperor his contemporaries understood better than we do where he looked for his ideal.

The Saxons of his day must have seen in the Emperor's plan something totally different from what has caught the attention of their descendants; for recent research has shown that the young Saxon nobles followed Otto III with enthusiasm, readily offered him their services, admired his brilliant gifts and with the Romans called him "the wonder of the world" (136). This hardly fits in with the notions of Otto's Renovation that have prevailed so far.

Nor is there any need for overrating the importance of some contemporary writers who bitterly criticised Otto III's work. We know now what we are to think of the so-called opposition of the German bishop of Posen, Unger; and Thietmar was too enamoured with his Magdeburg and her "rights" to lend approval to the Emperor's attitude towards his beloved ecclesiastical centre. Writing his Chronicle at a time when Boleslas the Great was on an equal footing with Germany and making an unsuccessful bid for a great Slavonic State, Thietmar, in common with his countrymen, felt all the bitterness of this national humiliation and was only too ready to accuse Otto III of harbouring that young Polish viper in his bosom, instead of drawing its fangs. As regards Bruno of Querfurt, who in his biography of Adalbert, says things that might be read as criticism of Otto's *Renovatio*, his words should be read in the light of his letter to Henry II of which we shall have something to say presently, and where he clearly shows his regard for Otto III and his principles.

*   *   *

The critical attitude of so many modern German historians to Otto's unfinished task cannot, for all its weight (137), alter historical truth; and

---

(136) Those who accompanied Otto III to Italy were mostly Saxons—nobles and bishops—and the young Emperor amply rewarded them with old Roman offices and dignities; such is the conclusion of researches made by M. Uhlitz "Die Italienische Kirchenpolitik der Ottonen," *Mitteilungen des Instituts für Oester. Geschichtsforschung* (1934) Bd. 48; *Idem*, " Das Deutsche Gefolge Kaiser Ottos III in Italien," *Gesamtdeutsche Vergangenheit. Festgabe für H. von Srbik* (1938).

(137) What is one to think, on reading in the *Volk und Rasse* (vol. XIV, February, 1939, p. 34), the severe judgement pronounced by W. Brewitz in his article on Kaiser Otto III, on this *Rassenbastard* (mongrel)? " It is amazing to see how the strong and essentially German stock of Ludolfing, of Henry I and Otto I ...... by a damaging mixture of blood, racially deteriorated and degenerated; and how Widukind could romance about his forefathers. . . . Otto III was an unlucky and double character, pulled hither and thither by his ambiguous blood, with no friends and no happiness, broken in body and soul, a poor, pitiful man and in no way the world's wonder."

it is no exaggeration to say that Otto III was the only German Emperor who succeeded in mapping out for Central and Eastern Europe a scheme acceptable to both German and the new Slavonic and other nations, and comprehensive enough to shape the fate of this part of Europe to the benefit of all peoples concerned.

But was it wise to strive for such an end ? It is easy for us to criticise it as a Utopia, but Otto III died in 1002 before he had time to see the result of his projects, before he could completely crush the revolt of the Romans. Who knows how things would have fared, had he reached his full manhood ? Europe was at the worst of her growing pains and anything might have happened. The first contact between West and East under Otto I and Otto II produced the Ottonian Renaissance; do we know what would have come to the West, if that contact had been intensified in accordance with Otto III's intentions and if Western Europe had come by the treasures of Plato, Aristotle and other Greek thinkers that were hidden within the walls of Constantinope some centuries earlier than it did ? What Western Europe needed in Otto III's time was a more frequent, close and friendly contact with the only centre where Greek and Roman civilisation was still fully alive; and this centre was Byzantium. It was severance from this centre, brought about in the seventh century by the Arab conquest of the main shores of the Mediterranean, which precipitated the barbarization of France and Italy, and prevented the remnants of the Roman Empire and of romanized Gaul from passing on the treasures of the Greco-Roman and Hellenistic culture to their barbarous German conquerors. The first consequence of this failure and decadence was that the centre of political power shifted from southern France to its less cultivated north. All that the north could produce was a Pippin, a Charlemagne and his successors, who by a disconcerting turn of fate, were to become the masters not only of the south of France, but also, at least nominally, of Italy, and the saviours of the Papacy(138). They did what they could to salvage what was left of Greco-Roman civilisation, but access to its source remained barred by the Arabs, by the Avars and the Slavs—who were holding Central Europe and the Balkans.

It was the destiny of a Slavonic tribe—the Moravians—to reopen the obliterated road and to resume direct contact with the city on the Bosphorus. Even this short period of cultural intercourse brought untold blessing to Moravia and Bohemia. Little as they could store in their own country of the Byzantine inheritance for want of time, the Czechs were yet able so to benefit by it as to force the pace and steal a march on the Germans in their cultural evolution. Throughout the tenth century their cultural level was unparalleled.

But as the bridge was in the process of building it was cut again by the new invasion of the Magyars, and Western Europe found itself again severed from its intellectual roots. The Germans, who had provoked the

---

(138) These ideas have been developed by the foremost modern historian of Belgium, H Pirenne, in his book *Mohamed et Charlemagne* (Paris, Bruxelles, 1937), also available in an English translation by B. Miall : *Mohammed and Charlemagne* (London, 1939).

destruction, stemmed the flood; but the pity was that the Magyars, next-door neighbours to Byzantium as they were, felt unable to take over the task of intermediaries and to transmit to the rest of Europe the treasures of Constantinople. This fell to the Germans' lot under the Ottos and the chances were promising. The German sword not only clove a path by land, but swept clear the maritime route into Southern Italy, forcing the Arabs to the defensive and helping Byzantium to regain access to Europe. By his *Renovatio Imperii* and his contact with Byzantium, Otto III bid fair to open a new phase in the history of Europe. His days seemed to offer the best opportunity for East and West to reunite in a common culture to the lasting benefit of the human race. But the opportunity was lost for centuries. After Otto's death a great ideal collapsed, and East and West once again fell apart to remain hopelessly separated to this very day.

The Emperor's death proved disastrous, since neither he nor his partner Sylvester II found successors in their common task. The way they had opened was soon lost, there being nobody with the intellect to understand where it led and the will to carry it to its final goal. Their dream remained a dream and Otto's death left Central and Eastern Europe strewn with hopes unfulfilled and chances for ever lost.

CHAPTER V

A POLISH-CZECH OR A CZECH-POLISH STATE

HENRY II BREAKS WITH OTTONIAN IDEALS—BOLESLAS THE GREAT SUPPORTS
OTTO'S IMPERIAL CONCEPTION—BOHEMIA, A POLISH-CZECH STATE REALISED—
FIRST CLASH BETWEEN THE EMPEROR AND THE POLE—THE EMPEROR'S
ALLIANCE WITH THE PAGAN VELETIANS DEALS DEATH BLOW TO OTTONIAN
IDEOLOGY—BRUNO OF QUERFURT'S MISSION TO HUNGARY AND POLAND
AND HIS DEFENCE OF BOLESLAS—BOLESLAS' BID FOR A WESTERN SLAVONIC
EMPIRE AND HIS SYMPATHISERS IN GERMANY—HENRY II AND BOLESLAS
BEFORE THE BAR OF HISTORY—POLISH KING SUCCEEDS TO THE ROLE RE-
LINQUISHED BY THE EMPEROR—POLAND, BOHEMIA, HUNGARY AND RUSSIA—
MIESZKO II AND CONRAD II—LAST BID FOR A PRZEMYSLIDE STATE—CONRAD'S
" DIVIDE ET IMPERA "—ABORTIVE CZECH-POLISH STATE—POLAND AND
BOHEMIA AT THE CLOSE OF A PERIOD.

Otto III was succeeded on the imperial throne by his cousin Henry II,
Duke of Bavaria. The main feature of the new reign was a complete
reversal of Germany's policy towards the Slavonic East beyond the Elbe,
with, as its natural sequel, a fierce struggle between the emperor and the
Polish duke, Patricius of the Roman Empire. For the first time the
imperial head of Western Christendom crossed swords with a Christian
country, the Christian character of which had been so openly and solemnly
blessed by his predecessor. This complete reversal bewildered many a
contemporary; and indeed the new Emperor's change of mind is strange
enough to call for closer examination. Evidently, a new factor had entered
the relationship between the Empire and the neighbouring Slavonic countries, weighty enough to make its influence felt for centuries; but so far no
satisfactory explanation has been forthcoming and the solution of some
collateral problems has scarcely been attempted. It is only too easy to
throw the responsibility on either German lust for power or on the arro-
gance of the Polish Duke deliberately severing all ties of friendship with the
Empire for an all-out effort to create a Slavonic empire in opposition.
Such conjectures too often overstep the limits set by historical science for
the unhistorical satisfaction of reading the present into the past and writing
history backwards.

However, before we attempt to explain how this revolution was
brought about, one point should be cleared up : the whole reign of
Henry II (1002-1024) seems on the surface of it to have been directly at
variance with whatever Otto III had done. Was Henry II then absolutely
and on principle antagonistic to Otto's concept of the " renovation," and
did he actually intend to put his own political ideology as more realistic,
in the place of his predecessors ? With so many arguments pointing
one way or another it is not easy to give a definite answer, but one thing is
certain: as Duke of Bavaria, Henry had been very closely associated with

Otto III and very helpful, as has been pointed out, in furthering the Emperor's designs in Hungary, when, together with his saintly relative S. Adalbert of Prague, he contributed his share to the christianisation of that country and probably paved the way to Stephen's embassy to Rome. He must, therefore, have been in sympathy with Otto's and Sylvester's intervention in Hungary and with the union of this new Christian country with the renewed Roman and Christian Empire. We should of course bear in mind that as Hungary was Bavaria's next-door neighbour, the Duke could not but be interested in that country's fate as a mere matter of policy.

Again, as a loyal vassal of his king and emperor, Henry did not stint military support and did not leave the young Emperor in the lurch at the most critical moment of his reign, with the result that when Otto III withdrew to Ravenna in 1002 he charged Henry with the duty of keeping watch over the rebellious Romans. Thietmar(1) frankly confesses that Henry refused the suggestion of some discontented elements in Saxony to join them in their revolt against Otto's policy and it was due to his refusal that the rebellion of some Saxon nobles, probably grouped round Giseler, the archbishop of Magdeburg, collapsed.

It is clear then that Henry was not opposed to Otto's imperial ideas on principle. Like many of his German contemporaries he would have been quite ready to accept them whole-heartedly if only Otto had been more successful in carrying them out, which unfortunately was not the case. The two events that checked Otto's dreams—the Roman insurrection and discontent among the Saxons—made Henry very cautious and all the more critical as he had personal knowledge of both incidents. The rebellious Romans wrested victory from Otto's grasp and his failure survived him to discredit his ideals with the coming generations. Henry was politically sensitive and shared in the general disillusionment.

At the same time, the jealous efforts of Eckehard, margrave of Meissen and after him, of Herimann, Duke of Suabia, in competing for the royal throne, coupled with the attempt by Arduin of Ivrea to proclaim himself King of Italy, were signs which Henry was not likely to misread or to forget and may have made him wary in pursuing the policy of Otto III. Not being gifted with the intellectual subtlety and the spiritual power of his Graeco-German predecessor, the practical and prosaic Henry II lacked the incentive

---

(1) Chronicon, IV, ch. 49, *M.G.H.S.* N.S. IX, p. 188. The reign of Henry II, unlike the reign of his predecessors, has failed to interest modern German historians and the fundamental study of his life and work still remains the *Jahrbücher des Deutschen Reichs unter Heinrich II*, written by Siegfr. v. Hirsch, H. Bresslau, H. Usinger and H. Pabst in 3 vol. (Leipzig, 1862, 1864 and 1874), as also W. von Giesebrecht's *Geschichte der Deutschen Kaiserzeit* (Braunschweig, 1875), vol II. The Life written by Deacon Adalbert in the XIIth century was published, by Pertz in *M.G.H.S.* IV, pp. 799 seq. The bibliographical indications in A. Pothast's *Bibliotheca Historica Medii Aevi* (Berlin, 1896), vol. II, 1363, may still be of some use. On Henry's marriage with Kunigunde, see A. Michel, "*Der Josefsche Kaiser Heinrich II*" (*Theol. Quartalschr.*, 1917) vol., 98, with more bibliographical information. On his relations with Poland : H. Zeissberg, "Die Kriege Kaiser Heinrichs II mit Herzog Boleslaw v. Polen" *Sitzungsber. Akad. Wien. Hist. Phil. Kl.*, vol. 57, 1868, and especially St. Zakrzewski, *Bolesłas the Brave, the Great* (in Polish, Lwów, 1924). The more recent works by H. Lesêtre (*Saint Henry*, Paris, 1897) and by H. Mueller (*Das Heilige Kaiserpaar Heinrich u. Kunigunde.*, Steyl, 1903) are of little use for scientific research. Equally disappointing is the publication issued to commemorate the 900th anniversary of Henry II's death ("Festschrift zum 900. Todestage Kaiser Heinrichs des Zweiten," *Heimatsblätter*, Bamberg, 1924, vol. IV).

to struggle for the realisation of ideals that hovered so high and lay so far beyond the ambit of daily life, and he lacked the enthusiasm and energy of youth to force them into a workable scheme of action.

There are documents to prove Henry's departure from Otto's imperial ideas. We know that at the beginning of his reign Henry II used a seal on which can still be read the inscription *Renovatio Regni Francorum* (Renovation of the kingdom of the Franks), which has generally been taken to stand for the programme of Henry's reign in contrast to Otto's *Renovatio Imperii Romanorum*. This reading, however, strains the implication, as Henry II could scarcely have been expected to use his predecessor's motto before his own imperial coronation. Nevertheless, the choice of this particular wording for the new Emperor's seal was suggestive of a different conception of the Roman Empire, as further demonstrated by the seal which Henry II adopted after his coronation. P. E. Schramm's fine book on German emperors in contemporary portraits enables us to draw comparisons between their respective seals[2]. Whereas Otto's seal bore the allegoric picture of Rome as it figured on ancient coins with the *Renovatio* inscription, Henry's seal was a replica of Otto's, except that instead of the allegoric representation of Rome, it had standing in the centre of the walled city of Rome, the figure of S. Peter holding two keys, and the inscription *Roma* and *S. Petrus*, a fairly clear indication that the new Emperor still regarded Rome as the centre of his Empire, but strictly viewed as a Christian Empire and a Christian Rome. All the antique reminiscences so dear to Otto had vanished.

These seals can thus be read as the symbols of the new emperor's political conceptions. Henry II was in reality sinking back from ideal heights to hard realities in his resolve to feel his feet on the soil of his Frankish-German kingdom, whilst keeping one eye turned in filial reverence towards the centre of Christendom. The incidents of his first Italian visit spoke for themselves. When he crossed the Alps for the first time as Emperor in 1004, Henry II contented himself with expelling Arduin of Ivrea, who had dared to pose as the king of Italy; and to forestall any repetition of a similar attempt, he allowed himself to be elected and crowned King of Italy in Pavia, thus setting a precedent at complete variance with the old imperial tradition[3].

When he was crowned emperor in 1014, the tradition created by Otto III was again revived and many instances can be quoted in evidence that Otto's notions were anything but dead in Rome[4] : only Henry II did nothing to lend them any prestige, contenting himself with leaving the actual power over Rome and over the Papacy in the hands of the influential family of Tusculum, whose leaders had contrived to oust the Byzantinophil Crescentii. The arrangement created an interesting *modus vivendi* : the Counts of

(2) P. E. Schramm, *Die Deutschen Kaiser und Könige in Bildern ihrer Zeit ; 751-1152* (Berlin, 1928), pp. 104 seq., Illustrations, nos. 79,80.

(3) Thietmar Chronicon VI, ch. 6, *M.G.H.S.* N.S. IX, p. 280. Cf. S. Hirsch, *Jahrbücher*, vol. I, p. 306, and A. Klippel, "Die Völkerrechtlichen Grundlagen der Deutschen Königsrechte auf Italien," *Hist. Studien* (1920), Hft. 140, pp. 21-8.

(4) P. E. Schramm, *Kaiser, Rome und Renov.*, vol. I, pp. 190 seq.

Tusculum, holders of secular and spiritual power in Rome, offered the Emperor their services in return for his indispensable backing. This situation was to endure in Rome throughout the reigns of Henry II, Conrad II and the first years of the reign of Henry III.

Henry II jettisoned Otto's ideas in other matters as well. The reader will remember how jealously the young emperor had asserted his right to keep control over the Patrimonium of S. Peter and how with the Pope's consent he inaugurated a policy calculated, if persisted in, to save Western Christendom from a conflict between the *Sacerdotium* and the *Imperium*, a conflct destined to sap its energies and especially those of Central Europe. Otto only tried to stem the tendency which could be traced within the papal Curia as far back as the end of the eighth century, and which evolved towards the substitution of the spiritual authority of the Papacy for imperial power in Italy, whether Western or Eastern. He even dared to call the notorious *Donatio Constantini* by the name it deserved and thereby cut from under the curialists' feet the best ground on which they could have erected their theories; and as he had found a powerful partner, perhaps a prompter, in the person of the Pope himself, he felt strong enough to brush aside the so-called *Privilegium Ottonis*, *i.e.* the Donation of S. Peter's *Patrimonium* made to the popes by Otto I, and assert his political supremacy over the *Patrimonium* and over the territory he personally conferred on the Pope.

This masterful assertion of imperial rights is still regarded by many historians as a kind of imperial *pronunziamento* against the established supremacy of papal power, but the diagnosis is not correct. Otto III was only returning to the old status which had existed since Constantine the Great—the real, not the legendary Constantine—and which even Charlemagne had in mind, although he failed in his lifetime to drive this policy home in Italy. The political supremacy of papal power was not yet an accomplished fact in the Ottonian period, notwithstanding the *Privilegium Ottonis*, which incidentally marked the steady progress the radical curialists had been able to make. And yet, the action of Sylvester II was evidence that all the curialists were not equally radical and that some avenues to a possible compromise between imperial and papal conceptions remained open.

Of course, Otto III's policy in Rome and in Italy was not welcome among the radical curialists who refused to accept defeat and after the death of Otto and Sylvester revived their views even within imperial circles. Henry II, who failed to realise the gravity of the stake, yielded and in 1020 confirmed the so-called *Privilegium Ottonis*. As Henry's charter did not even mention Otto III's document the curialists carried the day(5).

With Henry's successors following the precedent, this break with the past had far-reaching results, though it did not prevent succeeding emperors from trespassing on the spiritual domain in all practical matters and trying to usurp within their Empire the part that should have been the privilege of the

(5) *M.G.H. Dipl.* II, p. 427 ; *M.G.H. Const.* I, No. 33, pp. 65 seq. Cf. P. E. Schramm, *Kaiser Rom und Renovatio*, vol. I, p. 166.

Sacerdotium. In this and in other ways they copied Otto III, except that they neglected to back practice with theory and omitted to provide behaviour with a basis of thought. Otto III was at any rate consistent. Not until he had first erected his theoretical conception from its very foundation to its pinnacle and reached agreement with the representative of the Sacerdotium did Otto proceed to carry his notions into practice. There was no other possible way of realising the medieval conception of the dual role of the two powers over Christendom as embodied in the famous definitions of Gelasius and Augustine. Any retreat from the Ottonian ideology spelled concession to the rigoristic party of the Curia and strengthened its hands. It thus happened that when the clash between the Sacerdotium and the Imperium occurred in the second half of the eleventh century, the Papacy had the initial advantage, because its theorists had been given plenty of time to prepare the positions of the spiritual power. Henry II's equivocal policy was largely responsible for the handicap.

One may regret that Henry II was so unfamiliar with Otto III's system of political thought, as, appearances notwithstanding, the position was not quite as unfavourable to the growth of the imperial programme after Otto's death as has been generally believed. It must be remembered that after the final overthrow of the Crescentii, the Counts of Tusculum had been the warmest supporters of Otto's Renovatio ; and P. E. Schramm(6) in his book on the Renovatio has pointed out that in spite of Otto's setback in Rome, his notions on the renovated Roman Empire were not merely alive, but popular in Rome even under the regime of the Tusculan Counts. The two new editions of the old " List of Roman Judges "(7), composed in Rome about 870, should be dated not from the reign of Otto III, but from the beginning and the first half of the eleventh century. An even more important document—the Graphia Aurea Urbis Romae(8) — so full of reminiscences of the Roman Empire and inspired by the Renovatio of Otto III, was written in Rome not under the Emperor, but about the year 1030. Its influence was still felt by the successor of Henry II, Conrad II, the first Emperor to engrave on his seals the proud motto he had borrowed from the author of the Graphia Libellus : Roma caput mundi tenet orbis frena rotundi " (Rome, the capital of the universe, holds the reins of the whole world). For the first time in imperial history, his sceptre was adorned with the figure of an eagle, reminiscent of the legions, but revived and enjoined by the Graphia; and it was characteristic to see this Emperor, who certainly could not be accused of sentimentality, yielding to the charm of imagery that had cast its spell over his contemporaries after the reign of Otto III.

Nor could Henry II evade this influence. Thietmar(9) in his description of Henry's royal and imperial coronation, fairly accurately reflected the feeling inspired in his day by an emperor's high office and not so different

(6) loc. cit., vol. I, pp. 188 seq.

(7) Loc. cit., pp. 191 seq.

(8) The new edition of Graphia by P. E. Schramm, loc. cit., vol. II, pp. 68 seq.

(9) Chronicon V, chs. II, 16, 17, M.G.H.S. N.S. IX, pp. 234, 239 seq. ; VII, ch. I, loc. cit. p. 396. Cf. P. E. Schramm, Die Krönung in Deutschland, pp.283-90.

from the feeling once instilled and propagated by Otto III and Sylvester II, who expected an emperor to be S. Peter's advocate, the Patron and Defender of the Church. Similar notions ran through some of Henry's charters. We shall have further opportunities to examine some other contemporary witnesses showing how deeply the imperial idea, so accurately defined by Otto III, had sunk into the minds of Henry's age.

*   *   *

All this goes to show how the sudden break with Ottonian traditions, due to Henry's indolence, imperilled the imperial plans and thwarted the steady development of amicable relations between the *Imperium* and the *Sacerdotium*. Greater still was the loss resulting from this unexpected reversal in imperial policy to the relations between Germany and the Slavonic East, Poland in particular. Unfortunately we have to depend only on German writers, Thietmar and a few annalists, for information on these relations. There being no Polish contemporary sources to appeal to, the historian's task is made none the easier for the impossibility of confronting his informants.

We come across this difficulty at the very first contact between Henry II and the Duke Boleslas the Great. Thietmar(10) tells us that the Pole took advantage of the murder of the margrave Ekkehard to occupy, with the assistance of the Slavonic population, the major part of his possessions, including Lusatia, Milsko and Meissen, and this is regarded as the Duke's first opening of hostilities against the Empire. But critics overlook the fact that Ekkehard was Henry's most dangerous rival and that his suppression facilitated the Bavarian Duke's election and coronation. It is somewhat surprising to read in Thietmar's Chronicle that the Pole succeeded in allaying the apprehensions of the Saxon Counts of the territory he had seized by declaring that he had acted in connivance with the Bavarian Duke and that the final status of their country would be definitely settled after Henry's election in accordance with the new King's wishes.

This would mean that Boleslas the Great supported the Bavarian Duke's candidature—and small wonder, since the mighty margrave was the Pole's next-door neighbour, and where Poland was concerned, possessed more nuisance value than any other German duke. Thietmar reports these happenings with profound indignation, but he cannot disguise the fact that Boleslas the Great was one of the princes who greeted the new Emperor at Merseburg and that the fate of the country he had occupied was actually settled by the same Emperor. Boleslas the Great was allowed to keep Lusatia and Milsko by feudal tenure as the emperor's vassal, whereas Meissen was allotted to his relative Guncelin(11).

A comparison of all contemporary accounts points to the Polish Duke's firm intention to keep on friendly terms with the Empire, even after Otto III's death, and he actually continued to consider himself as Germany's

---

(10) Chronicon V, ch. 10. *M.G.H.S.* N.S. IX, pp. 230-2.
(11) Thietmar, Chronicon I, chs. 15-18. *M.G.H.S.* N.S. IX, pp. 236-41.

ally and a member of the Empire exactly as Otto III had visualised it. His intervention against Henry's rival was intended as a friendly act, calculated to restore order in a country the peaceful development of which served his own interests. Boleslas actually appeared at the new Emperor's court and paid homage to him, not as a vassal, but as a member of the Christian and Roman Empire, determined by his presence to strengthen the position of his ally and sincerely hoping that the " imperial status " of his country would remain as it had been defined by Otto III.

But Henry's attitude must have been a disappointment to him. No sooner did Henry II feel himself firmly in the saddle than he took his own line. Henry, the margrave of the Nordgau, who had been promised the Dukedom of Bavaria as a reward for supporting Henry's imperial candidature, was the first to be made to realise that the new Emperor was never in a hurry to honour his promises; and Boleslas must have gathered the same impression from pourparlers concerning the promised territory, although in his case the Emperor knew better than to make light of Boleslas' request. To all appearances, everything was allowed to stand as Otto III had left it, but the Pole had seen enough to suspect that in reality the Emperor had no comprehension of Otto's eastern policy.

The first disappointment over, things would probably not have moved so rapidly, but for an unfortunate incident. On leaving Merseburg, Margrave Henry and Boleslas were ambushed by a number of German knights and only escaped with their lives thanks to good swordsmanship and the assistance of Bernhard, Duke of Saxony. Even Thietmar(12), in reporting this assault, lent colour by his very protestations to contemporary public opinion which made the King responsible for the attack. Though it is impossible to unravel the plot that prepared the aggression, it is difficult completely to dismiss suspicions as to the new King's responsibility : some German knights needed very little encouragement and were sure of their reward, had they succeeded, for the King's relief would have been great.

However, nothing happened, except that as a result of the attack, Boleslas lost all confidence in the new Emperor and refused ever again to put any faith in his offers and pledges. Rightly or wrongly he took the incident as sufficient proof of the Emperor's bad faith and as an indication that he had seen the end of Otto's policy. The sequel proved disastrous. Still on his way home, Boleslas opened hostilities against the King and completed his plans to undermine his influence and domination in other ways. Relations with the Empire, or rather with this particular ruler of the Empire, were severed.

*　　　*　　　*

Fate seemed at first to favour Boleslas. Whilst his relations with Henry II were deteriorating and he himself felt released from his obligations to the new King and Emperor, the situation in Bohemia rapidly ripened for Polish intervention. The hour for which his father had been patiently

(12) Chronicon, V, ch. 18, loc. cit., p. 241.

waiting and the approach of which had been hastened by the conquest of Cracow and Silesia, was soon to strike and usher in the union of the whole Przemyslide State with Poland under the leadership of the great Piast.

Boleslas III of Bohemia (999-1002), successor to Boleslas II, proved unworthy of his father. The glory of the first Przemyslides completely flickered out during his reign. Contemporary sources, especially Thietmar(13), have much to say about his instability and cruelty. To make sure of his possession of the ducal throne, he had his brother Jaromir castrated, and attempted to murder his other brother Odalrich, but both made good their escape and, with their mother Hemma, found refuge with the Duke of Bavaria, the future Emperor Henry II. These incidents were to leave their mark on future events in Bohemia. We also read that Boleslas III got into serious trouble with his bishop Thiddag, who owed his high position to his vast knowledge of medical lore and, as a monk of Corbey, was promoted by Boleslas II to the see of Prague in acknowledgement of his skill. Cosmas(14) extols his science and piety, but Thietmar(15) paints him as a notorious drunkard and gives little credit to his medical capacity. He quotes the bishop's own opinion that nothing but heavy drinking would ever cure his illness, presumed to be chronic paralysis. But Thietmar could be fairly hard on his brothers in Christ. The bishop must have been interested in other than medical pursuits, since he was at constant loggerheads with the Duke, until he was finally, though not for the first time, driven from his see by Boleslas III. For protection, Thiddag went to Margrave Ekkehard of Meissen, who saw his chance to interfere in Bohemian affairs, restore order and reduce Boleslas III to vassalage.

This short statement by Thietmar has its importance, for it reveals a marked change for the worse in the relations between Bohemia and the Empire under Boleslas III. Until then Bohemia had been treated as part of the Empire, somewhat on the footing of a federated country. The duke was expected to attend the imperial assemblies and to contribute auxiliary troops to the emperor's military expeditions, though no reference is found anywhere to a tribute or to other obligations of a more substantial nature. The Duke succeeded to the throne without the Emperor's interference and he was the lawful ruler of his country before he rendered homage to the Emperor. Nor had he so far held his country as an imperial fief. Nothing but Boleslas III's incapacity must have given the Empire the welcome chance to tighten the bonds that united Bohemia to Germany and to treat the country not as a federated duchy but as a fief. This was a very serious matter which was to involve unexpected consequences.

Boleslas III's reckless behaviour and his blunders, alienated even the powerful aristocratic family of the Vrshovci, his erstwhile friends, and

---

(13) Chronicon V, II, chs. 23, 29, *M.G.H.S.* N.S. IX, pp. 232, 247, 253 seq. Cf. V. Novotný *Czech History* vol. I, part I, pp. 666-80.
(14) Chronica I, chs. 31, 39 ; *M.G.H.S.* N.S. II, pp. 56, 72 : This Thiddagus was a worthy successor of the saintly bishop Adalbert. He followed in his predecessor's footsteps, denounced the failings of the flock committed to him and suffered martyrdom, if not in the body, at least in mind. Nor did he die like other men, but having followed the Lord, he slept and rested in peace.
(15) Chronicon VII, ch. 56, *M.G.H.S.* N.S. IX, pp. 468-70.

successors in some respects to the Slavniks, and ended by provoking a revolution in the country. He was banished and his kinsman Vladivoj was recalled from Poland to succeed to the dukedom. Boleslas III took refuge with Margrave Henry who first treated him as a prisoner, later to surrender him to his kinsman Boleslas the Great of Poland. The election of a prince backed up by the Poles was to be the shadow which Poland's power was again casting over Bohemia. The new Duke possessed sufficient political wisdom to ask Henry II for recognition and thereby forestall further complications that might arise from the King's sponsorship of Jaromir and Odalrich, brothers of Boleslas III whom he kept in Bavaria as handy trump cards.

But the new Duke turned out to be a very poor acquisition, for he was no more capable than Boleslas III, and Thietmar(16), who had a flair for such details, reports that he could not remain sober for more than an hour at a time, which was more than even the medieval Czechs found it possible to put up with, though in matters of sobriety they were not exceptionally prudish.

He died a few months after his election, early in 1003. If the Vrshovci, the most influential aristocratic family in Bohemia, expected to secure succession to the Bohemian throne for one of their own stock, they were forestalled by their rivals who lost no time in recalling Jaromir and Odalrich from their exile in Bavaria.

This was not exactly the sequence of events as Boleslas of Poland had planned it. For him, Bohemia was an important stake which he badly needed, not only for the extension of his empire, but as a bridge to link up with the territory of Margrave Henry of Nordgau, whose alliance would be useful in the case of a clash with the Emperor. For this purpose he took advantage of Boleslas III's presence at his court as a refugee to hoist him back on a throne which he had lost so ignominiously.

But again Boleslas III proved impossible, and the only feat of the second instalment of his reign was the treacherous massacre of the most prominent Vrshovci at the Shrove Tuesday banquet of 1003. But this time, the Czechs approached Boleslas the Great directly with the request to rid them of their embarrassing duke. According to Thietmar(17) and to Cosmas(18), Boleslas the Great invited his protégé to an interview at Cracow, where the unfortunate Duke was treacherously blinded and cast into prison. A few days later, the Pole was in Prague, where he was hailed as a liberator. Only the castle of Vyshehrad, near Prague, remained loyal to the exiled Duke Jaromir and was the last stronghold to bar the way to Boleslas's warriors.

Thus, Mieszko I's plan was finally realised by his illustrious son, Boleslas I the Great, and the whole of the Przemyslide state was joined to Poland. Whereas Mieszko I annexed Cracow and Silesia, his brave son annexed Bohemia, Moravia and modern Slovakia, shifting Poland's frontiers southward to the banks of the Danube and the border of Hungary. Sobieslav, brother of S. Adalbert and the last of the Slavniks, accompanied Boleslas the

---

(16) Chronicon V, ch. 23, loc. cit., pp. 247 seq.
(17) Chronicon V, ch. 30, loc. cit., p. 255.
(18) Chronica I, ch. 34, *M.G.H.S.* N.S. II, p. 60.

Great into Prague and the fate of the Przemyslides seemed to be sealed for ever. A new phase in Poland's and Bohemia's growth to maturity was ushered in.

Echoes of Polish penetration towards the Danube are found in the *Hungaro-Polish Chronicle*, a compilation dealing with early Magyar history and particularly with the reign of Stephen I. The account is legendary to a great extent and few of its bold assertions can be verified from more reliable sources. It was written in the thirteenth century. Its authors delineate(19) the frontiers between Hungary and Poland in Stephen's time as follows :—" The lands of the Poles ended on the banks of the Danube near the town of Esztergom, whence the frontier ran to the town of Magri and the river called Tisza, and from there followed the course of the river called Topla as far as the town of Salis, to end there between the territories of the Hungarians, the Ruthenians and the Poles."

This extract from the chronicle is naturally treated with contempt by historians and, as a matter of fact, it is found sandwiched between statements that inspire anything but confidence. Still, we think it does reflect events of the early years in the eleventh century, though subsequent happenings may have obscured the tradition, since the Polono-Hungarian episode was a short-lived one.

*   *   *

This new development was naturally a heavy blow for the Emperor who must have seen the danger of letting Boleslas the Great, as master of Bohemia and ally of Henry of Nordgau, grow into a power to be reckoned with. It was high time he should secure possession of the two Przemyslides, Jaromir and Odalrich, who once again had to leave their country, though their idle presence in Bavaria was a waste of a good price to pay for the Pole's friendship. When Boleslas asked the Emperor(20) to confine Odalrich, the more dangerous of the two brothers, to prison, the Emperor was only too glad to oblige and even went so far as to signify his willingness to accept the *fait accompli* in Bohemia, if only the Duke would consent to take his country from the Emperor's hands as a fief of the Empire(21).

It is difficult to say wheter Boleslas the Great demurred to the offer and considered himself strong enough to bring the Emperor to terms, or whether he was ready to accept the offer, knowing as he did that the Emperor's claim to ascendancy over Bohemia rested on historical and juridical grounds. It is more likely that in the light of past experience he simply refused to trust Henry II(22). He might have discovered that whilst the King was despatching his message to Poland, he was in the act of securing a new powerful ally against him. Thietmar(23) reports that the Radarians, the

(19) Chronicon Hungarico-Polonicum, ch. 7. The latest edition is by Deér and is to be found in *Scriptores Rerum Hungaricarum* (Budapest, 1938), vol. II, pp. 310 seq.
(20) Cosmas, Chronica, 35, *M.G.H.S.* N.S. II, p. 63.
(21) Thietmar, Chronicon V, ch. 31, *M.G.H.S.* N.S. IX, pp. 245, 257.
(22) Cf. S. Zakrzewski, *Boleslas the Brave, the Great* (in Polish), p. 182.
(23) Chronicon V, ch. 31, loc. cit., pp. 255, 257.

most powerful tribe of the Veletian confederation, were at that moment sending an embassy to the Emperor, who of course received the envoys with unwonted friendliness.

So far, Boleslas' attitude could not be taken as aiming at complete severance of relations with the Empire. Like all his contemporaries, he was still professing his faith in the old imperial ideology and hoping that Otto's conception of the Empire and its relations with Poland, now enlarged by the recent acquisition of Bohemia, could still be saved ; only for this another emperor should have been at the head of affairs. And Boleslas had his candidate ready to do what was necessary—Margrave Henry of Nordgau, who could count on the support of some other rebel elements, including the Emperor's own brother Bruno.

It was the occupation of Bohemia by the Poles that encouraged the Margrave to hoist the flag of rebellion. But the Emperor had kept his eyes open and whilst his opponents were still busy consolidating their ranks, he marched from Saxony into Bavaria and fell upon the rebels with lightning speed and excellent effect. Boleslas, who had only sent an auxiliary corps in aid of his ally, soon received the defeated Margrave as a guest in his new Prague residence(24).

Having settled accounts with the rebels, Henry II proceeded to reconquer Bohemia; but instead of trying to seize the country by frontal attack and for his own profit, he shrewdly decided to approach it as a liberator and an avenger for the unselfish purpose of restoring the national dynasty of the Przemyslides. Accompanied by the Duke Jaromir and his brother Odalrich, he marched towards the Bohemian mountains. As Poland's grip on Bohemia was still loose and pro-Przemyslide sympathies still held the hearts of the local aristocracy, the rumour that the Czech princes were in the Emperor's train spread like wildfire among the Czech warriors who supported the Pole in defence of Bohemia, and it was this rumour which more than armed strength helped the Emperor in forcing the Bohemian passes. Taken aback by this initial success, Boleslas gave orders to evacuate Prague and withdrew with his troops in the direction of Poland. It was during the evacuation that Sobieslav, S. Adalbert's brother, the last Slavnik, was killed(25) and that the last hope for the restoration of the Slavniks under Poland vanished for ever.

Jaromir took possession not only of Vyshehrad, the garrison of which had remained loyal to him, but of Prague, where Henry II soon arrived to be received by the Duke with royal honours on September 8th. Naturally Henry took the opportunity to re-assert Bohemia's allegiance to the Empire, and at a meeting in Prague castle to hand over the country to Jaromir as an imperial fief. The worst danger to Henry had collapsed, his rival for the Empire was on the run and Bohemia was once again under Germany's masterful protection. Whilst Henry of Nordgau was in flight the margrave's friends in Prague took the first steps to bring about a reconciliation

---

(24) The main source for the history of the conflict is again Thietmar, Chronicon V, ch 32, seq. *M.G.H.S.* N.S. IX, pp. 257 seq.

(25) *Ibid.*, VI, ch. 12, p. 288.

between the Emperor and his rival, and succeeded. There only remained accounts to settle with Boleslas the Great, a task that was not so easy.

To attain his object, Henry II threw up every principle on which his predecessors had built their Empire: he concluded an alliance with the pagan Slavonic Federation of the Veletians. It was understood that the Czech Duke Jaromir would help the Emperor with his troops. As the different phases of the struggle and the military operations conducted by Henry II against Boleslas the Great have been described by Thietmar(26) and the Annals of Quedlinburg and Hildesheim(27), and as they were studied in detail in 1868 by H. Zeisberg(28), it would be superfluous to go over the same ground again. Suffice it to point to such features of this protracted struggle as are less well known.

For all the effective assistance given to the Emperor by the pagan Veletians, the results of the operations did not come up to his expectations. He did succeed in penetrating as far as Meseritz, the abbey believed to have been founded by S. Adalbert, which the Emperor had taken under his special protection, and thence to Posen; but the wily Pole, who believed in preparing his defences in depth, inflicted appalling losses on the imperial army.

Deeming the moment favourable, Boleslas offered a compromise, and the peace treaty of Posen (1005) must have disappointed the Annalist of Quedlinburg, who expected much more and called the peace " unsatisfactory " (*assumpta non bona pace*). Boleslas undertook to give up Bohemia and the territory of the Sorbian tribe of the Milzi, but kept Moravia and Slovakia together with his independence, not such a bad dénouement, considering the circumstances.

*　　*　　*

Henry's alliance with the pagan Veletians had far-reaching consequences. For one thing it broke away from the traditional notion of an emperor's position in Western Christendom and his duty to convert the pagans ; and Henry had to sanction his new allies' right to practise their religious rites freely and to carry their own pagan banners and gods in battle, a concession that puzzled and worried his contemporaries and even his own warriors. We can still see a reflection of what many a sincere Christian, even in Germany, was saying about this unheard of change of front in the writings of a great contemporary German figure, Bruno of Querfurt(29).

Bruno belonged, as already stated, to the group of enthusiastic reformers who had chosen S. Adalbert as their patron saint for being the embodiment of the two great ideals of this period, a perfect monastic life and martyrdom for Christ. The son of a Saxon count, he was born about

---

(26) In the VIth, VIIth and VIIIth Books of his Chronicle.
(27) *M.G.H.S.* III, pp. 81 seq., 92 seq.
(28) "Die Kriege Kaiser Heinrich II mit Herzog Boleslav I von Polen," *Sitzungsberichte Akad. Wien*, Hist. Philol. Kl., vol. 57. Cf. also V. Novotný, vol. I, I, loc. cit., pp. 681 seq. and Z. Zakrzewski, *Boleslas the Brave, the Great*, pp. 172-208, 252-96.
(29) A good biography of S. Bruno was written by H. G. Voigt, *Brun von Querfurt, Mönch, Eremit, Erzbischof der Heiden und Märtyrer* (Stuttgart, 1907).

the year 974 and educated in the same Saxon cultural centre as Adalbert—
in Magdeburg—where he met his young kinsman, Thietmar of Merseburg.
He then became chaplain to the Emperor, Otto III, probably in 997, the
year of Adalbert's martyrdom.   When in 998 he called, in the company
of the Emperor, at the convent of SS. Boniface and Alexius in Rome,
where Adalbert had been living, Bruno was so overwhelmed by the saint's
memory that he left the Emperor's service to join the monastery as a
monk.

Not content with the strict discipline of the monastery he, in the
year 1000, joined with some other monks the hermit Romuald of Ravenna,
who had come to Rome after his pilgrimage to Monte Cassino.   The
next year they all followed Otto III to Ravenna, in whose vicinity, i.e. at
Pereum, the Emperor undertook to build for their benefit a monastery
and a church dedicated to S. Adalbert(30).

It was there that Bruno's second ideal—missionary activity among the
pagans with possible martyrdom for Christ—came a step nearer to its
realisation.   In his biography of " The Five Brothers," Bruno reports(31)
how the Emperor intended to send to the Slavs some hermits for the purpose
of founding a monastery as a new missionary centre for the conversion of
the pagans, though Peter Damian(32) credits the initiative of the plan to
the Polish Duke Boleslas.   Bruno and two of his friends volunteered for
the mission, but Bruno first went to Rome, for the Pope's permission and
episcopal consecration, whilst the other two hermits were sent directly
to Poland to learn Slavonic and were cordially received by the Duke.

Otto III's death and the troubles that followed in Italy upset all these
plans.   Bruno did not reach Rome till the autumn of 1002, when he got
his permission from the Pope and then proceeded to Regensburg(33),
where he spent the winter.   Here Thietmar of Merseburg(34), in his short
but accurate statement on Bruno's fate, takes up and completes his
narrative to tell us that Bruno had also brought with him from Rome a
pallium, the archbishop's insignia of office, and that with the permission
of the new Emperor, Henry II, he was consecrated in Merseburg by the
new Archbishop of Magdeburg, Tagino (21st August, 1004).

This may sound strange, as one would rather expect the Pope to act
independently and consecrate the missionary bishop in Rome.   If it was
only a question of missions among the pagans, why did he refer the matter
to the Emperor ?   Only one explanation is possible—the notion common
to Otto III and Sylvester II of the co-operation between the *Imperium*
and the *Sacerdotium*.   In the scheme of things as Sylvester conceived it,
the emperor was the Protector of the Church and on him fell the obligation
of organising missions among pagans.   All important decisions concerning

---

(30) On S. Romuald, see the study by W. Franke, "Romuald von Camaldoli und seine
Reformtätigkeit zur Zeit Ottos III." *Hist. Studien* (Berlin, 1913), Heft 107 (on Pereum, pp.
222-37).

(31) Vita Quinque Fratrum, ch. 2, *M.G.H.S.* XV, ch. 2, pp. 719 (ed. R. Kade).

(32) In his Vita S. Romualdi, *P.L.*, vol. 144, col. 980, ch. 28.

(33) Vita Quinque Fratrum, loc. cit., p. 726, ch. 10.

(34) Chronicon, VI, chs. 94, 95, *M.G.H.S.* N.S. IX, pp. 386-8.

the Christian Church had to be endorsed by the emperor, whose business it was to help the pope in carrying them out and give him the necessary temporal backing.

This would explain why the Pope sent Bruno to the Emperor, but not why he sent him unconsecrated, gave him a pallium and let the Archbishop of Magdeburg do all the rest. There must have been more at stake than the mere appointment of a missionary bishop. In fact, Bruno and the late Otto III had been great friends and their friendship had something to do with the ecclesiastical organisation which both Otto and Boleslas the Great were planning for Poland. Polish sources assume the existence of two metropolitan sees in Poland under Boleslas. There is first of all Anonymus Gallus(35) who plainly states the fact. Then there is the Annuary of the Chapter of Cracow(36), which records for the years 1027 and 1028 the death of two archbishops, Ipolitus, who was succeeded by Bossuta, and Stephen. It is difficult to admit that these three archbishops could have occupied the same See of Gnesen in such a short interval. But the difficulty vanishes if the Annals of Cracow record the deaths of the incumbents of two different metropolitan sees and mention the successor in one case only. The metropolis of Gnesen seems to cover rather the western part of Poland, where all the known dioceses are situated, and this would suggest that Boleslas had planned two metropolitan sees for western and eastern Poland respectively. The prestige attached to S. Adalbert's name inclined Polish and German historians to assume that only Gnesen, where the saint's body lay buried, could be raised to metropolitan rank and made them overlook the statement by Anonymus Gallus(37). As western Poland was more thoroughly Christian, its ecclesiastical organisation could be completed in the year 1000. Eastern Poland was more of a missionary country and needed a metropolitan with a missionary temperament.

Otto III had the right candidate for this task, Bruno of Querfurt ; and Boleslas would be only too glad to accept him and possess two disciples of S. Adalbert in his kingdom. This would explain why Bruno was so keen on founding a missionary centre in Poland with the help of his friends of Ravenna, why he received the pallium and why his friends in Poland were so anxiously waiting for him in their provisional training centre at Gnesen.

Political events in Rome, Otto's death and the new Emperor's policy upset the scheme. Had Otto not died in 1002, Bruno would have been consecrated by the Pope and sent straight to Poland. But Sylvester II, not knowing Henry's attitude and policy, considered it more discreet to send Bruno to him, in the hope that Henry would honour Otto's and

---

(35) Chapter II of the first book. *M.P.H.*, I, p. 407.

(36) *M.P.H.*, II, p. 794.

(37) So far, only S. Laguna has advanced this theory in his study " The First Centuries of the Polish Church (1891, in Polish), *Kwart. Hist.*, vol. V. Recently S. Kętrzyński developed it in his work on "The Vanished Metropolis after Boleslas the Bold " (in Polish), published in 1947 by the *Historical Institute of the University of Warsaw* (vol. 1). See my review (in Polish) of the study in *Teki Historyczne* (Historical Files), London (1947), no. 2.

Boleslas' agreement. But Henry II did not and preferred to revive the scheme of Otto I who had planned to make Magdeburg the metropolis of the Slavonic lands. He therefore prevailed on Bruno to take his consecration at the hands of the incumbent of Magdeburg. Such a change of policy did not suit Boleslas who by that time had completely broken away from the Emperor. As he did not know Bruno's share in the arrangement, he proceeded with his own plan and chose a member of his own clergy to be the head of the second metropolis. This could only be Sandomierz, one of the commercial centres of White Croatia. Like Cracow, it must have benefited by the Christian influence that came from Moravia in the ninth century.

This sequence of events, though admittedly hypothetical, seems to fit best into the general historical frame and Bruno's chequered career. That is why Boleslas the Great took such a personal interest in the missionary centre which was being erected in Pereum near Ravenna. In his biography of S. Romuald(38), S. Peter Damian tells us that the saint received the gift of a fine horse from the Duke's son, who himself became the saint's disciple. He was probably a son of Boleslas by his first or second marriage which was later dissolved, and his name is not known. However that be, Romuald exchanged the horse for a donkey, declaring that when astride on this noble, though underrated, animal, he would feel more alike to Christ, who had entered Jerusalem on the back of an ass. This homely incident holds some significant information that might otherwise have been lost. Boleslas must have thought highly of that missionary centre to send his own son there. It embodied the ideas of Otto III and Sylvester II, and Boleslas must have treated it as a training ground for his own priests and for missionaries among the Balts and the Slavs.

It is a matter for regret that the two centres in Italy, Pereum and S. Alexius in Rome, failed in their purpose. The few writings that issued from them quiver with the freshness that must have pervaded the atmosphere of that period. They are inspired by the ideals for which S. Adalbert, Otto III and Sylvester II had lived, and if allowed to gather strength those centres would have left their mark on the history of Central and Eastern Europe. When S. Romuald heard later of the death of his disciple S. Bruno, he resolved to become a missionary in Hungary, the land nearest to Ravenna that needed preachers. But his health defeated his good will. S. Peter Damian(39) speaks of twenty-four disciples who offered to accompany the saint to Hungary. Bruno's example drew adepts not only from among the Italians; the Germans were equally well represented, for instance, by Gunther, a hermit, who also felt a longing for evangelising the same regions Adalbert and Bruno so loved—Hungary and the Slav basin of the Elbe. We read in the Life of S. Stephen(40) that he had some influence over Stephen of Hungary at whose court he lived for some time, and in *Annalista Saxo* (A.D. 1017) (41) that he planned to preach the Gospel

(38) Ch. 26, *P.L.*, vol. 144, col. 976.
(39) Vita S. Romualdi, ch. 39, *P.L.*, vol. 144, cols. 989 seq.
(40) *S.R.H.* II, p. 388.
(41) *M.G.H.S.* VI, p. 672 : Gunterus conversus abiit ad Liuticios causa praedicandi.

to the Veletians. According to the biographer of S. Godehard(42) his community in the Bohemian mountains was supported by the dukes of Bohemia and Poland and by the king of Hungary. But instead of becoming the apostle of the Veletians, Gunther settled down as a hermit in the Bohemian forest. Still, Gunther was one more answer to the call which S. Adalbert and S. Bruno had addressed to the Germans, especially the Saxons, urging them to great deeds in the evangelisation of their pagan neighbours. In all this, Otto III was the prime mover who found a greater response among the Germans themselves than is generally believed. It gives the lie to the pessimism prevailing among historians regarding the chances of success of Otto's political programme, if only death could have stayed its hand.

*   *   *

Bruno stood out as the best representative and boldest champion of those schemes even against Otto's successor Henry II. His *Life of the Five Brothers* is so interesting, just because it reveals how stubbornly Otto's devotees fought against endless odds to carry out their master's dreams. In the meanwhile, the two brothers Benedict and John set up another small centre where they waited for Bruno's arrival and were joined by four Poles, Antonius, Matthaeus, Isaac and the lay brother Christinus. After mastering the difficulties of the Slavonic language, Benedict worried over the uncertainty of Bruno's position and fearing for Boleslas' plans regarding the second metropolis, travelled as far as Prague(43), which at the time was in Polish hands. But Boleslas, who was busy with his war against the Emperor, feared for the Brother's personal safety and forbade him to enter Germany. Benedict returned to Poland whence he sent another monk on Bruno's trail with orders to find out if Bruno had the Pope's *licentia*, and if not, to send to Rome for it.

It looks as though the papal *licentia* meant more than an ordinary permission to preach among the pagans, which could have been granted by the metropolitan of Gnesen, and confirms the theory of a second metropolis. If Bruno is not more explicit in his account, it is because the scheme was carried out, though he himself never became archbishop of Eastern Poland.

His position was awkward. Unable to get into touch with his friends and to explain how the original plan had miscarried, he yet was under no illusion about the imperial alliance with the Veletians and the threat of war with Poland. He made a short stay in Hungary prior to his consecration, when unexpected circumstances released him from his obligation to inform his brethren of what had happened. Meanwhile, Benedict and his friends, after waiting in vain for their messenger's return,

---

(42) Wolpherii Vita Godehardi Episcopi, *M.G.H.S.* XI, p. 202, ch. 9. Cf. also Vita Gunteri Eremitae, *M.G.H.S.* VI, p. 277, a legendary account of Günther's stay at the Hungarian court.

(43) Vita Quinque Fratrum, ch. II, *M.G.H.S.* XV, pp. 727 seq.

decided to go to Rome to clear up matters. They had the good wishes of Boleslas the Great, who gave them a sum of money to speed them on their journey. The pious monks politely returned the money but some wicked men, who had heard of the gift, but not of its return, broke into their cells at dead of night and murdered the occupants (Nov. 11, 1003)(44).

Whilst waiting for his consecration after his return from Hungary, Bruno wrote his first edition of the Life of Adalbert. Then on learning that Boleslas refused to take his archbishop from Magdeburg, Bruno decided to leave for Hungary again, and during the spring·of 1005 went back to King Stephen to start missionary work in the territories governed by Achtum. They came under Stephen's suzerainty and included the lands between the Danube, the Tisza and Koros rivers and Transylvania. Achtum was a Christian of the Greek rite, but he and his subjects were only Christians of sorts. Bruno called his flock " the Black Hungarians " and never thought much of his success among them(45).

Once more could he observe at close quarters how the ideal of Christian unity was breaking up. At Stephen's court he met his name-sake, the Emperor's brother Bruno, who after his reconciliation with Henry II became bishop of Augsburg. There also he learned that the Emperor was planning to rally the pagan Veletians and the Hungarian king against the Polish duke by a new alliance. To see Christian unity disrupted by the very man who was supposed to uphold it, was too much for Bruno. But the Emperor's brother brought to the zealous missionary a message from Henry II warning him not to risk his life unnecessarily, which was probably only the King's polite way of telling him not to meddle in politics, well aware that the good prelate would do his best to interfere with the quarrelsome Christian princes.

But Bruno failed in his intervention and Stephen I joined his brother-in-law, the Emperor, against Boleslas. Disheartened, Bruno left Stephen I and went to the Duke of Kiev(46), Vladimir by name, who personally accompanied Bruno to the Lower Dnieper, where the Pechenegs(47), recent invaders of Turkish origin, had their seat. These Pechenegs were to succeed to the Khazarian empire in the south of modern Russia. An Arabian traveller, Gaihani, has described their home in the ninth century to the east of the Volga and extending from the north of the Caspian to the Aral Sea. In the second half of the ninth century they crossed the Volga and forced the Magyars, who were living there under the suzerainty of the Khazars, back towards the Dniester and the Sereth. Thus the settling of the Magyars in the Danubian basin was really due to the Pechenegs. At the request of the Bulgarian Tsar Symeon the Great (about

---

(44) *Vita Quinque Fratrum*, ch. 13, loc. cit., pp. 729-34.

(45) We gather the details of Bruno's work in Hungary and Russia from the letter sent in 1008 by Bruno to Henry II : Epistola Brunonis, *M.P.H.* I, pp. 224-8. See the German translation in Voigt, *Bruno von Querfurt*, pp. 436-45.

(46) Cf. the legendary account of Vladimir's conversion after Bruno (Bonifacius) had miraculously passed unharmed between two burning stacks of wood, as related in the Vita S. Romualdi, written by S. Peter Damian, *P.L.*, vol. 144, ch. 24, col. 977 seq.

(47) On the Pechenegs see V. J. Vasilievskii, Vizantya i Pechenezgi, *Trudy*, vol. I (St. Petersburg, 1908), and summary information in F. Lot, *Les Invasions Barbares*, pp. 108-10.

889) to lend him a hand against the Magyars who had attacked him at the instigation of the Byzantines, the Pechenegs defeated the Magyars and occupied their territory. Their neighbours and rivals, the Khazars, had their empire destroyed by the Russian Duke Svyatoslav in 965, whilst the Pechenegs made themselves the supreme masters of the steppes and cut off Kiev from the Black Sea. They were pagans and fire worshippers until Islam secured a footing among them in the tenth century, This, however, failed to soften their wild and fierce habits or stop them fighting the Russians. It was among these barbarians that Bruno decided to try his chances in spite of the duke's urgent appeal not to expose his life to certain death. The bishop did indeed have some narrow escapes, but he survived them and even registered some successes, of which the most outstanding was the restoration of peace between the Duke of Kiev and the fierce nomads. He consecrated a bishop to carry on his work among them.

But conversions among the Pechenegs so well begun failed to satisfy Bruno, whose mind was still haunted by his first ambition to go to Poland and evangelise Poland's neighbours, the Prussians and the Veletians. So he left Kiev and on arrival in Poland during the year 1007(48), explained to Boleslas what had happened and cleared past misunderstandings. The Emperor did not approve the bishop's co-operation with Boleslas ; and Bruno learned with whom the Emperor was then at war, and that Henry had spoken in that sense to his friends. Bruno then wrote him a letter to explain his attitude and to make a new effort to reconcile the Emperor with the Duke.

This letter reveals the utter consternation which the Emperor's change of front had provoked among the reformists of Otto's and Adalbert's school of thought; and as it affords the best illustration of the political programme advocated by Otto III and his followers, a few extracts will not be amiss. After expressing his gratitude to the Emperor for his solicitude concerning the writer's welfare, as conveyed to him by the Emperor's brother, bishop of Augsburg and ambassador in Hungary, Bruno reports at length on his missionary activities in Hungary and among the Pechenegs, obviously dilating on his performance, because he still looked upon the Emperor as the supreme head of Christendom and the protector of the Church, whose function it was to support and encourage every missionary activity and whose right it was to be informed of every endeavour in that line.

After this report, Bruno comes to the most ticklish point—his relations with Boleslas and his plan to work among the pagans with the Duke's assistance, the subject that had worried the Emperor and provoked his criticisms(49) : " If anybody states that I am harbouring fidelity to, and friendship for, this Prince, he is telling no more than the truth, for I love him as my own soul and more than my own life. But I appeal to our

---

(48) The dating of Bruno's stay in Kiev and in Poland given by H. Voigt (*Bruno von Querfurt*, pp. 95-125) needs to be revised. Cf. St. Kętrzyński, *The Vanished Metropolis*, p. 40.
(49) *M.P.H* I,. pp. 226 seq.: Voigt's translation, loc. cit., pp. 440 seq.

common God as the unimpeachable witness from whom nothing is hidden to testify that I do not love him in opposition to you, because I am only trying to do my best endeavour to rally him to your cause. But I hope I shall not forego your gracious feelings towards me if I take the liberty to state as follows : Is it right to persecute a Christian nation and to admit a pagan nation to friendship ? How can Christ truck with Belial ? How can we compare light with darkness ? How can Zuarasiz [the Veletians' supreme God] or the devil compound with the Duke of the saints, yours and our Mauritius ? How can the Holy Spear [of S. Mauritius] and the devilish, blood-soaked military standard be borne aloft together ? Do you not consider it a sin, O King, that the head of a Christian—dreadful thought—should be sacrificed under Satan's banner ? Would it not be far better for you to earn the loyalty of a man with whose aid and counsel you could levy tribute from a pagan nation and turn it into a saintly and godly people ? Oh, how I would love to find a faithful follower and not a foe in the Duke Boleslas, for of him am I speaking. Is it not better to fight the pagans for the benefit of Christendom than to wrong Christians for wordly honours ? Man thinks and God leads ; but has the King, for all the imperial forces he had, not entered this land with pagans and Christians ? What then has happened ? Have not S. Peter, whose tributary he claims to be, and S. Adalbert taken up his defence ? And if they refused their help, then the five martyr saints, who shed their blood and worked so many miracles to reveal God's dreadful greatness, would never have rested in this country. . . ."

After urging the King to show mercy and to remember that gentleness conquers more nations than force, Bruno continues : " Two great calamities are befalling the new Church which God and Peter the warrior have started building among the pagans, and the first is this : Duke Boleslas, who had undertaken to give me material and spiritual help for the conversion of the Prussians and decided to spare no money to gain this object, is now prevented from spending any time and resources on the preaching of the Gospel by a war that is forced on him by a wise King ; and the second is that as long as the Veletians are pagans and worshippers of heathen gods, God cannot plant in the King's heart a desire to fight these heathens with any glory and to benefit Christianity by their forced conversion in obedience to the Gospel's precept (Luke XIV, 23). Would it not be more honourable and salutary to yourself to promote the growth of the Church, to work for the baptism of the heathen, thereby deserving in the eyes of God the title of apostle and to leave in peace a Christian [prince] who is offering you his help ?

" But the root of the mischief lies in the fact that neither has the King any confidence in Boleslas, nor the latter in an angry King. After the saintly Emperor Constantine the Great and Charles [Charlemagne], both patterns of virtue, somebody can be found to persecute Christians, but hardly anybody to convert the pagans. Therefore, O King, if you will give peace to the Christians and give them time to conquer the pagans to

Christianity, you will find favour at the Last Judgment . . . The King has no reason to fear lest any man of religion [*i.e.* Boleslas] could ever make an alliance with pagans on any provocation. Only, you must not expect the impossible. At the same time, Boleslas is giving, as our King wishes, every assurance that he will never desert you, but will always zealously assist you in the conversion of the pagans and pledge his loyal service in all things. Think of the benefit that will accrue to you from your joint co-operation in the defence of Christendom and the conversion of the pagans if, as his father Mieszko and the late Emperor, so also the son Boleslas and you, our King, who are left to us as the last hope of the world, would live in concord.''

These eloquent words make it clear how deeply the Ottonian ideals had penetrated into the hearts of Henry's contemporaries and that even the Polish Duke Boleslas took his stand upon them. The same letter also proves that the Duke would never have fallen out with the Emperor had it not been for Henry's backsliding from his predecessor's ideals. Had he but followed them, the fate of Eastern and Central Europe might have taken a different course and Henry would have rallied the best minds of his age to his side.

We shall presently have occasion to see that the policy of collaboration with Poland in the conversion of the Veletians had the support of many followers, even outside the reformist circles, and among the German ecclesiastics and nobles, not excepting Saxony.

*   *   *

Hostilities between the Poles and the Emperor re-opened in 1007. It is fairly certain that Boleslas tried the political weapon by attempting to detach the whole Slavonic world from Henry's Germany and to bribe some of the lesser tribes. He almost succeeded with the Czech Duke Jaromir. The Czech Duke, who remembered that the struggle between Bohemia and Poland was at bottom only a feud between two dynasties, and that his own position was far less secure than the Pole's, mistrusted Boleslas. We must also remember that Jaromir had been mutilated by his brother Boleslas III and that his other brother Odalrich had no legitimate heirs. This left the way open to a fusion of Bohemia and Poland under the Piast dynasty.

The Veletians distrusted Boleslas even more than did the Czechs, and at least for the time being, their alliance with the Empire suited their book better. According to Thietmar(50) the whole plan was disclosed to Henry II by special Veletian and Czech envoys. Asked for an explanation and threatened with a new invasion, Boleslas had but one reply to give—a brisk attack on the Slavonic lands along the Elbe and a second occupation of Lusatia. The Duke was successful, and the King's retaliation, especially in 1010, was disappointing, whilst a second expedition against the Pole, first planned for 1012 then postponed till 1013, never came to anything, as

(50) Chronicon, VI, ch. 33, *M.G.H.S.* N.S. IX, pp. 313 seq. Cf. Novotný, loc. cit., vol. I, I, pp. 697 seq. ; St. Zakrzewski, loc. cit., pp. 252 seq.

Boleslas, who needed a free hand in the West to deal with Kiev, offered his own peace terms. Henry accepted the offer gladly, leaving Boleslas all the territory he had wrested from Germany on the condition of holding it as a fief of the Empire.

The war with Poland was apparently not popular in Germany, for we learn from Thietmar(51) that in 1012 the Bavarians sent an embassy, loaded with presents, to Boleslas, for reasons unknown, but certainly not in accordance with the King's wishes. As the Czech Duke Jaromir, through whose territory the Bavarian envoys travelled, guessed as much, he captured and massacred them to a man. But the exploit, though done to please the King, cost him dearly. When he was dethroned by his younger brother Odalrich and applied to Germany for help, the King, displeased at this encroachment on his rights to judge the Empire's citizens and probably anxious to discover the exact purpose of the embassy and its senders, kept Jaromir a prisoner and sanctioned the usurpation of the Bohemian throne by Odalrich. At the same time we learn again from the irate Thietmar(52) that the chronicler's own nephew, Wirinhar, and Ekkehard, brother of the margrave Herriman of Meissen, had also opened unlawful negotiations with the Polish Duke.

Another instance of Saxon sympathies with Boleslas is even more telling. Still clinging to his old idea of detaching the Slavs from Germany and incorporating them into his dominions by friendly negotiations, Boleslas, in 1014, sent his son Mieszko to the new Czech Duke Odalrich, asking him to sever relations with Germany and to form with the Poles an alliance against their common enemies, especially against Henry II. But again dynastic difficulties came in between to upset his plans. Odalrich had already a grown-up son of a woman whom he had come upon in one of his forest hunts. Cosmas(53) dwells with relish on this romance, little as it squared with existing ecclesiastical laws, and he contributed to its survival and popularity in Bohemia, where sentimental pictures are still popular showing the prince in admiration before the beauty of his Bozena as she stands in the prosaic garb of a washerwoman and bends over a brook in the act of rinsing her husband's laundry. The relationship was apparently regularised later and the position of the dynasty straightened out.

Odalrich not only refused the Pole's offer, but secretly instructed his knights to seize the Pole's son on his homeward journey. This was not exactly chivalrous, but that did not prevent the Emperor from claiming the prisoner and holding him as a hostage while bargaining with his foe, Boleslas of Poland. Strange to say, we read in Thietmar's Chronicle(54) that the Saxon nobles, following the lead of the new archbishop of Magdeburg, Gero, insisted on Mieszko's release and on his return to his father. The Emperor had no option but to give in.

The incident is significant, because Henry had at first intended to follow

---

(51) Chronicon, VI, ch. 83, loc. cit., pp. 272 seq.
(52) Chronicon, VI, ch. 90, loc. cit., p. 382.
(53) Chronica, I, ch. 36, M.G.H.S. N.S. p. 65.
(54) Chronicon, VII, chs. 10-12, M.G.H.S. N.S. IX, pp. 408-12.

a different line of action, going so far as to promise the Czech Duke help and support, should the Pole retaliate for the treacherous capture of his son and for his extradition to the German King. The Saxon nobility's insistence on Mieszko's release was not merely due, as Thietmar insinuates, to the soothing effect of Polish money; it rather proves that the great majority of the Saxon counts still preferred a peaceful settlement with the Pole and desired his collaboration in subduing and christianising the pagan Veletians(55).

The outcome of the war which flared up between Henry and Boleslas in 1015 was to prove that Gero and the Saxon nobles had been well inspired and that Germany would probably have fared better for a more faithful compliance with the Ottonian policy in the East. The German expedition was well planned. The Germans, reinforced by Veletian and Czech contingents, poured into Poland in three columns, the main army under the Emperor penetrating deep into enemy country well beyond the Oder. But Boleslas, who had again prepared his defences in depth, let the Emperor march in, whilst he concentrated all his efforts on the Saxons and the Veletians and by skilful manoeuvring prevented them from joining up with Henry. At the same time, a lightning attack from Moravia, still in Polish hands, kept the third southern army of the Bavarians too busy to join hands with the Germans. All they could do was to recover part of the rich booty which the Poles were carrying home. Only the Czech Duke Odalrich could report some success, when he attacked the Poles in Moravia and took a fortified locality, which Thietmar(56) calls Businc.

The place has not yet been identified, some suggesting Bzenec in South Moravia, and more recently, W. Semkowicz(57) proposing Pezinek near Bratislava as the more likely place. The detail has its importance as this is one of the rare instances to prove that in 1015 the Poles had still a grip, if not on Slovakia, at least on Moravia. Since the Czechs were on this occasion co-operating with the Bavarians, who supported them from the south, we must locate these operations somewhere near the Danube, very probably near, if not in, Bratislava. The name is mentioned for the first time by the newly discovered Annals of Salzburg(58) in 907 as Brezalauspurc, probably so called after its founder and first commander, either a Czech or a Slovak; but very early documents also call it Poznan-Pozon, which the Magyars transformed into Pozsony. However that be, the Czech Duke's side-show was of little use to the Emperor, who on realising his failure in welding his three armies into common action, preferred to fall back, suffering severe losses in the process. The young Mieszko distinguished himself during these operations.

---

(55) On this matter cf. H. Zeissberg, " Die Oeffentliche Meinung im XI Jh. über Deutschlands Politik gegen Polen," *Zeitschrift f. Oester. Gymnasien* (1868), vol. XIX, pp. 83-100.

(56) Chronicon, VII, ch. 19, loc. cit., p. 420 ; *ibid.*, VII, chs. 16-25, loc. cit., pp. 416-28, for detailed information about the expedition.

(57) " Geographical foundations of Poland under Boleslas the Great " (in Polish), *Kwart. Hist.* (1925), vol. XXXIX, p. 294.

(58) *M.G.H.S.* XXX, 2, p. 742 : Bellum pessimum fuit ad Brezalauspurc IV nonas Julii. Cf. J. Janko, " On the origin of the name of Bratislava " (in Czech), *Czech Hist. Rev.* (1927), vol. XXXIII, pp. 347-51.

Pourparlers for a peace settlement having come to nothing, Boleslas again opened hostilities in 1017 by an attack on Bavaria and Bohemia. This time the imperial armies came to a dead stop before the important Silesian fortress of Nimpsch (Nemzi) (59), which they besieged in vain, and as Boleslas had cut off their retreat towards the north-east, the Emperor was forced to find his way back to Germany via Bohemia, the country that suffered most in the course of these operations. Exhausted by his campaign, the Emperor was naturally more amenable to negotiation, but again Boleslas gave evidence of sound statesmanship by being the first, although virtually the victor, to submit terms for reconciliation. The offer (not a supplication, as Thietmar(60) has it)—could hardly be rejected, as the whole Polonophil '' party among the Germans '' urged the Emperor to make a virtue of necessity. Gero, Archbishop of Magdeburg, was found to be among the most zealous peacemakers and his opinion meant a great deal among the foremost ecclesiastical princes and nobles; and as he accompanied his master on these expeditions with his own men and realised the hopeless position he had got into, it was not to be expected that an ecclesiastical counsellor would not make the Emperor feel that such a fiasco would never have happened had Henry but listened to his archbishop's advice not to fight a Christian prince. This was the archbishop's peace, and Berno(61), the Abbot of Reichenau, another keen supporter of the peace proposals, praised him in his letter of congratulations as the ideal peacemaker.

All this goes to show how unpopular the change of Henry's eastern policy was among German ecclesiastical dignitaries and many nobles. It is therefore not right to speak of an insignificant minority and to take for granted that Thietmar's attitude to the Emperor and his policy was that adopted by the overwhelming majority of the German higher clergy and the nobility. Not even Thietmar could minimise the strength of the opposition which, for all its loyalty to the Emperor, more than once gave vent to its feelings in the course of those tiresome campaigns. But then, those critics did not reap such valuable rewards for their plans as did the learned chronicler, who was promoted to the See of Merseburg. It is true that episcopal sees on the eastern borders were not much of a gift—once the Veletians were German allies, their religion had to be respected and all missionary activity had come to a dead stop. It appears that from intercourse with their neighbours only the Christians learned something of the heathen gods and the Veletian rites(62), whereas the heathens carefully avoided every opportunity of learning anything about the German God. The bishops of Brandenburg and Havelberg looked with dismay in the direction of the east, where their dioceses lay and where they probably were never allowed to set foot.

(59) Thietmar, Chronicon, VII, ch. 59, loc. cit., p. 472.

(60) Chronicon, VIII, ch. I, loc. cit., p. 492.

(61) Bernonis Abbatis Augiensis Epistolae, *P.L.*, vol. 142, cols. 1159 seq.

(62) We owe to Thietmar, Chronicon, VI, chs. 23-25, loc. cit., pp. 302-4, a very important description of Veletian paganism. On the religion of the western Slavs, cf. the recent publication by E. Wienecke, '' Untersuchungen zur Religion der Westslaven,'' *Forschungen zur Vor- und Frühgeschichte,''* Heft. I, Leipzig, 1940.

Not only was the christianisation of the pagan Slavs made impossible as a result of this policy, but the converted Slavs were thereby exposed to attacks and persecution at the hands of their own pagan countrymen. Mistislav, the prince of the Slavonic Obodrites, whose seat was on the Baltic in modern Mecklenburg-Schwerin, was a Christian and naturally disliked the alliance with the Veletians. As he refused to join them with his own contingents, they invaded his country directly after the campaign, in the early spring of 1018 (63) and with the help of the local pagans forced him to flee and take refuge behind the walls of Schwerin. The bishop of Oldenburg, on hearing what had happened in his own diocese, was horror-stricken and reported the matter to the Emperor. Even Thietmar (64) could not tell the facts without deploring them and expressing the wish that the Emperor would, with God's help, come to a decision as he had promised to do at the Easter session of the Reichstag; but as he fails to tell us how the Emperor settled this humiliating affair, we must assume that Thietmar closed his chronicle before Easter, 1018, immediately after peace was signed in Budyshin (Bautzen) on February 3 of the same year.

The terms of the settlement justified the unwillingness of many nobles to have anything to do with the Emperor's new policy and Thietmar (65) had to confess that the peace was not what it should have been, only " as good as it could be under the circumstances." We are not told what the conditions were, but Thietmar's reticence and the annalists' discretion speak volumes to Boleslas' advantage.

As it is mentioned nowhere whether the Pole kept the conquered territories Lusace and Meissen as a fief of the Empire, we may at least presume that he achieved his main purpose—complete independence. It was the last bond of Poland's political dependence on the Empire that was dropped and thenceforth the Emperor, who refused Boleslas' alliance and help in subduing and christianising the pagan lands in the east, ceased to be in his eyes the venerable head of Western Christendom, to remain only a foreign monarch who in contests with Polish arms had repeatedly got the worst of it. In his second object, the union of all Western Slavs under his leadership, Boleslas found himself baulked; the Veletians preferred their alliance with the Germans, a strange instance of stubbornness and jealousy of a kindred nation, while the Czechs preferred their own private and local interests as embodied in their national dynasty; they refused to sacrifice it for the benefit of an alliance with a sister nation, though at this time the two neighbours spoke almost the same language. The Czechs did not see much in a Western Slavonic empire and Boleslas did too little to enlighten them. His policy in Bohemia, especially towards the Przemyslides, sometimes lacked subtlety and sometimes determination, which in the end proved fatal to his best laid schemes.

And yet we must admit that on the whole the Pole was far-seeing in his conceptions. Even if one chooses to be cautious and hesitates to

(63) Thietmar, Chronicon, VIII, ch. 5, loc. cit., p. 498.
(64) Chronicon, VIII, chs. 5, 6, loc. cit., pp. 498 seq.
(65) Chronicon, VIII, ch. 1, loc. cit., p. 492.

believe that Boleslas had any intention of building an empire comprising all the Western Slavonic tribes; if one feels inclined to see in his conquests only the design of creating around Poland a ring of border territories, of marches for the protection of Polish lands proper(66), one is led to conclude that even from such beginnings, in due course a Slavonic State was due to develop, the existence of which would have radically altered conditions in Central Europe. But though a system of marches on the German model might have seemed adequate to a Polish monarch of this time, it appears that Boleslas' ambition was loftier and worthy of his father Mieszko I who, acting according to his plan, steadily expanded his influence over all Polish tribes first and then over kindred Slavonic peoples.

Boleslas was the only prince to command all the conditions necessary for success. Statesman that he was, moreover faithful to Ottonian ideals in imperial and ecclesiastical affairs, it was easy for him to rally the sympathies of many German Church dignitaries and Saxon princes. As he still piously professed the necessity for all Christian princes to propagate the Gospel among the pagans, he won the support of the reformist party; and as he humbly declared his realm to belong to S. Peter and faithfully paid(67) his tribute to the Roman See (a very important consideration), he had all the necessary backing from the Papacy. Boleslas thus, in the estimation of many, slowly and almost imperceptibly took over the part that so far, according to general belief, could only be played by the emperor in Eastern Europe.

All this happened for no other reason but that Henry II had thrown up the Ottonian scheme of Empire. In doing so he only proved his practical and realistic temperament, guiding Germany along paths more appropriate to its immediate interests, whereas Otto III's policy let the Poles and the Hungarians slip away from the German grasp for the benefit of the Poles, Germany's foremost enemy. The view that has prevailed so far among German historians credits Henry II with having restored Germany's prestige in the East, blocked Polish advance towards the Elbe, prevented the formation of a big Slavonic empire on Germany's flanks and preserved her sacred right to expand eastward.

To-day we know better. Henry did not restore Germany's prestige in the East. He was on several occasions and despite his alliance with the fierce pagan Veletians, soundly beaten by the Poles. Poland broke off relations with the German-Roman Empire and German prestige deteriorated in proportion even among the subjugated Slavs on the Baltic, and among Germany's recent allies, the pagan Veletians, while the Slavonic East, recently christianised and deferential to the Christian imperial idea, was only puzzled by the sudden change of front of an Emperor so far regarded as the supreme secular head of Christendom.

Nor did Henry stop Polish expansion towards the Elbe. It remains

---

(66) Such is the opinion of W. Semkowicz, *Geographical Foundations* (in Polish), pp. 258-314. An interesting view, but his arguments are not convincing.

(67) On the growth of the Peter's Pence, see E. Maschke, "Der Peterspfennig in Polen und der Deutsche Osten," *Königsberger Hist. Forschungen*, (Leipzig, 1903), Bd. 5.

true, however, that Henry's policy did prevent the growth of a strong Slavonic State in the East, and German historians who praise him for it, view it only on the strength of the subsequent hostility that arose between the Germans and the Slavs. Boleslas' own attitude, the Saxons' sympathy and the Czech's friendliness proved that this new political centre was no threat to Germany.

We shall see in the last chapter what benefit the whole of Europe might have derived from such a centre had it been able to mediate between the culture of Byzantium, which found its channel through Russia of Kiev, and the Latin West. Germany would have been the first to benefit by such a process. At the same time, the Slavs were only too glad to adopt many German institutions and benefit by the German genius of organisation.

These prospects were ruined by Henry II when to the disappointment of many contemporary Germans, he jettisoned Otto III's views. Instead of a peaceful coming to manhood taking place, wars of conquest marred the relations between Germany and Poland and became a familiar feature of their history. The Germans prospered on their annexations. The Slavonic lands between the Elbe and the Oder and beyond were destined to become the new Germania which in the distant future was to subjugate the old Germania. If this is a great achievement, one need not wonder that German historians should be all praise for Henry II for embarking on a policy that has ruled centuries of German history. To-day we see which course would have been more beneficial to the German people, the policy inaugurated by Otto III, or its reversal by Henry II.

We must admit that Henry's decision exercised a paramount influence upon the subsequent growth of the imperial idea. Henry claimed that his own programme was the same as that drawn up by Otto III and Sylvester II; and he and his successors took good care to vindicate all the rights which the theory implied. But in practice they dealt it a blow from which it never recovered. Because of their ambiguous policy, the interests of Germany and of the Empire often, as in Henry II's time, proved to be mutually contradictory. This accounts for the lack of precision on the part of the imperial legists in defining the respective rights of the emperor and of the Church, whilst the theorists of the Curia were steadily elaborating the theory of the supremacy of the *Sacerdotium* over the *Imperium*. This prepared the fatal clash between the two the seed of which was sown at this period. It decided the fate of the two powers and ruined the ideals that had inspired medieval man ever since he was able to read S. Augustine's *De Civitate Dei*.

However, Henry's failure to see where his decision was leading the German nation and Central Europe does not belittle his personal moral integrity, though he has admittedly supplied the material for many legends, his beloved Bambergers being responsible for most of them. Overflowing with gratitude for an emperor who had spent his personal fortune on the magnificent cathedral he built in their city and on the episcopal see he had founded, they obtained his canonisation in 1152, an honour his private life certainly justified. But the biography of Henry II, written in 1170-1184 by a Bamberger, the monk Adalbert(68), is a legend which is in no way true to the real Henry as history knows him. The monks of his day did not like him, not so much for his attempts to reform them, as for the practical consequences of his reforms that did not suit them; the resources which their austere living had saved, were requisitioned for equipping an imperial army mostly recruited from among men who lived on lands belonging to monasteries and bishops(69). Some of the monks certainly overdid somewhat their dislike of the holy man and spread with no little satisfaction the sensational news that the devil had seized hold of the Emperor after his death. Even Thietmar disapproved of some of the Emperor's reforms.

It is, in any case, very strange that the supreme honour which was conferred on Henry II should have been denied to his predecessor Otto III, for there is no doubt that the young Emperor in many ways deserved the same distinction as his cousin. If there was anything that was not in absolute harmony with Christian principles in his personal behaviour—his ruthless severity in punishing rebels and the deposed anti-pope Philagathos, or his love affair with a Roman lady(70), doubtful as such gossipy rumours usually are—Otto III nevertheless did all he could to make amends for whatever he did by severe penance and the humble confession that he was but a weak human being. But posterity has been more lenient towards Henry, who also gave evidence that he was but a very imperfect man. Though comparisons may be odious, Otto III was far more inspiring, more imbued with the medieval Christian ideal, more anxious to promote the Christian faith and to reform the Church than his canonised kinsman, and he was gifted, as far as one can judge, with deeper religious feelings than his more realistic and practical-minded successor. There was about Otto a certain dramatic greatness, and his tragic and exemplary death (one cannot read the account of his last moments by Bruno in his *Life of the Five Brothers*(71) without emotion) offered a strong appeal to human feeling. Strange irony of fate that the medieval Church should not have adopted among her heroes the idealist(72) who understood the aspirations of the medieval Christian so well and tried so hard to realise them.

The explanation may lie in the fate that befell Otto's ideas. When subsequent developments took an unexpected course, and the two powers—

(68) Published by G. Waitz in *M.G.H.S.* IV, pp. 792 seq. and followed on pp. 821-8 by the *Vita S. Cunegundis*. Cf. Ibid., pp. 787 seq., the remarks by the editor on Henry's canonisation and on Adalbert. The other *Vita S. Henrici*, written by Bishop Adalboldus, about 1024, only covers the period till 1004. (Ibid., IV, pp. 679-95.) On Henry's marriage with Kunigunde see A. Michel, "Der Josefsche Kaiser Heinrich II", *Theol. Quartalschrift*(1916), vol. XCVIII, pp. 463-7. As may be concluded from Cardinal Humbert's "Liber III adversus Simoniacos" (*M.G.H.* Libelli de Lite, I, p. 217) nothing was known in Rome in the middle of the XIth century of the legend that Henry II and his wife were living as brother and sister. The cardinal merely attributes Henry's childless marriage to divine punishment for Henry's sinful exploitation of the Church. Cf. also S. Hirsch, *Jahrbücher*, vol. II, pp. 358-70 : Einige Bemerkungen über die Sagen von Heinrich II.

(69) Cf. what J. Haller (*Das altdeutsche Kaisertum*, Stuttgart, 1934, p. 39) has to say about Henry II.

(70) Cf. P. E. Schramm, *Kaiser, Rom und Renovatio*, vol. I, pp. 107 seq.

(71) *M.G.H.S.* XV, ch. 7, pp. 712-24.

(72) Cf. K. Hampe, "Kaiser Otto III und Rom," *Hist. Zeitschr* (1929), vol. CXL, p. 533.

the secular and spiritual—had imperceptibly drifted apart, Otto's notions must have sounded fantastic, whilst Sylvester's share in their formation must have been forgotten. How far Otto's and Sylvester's ideas were able to be fulfilled, is another question for which history has no answer; but they were lofty and generous and a perfect expression of the Christian conceptions such as the Middle Ages had crystallised them.

*　　*　　*

Henry II did not live to witness the last act of the estrangement between Poland and Germany, to which his policy had contributed so much. It was only shortly after his death that the severance of Poland from the Empire was sealed, when Boleslas I started using the royal title. It appears that he had been manoeuvring for this step for some time, for we read in the *Life of S. Romuald*, written by S. Peter Damian(73), that as early as 1005 Boleslas asked the Holy Brothers, as they made ready to start for Rome, to act as his envoys and to induce the Pope to send him a royal crown. This report ante-dates an event which actually happened much later, a detail which escaped the contemporary biographer of the Five Brothers, S. Bruno. It will be remembered that Boleslas' feelings towards the Empire evolved only slowly and gradually and that at the outset of Henry's reign it had never been his intention to sever relations with the Empire, least of all in the course of his first war, which was more like a bid for another emperor.

Henry must have been suspicious of Boleslas' relations with Rome. We have seen how Boleslas kept up contact with the reformist centres in Rome and Ravenna (one of his sons was a disciple of S. Romuald), and Peter Damian states (74) that the Emperor had issued orders to guard every road from Poland to Rome, with the result that an innocent traveller, the monk sent by Brother Benedict to look for Bruno, was arrested. On learning, after his return to Poland, of the tragic fate that befell his brothers, Bruno returned to Rome to further their canonisation.

It is impossible to say what Bruno's position in Poland was. It being generally believed that S. Bruno intended to start from Poland on his mission to the Prussians, many historians overlooked a significant eleventh-century account of his martyrdom. This narrative states that before leaving for Prussia, Bruno left his diocese and his flock(75). This would accord with the theory of a second metropolis for Eastern Poland for which Bruno was the candidate appointed by Otto III and Boleslas the Great. Because that metropolitan see was given to a native candidate, Bruno accepted a diocese created for him, probably in the country of the Polish Kuyavians or Mazovians, next-door neighbours to the Prussians. They would have been Bruno's next best objective, keen as he was on following Adalbert's footsteps in the Prussian mission(76). He opened his mission among the Prussians

(73) Ch. 28, *P.L.*, vol. 144, cols. 979 seq.
(74) Vita S. Romualdi, ch. 29, *P.L.*, vol. 144, col. 981.
(75) Historia de Praedicatione Episcopi Brunonis, *M.P.H.* I, pp. 229 seq. : Dimisso episcopatu una cum grege sibi credito. This short legend seems to be based on the writings of Wibert, a contemporary of S. Bruno.
(76) See S. Kętrzyński, *The Vanished Metropolis*, p. 40, and my review of this study in *Teki Historyczne* (1947), No. 2 (in Polish).

in 1009, but like S. Adalbert met a martyr's death after a promising start.

It was a pity that Bruno was not given time. As may be gathered from the report on his Kiev mission in his letter to Henry II, he had made his missionary plans on a generous scale, drawing into the scheme Prussians, Veletians and Swedes, *i.e.* the nations that mattered most along the Baltic Sea. His interest in Sweden is surprising. He must have learned about that country during his stay in Kiev where contacts with Sweden were still frequent. Bruno intended to win over that country to the faith, for he stated in his letter to Henry II(77) that he had already sent to the Swedish rulers one of his disciples whom he had consecrated bishop, together with the monk Rodbert. This mission was probably sent direct from Kiev.

According to Bruno the bishop succeeded in baptising the Swedish king, whose wife was already a Christian, and part of the population, and Bruno promised the Emperor to keep him informed of any further progress· Bruno's biographer, H. J. Voigt(78) is of opinion that the king mentioned could be none but the famous Olaf Skotkonung (995-1024) and that Bruno's mission to Sweden preceded the Anglo-Saxon mission headed by the second apostle of the north, Siegfried.

Poland proved an excellent choice as the centre for all these undertakings, as the Poles also were in constant touch with the Scandinavians. In this Boleslas only followed the policy of his father Mieszko I, and his friendship with Canute the Great, one of the most powerful rulers of the north, was no more than a shrewd bit of political foresight, as it insured him against attack in the rear during his struggle with the Emperor.

Though Bruno in his letter still acknowledges the Emperor's right, as the secular head of the Church, to be informed of all missionary enterprises, especially in the east and in the north, he nevertheless selected Poland as a jumping-off ground for his missionary expeditions. Did he expect to see the Emperor neglecting his duty and hampering all missionary work ? And did he read the signs of how things in the east and the north were gradually slipping from the Emperor's control to be gathered up by the Duke of Poland ?

* * *

The Slavonic country that suffered most in the end from the rivalry between Poland and the Empire was Bohemia. As the Przemyslide dominion had been broken up, the successors of Boleslas I had to content themselves with what was left, Bohemia; and their dependence on Germany hampered and sometimes humiliated them, creating a position, the danger of which the Bohemians were to feel for centuries. The Czechs fought on the side of the Emperor, but that did not help them to recover their lost territories. There is still some uncertainty as to the date when Moravia was retaken by the Czechs and once again joined to Bohemia; all we know is that in 1017 the Moravians were fighting the Czechs side by side with the Poles(79), one

---

(77) *M.P.H.* I, p. 228. H. J. Voigt's German translation (*Bruno von Querfurt*, p. 443).
(78) Loc. cit., p. 288.
(79) Thietmar, Chronicon, VII, ch. 61, loc. cit., p. 474.

more indication of how easy it must have been for the Poles to enlist the services of a kindred Christian Slavonic tribe and involve it in their own policies. Other indications would go to show that Moravia again belonged to Bohemia after 1021(80). It does not seem likely that this change came about in 1018 as a clause in the treaty of Budyshin, since the Moravians had been fighting the Czechs only the year before. The expedition of Odalrich's son, Brzetislav, into Moravia must have been in the nature of a raid rather than an occupation and the peace he concluded could hardly benefit the Czechs. The only document to date the recovery of Moravia before 1021, the Chronicle of Cosmas(81), is generally discredited, and as long as we cannot come by any new materials, we must hold to established tradition and date the re-conquest of Moravia after 1018 and before 1030.

There is also a doubt hanging over the relations between Poland and Hungary during Boleslas' reign. It will be remembered that Henry II was the brother-in-law of the Hungarian King Stephen I; and as we have seen, Bruno of Querfurt informs us in his letter to Henry II that the King had, in 1007, sent his own brother to Stephen, the purpose of this embassy being probably the conclusion of an alliance between Henry and Stephen against Poland. There being no reason to suppose that this alliance was not implemented, Stephen must have made some military demonstration against Boleslas. We also know that Boleslas occupied the whole of the Przemyslide dominions, modern Slovakia being of course included, and that later the author of the Chronicle of the Hungarians clearly remembered the Hungarian thirteenth century tradition of a common frontier between Hungary and Poland on the Danube. This is also recorded in Polish thirteenth century tradition, as reported by the Anonymus Gallus(82), the first Polish chronicle, and the Hungaro-Polish Chronicle(83).

It was this circumstance which prompted Henry II, as he was preparing a second thrust against Poland, to ask for his brother-in-law's help, while Stephen no doubt saw in the proposed combination an excellent opportunity for extending his realm towards the Carpathians. We have unfortunately no direct information as to the extent of the Hungaro-Polish hostilities or their results. Nor are we better informed of the progress of the Magyar infiltration towards the north-east and towards the east. Stephen certainly appropriated the territory beyond the Tisza, which before the Magyar invasion belonged to Bulgaria and was occupied by Bulgarian Slavs mixed with eastern Slavonic tribes, later called Ruthenians, who since the tenth century had been worming their way beyond the Carpathians(84).

---

(80) Cf. Novotný, *Czech History*, vol. I, pp. 723 seq.
(81) Chronica, I, ch. 40, *M.G.H.S.* N.S. II, p. 75.
(82) Anon.Galli Chronicon, I, ch. 6, *M.P.H.* I, p. 399. : "Did he not repeatedly defeat the Hungarians in battle, and has he not annexed the whole of their country as far as the Danube?"
(83) Chronicon Hungarico-Polonicum, ch. 7 (ed. J. Deér), *S.R.H.* II, p. 311. Reminiscences of Polish-Hungarian conflicts are also to be found in Anonymi Gesta Hungarorum, chs. 17, 18, 34, *S.R.H.* I (ed. A. Jakubovich), pp. 57, 75, 76.
(84) L. Niederle, " Origins of Carpathian Russia " (in Czech), in *Věstnik Národopisného Musea* (Prague 1922), dates the immigration of the Russian tribes beyond the Carpathians into the northern part of Hungary and into Transylvania from the Xth down to the XIIth centuries, the period marked by the pressure which the Pechenegs were exerting on the Russians. Some tribes may have penetrated into this region as far back as the VIIth century,

We are also in the dark with regard to the conquest of modern Slovakia by Stephen, erroneously attributed to Arpad by the thirteenth-century Hungarian Chronicle, an anonymous work(85). All we know is that modern Slovakia was in Hungarian hands in 1031, though it is impossible to tell in which period of Stephen's reign this happened. It is not likely that Stephen conquered it early after 1007, as it would have been difficult for Boleslas the Great to hold Moravia without having Slovakia under his control, and as Moravia was still under Polish domination in 1017 to become Czech again only later, about 1029, we must assume that Stephen annexed Slovakia after Boleslas' death(86).

In any case, the fact that the Emperor, as the secular head of Christendom, had asked a Christian king for help in crushing another Christian prince, also contributed to the further disintegration of the medieval outlook. The impression it created must have been disastrous, as all these princes were rulers of newly converted nations. If they had been made to believe that the Emperor had certain rights over all Christian nations, it must have occurred to them that he did not always behave in accordance with that privileged position. There is no doubt that under Henry II a new factor emerged in the relations between the Roman-German Empire and the non-Germanic neighbouring countries, a downright lust for domination, conquest and subjugation. The old ideology still existed, but mainly as window-dressing, to bolster up the emperor's pretended rights. And as its true purpose came to be known, opposition to the emperors grew in intensity both from non-Germanic neighbours and from the Papacy, which was soon to assert its claim to the *Imperium* in secular matters. It is in this crucial dilemma that one will find the key to the whole evolution of Europe in the Middle Ages and to the struggle that was to cast its shadow on later centuries and its gloom on our own days.

The reign of Boleslas saw a renewal of the old feud between Poland and Russia of Kiev, though one should not attribute undue importance to

---

when the Avars attacked some eastern Slavonic tribes. The writer successfully controverts the Magyar thesis as propounded by A. Bonkáló (" Die Ungarländischen Ruthenen," *Ungarische Jahrbücher*, 1921, vol. I), which would have it that the Russian Slavs came to those regions only after the XIIth century. Its weak spot is the gratuitous assumption that the country concerned was waste land in the early Middle Ages. The important trade route through the valley of Uh must have attracted the Slavs on both sides of the Carpathians in very early days. On this question, cf. H. Weidhaas "Zur Frage der Przemysliden Rundkirchen," *Kyrios* (1937), vol. II, pp. 291 seq.

(85) Anonymi Gesta Hungarorum, ed. E. Jakubovich, *S.R.H.* I, chs. 18-42, pp. 58-86. An account of the occupation of the Bulgarian territory beyond the Tisza is also to be found in the XIVth century chronicle called *Chronicon Pictum Vindobonense*, latest edition by A. Domanovsky in *S.R.H.* I, p. 305 (ch. 57).

(86) Such also seems to be the opinion of V. Chaloupecký as defended in his work *Old Slovakia* (in Czech), Bratislava (1923) ; unfortunately, I have been unable to consult the book in Great Britain. I have gathered his leading ideas from the reviews of his book, more especially V. Hrubý in *Časopis Matice Moravské* (1927), vol. LI, pp. 254-283 ; J. Pekař in *Czech Hist. Rev.*, (1925), vol. XXXI, pp. 595 seq. ; A. Brückner, "Zur Geschichte der Slowakei," *Ungarische Jahrbücher* (1927), vol. VI, pp. 460-2, and in some of his own studies published separately and previously quoted. Though unable to follow his line of argument and to accept all his opinions, I am glad to state that my research has led me to identical conclusions on several points. Nor did I come upon his studies on Carpathian Russia (Bratislava, 1925). Cf. also F. Hrushevsky, ("Boleslas the Great and Slovakia") (in Slovak), *Sbornik J. Skultétyho*, Matica Slov. (Turč. Sv. Martin, 1933).

Boleslas' intervention in Russia. The growth of Poland's power under Boleslas impressed the Russians and in 1013 Vladimir the Great (980-1015) negotiated the marriage of his son and heir Svyatopolk with a daughter of the Polish Duke(87). An embassy, headed by the bishop of Kolobrzeg (Kolberg), the German Reinbern, accompanied the princess to Turov, of which the young prince was the governor. But the German prelate must have lacked diplomatic skill, as friction soon arose between the prince, his Polish wife and the population. Some historians have attributed the misunderstanding to Reinbern's maladroit attempt to shift the allegiance of young Russian Christianity from Byzantium to Rome; but to impute such an intention to a Polish bishop in 1013 would argue a naive anachronism, as at that time disaffection between Eastern and Western Christianity did not yet exist. Remember how cordially Bruno was received by the Russian Duke and how Vladimir supported his mission to the Pechenegs; yet Bruno was also a German and of the western rite. What is more likely is that the bishop tried to turn Svyatopolk against his father, as it would have served Polish interests in Russia better to have the Polish princess installed with her young husband in Kiev. But Vladimir got to know of the plot and to cut short any possible intrigue, imprisoned bishop, princess and prince. The incident interfered with the Polish-German war, as the Duke hastened to make his peace with Henry II in 1013, hired some troops from Russia's sworn enemies, the Pechenegs, and made a demonstration on Russian territory; but all the satisfaction he got from Russia was the damage he wrought. The bishop died in prison, while Svyatopolk effected his escape with his wife.

The Russian Primary Chronicle completes Thietmar's story of Polish-Russian contacts after Vladimir's death(88). Vladimir made peace at the last minute with his son Svyatopolk who became ruler of Kiev in 1015. His cruel treatment of his brothers Boris and Gleb whom he had put to death provoked the Duke of Novgorod to avenge them. With his faithful Varyags, Yaroslav defeated Svyatopolk and occupied Kiev(89), where the Russian Duke had left his Polish wife. The fugitive appealed to his father-in-law, but Boleslas the Great, who had come to the conclusion that his Russian son-in-law did not come up to expectation, offered to recognise Yaroslav, if the Duke of Novgorod would let him have his sister in marriage. The Duke of Novgorod had a poor opinion of parental relationship with the Pole and refused.

Only war could decide the issue. Boleslas made a peace settlement with Henry II in Budyshin in 1018, thereby frustrating the Russian's plan of a German combination against Poland and even secured a German auxiliary corps for his expedition. To this we owe the first description of Kiev by Thietmar(90) who collected his information from the German soldiers when

(87) Thietmar, Chronicon, VII, chs. 72, 73, M.G.H.S. N.S. IX, pp. 486-8.
(88) Ad a. 6523 (1015). S. H. Cross, loc. cit., pp. 214-20.
(89) Ibid., ad a. 6524 (1015), loc. cit., p. 220.
(90) Chronicon, IX, ch. 32, M.G.H.S. N.S. IX, p. 530: " In this great city which is the capital of the realm, there are more than forty churches, eight market places and a countless multitude of population," exactly what must have impressed the Germans.

they returned, proudly displaying the rich booty they brought home.

Boleslas' expedition was a success. Yaroslav fled from Kiev to Novgorod, and so rapid and decisive was the victory that the Duke had not even the time to save his family. The Pole, however, returned the Russian's relatives in exchange for his daughter and only kept the sister whose hand he coveted. From Kiev, Boleslas sent letters to Henry II and to the Byzantine Emperor announcing his triumph.

And yet, the whole campaign never went beyond the adventure stage. As the native population objected to the Poles' prolonged stay in Kiev, various troubles, fomented by the son-in-law, soon made the place too uncomfortable for them and Boleslas, who had already sent his auxiliary troops, laden with booty, back to their homes, withdrew to Poland, leaving his son-in-law to fend for himself as best he could. Svyatopolk was again ousted (1019) by the Duke of Novgorod. The Pechenegs' help did not avail him. He was finally driven out of Russia and died in exile, leaving Yaroslav in sole possession of Kiev. The Pole's only permanent and territorial gain was the re-occupation of the border fortresses of Czerwien and Przemyśl(91).

Boleslas' excursion into Russia was thus only an episode provoked not by the Poles' desire for eastward expansion, as has sometimes been alleged, but simply by the domestic interests of the Polish ruling family. Nor did Polish intervention rouse, as far as can be ascertained, any serious anti-Polish animosity among the Russians. In reading the long report on this incident in the Russian Chronicle, one gathers the impression that public hatred in Russia did not settle on Boleslas, foreign ruler though he was, but on Svyatopolk for murdering his two brothers Boris and Gleb, two very godly persons, who were not in the least interested in politics, were soon honoured by public acclaim as saints and raised to the distinction of Patron Saints of Russia. Their fame spread into Poland and Bohemia and the worship they received in these countries still provides interesting evidence, as we shall presently see in detail, of the intellectual intercourse that drew Russia of Kiev and the Slavonic West together at a time when East and West were drifting apart. The Primary Russian Chronicle mentions Boleslas with detached feelings, picturing him as a stout man, too heavy for any but a draught-horse to carry, but physically fit and intellectually exceptionally clever.

*   *   *

For all his achievements, Boleslas fell short of his main ambition, the permanent union of the Przemyslide dominions with Poland, his failure being due not only to Henry II's astuteness, Boleslas' own strategical mistakes in the defence of Bohemia and his diplomatic shortcomings with the Czechs, but also to the Czechs themselves who failed to discern the importance of a

---

(91) The main sources for these incidents are Thietmar's Chronicle (VII, chs. 72, 73 ; VIII, chs. 31-34, loc. cit., pp. 486-8, 528-32), and Nestor's Annals (ad a. 6523-6527 ; loc. cit., pp. 212-22). Cf. also Anon. Gallus, ch. 7, *M.P.H.* I, pp. 402-4 ; Hirsch, *Jahrbücher*, loc. cit., III, pp. 89-93 ; Zakrzewski, *Boleslas the Brave, the Great*, pp. 300-8.

M.   H

permanent union with Poland and put their local interests above the Pole's imposing scheme. Indeed, their own local and dynastic concerns proved so attractive that in trying to escape from Polish designs, they flung themselves straight into the arms of Germany.

Whatever critics may say about Boleslas' schemes, we must admit that they were sound and could have been carried out, if only the Czechs had made common cause with him. Boleslas found an able successor in his son Mieszko II, also called Lambert, not his eldest son, as Bezprym was older, but Boleslas refused to acknowledge the latter as his legitimate son, having had his union with the boy's mother, daughter of a Hungarian duke, dissolved. In this respect, Boleslas had somewhat broad views and his private life was not as exemplary as that of his rival, Henry II. Their contemporaries must have been aware of it, since Thietmar(92) devotes a special chapter to Henry's morality; legendary tradition has since the twelfth century commended him for renouncing marital intercourse with his legitimate wife Kunigunde. Bezprym's mother was not Boleslas' first wife, for he first married the daughter of the margrave of Meissen; but only the third union, that with Ennilda(93), daughter of the chief of a Slavonic tribe on the Elbe, was regarded as legitimate, and not until after her death did Boleslas, in 1018, marry the German Oda(94).

Mieszko II's capacity has been commonly underrated, for as a successor he was a credit to his father, noted not only for his military skill, but for his political versatility, an educated man keenly interested in cultural matters. Of this, a curious confirmation is to be found in a letter which Mathilda, the Duchess of Lotharingia and daughter of Heriman, Duke of Suabia, sent to Mieszko II about the year 1027 together with a liturgical book. Therein(95) she praised the Pole's philological gifts and his knowledge of the Greek language, an exceptional accomplishment for a Polish king of that period, proving, as we shall see later, that as a result of frequent contact between Poland and Russia of Kiev in Boleslas' reign, the cultural influence of Greek clergy working in Kievan Russia had reached even some Polish circles.

The letter also lavishes praise on the King's piety and humane feelings, and on his father's memory : '' You are all but wholly devoted to heavenly things, inspired by the exemplary deeds of a father, who in the part of the world you are governing, became so to speak the fountain head of our Holy, Catholic and Apostolic faith; for such barbaric and ferocious nations as proved refractory to the saintly preachers' words were soon compelled by his sword and brought to the Lord's table.''

It is interesting to find in this letter additional evidence of how much the fame of the valiant Pole had spread in Germany and of how the old notion,

---

(92) Chronicon, VII, ch. 74, loc. cit., pp. 499 seq.
(93) Ibid., IV, ch. 58, p. 198.
(94) Ibid., VIII, ch. I, pp. 492 seq.
(95) Published in M.P.H. I, pp. 523-4 : "Who has brought together so many languages for the glory of God ? Though you could worship God worthily in your own tongue and in Latin, you were not content with this and preferred to add Greek." Mieszko II would deserve more appreciation on the part of Polish historians. There is only one monograph about his reign, and that out of date, but still useful.—A. Lewicki, "Mieszko II," Rozprawy Akademii (Hist. Phil. Section, Cracow, 1876), vol. V. pp. 87-208.

recently discarded by the new Emperor, concerning a Christian ruler's duty to convert the pagans by every possible means, was still deeply embedded in some German minds.   Even after his death Boleslas remained for many the personification of a Christian prince, keen on the pagans' conversion.   It is also noteworthy that the German lady should call Mieszko II " invincible king," who received royal title and honours through the grace of God.

This letter also calls attention to the fact that the young King, whose wife was a German, was not deliberately hostile to Germany.   All he meant was to take over his father's task of protecting the Church and of propagating the Christian faith.   He had of course no intention, after his father's unpleasant experiences from the first years of his reign, of altering Poland's new status and its relationship with the Empire.   Poland was now an independent country.   And Mieszko II was fully determined to maintain and defend his country's new position.

He himself was, however, severely handicapped by his elder brother Bezprym's refusal to stand back in accordance with his father's wishes. With Germany's connivance, Bezprym intrigued against the King, was banished from the country and fled to Russia.   For a while the danger was averted, but remained a threat for the future.

Mieszko's royal partner in Germany was Conrad II (1024-1039), founder of the Salian dynasty and a relative of the late Henry II.   A handsome man in the prime of life, overflowing with vitality, the new king was, from an exaggerated sense of justice, prone to savage autocracy.   He had never qualified for his imperial dignity and his education had been neglected. Had it not been for the famous German canonist Burchard, bishop of Worms, who took the neglected orphan in hand(96), Conrad would have remained illiterate all his life.   With a king of this type, there could be no question of any Ottonian theories, for he lacked his predecessor's piety and had not the slightest notion of what an emperor's sacred character stood for, of what was expected from the Protector of the Church and the secular head of Christendom.   He upheld the Ottonian system as founded on the alliance with the Church, but did all he could, not deliberately, but for sheer lack of understanding and religious feeling, to belittle the old ideals in the eyes of his contemporaries.   Small wonder then that in Conrad's reign, Germany's behaviour to Poland grew more aggressive than ever.   Imperialism and conquest became the watchword and the last remnants of the old regime collapsed for good.

It was only to be expected that an emperor of Conrad's mettle should from the first be anxious to restore the Empire's prestige in the East, but Mieszko II was ready for it and took good care to see to his fortifications and to get rid of his enemies and potential allies of the Empire, the Veletians. His successful raid into Saxony and the Veletian country in 1028 prompted

---

(96) Vita Burchardi Episcopi (ed. G. Waitz), *M.G.H.S.* IV, ch. 7, p. 835.   On Conrad's reign cf. H. Bresslau, *Jahrbücher des Deutschen Reichs unter Konrad II*, vol. 2, (Leipzig 1879, 1884) ; J. R. Dietrich, *Die Polenkriege Konrad II u. der Friede von Merseburg*, (Giesen 1895) (not available) ; E. Brandenburg, "Probleme um die Kaiserin Gisela," *Berichte über die Verhandl. d. Sächs. Akad. d. Wissensch.* (Phil.-Hist. Kl.), vol. LXXX (Leipzig, 1928).   Main source : Wipponis Vita Cheronradi Imp., *M.G.H.S.* XI, pp. 254-75.

the Emperor to speed up his preparations, whilst relying on the Veletian envoys for support.

The Emperor's chances happened to be improved by his expedition to Italy, his coronation in Rome in 1027 and the success he scored in the north, where a new empire was in the process of building. The Dane, Canute the Great (995-1035), whom Conrad had met in Rome in 1027, besides conquering England, annexed Norway in 1028 and Scotland in 1031. As he was equally interested in the Baltic coast(97), then occupied by the Veletians and other Slavonic tribes under the aegis of Poland, Conrad II ceded to him all German rights over the border March of Schleswig(98) in return for Canute's daughter Gunhild as a bride for his son Henry. The support and friendship of the conqueror of the north and founder of the second greatest empire after Germany in the West was a valuable prize for the time being, as Conrad II knew that he would be unable to deal with the Slavonic East without the necessary cover for his northern frontier.

Both Veletians and Czechs were enlisted into Conrad's expedition against Poland. Udalrich's son, Brzetislas, must have been keen on Germany's favour, judging from the sensational manner in which he married Judith, sister of Otto of Schweinfurt, a Babenberger and the future Duke of Suabia. He secured his bride by a romantic *coup de force*, when he kidnapped her from a convent school in Schweinfurt. Again, our good canon Cosmas(99) rescued the details of this spirited abduction. So eager was the young prince to escape with his maiden that with his sword he cut an iron chain with which the guards had barred his way. It was a deed to impress the stoutest German. Such was the hero who offered to command a Czech contingent and attack the Poles from the south. This partnership may have been negotiated by the German hermit Gunther, who said his prayers in the Bohemian forest whilst keeping in constant touch with the Central-European courts(100).

The Emperor was again foiled in his schemes. Mieszko skilfully adopted his father's favourite tactics, defence in depth, with excellent results. The Emperor suffered heavy losses and was forced to retreat and abandon the campaign(101), the only success being scored by the Czechs, when Brzetislas conquered Moravia in the course of the 1029 expedition and annexed it once more to Bohemia. There is no absolute evidence for the date, but so far we have been unable to time the feat better. In comparing the different accounts, Cosmas(102) being again our main witness, one

---

(97) On Canute and his relations with the Baltic Slavs and with Conrad, see Dahlmann *Geschichte von Dänemark*, vol. I, p. 106 ; E. A. Freeman, *The History of the Norman Conquest of England* (London, 1877), 3rd ed., vol. I, pp. 455 seq.

(98) H. Bresslau, *Jahrbücher*, vol. I, p. 104 ; vol. II, pp. 104 seq.

(99) Chronica, I, ch. 10, *M.G.H.S.* N.S. II, pp. 73 seq. Cosmas's account bears the romantic heading : Omnia vincit amor : rex et dux cedit amori. Fluctuat mens iuvenis igne succensa Veneris velut ignibus estuat. . . . Then follows a pointed remark about the Germans and their contempt for the Slavs : " For he thinks of the pride so natural to the Germans and their arrogant habit of despising the Slavs and their language " ; which remark denotes, if not the position of Brzetislav and his Czechs, at any rate the Canon's patriotic feelings.

(100) See H. Bresslau, *Jahrbücher*, vol. I, pp. 266 seq.

(101) For details, see H. Bresslau, loc. cit., vol. I, pp. 277 seq.

(102) Chronica, I, ch. 40, loc. cit., p. 75. Cf. V. Novotný, *Czech History*, vol. I, pp. 723 seq.

gathers the impression that it was only Brzetislas' participation in the Emperor's expedition that prompted the German nobles to overlook the Schweinfurt incident instead of resenting it. Udalrich placed the conquered territory under the government of Brzetislas who hastened thither with his beloved Judith.

The following year Conrad II had his hands too full with Hungary to make good his Polish failure. Stephen I, who went on quietly with his policy of building a powerful Danubian State, was for years in complete control of the greatest part of the basin, having in 1003 annexed the territory of Transylvania together with the region north-east of Hungary, then governed by Gylas. He was supreme judge, the highest Magyar distinction, and must be identified with Achtum and Prokui, mentioned by some sources. At any rate, the annexation set the stage for the final unification of all the Magyar tribes. Relations with Germany grew strained after the death of his brother-in-law, Henry II. Seeing the Empire governed by a man who had no time for a policy after the Ottonian style and who seemed determined to bring all his neighbours under his sway, Stephen could not trust Conrad. No more did the latter trust his Hungarian neighbour, and this for good reasons, as the activity on the German-Hungarian border pointed to a desire on the part of Stephen to extend his territory westward at the expense of the Bavarian March. But it was the growth of Stephen's power rather than a few border incidents that prompted the Emperor to organise a military expedition against Hungary. At the outbreak of hostilities in 1030, Stephen was certainly already in possession of the north of Hungary, i.e. of modern Slovakia. This could hardly have been the case in the reign of Boleslas the Great. If any successful Hungarian occupation at the expense of Poland did take place after 1008, when Stephen had been won over to the side of Henry II, it must have been that of some such locality as Gran (Ezstergom), if this town was still lying outside Hungarian territory in 1008. This would explain why Stephen started building the Gran cathedral only in 1010. But the whole of the territory could scarcely have been annexed, as this would have rendered the Polish occupation of Moravia between a Czech Bohemia and a Magyar Slovakia too precarious, if not impossible. It seems, however, that the Poles remained in possession of Moravia till the year 1029(103).

One feels tempted to suppose that the same year which saw the reconquest of Moravia by the Czechs also witnessed the occupation of modern Slovakia by the Magyars. For it is quite possible that on seeing the Czechs re-enter Moravia, Stephen marched his troops to the north and occupied the territory between the Danube and the Tatras as a precautionary measure against the Czechs who, be it remembered, acted in collusion with the Emperor. Nor should we forget that the same territory, modern Slovakia, had belonged years before to the Przemyslide State. It was thus obvious that the Czechs would never stop between the Morava and the Vag

---

(103) Legenda S. Gerhardi Episcopi, ed. E. Madzar in *S.R.H.*, chs. 5, 8, vol. II, pp. 487, 489, 490-2. Annales Hildesheimenses ad a. 1003, *M.G.H.S.* III, p. 92. Cf. K. Schünemann *Die Deutschen in Ungarn*, pp. 29-33.

rivers, should their operations turn out successful. This did not require any previous understanding between Mieszko and Stephen I, although the hypothesis has been put forward by some historians, but we have no evidence for it. It is more likely that Stephen acted on his own, anxious to bring the whole Danubian basin under his control.

This supposition finds corroboration in the attitude of Brzetislas. In him, the Emperor found again in 1030 a helpful ally, this time against the Hungarians. The Czechs joined Henry in such strength that they were left to advance against the Hungarians as an independent army, and whilst the Emperor was marching his German troops along the right bank of the Danube, Brzetislas moved with his Czechs on the left bank from Moravia, an obvious sign of what he had in mind. As the last scion of the Przemyslide dynasty, he was anxious to redeem the family's prestige which for the last decade had come on such evil days, and to reinstate the Przemyslide State in its old glory. It was indeed the very reason why he had joined the Emperor on his expedition to Poland.

It should be remembered that Boleslas I, as the Emperor's ally, had also conquered Moravia, modern Slovakia and the region of the Upper Vistula as soon as Otto I's decisive victory over the Magyars at Lechfeld made that conquest possible; and it was certainly this ancestral precedent that inspired the romantic and impulsive prince, not to mention his secret anxiety to remove, by winning military fame, the stain of his illegitimacy.

At first, Brzetislas' expectations were all but foiled by the Hungarians. It is true, he conquered Moravia, but before he had time to complete the occupation of the country and push further eastward, the Magyars stepped in and took the very territory he had been coveting between the Danube and the Tatras. As the Emperor at that moment was not lucky in his Polish campaign, Brzetislas had to rest content with what he had and wait for better days.

All this should be kept in mind if we wish to understand the Czechs' readiness to help the Emperor against the Hungarians. The Czech expedition against the Magyars was meant to be an all-out attempt to revive the old Przemyslide State. Once again the Czechs had better luck than the Germans. Brzetislas defeated the Hungarians and, according to Cosmas(104) continued his victorious march as far as Gran on the Danube. It almost seemed as though the young prince's dream had come true, but unfortunately the Emperor again came to grief. After penetrating as far as the Raab, his warriors found their match and failed to withstand the Hungarian onslaught. Brzetislas ordered the withdrawal, as without the Emperor's support his own successes would have lost their military value.

The Magyars pursued the Emperor well beyond the frontier of the Ostmark and occupied a long strip of German territory with the inclusion of Vienna. Not until 1031, by the intervention of the young Henry, the Emperor's son, was peace concluded between Stephen and Germany, the Hungarians keeping most of their gains of the previous year(105).

(104) Chronica, I, ch. 41, *M.G.H.S.* N.S. II p. 76. Cf.Wippo, Vita Chuonradi, ch. 26 *M.G.H.S.* XI, p. 268, Annales Hildes., *Ibid.*, III, p. 97, Annales Althan., *Ibid.* XX, p. 791.
(105) H. Bresslau, *Jahrbücher Konrads*, vol. I, pp. 312 seq.

The initiative of the peace treaty came from Stephen and as the Emperor found himself involved in another war with Poland, the offer was accepted. Mieszko II, after his victory of 1028, in 1030 invaded Saxony, and judging from the chroniclers' dismay in reporting it, the raid wrought great havoc. The Emperor could not retaliate till 1031; but in the meantime, the position of the young Polish King was considerably endangered by his elder brother's renewed intrigues(106). Bezprym had been in Russia waiting for the moment to strike and seize the reins of government with the support of the Russian Duke Yaroslav who had old accounts, dating from Boleslas' days, to settle with the Poles.

This was a godsend for Conrad. When Mieszko II learned that Bezprym was marching against him at the head of a Russian army, he was ready to come to terms with Conrad at any price, so as to have a free hand to deal with the danger threatening him both from the south-east and from the interior, where Bezprym had his local supporters. In league with Bezprym though he was and the instigator of his coup, Conrad saw no advantage in refusing the proferred offer of peace, which gave him as a gift what he would otherwise have had to fight for. The Polish King not only promised to return all the booty he had carried off from Germany the year before, but ceded the two Marches of Lusatia (Lausitz) which his father had conquered. This meant the end of Polish expansion in the lands of the Polabian Slavs.

But the sacrifice did not benefit Mieszko: his brother with his Russians proved too strong; the young King had to flee from the country and to seek asylum in Bohemia, leaving his brother to do as he pleased with Poland. The new ruler, in order to curry favour with the Emperor, sent him the royal crown of Boleslas the Great with all the insignia of his royal dignity, declaring himself content with the ducal title and promising to be a faithful vassal of the emperor. As compensation for their assistance, the Russians helped themselves to booty in plenty and to the territory of the Red Cities(107).

The question now arises—why did Mieszko II take refuge in Bohemia? After his experience of Duke Udalrich's treachery on a previous occasion, how could he expect better treatment this time? The fact is, the Polish King may have been influenced in his decision by rumours originating in Germany to the effect that the Emperor was not on the best of terms with the Czech Duke. Conrad's biographer, his faithful Wippo(ch.29), has recorded some of these rumours. Yet there was nothing to justify Conrad's anger with the Czech Duke, except Bohemia's growing power. The Czechs had been so far the only soldiers in the imperial army to lay claim to any military success and the occupation of Moravia must have been enough to make the Emperor suspect that Czech ambition aimed at expansion

---

(106) Cf. *Ibid.*, vol. I, pp. 328 seq.

(107) Annales Hildesh., *M.G.H.S.*, III, p. 98. Wippo, *Vita Chuonradi*, ch. 29, *ibid.*, XI, pp. 269 seq. Cf. Nestor's Chronicle ad a. 6339 (1013), S. H. Cross, loc. cit., p. 225. Interesting particulars on Bezprym's invasion will be found in M. Gumowski, " The Bishopric of Kruszwicsa in the eleventh century " (in Polish), *Towarz. Prz. Nauk* (Kom. Hist., Poznań, 1921), t. III, 3, pp. 18 seq.

towards the south-east and the north-east. That the Emperor was displeased became obvious when in 1031 he marched against Hungary and Poland, not a word being said about a Czech contingent. Evidently the Emperor meant this time to rely on himself alone, and to share with no one the conquest and the spoils he was promising himself. It may be that this rumour had raised hopes in Mieszko to see Bohemia on the cross roads of its policy towards Germany and to count on Czech assistance for the recapture of his throne.

If this was the reason which decided the choice of his sanctuary, the event showed that Mieszko had over-estimated his neighbour's chivalry. Udalrich, who looked upon Mieszko's arrival as a heaven-sent gift wherewith to appease the Emperor, imprisoned the refugee and offered him to Conrad. But the Emperor saw no advantage in accepting the bargain—Poland had already made its submission—and declared to the Czech envoys that he had no wish to buy one enemy from another, hoping at the same time that the Czech would keep the Pole in confinement. Deeply hurt by the Emperor's answer, Udalrich ordered Mieszko's release, which, of course, did not improve the Emperor's temper(108).

However, Mieszko II unexpectedly met with his chance: his brother Bezprym, whose cruelty had sickened the nation, was murdered in 1032, not without the knowledge of his brothers Mieszko and Otto. It was then that the Emperor bitterly regretted, but too late, his refusal of the Czech's bargain. Mieszko II, who recovered his throne, offered to come to terms with him but to no avail, and another German expedition was set on foot against Poland with the usual abortive result. Conrad then was only too glad to accept Mieszko's new offer of peace (1033). The Emperor's conditions were harsh: Mieszko was asked to renounce his royal dignity and to share the government of Poland with his brother Otto and apparently some other relatives. This was the start of Poland's subsequent partition between the members of the Piast dynasty, the system that was to sap Poland's strength. The country was made a German fief as a matter of course(109).

Here we observe again how astutely the Germans were paving the way for a future push towards the Polish coast of the Baltic. According to the Annals of Hildesheim(110) (a. 1032) part of these Polish possessions was given to Mieszko's first cousin Theodoric, identified by some historians as the descendant of one of the three sons born to Mieszko I by his second wife Oda, daughter of Theodoric of the northern Marches, possibly Swientopolk. Boleslas the Great naturally disliked internal complications over any possible competitors for the ducal throne and he soon got rid of his stepmother and step-brothers. As they had found refuge in Germany, in Quedlinburg, they were understood to be more in favour of German interests than anybody else. It was thus a clever move on the part of Conrad to produce

<hr>

(108) These problems have raised lively discussions among Czech and German historians ever since the days of F. Palacký (*Geschichte von Böhmen*, Prag, 1836-1867, vol. I, pp. 275 seq.). Cf. on the discussion V. Novotný, loc. cit., vol. I, pp. 731 seq. and A. Lewicki, *Mieszko II*, pp. 174 seq.

(109) For details, see H. Bresslau, *Jahrbücher Konrads*, vol. II, pp. 8 seq., 79-81, 481-483.

(110) *M.G.H.S.*, III, p. 98.

one of these exiles and force Mieszko II to share his lands with his forgotten cousin. The probabilities are that Theodoric got Pomerania as his share, a country politically as important to Germany as it was economically vital to Poland. It was to be organised into a March against the Veletians. Conrad was thus, after Gero under Otto I, the first German statesman to show an interest in this part of Poland and to take the first active steps to secure this country to German interests.

It is possible that the Polish hold on Pomerania had to some extent been relaxed under the pressure of Canute the Great's progress in these parts, though his interference in Polish Pomerania has been exaggerated. The truth is that in the years 1026-1030, when he was generally supposed to be extending his dominion over the Polish Baltic Sea, Canute was kept too busy in Denmark, Norway, and after his pilgrimage to Rome, in England and again in Norway(111). There seems to be only one piece of evidence for Canute's connection with the history of the Slavs on the Baltic and even that is not conclusive: it is found in Henry of Huntington's History of England— not a likely source of information on Slavonic history—where we read that the English hero Godwine played a conspicuous part in this strange association.

Archdeacon Henry of Huntington(112) records that in 1019 Canute returned to Denmark with a mixed army of Danes and English to settle some rebellion. The insurgents are called Vandales, which might perhaps stand for Venedes. On this expedition Godwine gave evidence of such military distinction (acting on his own initiative, he defeated the enemy before the King got knowledge of the engagement) that Canute admitted him to the circle of his most intimate counsellors, gave him his own sister in marriage and promoted him to a West-Saxon earldom.

This account and the assumption that Henry may have had in mind an expedition against the Veletians find corroboration in the fact that the State papers of Canute the Great(113) mention in 1026 the name of Wrytsleof Dux, possibly identical with Wyrtgeorn, King of the Wends, who is also mentioned elsewhere(114), and was the Slavonic chieftain who spent some time with Canute in England. It is somewhat difficult, if not impossible, to identify this mysterious personage(115), but I am inclined to see in him a Pomeranian prince. We know that at a later period there were several princes ruling over small districts under the suzerainty of a duke who in turn acknowledged Polish overlordship, which may point to similar

---

(111) Cf. E. A. Freeman, loc. cit., pp. 454-479, and the more recent book by L. M. Larson, *Canute the Great* (New York-London, 1912), pp. 197-257.

(112) Henrici Archidiaconi Huntington, *Historia Anglorum*, lib. VI, *P.L.*, vol. 195, cols. 917, 918 : Cnut tertio anno regni sui ivit in Daciam, ducens exercitum Anglorum et Dacorum in Wandalos. Cf. E. A. Freeman, loc. cit., pp. 422, 743-7 on Godwine's exploits.

(113) J. M. Kemble, *Codex Diplomaticus Aevi Saxomici* (London, 1839-1847), No. 743 vol. IV, p. 34.

(114) *Florentii Wigormiensis Chronicon*, ed. B. Thorpe (London, 1848), vol. I, pp. 184, 199. Cf. L. M. Larson, loc. cit., p. 263.

(115) E. A. Freeman, loc. cit., vol. I, pp. 747-9, identifies him with Godescalc, Prince of the Obodrites, which is scarcely admissible. The name of that prince was in all probability Warcislaw. For details, see Z. Wojciechowski, *Mieszko I*, pp. 150-72, where he goes over the whole discussion among Polish scholars about the origin of the West-Pomeranian dynasty.

conditions in earlier days. At any rate, he must have been a prince ruling over a territory near the Baltic Sea, probably near the mouth of the Oder in whose control Canute was interested. There was on the island of the same name a Scandinavian settlement called Wollin (Iomsburg) which was a protectorate of his, and Canute's interest could scarcely extend beyond, so that if there is any truth in Henry of Huntington's account, we must assume that the English under Godwine were fighting in 1019 somewhere near the mouth of the Oder, not far from Stettin or Wollin. This rectification does not, however, depreciate what the alliance with Canute the Great meant for Conrad and his schemes, for it protected the German flank and allowed him free play in Pomerania.

Mieszko II must have been aware of what was brewing. He was an exceptionally able ruler, whose energy was equal to every strain and the bitterest humiliation. This time fate was on his side, when his brother Otto's death gave him the chance to endeavour to recover all Polish lands. According to the same source, the Annals of Hildesheim, he succeeded in breaking up Conrad's new order in Pomerania and forcing Theodoric to return to Germany. Later, the Germans made use of Theodoric's son Zemusil to renew their attempt on Pomerania(116) but meanwhile the Pole did so well that he recovered from the Germans the territories he had lost by the last peace treaty. But Mieszko never restored his independence completely. Few medieval kings were destined to go through experiences more disappointing, yet to display more undaunted energy than this ill-fated son of Boleslas the Great. His nerves broke under the weight and he lost his reason, but death released him on May 17, 1034.

After disposing of Poland in 1033, Conrad turned to the Czech business, resolved to settle it once for all. In the autumn of 1033, Udalrich had to appear before the Emperor's court in Werben on the Elbe and to account for his past behaviour, probably the release of Mieszko. He was deprived of his dukedom and confined to some unknown place in Germany. Brzetislas, who was ruling the duchy with his father's consent, experienced bitter disappointment when he realised at last that Conrad was not the man to allow him to rebuild a Przemyslide State under German control. He at least made an attempt to defy the Emperor who had placed the old Jaromir, his uncle, on the ducal throne. Though he was allowed to retain Moravia as in the past, he was not likely to forget his first experience of the German army and Henry, the Emperor's son.

Udalrich was eventually set free by the good offices of the Empress and the hermit Gunther, but soon challenged the Emperor's decision to share his government with his brother and his son by blinding and imprisoning Jaromir. Even Brzetislas found it advisable to flee before his father's wrath, when Udalrich's death (9th November, 1034) straightened out the tangle. The old blind Jaromir having renounced his right to the throne, Brzetislas succeeded to the dukedom. Conrad was not pleased with developments in Bohemia, but he made the best of them, since Brzetislas

---

(116) Z. Wojciechowski, op. cit., pp. 162 seq.

had made his submission and promised to hold Bohemia as a fief of the Empire(117).

Conrad had to thank not his military prowess so much as his luck in the East, where he gained complete control over Poland, aided and abetted by Mieszko's son and successor Casimir who under the matriarchate of his German mother Richenza was playing a pro-German game. Bohemia also was firmly welded to the Empire. This left only the Veletians to deal with. As for the moment their assistance was of no use to the Empire, their forcible subjection was worth trying. The Saxons, their next-door neighbours, were growing impatient and bloody clashes between yesterday's allies were of frequent occurrence. On one occasion, Conrad had to accede to their request for a Saxon and a Veletian to meet in single combat and let God decide between the two; but to the bitter disappointment of the Germans, who were sure that God would never help a pagan against a Christian, the Veletian got the better of his opponent. It was a public scandal.

To make an end of all these disturbances on the Veletian border, Conrad, after successfully terminating his war over the succession to the Burgundian kingdom(118) in 1035, marched against the Veletians. In spite of widespread devastation and great deeds of valour displayed by the Emperor and by the Czech Duke Brzetislas, whose contingent accompanied the imperial army, the Veletians held out, to make their submission only the following year, when they were condemned to a heavy tribute and brought under closer dependence(119).

That is how German influence and power struck roots on the other side of the Elbe; only, this time what was meant was political influence and physical power at the expense of Slav freedom and independence, marking the end of all Ottonian ideals of combined expansion and collaboration. The old idea of the emperor's sacred duty to convert the pagans seemed to be lost, for Conrad II never gave the christianisation of his subject tribes a single thought, except once, when, as reported in Wippo's biography of the Emperor, he attempted to raise the prestige of the Christian faith in the eyes of the pagans after his own peculiar manner. Conrad had been informed that in the course of the Veletian campaign some pagans had come into possession of a crucifix, and to show their hatred for the German God, had treated the symbol as a living being by mishandling it, putting its eyes out and cutting it to pieces. To avenge this affront, Conrad ordered a number of Veletian prisoners (maximam multitudinem pro una effigie Christi) to be subjected to exactly the same treatment as their compatriots had inflicted on the wooden figure of Christ. And Wippo who reports the atrocity, holds it up as an example of piety and praises Conrad for his righteous retribution.

That was as far as the Emperor's religious zeal could go. Even among the Sorbs, who after the death of Mieszko II were drawn into complete

---

(117) Main sources : Annales Hildesheim. ad a. 1032, 1034, *M.G.H.S.*, III, pp. 98, 99. Annal. Althah., *ibid* XX, p. 791. Cf. Novotný, loc. cit., vol. I, part I, pp. 733-7.

(118) For particulars, cf. L. Weingartner, *Vereinigung Burgunds mit dem Deutschen Reiche unter Konrad II* (Brünn, 1880).

(119) Wippo, *Vita Chuonradi*, loc. cit., XI, ch. 33, p. 271.

dependence on the Empire, Christianity had proved a dismal failure. Magdeburg's role as a missionary centre for the East had come to an end and its ecclesiastical influence on Poland was but a memory of the past. In vain did the archbishops try to gather at least Posen under their jurisdiction after the faithful Unger's death (1012). Gone also were the ideals of Bruno and his companions, and the new centres in Rome and near Ravenna for the training of missionaries to the Slavonic East were closed. A new factor had poisoned the relationship between the Empire and the East, the spirit of domination and bloody subjugation to Germany(120).

*   *   *

If anybody among the Slavonic nations at this time was able to grasp the wheel of fate that was driving the Slavs to complete subservience under the German heel and give it a jerk backward, it was the young Czech Duke Brzetislas. So far he had proved himself a man of outstanding merit, fearless and extremely enterprising. He firmly seized the reins of government and was soon absolute master of Bohemia and Moravia. Hesitations and political weaknesses were things of the past and the road once more lay open for further expansion. At that moment Poland was again in a bad way. Mieszko II's son and his German mother were driven out of the country by a strong national reaction against their blatantly pro-German tendencies, and from the political sphere the revolt spread over the cultural and religious fields, when the half-converted pagan elements rose against the Christian institutions imposed on their country, and a period of absolute anarchy followed in the wake(121). At that particular moment, in 1038, the Emperor was too busy with his Italian expedition to intervene. Stephen I of Hungary died the same year, and conditions in his country were not much better than in Poland.

It was during this upheaval that the second Polish metropolis of Sandomierz, if it ever existed, and its suffragan sees(122) vanished for good. The pagan reaction was worst in eastern and northern Poland which was only half christianised, and the havoc wrought there was so great that Casimir the Renovator, who pacified these districts, considered it useless to revive the sees and allowed the dioceses of Gnesen and Cracow to exercise their jurisdiction over the reconquered lands.

Brzetislas was the last man to miss an opportunity for aggrandisement. He summoned his soldiers and threatened them with the gallows should they refuse to join him—a superfluous threat, since the Czechs were always spoiling for a fight, especially with the expectation of rich booty in the offing. In the autumn of 1038 the Czech army moved towards the Polish borders. Judging from the lengthy and vivacious account left by our old acquaintance,

---

(120) P. Kehr, *Das Erzbistum Magdeburg*, pp. 46 seq. We lack information on Unger's succession. V. G. Sappok, *Die Anfänge des Bistum Posen*, pp. 78 seq.
(121) For details, cf. S. Kętrzyński, "Casimir the Renovator" (in Polish), *Rozprawy Akademii* (Hist. Filol. Sect.), Cracow, 1899, vol. XIII, pp. 302-12.
(122) Kętrzyński (*The Vanished Metropolis*, pp. 18 seq.) thinks that the suffragan sees were situated in Płock, Kruszwica, Łęczyca and perhaps somewhere in the country of Chełmno.

Canon Cosmas(123), the expedition must have deeply stirred the whole nation. Brzetislas first invaded Silesia to push on as far as Cracow which was completely destroyed and where he found sufficient treasures to reward his men.

From Cracow the Czechs marched on the capital of Poland, Gnesen, the resting place of S. Adalbert's body, without meeting with any opposition, the population fleeing in terror before the onslaught. The inhabitants of Giecz, for sheer panic, even went so far as to ask the Duke to settle them in Bohemia. Posen was captured with all its treasures and Gnesen, though well fortified, was left without cover, and occupied. Cosmas reports with no little emotion how the Czech soldiers dropped all their rich booty in trying to be the first to kiss the place where the great saint lay buried.

Only the intervention of the bishop Severus prevented the soldiers digging up the body and carrying it away. With infinite tact he persuaded his flock to observe a three days' fast, after which S. Adalbert appeared, at night of course, to his successor and gave his consent to the transfer of his body from Gnesen to Prague on condition however that the Czechs would solemnly promise to avoid all the great sins that had driven Adalbert out of Bohemia. Brzetislas and the bishop then announced the news to the pious crowds and all vowed that they would in future live in accordance with the great saint's wishes.

The sins to be shunned are detailed by Cosmas together with the punishments to fit them, an interesting catalogue that opens a glimpse on the moral standards of the period in Bohemia. The first three prescriptions aimed at uprooting all sins against the sanctity of marriage, all polygamists to be sold as slaves, not in Bohemia, but in Hungary. Other clauses forbade the killing of innocent people. But the most unpopular restriction must have been the prohibition to open any new public houses, with all the punishments that awaited drunkards. Sunday rest and the veto on all burials in private places were also stressed. In this, the Duke loyally co-operated with the bishop and threatened all trespassers with short shrift. Not until the whole army had made the promise to respect the saint's wishes was S. Adalbert's coffin opened by the bishop and the clergy. Together with the relic of the saint, the Czechs also took away the remains of the first Polish archbishop Radim-Gaudentius and those of the Five Brothers, who had died some thirty years previously and were held in great veneration.

By the end of August, 1039, Brzetislas and his victorious army entered Prague in triumph, displaying before the eyes of a delirious population all the treasures they had looted from Poland, amongst them the golden cross which Boleslas the Great had erected over Adalbert's grave. Twelve priests were hardly able to carry it, as the generous Pole had ordered a cross three times his own weight and we know that Boleslas was not of negligible stature.

Brzetislas' success was astounding enough for many historians to proclaim

---

(123) Chronica, II, chs. 2-8, *M.G.H.S.* II, pp. 82-93. Cf. also Anonym. Gallus *M.P.H.* I, p. 416. On the expedition cf. S. Kętrzynski, loc. cit., pp. 302 seq. and V. Novotný *Czech History*, vol. I, part 2 (1913), pp. 15-26.

him the spiritual successor of Boleslas the Great, whose ambition to create a Slavonic State on the eastern borders of Germany was his inspiration for the rest of his life(124). It was, in their estimation, a new attempt to unite Poland and Bohemia under one sovereign and to found a Czech-Polish State with sufficient vitality further to develop into a great Central European and Eastern power. There are, of course, various aspects to give colour to the theory and to explain the general persistence of the opinion. We can share it, provided we introduce a slight correction into the assessment of motives that prompted Brzetislas. It was not so much the example of Boleslas the Great of Poland as that of his forefather Boleslas I which inspired the Czech Duke. The conviction that Bohemia and its rulers were the legitimate heirs of the Moravian Empire survived the catastrophe under the successors of Boleslas I and reasserted itself under Brzetislas. That is what drove him first to try and re-conquer Moravia and Slovakia. In Poland, his first objective was Silesia and the region of Cracow, as these countries had been the mainstay of Moravian power in the past. His campaign against Gnesen was more in the manner of a raid for the capture of the relic of S. Adalbert. It is not likely that he intended, at least at that moment, to occupy the whole of Poland for good. Following the tradition of Great Moravia which had also annexed White Serbia (modern Saxony), the Przemyslides were always more interested in expansion towards the north.

What is certain is that if Brzetislas had succeeded in holding Silesia with the region of Cracow, Poland would sooner or later have shared the same fate and the road to the Sorbish country would have lain open, exactly what happened under Svatopluk of Moravia and Boleslas the Great of Poland. But Brzetislas was an astute statesman, and if for the time being he waived his claim to the rest of Poland, it was in deference to the Emperor and the German King, whom it would have been bad policy to alarm. However, Prague was now in possession of Adalbert's relic and this was proof sufficient in the eyes of the Czechs and perhaps of many Poles that the gallant Przemyslide had inherited Boleslas the Great's ideas and ambition.

The possession of Adalbert's relic also convinced Brzetislas of his right to have his episcopal city raised to a metropolis, as had been the case with Gnesen, and he sent, according to our sole informant, Annalista Saxo(125), a message to Rome, requesting the Pope to bestow on his bishop the pallium as an archbishop's insignia, but without any ulterior political motive. Brzetislas simply hoped, somewhat naively, that the distinction would crown his life's work and outdo even his forefather's achievements. The move was not necessarily aimed against the Empire. We know that the strongest opposition to the creation of new bishoprics and metropolitan sees used to come not from the emperor so much as from the bishops and archbishops

(124) This was the opinion of the older school of Czech and German historians, for instance, of F. Palacký, loc. cit. vol. I, pp. 277 seq.; W. v. Giesebrecht, *Gesch. der Deutschen Kaiserz.*, vol. II, pp. 771, 775 seq. (5th edition); A. Huber, *Gesch. Oesterreichs* (Wien, 1892), vol. I, p. 170. This view has so far prevailed: V. Novotný, loc. cit., vol. I, 2 (1913), p. 9 seq.

(125) *M.G.H.S.*, VI, p. 685.

themselves; but once he had secured the Pope's consent, he relied on Polish gold and silver to do the rest and bring the Emperor and the metropolitan to a better frame of mind.

Luckily, he had abundantly provided his envoys with Polish treasures, for according to Canon Cosmas(126), they soon needed them, but only to avert the storm that threatened him and his bishop. The Polish clergy also sent their envoys to Rome with a long recital of all the depredations committed in Poland by the Czechs, heading the list with the translation of Adalbert's relics, naturally regarded as the worst crime, since his memory was particularly dear to the Romans. Some bishops summoned to the local synod even insisted on excommunication as the fittest punishment for the duke and his bishop.

There could of course in these circumstances be no question of any archbishopric for Prague, as all the envoys could do was to smooth ruffled feathers. Cosmas innocently confesses with satisfaction that Brzetislas' gold had the desired effect and that the duke and the bishop were let off with a severe admonition and the injunction as a penance to erect a new chapter in Bohemia, the church and chapter of Stara Boleslav, the place where S. Wenceslas had been murdered and which owes its survival to this memorable event.

The Polish campaign was never intended as a demonstration against the Empire, since Brzetislas never had any intention of rebelling against the Emperor, merely hoping that he would acquiesce in the arrangement, provided the conquered territories were held as a fief of the Empire, while forming part of the Przemyslide dukedom. But there he made a mistake. Conrad II died during Brzetislas' campaign and his son Henry III, who regarded the incident as a serious violation of the rights of a neighbouring fief and moreover feared the Duke's growing power, was not going to be hoodwinked; he stood by his father's policy and made military preparations against Brzetislas.

The Czech did his best to avoid open hostilities. He sent his own son as hostage and offered to appear at the Emperor's court and to accept all his lands as a feudal benefice. Cosmas(127) reports with obvious lack of precision that Henry III claimed all the gold that was part of the Polish booty and quotes the declaration which the Czechs sent in reply to the Emperor's claim, a document of exceptional interest for its definition of the Czech position in the Empire. The Czechs said : " We have always belonged, and to-day, however, still belong, without any prejudice to our own law, to the Empire of Charlemagne and his successors. Our nation never rebelled; it has always remained and will ever remain loyal to you in all your wars, provided you treat us justly. Pippin, son of Charlemagne, put us under the obligation of paying to the Emperor's successors an annual tribute of 120 fat oxen and 500 Marks . . . This we unhesitatingly pay to you and will pay to all your successors every year; but if it is your intention to impose on

---

(126) Chronica, II, chs. 6-8, *M.G.H.S.* N.S. II, pp. 91-3.

(127) Chronica, II, chs. 8, loc. cit., pp. 93 seq. Cf. also Herimanni Augiensis Chronicon, *M.G.H.S.* V, p. 123, and Annal. Althah., loc. cit., vol. XX, p. 24 (ad a. 1041).

us a heavier burden in violation of our ancient law, then we prefer to die rather than bear a yoke to which we have not been used.''

This was to some extent a definition of Czech constitutional law(128), of course as viewed by Cosmas; but the tribute mentioned was never imposed by Charlemagne or any of his immediate successors. It was Cosmas' own invention. When it was imposed on Bohemia in this form is not known, unless it was perhaps exacted in the reign of Boleslas III. Cosmas undoubtedly revealed Brzetislas' mind; without ever questioning his links with the Empire, he was determined to defend the existence and the self-government of his State and in this respect his was a manly and loyal reply.

But Henry III clung to his resolve to overthrow the Duke and to his father's scheme of partitioning Bohemia into several dukedoms, though his first expedition into Bohemia ended in failure. There still exists at Brodek (Fürtel) in the Bohemian forest a church of S. Wenceslas built by the Duke in memory of his victory over the Emperor. Only the following year (1041) did the King meet with success when after by-passing the fortifications in the forests he penetrated as far as Prague. Even then the Duke, abandoned by his bishop, who for fear of his metropolitan the archbishop of Mainz' retaliation for the Roman embassy, had thrown in his lot with the Germans together with some other nobles, persisted in his resistance and only offered to submit when he saw his country devastated. As winter was near, the offer was accepted. The Duke was summoned to appear at the Emperor's court, to make his public and unconditional submission, to pay a large indemnity and hand over his own son, with some nobles, as a guarantee of good behaviour.

The Annals of Altaich and the Annalista Saxo(129) describe at length the scene of the Duke's humilitation and the Emperor's characteristic attitude. Satisfied with the sight of the Duke walking barefooted between two lines of German nobles up to the throne and imploring on his knees the Emperor's mercy, the monarch bestowed on the Duke Bohemia as an imperial fief, reduced the indemnity by half and gave his consent to Moravia being united to Bohemia with the addition of Silesia which had been wrested from Poland.

It thus happened that the Duke could in the end keep the most important proceeds of his daring raid and witness the partial revival of his forefathers' State. He only failed in his attempt to obtain an independent ecclesiastical organisation of his own, being outmanoeuvred in Rome by the Poles and at the imperial court by the metropolitan of Mainz, who was not going to have

---

(128) On the relations between Bohemia, Germany and the Empire, cf. Novák's study published in *Le Monde Slave*, vol. II (1925): " L'ideè de l'Empire Romain et la Pensée Politique Tchèque au M.A." ; also, A. Koester, " Die Staatlichen Beziehungen der Böhmischen Herzöge und Könige zu den Deutschen Kaisern von Otto dem Grossen bis Ottokar II " (O. von Gierke's *Untersuchungen für Deutsche Staats und Rechtsgeschichte*, Heft 114, 1912). This work was not available. Cf. also C. Bachmann's *Böhmens Staatsrechtliche Beziehungen* (Deutsche Arbeit in Böhmen, Berlin, 1900), pp. 74-106.

(129) *M.G.H.S.* XX, pp. 28, 29, *ibid.*, p. 686. Both Annals together with Cosmas (II, chs. 9-14, loc. cit., pp. 95-100, are our main sources for the campaigns. For details, see Novotný, loc. cit., vol. I, 2, pp. 45-55.

his metropolitan rights ignored. But after his experience with his own bishop Severus, Brzetislas had lost all interest in ecclesiastical privileges. He had of course to take Severus back to his see and get on with him as best he could. The bishop apparently was not very popular with his own clergy; at any rate a monk from Bohemia had a very comforting vision, the account of which has been preserved in Othlo's *Collection of visions*(130), when he had the satisfaction to see the red hot and blazing chair which the devil was keeping ready in Hell to seat the bishop for neglect of duty. Of course these over-zealous monks did sometimes exaggerate.

It may be that his disappointment with his bishop made Brzetislas such a friend of the Czech Abbot Procopius(131), for whose benefit his father, or he himself, had helped to build the Abbey of Sazava, near Prague. This abbey was one of the refuges of the Slavonic liturgy in Bohemia whilst it was still popular in many parts of the country, together with Slavonic literature, as was pointed out in the third chapter. So wide-spread in the lands of the Przemyslides was that liturgy, that Brzetislas is supposed by many to have harboured the idea of introducing it to the rest of his realm. This is perhaps an exaggeration, but it is true nevertheless that such was the intention of his successor Vratislav. It only shows that there was a good deal to be said for the schemes of Boleslas the Great and Brzetislas, since they had the sense to see as early as the eleventh century, that a Slavonic empire rising on the eastern boundaries of Germany could derive strength and compactness from a common Slavonic culture based on Greek and Latin traditions. We shall see in the next chapter what possibilities lay hidden there, had political circumstances only been more favourable.

Through the opposition of the Emperor Henry III, Brzetislas' plans miscarried. Moravia and Silesia were the only acquisitions he managed to keep. It appears that Brzetislas renounced the idea of recovering for Bohemia the territory which had been seized, probably in 1029, by Hungary. As a good statesman he could not expect the Emperor to consent to any further Czech depredations. Not that he meant to keep his hands off Hungarian affairs altogether. On the contrary. King Peter, Stephen's successor, even joined him as an ally in his war with Henry III, raided Ostmark towards the end of 1039, and in 1040 sent a detachment of cavalry to help Brzetislas. But King Peter made himself unpopular, was banished in 1041 by Aba-Samuel and found refuge at Henry's court. Provoked by another Hungarian raid, the Emperor prepared a punitive expedition to teach Hungary a lesson, when the Czechs joined him in considerable numbers, and Brzetislas distinguished himself on a terrain he knew well. When the defeated Hungarians refused to take Peter back and asked the Emperor to choose them another king, Brzetislas made the interesting attempt of placing on the throne of Hungary a protégé of his, a relative of the late Stephen who lived in Bohemia. The Emperor agreed to the candidate, but the combination did not work and Aba-Samuel regained his throne. Again Brzetislas

---

(130) Othlonis Liber Visionum, Visio 14, *M.G.H.S.* XI, p. 384.
(131) Annals of Sazava, *F.R.B.* II, pp. 244, 245.

came forward with Peter's candidature to the Hungarian throne(132) during the last imperial expedition in 1044.

The future was to justify Brzetislas' intervention in Hungarian affairs. The position in Poland had altered in the meantime and the state of anarchy so cleverly exploited by the Czechs in 1038 had come to an end. It had been provoked by chiefs of various tribes who wished to get rid of the central power of the Piasts, but the grave consequences of the outbreak opened their eyes to the necessity and the blessings of a central authority. With the young Emperor's assistance Casimir returned to Poland in 1039 and was everywhere hailed with relief, except for two centres which refused to acknowledge his authority : Mazovia, where Maslav, of the old dynasty of a local Polish tribe, was supreme master, and Pomerania, where Ziemuzil or Ziemomysl, son of the Duke Dietrich, who had been expelled from Pomerania by Mieszko II, was the ruler. These two parts of Poland had only been superficially touched by Christianity.

With the assistance of the Russian Duke Yaroslav, who had given him his sister in marriage in return for Casimir's sister, the bride of his son Izyaslav, Casimir succeeded in defeating the Mazovians, whose Duke was slain on the field of battle, and soon after, the Pomeranians. Pomerania was Polish again and Casimir well deserved the title of Renovator which posterity conferred on him(133).

It was only to be expected that after this first success Casimir should be planning again to restore Silesia to his dominion; but Henry III saw the complications that would arise and induced the Duke in 1046 to keep the peace in the interest of his Roman expedition. But already in 1050 we hear that Casimir attacked the contested country and took it. Followed trouble in Hungary where Peter once more found himself expelled and Andrew, who was living with his brothers in Bohemia and in Poland, was called to the throne of Stephen. In 1051 the Czech and the Pole were fighting side by side in the imperial army, as it tried in vain to restore "imperial order" in Hungary, a sign that the previous year's incident had been forgotten. Only in 1054 was a final arrangement come to at Quedlinburg, when Brzetislas ceded Silesia and Breslau to Poland in return for an annual payment of 500 lbs. of silver and 30 lbs. of gold(134).

This compromise was the milestone that closed the first stage in the political evolution of Bohemia and Poland, a period in many respects as vital to Poland and Bohemia as it was to Germany, Hungary and the whole of Central and Eastern Europe. It witnessed two important attempts to set up along the eastern borders of Germany a Slavonic Centre, a *Sclavinia*, that could be left to itself to develop into a free and independent State. The first attempt—the Moravian empire, the ambition of which lay not only further to the north along the Elbe, but also towards the Vistula and the Danubian Basin—was broken up by a combined attack of Magyars and Germans; the second, first started by Mieszko I and carried on by his son

---

(132) The detailed discussion of these events in Novotný, loc. cit., vol. I, 2, pp. 59-67.
(133) For more details, see S. Kętrzynski, *Casimir the Renovator*, (in Polish) pp. 333-7.
(134) S. Kętrzynski, loc. cit., pp. 337-43 ; Novotný, loc. cit., vol. I, 2, p. 71.

Boleslas the Great, although better designed than the first, failed too, undermined not so much by the Germans as by the rival Czech dynasty of the Przemyslides. Yet Boleslas' plan was sound, since the Piasts were at that time the only Slavonic dynasty able to tackle such an undertaking with any hope of success. They had four able rulers in succession, Mieszko I, Boleslas the Great, Mieszko II and Casimir, to assure the necessary continuity of effort; but directly Boleslas lost control over Bohemia, the whole plan was put out of gear and headed for failure. And yet, nothing but the union of Bohemia and Poland could have supplied the indispensable corner-stone for the building of such an empire. Unfortunately it was not to be.

A Polish-Bohemian State would have had incalculable consequences for the subsequent growth of Europe. It seems that Boleslas had planned to make Prague the centre of his empire and Bohemia his jumping-off ground for the further expansion of his dominions, if possible, across the lands of the Slavonic tribes living between the Elbe and the Oder,—and the formation of such a nation was all but realised. At that time the difference between the Czechs, the Poles and the other Slavonic races was not so deep-seated as to preclude a speedy amalgamation into one linguistic bloc, and one can easily imagine how differently the fate of Europe would have shaped had the scheme succeeded.

It failed, and by the close of this period Poland and Bohemia remained standing side by side, but not united, not even as good friends, only as benevolent neighbours, each recovering from a spell of internal troubles and both dependent on the German Empire. Thus placed, they were powerless to arrest the fate that awaited the many Slavonic tribes living between the Elbe, the Oder and the Baltic Sea, when nothing short of joint action between the Czechs and the Poles could have exercised any beneficent influence on the destiny of this part of Central Europe. As things had developed politically in the previous decades, neither the Przemyslides nor the Piasts were willing to make common cause for their mutual benefit, if ever they did see where the common interests of their peoples lay. Slight as prospects were at the close of this period, the future still held possibilities for the better. In the meantime, Germany remained the only decisive factor in Central Europe and the emperors had at last a free hand to expand to the East.

CHAPTER VI

KIEVAN RUSSIA AND CENTRAL EUROPE

KIEVAN RUSSIA'S CULTURAL ACHIEVEMENTS—RUSSIA, A NEW CHANNEL BETWEEN BYZANTIUM AND THE WEST?—WESTERN SAINTS AND THE RUSSIAN CHURCH—PENETRATION OF WESTERN SLAVONIC LITERATURE FROM BOHEMIA INTO KIEV—MAGYARS, CZECHS, CROATS, GERMANS AND RUSSIANS IN THE ELEVENTH CENTURY—POLAND AND KIEVAN RUSSIA—RURIKS AND THE COURTS OF WESTERN EUROPE—WESTERN INFLUENCE IN KIEV—GREAT POSSIBILITIES FOR EUROPE—CONSEQUENCES OF A FATEFUL DEVELOPMENT.

In the meantime, the young Russian Christian State was making rapid strides in its literary education. Soon after the introduction of the Slavonic liturgy into the Russian Church, when the Russian Slavs came into possession of all the treasures of Old Slavonic literature bequeathed by S. Cyril and S. Methodius to Moravia(1), and which their disciples salvaged and brought over to Bulgaria, the benefits of the Byzantine missionary methods in the upbringing of the converted nations became apparent. Bulgaria made excellent use of the gift during the last decades of the ninth and the first of the tenth centuries and reached her " golden age " under Tsar Symeon the Great(2). But as we have seen, Slavonic literature did not vanish from Central Europe altogether with the departure to Bulgaria of Methodius' leading disciples, for it continued to flourish in Bohemia right through the tenth and eleventh centuries. The bulk of Slavonic literature,—translations from the Bible, from Greek liturgical and theological texts, from Latin and other writings as well as valuable original works—found their way into Russia of Kiev through the agency of Bulgarian refugees. This was indeed a godsend for a young nation to come by, on the very threshold of its cultural and intellectual career and the Russians were fortunate in being able to start from such promising beginnings.

These were based on Graeco-Roman civilisation transmitted by Constantinople, so that Russia in the first years of its Christianity, received a present that had been denied to the Western nations and got the start of the rest of Europe. Christian Russia then proceeded to build up a literary record which other nations would have had good reason to envy. Let us single out a few of its best productions.

First, the work of the metropolitan Hilarion who lived in Kiev about the year 1050. There is majestic sonority about his discourse on S. Vladimir, in spite of a few touches of naïveté peculiar to early Christians;

(1) On the literary work of SS. Cyrillus and Methodius, see my brief indications in *Les Slaves, Byzance et Rome*, pp. 164 seq., 283 seq.

(2) On the literary productions of the " Golden Age " cf. *ibid.*, pp. 313-8. As far as I know, the best account of this literature was written by the late M. Weingart, *Bulgars and Constantinople a Thousand Years Ago* (in Czech) (Prague, 1915).

and his discourse on the Old and New Testaments recalls the style of the Greek Fathers. His originality shows how quickly the Russians were assimilating Graeco-Byzantine culture and drawing nourishment from its treasures.

At the beginning of the twelfth century the famous Chronicle of Kiev, whose anonymous author used to be called Nestor, was given its final shape, and its fluent narrative, its raciness and freshness are a delight to the reader. It is written in the best Byzantine tradition and the author's erudition is striking. Though a Byzantine by training, the writer is patriotic enough to be conscious of the unity of the Slavonic nations and of their common origin, a sure instance of national awareness at so early a period. No doubt the Russians of the time had access to the historical works of the Byzantines, and one of these, the Chronicle of George the Monk(3), of which a Slavonic translation had been made, probably in Bulgaria in the tenth century, and brought to Russia of Kiev, had an immense vogue among the Slavs. The author of the Primary Russian Chronicle must have known of it, judging from his quotation from George in the introductory chapter of his work(4).

At the same period the Duke, Vladimir Monomakh, who died in 1125, left to his children a book of Instructions in terse and telling style the manner of which revealed close familiarity with Holy Scripture(5). Not many Western princes would have dreamt of attempting such a thing in the vernacular. Even more original is the account which the Abbot Daniel, a contemporary, wrote of his pilgrimage to the Holy Land and of the conditions in Jerusalem in the reign of the Latin King Baldwin(6), whom the Russian monk accompanied on his campaign against Damascus. He covers more ground than his predecessors Arculf, Willebald, Bernard the Wise, though their works are mines of information on the archeology of the Holy Land; and he also completes the accounts by his contemporaries Saewulf, Eugesippus and Epiphanius(7). There are in his book pages of unusual charm and beauty that make it rank high in Russia's early literature.

For original work, we may place beside the metropolitan Hilarion two other bishops, the Metropolitan Clement Smolyatich and Cyril, Bishop of

---

(3) Cf. M. N. Speransky, *History of Early Russian Literature* (in Russian, Moscow, 3rd ed., 1920), pp. 215-22. On the Primary Russian Chronicle, *ibid.*, pp. 323-45. On the Slavonic translations of Byzantine chronicles, see M. Weingart, *Byzantine Chronicles in Slavonic Ecclesiastical Literature* (in Czech), Publications of the Faculty of Phil. of the Univ. in Bratislava (1922-1924). See R. Jakobson, " The Beginnings of National Self-determination in Europe," *The Review of Politics* (1945), vol. VII, pp. 29-42, on the influence of Moravian culture on the national consciousness of Hilarion and the first Russian chronicler.

(4) S. H. Cross, loc. cit., p. 142.

(5) I. M. Ivakin, *Duke Vladimir Monomakh and his Instruction* (Moscow, 1901).

(6) A. de Noroff—*Pélerinage en Terre Sainte de l'Igoumène Russe Daniel au commencement du XIIe siècle*, St. Pétersbourg, 1864 (French translation and Russian text). The English translation was made from the French version by C. W. Wilson " The Pilgrimage of the Russian Abbot Daniel in the Holy Land, 1106-1107" (London, 1888), *The Library of the Palestine Pilgrim's Text Society*, vol. IV.

(7) The works of S. Adamnan, Abbot of Hy (c. 670), Willebald of Eichstätt (c. 728), Bernard the Wise (c. 870) and of Saewulf (c. 1102) can be read in an English translation in the same collection, vols. III, IV ; those of Eugesippus (c. 1155) and Epiphanius (c. 1170) in *P.G.*, vol. 133, cols. 99 seq. and vol. 120, cols. 259 seq. For summary indications on texts containing descriptions of the Holy Land, cf. T. Tobler, *Bibliographia Geographica Palaestinae* (Leipzig, 1867), pp. 5-18.

Turov. Those of Clement's letters that have been preserved show, with their references to Homer, Aristotle,and Plato, that at that early period the Greek classics were known in Russia of Kiev, while Cyril, who died in 1185, evidences how soon after the nation's conversion its clergy mastered the works of the Greek Holy Fathers and imitated them intelligently. His contemporaries and followers credibly compared him with S. John Chrysostom. Of other Russian original writers whose works have partly survived, we may single out the two bishops of Novgorod, Lucas and Elias, and the Abbot Theodosius of Pechersky Monastir(8).

But they do not exhaust the list. Besides numerous translations of Greek hagiographic writings, original Legends issued from Kiev such as the life of S. Vladimir, from the pen of the monk Jacob; two lives of S.S. Boris and Gleb (1015), one by the monk Jacob and the other by Nestor, monk of Pechersky Monastir; the life of S. Theodosius of Perchersky, the founder of Russian monasticism (1074) by the same Nestor and of S. Mstislav of Kiev (1132)(9). One important contribution, typical of this kind of Russian literary activity in the first centuries after Russia's conversion is called *Pechersky Paterik*, a collection of translated and original lives of saints drawn up in the famous abbey, including some original items of information on that celebrated centre of ascetic life. The collection can be traced to the beginning of the thirteenth century(10).

Juridical literature is also well represented by some original works such as the *Greek and Russian ecclesiastical Rule* (about 1089) by the metropolitan John II, and *Voproshchanie* of Kirik (about 1130-1156), of which we know very little(11). The first codification of Russian customary law attributed to Yaroslav the Wise and called *Russkaya Pravda*, long believed to have been written only in the thirteenth century, also belongs in its original form to the eleventh century, according to the latest discoveries concerning it.

Such are the outstanding works of early Russian literature, written in Old Slavonic which SS. Cyril and Methodius first based on the Macedonian dialect and developed into the national medium of the Slavs' self-expression, but which already then bore the stamp of Russian originality. It should be noted that all these works were written in prose(12), a remarkable achievement at that time, since we know that the Western nations started writing in vernacular prose in the thirteenth century at the earliest, and most of them only in the fourteenth(13).

(8) On the lives and works of the said writers and the editions of their writings consult M. V. Speransky, loc. cit., pp. 299-314.

(9) Cf. M. V. Speransky, loc. cit., pp. 319-21.

(10) For details, *ibid.*, pp. 214, 321.

(11) *Ibid.*, pp. 316-9.

(12) On the most striking poetical production of the Kievan period, Slovo o Polku Igorovym, *The Tale of the Host of Igor*, see R. Jakobson's studies in (*Annuaire de l'Inst. de Phil. et d'Hist. Orient. et Slaves*). (New York, 1945-7), vol. VIII.

(13) Cf. the appreciation of early Russian literature in " Les Conséquences de l'Evangélisation par Rome et par Byzance sur le Développement de la Langue Maternelle des Peuples Convertis," *Bulletin de la Classe des Lettres* . . . de *l'Académie Royale de Belgique* (1903), pp. 746 seq. The author was an expert in Germanic literature and his essay was no more than a digressional glimpse into Russian literature, but his enthusiastic surprise at his findings was significant in a writer so familiar with the literary products of the Western nations.

The little I have said about Kievan Russia's literary achievements from the tenth to the thirteenth century does not do justice to the subject, but should be enough to help us in estimating the transformation which close contact with the greatest cultural centre, Byzantium, had worked in the midst of a barbarous people. This young Christian nation had made such progress in so short a time that it, in many ways, outstripped Western nations converted centuries before the Russians by Roman missionaries. They were not in a position to give their converts the benefits conferred by Byzantium, since, after the destruction of the western part of the Empire, the cultural level of Rome had sunk far below the standards of the rival city(14).

And Byzantium's legacy to Russia was as generous in art as in literature. The church of Holy Wisdom (S. Sophia) erected by Yaroslav the Wise in Kiev in 1017-1037 was a marked improvement upon the Church of the Assumption erected in 989 by his father Vladimir and destroyed by the Mongols in 1240. It is a jewel of Byzantine art built and decorated by Greek artists, and there are few samples of Greek architecture of this period left even on Greek soil to equal it. Vladimir's church of the Assumption in Kiev and the wooden structure which he erected in Novgorod must have been in the same style. The church of Holy Wisdom of Novgorod (1045-1052) as well as the Nereditsa church (1198) followed the pattern of Holy Wisdom in Kiev. Its bold lines converging on a crown of thirteen cupolas must have appealed strongly to the taste of the Russians since they made it the characteristic feature of all their subsequent religious architecture.

Yaroslav the Wise so enriched Kiev with churches and monasteries that the city became the queen and centre of Russian religious art ; and Greek influence so dominated it that Adam of Bremen, on the strength of its reputation, called it " the peer of Constantinople's splendour and the shining credit of Greece "(15). It will be remembered that the German soldiers who invaded Russia under Boleslas the Great marvelled at the beauty of Kiev and its numerous ecclesiastical buildings; whilst Thietmar of Merseburg registered the impression which the city had made on his countrymen, when he described it as the city of 400 churches and eight squares(16). Some of its monuments, such as the church of S. Cyril, the church of S. Michael of the Golden Heads and chiefly S. Sophia, still recall this splendid past. Second to Kiev, Novgorod-Pskov developed into another such centre, to be followed by Vladimir-Suzdal.

---

(14) For further information on this topic, besides the work of Speransky, the following studies may be consulted : A. S. Orlov, *Drevniaya Russkaya Literatura XI-XVI·vv.* (Ancient Russian Literature of the eleventh and twelfth centuries), Moscow-Leningrad, 1937. (Akademiya Nauk SSSR, Nauchno-Popularnaya Serya) ; A. S. Orlov, V. P. Adrianov-Perets, N. K. Gudzy, *Istoriya Russkoy Literatury*, vol. I (Moscow-Leningrad, 1941). (Akademiia Nauk SSSR, Institut Literatury), especially pp. 257-375. A chrestomathy of ancient Russian literature was recently published by N. K. Gudzy, *Khrestomatiya po drevney Russkoy Literature XI-XVI vekov* (Moskva, 1938).

(15) Gesta Hammaburg Ecclesiae Pontificum, ed. B. Schmeidler, p. 80 ; Analista Saxo ad a. 983, ed. G. Waitz, *M.G.H.S.* VI, p. 631.

(16) Chronicon. VIII, ch. 32, *M.G.H.S.* N.S. IX p. 530 ; cf. also Analista Saxo ad a. 1118, loc. cit., p. 674. See above, p. 206.

The mosaics and the frescoes of S. Sophia in Kiev were discovered in 1843 and have attracted the attention of historians of art ever since, and with reason, for they are of singular beauty, some of them exceptionally striking for their vigorous design and their expressive realism. In the evolution of Byzantine art between the tenth and twelfth centuries the decorations in S. Sophia of Kiev certainly represent an indispensable link ; and from what has been preserved in Kiev and in Novgorod we can gather how lavishly Byzantium shared with its converts all that Greek genius at its best had produced in the city on the Bosphorus " Protected by God "(17).

*   *   *

This is not the place to treat this aspect of Kievan Russia's progress in detail. Adequate appraisal of the frescoes preserved in the churches of Novgorod (twelfth century) and Vladimir, of the icons of Byzantine origin (the touching and unaffected beauty of Our Lady of Vladimir, an icon of the eleventh century, has inspired millions of Russians), and of the plastic works of art of Russian inspiration belonging to the same period would lead us too far afield(18). I only mention them for the purpose of showing that in the tenth eleventh and twelfth centuries Kievan Russia grew into a centre of culture far ahead of anything similar in the Latin West at that time. Byzantium, the world centre of classical and early Christian culture, which had survived the worst upheaval that destroyed the western part of the Roman Empire and which was being held apart from the West by the Arabs, seemed at last to have discovered a channel to convey its treasures of science, art and literature to the West.

It is because this aspect of Russia's cultural development in the Kievan period has been missed by most historians that its extraordinary possibilities and Europe's lost opportunity have been so often overlooked. More significant and less appreciated still is the fact that Kievan Russia was ready and willing to act as intermediary between Byzantium and the West, and better still, that in the eleventh and twelfth century she was, by every indication, qualified to play that part. The opinion so widely current that in the Kievan period Russia was closed to any influence from the West, lived its own life and cared little about its Western neighbours is largely

---

(17) The predominance of Byzantine influence in Kievan Russia is now generally admitted by historians of art and the opinion, once popular among specialists, that the first artistic impulse in Kiev originated rather from the Caucasus and Armenia through the imaginary link of Tmutarakan has been abandoned. The Byzantine character of Russian art in the Kievan period is too evident to be questioned, though the possibility of Armenian affinity need not be excluded. On this controversy cf. P. Schweinfurth, *Geschichte der Russischen Malerei im Mittelalter* (Haag, 1930), pp. 25-38. On the Byzantine character of Kievan art, consult Ch. Diehl's *Manuel d'Art Byzantin* (Paris, 2nd edition, 1926), pp. 513-18.

(18) The following are among the best detailed and easily accessible studies on Russian art : Ph. Schweinfurth, loc. cit., pp. 38-156 ; L. Réau, *L'Art Russe—Des Origines à Pierre le Grand* (Paris, 1922) ; D. R. Buxton, *Russian Medieval Architecture* (Cambridge, 1934). A brief but useful survey of the art of Kievan Russia is to be found in A. S. Orlov, V. P Adrianov-Perets, N. K. Gudzy, *Istoriya Russkoy Literatury* (Moscow-Leningrad, 1941), vol. I, pp. 24-39 (Akademiya Nauk SSSR, Institut Literatury). For a rapid survey, see my short studies " Byzantium and the North," " Byzantine Influences in Russia," published by the *Geographical Magazine* (London, 1946, 1947), vol. XIX, No. 9 ; vol. XX, No. 1.

responsible for our ignorance in this matter. But recent discoveries in the early medieval history of Europe have enabled us to correct this erroneous impression ; Russia was not isolated from the West. All that has been said about the Ottos' policy with regard to Russia goes to prove that the West was to some extent aware of the rise of the new Eastern State and was trying to make contact, the obvious gateway linking Germany and the rest of the West with Russia of Kiev being the lands under Przemyslide rule. It will be remembered that a number of problems in connection with the building of their dominion by the Przemyslides have so far not been cleared up, that its extension is still a subject of debate and especially that the political conditions of the regions north-east and south-west of the Carpathians are shrouded in mist which few historians have ventured to pierce. The Magyar invasion of the Danubian plain was alleged to have brought about, with the destruction of the Moravian Empire, the complete isolation of the Western from the Eastern Slavs ; and as it was thought that the whole of modern Hungary was occupied by the Magyars from the moment of their entry into the Danubian Basin, any direct contact between Bohemia, the heir of the Moravian Empire and Russia of Kiev seemed out of the question. Such guesses naturally misled many specialists and stopped all further research.

But those guesses are not history. The genesis of the lands south-west and north-east of the Carpathians can be easily traced through the fog of legend. The Magyars, after breaking up the centre of the Moravian Empire, seem to have left its borderlands in peace, resting content with extracting tribute and other services from the subjugated tribes and finding better profit in harassing the Carolingian Empire. The defeats they suffered at the hands of Henry I and Otto I then enabled Boleslas of Bohemia to step in and make a bid for the recovery of the lands that were part of the Moravian Empire ; and as his move benefited the King of Germany as well the future Roman Emperor, Otto I gave his assent to the operation. Such was the origin of Przemyslide power which lasted, in spite of its decline, till the end of the reign of his successor, Boleslas II. But the consequences to the Hungarians of the defeats should not be underestimated.

The latest discoveries have had repercussions in other fields. Not until our notions on the relations between Kievan Russia and Bohemia, which at that period was considered part of the German Empire, be revised, shall we understand certain facts long familiar to Slavonic philologists, but puzzling for being at variance with the political history of the tenth-twelfth century interval period. First of all, on examining the first original writings in Old Slavonic, *i.e.* the Lives of SS. Cyril and Methodius, we are surprised to discover that the Life of S. Cyril was well known to the southern Slavs, yet not one manuscript of S. Methodius' Life was ever heard of. This would mean that S. Cyril's Life was brought to Bulgaria by his disciples immediately after S. Methodius' death. As regards the Life of Methodius it is impossible to say when and by which of his disciples it was written—possibly after the expulsion of his Byzantine disciples(19) ;

---

(19) The Moravian origin of both Legends seems now to be definitely established.

and as soon afterwards the Magyars severed all intercourse between the shattered Moravian Empire and the south, it is pretty obvious why no copy of Methodius' Life could be brought to Bulgaria. This is none the less surprising, as a number of works known to have been written in Moravia in S. Methodius' lifetime are now found in Bulgarian manuscripts. Curiously enough, the Life of Methodius has survived to our days only thanks to copies made of it in Russia. There exist of this Legend no less than eight manuscripts all of Russian origin, which would imply that when the Magyar invasion severed Bohemia and the rest of the Moravian Empire from Bulgaria and the Croats it did not cut them off from Russia.

*   *   *

And yet, there is amongst the Serbs and the Bulgars not a trace of any cult of the Czech saints of the tenth century, S. Wencesl s and S. Ludmila, although they still figure in the Calendar of the Russian Church. Their cult must therefore have been imported from Bohemia soon after their canonisation. Not only these Czech saints, but S. Vitus, the Patron Saint of Saxony, who certainly had nothing to do with the Slavs, was known and revered in Kievan Russia, and his Latin Legend(20), once popular in Bohemia, where it was translated into Old Slavonic, probably in Prague, whence it was taken to Kiev, is found in a Russian Collection dating from the twelfth century and called the " Uspenski Sbornik," together with the Legend of S. Methodius.

We also find in Kievan Russia, besides the knowledge of these popular saints, traces of the cult of S. Adalbert, the Slavnik prince who once studied in Magdeburg, was a close friend of Otto III and ended his public career in Prussia as a Polish missionary. An interesting document in this connection is a prayer to the Blessed Trinity, of Western origin and belonging to the eleventh century, which could have found its way into Kievan Russia from nowhere but the Przemyslide dominion. That a prayer of Latin origin should have been popular in Russia at the end of the eleventh and in the twelfth century, has its bearing also on the general issue of the religious relations between East and West. Here then are the names of the Western saints whose

---

Cf. what I say about this in my *Légendes* . . . loc. cit., pp. 334 seq., and *ibid.*, pp. 339-42, a short list of the MS texts of the Legends. The author of the Russian Primary Chronicle seems to have had knowledge of the *Vita S. Methodii* (6396-6406-888-898, S. H. Cross, loc. cit., pp. 147 seq.). The Bulgarian author of the Life of S. Clement, one of S. Methodius' leading disciples, certainly knew the Legend of Constantine-Cyril, but it is not possible to say with any certainty whether he knew of Methodius' Life or not. His confused account of the events would indicate that he knew of it only from oral tradition ; but this is not convincing, since we only know the Life of S. Clement in a Greek version of later date (Vita S. Clementis Ochridensis, *P.G.*, vol. 126, cols. 1194-1240). The author of the Russian Primary Chronicle seems to have had knowledge of the Legend of S. Methodius, as has been demonstrated by A. Shakhmatov, " Povest Vremennikh Let i ee Istochniki," *Akademiya Nauk SSSR, Trudy otdela Drevney-Russkoy Literatury* (1940), vol. IV, pp. 81-92). In the same study Shakhmatov proved that the author took his information on the invention of Slavonic letters and on the origin of Slavonic literature from an Old Slavonic writing produced in Bohemia at the beginning of the tenth century and known in Russia at that time.

(20) Published by A. Sobolevsky, " Muchenie sv. Vita v drevnem tserkovno-Slovyanskom perevode " in *Izvestiya Otdeleniya Russk. Yazyka i Slovesnosti Imp. Akad. Nauk* (1903), vol. VIII, Book I, pp. 278-96.

intercession is asked for in this prayer(21) : SS. Magnus, Canute, Olaf, Alban, Botulf, Martin, Victor, Vitus, the Popes Linus, Anacletus, Clement and Leo, the saintly brothers Cyril and Methodius, SS. Wenceslas and Vojtiekh (Adalbert).

The composition or the translation of this prayer probably belongs to the end of the eleventh century, since S. Canute and S. Olaf died in 1086 and 1072 respectively, and it has come down to us in different versions found in Russian MSS. dating from the fourteenth-sixteenth centuries ; but as A. I. Sobolevsky rightly points out, it has kept words that betray lineage from the Old Slavonic period.

This choice of saints, whose protection is invoked, should help us in dating the composition of the prayer with greater precision. S. Magnus, Abbot of Fuess in Suabia, who died about the middle of the seventh century, was a disciple of SS. Columban and Gall and was held in great veneration in Germany at the time the prayer in question was composed. The legendary Life attributed to the hermit Theodore, a contemporary of Charlemagne's father, Pippin, pretends that Magnus was of princely origin and belonged to the Scots royal family, but it is more likely that he was of German origin. The Life was written in the tenth century, probably anonymously, by an author who used as his main source the Lives of SS. Columban and Gall. In the eleventh century, Othloh of S. Emmeran in Regensburg wrote another Life of the same saint(22).

The cult of Canute of Denmark(23) and of the Norwegian King Olaf(24) must have spread rapidly to Germany. The interest which the German, especially the Saxon, clergy took in the conversion of Denmark (one has only to recall the part played in it by Hamburg) would be enough to account for the popularity of those saints. Semi-christianised Norway, as was to be expected, also came uppermost in the German clergy's attentions. This would explain the juxtaposition of these two Christian heroes with another German favourite saint in a prayer composed at the end of the eleventh century.

S. Alban (martyred in 406) is a Patron Saint of Mainz whose Life was written about the year 1062 by Goswin, Canon of the same city(25). Botulf is an Anglo-Saxon saint who died at the end of the seventh century as

(21) This prayer was published for the first time by A. S. Arkhangelsky in the *Pamyatniki Drevney Pismennosti* (1884). The same year another copy was made available by I. A. Shlyapkin (*Zhurnal Ministerstva Narodn. Prosveshcheniya*, 1884, No. 12, pp. 267-69), and a third copy, made from a fourteenth century MS., was published by A. Sobolevsky " Russkiya Molitvy s upominaniem Zapadnykh Svyatykh " (Russian prayers that mention western saints) in *Sbornik otdelenia Russkago Yazyka i Slovesnosti Imp. Akademii Nauk*, t. 88, No. 3 (St. Petersburg, 1910), pp. 36-47. None but the MS. published by Arkhangelsky mentions the names of the Popes, whereas the two other versions leave out Linus and Anacletus and put the general invocation instead : O Holy Order of the Popes (Sv. lik papezhiu). After enumerating the Popes, the three versions add the Latin greeting—*Ave papa*—transliterated in Slavonic characters. In the MS. the prayer is attributed to either S. Cyril or S. Chrysostom.

(22) *A.S.*, 6th September, II, pp. 735-59. Cf. *Bibliotheca Hagiographica Latina* (Bruxelles, 1898-1911), vol. II, p. 767.

(23) *A.S.* Julius, d. 10. Cf. also *M.G.H.S.* XXIX.

(24) *A.S.* Julius, d. 29.

(25) Junius, d. 21 ; *M.G.H.S.* XV, pp. 985-90.

abbot of Ikanhoe(26) and his cult must have been revived in the tenth century when his relics were translated in the reign of King Edgar.   S. Martin can be none other than the bishop of Tours(27), whose cult became and still is popular throughout Central Europe.   S. Victor should probably be identified with the famous martyr of Solodurum in Switzerland, where he is venerated in association with S. Ursus and the soldiers of the legendary legion of Thebes, especially at the religious centre of St. Gallen(28).

Bearing in mind Bohemia's relations with Saxony, Mainz and Regensburg, we can imagine how the devotion to those saints found its way into that country.   It was there, then, that the prayer we are examining was, if not written, certainly translated from the Latin into Old Slavonic, since such a selection of Germanic, Roman and Slavonic saints could only have been made in eleventh century Bohemia.   There exists no acceptable reason for inventing direct penetration into Russia from Scandinavia ; we are dealing only with a curious instance of Christian interaction at a time when Eastern and Western Christianity are supposed to have drifted apart.   This is but another instance which calls for the radical revision of the generally accepted opinion on the origin of the Eastern Schism.

The Western saints who, as this prayer shows, were venerated in medieval Russia, are not mentioned in the Offices of the Eastern Church ; and it should be pointed out that not even S. Adalbert (Vojtiekh), although mentioned with SS. Cyril, Methodius and Wenceslas, was included in the .Calendar of the Russian Orthodox Church(29).

Another interesting prayer, preserved in a MS. of the thirteenth century, which similarly points to an Old Slavonic origin, also mentions S. Vitus, a sign that it came to Russia from Bohemia.   It implores protection against the Devil and bears the title—*Molitva na diavola*(30).   Among the many saints invoked by the author, we find S. Florian, a saint popular in Austria and among the Czechs, S. Vitus, SS. Lucy, Cecilia (Kalikyia), Valpurga and Margaret.   Another prayer of the same class is found in a MS. of the Typographical Library of Moscow (No. 388, fourteenth c.)(31), in which S. Vitus is invoked together with SS. Lucy, Felicitas, Valpurga, Margaret, Martina, and with the Popes and Patriarchs Sylvester, Damasius, Celestine, Leo, Vigilius and Agatho.

The Collection which contains the prayer against the Devil has other prayers which also may be translations from a Latin text in the opinion of

---

(26) *A.S.* Junius, d. 17.

(27) *A.S.* Novembris, d. 11 ; *Biblioth. Hagiogr. Latina*, vol. II, pp. 823-30.

(28) *A.S.* Septembris, d. 30.

(29) The Russian tradition which makes Adalbert a bitter enemy of Slavonic letters and attributes to him the suppression of the Slavonic liturgy in Poland and Bohemia is of much later origin.   It could not have been put about before the twelfth century and it has come down to us from the fifteenth, sixteenth and seventeenth centuries in Russian chronograph MSS. (Complete publication by A. Bielowski in *M.P.H.* I, p. 89.)   The discovery of this short notice of Adalbert in 1825 by Pogodin has to a great extent influenced historical research on this period and contributed to the misjudging of Adalbert's character and work.   On this controversy, cf. V. Chaloupecký, *S. Adalbert and the Slavonic Liturgy*, loc. cit.

(30) A.I. Sobolevsky, loc. cit., pp. 41-5.

(31) Idem, pp. 38 seq.

their editor N. Sobolevsky(32), especially the one attributed to S. Gregory the Great and addressed to S. Ambrose in the manner of the Latin Confiteor. As the MS. belongs to the thirteenth century, there should be no difficulty in dating it from the twelfth when other prayers of Western origin found their way into Russia.

Another Western saint whose biography may have been known in Kievan Russia is S. Ivan, first hermit of Bohemia, who seemingly was not the legendary figure he is supposed to have been, though not all the problems connected with his existence are yet cleared up. According to J. Vašica(33), he was of princely origin, perhaps the son of the Obodrite prince Gostomysl, and became a monk at Corvey from where he proceeded to Bohemia. He lived in the ninth century. If these new findings on S. Ivan could be confirmed, we would find in him another interesting link between Germany and Russia via Bohemia. In Corvey, too, and in the ninth century we can trace the existence of a monk called Unwanus, a name that recalls the Anglo-Saxon name of Iwein. This Unwanus or Iwein is possibly identical to the Czech saint Ivan.

An old Slavonic Legend on S. Ivan has been preserved by a thirteenth century Russian chronicler(34). It reads like an abbreviation of a Life of the saint originally written in Old Slavonic : numerous Bohemianisms in this document suggest that the original must have been written in the tenth century in Bohemia whence it passed into Russia. There also exists a Latin Legend written in Bohemia in the fifteenth century(35) which would seem to presuppose the existence of the Old Slavonic document.

*   *   *

But this is not all. Other Western religious literature penetrated into Kievan Russia and has been preserved in Old Slavonic translations. We have mentioned the Life of S. Vitus. The account of the martyrdom of S. Apollinarius of Ravenna was translated into Old Slavonic and is found in a Russian MS. of the fourteenth century(36). The translation of the Life of S. Benedict of Nursia can be read in a MS. of the same century(37) and the Martyrdom of Pope S. Stephen in another of the fifteenth century(38).

---

(32) " Neskolko riedkykh molitv iz Russkago Sbornika XIII vieka " (Some Rare Prayers from a Russian thirteenth century Collection), *Izvestiya*, loc. cit. (1905), t.X, No. 4, pp. 66-78,

(33) See his book *Frederick Bridel's Life of S. Ivan* (in Czech) (Praha, 1936). Cf. my review of a previous study on the subject by the same author in *Revue d'Histoire Ecclésiastique* (1935), pp. 709 seq.

(34) J. Jireček, " Old Slavonic Biographies of S. Ludmila and S. Ivan " (in Czech), *Časopis Musea Král. Česk.* (1862), vol. XXXVI, pp. 318-22.

(35) *F.R.B.* I, pp. 112-20. This Legend pretends that Ivan was a Croat from Bohemia. This was also the opinion of M. Weingart, *Anthology of S. Wenceslas*, vol. I, p. 1029. There may be some other problems of the same kind which are still awaiting a solution, as this field of research has scarcely been touched.

(36) A. Sobolevsky, " Muchenie sv. Apollinariya Ravenskago," *Izvestiya*, loc. cit. (1903), vol. VIII, No. 2, pp. 103-22.

(37) *Ibid.*, pp. 121-37.

(38) Published by A. I. Sobolevsky in *Izvestiya*, loc. cit., t.X. No. 1, pp. 105-35.

Other texts of early Old Slavonic origin have been published by A. I. Sobolevsky from MSS. of Russian provenance, which also raise the question as to where they were written and how they came to Russia. Cases in point are a short homily on the feast of SS. Peter and Paul, a short sermon for Easter on the Baptism and the Ascension of Jesus Christ and another homily on S. John the Baptist and SS. Cosmas and Damian(39).

Some of these texts may be credited to Methodius' favourite disciple, S. Clement who fled to Bulgaria, as for instance the sermons on SS. Peter and Paul, on S. John the Baptist and the Easter sermon. In their case the question as to how the texts came to Russia makes no difficulty, since the Russians were indebted to Bulgaria for many literary treasures. The case with other texts is more obscure. As regards the translation of Pope Stephen's martyrdom, the editor discovered similarities of style between the translator and the author of the Life of S. Methodius. Another relic of Old Slavonic literature, the sermon by S. Gregory the Great(40), translated from the Latin and found in a Russian MS. of the thirteenth century, offers many similarities with the style used in the so-called Glagolitic Fragments of Kiev, which contain a portion of the Mass formulary of the old Slavonic liturgy used in the Moravian Empire and, after its destruction, in Bohemia. Should this be correct, the Moravian, or rather the Czech origin of both documents would be undeniable.

What is more, a similar affinity of style is found to exist between the writers of those documents and the author of the Old Slavonic Life of S. Wenceslas. This Life, as already stated, is a Slavonic translation of the Latin Legend written by Gumpold, enlarged with many additions, and nowhere could it have been written but in Bohemia either at the very end of the tenth century or at the beginning of the eleventh(41). That Wenceslas'

(39) *Idem*, " Iz Oblasti Drevney Tserkovno-Slavyanskoy propovedi " (From the Field of Old Church Slavonic Homiletics), *Izvestiya*, loc. cit. (1906), t.XI, No. 1, pp. 44-52, No. 2, pp. 144-54.

(40) Cf. A. I. Sobolevsky, " Ecclesiastico-Slavonic texts of Moravian origin " (in Russian), in *Russkyi Filologicheskyi Viestnik* (1900), No. 1 ; but I have not been able to consult this study. Cf. also the liturgical prayers " pro diversis necessitatibus " with the rubrics on the time and manner they should be said, extracted by A. I. Sobolevsky from the *Sinaisky Trebnik* and published in his study (in Russian), "The chronology of some old Ecclesiastico-Slavonic literary relics," *Izvestiya*, loc. cit. (1906), t.XI, No. 2, pp. 9-14. Cf. also the Old Slavonic Apocryphal Gospel of Nikodemus, translated from the Latin in Bohemia, probably at the same period as the sermon by S. Gregory the Great, but preserved in Russian and Serbian MSS. Cf. J. Polivka, " Nicodemus' Gospel in Slavonic Letters " (in Czech), *Časopis Českého Musea*, vol. LXIV, LXV, 1890, 1891 ; A. I. Sobolevsky, " Some Materials and Studies from the Field of Slavonic Philology and Archeology " (in Russian), *Sbornik Otdel. Russk. Yazyka i Slov. Imp. Akad. Nauk* (1910), LXXXVIII, No. 3, pp. 52 seq., 81-91.

(41) A. I. Sobolevsky, loc. cit. (*Izvestiya*, 1906, t. XI), pp. 8, 15-19. Cf. the latest edition of the *Vita* by V. Vajs, previously quoted, and also what M. Weingart writes on the composition of the first Slavonic Legend of S. Wenceslas and its relation to the Old Slavonic translation of Gumpold's Legend in his edition published in *Anthology of St. Wenceslas* (in Czech), loc. cit., pp. 863-904. This Legend also was known in Russia (*Ibid.*, pp. 962-66). Cf. *Ibid.*, pp. 941 seq., what he writes on the cult of S. Wenceslas and S. Ludmila in Russia. The official Russian *Prologus* which contained the Lessons of the Lives of the saints, did not include those of Wenceslas and Ludmila till the twelfth or thirteenth century. Yet, the cultus must be older, since the name Wenceslas was used by the Russian ducal family, a son of Yaroslav the Wise, born in 1034, being called Vyacheslav, *i.e.* Wenceslas, a name of Czech origin. The first Lesson for the feast of S. Wenceslas must have been a Russian composition taken from the Slavonic translation of Gumpold's Legend well before the year 1095, and it reveals traces of the Slavonic Legend of S. Ludmila, now lost, being known in Russia in the eleventh century.

first original Life, written in Bohemia soon after 929, the date of his death, was saved for future generations was mainly due to the fact that it found its way to Russia and became a great favourite there. Besides the Russians, only the Croats, who used the Slavonic liturgy, have preserved the Legend.

*   *   *

All this leads to the one conclusion that contact between Bohemia and Kievan Russia was frequent in the eleventh century; nor did the occupation of modern Slovakia by Boleslas the Great and after him by Stephen I of Hungary suspend these relations. At that time Bohemia still prided herself on an active centre of Old Slavonic liturgy and literature in the Abbey of Sazava, near Prague. It became famous under its first abbot S. Procopius and was the proud possessor of some of the relics of the Russian saints Boris and Gleb(42), who were canonised by the Russian Church in 1071. In 1096 the abbey lost its Slavonic character for good. At their first expulsion in 1055 the Sazava monks took refuge in Hungary, as stated in the Latin Legend of S. Procopius(43); but it must have been the northern part of Hungary, or modern Slovakia, where the Slavonic liturgy survived after the Moravian disaster. Quite possibly some of the monks found refuge again in Slovakia in 1096, when they were finally expelled from Sazava and replaced by Latin monks. That territory was in some ways the most cultured part of the Magyar realm and as it was the main preoccupation of eleventh-century Hungary to intensify Christian life, we can imagine that if there was any Christian centre left from bygone days, the Magyars allowed it to carry on in peace. As already stated, the mere use of a different liturgical language in those centres could not possibly distress the Magyars, as at that time they were still wavering between Byzantium and Rome.

When the Magyars adopted Christianity, contact between Bohemia and Croatia was renewed. We know, for instance, that the Glagolitic "*Fragments (Leaflets) of Kiev,*" which were written in Bohemia in the tenth century, have a supplement that was written in the eleventh century in Croatia. Another Glagolitic document called the "*Fragments* (Leaflets) *of Vienna,*" is only an eleventh or twelfth-century Croat copy of the Old Slavonic Missal composed in Moravia in the ninth century. The Glagolitic Fragments or Leaflets of Kiev are also a copy of a Moravian Missal of the ninth century(44). Relations between the Bohemian and Croat remnants of Methodius' inheritance, suspended by the Magyars after the destruction of the Moravian Empire, must therefore have been resumed in the eleventh century when the Magyars altered their attitude to Christian civilisation. Other Old Slavonic documents found their way into Croatia, as when the Croats received from Bohemia the Lessons for the feasts of SS. Cyril and Methodius and the cult of S. Wenceslas. Thus much can be gathered from

---

(42) This is confirmed by the *Annals of Sazava*, the continuation of Cosmas' Annals for the year 1095, *F.R.B.* II, p. 251.

(43) Vita S. Procopii, ch. 8, *F.R.B.* I, p. 366.

(44) M. Weingart, loc. cit., p. 962.

the existence of manuscripts of Wenceslas' Legends of Croat origin(45) and from the inclusion of SS. Wenceslas and Ludmila in the oldest Croat Calendars. Nor were those the only Slavonic texts that crossed Hungary into Croatia at that period(46). We can assume that the Old Slavonic centres which had survived in later Slovakia served as half-way transmitting centres in those transactions, since they came under the direct control of Hungary.

It looks then as though commercial exchanges between Russia and Central Europe, which for the ninth century and the beginning of the tenth find confirmation in the document of Raffelstetten described below in Appendix III, went on via Bohemia in the second half of the tenth and in the eleventh century. It appears that in the eleventh and in the twelfth century, when Bohemia was made part of the Empire, the commercial route crossed Hungary towards the Danube, where Regensburg became the main clearing house for Kievan goods imported into the rest of Germany and into France. In fact, we read in the *Life* of S. Marianus, Abbot of Regensburg, of German merchants travelling from Kiev to Regensburg, an interesting instance showing that the German monks of the abbey kept in close touch with Kiev, notwithstanding the eastern schism. Moreover, as the gifts of the city merchants were inadequate for the completion of the abbey, the monk Marianus conceived the idea of collecting contributions in Kiev. Thither he went, accompanied by a boy of the abbey and received from the king and from the principal burghers of the city a number of valuable furs worth 100 marks. On his return home he joined a caravan of merchants on their way to Regensburg(47).

We may in this connection mention another case to show that in the twelfth century Kiev and Germany kept in religious contact. We read in in the *Translation of the relics of S. Godard* that a number of pilgrims returning from Russia (quidam peregrinantes de Ruzia) were attacked by robbers and rescued by the intercession of S. Godard(48). The expedition was apparently a religious pilgrimage made for no commercial motive. Was it to the shrines of Kiev ? We do not know, but the fact is significant. As the translation was written after 1132, the incident could be placed within the first decades of the eleventh century. It throws an unexpected light on the relations in the religious field between Kiev and Germany at a

---

(45) *Idem*, loc. cit., pp. 864 seq., 904 seq. That the *Vita Methodii* should not be traceable in Croatia only deepens the mystery. Many MSS., it is true, must have perished in that troubled period and it is also possible that the *Vita* never reached Croatia at all, as suggested before. When Bohemia and Croatia resumed intercourse in the eleventh century, the Czechs had come by a new saint, S. Wenceslas, whose popularity cast the two saints of the Moravian period, SS. Cyril and Methodius, into the shade. The Czechs naturally advocated their own.

(46) Such seems to have been the case with the *Gospel of Nicodemus*, judging from I. Polivka's study.

(47) Vita s. Mariani, Abbati Ratisponensis, *A.S.*, February, vol. II (dies 9, ch. IV, p. 368).

(48) Translatio S. Godardi, *M.G.H.S.* XII, p. 647. On the trading between Russia and Regensburg, see the study by V. G. Vasilevsky, " Drevnyaya Torgovlya Kieva s Regensburgom " (*Zhurnal Minist. Narodn. Prosv.*, (1888), vol. VII, July, pp. 121-50). Cf. *ibid.*, p. 140, on the German trader Hartvic, from Regensburg, who settled in Kiev and grew rich by trading in furs with Germany. As he could not get his due from some burghers who owed him the price of some valuable Russian furs, he credited the sum to the abbot of S. Emmeram (Codex Traitidonum s. Emmeramensium in Pez, *Thesaurus Anecdotorum Novissimus*, Augsburg, 1721-23, t. I, part 3, p. 173).

time when the two, as is generally believed, were held apart by an official schism(49).

The Croatian instance lends colour to the assumption that the political changes which came over the lands south-west of the Carpathians did not interfere with the cultural intercourse between Russia and Bohemia via Slovakia ; and only some prejudiced notions on the Magyars' alleged hostility to the Slavonic liturgy, due to the ante-dating of later happenings, prevented specialists from looking more closely into the political and religious developments in this corner of Central Europe. The part played by the Old Slavonic liturgy and language in the christianisation of the Magyars has still to be defined(50).

This contact between Kievan Russia and Bohemia in the eleventh and even the twelfth century receives additional confirmation from archeology ; many ancient tombs in Bohemia have yielded a number of articles such as bracelets, rings and buttons that were either imported from Byzantium through Russia or manufactured in Kiev in the Byzantine style(51). They bear witness to the trade relations that existed between Russia of Kiev and Bohemia and made the latter the agent needed to link the new Byzantine commercial branch in Eastern Europe with the Latin West(52).

*   *   *

There existed an alternative line of communication between Kievan Russia and the West, namely through Poland, though few documents could be quoted in support of its existence owing to the lack of genuine Polish sources, the first Polish Annals having been written only in the twelfth century. But what has been said on the history of White Croatia in the ninth, tenth and eleventh centuries rather favours our assertion. The Slavonic liturgy must have been introduced into what was once White Croatia in Methodius' time, since that country must have been open to

---

(49) On similar points of contact between Novgorod and the Latins of Scandinavia and Germany, see B. Leib, *Rome, Kiev et Byzance à la fin du XIe siècle* (Paris, 1924), pp. 90 seq. Details of this intercourse will be found in my paper " The Kiev State and Western Europe," *Transactions of the R. Hist. Soc.* (1947), vol. XXIX, pp. 40 seq.

(50) The wealth of words derived from the Old Slavonic in the Magyar language points to the part played by the Slavonic Church in Bohemia and in the North of Hungary in the christianisation of the Magyars. Cf. F. Miklosich, *Die Slavischen Elemente im Magyarischen* 2nd ed. by L. Wagner (Wien, Teschen, 1884), pp. 41 seq. Cf. also the remarks by Chaloupecký on this problem in his " The Czechoslovak History," *Czech History. Review* (1922), vol. XXVIII, pp. 13 seq.

(51) Cf. J. Schránil, *Die Vorgeschichte Böhmens und Mährens* (Berlin, 1928), pp. 288-322, tables 64-74.

(52) I regret my inability to consult the book published by A. V. Florovsky, *The Eastern Slavs and Czechs. Essays on the History of Czecho-Russian relations during the tenth to eighteenth centuries* (i Russian) (Prague, Slov. Ustav, 1935). According to the reviews of this book published in *Czech Hist. Rev.* (1936), vol. XLII, pp. 363 seq., and in the *Jahrbücher für die Geschichte Osteuropas* (1935), vol. I, pp. 280 seq., the author finds in the good relations between Bohemia and Russia of Kiev in Vladimir's time evidence that the Grand Duke of Kiev had concluded an alliance with the Czechs against the Poles. I have found nothing that could be advanced in favour of this hypothesis : there is no indication pointing to such a political combination and there does not seem to have been any reason for it. The way the history of this part of Europe at this period has been treated so far must have influenced such conclusions and we have seen that in reality things happened very differently.

M.   I

Methodius' disciples after the prince of the Vistulanians had been defeated by Svatopluk. As the Polish religious terminology implies that the Old Slavonic as used in Bohemia was taken as the basis of its formation, we must infer that the Slavonic religious element had more to do with the conversion of Poland than experts have been willing to acknowledge. Sobolevsky(53) even went so far as to see in the Glagolitic "Fragments of Kiev" the copy of a Bohemian original of the Slavonic Mass formulary ; and he was of opinion that this copy was made in Poland, as it contains words which he believed to be spelt after their Polish pronunciation. The document belongs to the eleventh century. The cult of the Czech saint spread to Poland and provided the three Slavonic neighbours with a common link. We should also underline the fact that S. Adalbert, in the course of his Polish ministry, offered no objection to the Slavonic liturgy and cannot be regarded as an intransigent Latin, antagonistic to whatever was not strictly "Roman." It would therefore be unfair to his memory to attribute to the spread of his cult to Poland, Bohemia and Russia the motive of anti-Slavonic animus.

Religious architecture popular in Bohemia and perhaps also in the Moravian Empire, which had a preference for the small rotunda as the prevailing architectural feature of its churches, was adopted by Poland where it was still popular in the eleventh century, as evidenced by the church of S. Mary's (to-day SS. Felicitas and Adauctus), built on the Wawel in Cracow in the eleventh century ; and a similar structure was erected in Teschen, in Silesia—the church of S. Nicholas, now dedicated to S. Wenceslas(54). It is also remarkable that we find in the region of Cracow churches dedicated to S. Clement, the favourite saint of the Cyrillo-Methodian tradition, whose relics were brought by the Greek brothers from Byzantium to Moravia and then translated to Rome where they still rest(55). It is true that most of those churches are of much later origin(56), but the fact that S. Clement remained a favourite around Cracow so long ; shows that Slavonic traditions penetrated from the Moravian Empire into what was once White Croatia and struck root there.

Another fact deserves consideration. The catalogue of the bishops of Cracow, drawn up about the middle of the thirteenth century, mentions two bishops before Poppo who occupied the see the year of the " Act of Gnesen." Their names are Prohorius and Proculphus, both names

(53) " K Khronologii drevneyshikh tserk. Slav. Pam.," *Izvestiya,* loc. cit. (1906), t. XI, p. 19. Sobolevsky's opinion about the Polish origin of the Glagolitic Fragments of Kiev is not shared by modern Slavonic philologists.

(54) Cf. the study by H. Weidhaas on " The Round Churches from the time of the Przemyslides," loc. cit., *Kyrios* (1937), t. II, p. 308. I repeat again that Weidhaas's opinions deserve the archeologists' closest attention. I lack sufficient knowledge of the history of church architecture at this period to pronounce on the value of his study, but many of his statements are corroborated by the historical facts I have tried to elucidate in this book. On the other hand, his other study ("Methodius und die Mährer," *Jahrbücher für Gesch. Osteuropas,* 1937, t. 11, pp. 183-200) is somewhat disappointing, as A. Brückner's opinions on SS. Cyril and Methodius have made him see things in the wrong light.

(55) My book *Les Légendes,* pp. 190-7, has demonstrated, I think, that the relics of S. Clement are not genuine. S. Cyril found in Kherson the relics of a local saint whom a legendary Life of S. Clement wrongly identified with the third successor of S. Peter.

(56) On those churches and on S. Salvator, cf. K. Potkanski, *Cracow before the Piasts* (in Polish), pp. 193 seq.

unfamiliar in the Latin West but common in the Greek East(57). This would show that like the cult of S. Clement in the Cracow region later known as Little Poland, Greco-Slavonic traditions survived the Moravian disaster.

But there is more behind this tradition. We know that at the request of Mojmir II, a papal legation was sent to Moravia in 889 to reorganise the Moravian Church. How far it succeeded and who were the bishops consecrated by the papal legates we have no direct means of knowing, as the Moravian Empire was destroyed a few years later ; only, Pilgrim, the bishop of Passau, gives a vague hint that some Moravian bishops survived the catastrophe. If there is any truth in the tradition, they could have come only from the periphery of Moravian power. This would best apply to Cracow, the capital of White Croatia, which probably was still part of Moravia about the year 900. It was certainly entitled to have its own bishop as the country had preserved its autonomy under Moravian overlordship. Taking into consideration what has been said on the subsequent fate of White Croatia, Cracow could have no difficulty in carrying on its religious life under its bishop Prohorius–Prochoros, a very suitable name for a disciple of S. Methodius. If so, Proculphus, or another member of the Moravian hierarchy who had found refuge in Cracow, would fit into the scheme as Prohorius' successor, since White Croatia must have carried on on its own, may be as a Magyar tributary, till 955 when it was re-conquered by Boleslas I of Bohemia. It being scarcely possible that only two bishops should have occupied the see for a century, from about 900 to 1,000 when Poppo became bishop of Cracow, we must assume a vacancy, presumably after 955 when Cracow became part of the Przemyslide dominion and later, of the diocese of Prague. Planned in 967, its foundation only took place in 973. The dates proposed by the *Annals of Traska*—970 for Prohortus (*sic*) and 986 for the consecration of Proculfus (*sic*)—do not tally with the facts as we know them. It is at best the speculation of a thirteenth-century annalist who, to fill in the gap in the succession, inserted a third bishop, Lampertus by name and ordained in 995(58). He evidently meant to square things with the tradition recorded by the catalogue of Cracow with reference to the first two bishops who preceded Poppo.

This local tradition, though its record dates only from the thirteenth century, should not be lightly discarded, for it at least points to the conclusion that the Christian mission of the Cracow region was directed by two men whose names were associated with the Graeco-Slavonic culture introduced into Moravia by SS. Cyril and Methodius.

---

(57) Prohorius (Prochoros in Greek) was one of the seven deacons chosen by the Apostles from among the seventy disciples of the Lord. According to Greek tradition, he became bishop of Nicodemia in Bithynia (Asia Minor) and was venerated on the 28th July (see Synaxarium Constantinopolitanum, *A.S.*, Nov., p. 851). Proculphus can be identified with Proculos, alias Proclos, deacon of Puteoli, who was venerated together with the famous Patron Saint of Naples, Januarius, on the 21st April (*ibid.*, pp. 59, 169). That Proculus should have been a common name in medieval Italy ought not to mislead us, since southern Italy was under Byzantine supremacy. That was why saints used to be common property in this part of the Empire and in Byzantium. Cf. K. Potkanski, loc. cit., pp. 189 seq.

(58) *M.P.H.*, II, pp. 828 seq.

Corroborative of the survival of this culture in Cracow in the tenth and eleventh centuries is the discovery of coins with Slavonic inscriptions and dating from the reign of Boleslas the Great. The denarii bear on the obverse the effigy of the prince with the name Boleslav in Slavonic letters, and on the reverse a Greek cross with the same inscription. Their style recalls the Byzantine silver coins of the tenth century, especially those of Constantine VII Porphyrogennetos, of Romanus II (959-63), of Basil II and Constantine XI (976-1028). The Greek cross follows the pattern of the Byzantine coins(59). It all goes to show that these denarii were issued by the Cracow Mint before the year 1,000, a sign that Greco-Slavonic culture still flourished in Cracow at that time.

The difficulty, however, is that one would expect the inscriptions to be written in S. Cyril's glagolitic lettering as used in Moravia, but not in the cyrilic lettering which in the tenth century replaced the complicated glagolitic alphabet in Bulgaria and from there was passed to Russia. One would have expected Cracow to use the glagolitic alphabet. But the similarity in style of the denarii with the Byzantine currency of the tenth century may be due to the fact that the governor of the Cracow Mint was familiar with matters Byzantine and Bulgarian, possibly as a refugee from Bulgaria after that country's submission to Byzantium under Basil II, the Slayer of Bulgarians. As a commercial centre, Cracow must have attracted refugees in search of security. As stated before, the road via Hungary was cleared again after the Magyar defeat of 955(60), and there was the alternative route via Kiev.

It is likely that Boleslas' acceptance of Otto's Renovation of the Roman Empire and the setting up of an independent Polish hierarchy affected the chances for the spread of the Slavonic liturgy over Poland(61), but this did not mean its end. Poland's progressiveness and new contacts with Russia under Boleslas created alternative possibilities for Slavonic culture by clearing access to Kiev where Greco-Slavonic culture had found a home. A reference to this effect is found in the Life of S. Moses(62), where we read that the saint, who had been brought over with other boyars from

(59) A similar cross is found on the Polish coins issued at the same period by the Mint of Gnesen ; also, on some Danish coins of the tenth century. On the denarii of Boleslas the Great, consult the thoughtful study by M. Gumowski, "Numismatic and historical essays on the eleventh century" (in Polish), *Poznan. Tow. Przyj. Nauk.* (Kom. Hist.), t. III (1924), ser. 2, pp. 80-108.

(60) See what the *Russian Primary Chronicle* has to say about trade between Bulgaria, Bohemia and Hungary in Svyatoslav's time (6477—969—S. H. Cross, loc. cit., p. 173) :— "Svyatoslav announced to his mother and his boyars : I do not care to remain in Kiev, but would prefer to live in Pereyaslavets on the Danube, since that is the centre of my realm, where all wealth is concentrated : gold, silks, wine, and various fruits from Greece, silver and horses from Hungary and Bohemia, and from Rus, furs, wax, honey and slaves."

(61) There may be a reference to this in the legendary and perplexing statement in the *Russian Primary Chronicle* (6538-1030—S. H. Cross, loc. cit., p. 225) that after the death of Boleslas a pagan reaction set in in Poland. This report is repeated by Polycarp, author of the Life of S. Moses, written at the beginning of the thirteenth century (*M.P.H.* IV, p. 815, ch. 11) who states that Boleslas drove all the monks out of his country and that this was God's punishment for his misdeeds. The statements are confused and are not substantiated by any more reliable source.

(62) *M.P.H.*, IV, p. 810 (ch. 6).

Russia to Poland by Boleslas, received, whilst in prison, the monastic habit from the hands of a monk who had come to Poland from the Holy Mount. This could be no other than Mount Athos.

The oldest Polish chronicle, the *Anonymus Gallus*, confirms the existence of the Slavonic liturgy in Poland under Boleslas the Great. In recording the death of the King, the chronicler states that Boleslas was mourned by the whole Polish population of the Latin and the Slavonic rites(63). The statement can only imply that in Boleslas' days Poland, like Bohemia, was still bi-liturgical.

Another document dating from the year 1027 shows that there was more than met the eye in Boleslas' contact with Kievan Russia. It is the letter addressed by Matilda, daughter of Herimann, Duke of Suabia, to Mieszko II, and accompanied by a liturgical book, the *Ordo Romanorum*, as a presentation to the King. The German lady praises the Polish King's piety and his capacity to praise God in several languages(64) : " Who ever mastered so many languages to God's glory ? Though able to worship God worthily in your own tongue and in Latin, you did not consider this enough and chose to add Greek." Since the lady was referring to divine worship, " your own tongue " could only mean the Old Slavonic. which was the liturgical language in use among many Czechs and Poles in the official worship of the day.

But Mieszko's knowledge of Greek is even more apposite to our purpose, for he could only have learnt it from the Greeks who lived in Kievan Russia, so that his father's personal contact with Kiev, whatever its military and political consequences, turned out to be culturally fruitful. The son seized the opportunity and his Greek is evidence that in the eleventh century Byzantine culture had found its way to Poland via Kiev.

Thus at that time Poland was qualifying as an intermediary to hand on to the West the culture of Byzantium in its Slavonic form. If a Suabian lady could be found to admire the young Polish King for saying his prayers in Greek it is likely that, given the requisite conditions, Germany would have welcomed an extension of such classical imports to other Western countries as well.

*   *   *

In evidence of this it is good to remember that the ducal family of Kiev was matrimonially connected with every court of eleventh and twelfth-century Europe. Vladimir gave away the sons and daughters of his last liaison to Western princes and princesses : Svyatopolk to a daughter of Boleslas the Great, Premislava to Ladislas the Bald of Hungary, Yaroslav to

---

(63) Anonymi Galli Chronicon, I, ch. 16, *M.P.H.*, I, p. 413 : " Tanti viri funus mecum, omnis homo, recole, dives, pauper, miles, clerus, insuper agricolae, Latinorum et Slavorum quotquot estis incolae." The study of Old Polish ecclesiastical terms also reveals the marked influence of the Old Slavonic on Polish Christian terminology. Cf. E. Klich, *Polish Christian Terminology* (in Polish) (Posen, 1927). (Unobtainable in England.)

(64) *M.P.H.*, I, p. 323 : Quis in laudem Dei totidem coadunavit linguas ? Cum in propria et in Latina Deum digne venerari posses, in hoc tibi non satis, Graecam superaddere maluisti.

Ingegerde of Sweden, Mary to Casimir I of Poland and it is suspected that in 1025 Boleslas the Great married Vladimir's daughter Predslava. Yaroslav followed his father's policy. His son Izyaslav married a sister of Casimir I of Poland ; his daughters Elizabeth, Anne and Anastasia married Harald of Norway, Henry I of France and Andrew of Hungary respectively, and his sons Igor and Svyatoslav married Kunegunde of Germany, daughter of Otto, Margrave of Meissen, and the German Oda whose mother may have been a daughter of Henry III's brother. Yaroslav's successor Vsevolod broke with the habit and turned east by marrying a daughter of the Emperor Constantine Monomakh, but his daughter Eupraxia went to Germany to become first the wife of Henry von Stade, Margrave of the Nordmark, and after the Margrave's death, of Henry IV, whilst his son and successor, the famous Vladimir Monomakh, found his wife in distant England when he married Gytha, daughter of Harald, the last Saxon king and niece of Svean the King of Denmark. Two Polish princes, Boleslas II and Mieszko, married Russian princesses, the former, Vicheslava, daughter of Yaroslav's son Vladimir, and the latter, Eudoxia, daughter of Izyaslav. Boleslas III of Poland also married a princess of the Izyaslav line Zbislava, daughter of Svyatopolk and sister of Predslava, who married a son of Coloman of Hungary. Vladimir Monomakh's children followed the tradition, Euphemia marrying the Hungarian King Coloman, and Mstislav, Christine of Sweden. Lastly, his daughter Malmfrid married Sigurd of Denmark, and her sister Ingeburge married S. Canute of Denmark(65).

To appreciate the bearing of these intermarriages on the interests of Russia of Kiev and the rest of Europe one should bear in mind what they meant in the medieval world. . It need not surprise anyone that Kiev should have kept contact with the Scandinavian countries since in this it remained true to tradition dating from pagan days ; but these new contacts with the neighbouring nations of Poland and Hungary were a significant demonstration of friendly feelings. Suggestive, too, were Kiev's relations with Germany(66) and the deference paid in France(67) and Saxon England to the prestige of the court of Kiev. One can then well imagine that, had fate been kinder, Kiev might have been the carrier of a treasure more enduring, the refinement and culture of ancient Byzantium.

*   *   *

---

(65) On these relations, cf. B. Leib, *Rome, Kiev et Byzance à la fin du XIe siècle* (Paris, 1924), pp. 143-69, 322. F. Braun, "Russland und die Deutschen in alter Zeit" (*Germanica, E. Sievers zum 75. Geburtstage*, Halle, 1925), pp. 683 seq. ; A. Bloch, "Verwandschaftliche Beziehungen des Sächsischen Adels zum Russischen Fürstenhause im XI Jh." *Festschrift A. Brackmann* (Weimar, 1931), pp. 185-206 ; N. de Baumgarten, "Généalogies et mariages occidentaux des Rurikides Russes du Xe au XIIe s,." *Orientalia Christiana*, Nos. 35, 94, Roma, 1927, 1934.

(66) For further details, cf. M. E. Shaytan, "Germaniia i Kiev v XI v." (*Letopis zanyatyi postoyannoi istoriko-arkheograficheskoi komissii*, vol. XXXIV (Leningrad, 1927), pp. 1-26.

(67) Cf. G. Lozinski, "La Russie dans la Littérature Française du Moyen Age," *Revue des Etudes Slaves* (1929), vol. IX, pp. 71-88, 253-69. Note that the name of Russia appears in the "Chansons de Geste" more often than that of Poland. To the French of the eleventh to thirteenth centuries, Russia was not known as a legendary country, but as a nation whose geographical position must have been quite familiar, and whose wealth especially was appreciated. Cf. *ibid.*, pp. 258-65, interesting and numerous indications of the place Russia of Kiev occupied in the trade of the West, especially France. Cf. my study, *The Kiev State*, pp. 42 seq.

These investigations throw a sidelight on one particular problem of the early history of Russian Christianity. Many specialists have puzzled over the introduction of some western practices into the Russian Church. Of these the first, which can be traced to Vladimir's time, was the tithe. Unknown in the Byzantine Church, it was a Frankish invention which had spread from Frankish territory to Western Christendom. As we learn from the *Primary Russian chronicle* attributed to Nestor, Vladimir ordered a tenth of his income to be earmarked for the church of the Holy Virgin, his own foundation, which from that time came to be called " Desiatinnaya," or Church of the Tithe. Other canonical customs that were definitely Western are listed in the *Ustav* of S. Vladimir. For instance, transgressions of the moral code and of ecclesiastical prescriptions are, according to this document, to be referred to ecclesiastical courts ; even some civil cases and whatever had any connection with hereditary rights came under the jurisdiction of the Church authorities.

Experts are still debating the authenticity of this statute. Its oldest manuscript only dates from the thirteenth century and in most manuscripts Vladimir is quoted as saying that he received baptism from the holy Patriarch Photius, which is of course no proof of authenticity. Many of the ordinances attributed to Vladimir by the manuscripts are wholly alien to Byzantine mentality and were doubtlessly foisted into Russian ecclesiastical legislation under Western influence, but there is nothing to prove that they came from Vladimir. That the first Russian duke who happened to be a Christian, should have introduced into Russia the system of tithes, unknown in Byzantium and of Western origin, is also no evidence. Vladimir only ordered the tenth of his revenues to be reserved for the church of Our Lady, which was at the same time the cathedral of Kiev, as an endowment, but we have no evidence that the system was extended to the whole of Russia as it was in the West. Nor is it justifiable to see in the person of Anastasius who was charged by the Duke with the collection and the administration of the tithe, a sort of " Vogt " or Lord Protector, such as officiated at the time in the German Church.

In any case it is certainly an exaggeration to infer from these premises that Russian Christianity was of Western origin, whether Roman or Scandinavian. That Western influences should have found access to Russia in the early stages of her christianisation is not so extraordinary, since her doors were wide open and in the tenth century Bohemia provided a convenient approach. It should also be remembered that before Vladimir's conversion two of his wives were Czechs. When Poland became Christian the Bohemian thoroughfare was considerably widened by this accession, so that in the eleventh century the mutual exchange of Western and Eastern influences between those three countries must have proceeded well-nigh unhampered. It is significant that the oldest collection of Russian law, the *Russkaya Pravda*, attributed to the Duke Yaroslav the Wise, bears traces of Czech influence(68).

---

(68) I am unable to pronounce on these Western influences more fully, as the relevant books were not available : N. S. Suvorov, *Western Influences on Ancient Law* (Yaroslavl, 1892) ;

In view of all that has been said about the political and cultural development of Kievan Russia and its relations with Poland, Bohemia, Germany and the rest of Europe, one must admit that in the eleventh century Europe was standing on the threshold of great possibilities. It was the period—the only one in European history— when Russia was fully conscious of belonging to Europe and at the same time able to offer her the service of a passage for the free transmission to the West of Byzantine civilisation, that harmonious blend of classical, Hellenistic, Roman and oriental traditions ; and Europe at this time was only too anxious to enrich its Roman inheritance and the traditions of the Germanic conquerors with the treasures of the great classical and Hellenistic age of which the few remnants saved by Rome had given her only a foretaste. In this process, two Slavonic nations, the Czechs and the Poles, seemed to be destined to act as intermediaries, all the better qualified for their task as they were still in possession of the remnants of the Graeco-Slavonic culture which the two Greek brothers Cyril and Methodius had founded in the ninth century in Great Moravia. With this culture still flourishing among the Bulgars, the Serbs and to some extent among the Croats, Europe's eastern windows opened on vistas of an intellectual renascence full of promise.

And Western Europe stood in urgent need of new incentives coming from the only centre that had kept the old Hellenistic and Christian culture unblemished. For the fusion of the old Roman legacy rescued by the Church with the traditions of the new masters of the Western parts of the Roman Empire were not an unmixed blessing. Many features of primitive and Roman Christianity which had evolved in an atmosphere of Hellenistic cultural traditions were either slowly vanishing or revealing aspects at variance with the traditions so dear to early Rome and giving birth to a sort of Germanic Christianity the novelties of which, especially in Church administration and canon law, gradually took hold of the West. But the old Roman spirit was still alive, gathering strength for a last stand. The conflict that ensued at the end of the eleventh century ended in disaster. Europe and the world were the losers. And yet the struggle, which practically lasted for over a century with its intervals of calm and attempts at compromise and was to persist in other forms till the end of the Middle Ages, would have lost much of its bitterness, if before hostilities broke out or minds on both sides had time to harden into fanaticism, some fresh air had been let in from the East to cool the hot heads with a better knowledge

idem, *Traces of Western Catholic Canon Law in the Monuments of Ancient Russian Law*, (in Russian, Yaroslavl, 1888) ; K. Fritzler, *Zwei Abhandlungen über Altrussisches Recht ; Die Sogenannte Kirchenordnung Yaroslavs ein Denkmal Russisch-Germanischen Rechts* (Berlin, 1923). Western influences in Russian canon law notably increased in the twelfth century through Novgorod and are noticeable in the *Ustav* attributed to the Duke Yaroslav. Both documents are to be found in V. N. Beneshevich, *Collection of Records touching on Canon Law* (in Russian, Petrograd, 1914), vol. I, pp. 59-89. A new edition of the *Russkaya Pravda* is being published under the supervision of B. D. Orlov, by V. P. Lyotimov, N. P. Lavrov, M. I. Tikhomirov, G. L. Gegermans, G. E. Kochin (*Akad. Nauk. Inst. Istorii*, Moscow, 1939, vol. I). Cf. also L. K. Goetz, " Kirchenrechtliche und Kulturgeschichtliche Denkmäler Altrusslands," *Kirchengeschichtliche Abh.* (U: Stutz), Stuttgart, 1905, Heft 18, 19, pp. 1-62. It contains a translation of S. A. Pavlov's Course of Canon Law (1902) ; Canonical Advice of the metropolitan John II, pp. 98-171 ; Questions of Kirik Sabbas and Elias, pp. 172-342 ; the Exhortation of Archbishop Elias of Novgorod, pp. 343-89.

of the methods applied by Eastern Christianity to problems that so upset the West. But when the West reopened contact with the East at the time of the Crusades it was too late ; for the Western theologians had made up their minds and the more or less pious pilgrims and liberators of the Holy Land soon deteriorated into conquerors, more interested in Byzantium's gold and jewels than in her letters and culture. A more discreet contact through neutral intermediaries would probably have profited Western Europe better and given her more leisure for quiet assimilation.

Unfortunately, things happened otherwise, and Russia of Kiev was never allowed to play the part that might have been expected from her in the eleventh century. The distance between Kiev and Western Europe was so great that an extension of that channel through Bohemia and Poland reaching the German frontiers seemed indispensable. The extension was being made, but it could never have functioned unless the countries concerned remained sufficiently independent to do their share and were not unduly implicated in the Western transformation of Christianity. This would have been possible on the one condition that there stood between Germany proper and Kievan Russia a political power strong enough to withstand the tidal wave of the Germanic onrush towards the East and enlightened enough to keep its cultural atmosphere open to the Latin world without closing it to the Greek. I have pointed out that something of the sort was attempted. The Moravian Empire all but achieved this object and after its collapse the Czech Przemyslides made some effort to carry on the work, but were foiled in their attempt by the proximity of their lands to Germany. The Magyars, who were responsible for the fall of Moravia, far from lending their assistance, thwarted every move in that direction in their own national interest. Poland came forward under Mieszko I and bid fair under Boleslas the Great to set up the independent State that Central Europe so badly needed. His Polish-Czech State would have fulfilled this mission, since the fusion of the Polish and the Czech tribes would have sprung from their ethnical roots. But the project failed and all hopes of seizing an opportunity that seemed within grasp and would have enriched the whole of Europe were dashed to the ground. The collapse was followed by the disappearance of every element that could have supplied such a political combination with its own cultural and national basis. At the end of the eleventh and in the twelfth century what remained of the Slavonic liturgy in Bohemia was hounded out of the country and condemned to final extinction. So radically did the situation alter that at the beginning of the twelfth century Cosmas, the first Czech chronicler, who wrote his work between 1119 and 1125, was for all his loyalty and patriotism a convinced Latin and a sworn foe of the Slavonic liturgy and letters. Byzantium and its culture were irretrievably banned from Central Europe, leaving Latin and Roman civilisation the undisputed master of the field. Germany had scored a complete political victory and dug herself in for centuries as the paramount political factor in that part of Europe. She also remained, as a result, the only representative of Roman Latin culture, which she had received from the Franks just as the Franks had received it from the Romans and the Latinised Gauls. But past intermediaries were soon forgotten in Central Europe where Germany remained the only cultural power to be reckoned with. Thereafter, the nations of Central Europe had no choice but to accept Latin culture at Germany's hands and be content with its German version.

*   *   *

The failure to create in Central Europe an independent political centre on a level with Germany also powerfully influenced the subsequent course of events in Russia which, as time went on, tended to incline towards the East. Of course the political system introduced by Yaroslav the Great (1054) by dividing the realm between his five sons, leaving Kiev and Novgorod to the eldest, substantially contributed to this new orientation. It was the beginning of a gradual disintegration of the Russian State, a process only slowed down by the prestige of Kiev and the attitude of the Church, which took no notice of any partition and continued to treat all Russian lands as one. The succession to the throne was governed by the old Germanic system of " tanistry," as practised also by the Vandals in Africa, the Grand Duke of Kiev being succeeded at his death, not by his son, but by his brothers, the youngest of them being followed by the eldest of his nephews. Izyaslav I (1054-1073) was succeeded by his brothers Svyatoslav (1073-1076) and Vsevolod I (1078-1093); these were followed by Izyaslav's son Svyatopolk II (1093-1113), who in turn was succeeded by Vsevolod I's son, Vladimir II Monomakh (1113-1125)), one of the greatest of the Kievan Grand Dukes. After Monomakh's death, this system of succession was abandoned and instead the Grand Duke was succeeded by his sons. Grand Duke Mstislav (1125-1132) was a capable ruler, but on the accession of his brothers, rivalry broke out among the Princes, and their internecine wars, together with repeated incursions by the Kumans, successors of the Pechenegs in modern South Russia, brought about the political and economic downfall of Kiev(69).

But this was not the end of Russia. Cultural and economic conditions progressed in other principalities, and these were many : Smolensk, Chernigov, Seversk and Pereyaslav were carved out of the territories of the Radimichians, the Severians and the Vyatichians ; to the south-west the Buzhanians, the Luchanians amalgamated with the Volhynians and together formed the principality of Volhynia which became in the beginning of the thirteenth century part of the principality of Galicia, called after Halicz, a stronghold built by the Duke Vladimir in 1140. This was the only part of Russia which, owing to its proximity to Poland, remained in contact with the West. But the partition of Poland into a number of principalities after the reform of the law of succession introduced by Boleslas III, a change similar to that which occurred in Russia, had left Poland considerably weakened and made it difficult for her to take advantage of the deep transformations on her eastern borders ; and though the senior duke was

---

(69) For more details on this period, see S. F. Platonov, *History of Russia* (London, 1925), translated by E. Aronsberg, pp. 44-81 ; M. Hrushevsky, *A History of the Ukraine* (ed. by O. J. Frederikson, Newhaven, 1941), pp. 76-95.

258

also the ruler of Cracow, he never succeeded in rousing the other dukes to common action in that quarter. The result was that not only was Poland unable to recover the territory that was originally Polish and had been a bone of contention between Poland and Russia since the first Mieszko's days, but the Polish dukes' attempts at mediation in the local quarrels of Galicia and Volhynia lacked the necessary backing to produce any results. Not until a reunited Poland rose to new endeavours under Casimir the Great was Galicia restored to Poland and together with Volhynia shared in her destiny till the year 1772. But the cultural profit of this development to the rest of Europe fell short of what it should have been, had the possibilities of the eleventh century been realised.

There remained another principality to link up Russia with the West and that was Novgorod, the geographical position of which made it Russia's natural gateway to Germany, Scandinavia and the Baltic. Originally under the Grand Duke of Kiev, the city had for all practical purposes won its political freedom, including the right to choose its own prince, as a reward for its prosperous trade with the West, especially Germany, and Western influence had settled within its walls without marring its Russo-Byzantine features. And yet the city, which owed to its Western trade its membership of the Hanseatic League, failed to leave any deep cultural mark on the countries which it had benefited economically.

With no power on her Western frontiers to keep her, by prestige or expansion, in touch with the West, Russia lost interest in her Western neighbours and gradually drifted towards the East. Then a new principality came into being in the north-east, on territories lying between the upper Volga, the Oka and the Moskva rivers, that of Suzdal. It had been colonised from the middle Dnieper and rose to fame in the twelfth century. New cities sprang up alongside Rostov and Suzdal—Tver, Vladimir, Yaroslavl, Moscow, Nizhni Novgorod, Ryazan—and a brisk trade with the Bulgars on the Volga and the countries beyond brought in wealth and prosperity. Again, the East invitingly lay open to allure the Russians. They must have yielded to its attraction, for the beautiful churches in Vladimir and Suzdal, though inspired by Byzantine ideals of style, show undoubted affinity to the twelfth-century architecture of Armenia and Georgia and their stones were quarried in the Urals. The Volga and the Caspian resumed their activity as trade arteries and links with the civilised Arabian world.

However, all this did not imply that relations with the West were in danger of being severed. As Russia's culture and economic interests were still in the making, the possibility remained open for Central and Western Europe to profit by the new connections created by the great Eastern Russian principality, in spite of the many centrifugal forces that were later to enter into play. Western influences still reached Russian soil through the gates of Chernigov, Halicz and Novgorod. But the East beyond the Volga lay open through Vladimir and Suzdal, inviting Russia to carry into the interior of Asia her hybrid culture enriched by Byzantium and the West.

At this stage a new factor intervened and ruined every prospect for centuries to come—the Mongols. Their first invasion started when in 1224

Genghis Khan sent an army against the Kumans. The southern princes scented danger and despatched troops in support of their neighbours with whom they were then on more friendly terms. But the Russo-Kumanian army was routed. One disaster followed another. In 1236, Batu, grandson of Genghis Khan, defeated the Bulgars and attacked the eastern principalities ; all the north-eastern princes were defeated and made to pay tribute : only Novgorod escaped. In 1240, Batu was on the march again for the conquest of the southern principalities and Central Europe. Kiev was captured and destroyed, Volhynia and Galicia devastated. The Polish army which tried to stem the avalanche near Lignica (Liegnitz) was cut to pieces and the Duke Henry II fell with thousands of his gallant knights. Only the death of the Great Khan, which forced Batu to double back and make sure of his share in the partition of the empire, saved Hungary from utter destruction and the rest of Europe from the worst. But this was no relief to Russia. Batu received as his share the north-west of the Mongol Empire, including the whole of Russia, and founded the Empire of the Golden Horde, called Kipchak by the Mussulmans, which held Russia under its sway.

Then darkness fell over Russian lands and there was none to stretch out a helping hand to the Russian princes and release them from their humiliating position. Central Europe gradually fell to pieces; Poland writhed in the throes of internal strife between the dukes; Bohemia, severed from Russia by Hungary, fell back upon herself and tried to live her own life within the orbit of the Empire; Germany disintegrated into sovereign principalities whilst the Emperor Frederick II was absorbed in his conflict with the popes and in his dreams of a new Roman Empire revolving round Italy and Sicily along the Mediterranean coasts. It was then the void was felt, as Russia had not on her western borders an empire strong enough to fight its own battles and near enough to realise that any help given to her in her distress would turn to its own profit. The fate of Galicia was a striking case in point. As his country lay on the rim of the Tartar Empire, Daniel of Galicia found it possible to preserve some autonomy under Tartar supremacy, and he did all he could to elicit some help from the Westerners, to the extent of even offering to the pope to embrace Western Christianity. Innocent IV tried in vain to rouse Daniel's neighbours and to convince Poles and Hungarians that it was in their own interest to go to his rescue. Neither of them was strong enough to be useful and lofty-minded enough to look beyond his petty interests. All the satisfaction Daniel got was' a royal title conferred on him by the Pope, which since then was adopted by successive rulers of Galicia. In 1282, a second Tartar invasion made an end of Galicia's privileged position; the country was devastated and turned into pastures for the nomads' horses. They were given free run of the whole country between Lwów and Kiev to graze in peace.

For two centuries Russia fell out of European history—a long stretch in the life of any nation. At the same time the Byzantine Empire, as a result of the Latin conquests, was sinking to its dissolution, so that Russia had little to expect from a quarter that was once the main source of her cultural inspiration. When at last Russia emerged from obscurity she could scarcely recognise the West which had in the meantime made long strides towards cultural maturity and grown equally ignorant of the East. Russia did her best to make up for lost time, but the difference had struck too deep to be levelled out completely. To a certain extent Russia has ever since remained a stranger to the European family of nations. Her aloofness, her idiosyncracies date from that period. Her only chance of evolving in harmony with the rest of Europe occurred in the eleventh century and the opportunity was lost at the expense of both.

CONCLUSION

CENTRAL EUROPE'S FATE

We may therefore hold for sufficiently good reasons that during the period which we have treated, Central Europe took in rough outline the final shape it was to maintain and to work upon in the coming centuries. The tenth and eleventh centuries marked the making of Central Europe and another stage in the evolution of Europe, following upon the collapse of the Roman Empire, and Charlmagne's abortive attempt to revive it was brought to a close. Despite Germany's efforts to recondition the old Roman principle of political unity, the process of Europe's fragmentation into smaller political units went on steadily. Some sort of Roman unity might have been retrieved from the breakdown, but only on the lines of Otto III's plan, and his death wrecked it. A failure, too, was the attempt to set up in the huge area of Central Europe, between Germany and Russia, a great empire the existence of which would have simplified the process of Europe's growth. There only remained then the Roman imperial idea, worn to a shadow in the West, but still spelling danger to the lands beyond the Elbe where there existed no power in a position to curb greed and ambition or clip them to reasonable proportions ; and under the gathering gloom of that threat the stage was set.

At the close of this period, the Slavonic peoples between the Elbe, the Baltic and the Oder, with no power to afford them protection and nerve them in their uneven struggle with the emperor, Propagator of the Faith and Protector of the Church against the pagans, or with the German margraves all out to magnify their power and their domination, were virtually condemned to extinction. Thus the race for the creation of a new Germany between the Elbe and the Oder opened in the twelfth century under easy conditions and culminated in the foundation by margrave Albrecht the Bear of the March of Brandenburg. Colonisation completed the work done by conquest ; but what accelerated it was the entry of the Teutonic Order into Prussia. Little did the Polish Duke, Conrad of Mazovia, who had summoned the knights, suspect that his invitation would cost Poland the loss of Pomerania ; that a king of Prussia would replace the Grand Master of the Order, annex and Germanise the rich Polish lands of Silesia ; that the insignificant Slavonic village of Bralin on the Spree would under Prussian rule expand into the mighty metropolis of a new Germany, Berlin, and in addition gather under its sway the territory of old Germany from the Rhine to the Elbe.

And yet, in spite of the new turn of events and so many frustrations, the notion of a big political unit occupying Central Europe by the side of Germany never died. Again and again, at different periods, under different designations and disguises, it rose as though prompted by the sub-conscious feeling that in this direction lay the only hope of this part of the world. Sometimes, a sort of nostalgia for bygone days, with all their hopes unfulfilled and their wishes left unspoken, seemed to seize the conscience of its nations. Even the Przemyslides who in the eleventh century had been in part responsible for the failure of Boleslas the Great of Poland to set up his empire, at last gave the Polish plan a trial and almost succeeded where the Piasts had failed.

This happened at the beginning of the fourteenth century when, taking advantage of the state of exhaustion to which the struggle with the Papacy had reduced the Empire, and making the most of the silver mines they had struck on their territory, the Przemyslides rose to first rank among the Princes and became the wealthiest kings of Europe. Wenceslas II (1278-1305), was the son of the ill-fated Przemysl Otokar II who, by imposing his authority on Alpine lands, was the original founder of Austria, then lost his acquisitions to his rival Rudolph of Habsburg and his life at the battle of Marchfeld. Unlike his father, Wenceslas II looked for elbow-room outside the Empire ; but he took advantage of his father's footing in Silesia, eventually annexed the greater part of Poland and was crowned king of Poland at Gnesen, in 1300. Many Poles, who felt that their country had suffered grievously from divisions and internal strife, hailed the Czech King as a Liberator. Practically the whole of Poland was united again.

Poland's unification looked promising in many ways. It is true that King Wenceslas II felt the attraction of German culture and that his court was the favourite resort of the German *Minnesinger* or wandering minstrels ; and that Bohemia was in danger of losing her national characteristics and of being swamped by German colonists who poured into the country for several decades, but she found ample compensation in the influx of Slavonic elements from Poland where at the time national feelings were very much alive. On balance, Poland was not the loser. The new king introduced order into Polish financial and economic affairs, a timely service when Europe was transforming her economic system, and his monetary reform gave Poland the necessary start for action. On the whole, the reign of Wenceslas II, little as it has been thought of until recently, did benefit Poland and prepared the ground for the unification which the Poles were to work out later for themselves(1).

It was also the Czechs' and the Poles' last chance to fuse into a single nation at a time when the language difference offered no serious obstacle. Had the two nations been united for some time under one dynasty, their lingual fusion would have recalled a similar phenomenon which occurred in France, where the dialect used at the centre was adopted for general use and superseded among others the southern dialect, though it had already matured into a distinct language.

The fame of the Bohemian King's experiment must have attracted attention in Hungary, as after the extinction of her national dynasty, the Arpads, part of the nobility offered the Hungarian crown to his son Wenceslas III, who was crowned King of Hungary and Croatia at Buda in 1301. The establishment of a vigorous State in Central Europe, grouping

(1) New light was recently shed on the reign of Wenceslas II and his father by J. Šusta, professor in the Charles IV University of Prague, and one of the best Czech historians, in his excellent work *The Twilight of the Przemyslides and their Legacy* (in Czech) (Prague, 1935), vol. II, Part I of the *History of Bohemia* (České dějny), which was started by V. Novotný.

together the principal nations on Germany's borders—Poles, Czechs, Hungarians and even the Croats who since 1102 had acknowledged the king of Hungary as their own, seemed then within sight. Wenceslas II was still young; he had displayed marked ability, and Germany, which was frittering away into principalities that took notice of the emperor's authority only to a limited extent, could only stand by and let events take their course.

But fate frowned on the project. Wenceslas II died; the Hungarian crown was seized by the Anjou dynasty; a dangerous competitor, Ladislas the Short, was putting in his claim for Poland, and the young King Wenceslas III, on his way to Poland to assert his right, was slain by an unknown assassin at Olomouc in 1306. Who could refrain from seeing in this tragedy the long shadows of another drama enacted at Libice when the Przemyslides, to secure exclusive power over Bohemia, exterminated the Slavniks; and now the last of the Przemyslides, at the moment of accomplishing what his dynasty had prevented the Piasts from carrying out, fell to the assassin's dagger in his turn. Nemesis finds grim satisfaction in history.

The dynasty of Luxemburg which succeeded the Przemyslides on the throne of Bohemia continued the policy of the last Przemyslide and used Bohemia as a basis for expansion over Central Europe. Charles IV (1346-1378) succeeded where the Przemyslides had failed. He extended Czech influence to the north; he obtained possession of Lusatia, Meissen, the whole March of Brandenburg together with the late margraves' recent acquisitions in Pomerania and in the Polish district of Lubush. Brandenburg was to remain an inalienable part of the Bohemian crown, but in 1411 it was lost to the Hohenzollerns, and with it went the last hope for a slowing down of the Germanising process among the once powerful Veletians. Brandenburg then followed its destiny as the cradle of modern Prussia. The same Charles also realised the dream of Przemysl Otokar II, one of his predecessors on the Czech throne, and became Roman Emperor; he also gained possession of the kingdom of Hungary for his son Sigismund (1387). Unable to keep Poland, the last great acquisition of his predecessor on the Hungarian throne, Louis the Great of Anjou, who became king of Poland after the death of Casimir the Great in 1370, Sigismund secured the next best prize—the succession to his brother Wenceslas IV of Bohemia (1419) and his election as king of the Romans.

But by far the best chance for a re-grouping of Central Europe and part of Eastern Europe as well came the way of Poland when Hedwig (Jadwiga) of Anjou, daughter of Louis the Great, King of Hungary and of Poland, came to the throne and was made Queen of Poland. In 1386 she married Jagello, Grand Duke of Lithuania, the last country in Europe to cling to paganism, and this union brought about its conversion to Christianity. At that moment Lithuania was already a power in Eastern Europe. This Baltic people, under constant pressure from the Teutonic Order, had developed a military tradition, and Jagiello's predecessors, with the help of many Prussian refugees, men hardened by suffering, had considerably expanded their power towards the south. Acting as liberators of the Russian princes from the Tartar yoke, they conquered White Russia,

Volhynia and a goodly portion of Lesser Russia, including Kiev, leaving to the Poles the task of liberating and occupying Galicia. The political formation emerging from this union between Poland and Jagello's State represented a sort of federation between three nationalities, the Poles, the Lithuanians and the Russians, *i.e.* the White Russians and the Ukrainians, and a constitution governing their relations was finally agreed upon at Lublin in 1569. The new Union was not long in gaining control over that part of Europe. The two provinces that formed the nucleus of modern Roumania —Moldavia and Valachia—became the vassals and the allies of Poland— Lithuania and even the Czech Hussites felt inclined to choose Jagello as their king. As King Vladyslav II of Poland, Jagello put a stop to the Teutonic Order's predatory activities and defeated them at Grunwald in 1410, though it was not till 1454 that the conflict ended, when Poland recovered the old province of Pomerania with Danzig, which had been seized by the Order, and when Eastern Prussia became a vassal State of Poland and severed connections with the Empire. It was only a matter of time for the Latvian lands to come within the sphere of influence of the Union.

The advantage to the Czechs of belonging to a strong federation was best appreciated by the Czech King, George of Podiebrady (1458-1471), who advised the Czech nobility to offer the Czech crown, after his death, to a prince of the Jagellon dynasty. Thus, for half a century Bohemia came to be ruled by descendants of Jagello : Vladislas II (1471-1516) and Louis (1516-1526), and the Jagellon Federal Union, later reinforced when Vladislas II was made King of Hungary in 1490, came into direct contact with Central Europe.

The federation, whose sway stretched from the Baltic to the Black Sea, recalled in many ways the ambitious schemes of the Przemyslides and the Piasts as well as the achievements of Kiev in its early days. More solid than the ephemeral empire of the Goths under Vitimir, set up a thousand years before in the same country, the federation had every chance for further development. And yet it could never muster the strength which a similar federation would have commanded in those parts of Europe in the eleventh or twelfth centuries. Given time, it might have learned to compose its differences and blend its heterogeneous elements, but religious disunion wrecked the prospect. East and West had too long followed each their own ways for Catholics and Orthodox to come to mutual understanding and save the Jagellon Union. Meanwhile the princes of Moscow were grouping around them the population of Russia, and the Church, whose representative, the metropolitan of Kiev, had transferred his residence to Moscow, gave them full support. Religious co-operation thus enabled the princes to prepare the blow that knocked out the Tartars, and gave them the freedom and power to re-conquer their country.

But a new foe loomed over the south, the Ottoman Turks, and it will always be remembered how the Jagellons understood their duty and gallantly came forward to defend Christianity against Islam. Once more, as in the day of Boleslas the Great, princes of the Polish dynasty, though relentless opponents of the Empire, tried to play the part assigned to the emperors by the Middle Ages and led their troops to battle. Two of them perished in the defence of Christian civilisation—Vladyslav III at the disastrous battle of Varna on the Black Sea (1444) (2) and Louis, King of Bohemia and Hungary, at the battle of Mohacz on the Danube (1526), both in an attempt to bar the progress of the Turks into the heart of Europe. Long after the extinction of the Jagellon dynasty and the collapse of its political legacy, the duty of defending Christian civilisation which its imposing rise to political power had assigned to it, was remembered in the lands of the Vistula, and its last echo thundered under the walls of Vienna in 1683 when the Polish army, under the command of its King, John Sobieski, charged the Turks who invested the city, wrested it from the armies of Mohammed and removed the menace of Islam for ever from Europe.

The Jagellons failed to erect a durable political structure in Central-Eastern Europe, but the ideal which inspired it remained part of the Central European atmosphere long after the disappearance of this remarkable Lithuanian-Polish dynasty. The Habsburgs then came forward from Austria and after securing the long coveted crown of Bohemia proceeded to build up their own empire in Central Europe on the lines traced by the Piasts, the Przemyslides, the Luxemburgers, the Arpads, the Anjous and the Jagellons, and despite appearances, they had every chance of completing the work of their forerunners on the thrones of Bohemia, Poland and Hungary. Only, just as the centre of gravity of Jagellon power leaned too far to the East, that of the Habsburgs, based as it was on Alpine lands, swayed too far back to the West. This lack of balance prevented them from devoting sufficient attention to the problems of the East, especially of Poland, which stayed outside their particular sphere.

Worse than this—they had to carry over the long stretch of their history the dead weight of the "imperial idea," which hampered them at every step. As their power had its roots in German territory, they could never get rid of the obsession which this hollow but still glamorous notion exercised on every German prince. Instead of boldly facing south where Hungary and Croatia had spent their best on resisting the Turks, and setting the Balkans free; or instead of turning East and helping the Poles in their difficulties with the rising Prussian monarchy, offspring of the union of East Prussia with Brandenburg under the Hohenzollerns, they never could make up their minds to get rid of the obsolete imperial notion and stop spending time, money and armies on endless efforts to re-create the Roman Empire of the German nation. Eventually, forced to share the imperial title with the Hohenzollerns and failing to understand their true mission in Central Europe, they forfeited their throne, and their empire fell to pieces. This disaster concluded a long history of trial and failure round the original scheme of the Piasts in the tenth and eleventh centuries.

---

(2) See the recent article by O. Halecki, "The Crusade of Varna, A Discussion of Controversial Problems," *Polish Institute Series* (New York, 1943), No. 3.

Now the liberated nations started rebuilding their homes with the eagerness of youthful enthusiasm, but their leaders omitted to learn the lessons of history. There they would have read that it is only by uniting and defending each other's rights that small nations can preserve their character and freedom. The German *Drang nach Osten* was only temporarily checked and Russia only took a moment's breath before resuming its endeavour to make Ivan the Terrible's dream of a Third Rome come true. History shows how inexorable its laws and those of geography can be. Whenever a political vacuum is created in the vast spaces between the Baltic, the Adriatic and the Black Sea, one of the two giants of West or East will step in to upset the balance of Europe. This evolution was set going in the eleventh century when all hopes for a great Central European power were dashed to the ground.

Should this be Central Europe's irrevocable fate ? Only future historians will be able to tell. Some ideas never die. So often did the idea of unification lie buried under the debris of Central European cataclysms, only to re-emerge in different forms. Perhaps the door is not closed on its last revival.

APPENDIX I

BYZANTINE, ARAB AND ANGLO-SAXON TRADITION ON WHITE CROATIA AND WHITE SERBIA—ORIGINS OF THE CROATS AND THE SERBS

CONSTANTINE PORPHYROGENNETOS—MA'SUDI, THE PERSIAN GEOGRAPHER AND KING ALFRED—THEORIES ON THE ORIGIN OF THE CROATS AND THE SERBS.

Only of recent years have specialists devoted some attention to the existence of White Croatia, north of the Carpathians, to White Serbia, north of Bohemia and to the racial origin of the Croats and the Serbs. This major problem still remains unsolved, but its discussion is a necessary preamble to the history of the tenth and eleventh centuries which were so decisive in the making of Central and Eastern Europe.

The tradition on those two countries is anything but negligible and we owe a most exhaustive account to the Emperor Constantine VII Porphyrogennetos. His statement provides us with a most convenient starting point. The Emperor found reliable information on foreign countries in the Archives of the Logothet of the Dromos. It functioned as the Foreign Office where the reports of the Byzantine ambassadors were filed (1).

This is what Constantine has to say about the Croats and the Serbs whom he locates north of the Carpathian Mountains (2) : " The Croats at that time dwelt on the other side of Bavaria where to-day we find the White Croats. One tribe detached itself from the rest, namely, the five brothers Klukas, Lobelos, Kosentzes, Muchlo, Chrobatos, and the two sisters Tuga and Buga. They came with their people to Dalmatia and found the Avars in possession of that land. After some years of war between Croats and Avars, the Croats remained victorious ; of the Avars, some were massacred, others forced to submission. Since then, the country has been ruled by the Croats. But there still remain in Croatia some descendants of the Avars, identifiable as such.

" The other Croats live in the neighbourhood of Francia [i.e. Germany] and they are called to-day Belochrobati, i.e. White Croats. They are ruled by a prince in subjection to Othon the great King of Francia and of Saxony and are not baptised. They make matrimonial alliance and friendly treaties with the Turks (i.e. the Magyars). From the Croats who went to Dalmatia, one portion broke away and occupied Illyricum and

---

(1) His most important book from our point of view is *De Administrando Imperio*. Its best studies are by G. Manojlović " Studies on De administrando imperio, Emp. Konstantine VII Porphyrogennetos' work," *Rad jugoslov. Akademije* (in Croat) (1910-1911), vols. 182, 186, 187, and by J. B. Bury ("The Treatise De Administrando Imperio", *Byzant. Zeitschrift* 1906, vol. XV).

(2) *De adm. imp.*, ch. 30, 31, Bonn, pp. 143, 144, 147, 151. Cf. J. B. Bury, *The Early History of the Slavonic Settlements in Dalmatia, Croatia and Serbia, Constantine Porphyrogenetos, De Adm. Imp., chs.* 29-36 (London, 1920).

Pannonia. They also had an independent prince and kept on friendly terms with the prince of Croatia.

" For some time, the Croats of Dalmatia remained subjects of the Franks, as they used to be in their previous habitat. But the Franks treated them so cruelly that they killed babies at the breasts of their Croat mothers and threw them to the dogs. Unable to put up with such treatment the Croats rebelled and killed the chiefs appointed by the Franks. Thereupon the Franks sent a strong force against them. War followed, which lasted seven years and eventually the Croats got the upper hand with great difficulty and massacred all the Franks with their prince Kotzilis. Since then they have been their own masters, were governed by their own laws and they asked the Pope of Rome to be baptised. Bishops were sent to them under their prince Porinos. And their country was divided into eleven Zhupanies [counties.]"

The above information is completed in chapter XXXI, where we read that " the Croats who to-day occupy the region of Dalmatia originated from the non-baptised Croats, called also White. The latter live on the other side of Turkey (i.e. Hungary) near Francia (Germany) and are neighbours to the non-baptised Serbs." In the following chapter, Constantine placed the migration of the Croats to the south under the reign of Heraclius. The Serbs followed the Croats. Heraclius made use of them against the Avars and settled them on the lands from which the Avars had been expelled. Their prince was at that time Porga. Under him they were christened by priests sent from Rome at the request of the Emperor. After a few details about the pacification of the Christian Croats, the emperor concludes his account by distinguishing again between White Croatia and Southern Croatia : " Great Croatia, also called White, remains non-Christian like the Serbs who live in its neighbourhood. This Croatia possesses fewer cavalry and infantry than Christian Croatia, as it is harassed by frequent incursions of Franks, Turks and Pechenegs . . . It has no fleet . . . being far from the sea. It lies a thirty days' journey away from it and this is the Black Sea."

In chapter XXXII, Constantine deals with the Serbs : " We should know that the Serbs originated from the non-baptised Serbs also called White. These live on the other side of the Turks (Magyars) in a region they call Boiki, also neighbouring on Francia and on Great Croatia, non-baptised and also called White. It was there the Serbs originally lived. When the government of Serbia passed from the father to the two sons, one of these, accompanied by half the population, took refuge with Heraclius, the Emperor of the Romans. The same received him and allowed him to settle in the thema of Thessalonica, in a place which since then has been called Serblia." Not satisfied with this settlement, the Serbs thought of turning back, but accepted instead the present territory of Serbia, from which they expelled the Avars. They were then baptised by priests summoned from Rome by the Emperor and became subjects of the Byzantines.

Constantine must then have had definite knowledge of the existence of a political formation founded by the Croats on the northern slopes of the Carpathians, which extended from the steppes then occupied by the Pechenegs to a similar state founded by the Serbs and identified with Bohemia. This could be no other than the land lying between the Saale, the Elbe and the Havel, where remnants of the Serbs are still found to this day.

It was this part of Constantine's account that provoked the sharpest criticism, as it was taken for granted at the end of the nineteenth century (3) that the Slavs' southward migration could not have taken place in two distinct waves. This objection seemed well founded, as what the imperial writer states further about the christianisation of the Croats and the Serbs in Dalmatia was generally regarded as untrue(4). Heraclius, so it was argued, could not possibly have asked the Pope to send missionaries to Illyricum, as reported by Constantine, since his relations with the Pope were not satisfactory and because such a move on the part of a Byzantine emperor would have been against the interests of Byzantium. On this ground very few attempts(5) were made to rehabilitate Constantine's story of the settling of Croats and Serbs in the south, to the consequent detriment of other details in the Emperor's account. In dealing, however, with the christianisation of the Croats and the Serbs, we have been able to prove(6) that Constantine's account of the part which Heraclius asked the Pope to play, was quite consistent with the general situation, since Heraclius and Honorius were on friendly terms, and Byzantium at that period still respected Rome's jurisdiction over the Roman province of Illyricum. This finding lends weight to Constantine's evidence and makes his account, however confused it may be in its details, more reliable in view of the solid tradition behind it, as preserved in the imperial Chancellery of Byzantium.

*   *   *

This Byzantine tradition is confirmed by Arab sources on which experts have drawn only recently. The Arab Ma'sudi described the Slavs in northern Europe in 943 on the basis of information he gathered on his travels(7). Among indications which are debatable, one point is clear : he includes in his enumeration of the principal Slavonic tribes of Central Europe the Surbin (Serbs), a people feared by "the Slavs for reasons too long to enumerate, owing to characteristics it would be too digressive to

---

(3) See a detailed account of this controversy in L. Niederle, *Slav. Antiquities* (in Czech) Part II, vol. I, pp. 250-62, in Niederle's *Manuel de l'Antiquité Slave* (Paris, 1923), vol. I, pp. 88 seq., and a short summary in my book, *Les Slaves, Byz. et Rome*, pp. 7 seq.

(4) Especially by C. Jireček, *Geschichte der Serben* (Gotha, 1911), pp. 107 seq., whose authority on the history of the Serbs is universally acknowledged.

(5) Made chiefly by N. Županić, "White Serbia" (in Croat), *Narodna Starina* (1922), vol. I, pp. 107-18, and by L. Hauptmann, "The Migration of the Croats" (in Slovene), *Strena Buliciana* (Zagreb, 1924), pp. 515-45, and reprinted in Croat in *Zbornik Kralja Tomislava, Opera Academiae Scientiarum et Artium Slavorum Meridionalium separatim edita*, vol. XVII (Zagreb, 1925), pp. 86-127.

(6) See my book, *Les Slaves, Byz. et Rome*, pp. 71-4. Cf. *ibid*, pp. 7 seq.

(7) I. Marquart, *Osteuropäische und Ostasiatische Streifzüge* (Leipzig, 1903), pp. 101 seq.

explain and also because they have no religion to submit to," the Morawa (Moravians), the Chorwatin (Croats) and the Cachin (most probably not the Saxons but the Czechs). He also gives information on the Serbs and describes some of their funeral customs which he compares to those of the Hindus and which are common in the Caucasus and among the Khazars(8). What Ma'sudi says of the Croats and the Serbs can only refer to the Croats north of the Carpathians and to the Serbs living in the Czechs' neighbourhood.

There are other Arab writers, particularly Ibn Rustah, al Bekri, Gardizi and the Persian Geographer belonging to the tenth century, but their information is probably derived from Al Djarmi's lost work. (9) Though the affinity of these writings is not quite established, it is generally agreed that all these accounts are indebted to an older source belonging to the first half of the eleventh century, if not earlier, and attributed to an Armenian or a Persian who visited the country of later Russia and kept an interesting record of his findings on the tribes living there, especially the Slavs. According to these reports the country of the Slavs was a fourteen-day journey's distance from that of the Pechenegs. The first Slavonic city is called Va-it by Ibn Rustah, Vantit by Gardizi and Vabnit by the Persian Geographer(10). After that, another Slavonic land is mentioned as being governed by a king who, after the custom of the Turco-Tartar nomadic tribes, lived on mare's milk(11). The capital is alternately called Jrvab, Khurdab or Jravt, in which it is easy to detect the national name of Hrvat or Croat(12). The king is called Swet Malik, who has a viceroy called Supandj (zhupan). For all its obscurities, this source, too, confirms the existence of quite a respectable State created by the Croats on the northern slopes of the Carpathians.

The identification of the first Slavonic city mentioned in the previous paragraph will be discussed presently. As to the King called Swet Malik, it is possible that those Arab texts perpetuated the name of one of the Croat rulers, Svatopluk(13), under the guise of Swet Malik, not, however, to be confused with Svatopluk of Moravia; but as he conquered the country of the Croats, the Arabian writers of the tenth century may have mixed up the facts, unless perhaps there did exist a Croat ruler in the eleventh century called Svatopluk, a name fairly common among Slavonic chiefs of the western tribes.

The translator of the Persian Geographer(14), V. Minorsky, favours, not without hesitation, the contention that the Croats mentioned by the Geographer were the Croats of the south who to some extent also came

(8) Cf. also Ibn Ja'cub's transcription of Ma'sudi's account, Hirsch, *Widukinodo, Sächsische Geschischten*, pp. 192 seq.
(9) J. Marquart, loc. cit., pp. 466-73.
(10) See comparison of the three accounts in V. Minorsky's Edition of the Persian Geographer (*Hudad al—Alam*, " The Regions of the World," *a Persian Geography*, London, 1937, p. 428).
(11) J. Marquart, loc. cit., pp. 466 seq.
(12) See the various interpretations in L. Hauptmann, *Germanoslavica* (1935) vol. III, pp. 534-40.
(13) Loc. cit., p. 431.
(14) V. Minorsky, *The Regions of the World*, pp. 159, 430.

under the rule of the Moravian Svatopluk. But this would hardly fit the facts as we know them. The conquest of White Croatia by Svatopluk must have impressed the Arab world much more than his raids into distant Pannonia. We do know that Svatopluk annexed White Croatia. but we know nothing definite about his Pannonian campaign. As regards the capital of these Croats there is nothing to show that the Geographer was referring to a Croat city on the Danube. The Pannonian Croats, as far as we know about their country, had no city on the Danube. Besides, the tract between the Danube and the Drava rivers, which formed the bulk of Svatopluks conquest in Pannonia, could hardly be called Croatia. It was Frankish territory. Nor could they claim any city further along the Danube, since Sirmium, with the territory between the Danube and the Lower Sava river, belonged to the Bulgars.

The river Ruta on which the Persian Geographer in another passage(15) locates the Slav town of Khurdab, cannot therefore be taken in this case for the Danube. His indications are not clear, but they fit the Vistula-San better than the Danube. His Ruta flows to the west, which the Danube does not. The town in question could then be Cracow on the Vistula. But he may have taken the San for the upper reaches of the Vistula. Such a mistake would be natural to a foreigner not well acquainted with local names. The Geographer's location of the sources of the river " on the frontier between the Pechenegs, the Magyars and the Rus " points to such a possibility. The next detail—" then it enters the Rus limits and flows to the Saqlab "—would also apply to the river San-Vistula, since it touches the territory of the Red Cities, the possession of which was contested by Russians and Poles and which at the time (after 981) belonged to the Russians. In this case the city in question could be Sandomierz. Its position on the confluence of the San and the Vistula marked it out as a natural centre of commerce. The Vistula gave access to Cracow and the Baltic and the valley of the San linked it with the Red Cities including Przemysl and with the Black Sea and spread its fame to the Arab commercial world as the emporium of White Croatia.

We may take it then that the Arab sources and the Persian Geographer described the same country north of the Carpathians as did Constantine Porphyrogennetos, and that was White Croatia.

Here we may note that the existence of the Croats north of the Carpathians in the tenth century was also known to King Alfred. In his Anglo-Saxon translation of Orosius' *History of the World*, Alfred, describing the nations of Central Europe, writes (16): " To the east of the country of

---

(15) V. Minorsky, loc. cit., p. 76 (par. 6, ch. 45, of the translation): "Another river is the Ruta (?), which rises from a mountain situated on the frontier between the Pechenegs, the Magyars and the Rus [this description would fit the Carpathian Mountains]. Then it enters the Rus limits and flows to the Say hab. Then it reaches the town of Khurdab belonging to the Saqlab. . . ."

(16) J. Bosworth, *A Literal Translation of King Alfred's Anglo-Saxon Version of the Compendious History of the World by Orosius* (London, 1855), p. 37 (Book I, ch. I, par. 12). The Anglo-Saxon text published by J. Bosworth (*A Description of Europe and the Voyages of Ohthere and Wulfstan, written in Anglo-Saxon by King Alfred the Great*, London, 1855 p. 2).

Morava is the country of the Wisle [Vistula], and to the east of them are the Dacians, who formerly were the Goths. To the north-east of the Moravians are the Dalamensan [the tribe of the Daleminzi, on the Elbe], and to the east of the Dalamensan are the Horithi [Croats], and to the north of the Dalamensan are the Surpe [Serbs] . . ."(17)

The existence of a Croat State north of the Carpathians is thus placed beyond any possible doubt, though the acceptance of this fact does not clear all the difficulties. Who were those Croats and those Serbs ? First of all, the names of Serbs and Croats find no explanation in Slavonic philology ; they are not Slavonic and considerably differ from the names of all the other Slavonic tribes. We have seen that Ma'sudi described some funeral customs observed by the Serbs on the Saale and the Elbe which were not common to the Slavs, but were found in the Caucasus and among the Khazars. The king of the Croats was stated to be feeding on mare's milk, not a Slavonic diet, but one popular among the Turco-Tartar nomads. The names of the Croat chiefs who led their people to the south, as recorded by Constantine, are not Slavonic; and some names of the Croat zhupas or counties into which the territory they occupied was divided in the tenth century, as found in Constantine's Treatise(18), are also non-Slavonic. For one thing he calls the ruler of the southern Croats " Banus," which is not a Slavonic name. The vice-regal function in White Croatia mentioned by the Arab cannot be traced among other Slavs, though it was familiar to many tribes and nations of Asiatic origin. Finally, the zhupan who represented the king in various parts of the realm is reminiscent of a similar Asiatic institution, which the Serbs between the Saale and the Elbe preserved in an adapted form throughout the Middle Ages, whilst their neighbours, the Veletians and the Poles, professed to know nothing about it. All this, together with the analogy between the Bulgarians and the Varyags, would seem to point to the conclusion that the original Croats and Serbs were of non-Slavonic stock and that they imposed their dominion on Slavonic tribes which ended by absorbing them and adopting only their name.

*   *   *

These findings have startled many historians and set them on the trail to discover the first origins of the Croats and the Serbs. The first to publish the theory of the Croats' non-Slavonic origin was an English scholar, H. Howorth(19), who was of opinion that the original Croats were of Bulgarian descent; but his attempt to trace them to the Bulgarian chieftain Kuvrat was

---

(17) On this passage cf. H. Geidel, "Alfred der Grosse als Geograph," *Münchener Geograph. Studien* (1909), vol. XV (Alfred's Germania, pp. 25-99, esp. pp. 35 seq.), and J. Marquart, *Streifzüge*, p. 130. See the study by K. Malone, " King Alfred's North, A Study in Medieval Geography,"*Speculum*(1930), vol. V, pp. 139-67. Malone (p. 153) corrects the fact and locates the Croats south-east of the Daleminzi in Bohemia. Even if the correction is warranted, it implies that the existence of Croats, not only in Bohemia, but beyond—in Silesia and Western Galicia —was known to Alfred.

(18) *De adm. Imp.,* ch. 30, Bonn, p. 145.

(19) The Spread of the Slavs. Part IV—The Bulgarians : *The Journal of the Anthropological Institute of Great Britain and Ireland* (1882), vol. XI; pp. 224 seq.

not a success and his theory was abandoned., It was recently revived by
H. Gregoire(20). A Polish scholar(21) took the Croats to be Goths or their
scattered remnants who fled before the Huns, a theory that found favour
with some(22), but could scarcely be defended in its entirety. Institutions
and customs found amongst the primitive Croats and Serbs and such words
of their primitive language as have survived, exhibit no German characteristics and are rather Asiatic. The "Germanic" theory was recently
exploded by the German Slavist M. Wasmer,(23) which, however, does not
preclude the possibility of there having been some implanting of Germanic
elements into the primitive Croats.

Some scholars have also tried the theory of Avar and Turkish origin(24),
but again without success(25). It all shows at any rate that the "Slavonic
theory," which was still defended by two experts in Slavonic philology, i.e.
V. Jagić and A. Brückner, is now being abandoned by philologists, and that
the impossibility of tracing the Croat name to any Slavonic root is now generally admitted.

But an approach to more promising results was cleared by A. Pogodin(26),
who from the Greek inscriptions of the second and third centuries of our era,
found on the emplacement of the ancient Tanais at the mouth of the Don,
and which mention the name Choroathos or Chorouathos(27), derived the
Iranian origin of the name, since that region was considered by the Greeks of
those days to belong to Asiatic Sarmatia(28). This theory was accepted by
the German Slavist M. Wasmer(29), A. Sobolewski(30), the French linguists

---

(20) "L'Origine et le nom des Croates et des Serbs," *Byzantion* (1944-5), vol. XVII.
(21) L. Gumplowicz, *Chorwaci i Serbowie* (Warsaw, 1902). *Idem*, "Die politische
Geschichte der Serben und Kroaten," *Polit. anthrop. Revue* (1903), vol. I, pp. 779 seq.
(22) For instance, J. Rus, *King of the autochthonous dynasty* (Ljublana, 1931, in Slovene),
idem, "The Slavs and the Croats on the Vistula from the sixth to the tenth century," *Etnolog*
(1933), vols. V-VI, pp. 31-44 (in Slovene).
(23) *Die Urheimat der Slaven* (Breslau, 1926), pp. 126 seq., and especially in *Zeitschrift
für Slav. Philologie* (1936), vol. XIII, p. 329.
(24) The foremost champion of the "Turco-Avar theory" was J. Peisker, whose contributions to the *Cambridge Medieval History* ("The Asiatic Backgrounds," vol. II, pp. 323-59,
and "The Expansion of the Slavs," vol. III, p. 418-58), misconceive the Slav problem and have
been repudiated by the great majority of experts in Slavonic archeology. They are now
obsolete and have been superseded by the works of other Slavonic scholars. Cf. also I.
Mikkola, "Avarica," *Archiv. f. Slav. Phil.*, vol. XLI (1927), p. 158.
(25) L. Niederle, *Slav. Antiquities*, vol. II, 2, pp. 484 seq., shortly reviews the various
attempts at explaining the origin of the name Croats. The complexity of the problem is
clearly demonstrated in a historical and systematic survey of the controversy by R. Nachtigal,
"A Contribution to the history of the problem of the name of the Croats" (in Slovene),
Etnolog (Ljubljana, 1937-9), vols. X-XI, pp. 395-409, where also are to be found the main
bibliographical indications for the various theories. In the same study the author published
a German letter sent in 1915 to prof. J. Peisker on the origin of the Croats' name, but he
remains cautiously inclined to regard the name as of Sarmatian origin.
(26) "Epigraphic documents on the Slavs" (in Russian), *Russ. Filol. Vestnik* (1901),
vol. XLVI.
(27) V. Latyshev, *Inscriptiones Antiquae Orae Septentrionalis Ponti Euxini* (Petropoli,
1890), vol. II, Nos. 430, 445.
(28) On the Sarmatians in this region at that period consult M. Rostovtzeff, *Iranians and
Greeks in South Russia* (Oxford, 1922), pp. 143 seq. Cf. also G. Vernadsky, *Ancient Russia*,
loc. cit., pp. 84 seq.
(29) *Deutsche Literaturzeitung* (1921), col. 508 seq. and in his work—*Untersuchungen
über die ältesten Wohnsitze der Slaven, I. Die Iranier in Südrussland* (Leipzig, 1923), p. 56.
(30) "Russian-Scytic Studies" (in Russian), *Izvestiya Otd. Russ. Yazyka i Slov.* (1921),
vol. XXVI, p. 9 (Leningrad, 1923).

A. Meillet and A. Vaillant(31) as well as by several south Slavonic philologists(32).

N. Županić(33) has adduced many arguments in favour of tracing the origin of the Croats and the Serbs from the North of the Caucasus. They would have belonged to the autochthonous occupants of the Caucasus and been neighbours of the region that lies between the Sea of Azov and the western chain of the Caucasian mountains. Racially and linguistically he classes them with the Alarodian group to which also belonged the Pelasgians and the Etruscans.

Županić's daring theories gave a strong impetus to the study of the problem and he was followed by another Yougoslav historian, L. Hauptmann(34). From all these studies it follows that the non-Slavonic origin of the primitive Croats and Serbs can be taken to-day for a fact having most of the arguments in its favour. At the present stage of research it cannot yet be established with certainty to which linguistic and racial group either nation belonged, but everything seems to converge on the fact that they were originally living between the northern slopes of the Caucasus, the Black Sea, the Sea of Azov and the lower Don and that they were of Sarmatian stock. The discovery that both Croats and Serbs are of non-Slavonic stock(35) provides the only means of lending consistency to Constantine's account of the Croats' and the Serbs' arrival in the south. It also explains how their coming amongst the southern Slavs already settled on the spot left no impress on their linguistic evolution. If we assume that the Croats and the Serbs were of non-Slavonic origin and settled among the western Slavs north of the Carpathians as a military and ruling class just as the Bulgarians did among the Danubian Slavs and the Varyags among the eastern Slavs, giving them their names but unable, owing to their limited numbers, to influence their racial and linguistic evolution, the difficulty raised by the Slavonic philologists against the emigration of the Croats and the Serbs to the south,

---

(31) A. Meillet-A. Vaillant, *Le Slave Commun* (Paris, 1934), pp. 507 seq.

(32) Especially F. Ramouš, "The Primitive Slav name of Kasęg-Edling," *Razprave znanstv. drušstva za human. vede* (Lyublyjana, 1925), vol. II, pp. 317 seq. (in Slovene).

(33) "White Serbia," *Narodna Starina* (1922), vol. I, pp. 107-18; "The Serbs of Plinius and Ptolemy," *Zbornik J. Cvijić*, Beograd, 1924 (in Croat, with a summary in French); "The Primitive Croats" (in Croat), *Zbornik kralja Tomislava, Opera Acad. Scient. Slavorum Meridionalium*, vol. XVII (Zagreb, 1925), pp. 291-96; "The Harimati: a study on the problem of the primitive Croats" (in Slovene), *Etnolog*, vol. I (1926-27); "The Significance of some old geographical and ethnical names in the Balkan peninsula," *Etnolog* (1933), vol. V, pp. 98-112; "The first bearers of the names—Serb, Croat, Czech and Ant" *Etnolog* (1928), vol. II, pp. 74-79 (in Slovene).

(34) "Kroaten, Goten und Sarmaten," *Germanoslavica* (1935), vol. III, pp. 345 seq.; "Migration of Croats and Serbs," *Yugoslav Historical Review* (1937), vol. III, pp. 30-61. Equally interesting are the linguistic researches of K. Oštir, but I have been able to read only his study "A Contribution to the pre-Slavonic ethnology of the region beyond the Carpathians" (in Slovene), *Etnolog* (1926-1927), vol. I, pp. 1-35. His Illyrico-Thracian theory, however, is, in the opinion of historians, less satisfactory.

(35) The Serbian problem seems to many scholars to be less evident than the corresponding problem of the Croats. L. Niederle, *Slav. Antiquities*, vol. II, 2, p. 486, is of opinion that the name "Serbs" is of Slavonic origin. N. Županić provides sufficient material in the study quoted above to prove that the Serb and the Croat problems are parallel. He identifies the primitive Serbs with the "Serbi" found by Pliny and Ptolemy in Caucasia or on the eastern shores of the Sea of Azov. It is evident from Constantine's account that the two questions are inseparable: if the early Croats were non-Slavonic, early Serbs could not be Slavonic either.

as reported by Constantine Porphyrogennetos, vanishes(36).   Such a
numerically small body of half-slavicised Sarmatians or Caucasians, whatever
may have been their military efficiency, could not have affected to any noticeable extent the growth of the southern Slavonic idioms.

---

(36) The founders of Slavonic philology—J. Kopitar (1780-1844) and F. Miklosić
(1813-1891)—favoured the dualistic theory of the settlement of the Slavs in the old Roman
province of Illyricum, as propounded by Constantine ; but it was V. Jagić who raised the
objection that the organic philological unity of the Yugoslav languages would have been broken
by the late arrival of the Croats and the Serbs who belonged to the western Slavonic group
("Ein Kapitel zur Geschichte der südslavischen Sprachen," *Archiv für Slavische Philologie*,
1895, vol. XVII, pp. 47-87). Jagić's authority prevailed, causing Constantine's account to
be relegated to the lumber-room of dreams and fantasies by almost all the Slavonic historians
and philologists.

FORGOTTEN EMPIRES ; THE EMPIRE OF THE ANTES, WHITE CROATIA, WHITE SERBIA.

SARMATIANS AND SLAVS IN SOUTH RUSSIA—THE SPORI (SPALI) AND THE EMPIRE OF THE ANTES—CROATS AND AVARS—MIGRATION OF THE CROATS AND THE SERBS TO THE SOUTH—NATURE OF CROATIAN AND SERBIAN ORGAN-ISATION—HISTORY OF WHITE CROATIA AND WHITE SERBIA TILL THE TENTH CENTURY—CROATS, SERBS AND BOHEMIA—WHITE CROATIA AND THE MAGYARS.

The part played by the Iranians in South Russia before the Slavs had settled in the Russian steppes lends probability to the Sarmatian origin of the Croats and the Serbs. The history of the Iranians, *i.e.* the Scythians and Sarmatians in South Russia, has been written by M. Rostovtseff(1). His disclosures concerning their trade with the Greek cities in the Crimea and the Taman Peninsula and with the populations of the interior of modern Russia and the Baltic shores, lay stress on the geographical elements that stimulated the economic instincts of the Scythians, the Sarmatians and other nomads. First of all, the steppes of South Russia offered rich grazing facilities for the herds of those nomadic tribes with an easy access to the Black Sea and the Lower Danube and to points where they were bound to contact Greek and later Roman cultural spheres. Again, the large water-ways of this region linked the Baltic and the North Sea with the Black Sea and the eastern frontier of the Roman Empire,along the Dvina, the Niemen and the Dnieper in one direction, and in another, through modern Galicia along the Vistula, the San and the Dniester around the Carpathians. Historians have concentrated so much on the West that they have overlooked these geographical features which explain so much of the history of Eastern Europe.

The Scythians availed themselves of all these facilities when about 500 B.C. they carved their way through Galicia and the valleys of the Morava, the Vltava and the Elbe into the heart of Central Europe. The Germans also used them in their migration from the Baltic to the Black Sea. In the first and second century A.D. a large Germanic population settled on the Dnieper and the Gothic invasion about 165-80 A.D. was only a last act of an age-long Germanic trek towards a warmer climate and more cultured lands. The route was well known to traders, and the Slavs had used it in their drive through Galicia towards the lower Danube and the Black Sea and from the Bug towards and along the Dnieper.

When the Slavs reached the southern steppes, they came upon the Sarmatians who had taken over from the Scythians their control of the local tribes. Having to deal with farmers and half-nomadic hunters, the

---

(1) Cf. his book *Iranians and Greeks in South Russia* (Oxford, 1922).

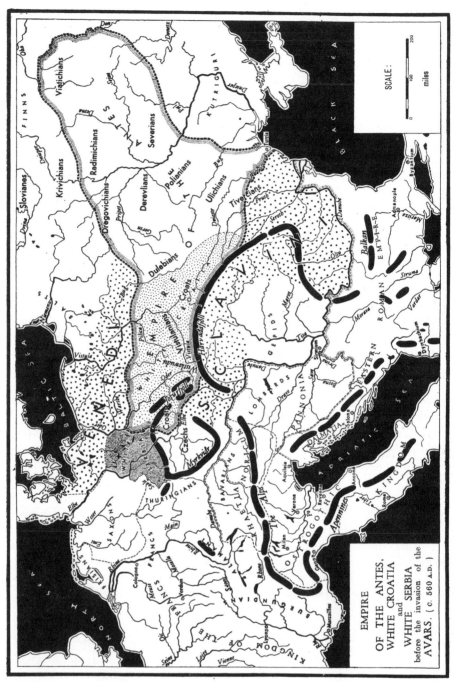

EMPIRE
OF THE ANTES,
WHITE CROATIA
and
WHITE SERBIA
before the invasion of the
AVARS. (c. 560 A.D.)

Sarmatians found no difficulty in dominating them; and the Slavs, used as they were to easy geographical conditions and eager to exploit them for trade and agriculture, were only too glad to place themselves under the protection of a military class instead of developing their own military traditions.

278

First evidence of the Slavs coming under the authority of the Sarmatians comes from the Byzantine sixth-century writer Procopius(2). He calls them *Sclaveni* and *Antes*, but alleges that these names were new and that in olden days all the Slavs went by the name of Sporoi or Spori. These Sporoi should probably be identified with the Spali mentioned by Jordanes(3), whilst his Spali seem to be the same as the Spalei mentioned by Pliny(4).

The Spalei or Spali, as stated by Pliny, crossed the Don-Donets into the Dnieper basin where they collided with the Goths, who also were on the move in search of a new home and had just struggled through the Volhynian marshes. Jordanes places the encounter in the reign of the third Gothic King, Filemer, therefore, in the second century of our era. After defeating the Spali, the Goths had a clear run to the shores of the Black Sea.

The Spali, most probably indentical to the Spalei, were then living in the Donets-Don-Dnieper basin and must have belonged to the Alanic group of the Sarmatians; only, as we know from other evidence that the region where the Goths came upon the Spali was at the time occupied by Slavonic populations, Jordanes' statement can only lead to the conclusion that the Alanic Spali were in control of the Slavonic tribes of the Donets and the Dnieper basins. Additional confirmation is yielded by the fact that in old Slavonic the word *gigas* or giant is rendered by the word *spolin* (in Russian, *ispolin*; in Polish, *stolin* or *stolim*), a word that closely resembles Spali. If then the Spali were for some time the rulers of the primitive Slavs in the country that is now the Ukraine, it is quite understandable that their subjects honoured them with a name that expressed their concept of a giant and a super-man. These conjectures would lend a new significance to Procopius' statement. It seems that there really was a time in primitive Slavonic history when the Slavonic tribes of the Dnieper and Donets basins were called Spali, Spoli or Spori after their Alanic masters.

This situation did not last. We have already noted that the two writers, Jordanes and Procopius, divide the Slavs into various groups—Jordanes(5) into Sclaveni, Antes and Venedi; Procopius into Sclaveni and Antes, Procopius being naturally interested only in those Slavs who had come into contact with the Byzantine Empire, *i.e.* the Sclaveni and the Antes. The Venedi who according to Jordanes lived north of the Vistula were of no interest to the Byzantines; but Jordanes had learned to know them from the Gothic

---

(2) *De Bello Gothico*, III, ch. 4 (Bonn, vol. II), p. 332, ed. I. Haury (Leipzig, Teubner, 1905), vol. II, p. 358.

(3) Getica, ch. 4, section 29, *M.G.H.* Auct. Ant. V, p. 61.

(4) *Historia Naturalis*, VI, ch. 7, ed. C. Mayhoff (Leipzig, 1906), vol. I, p. 438. Županić in his studies on " The Serbs of Plinius " (in Croat), in *Zbornik J. Cvijić* (Beograd, 1924), and in " Dobrovskj's Opinion on the Spori and Later Ideas about them " (in Slovene), published in *Sbornik J. Dobrovskj* (Prague, 1929), identifies Procopius' Sporoi with the Serbloi, who according to him were Caucasians of Allorodian origin, driven out by the Hunnic invasion. This theory is difficult to reconcile with the facts, as in that case the Serbs could not have stayed sufficiently long north of the Danube to substantiate Procopius' statement. For he supposes a long period of submission of the Slavs to the Sporoi. In general, Županić disregards the importance of the Sarmatians in South Russia. If there is any evidence for the non-Sarmatian origin of the primitive Antes, Serbs and Croats, they must at least have made common cause with the Sarmatians and shared with them in one common State.

(5) Getica, ch. 5 sectio 32-37, *M. G. H.* Auct. Ant, V. pp. 62 seq.

tradition. In the light of our comments on Procopius' first statement about the Spori it would seem that the Antes succeeded to the Alanic Spori and contrived to impose their authority on at least some of the Slavonic tribes that had previously been under the rule of the Spori. About this there could scarcely be any doubt left.

But, as stated, the Spori were of Alanic, and therefore of Iranian, origin. With regard to the Antes it would be more logical to suggest that they were not one of the autochthonous tribes originally living north of the Caucasus(6), but simply another Iranian or Alanic tribe distinct from the Spali or Spori. The Alans made their appearance on the confines of modern Europe in the first century of our era whilst the Antes were located in the neighbourhood of the Sea of Azov first by Pliny(7), then by Pomponius Mela(8) and by Ptolemy(9); and they must have spread to the neighbourhood of the Crimea fairly early as indicated by some Greek inscriptions(10) discovered there. It would have been easy for a different Alanic tribe to supplant the defeated Spoli amongst the Slavs. As the foreign masters constituted the upper classes in Slav society and did most of the fighting, it is conceivable that the Spoli-Spori were considerably weakened by the Goths and made it easy for another Alanic tribe to take their place. We may also assume that the Antes, at any rate some of them, penetrated into the Donets basin already in the second century of our era.

Which were the Slavonic tribes subjugated by the Antes? Jordanes seems to locate the Antes on the bend of the Black Sea shore between the Dniester and the Danube, the home of the Tivercians and she Ulicians; but Procopius also mentions Antes as present in the Donets basin. Turning then to archeological data, we find that some eastern Slavonic tribes observed Iranian customs in their burial rites and in their divine worship. Amongst the divinities worshipped by the pagan Slavs, the first Russian Annals(11) mention a deity called Simargl, which can be none other than the Bird-Dog Senmurv, the guardian, in Alanic mythology, of the tree that supplied the seed for every plant. The practice of inhumation as observed by the Sarmatians apparently prevailed among the Vyatichians, the Radimichians, the Dulebians, the Derevlianians and the Dregovichians, whereas, judging from archeological finds, cremation, an old Slavonic custom, prevailed among the Krivichians and the Slavs in the neighbourhood of Novgorod(12). We may then assume that the Slavs between the Dniester, the middle Dnieper and the Pripet basin remained for a long time under the influence of the Alans, in this case in all probability the Antes.

---

(6) This is the opinion of N. Županić, " Der Anten Ursprung und Name," *Actes du IIIe Congres Internat. des Etudes Byzantines* (Athens 1932), pp. 331-9.
(7) *Natur. Hist.*, VI, ch. 35 : Cissi Anthi (ed. C. Mayhoff, Leipzig, 1906, vol. I, p. 443).
(8) *De Chronographia libri tres*, I, ch. 13 : Cissiantes, (ed. C. Frick, Leipzig, 1880, p. 4).
(9) *Geographia*, V ch. VII, 10 : Asaioi ; (ed. C. Müller, vol. I, 2, pp. 915).
(10) Latyshev, *Inscript. Antiquae*, loc. cit. vol. II, pp. 20-9. Cf. G. Vernadsky, *Ancient Russia*, pp. 106 seq.
(11) 6686-6688 (978-980), S. H. Cross, loc. cit. pp. 180.
(12) For more details see Vernadsky, *Ancient Russia*, pp. 327 seq. As concerns the Polianians and the Severians, the evidence for cremation refers only to the tenth century. In the earlier period they might have also practiced inhumation.

This conclusion seems to be endorsed by Procopius' and Jordanes' classification of the Slavs. Both clearly differentiate between the Slavs (Sclaveni) and the Antes, and from Procopius' statement we may conclude that the Antes only succeeded in forcing their rule on the tribes enumerated above and living mostly in the Dnieper and Pripet basin, whilst the tribes living in the Dvina, Lovat and upper Volga basin maintained their own tribal organisation. The " empire " of the Antes was therefore probably far more extensive than would appear from the description of the Byzantine writers who were only interested in the regions adjacent to their Empire, and never intended to be exhaustive in their enumerations of the Slavonic tribes. More than others, the Slavs, who by that time had already crossed the Carpathians into north-eastern Hungary and Transylvania and advanced towards the Danube, must have remained outside the Antes' sphere of influence: and they were the Sclaveni mentioned by Jordanes.

The position was again upset by the Goths whose king Ermanrich (Ermanaric) (350-370) took the offensive and proceeded to carve out his empire. After subjugating the Heruls in the Azov region and making an end of the Bosporan kingdom which relied for its security on the Roman protectorate, he first attacked the Antes and overthrew them, then turned against the Sclaveni and forced some of them to migrate northward and settle round Novgorod, and finally marched north, where he defeated the teeming tribes of the Venedi—the future Poles—thence to extend his sway over the Balts and some Finnish tribes(13). For the first time in history an empire stretched from the Baltic to the Black Sea, an achievement emulated only many centuries later when the Poles under the Lithuanian dynasty of Jagiello reached the Baltic and held power as far south as the Black Sea.

It looked as though the Goths were about to take over among the Slavs the role which the Spali had relinquished, the Antes were about to lose and which other nations, namely the Russians and the Bulgars, were destined to take on in later years, when other invaders—Huns of Turkish stock, with ranks swelled by Ugrian and Mongol tribes—once again broke in. After defeating the Alans and forcing some of them to join the main body of the horde whilst others fled to the North-Caucasian area and to the upper Donets region, the Huns attacked the Goths. King Ermanrich either committed suicide or was otherwise disposed of by rebels, and whereas some of the Ostrogoths submitted to Hunnish supremacy, others, joining forces with two Germanic nations, the Heruls and the Burgundians, settled on the shores of the Azov Sea, then retreated towards the middle Dnieper. Finding his way barred by the Antes in revolt, the new Gothic King Vinitharius or Vitimir won the battle and crucified their King Boz with seventy other chieftains (375)(14). But the following year the Goths were in their turn beaten by the Huns, or more precisely by the Alans, who formed an important contin-

(13) Jordanis, Getica, ch. XXIII, M. G. H. S. Auct. Ant. V, pp. 88 seq. Cf. the recent publication by C. Brady, The Legends of Ermanaric, University of California Press, 1943, which has a complete bibliography of the works dealing with Ermanrich. On "the Gothic Ermanric Legend known to Jordanes," ibid., pp. 1-22.

(14) Jordanis, Getica, ch. 48, loc. cit., p. 121.

M.   K

gent of the Hunnish hordes on the Erak river, as was recently established(15). The Antes breathed again and when the Hunnish empire founded by Attila with its centre in later Hungary, disintegrated after his death (453), the Antes retrieved their position and moved the frontiers of the " empire " they had founded among the Slavs nearer the lower Dniester and the lower Danube. That is how they came into contact with the Byzantine Empire and attracted the attention of the Byzantine writers of the fifth and sixth centuries, when Byzantine diplomacy occasionally used their services against the Sclaveni and other invaders. By the sixth century, the slavicisation of the Antes had been completed, though some knowledge of their non-Slavonic origin must have been extant amongst their contemporaries at the time(16).

The existence of the "empire" of the Antes is no mere matter of speculation since Byzantine historians have recorded at length the phases, friendly or otherwise, of their relations with the Byzantine Empire. Not that we learn from these records many details of the organisation of the Antic State. Only a few incidents have come down to us marking the last phase of Antic history, when the Antes fell under the onslaught of the new invaders, the Avars, a combination of united clans of Turkish, Mongolian and probably also Manchu stock, which in 558 made its appearance in the northern Caucasus.

After playing off the Avars against the Bulgars the Byzantines were only too pleased to see the Avars and the Antes at grips, when the latter attempted to bar the way into the country known to-day as Bessarabia. Defeated, the Antes despatched Mezamir, son of Idarisius and brother of Kelagast(17) as envoy to the Avar Khagan. The envoy was killed, but that did not put an end to the Antic power. Only when the Avars realised they had no hopes of being allowed to settle on imperial territory did they decide to go to Pannonia, probably by way of the Pruth and the Dniester to reach, as it seems, the centre of Antic power on the upper Dniester. The Russian Primary Chronicle in its introductory chapter(18) dwells on the sufferings which the Dulebians had to endure at the hands of the Avars, and as these concentrated their hostilities on the Dulebians it seems likely that this tribe formed the backbone of the Antic empire. However that be the Avar onslaught had very serious consequences for this vigorous slavicised tribe. After its defeat some of the tribesmen retreated to the north beyond the Pripet and the rest of them disintegrated, later to go by the name of Volhynians, or Buzhanians—the name of the riparians of the Bug—or Luchanians(19). A number of them served the Avars as slaves and were settled by their masters on the Tisza river.

---

(15) N. Županić, "The Erak River" (in Slovene), *Etnolog* (1930), vol. IV., pp. 113-21.

(16) This can be inferred from Procopius' insistence on the fact that the Antes and the Slavs spoke the same language.

(17) I quote these names designedly to illustrate the mixture of Slavonic and foreign elements amongst the Antes of this period.

(18) S. H. Cross, loc. cit., p. 141.

(19) Cf. L. Niederle, *Slav. Antiquities*, part I, vol. IV, pp. 173 seq.

A trace of these happenings is found in Ma'sudi's account of the Slavs, where he says(20) : " The Slavs consist of several nations. Among them there is one which in earlier days wielded power. Its king was called Magak. This nation is called Valinjana and the other Slavonic tribes used to take their orders from it because it was in power and the other Slavonic kings obeyed it." The passages can only refer to the Dulebians, since the Volhynians (Valinjana) were only a portion of the disintegrated tribe(21) and were in Ma'sudi's days the most developed of the three branches of the erstwhile Dulebians. It is also possible to detect in King Magak's name that of the Slavonic chieftain Musokios, who lived on the lower Danube and is mentioned in 593 by some Greek sources(22).

After their disaster, the Antes completely vanished from history and what the Arab writers, previously mentioned, state about the first city among the Slavs cannot be used as evidence for the survival of the Antes' till the ninth century. The mysterious name Va-it, Vantitt or Vabnit, though somewhat reminiscent of Antic nomenclature, probably disguises the name of the Vyatichians(23) who lived nearest to the Bulgarians on the Volga and may therefore have been the first Slavonic tribe met by an Arab traveller coming up the Volga.

*   *   *

As regards the Croats of the northern Carpathians, everything points to their history being closely linked with that of the Antes. Here we may repeat that though the Croats were possibly an autochthonous tribe hailing from the region north-east of the Caucasus and joining the Antes as they headed north-east away from the Hunnish menace, it seems to be more of a piece with the facts as we know them to see in those Croats only another Alanic tribe akin to the Spali and the Antes. It has been shown in

---

(20) Marquart, *Streifzüge*, p. 101.

(21) Another instance of how the name of a tribe could be adopted by the confederation of which it was a member is found in the so-called *Anonymous Geographer of Bavaria*, whose work is generally attributed to the IXth century. He speaks of a tribe called Zeriuani (quod tantum est regnum ut ex eo cunctae gentes Slavorum exortae sint, et originem, sicut affirmant, ducunt). The Zeriuani may have been the inhabitants of the Czerwień or Red Cities' territory, which was once part of the Dulebian State. As the Dulebians were the backbone of the Antic dominion, a tradition to that effect may have survived. The Czerwień were a trading centre in the Geographer's days, both Poles and Russians laying claim to their possession. See the edition of the Geographer's writings by S. Zakrzewski, "Geograf Bawarski," *Archiwum Naukowe* (Lwów, 1917), dzial I, t. IX, p. 4. I have not seen the more recent edition by J. Schnetz (*Itineraria Romana*, vol. II, Leipzig, 1940).

(22) On the Dulebians, see Niederle, loc. cit., pp. 172-7. Moving from the Bug, they entered modern Galicia from one side, and the province of Minsk from the other, as evidenced by local names. This would vindicate the Primary Chronicle's report on the existence of Russian Dulebians (S. H. Cross, loc. cit., p. 141). Cf. my book *Les Slaves, Byzance et Rome*, p. 5. Cf. what A. Shakhmatov says on this passage of the Chronicle about the Dulebians in his " Povest Vremennikh let i ee Istochniki " (The Russian Primary Chronicle and its Sources), *Trudy Otdela Drevney-Russokoi Literatury, Akad. Nauk SSSR* (1940), vol. IV, pp. 91 seq.

(23) L. Niederle, *Slav. Antiquities*, part II, vol. I., pp. 269 sq. was rather inclined to see in the passage in question a reference to the Antes ; but in 1924, when he published the 4th volume of the Ist part of his Slavonic Antiquities (pp. 80 sq.) where he deals with the origin and the primitive history of the eastern Slavs, he gave up his opinion and pronounced himself in favour of the alternative rendering mentioned above.

Appendix I that the existence of the Croats somewhere on the northern slopes of the Carpathians must be stated as a fact. But when did they arrive there and in what relation did they stand to the Slavonic tribes found on the spot and to the Antes?

Two sources of the history of the Langobards may throw some light on these queries. The *Origo Gentis Langobardorum*(24) records that on moving from the Elbe to the lands of the Rugii (another Germanic tribe destroyed by Odoacer which probably also occupied modern Lower Austria), the Langobards had to force a passage through *Anthaib et Bainaib seu et Burgundaib*. Bainaib(25) is the country of the Banings, who must be located in the neighbourhood of the Burgundians, while Burgundaib designates Lower Lusatia and northern Silesia, where this Germanic tribe was living before migrating to Gaul, whereas Anthaib would point to the lands of the Antes. In that case, since the Langobards must have touched on their route the region of Silesia and of the Upper Vistula, presumably the country named Anthaib, the dominion of the Antes must have extended at the end of the fifth century over the whole of that tract. The conclusion, without being absolutely evident, is yet quite reasonable and is at any rate the only possible reading of the names.

But we may go further. Paulus Diaconus(26), the historian of the Langobards, states that before settling in the land of the Rugii, the Langobards joined battle with the Bulgars about the year 450; but this cannot be taken literally, since the Bulgars were stated at the end of the fifth century to be living round the Sea of Azov. The Avars defeated them in the middle of the sixth century and settled some of them along the middle Danube: not until then could any clash have taken place between the Langobards and the Bulgars. Fredegar(27) has also some knowledge of this, as he refers to a conflict between the Langobards and the Huns, probably meaning the Kutroguri who were part of the Hunnish hordes and were Bulgars by race.

The same battle may be recorded also in the Old English poem Widsith(28) and in the Nordic Hervarar saga(29), though the reference is necessarily vague and the event is given different dates. As described in the Hervarar saga, it took place between the Hercynian Forest (Myrkuidr), the Vistula-Oder Forest (Wistlawudu), the Carpathians (Harvadja) and the Jósurfjöll which can only be identified with the Gesenke Forest in Silesia, called in Czech Jeseniky(30), and must be the same as that recorded

(24) Ed. G. Waitz in *M.G.H.S. Rer. Lang.*, ch. 2, p. 3.
(25) F. Westberg ("Zur Wanderung der Longobarden," p. 28, published in the *Memoirs of the St. Petersburgh Imperial Academy of Sciences*, VIIIth series, Hist. Phil. Cl. vol. VI, No.5, 1904) reads *Banthaib* and sees in it the name of the Slavonic Vends. This reading would fit into our hypothesis, as the Vends were neighbours to the Banings. According to Westberg (loc, cit., p. 31) the Langobards were on their way to Pannonia in 546.
(26) Pauli Diaconi *Historia Langobardorum*, ibid., I. ch. 18, p. 56.
(27) Fredegarius Scholasticus, Historia Francorum, lib. III, ch. 65 ; *P.L.*, vol. 71, col. 596.
(28) The latest edition by Kemp "Malone," Widsith, *Methuen Old English Library* (London, 1936).
(29) S. Bugge, *Det. Norske Oldscriftselskabs Samlinger*, vol. VIII. (Christiana, 1865.)
(30) Cf. the discussion and identification of the names in R. Heinzel's study, "Über die Hervararsaga," *Sitzungsberichte of the k. Akademie Wien, Hist.-Philol. Kl.*, vol. 114 (1887), especially pp. 469 seq, 483 seq., and 499 ; R. Much, "Ascriburgion Oros," *Zeitschrift für*

by Paulus Diaconus and Fredegar. To the Langobards the Sagas substituted the Goths owing to their renown in Germanic legendary tradition which they owed to their gallant engagements with the Huns. All other attempts made so far to locate and to date this famous battle have proved fruitless.

The reference to a Harvardjafjöll in the Hervarar saga(31) is very pertinent to our investigation. The place can be none other than the Carpathians, which point to the conclusion that those mountains were known in Langobard national tradition as the Harvata Mountains, *i.e.* of Harvati or Croats(32). It confirms the historically known fact that the Croats were settled on the northern slopes of the Carpathians.

Piecing all these data together, we come to the conclusion that the Croats also belonged to the Anthaib and that therefore the empire of the Antes stretched as far as Silesia(33). This may seem surprising, but if our data are correct, the Croats were originally an Iranian tribe—another branch of the Alans—which together with the Antes settled among the Slavs, stole a march upon its racial brothers, reached eastern and western Galicia and got as far as eastern Bohemia. We shall discuss in Appendix III the problem of those Croats who settled amongst the eastern Slavs in the neighbourhood of the Dulebians. As regards the Serbs, it is more consistent to see in them an Alanic tribe which, on finding in the Slavs an easy prey, wedged itself between the Saale and the Elbe and founded there the power called White Serbia.

After what has been said about the traffic value of the Dniester-San Vistula waterway between the Baltic and the Black Sea coastal regions, one can understand why the Sarmatians penetrated so deeply into Slavonic lands. Antes, Croats and Serbs only followed the route traced by the Scythians. There was no difficulty in reaching the Oder from the Upper Vistula and thence reaching the Middle Elbe through Moravia and Bohemia, or through Silesia ; and nothing to prevent a foreign element, most probably Iranian—Spali, Antes, Croats and Serbs—from setting up the first organised States among the Slavs.

* * *

It appears then that not till the defeat of the Antes by the Avars did the Croats emerge as a leading factor in Slavonic history. Though they must

Deutches Altertum, vol. XXXIII (1889) pp. 1-13 ; Idem, *Widsith*, ibid., (1925), vol. LXII pp. 112-50. R. Much there comments on R. W. Chambers' study of the Saga (*Widsith. A Study in Old English Heroic Legend*, Cambridge, 1912) ; cf. the discussion of the various locations of the battle by L. Hauptmann, *Migration of the Croats and the Serbs*, pp. 56-8.

(31) S. Bugge, loc. cit., p. 265. Cf. Heinzel, loc. cit., vol. 114, p. 499.

(32) The attempt by some scholars to derive this name from that of a Gothic tribe, called Hreidgotar (cf. for instance J. Rus, "Slavs and Vistulanian Croats," *Etnolog*, 1933, vols. V-VI, pp. 31-44) was lately discredited by the German Slavist M. Wasmer in *Die Urheimat der Slaven* (Breslau, 1926), pp. 126 seq., and especially in *Zeitschrift für Slavische Philologie*, (1936), vol. XIII, p. 329.

(33) As regards Silesia, I would call attention to a recent study by M. Rudnicki, "Discussion on the name of Silesia," *Slavia Occidentalis* (1938), vol. XVI. The author is of opinion that the name is not derived from the German tribe of Silings mentioned by Ptolemy, but from the Old Polish word *ślęza*, which comes from the Old Slavonic root *slenk, sleng*, and denotes a muddy brook. I have not been able to consult this study.

have shared in the sufferings inflicted by the Avar onslaught, it was thanks to their geographical position coupled with the fact that the Avars moved into modern Hungary (it was an easy proposition to seal off the passes that led from Hungary into Galicia and nomads were not fond of mountains) that they regained their independence and continued to rule over the Slavs. Such was the origin of what Constantine Porphyrogennetos called White Croatia. But not unlike what had happened to the Antes, the probable heirs of the Spoli, the Croats, heirs of the Antes, were not able to supplant the Antes among all the Slavonic tribes that were subject to Antic supremacy. The Avars had seen to that by destroying the centre of Antic power on the territory of the Dulebians(34) and by reducing the Slavs east of the Bug to subjection. As the Croats were more densely settled in the Upper Vistula region, they established their political centre there. This gave Cracow its chance to rise to prominence and created a State that stretched from the Bug and the Styr over the whole of Galicia, Silesia and part of Bohemia. All these tribes—the future Poles and Czechs—belonged to the western Slavonic branch. As far as can be ascertained only one eastern Slavonic tribe belonged to this dominion, probably one settled in the neighbourhood of the Dulebians.

*   *   *

The Avars, who occupied the Danubian basin of modern Hungary, directed their efforts to the acquisition of the rich provinces of Illyricum and Thrace and to the capture of Constantinople. They gained a hold on the Slavs who had overrun Pannonia and Illyricum and with their help and that of their allies, the Persians, they encircled Constantinople in 626.

At that moment matters looked critical indeed, and the Porphyrogennetos' account of Croat and Serb migrations to the south would fit in with the desperate position in which the Emperor Heraclius found himself. As he looked about for help, the successes of the Croats' against the Avars must have given him the idea of calling them to his assistance. The half-slavicised Croats, eager to settle some accounts of their own with the Avars, welcomed the Emperor's request and some of them, a body of well seasoned troops, entered Illyricum, vanquished the Avars (the bulk of their army may have been pinned down under the ramparts of Constantinople or disorganised after their defeat), and were then settled by a grateful Emperor in the liberated province of Illyricum. From the Avars they took over the leadership of the Slavonic masses that had been in occupation since the end of the sixth century.

Meanwhile some Serbs from Constantine's White Serbia(35) possibly

(34) Cf. what L. Hauptmann (*Migrations of Croats and Serbs*, pp. 55-61) says about the Dulebians.

(35) It seems that some of the Serb tribe either halted on the Vistula or advanced west or north ahead of the main body. There certainly existed a Serb settlement in the region to-day called Zerbst on the right bank of the Elbe in what used to be the dukedom of Anhalt ; but the main Serb settlement lay between the Saale, the Schwarze Elster and the borders of Bohemia as far as the Bober river. Constantine VII says in ch. 31 of his treatise on the administration

arrived on Byzantine soil before the Croats and under the command of a son of the late chieftain of the White Serbs. According to Constantine VII he had quarrelled with his brother over his share in their patrimony and preferred to apply with his followers to the Emperor Heraclius for a new settlement. It appears that they were assigned a place in Greece since called Serblia, north of Mt. Olympus and were later employed by Heraclius(36) to help the Croats against the Avars. Their fewness sufficiently explains why the Croats came to the fore in Illyricum, the Serbs coming into their own only much later.

However much Constantine's account of the Serbs' southward migration be frowned at by historians, there is one detail, reported in Fredegar's chronicle, (37) which proves that Heraclius did take an interest in those remote lands. Fredegar reports that Dagobert, King of the Franks, and the Emperor Heraclius exchanged embassies and concluded a treaty of friendship in 629 against their common enemy the Avars(38). This must have interested the Serbs. Constantine's White Serbia had, it is true, escaped Avar authority, as had the Croats, but after the Franks' conquest of Thuringia which bordered on White Serbia, they could not shake themselves free from Frankish suzerainty. Frankish pressure and the knowledge that Heraclius was looking for allies against the Avars would have been enough to justify the migration of part of the Serb population to Byzantium.

So far the facts accord with Constantine's account ; Croats and Serbs combined to destroy the Avar power, and their intervention coincided with the emancipation of the Bulgars under their Khagan Kuvratos, nephew of Organa. Because of this coincidence and the similarity between the names of Kuvratos and Chrovatos, who is numbered by Constantine among the chiefs of the Dalmatian Croats, the attempt was recently renewed(39) of deriving the name "Croats" from Kuvratos. But the coincidence and the similarity do not call for such a hypothesis. All there is to it is that

---

of the empire (Bonn, p. 160) that the forbears of the prince of the Zachloumians, Michael Bousebouce, came from the pagan Serbs on the Vistula, *i.e.* the region called Ditsike. Niederle, *Slav. Antiquities*, vol. II, 1, p. 276, thinks that the latter name should read Litsike, which would recall the name Visla, Vislitsa, or else the name of the Slavonic tribe of the Licicaviki, who were settled on the Oder near the mouth of the Varta river ; but the generally accepted derivation of this tribe's name is from an ancestor Lestka whose descendants were called Lestkovici, and it sounds plausible enough. Amongst the towns of the Zachloumians, Constantine mentions one called Galumaenic, which shows a curious similarity to the name of a Slavonic tribe of White Serbia, then under the Serbs—Glomachi. On the other hand, some Croats must have accompanied the Serbs, as we find between Merseburg and Halle a locality called Klein Corbetha, which in the Midlle Ages was called Chruvati Vicus. Names of localities of Croat derivation are also found in northern Hungary. Cf. Niederle, loc. cit., vol. I, 4 (1924), p. 156. L. Hauptmann, *Migrations of Croats and Serbs*, p. 48, places the Serbs on the upper Vistula.

(36) Cf. N. Županić, "The Serb Settlement in the Macedonian town of Srbčište in the VIIth century and the Ethnological and Sociological moment in the report of Constantinus Porphyrogenetus concerning the advent of Serbs and Croats," *Etnolog* (1928), vol. II, pp. 26-35.

(37) *M.G.H.S. Rer. Merov.* II, book IV, chs. 48, 62, 68, pp. 144, 151, 155.

(38) V. N. Zlatarski ("Die Besiedelung der Balkanhalbinsel durch die Slaven," *Revue Internationale des Etudes Balkaniques*, 1936, vol. II, p. 374) is of opinion that one of the stipulations of the treaty concerned the settling of the Serbs and the Croats in the south. The opinion is unfounded. Nor can it be said that the treaty was aimed at Samo, the liberator of the Bohemian and the Carantanian Slavs, for the Serbs' migration was anterior to this liberation.

(39) By H. Grégoire, " L'Origine et le Nom des Croates et des Serbes," *Byzantion* (1944-45), vol. XVII.

Heraclius looked for allies where he was most likely to find them, and that was amongst the Croats, the Bulgars, the Franks and the Serbs.

Besides, the similarity of names may be only apparent. The name Kuvratos and that of his father Organa were most probably the Greek forms of proto-Bulgarian names which were lost and may have sounded differently. In reality we find in the list of Bulgarian rulers, the *Immenik*(40), which for all its inaccuracies, rests on sound national tradition, only the names Irnik and Kurt, which the author of this theory identifies with Organa and Kuvratos. But it needs imagination to identify Porga with Irnik-Ernik-Organa (Kernaka in Syriac Tradition) and Chrovatos with Kurt and Kuvrat.

The weak link of the hypothesis is that it fails to tally with Constantine's account of the Croat settlement in the south. He states that the Croats first liberated Dalmatia after a hard fight ; and not till later did they overrun the rest of Illyricum and Pannonia. The action of the Serbs against the Avars was also confined to the south and to the Roman province of Praevalitana, near Dalmatia. It was sound strategy to start operations from the southern bases, which were on imperial soil, and to clear the maritime region where the imperial navy could be of assistance and where the refugees from the Dalmatian towns could be set free and released from the Adriatic islands where they had taken shelter. This makes Constantine's story intelligible. The Croats and Serbs therefore operated miles away from Kuvrat's theatre of war against the Avars.

The Croats' success in Dalmatia brought about the downfall of the Avars in Pannonia. A significant episode is related by the *Miracula S. Demetrii*(41). About the year 640, Kuver was charged by the Khagan with the governorships of the Greek, Slav, Roman and Bulgarian prisoners of war settled in Pannonia near Sirmium. He revolted and returned to imperial territory with his heterogeneous troops after defeating the Avar army. The fact is that being nomads, the Avars settled their prisoners on fertile land, because they needed agricultural workers and Greek artisans. The Danube and the Sava rivers, which enclosed the plain of Sirmium, made it a safe concentration camp for such a population. The collapse of the Avars, brought about by the combined forces of Samo, Kuvrat, the Byzantines, the Croats and the Serbs, was the signal for the revolt and the escape of the prisoners.

However, there is no sufficient evidence for identifying the names of Kuver and Kuvrat, though their fate was the same ; and still less for identifying the names of Kuver and Chrovatos. Constantine attributes the leading role in the subjugation of Dalmatia by the Croats to Porga, not to

---

(40) On this list cf. S. Runciman, *A History of the First Bulgarian Empire* (London, 1930), pp. 272-81. The resemblance of the name Irnik with Ernach, Attila's youngest son, is certainly striking. Identity being granted for the sake of argument, there still is a long cry to a resemblance between Ernach-Kernaka in the Syriac transcription by he chronicler John of Nikiu—and the Croat chieftian's name of Porga. Identity between Irnik and Ernach is probable, not so between Irnik-Ernach-Organa and Porga.

(41) A. Tougard, *De l'Histoire profane dans les Actes Grecs des Bollandistes* (Paris, 1874), pp.186-204.

Chrovatos. H. Grégoire gives it to Chrovatos in one passage(42), but else-where puts forward the theory that Chrovatos was a minor, for the purpose of bringing his theory into line with Constantine's statement. But it is difficult to see how a minor could give his name to a great people and become the hero in a great campaign when the only historical evidence we possess on this migration gives the credit for it to his father Porga. Nor is there any evidence to show that Kuver, *alias* Kuvratos, *alias* Chrovatos was the founder of a Slavonic State covering all the lands where the name of the Croats is recorded and that the border districts of this state perpetuated his name. But how could such a state have held out for decades, as it is alleged, with the Avars commanding the Danubian basin till the beginning of the ninth century ? Let the facts as we know them suffice : the existence of White Croatia and White Serbia and the migration of the Croats and Serbs to the south under Heraclius, as we find them in Constantine's book.

*   *   *

A classical example may perhaps help us to understand how the non-Slavonic tribes succeeded in forcing their authority on so many Slavonic tribes. The Slovenes of Carinthia were also set free by the Croats, since Constantine Porphyrogennetos explicitly affirms that some of them left Dalmatia for Illyricum and Pannonia. As L. Hauptmann(43) has shown in his study on the free peasantry of Carinthia, the existence in Carinthia can be traced from the fifteenth century onward of free peasants called *Edlinger* (from the German *edel*, *i.e.* noble) or kasa(n)z. Their position gradually deteriorated, but originally they formed a class of a free aristocracy deriving its origin from the Croats settled among them as masters and aristocrats after the liberation of the Slovenes from the Avars. Numerically insignificant they lost their racial identity and got absorbed into the autochthonous element. Only a number of localities in Carinthia which inherited Croat names still reveal their places of residence.

Another detail. The word kaza(n)z, which in the light of the research work we mentioned is identical with the German word *Edlinger*, recalls the name of one of the seven brothers who according to Constantine led the Croats to the south—Kosentzes. Would it be admissible to suggest that the Croat tribe which left the main body in Dalmatia after the defeat of the Avars and penetrated " into Illyricum," as Constantine has it, was the tribe whose leader was Kosentzes or, if the names recorded by the imperial writer should rather be tribal or clannish, the tribe called Kosentzes ? If so, the original form of kaza(n)z, which in old Slavonic must have sounded like karenz, would be strikingly similar to Kosentzes and identification with the German word *Edlinger* (noble) would be easier still ; the free peasants of medieval Carinthia would have been the descendants of the

(42) Loc. cit., pp. 95, 100.

(43) " Carinthian Crotia," *Zbornik'kralja Tomislava*, pp. 297-317 (in Slovene).

Croat clan Kosentzes(44) that helped the Slavs of Carinthia in their emancipation from the Avars and settled among them as the ruling class.

The finding on the origin of the Carinthian free peasants may also help us with the solution of another social problem—the origin of the numerous class of " petty gentry " in Poland. On the supposition that Cracow was the capital of White Croatia and that the lands destined in later years to become Lesser Poland formed the centre of the empire, the primitive Croats must have populated the territory to a fair density ; there we,might find the clue to the origin of the Polish *szlachta* which so increased during the Middle Ages down to more recent times. The 'same may be said of the origin of the social distinctions among the Serbs of later Saxony in medieval days, who besides the ordinary peasants called *smerdi* prided themselves on belonging to the two classes called *vitaz* and *zhupans*. But these are problems that interest not only historians(45).

The Polish problem is of course more complex, as another process went on in the heart of the country parallel to the evolution in White Croatia. We have seen Mieszko emerging into history surrounded by his 3,000 well-armed and well-paid warriors on whom he could depend for his military adventures. The old Slavonic social organisation must have found in his lands the best chance for reaching maturity, since Mieszko's country occupied the centre of what was the cradle of the Slavonic race where it was left free to develop unhampered and take advantage of the example set by neighbouring nations(46).

Constantine's account also shows how Croat domination spread over the south and how the Croats gradually encroached on adjacent territory ; and what he has to say about the Serbs is even more significant. In time the various Slavonic tribes shed their tribal individuality and adopted the

---

(44) This without prejudice to the possibility of the Kosentzes being a Gothic band which joined the Croats after the destruction of their empire by the Huns and went shares in their authority over the Slavs. The presence of some Germanic elements in White Croatia is a problem that has not yet been cleared up. According to L. Hauptmann, *Migration of Croats and Serbs*, pp. 60, 61, the word *Kaza(n)z* is derived from the Sarmatian *Kasagos* which points to the Cherkess origin of the tribe. P. Skok, " Some Items from the Toponomastik of Slovenia" (in Croat), *Etnolog* (1934) vol, VII, pp. 80 seq., favours an Avar origin of the five brothers mentioned. This seems inadmissible. See also Hauptmann Die Herkunft der Kärtner Edlinge, *Vierteljahrschrift für Sozial und Wirtschaftsgeschichte* (1928) vol. XXI, pp. 245-79, and bibliography.

(45) Cf. the important work on the history and settlement of the Serbs in modern Saxony by E. O. Schulze " Die Kolonisierung und Germanisierung der Gebiete zwischen Saale und Elbe," *Preisschriften der Jablonowskischen Gesellschaft* (Hist.-Nationalökonom.   Sect.) No. XX (Leipzig, 1896). In the first part of the book (pp. 1-78), the author gives the history of the Serbs down to the time of their country's subjugation by Otto I. On the zhupan, the vitaz and the smerdi see ibid., pp. 98-116. Some other minor problems must be left to philologists, for example the adoption by the Croats and the Serbs of apparently Turco-Tartar customs, Avar influence on Croat institutions, especially that of the Ban, the zhupan and others. Cf. P. Skok, " Southern Slavs and Turkish Nations" (in Croat), *Yugosl. Hist. Rev.* (1936), vol. II, pp. 1-15, who favours the Avar origin of the words *Ban* and *zhupan*.

(46) As I cannot enter into details here, I leave this problem to other specialists. The various theories on the origin of the Polish gentry have been discussed by F. Piekosinski, *Polish Knighthood in the Middle Ages* (in Polish) (Cracow Academy, 1896), vol. I, pp. 5-59. The possibility of a foreign origin of the Polish nobility has not been overlooked, though varying points of view alter problems. I have been unable to read T. Wojciechowski's book —*Chrobacya* (Cracow, 1873).

name of the Serbs.   The Zachlumians are a case in point.   Their chieftain
came from White Serbia and in all probability forced his rule on a Slavonic
tribe already settled in the south, exactly the situation as it arose among the
Trevunians, the Canalitans, the Diocleans and the Narentanians(47), and a
process that should help us to visualise the growth of Croatian and Serbian
power in Central Europe.   Their political organisation was presumably
loose, since Constantine speaks of the rival principalities of the southern
Serbians and Croats, but as in the south the tribes submitted to the authority
of a supreme leader or duke, some central suthority must have been part
of their system.

The settling of the Croats and Serbs in Central Europe must have
proceeded on similar lines, with only this difference that in the first stage
of their conquests Croats and Serbs remained more distantly aloof from the
population.   Such was also the case of the primitive Bulgarians in the State
they founded on the Danube(48).   This would explain the facility with
which some of them could walk out of the countries they had conquered to
combine and emigrate into territories of the Roman Empire as a com-
pact military body.

*   *   *

Let us see now what can be gathered from various sources on the
history of White Croatia and White Serbia from the seventh to the tenth
century.   As regards White Serbia we find a few interesting indications in
Frankish chronicles.   We learn from Fredegar(49) that the Serbian prince
Dervan of his own accord joined the state of Samo who had liberated the
Slavs of Bohemia, Moravia and Carenthania from the Avar yoke, after his
defeat of the Frankish king Dagobert in 632.   Meanwhile the emigration to
the south of an important contingent naturally crippled the power formed by
the Serbs among the Slavs between the Elbe, the Saale and the Bober, and as
Samo's ill-jointed government did not survive him, his alliance failed to make
good the Serbians' loss.   They then ceased to be the formidable power
which, according to Ma'sudi, was dreaded by all the Slavs, and experienced
the mortification of having once again to make their obeisance to the Franks.
But they did not cease to be a nuisance, for we hear from the Frankish
chronicles of repeated Serb raids into Thuringia and rebellions against Charlemagne and his successors.   In the same source we incidentally learn the
names of one of the dukes, Miliduch, who was killed in battle in 806(50)
and of one of their rebel chieftains, Tunglo(51) (826).   White Serbia thus
continued to exist and even took an active part in the conflict between the
Franks, the Czechs and the Moravians.   We learn for instance from the

---

(47) *De Admin. Imp.*, ch. 32-37, Bonn, pp. 152-164.
(48) Cf. N. Županić " The Serb Settlement in the Macedonian town of Srbčиšte in the
VIIth century ; The Ethnological and Sociological implications of Constantine Porphyrogenetus' account of the Serbs and the Croats," *Etnolog* (1928), vol, II, pp. 26-35.
(49) *M.G.H.S.* Rer. Merov., II, book IV, ch. 48, pp. 144, 154.
(50) Einhardi Annales, *M.G.H.S.* I, p. 193.
(51) Ibid., p. 124.

Annals of Fulda that in 856 the Serbs were asked to accompany Louis the German on his expedition to Bohemia where he subjugated a number of tribes ; and the following year on another expedition against the chieftain called Slavitah, of a Bohemian tribe, who had ejected his brother and risen in rebellion.   The aggrieved party took refuge with the Serbian prince Zistibor, but was recalled to his country by the Franks after they had defeated the rebel.   He got away and was received by the Moravian Duke Rastislav ; but his pro-Frankish brother was killed by his people.   Another anti-Frankish revolt followed in 858(52).

These casual statements by Frankish annalists are all we learn on the growth of Constantine's White Serbia during the seventh, eighth and ninth centuries, while meagre reports on further clashes between Serbs and Franks show that animosity towards the Franks(53) did not abate during the succeeding period when the Moravian Empire came into being and reached its zenith at the annexation of White Croatia.   Though there is no direct evidence to show that Svatopluk imposed his authority on the Serbs(54), the spread of Moravian influence over the lands between the Saale, the Elbe and the Bober may be taken for granted ; only, death prevented Svatopluk from consolidating his growing empire after he had gathered both White Serbia and White Croatia under his rule(55).

The departure to the south of so many Croat chieftains with their followers also weakened White Croatia, with this difference, however, in favour of the Croats who stayed behind that Frankish expansion towards the Carpathians had been stopped by the Moravians and all danger from that quarter had vanished before any serious damage was done.   The Croatian State thus weathered its crisis and was left in undisturbed possession.

But when the Moravians had organised their State their next step was to annex their peaceful neighbour.   It will be remembered that Svatopluk, as confirmed by the Legend of S. Methodius, defeated a Vistulanian prince and forced him most probably to adopt the Christian religion, and from what we know of the political situation in those parts, that same prince must have been the head of the Croatian State.   Assuming then that the whole of White Croatia, from the Serbian borders to the Bug and the Styr rivers, was incorporated into Moravia, we must suppose, since the foundation charter of Prague mentions the Croats of Bohemia, that the eastern part of Bohemia also belonged to White Croatia and became part of the Moravian State.

(52) Annales Fuldenses, *M.G.H.S.* I, pp. 370-2.

(53) Ibid., pp. 380, 381, 387, 393 (the years 869, 874, 880).

(54) It is interesting to note that the Fulda annalist records in the same year after Svatopluk's death the submission of the Czechs and the Serbs' mission to Arnulf to assure him of their fidelity.   The coincidence would seem to indicate that the Moravians had something to do with the Serbs as well as with the Slavs of Bohemia (*Ann. Fuld.*, loc. cit., p. 413).

(55) Part of the Serbs must have been subject to Svatopluk of Moravia, as Thietmar (Chronicon VI, ch. 99, *M.H.G.S.* N.S. IX, p. 392) says of his ancestors : " In the reign of the Duke Svatopluk we were ruled by Bohemian princes.   Our ancestors paid him an annual tribute and he had bishops in his country, then called Marierun [Moravia] ; all this, he and his successors lost in their pride." It is probable that Svatopluk annexed the whole of White Serbia to his Moravian Empire and what confirms the assumption is that Thietmar's statement concerns the territory of the Thuringian March, the westernmost portion of White Serbia. Cf. also W. Boguslawski, *History of the Nord-Eastern Slavs* (in Polish) vol. III, pp. 122 seq

This would be enough to decide the leading tribe of Bohemia, the Czechs, who by their geopraphical position were rather within the Frankish sphere, to throw in their lot with the Croats and acknowledge the supremacy of Svatopluk of Moravia.

This process would explain the rise of the Moravian State in Central Europe. The existence of a State north of the Carpathians—Constantine's White Croatia, and in modern Saxony—White Serbia, facilitated the Moravians' eastward and northward expansion. Great Moravia, as Constantine VII called it (ch. XIII), was a federation of a sort under the authority of the Moimir dynasty of Moravia. The unification by the Serbs and the Croats of these loose Slavonic tribes lent solidity to the new state and gave it fairer prospects than many historians have been ready to admit.

But the union did not last. After Svatopluk's death trouble started between his sons, which caused the newly acquired territories and Croatia to cut themselves adrift. But the old Croat power never completely recovered after that. It appears that the Croats of Eastern Bohemia concluded an alliance with the leading tribe of the Czechs who occupied the centre of the country, kept the tribes north-west, west and south of the old land of the Boii under some sort of control and, as the Annals of Fulda seem to suggest(56), made overtures to the Bavarians who represented the Frankish Empire. Duke Witizla, who accompanied the Czech Spytihniev to Regensburg in 895 with several other princes of the Slavonic tribes of that country, must have been the leading prince of the eastern and the south-eastern part of Bohemia, very probably the leader of the Croats who controlled the minor Slavonic tribes of the eastern half of the country. The dukes of this part of Bohemia are believed to have belonged to the ducal house of the Slavniks. But the designation is not accurate. We do not know the founder of the dynasty, but its name has become familiar to all specialists in the history of Bohemia only because the best known duke of that house and the father of S. Adalbert was called Slavnik.

If this reading of the few facts that concern the early history of the Bohemian Slavs is right, then the conclusion that the Moravian episode contributed to the final amalgamation of the Slavs of the old land of the Boii into one single political group is justified. No doubt the Slavs of Bohemia are often mentioned, even before the Moravian period, on account of their contacts with the Franks(57); but the question is whether the annalists invariably had in mind the whole of Bohemia as we know it, or only that part of it which lay nearer to the Franks. All the Slavonic tribes that occupied the former country of the Boii could not be regarded as subject to tribute(58); nor do the Annals, in referring to the subjugation of the Bohemian Slavs by Charlemagne, mention the Croats who lived in

---

(56) See above, ch. I p. 11 seq.

(57) The different references to the Slavs of Bohemia by the early chroniclers have been collected by H. Jireček, *Antiquae Bohemiae usque ad exitum s. XII Topographica Historia* (Wien, Prag, 1843), pp. I-XXVIII.

(58) Cf. Novotný, loc. cit., vol. I, 1, pp. 270-84, especially p. 280. Cf. also J. Lippert, *Sozial-Geschichte Böhmens* (Wien, Prag, 1896), vol. I, p. 138.

the eastern part of the country. This makes it difficult to say if this part of Bohemia also came under the Avars and under Charlemagne who vanquished them, or whether it was still part of the Croat country which had escaped the rule of both the Avars and of Charlemagne. The latter alternative seems more likely, and in this case Bohemia's political unity would have been due to Moravian intervention.

*　　　*　　　*

Such a conclusion would also follow from what we know of the occupation of Bohemia by the Slavs. They infiltrated into the country perhaps while it was still occupied by the Germanic tribes, but mass immigration certainly did not take place till after the Germans' departure, i.e. at the end of the fifth century when the exodus started from Lusatia and Silesia(59), held at that time respectively by the Serbs and the Croats, already slavicised to a certain extent.

Evidence in favour of our view on Bohemia's occupation by the Slavs comes from Constantine Porphyrogennetos who, in referring to the Serbs' original seat on the Elbe river, seems to identify their country with the land of the Boii(60). The location of the Serbs of Lusatia in Bohemia has intrigued many historians ; but if we remember that the occupation of Bohemia, especially its western half, started from Lusatia which then became the centre of a State controlled by the Serbs, the occupation of central and western Bohemia could be regarded as the normal expansion of White Serbia. This would make Constantine's statement intelligible. If moreover the Czechs, who were the leading tribe in the western half of Bohemia, were somehow associated with the Serbs, then the identification of White Serbia with the country of the Boii would be more intelligible still. There is evidence for this association. It is, however, not necessary to suppose that the Czechs, the tribe which according to a national tradition handed down by Cosmas(61) took a lead in the occupation of Bohemia, were Serbs, or a tribe racially akin to them. The etymology of the name "Czech" has troubled Slavonic philologists(62), and we have been given theories on the non-Slavonic origin of the Czechs(63), but so far with little success. Yet we find indications in the national tradition to the effect that

---

(59) L. Niederle, "On the early history of Czech lands," *Czech. Hist. Rev.* (1900), separate edition, p. 49.

(60) Loc cit., ch. 32, Bonn, p. 152. See Appendix I, p. 268.

(61) Chronica, I. ch. 2, *M.G.H.S.* N.S. II, pp. 5 seq.

(62) Cf. what V. Novotný writes on the origin of the Czech name in *Czech History* (in Czech), vol. I., pp. 235 seq. After reviewing the theories advanced prior to 1912, he arrives at the conclusion that the name "Czech" was originally synonymous with the word "man." R. Jakobson in his study "Die Reimwörter Czech, Lech," *Slavische Rundschau* (1938), derives the name from the Old Slavonic root cęd, a derivation that has found favour with leading Czech philologists.

(63) Cf. the daring suggestions offered by N. Županić in his studies "Harimati," *Etnolog* (1927), vol. I, pp. 131-8: "First Bearers of the ethnical names of the Serbs, Croats, Czechs and Antes" (in Slovene) ibid., vol. II (1928), pp. 74-9, with a summary in French. The author believes that all those nations were originally autochthonous and belonged to the Alarodian group akin to the Pelasgians.

294

the Czechs lived originally in White Serbia, probably as one of the tribes under Serbian sway. It was to escape from it that they moved to the south. Cosmas has nothing to say about this tradition or about the legendary Czech ancestor of the nation, or his past, but the Czech chronicle of Dalimil(64) which was set in verse in the first half of the fourteenth century, completes Cosmas' account and presents the ancestral Czech as coming from " Serbian lands where there is a country named Croatia." Having committed a murder in his country and feeling unsafe there, Czech emigrated with his six brothers and all his men and left the land " which, as stated, is called Croatia (Charvaty)."

This passage has been too lightly dismissed, it being alleged that Dalimil was one of the first holders of the so-called autochthonous theory, which made the Slavs come from the south, the country of the modern Serbs and Croats(65). But this is untenable, for on reading the account with closer attention one has to admit that Dalimil rather heard something about the migration of the Serbs " to the land where the Greeks live, near the sea, from where they spread as far as Rome," as he writes previous to his account of the Czech's arrival in Bohemia. He did not quite know what to make of the tradition as he received it, but he faithfully handed it on in his rhymes, though not in its right place, for he couples it with the dispersal of the human race after the erection of the Tower of Babel.

It is not without significance that the contemporary German translator of the Czech chronicle should have preserved the same tradition, for he translates the name of the Serbs by Windin, Winden(66), as the Germans always called the Slavs on the Elbe, as well as the Slavs between the Saale and the Elbe. This must have been more than a mere coincidence. The translator was a German from Bohemia and a Bohemian patriot who thoroughly disliked the presence of foreigners in his native land and classed among them even his own countrymen from Germany. He was therefore well placed to know at least something of the local tradition(67).

---

(64) *F.R.B.*, III, p. 6.

(65) Niederle, *Slav. Antiquities*, vol. II, p. 265. Novotný, loc. cit. vol. I, 1, p. 232 rightly points out that Niederle's reading of the passage is wrong.

(66) *F.R.B.*, III, p. 6.

Dy Windin by den andirn	The Wendes among others
da nun dy Grichin wandirn,	Migrate to the Greeks
dy sich saczten by das mer . . .	Who settled near the sea . . .
Czu Winden ist ein ·gegent,	In Windenland, there is a country
di is Grauacia genennt.	Called Croatia.

The other German version, also contemporaneous, but in prose, renders Dalimil's Czech tradition as follows (ibid., III, p. 257) : Unter den sprachen und czungen was ein czunge und sprach, die die Wynden genannt sein, von dannen wo die Recken [Greeks] wonten. Die saczten sich nebem das mer und waren sich heren und preytten pys gen Rome. Und in der-selben windischen czungen ist ein land Charwat genannt. (Amid the languages and nations there was a nation and a language called Wendes from the land where the Greeks lived. This nation settled near the sea, multiplied and spread as far as Rome. And in the same Windish nation there is a country called Charwat, *i.e.* Croatia). In all passages where Dalimil mentions the Serbs the translators use the same name for the Serbs, namely Wendes. The tradition may be slightly confused, but is clear enough for the purpose.

(67) Even a literal interpretation of Dalimil's and his translator's passage is plausible enough, since we know that there were some Croat settlements in the country occupied by the Serbs.

In any case, the Czechs, little as we know about them or about the origin and rise of their ducal family, the Przemyslides(68), must have been a go-ahead tribe. The fact that the Annals of Fulda in 895 give precedence to the duke of the Czechs over Witizla is some indication that the Czechs began at that time to exercise some sort of a political power over the country. Not that I use this as evidence, since the Franks were naturally more interested in the attitude of the Slavonic tribes of western Bohemia than in the attitude prevailing in the east, so that the annalist could easily have lent greater importance to the duke of the Czechs ; but the fact is that the Przemyslides' drive for power and fame did start in 895.

This view of Bohemia's early history explains at the same time why the linguistic characteristics of the Bohemian Slavs remained unchanged. The Slavonic tribes that lived under Czech and Croat rule belonged to the western branch, closely akin to the Polish group from which they issued, obviously enough, since they remained so long near the Slavs' original home and were the last Slavonic group to migrate south. The same must be said of the group of tribes settled in the valley of the Morava, along the Vag, the Hron and the Danube, except that these were never subject to Croats, Serbs or Czechs and were able to carry on their own political existence, probably under pressure from the Franks whose expansion in the eighth and chiefly at the beginning of the ninth century bore very much to the north-east, north of the Danube.

*   *   *

What then became of the rest of White Croatia after the fall of the Moravian Empire ? The question is not easy to answer, as we are again left without any contemporary information on the subject. That the Croats of Bohemia pursued an independent policy and entered into an alliance with the Czechs would suggest that the rest of White Croatia continued for some time under the rule of Moimir II, Svatopluk's successor. We may at least suppose that the Bohemian Croats, who had made up their minds to break loose from Moravia (if this interpretation be admissible), would remain associated with the other Croats, if the latter had severed relations with Moravia at the same time.

Since nothing is known of the happenings in what was once White Croatia it seems only logical to assume that the territory of Cracow, which was the centre of White Croatia, Silesia and Western Galicia, resumed its

---

(68) What Cosmas (Chronica I, chs. 14-7, *M.G.H.S.* N.S. II., pp. 11-18) writes about the origin of the House of the Przemyslides and the marriage of Libusha, daughter of the legendary Krok, of the Czech tribe, with Przemysl is çertainly legend. Cf. Novotný, loc. cit., vol. I, pp. 247 seq., who finds there a trace of the reunion of the Czechs with the tribe of the Lemuzi in northern Bohemia, whose seat lay nearest to White Serbia. At the same time, it is not without interest that ladies of princely lineage among the Croats seem to have been given places of distinction, as can be gathered from Constantine's statement (ch. 30, Bonn, p. 145) pointing out as leaders of the Croats who came south Klukas, Lobelos, Kosentzes, Muchlo, Chorvat—and two sisters, Tuga and Buga. Be it noted again that none of these names is Slavonic. On the Sagas concerning Przemysl, Libusha, Krok and Piast, see A. Brückner, " Fälscher an der Arbeit," *Jahrbücher für Geschichte Osteuropas* (1937), vol. II, pp. 596-619.

individual existence after the defeat of the Moravians. Then how did they stand with the Magyars ? Did they pay tribute to the new invaders ? Circumstances would suggest that they did, as the Magyars made themselves masters of Moravia and probably of the whole Moravian Empire ; and through Moravia, which was completely at their mercy, they were within striking distance of the heart of White Croatia and Cracow. This city was a flourishing commercial centre at that period and the Magyars were not so barbarous as not to see it.

On this particular matter we have no direct information, except that what Constantine records on the relations between the Croats and the Turks (Magyars) might be read as a hint in that sense. The imperial writer says in fact that the Croats were on friendly, even intermarrying terms, with the Magyars. The passage, no doubt, is obscure, as the Emperor seems to be telescoping bits of information that belong to different periods. At the time Constantine was writing, the Croats of White Croatia were certainly not pagans, as he states, and they could not have been subjects of Otto I, as he has it, till after the occupation of Cracow by Boleslas I of of Bohemia, who was Otto's liege. Nevertheless, as almost all Constantine's information has a certain amount of reality behind it, we could relate this passage on the Croats' relations with the Magyars, to the time after the destruction of the Moravian Empire. In this case the statement would lend substance to our assumption that White Croatia carried on its independent existence for some decades, while the Magyars contented themselves with the payment of a tribute and even opened friendly relations with the Slavs on the Vistula, a compromise sealed by a marriage between the leading Croat prince and the house of Arpad. However, as Constantine refers elsewhere to Magyar incursions into White Croatia, we must make the additional supposition that the compromise was reached after some fighting between the Croatian Slavs and the Magyars. Their *modus vivendi* would have lasted till 955 when Otto I broke the Magyar power and when Poland and Bohemia joined in the fray to make sure of the spoils of the late dominions of White Croatia and Moravia.

APPENDIX III

POLISH AND RUSSIAN CONFLICT OVER THE REMAINS OF WHITE CROATIA

THE CROATS IN THE RUSSIAN ANNALS—MA'SUDI'S STATEMENT—THE RUSSIANS IN THE DOCUMENT OF RAFFELSTETTEN.

The tradition on the existence of a Croatian State in modern Galicia must have long survived in Kiev. This much can be gathered from the Russian Primary Chronicle, the so-called Annals of Nestor, which mentions the Croats. These could only belong to Constantine's White Croatia, to which the author refers on three occasions. As these passages have been differently interpreted and bear directly on the origin of the Polish-Russian contest over Galicia, they deserve examination.

First, at the beginning of his work, in speaking of the various Slavonic tribes, the chronicler writes(1) : " Thus, the Polianians, the Derevlians, the Severians, the Radimichians, the Vyatichians and the Croats lived at peace." As the tribes mentioned are all eastern Slavonic, the obvious explanation would be that there existed among them one tribe that had also been subject to the Croats and this could only be a tribe of the upper Dniester. As a matter of fact one passage in Constantine's account(2) would seem to connote that White Croatia extended as far as the upper Dniester for, after reporting on the military strength of White Croatia, he states that that country was suffering from frequent raids by Franks(3), Turks (Magyars) and Pechenegs, and that it was situated a distance of a thirty days' journey from the Black Sea(4). At that time, the Pechenegs occupied the south of Russia and if White Croatia included the territory of the Upper Dniester, Constantine's description corresponded to facts.

The other reference to the Croats by the Russian Primary Chronicle(5) belongs to the year 907 and concerns the attack launched by Oleg against Byzantium : " Leaving Igor in Kiev, Oleg attacked the Greeks. He took with him a multitude of Varangians, Slavs, Chuds, Krivichians, Merians, Polianians, Severians, Derevlians, Radimichians, Croats, Dulebians and

---

(1) S. H. Cross, loc. cit., p. 141.
(2) *De admin. Imperio*, ch. 31 (Bran, pp. 151 seq.)
(3) Attacks by the Franks can only be understood in connection with the Bohemian Croats, because in trying to subjugate the Slavs of Bohemia, the Franks may likewise have drawn the Croats of Eastern Bohemia into the conflict. These Croats probably belonged to White Croatia, even when the rest of Bohemia was under the Avars and at that time White Croatia was in fact a pagan country. It was this part of White Croatia which the Franks attached to their Empire, when the Czechs and the Croats made their submission in 895. We find then that Constantine's statement, though it upsets the historical sequence of events (an excusable slip, as the Emperor was writing about distant countries of which the Byzantines knew very little), was on the whole based on fact.
(4) The sea which is a thirty days' journey distant from White Croatia is called *Skoteine* or Black by Constantine, though the name " Black " would have fitted the North Sea better in the minds of the Greeks. They used to call the Black Sea " Pontos Euxeinos."
(5) S. H. Cross, loc. cit., p. 149 (ad a. 6412-6515, 904-907).

298

Tiverchians.'' This nomenclature may suggest that Oleg's Russian State included also a Slavonic tribe called Croats. Did it belong to the eastern Slavonic branch which the Croats had incorporated into their state and which, after the destruction of the Moravian Empire by the Magyars, drifted away from the bulk of what was White Croatia ? On first inspection this would seem to come near the truth.

But the third reference to the Croats by the Chronicler upsets our calculation. Referring to the year 6500 (992)(6), he writes : ''Vladimir attacked the Croats. On his return from the Croatian war, the Pechenegs appeared on the opposite bank of the Dnieper from the direction of the Sula (river).'' At a first glance this statement looks reconcilable with previous assertions ; it may have been an expedition against the tribe that once belonged to White Croatia and showed a desire to sever relations with Vladimir. Such things did happen in the early years of Russian history.

But the difficulty is that there seems to have been a war on between Russia and Poland at that very moment. The Russian Chronicler, curiously enough, knows nothing about it, but details are supplied by the German Annals. With reference to King Otto III's campaign against Brandenburg in 992 the Annals of Hildesheim mention the presence of Boleslas II of Bohemia and his contingent and add that Mieszko's son, Boleslas the Great, was unable to attend in person and sent only some troops because of a threat of war from Russia(7) : '' because a great war with Russia was impending.'' Taken literally this statement would imply that Russia and Poland were at war in 992 or 993, in which case the issue must have been something more important than a Russian tribe that formerly belonged to the Croatian Empire. Was it perhaps the capital of White Croatia, the region of Cracow ?

Corroboration for this conjecture may be found in the fact that Cracow, as we know from Arab sources already quoted, had developed into a great trading centre, a link between West and East that threatened Kiev and the old commercial route from the Baltic Sea over the Dnieper as a dangerous competitor and rival. As Cracow at that time already belonged to Poland it would have been the expected thing for Vladimir to cast longing eyes on such a prize, to take advantage of the change on the Polish throne after the death of Mieszko I and to attack Boleslas the Great in order to capture the wealthy city.

Such is the hypothesis that has been put forward and it has a fair amount of probability to its credit(8). It has even been suggested that Russia's interest in Cracow and in old White Croatia was not so sudden and inexplicable as would appear at first. After the collapse of Moravia the remnants of White Croatia had acknowledged the supremacy of Oleg's rising state, probably with a view to obtain security against the Magyar

(6) S. H. Cross, loc. cit., p. 207.

(7) *M.G.H.S.*, III, p. 169.

(8) L. Hauptmann, " The Arrival of the Croats " (in Croat), *Strena Bubliciana* pp.528 seq.

invading hordes. Ma'sudi's account of the Slavs referred to above is quoted, with some slight retouches that are not unreasonable, at least in some details, in favour of the view that about the year 943, when Ma'sudi was writing his account, Russia of Kiev was neighbour to Bohemia on the Giant Mountains (Riesengebirge—Krkonose), as the whole Croatian Empire had bodily joined Oleg. Thus the Croats who accompanied Oleg in his campaign against Byzantium in 907 were not a Russian tribe, but the Croats of Cracow. Czech expansion towards Silesia and Cracow started only about 960 when Svyatoslav was so engrossed in his adventures in the East that he lost all interest in the distant western part of his dominion. The Polish occupation of the Red Cities should also be dated from that period. In the light of this theory Vladimir of Kiev only tried in 992 to carry on an experiment started in 981 and to recover the rest of White Croatia, especially Cracow, which was then in the possession of the Poles.

This reading would also be suggested by the reference in the German Annals to the imminence of a bitter Russo-Polish conflict in 992; but, attractive as it is, there are difficulties that should not be overlooked. The main evidence, coming from the Annals of Hildesheim, is not convincing. The annalist himself says nothing about a Polish-Russian war ; he only quotes the answer sent by Boleslas the Great to the Emperor, apologising for his failure to lead his auxiliary troops in person on the plea of impending trouble with Russia. He must have ascended the throne about that time, a very tempting occasion for any neighbour to try experiments of the kind. It is also possible that a Russian tribe, which years before had belonged to White Croatia and lived somewhere on the upper Dniester, felt a desire to join Poland which at the time had the whole of the former White Croatia in its power, and that Boleslas the Great supported the Russian tribe in the hope that Russia of Kiev would be too busy in the East to worry about the West. It was a fascinating proposition to gather the Croat empire, including Przemysl, the Red Cities lost by Mieszko I, right down to the upper Dniester, under Polish power. But the new duke was different from Svyatoslav and his successor ; he acted swiftly, crushed the Croat rebellion on the upper Dniester and taught the Poles to go more warily(9).

It looks on the other hand as though the author of the Russian chronicle discriminated on the three occasions we have mentioned between the Southern Croats and the White Croats. In explaining how the Slavs had spread from their original seat, which he wrongly locates on the Danube to make it nearer Babylon, the starting-post at the dispersal of the human race, he writes(10) : " For many years the Slavs lived beside the Danube, where the Hungarian and Bulgarian lands at present lie. From among these Slavs, parties scattered throughout the country and were

(9) Nestor's Annals, ad a. 6500 (992), S. H. Cross, loc. cit., p. 207.
(10) Ibid. pp. 137 seq. The author of the Russian Primary Chronicle most probably took his account on the unity of the Slavonic race and on the various Slavonic tribes from a lost report "on the translation of the books into Slavonic," written in Bohemia in the Xth century, which thence reached Russia. On this lost source see A. Shakhmatov, " Povest Vremennikh let i ee Istochniki " (The Russian Primary Chronicle and its Sources), *Trudy Otdela Drevne-Russkoi Literatury Akad. Nauk SSSR* (1940), vol. IV, pp. 80-92.

known by appropriate names according to the places where they settled. Thus some came and settled by the river Morava and were named Moravians, while others were called Czechs. Among these same Slavs are included the White Croats, the Serbs and the Khorutanians. . . . '' The chronicler therefore knows of the existence of White Croatia, and perhaps also of its historical connection with the Moravians and the Czechs since he locates it in the neighbourhood of those Slavonic nations.

As after their unfortunate experience the Croats disappeared from Russian history the obvious explanation is that they forfeited their right to their own duke and were attached to the Duchy of Kiev, as happened to other Russian tribes whose rebellions had misfired. In this case the episode was only of local consequence and need not have troubled the annalist who in fact knew nothing of a war between Poland and Russia. Boleslas the Great may have exaggerated the threat from Russia to make the excuses for his absence more palatable to the German court.

The reticence of the Russian Annals on the incident could, it is true, be explained on the ground that the operations against the country that was White Croatia yielded such poor results ; but even then the annalist's silence on Russia's extraordinary expansion after the destruction of the Moravian Empire remains to be accounted for. Moreover, among the Slavonic tribes he refers to as belonging to the Russian State he includes some that belonged to the eastern Slavonic group, whereas the tribes that were part of White Croatia and would have been the bone of contention in the contest were definitely western and Polish. On the other hand, the Russian annalist carefully specifies the Poles, calling them Lyakhs and insists that they, too, belong to the Slavonic race, but he is perfectly aware of their difference from the Russian tribes. This would rather suggest that the Croats he mentions were a Russian tribe which had borrowed the name of those Croats who had been their masters but lost their identity through absorption. Ma'sudi's statement, important as it is, is unfortunately too summary and vague to serve as the basis for a solution.

*   *   *

This is what he says after the description of the Serbs' strange customs previously quoted(11) : '' The first of the Slavonic States is that of Ad Dir which owns large cities, rich fields, vast armies and numerous armaments. Muslim merchants visit its capital with various kinds of merchandise. Nearest to this Slavonic State is that of Al Firag [Prague] which owns gold mines, towns, many fields, enormous armies and wields great military power. It makes war on the Ar Rum, the An Nukubarda and other nations, and their battles sway between failure and success. Next to this Slavonic State lies that of the Turks, a nation of handsome manhood, the most numerous and bravest of the Slavs(12).

---

(11) Appendix I, p. 270.
(12) Marquart, *Streifüzge*, p. 102.

The Arab traveller's inaccuracies are patent and his account abounds in misstatements which he could have taken the trouble to correct. This is nothing new, as Ma'sudi is notorious for his carelessness ; but he also offers good value and precious information. The State of Ad Dir is generally taken to be Russia of Kiev as the dynasty which governed this city had been founded by Dir. But this is not quite evident and the identification is somewhat forced ; for it is difficult to see why the name of the defeated Dir should be given prominence while that of Oleg, conqueror of Kiev and founder of a great State, which happened to be nearer to the Arab world, or the name of Igor, who ruled in Kiev in Ma'sudi's time, should be left in the shade. Marquart(13) himself admits that he would have no hesitation in seeing here a description of White Croatia and in Ad Dir the name of its ruler, if only we could be certain that Cracow, *i.e.* the '' land of the White Croats, still had rulers of its own before its conquest by Boleslas I of Bohemia.'' After what has been said in Appendix II this seems quite likely. Ma'sudi's words would then refer to White Croatia and its capital Cracow, which is pictured as a great commercial centre by Ma'sudi just as it was by Ibrahim Ibn Ja'cub, in which case the Slavonic State's proximity to Bohemia, as affirmed by Ma'sudi, would make sense. It would then be admissible to read the extract as the only vestige left of the existence of White Croatia after the destruction of the Moravian Empire and of one of its rulers, though the name be given in a mutilated form.

But even if this interpretation is not accepted, the passage cannot be taken as evidence that Russia was master of the whole territory that once belonged to White Croatia as far as White Serbia, for it may mean that Bohemia, by annexing White Croatia, became a neighbour of Russia. In this case the occupation of Cracow by Boleslas of Bohemia should be dated before the year 943 when Ma'sudi was writing his memoirs ; such ante-dating may be inadvisable, but the passage is hopelessly confusing. The Turks or Magyars are classed among the Slavs ; Prague is alleged to be fighting Ar Rum, the Arab equivalent for Byzantium. To reconcile this statement with facts in history that are known, Marquart(14) makes Ar Rum stand for Otto I's renovated Roman Empire, as in his opinion the designation is often used by Ma'sudi and by Spanish Arabian writers in a wider sense designed to cover also the Christian nations of Western Europe. Instead of the reading An-Nukubard, he proposes that of Al Bazkarda, *i.e.* Magyars, which would make Prague fight Otto's Empire, the Franks and the Magyars instead of Byzantium.

But the explanation does not hold water. As the Franks are specifically mentioned in the passage there is no reason why Ma'sudi should refer to them twice in the same sentence. It is preferable then to read Byzantium for Ar Rum ; but how does Prague happen to be fighting Byzantium ? This difficulty would vanish, if we could suppose a misplacing of the clause—

(13) Loc. cit., p. 145.
(14) Loc. cit., pp. 142 seq.

" It makes war on. . . " etc., and shift it to the end of the passage so as to make it follow the sentence about the Turks or Magyars(15). The Magyars were in fact at war with Byzantium, the Franks and An Nukubard or the the Langobards of Northern Italy. Having gone so far, what is there to stop one shifting the whole statement about the Magyars back to the second place in the passage, after the statement on Ad Dir ? Then nothing could be inferred from Ma'sudi's account either for or against the theory under discussion, it being evident that the Arab writer was concentrating on Russia, Hungary and Bohemia and simply omitted to mention White Croatia and Poland. So, even if one feels reluctant to find in Ma'sudi's description proof for the existence of a White Croatia with its independent prince before the year 943, one cannot at any rate use it as evidence in favour of a Russian occupation of White Croatia after the Moravian catastrophe.

* * *

The weightiest argument in support of the assertion that Russia of Kiev was master of Silesia and Western and Eastern Galicia in the first half of the tenth century comes from a document of Raffelstetten on the Danube, which imposes customs tariffs on foreign goods entering Ostmark and Bavaria, with a special tariff on goods brought by Slavonic traders from Bohemia or the land of the Rugi(16). The latter designation is mostly interpreted as Russia ; but as it seemed difficult to many historians to believe that the Russians could have traded with Bavaria at such an early period, the passage has been explained away in other ways(17). On first inspection the suggestion that the " Rugi " may have been the White Croats of Cracow who at that time were under Russia of Kiev looks very attractive and disposes of every difficulty(18), but on second thought the suggestion is unacceptable.

The document was issued about the year 904 and its special stipulation for merchants from Moravia supposes the existence of the Moravian Empire, whether decadent or not. As we pointed out before, it seems unlikely that White Croatia should have drifted away from Moravia before its final destruction by the Magyars. Moreover, the document is based on experience gathered from the past and supplies the high-water mark of commercial activity as it had developed in that part of Eastern Francia under Louis the German (d. 876), Carlomann (d. 880) and Arnulf (d. 899)(19). This makes it doubtful that a document such as was designed to correct irregularities that had occurred over a space of thirty years in the

---

(15) As proposed by L. Hauptmann, loc. cit., pp. 530 seq.
(16) *M.G.H. Leges*, II, 250 Capitularia Regum Francorum, K. Schiffman, Die Zollurkunde von Raffelstetten, *Mitteilungen des Inst. f. öster, Gesch.* (1917), vol. XXXVII, pp. 479-88 : Sclavi vero, qui de Rugis vel de Boemanis mercandi causa exeunt.
(17) Cf. V. Novotný, loc. cit., vol. I, p. 433.
(18) Hauptmann, loc. cit., p. 529.
(19) Cf. what Arnold Luschin von Ebengreuth says about this in his *Geschichte der Stadt Wien* (Wien, 1897), vol. I, p. 402 (edited by H. Zimmermann and published by the Alterthumsverein zu Wien).

collection of customs tariffs on the Danube, should take such prompt cognizance of a political change in White Croatia which had scarcely had time to take effect and of which many nobles, on being consulted in connection with the issue of the document, probably knew little if anything(20).

This throws us back on the widely prevailing opinion that the " Rugi " were none but the merchants of Kievan Russia, the White Croats of Cracow being included among the Moravians in the document, as their country had been part of the Moravian Empire since about 880. The reference to the Russians has its importance in the history of the Kievan State as evidence that even at such an early date Scandinavian and Slav traders from Kiev were in commercial contact with Eastern Francia.

There is one piece of evidence left that may dispel any lingering hesitation—Constantine's statement on the relations between the Croats and the " Turks " or Magyars. If there is any truth in what he says about the friendly relations existing between the destroyers of the Moravian Empire and the White Croats, his statement can only be linked with the position as it arose in those parts from the dismemberment of Moravia. To say that Constantine confuses White Croatia with Bohemia, because White Croatia had been annexed by the Czechs, and that Bohemia's friendship may have started under Wenceslas who gave his sister in marriage to a Magyar chieftain(21), explains nothing, for there is no evidence for it. Besides, White Croatia did not belong to Bohemia in Wenceslas' time. No doubt Constantine confuses many things and we readily excuse him, because he was dealing with things that were confusing ; but this does not justify us in drawing from his statements such conclusions as only make the confusion worse confounded. There is some truth at the back of all his accounts.

Having examined the problem in all its aspects, we are now in a position to discover in Nestor's Croats an eastern Slavonic tribe which the warlike Croats had brought under their power. After the fall of Moravia only the Croats of Bohemia and of the upper Dniester definitely remained outside White Croatia. It carried on a more or less independent existence round Cracow as its capital and other important centres known to us as Przemysl and Czervien until it was again subjugated by the Czechs who looked upon themselves as the trustees of Great Moravia, and by the Poles who under Mieszko I were bent on gathering all the Polish tribes into one State. The Poles secured for themselves the lands round Sandomierz and the Red Cities, and it was this part of White Croatia which became the object of the contest between the Poles and the Russians of Kiev. The Russians were interested in it because one of the eastern Slavonic tribes was at one time under the political supremacy of the Croats. As the tradition of White Croatia was still alive in the tenth century and as possession of the Red Cities gave control over the trade that centred on Cracow, it was only to be expected that Kiev's expansion should lie in that direction.

---

(20) K. Schiffmann, loc. cit., p. 488, is rather inclined to identify the land of the " Rugi ' with Bohemia, Russia being too distant from the Danube.
(21) As Marquart suggests, loc. cit., p. 132.

PRIMITIVE RUSSIANS OF SARMATIAN ORIGIN?

THE RHOS IN EZEKIEL—THE RHOS IN ZACHARIAS THE RHETOR—RHOS AND RUKS-AS.

The part which the Sarmatians played in the early history of Southern Russia and of the Slavs, raises the question of the origin of the Russians and the Russian State. Were the Russians originally not an Iranian tribe which took over the succession of the Antes, the Avars and the Khazars among the eastern Slavonic tribes?

The most generally accepted etymology of the name " Russian " derives it from the Finnish word *ruotsi* applied by the native population to the Swedish newcomers. The difficulty is that the Byzantines called the Russians " Rhos," but it appears that the Rhos were known to the Byzantines long before the advent of the Scandinavians into northern and southern Russia. Two instances are quoted in evidence. The Patriarch Proclus, as reported in Socrates' Ecclesiastical History(1), commenting on the extermination of the barbarians who supported the usurper John against the Emperor Theodosius, quotes Ezekiel, XXXVIII, 2, 22, 23 : " And thou, son of man, prophesy against the princes Gog, Rhos, Misoch and Thobel . . ." On first inspection it looks as though Proclus were classing the barbarian invaders with the Rhos, a people which in the fifth century inhabited some part of Southern Russia. Another ecclesiastical historian, Zacharias the Rhetor(2), a Syrian, who wrote in the second half of the sixth century, mentions among the populations li ving north of the Caucasus one he calls " Heros," which looks like a Syriac transliteration of the Greek named Rhos. Both instances were known to the scholars who dealt with the problem and variously explained(3), but they were recently(4) produced as evidence to prove that the name Rhos for Russian is not of Finnish-Scandinavian, but of Sarmatian origin. Let us now weigh the evidence.

As to the first quotation, we need to read carefully what Socrates writes about the barbarians who supported the usurper and this is what he says: " Chapter 43. On what the Barbarians, the allies of the tyrant John, had to suffer. After the tyrant's death, the Barbarians whom he had summoned to his aid against the Romans, prepared to devastate the provinces of the Romans. When the Emperor Theodosius heard of it, he left the care of this matter to God, as he was wont to do; and when he had finished his prayers, he soon obtained what he had prayed for. It is truly worth

---

(1) *Socratis Historia Ecclesiastica*, Book VII, ch. 43, *P.G.*, vol. 67, col. 833.
(2) Translated by K. Ahrens and G. Krüger, *Die Sogenannte Kirchengeschichte des Zacharias Rhetor* (Leipzig, 1899, Teubner), book VII, ch. 7, p. 253.
(3) Cf. Niederle, *Slav. Antiquities*, part I, vol. IV, p. 93.
(4) Vernadsky, *Ancient Russia* loc. cit., pp. 258 seq.

hearing what befell the Barbarians. Their leader, whose name was Rugas, died struck by lightning. Then pestilence broke out and the majority of those who were under him perished. But this was not all: fire came down from heaven and consumed a multitude of those who had so far been saved. All this left the Barbarians terror stricken, not so much because they had dared to take up arms against the warlike nation of the Romans, but because they realised that God Almighty was on their side. Then, when bishop Proclus had preached in the church and applied Ezekiel's prophecy to the recent liberation God had brought about, he was received with great applause and admiration. And this is what the prophecy says : ' And thou, son of man, prophesy against the princes Gog, Rhos, Misoch and Thobel . . . I will visit him with death, and blood, and sweeping rain, and hailstones. And I will rain fire and brimstone upon him and all those with him, and upon the many nations with him. And I will be magnified, and sanctified, and glorified; and I will be known in the eyes of many nations, and they shall know that I am the Lord! ' Thus, as I have said, it came to pass that Proclus was hailed with admiration by all . . .''

The leader Rugas is identifiable with Ruas(5), Khagan of the Huns and Attila's predecessor. Jordanes(6) knew of him too and called him Roas, adding that he was brother of Octar and Mundzucus, therefore Attila's uncle, the latter being Mundzucus' son. The name has certainly very little in common with Rhos, the more so as the Barbarians who had made common cause with the usurper John were Huns. Even taking into consideration that a portion of the Alan tribe had joined the Hunnish hordes, we could scarcely infer from the quotation that there must have been amongst the Alans a clan called Rhos which joined in the Hunnish attack under Theodosius II. Socrates and Proclus, in quoting Ezekiel's prophecy, were not referring to any particular nation, but to the chieftain Rugas; his name vaguely recalled that of the Rhos whose prince is mentioned by the prophet and whose destruction, as well as that of his people, recalled the destruction of nations that had arisen against the Lord, as predicted by Ezekiel.

As to the nation of the Rhos mentioned by the Prophet, there appears to be in the translation an error which can be traced back to the Septuagint(7). The Hebrew word *nesi rosh* was taken by the first Greek translators to mean '' Prince of the Rhos,'' and the error was repeated by many subsequent translators. We may, however, observe that St. Jerome did not follow the Greek translators in his Vulgate(8) and rendered the words *nesi rosh* by

(5) Priscus Historia Gothica, *Excerpta e Prisci Historia*, ed. L. Dindorf, Bonn, (1829), p.p. 166 seq., published by C. Mueller in *Fragmenta Historicorum Graecorum*, p. 91.
(6) Jordanis Getica, ch. 35, *M.G.H. Auct Hist*, V., pp. 105, 154.
(7) Cf. the English translation of the Septuagint—Lancelot Charles Lee Brenton, *The Septuaginta Version of the Old Testament . . . translated into English* (London, 1844), vol. I, pp. 842 seq.
(8) Ez. XXXVIII, 2, 3 : Fili hominis, pone faciem tuam contra Gog, terram Magog, principem capitis Mosoch et Thubal, et vaticinare de eo. Et dices ad eum : Haec dicit Dominus Deus : Ecce ego ad te, Gog, principem capitis Mosoch et Thubal . . . XXXIX, 1 : Tu autem, fili hominis, vaticinare adversum Gog, et dices: Haec dicit Dominus: Ecce ego super te Gog, principem capitis Mosoch et Thubal. S. Jerome is perfectly convinced that this is the only possible translation and he explains his reasons in his Commentaria in Ezechielem, *P.L.*, vol. 25, col. 357 : "Aquila translates" 'primam gentem Ros' as head and we have

" princeps capitis." E. König, in a short study(9), pointed out the mistake and proposed the word " Oberfürst " or supreme prince as the best rendering of the words *nesi rosh*, making Ezekiel read as follows: " Gog, the ruler of the land Magog and supreme prince of Meshech and Tubal." This would make the passage more intelligible than what it reads in the translation of the Vulgate. The nations mentioned by Ezekiel would stand for the Scythians (Magog, Massagetes), the Moschoi on the south-eastern coast of the Black Sea, and the Tibarenoi of the eastern part of Asia Minor, both these nations being mentioned by Herodotus (III, 94 sq., VII, 78). This robs the Russians of the honour of seeing their name mentioned in Holy Scripture, but the prophet Ezekiel and his contemporaries knew nothing of a people called Rhos and all the trouble interpreters of Holy Scripture spent on discovering this nation has been wasted.

This does not mean that at the time the first Greek translation of Holy Scripture was being made, *i.e.* in the second and third centuries B.C., or more precisely in the second, since the writings of the Prophets seem to have been translated only then, there did exist such a people as the Rhos. Assuming that it should have lived not too far from the neighbourhood of the Scythians, such a nation as the Rhos, if ever it did exist, must have lived somewhere in later southern Russia, in the Caucasian region or in eastern Asia Minor. But may we assume that the translators of the Prophet Ezekiel knew of such a people ? Did they not simply make the very excusable mistake of taking the word *rosh* for the name of a nation, unknown in their time, but known, as they thought, to Ezekiel ?

*   *   *

The second instance we quoted—Zacharias the Rhetor—obviously points to the existence of a nation called Rhos, but it belongs not to the time when the prophecies of Ezekiel were translated into Greek, but to the sixth century of our era. After a list of thirteen different nomadic tribes living north of the Caucasus which are almost identifiable, Zacharias the Rhetor describes the fabulous race of dog-men and Amazons, gives an account of those ladies' customs and adds : " Next to these there live the Heros, men with long limbs who carry no arms and the size of whose limbs makes it impossible for horses to carry them. Towards the east, at the approaches of the north, there still exist three black races."

Even admitting the name Heros to be a Syriac transcription of the Greek word Rhos, Zacharias's description of those people is highly unsatisfactory; too fantastic, in fact, to pass for historical information. And what deepens the puzzle is that he knows all about the Alanes, mentions their

---

followed him, so that the meaning would be : the head of Mosoch and Thubal. In fact, neither in Genesis, in no other part of Scripture, nor even in Joseph, who gives the names of all the Hebrew nations in the first book of his Antiquities, have we been able to find this nation. This makes it evident that Ros does not mean a people, but a head [king]."

(9) E. König, "Zur Vorgeschichte des Namens ' Russen,' " *Zeitschrift der Deutschen Morgenländischen Gesellschaft* (1916), Band LXX, pp. 92-6.

five cities and is fairly well acquainted with the names of the populations living north of the Caucasus. But was he not influenced by the current reading of Ezekiel's prophecy about the Rhos and trying to locate them somewhere in the neighbourhood of the Scythians? He was a Syrian, but the Septuagint's tradition concerning this passage must have penetrated everywhere throughout the Eastern World, even amongst the Syrians. Thus the two main quotations proving Byzantine knowledge of a Russian nation before the ninth century dwindle to very little and can hardly serve as evidence in its favour.

What makes one sceptical is the lack of confirmatory evidence of the Rhos at the time the Old Testament was translated into Greek. The geographical work that comes nearest to that period is that of Strabo (born 63 B.C.) which was finally revised between A.D. 17 and 23(10). Though the author sojourned in Egypt and must have been acquainted with the geographical notions current in the intellectual world of Alexandria, there is not a word in his book that might serve as a clue. Herodotus (c. 484-425 B.C.)(11), whose book must have been in the hands of the translators of the Hebrew Old Testament, also leaves us in the dark as to how they came to discover a nation called Rhos; and Ptolemy who flourished about 100 and 170 A.D. is not more helpful. A nation called Rhos is unknown to Greek geography, which seems extraordinary since the translators of the Old Testament were all working in the same city as Strabo and Ptolemy, i.e. in Alexandria. If in the lands known to the translators as Scythia and called Sarmatia by Ptolemy there really did exist a nation called Rhos and generally known in Alexandria in the second century B.C., why did the geographers not mention it? Did it vanish from the map in the centuries intervening between the composition of the two works, or did it never exist?

There is in Strabo's and Ptolemy's accounts only one name that is a near approach to that of the Rhos, the Roxolani, who according to Strabo(12) dwelt between the Dnieper and the Don, whereas Ptolemy(13) places them on the north-west coast of the Sea of Azov. The latter location is something of an anachronism, as we know from Tacitus(14) that they invaded the Roman province of Moesia in 69, when at least the bulk of the Roxolani must have moved from the Don and the Sea of Azov to the lower Danube. Tacitus classes them as Sarmatians, but it would rather seem that the Roxolani joined another Sarmatian branch which Ptolemy located in their neighbourhood on the Sea of Azov, the Yazygians, who in the first half of the first century of our era were found on the lower and middle Danube. Ptolemy must therefore have taken his information from an older Greek

---

(10) Ed. Meiricke (Leipzig, Teubner, 1852-53).
(11) B. G. Niebuhr's *A Dissertation on the Geography of Herodotus. Researches into the History of the Scythians, Getae and Sarmatians* (Oxford, 1830). A useful account of Herodotus', Strabo's and Ptolemy's geographical indications is to be found in Niederle's *Slav. Antiquities*, part I, vol. I, pp. 233 seq., 320 seq., 347 seq.
(12) Strabo, II, 5, 7. *Geographica* II, ch. 114, ed. A. Meine, vol. I, p. 152.
(13) Ptolemy, *Geographica*, III, ch. 7, ed. C. Müller, vol. I, p. 423.
(14) Tacitus, *Historia*, I, ch. 79. Ed. E. Koester, Mann (Leipzig, Teubner, 1936), p. 42 Pliny also mentions them in his *Naturalis Historia*, IV, ch. 12, ed. C, Maryhoff, vol. I, p. 337.

geographical source. To-day the name Roxolanes is still explained(15) by commentators of Ezekiel's prophecy as the compound name of Rhos and Alanes, a dissection which is open to serious doubt(16). If the Rhos were only a Sarmatian people akin to the Alanes, or a branch of them, and were known as such to the Alexandrians of the second century B.C., one would rather expect the compound name of Rhosalanoi, not Roxolanoi. It is far more probable that the nation of Rhos existed only in the imagination of Ezekiel's translators who misinterpreted the Hebrew word *rosh*, and finding it difficult to transliterate it into Greek, made it the name of a nation, unknown to them but known, so they assumed, to Ezekiel. Remembering how Jerome translated the word—*princeps capitis*—we can quite understand, nay excuse, the translators' embarrassment at a passage which puzzled so accomplished an Hebraist as St. Jerome. It remains, however, that their mistake was responsible for the Byzantines' belief in the existence of a people called Rhos and for Zacharias the Rhetor's effort to locate it somewhere north of the Caucasus, where the Scythian Magog (Massagetes) were living in Ezekiel's days(17).

*   *   *

But still another theory was recently framed to explain the Sarmatian and Alanic origin of the Russians' name. It is suggested(18) that according to Ibn-Rusta(19) a portion of the Antes in the northern Caucasus were called Rukhs-As, which may be interpreted as the Light As. If the information is correct, we must take it that they were part of the Alans who stayed behind in the region north of the Caucasus and failed to set out for the upper Donets and the middle Dnieper with the majority of the Antes. In that

---

(15) Cf. G. Gesenius,*Thesaurus Linguae Hebraicae et Chaldeae Veteris Testamenti* (Lipsiae, 1835-1853), p. 1253 ; and E. K. König "Zur Vorgeschichte des Namens 'Russen'," p. 92.

(16) See E. König. loc. cit., 95.

(17) A. P. Dyakonov recently called attention to a passage in S. Ephrem of Syria's commentary on Genesis where the Syriac Father also seems to know of a people called Rhos, stating that they are the sons of Cethim, a descendant of Japhet "Izvestiya Pseudo-Zakhari, o drevnikh Slavyanakh," *Vestnik drevney Istorii, Instit. Istorii Akademii Nauk SSSR*, Moskva, 1939, vol, 4., p. 87). But the interpretation of the passage is questionable, since everything depends on the right transcription of the Syriac words. D. A. B. Caillau (*Sancti Patris nostri Ephraem Syri Opera*, Parisiis, 1842, vol. I, p. 208) reads Cethim pater " *Romaeorum*," instead of " Rosaye." This would answer better, as Rhodanim is supposed to have been the ancestor of the inhabitants of Rhodos (pater Rhodiorum Rhodanim, qui postmodum Rhodum insulam occuparunt). The question can only be decided by experts in oriental philology ; but even if we had to read " Rhos," the passage would only afford additional evidence of how much one mistake by the translators of the Septuagint could be responsible for. Once the Rhos were believed to be mentioned in Holy Scripture, there was nothing to prevent S. Ephrem trying to find a place for them in his legendary genealogy.

(18) G. Vernadsky, *Ancient Russia*, pp. 82 seq., 106 seq.

(19) V F. Minorsky, *Hudud al-Alam*, p. 445. Cf. Vernadsky, loc. cit., pp. 146 seq., 259. See, however, Minorsky's review of Vernadsky's book in the Slavonic Review (1945), pp. 551 seq. " The Arabic source which gives this name has D. Xsas and I tentatively restored it as R. Xsas (the letters D. and R being easily confused) and compared it with the ancient Roxolana (Ruxs-alan, the terms Alan and As being practically interchangeable). Personally, I should not carry the restoration any further in view of the uncertainties of the Arabic script. Still more should I hesitate to follow Professor Vernadsky in bridging Ruxs with Rhos . . . An Ingenious hypothesis, but already the third (Antae-As ; Ruxs-as) Ros and the Swedes assuming the name Rhos, and there is no reason for the disappearance of an X at such an early date . . ." Cf. also V. F. Minorsky's article in The Encyclopaedia of Islam; vol. III, pp. 1181 seq.

case we would have to admit that the Antes, the Antsai, the Assaioi and the Ants-As were one and the same people.   There is a suspicion of trickery in this philological modulation, but strictly speaking not only the credulous, but philologists might find it acceptable.   We know that there did exist Alans in that quarter.   The Iasi of the Russian medieval chronicles are the descendants of those Alans and the modern Ossetians of the Caucasus region are all that is left of that great Sarmatian tribe.

Those Rukhs-As are identified by G. Vernadsky as the Rogas, a nation which according to Jordanes was subjugated by Ermanrich together with the Rosomoni, also mentioned by Jordanes who states that two brothers belonging to this tribe killed Ermanrich(20); but it is difficult to see in this story any evidence for a revolt of either the Rogas or the Rosomoni against Ermanrich, as the alternative tradition according to which the king, on hearing of the approach of the Huns, committed suicide, seems more reliable.   The Rosomoni are said to be the same people as the Roxolani(21).

The equation of such different names will certainly raise apprehensions (22), especially among philologists.   Jordanes, for instance, differentiates between the Rosomoni and the Rogas, assimilating the latter rather to the Finns of the upper Volga.   But as the names of nations and places are but very imperfectly recorded by the early Greek and Latin geographers and historians, one may not rule out such identification as impossible; only, in this case, we should admit that the Roxolani, who would have been brought under Ermanrich's rule, were not settled north of the Caucasus, nor on the lower Don, but somewhere on the lower Danube or in the Dacia, since it will be remembered that they joined their racial brothers the Yazygians and followed them to that country.   The difficulty is serious enough to compromise the whole theory.   Then, how is it possible to identify the Roxolani with the Rukhs-As, supposing this people ever existed ?   No combination is admissible, which connects them with the northern Caucasus, since they left the country long before, unless we assume that some of them clung to their home, for which there is no evidence.   They probably shared the fate of the Yazygians with whom they had thrown in their lot and vanished from history.   That the Anonymous Geographer of Ravenna(23) of the seventh century should mention them and place them north of the Don opposite the island of Scanza on the Lutta river and between the Sarmatians and the legendary Amazons is no proof that they were still living near the Sea of Azov in the seventh century ; for it is evident from the Geographer's account that he is not drawing on his own knowledge, but on a much older source, probably Ptolemy who, as we know, did the same thing and located the Roxolani near the Sea of Azov when they were no longer there.

(20) *Jordanis Getica*, ch. XXIII, XXIV, loc cit., pp. 88, 91.
(21) Vernadski, loc, cit., pp. 106 seq.
(22) Cf. what M. Hrushevsky has to say on the impossibility of this identification in his *Geschichte des Ukrainischen Volkes*, Leipzig, vol. I, p. 569.   G. Brady (*The Legends of Ermanric* p. 10), also hesistates to advise this identification.
(23) *Ravennatis Anonymi Cosmographia et Guidonis Geographica*, ed. M. Pinder & G. Parthey (Berlin, 1860), pp. 29, 175, 324, 417, 421, 552.

The new theory also associates the Rukhs-As with the Slavs of the lower Don as rulers who bequeathed their name to the Slavs of the northern Caucasus, a mere hypothesis that rests on nothing. All we know is that the Antes ruled over Slavs who adopted their masters' name, the same applying to the Croats, the Serbs and possibly the Spali; but there is no evidence for attributing the same role to the Rukhs-As. We also know that the Slavs, probably the Severians, spread between the end of the seventh century to the beginning of the ninth as far as the lower Don, the middle Volga and possibly the Caucasian region, but this expansion was due to the mild Khazar régime which respected the rights of every population of the Empire. But at that period Antic ascendancy amongst the Eastern Slavs had gone down before Avaric power and we have no evidence to show that the Slavs had colonised the lower Don and the lands north of the Caucasus previously to that time. Why then should the Slavs, whilst they were under the Khazars, accept the Rukhs-As as their second masters? Conditions were different when the Arabs started their attacks on the Khazars. We learn that in 724 the Arabs captured 20,000 Slav families which the Khalif Marvan settled in Asia Minor(24). These Slavs cannot have been living in the Caucasus in 724, even for the benefit of association with the Rukhs-As. As the Khazars ruled over the Slavs from the Don to the Dnieper and beyond, they must have been drawing their auxiliary troops from the population and the Khalif Marvan had to invade that country. Once the Arab invasion started, followed by the Magyar and the Pecheneg migrations, the Slavonic element withdrew to its old centres.

All this rather damages the theory that in the north of the Caucasus there rose in those years a solid Slavo-Alanic bloc, held together by the Rukhs-As and being the seed of modern Russia. In order to explain why the West called the Scandinavians " Russi," whereas the Byzantines called them " Rhôs," it is easy to say that the name Rukhs may have sounded Rohs, Ross, Rus in some local dialects. It may and it may not. Such postulates land one nowhere. The quotation of Proclus from Socrates' Church History and the extract from Zacharias Rhetor promised some sort of a foothold, but proved disappointing.

A passage in the Arab writer Tabari (about 838-923) would seem to betoken that the " Rus " nation was known to the Arabs already in 644, but it could hardly serve as evidence. Tabari's work is only known through Balami's Persian translation which, with all its additions and omissions, is anything but reliable. Harkavy(25) states that the Turkish translation of the same work has " Tartars " instead of " Rus." As at the time the translation was made, i.e. fifty years after the original had been written, the Russians were known to the Arabs and the Persians as living beyond the Volga

---

(24) See Niederle *Slav. Antiquities*, part I, vol. IV, pp. 132-6 about the Slavs on the Don, the Volga and in the Caucasus. The Arab sources are found in A. Harkavy, *Skazaniya Musulmanskikh Pisatelei o Slavyanakh i Russkikh* (Reports by Moslem Writers on the Slavs and the Russians) St. Petersburg, 1870, pp. 38, 41, 42, 49, 55, 76, 80, 140, 251, 254 ; Marquart, *Streifüzge* pp. 31, 199.

(25) *Skazaniya Musulm. Pisateley*, p. 74.

and the Caspian Sea, it was only to be expected that a translator, who could take such liberties with the original, should have mistaken the Tartars or some other nation mentioned in the original for Russians.

No more reliable is the induction based on the existence of a certain Khaganat of the Slavicised Rukhs-As, alleged to have severed itself from the Khazar empire, established its centre in Tmutarakan, received consolidation from the Scandinavians who conveniently turned up under the name of Rhôs, and then made its first official contact with the Byzantines in 837. I have already stated my opinion on this embassy; there is no trace left of such a Khaganat and I have discussed the only " solid " argument that is offered for its existence, the Russian embassy, as reported by the Annales Bertiniani(26). Tmutarakan did not rise to any degree of prominence till the tenth century. I admit the possibility of a Varyago-Slav colony having existed at an earlier period, but it could never have played a conspicuous part in the attack on Constantinople in 860(27); nor could the Varyago-Slavs, who were still pagans, have had their own alphabet, since it was composed by the Slavonic apostle, S. Cyrillus(28), who spent some time in Kherson in 861 on his way to the Khazar Khagan(29).

This conjecture, which would give the credit for inventing the first Slavonic alphabet, the Glagolitsa, to pagan Rukhs-As-Russians and attribute the invention of the Cyrilitsa as it is still used by the Orthodox Slavs to S. Cyrillus, will shock Slavonic philologists. They are so proud of the Glagolitsa which renders to perfection every sound of the Slavonic tongue that in their estimation only a philological genius could have devised such an alphabet: how then could they tolerate the mere suggestion that the Glagolitsa must be credited to a pagan Alano-Slavico-Varyag nation ? But this issue can safely be left to the philologists to settle among themselves. But the suggestion is ingenious and would appeal to many, were it not that there is little evidence to support it. This throws us back on the solution proposed recently, which would find an error in this particular passage of the old Slavonic Legend due to a later transcription of the work. Writing at a time when Russia was a respectable State, one of the copyists altered the words " Syriac letters " into " Russian letters"(30).

---

(26) See above, p. 63.
(27) Vernadsky, loc. cit., pp. 342 seq
(28) Ibid., pp. 355 seq.
(29) Cf. A. Soloviev, He exo Rosia, *Byzantion* (1938), vol. XIII, pp. 226-232. The fact that Constantine VII Porphyrogenetus writes about an "external Russia " (*De Adm. Imp.* ch. IX, Bonn, p. 74) lends no support to this theory. Even if we do not admit that the Emperor had in mind the Russia of Novgorod, distinct from the Russia proper of Kiev, and if we insist that he meant the Russian colony of Tmutorakan, we must none the less bear in mind that Constantine was writing at a time when Tmutorakan was already known in Byzantium as a Russian settlement. Byzantine ignorance about the so-called " Tmutorakan Russia " before the Xth century strongly militates against any theory that makes of this city a Russian dependency.
(30) A. Vaillant, Les " Lettres Russes de la Vie de Constantin," *Revue des Etudes Slaves* (1935), t. XV, pp. 75-7. This theory, now largely accepted, is preferable to the explanation I offered in my book, *Les Légendes* . . ., pp. 185 seq., where I see in the Psalter written in " Russian letters " a Gothic book written in the alphabet invented by Ulphilla. It does seem admissible that the word in the Legend " surskimi " was altered by the copyist into " ruskimi," a slip that raised a problem on which much thought and ink have been wasted.

As regards Tmutorakan I have touched on this problem elsewhere(31), but see no reason for departing from my attitude towards this Slavo-Varyag colony and its rôle in the history of the Russians, the Khazars and the Byzantines in the ninth century.

At the close of this inquiry, I must confess that I have not succeeded in discovering the Alanic clan alleged to have bequeathed its name to the Slav tribes that were destined to grow into the Russian nation and all efforts in this direction have so far been unsuccessful (32). There remains then to be content with the most generally accepted theory which looks for the origin of Russia's name among the Finns and the Scandinavians. To this day the Finns call the Swedes " Ruotsi," and the Estonians call them " Rootsi." The name certainly shows affinity, though undefined, with the Old Swedish word " rodi " or " rodhsi," in modern Swedish, ro, ros and rod, meaning rowing or sculling. From this word is formed the name " Roslagen," in older documents " Rodslagen," which is applied to part of the coast of Upland(33). This part of Sweden was probably the first with which the Finns became acquainted and the name of the coast and its inhabitants was extended to the whole country. When the Swedes began to settle among the Finnish population of later Northern Russia, they were naturally called " Ruotsi " and the Slavs transformed the name, probably as early as the eighth century, into Rus, Rusi.

To explain the Byzantine variant of Rhos, we must remember that the name was known to the Byzantines through the Septuagint version of Holy Scripture. The prophecy of Ezekiel was read long after Proclus' time and

---

(31) See my book, *Les Légendes*, pp. 166 seq., 179 seq. Since that time the study by Germaine da Costa-Louilet, Y Eut-il des Invasions Russes dans l'Empire Byzantin avant 860 ? *Byzantion* vol. XV (1940-1941 New York), pp. 240-248, has shed more light on the whole problem. The author has produced good evidence against dating the life of S. George of Amastris from the IXth century, as was generally done. The Russian invasion mentioned in this Legend did not take place in 835, but in 941, and the Life was written in the Xth century. Only two Russian attacks on Constantinople can be proved—those of 860 and of 941. These findings have robbed the supporters of the Tmutorakan theory of their last serious argument. Instead of being dismissed with a casual remark (Cf. Vernadsky, 1. c., p. 280), they are serious enough to deserve, if not full credit, at least serious examination. Cf. also H. Grégoire, La Legende d'Oleg et l'expédition d'Igor, *Bulletin de la Classe des Lettres, Acad. Royale de Belgique*, vol. V. 23, 1937, pp.80-94.

(32) It is not implied here that G. Vernadski, who devoted a large portion of his book to this problem, did not contribute to the early period of Russian history a mass of valuable findings and interesting details. His book, which testifies to the mastering of an enormous number of sources and works dealing with this period, cannot but command the greatest respect. It marks the high level of modern American scholarship and every specialist will be grateful to the author for his masterly contribution to the early history of Eastern Europe. It is a great satisfaction to us that American science and especially Yale University should devote increasing attention to the medieval history of Europe.

(33) Cf. the study written by A. Pogodin, " Les Rodsi : un Peuple Imaginaire," *Revue des Etudes Slaves*, 1937, t. XVII, pp. 71-80, where the reader will find a short survey of the different theories elucidating this problem. It is interesting to note that the Finns still call Estonia " Viro," this being the name of the province nearest to Finland (Virumaa), and it was extended to the whole nation. Germany is called Saksa by the Finns and Saxony was also the nearest and only part of Germany with which the Finns could be in touch through the Baltic, the other parts of the northern coast of the Baltic being occupied by Slavs, Balts and Finns. Russia is called " Venaja," in which designation we find the old name of the Slavs, " Venedi," whose origin is not yet clear, or better still, the name of the Vyatichians, the easternmost Russian tribe with which the Finns were in constant touch. It looks as though the Finns generalised the name of this one tribe and used it for all the Slavs.

M.   L

one may suggest that this special passage of the Septuagint facilitated the acceptance of the invaders' new name and was responsible for the Byzantine form of Rhos(34). The name was already known to Byzantine intellectuals and prevailed over the Slavonic form Rus, Rusios, which apparently was in common use(35), to be accepted as the classical designation. Such transformations were true to Byzantine mentality and to the manner of the period.

Should anybody feel surprised that the Slavs, at the dawn of their political life, submitted to the leadership of foreign conquerors so easily, it must be stressed that this was not peculiar to the Slavs only. Does the name of a great western nation—France—not recall that of the Germanic Franks who conquered Romanised Gaul or ancient Gallia? The conquerers were absorbed into the mass of a non-Germanic population, and yet Gauls went on proudly calling themselves French, though there is very little Frankish blood in their veins(36). Two parts of ancient Gallia adopted the names of other Germanic tribes that established their rule there, Normandy and Burgundy. The Angles imposed their name on England, the country they wrested from the Britons. The Latins of northern Italy took their name from their conquerors, when they styled themselves as Lombards. Finally, the Vandals in Spain are still remembered thanks to the name of a Spanish province, Andalusia.

The Slavs were living on the borders of Asia and were the first to be swept off their feet by the successive waves of Asiatic invaders as they surged from the steppes and came rolling over them in the direction of western Europe(37). Most of the Asiatic peoples were well drilled warriors, gifted with a native sense of discipline and military rule. Such was the case with the Iranians, the Scythians and the Sarmatians. The cultural life of the Iranians was on a high level through contact with Greek civilisation in its outposts of the Crimea and the Taman peninsula.

As the Slavs inherited the Sarmatian trade between the North Sea, the Black Sea, Byzantium and the East, a friendly understanding with the Scandinavian traders followed as a matter of course. It was this co-operation which laid the foundation of the Eastern Slavs' subsequent prosperity.

---

(34) It seems that according to the Russian orientalists Harkavy and Chvolson, the Arabs made use of the Slavonic form. Only Marquart (*Streifzüge*, pp. 149, 383) gives the Byzantine form Rhos in his translation of the Arab texts. His attempt (loc. cit., pp. 355 seq.) to trace in the Rhos of Zacharias' Ecclesiastical History a last vestige of the Herules north of the Caucasus has not been repeated by any expert.

(35) This seems to be confirmed by Liudprand who writes in his Antapodosis (V, ch. 15): Gens quaedam est sub aquilonis parte constituta, quam a qualitate corporis Graeci vocant Rusios, nos vero a positione loci nominamus Nordmannos (*M.G.H.S.* III, p. 331). Cf. also ibid., I, ch. II, loc. cit., p. 277 and his Relatio de Legatione Constantinopolitana, ch. 29, loc. cit., p. 353. The Annales Bertiniani, in the famous passage quoted above (*M.G.H.S.* I, p. 434), the first reference to the Russians in a western source, have kept the Byzantine form Rhos, probably copied from the imperial letter sent by Theophil to Louis II. We may also note that in the Xth century the Byzantines were so struck by the Russians' flexible movements that they called them Dromitai or runners (*Theophanes Continuatus*, ed. Bonn, p. 423. *Simeon Magister*, ed. Bonn, p. 707, 746), an interesting instance of popular designation that may similarly account for the Finnish name Ruotsi, when the Finns were struck by the Swedes' dexterity in plying their boats.

(36) Cf. F. Lot, *Les Invasions Germaniques* (Paris, 1935), pp. 217-71.

(37) G. Vernadsky has drawn a remarkably clear picture of this complicated period in his *Ancient Russia*.

APPENDIX V

THE DONATION OF POLAND TO THE HOLY SEE BY MIESZKO ACCORDING TO THE "DAGOME IUDEX"

One of the most controverted documents in early Polish history is the donation of Poland to the Holy See, as contained in the collection of canon law written by cardinal Deusdedit at the end of the eleventh century(1). It opens with the words *Dagome Iudex*. As its right reading is essential to an understanding of Poland's early history it is worth a careful examination.

The Cardinal's Collection, besides being valuable for the study of the evolution of Canon Law, constitutes a mine of first-hand historical information. Having had free access to the Lateran Archives and bent upon enriching the documentation of canon law with a view to popularise the ideals of the reformist party in Rome, Deusdedit copied from the Archives many documents of historical value which have perished since. Among these we find a copy of the Act by which the Polish Duke Mieszko I and his wife declared the whole of Poland to belong to the Holy See.

The document starts with the words " *Dagome (Dagomae) Judex,*" Dagome (some manuscripts have Dagone) being generally taken for the name by which Mieszko was known to the Scandinavians(2). The document was handled by a copyist who obviously was not familiar with its foreign terms. It says : " In another volume bearing the date of John XV, one can read that Dagome the Judge, Ote the senatrix and their sons Misica and Lambertus (the latter two being issue from the Duke's second marriage with Oda), I do not know of what nationality, but I think they were Sardinians, as these were governed by four judges, presented to S. Peter an entire city (civitas) called Schinesne with all its territory as enclosed within the following frontiers : starting first from the long sea shore as far as

---

(1) This collection was published for the first time by P. Martinucci just before the meeting of the Vatican Council (*Deusdedit Presbyteri Cardinalis Collectio Canonum*, Venice, 1869), but at the time nobody grasped its importance. The second edition, published by Wolf von Glanvell (*Die Kanonensammlung des Kardinals Deusdedit*, Paderborn, 1905) met with a similar fate. The latest edition of the Polish document is to be found in B. Stasiewski's " Untersuchungen über drei Quellen für älteste Geschichte und Kirchengeschichte Polens," *Breslauer Studien für Historische Theologie*, Bd. 24 (Breslau, 1933), pp. 29 seq. This publication contains a complete bibliography of the problem and details concerning all the studies that deal with the Polish document, but we cannot accept the solution offered by the author. I am dealing with Deusdedit's Collection and with some other documents of importance, preserved only by the Cardinal, in my book—*The Photian Schism, History and Legend* (Cambridge, 1948), pp. 297, seq. I have not been able to devote a sufficiently close examination to two works dealing with this problem : J. Ptaśnik, *Dagome Judex* (Cracow, 1911) and St. Zakrzewski. The oldest Bull concerning Poland ? (in Polish), *Archivum Naukowe* (Lwow, 1921).

(2) Cf. the analysis of the various theories by Stasiewski, *Untersuchungen über die drei Quellen*, pp. 85-93. The most widely accepted theory is that the Polish duke was called Dagome by the Scandinavians, chiefly the Danes. Thietmar only knows the Polish name Misica (Mieszko), which at any rate makes it rather difficult for those who would use this as an argument in favour of the Scandinavian origin of the Piast dynasty, although the existence of Scandinavian influences in Poland cannot be denied.

Pruzze (land of the Prussians or modern Prussia), running thence to a country called Russe (the Russian border) and extending as far as Craccoa (the region of Cracow), thence to the river Odere (Oder) and straight on to a place called Alemure (probably the stream Mora, in German Mohra, which joins the Opava river, a tributary of the Oder on its left bank), and from Cracow to the land of the Milze (the Serbian tribe of the Milzians); from Milze right on to the Oder and along its banks as far as Schinesne, mentioned previously."

As stated before, there are many theories to explain why the Polish duke is called Dagome, and one is left to wonder whether the theory which gives the name a Scandinavian origin and is most widely accepted, is sound. It should be remembered that Deusdedit very probably copied the document from a *Breviarium* called also *Censualium*, which contained records of title deeds connected with the properties of the Holy See; and those records appeared in the *Breviaria* or *Censualia* mostly as extracts(3). In the present case it is not likely that Deusdedit ever saw the original, and his transcription was probably an extract from an extract, a process that calls for the utmost caution in the reading of the document. As the names recorded in the original were unfamiliar to the copyists (the numerous mistakes in the transcription of the names mentioned in the document proves it), one may wonder whether the name "Dagome" is not a mistake made by the first copyist who made the extract from the original document for the *Breviarium*. This brings us back to the original suggestion made by O. Balzer(4); only I feel inclined to go further than he did and to complete his suggestion.

I think that the name Dagome (Dagomae) can be read as the faulty transcription of the beginning of the document which contains the "Donatio" and very probably started with the words : "(Chrismon) Ego Mesico Dux cum Ote uxore mea." The chrismon which used to be placed before the first sentence in documents of this kind assumed different forms and one of them could have been easily mistaken for the letter D. An E could also pass for an A and the letters following ME for IU, which would be enough to account for the *Dagomae iudex*. Once these mistakes were made it was only logical to give Ota the title of *senatrix*, though the original probably gave her no title at all. As the copyist and Deusdedit after him took Dagome to be one of the four *iudices* who were governing Sardinia, they gave his wife the title of *senatrix* as a matter of course. It is also to be noted that the document is classed with title deeds of the Holy See in Italy, a peculiar mistake which does little credit to the geographical knowledge of the copyist, but one need not be too hard on him. Mieszko's donation was the first of its kind, previous instances known to the curialists being limited mostly to churches, abbeys and property situated in either Italy or Germany.

---

(3) Cf. B. Stasiewski, loc. cit., p. 42.
(4) *Genealogy of the Piasts* (Cracow, 1895), p. 24 (in Polish).

No doubt the theory has its weak spots and there are many. For one thing we do not know how Mieszko's name was recorded in the original document, and there is the additional fact that the name of his son is given as Misica instead of Mesico. We know that Balzer's proposal was rejected by every historian, but this was due to the obsession of the Scandinavian theory which left no room for any alternative explanation. However, palaeographists will have the last word on the theory; and even if it is not accepted one thing remains beyond dispute, that the tradition that has gathered round the name Dagome (Dagomae) has lost much of its value. The document passed through the hands of two writers and there is no certainty that the name Dagome escaped manipulation, no guarantee that the reading is not based on the mistake of either the first or the second copyist. The first part of the document, which is evidently an abbreviated extract, must therefore be treated with caution; nor is it fair to base on a name of doubtful tradition theories that are so radical and far-reaching(5).

We may now examine the second part of the document which lays down the boundaries of the territory concerned in the donation. There also, the names which must have sounded foreign to both copyists, are recorded in forms more or less mutilated, though it appears evident that the first copyist tried to be as accurate as possible and to give the delineation of the frontiers as he found it in the original document. This for obvious reasons since it mattered most in a *Breviarium* to define as correctly as possible the extent of the territories surrendered to the Holy See.

One thing should be pointed out: from the way the document refers to Schinesne, one may infer that this city was mentioned in the original document with special emphasis, designed to underline its transfer to the Holy See ; and one has the impression that this insistence misled the copyist into believing that the Donation included a *civitas* with territory attached, as was the case with some Italian city-republics. The analogy must have induced him to place the *Donatio* somewhere in Sardinia of which he probably did not know much more than he knew about Poland.

---

(5) One more thing to be noted : I have translated the text from the edition of Wolf von Glanvell, p. 359 and I am of opinion that the tradition represented by the MS. of the Vatican (Cod. Vatic. Lat. 3833), on which Wolf von Glanvell based his edition, comes nearest to the original ; whereas the tradition represented by the *Polypticon* of canon Benedict (written between 1140 and 1143) or by the *Gesta pauperis scholaris Albini* (written between 1185 and 1189), repeated in Censius' *Liber censuum* (about 1192) are, so I think, in no way preferable to the text of the Vatic. Latin. 3833. The latter tradition only reveals that the error made by the first two copyists was partly discovered in the XIIth century. Albinus found out that this particular donation had nothing to do with Sardinia, but only concerned Poland and he inserted his suggestion into the text (de provincia Polonorum) just as the first or second copyist had inserted his own suggestion that the document concerned a city in Sardinia. The Vatic. Latinus 3833 is the only complete MS. of Deusdedit's Collection and as it was written in 1099-1118, it is almost contemporary to Deusdedit who died between 1098 and 1100. This MS. should therefore serve as the basis for all investigations. The name Dagome is given by this MS. (spelled Dagomae) and by two other MSS. of the middle and the second half of the XIIth century which contained parts of the Collection. This reading is therefore preferable to Dagone. Details on the various MSS. can be found in Wolf v. Glanvell, loc. cit., pp. XIX-XLIV ; R. Holtzmann, *Böhmen und Polen im 10. Jh.*, pp. 14-19 ; B. Stasiewski, loc. cit., pp. 32-44. I have not been able to see I. Ptasnik, *Dagome iudex*, Cracow, 1911) and Zmigród-Stadnicki, *Die Schenkung Polens an Johann XV. um das Jahr* 995 (Freiburg, Schweiz, 1911), but Stasiewski gives a good summary of the opinions of all the experts who dealt with the problem.

This part of the document has also been variously interpreted by scholars interested in the problem, and it once more set Germans and Poles at variance. The German school, which holds that Poland did not reach the Baltic under Mieszko I and that Pomerania could not possibly have belonged to Poland at so early a date, has tried to identify the enigmatic name of Schinesne with Gnesen. This view cannot be accepted, because Gnesen does not lie on the Oder, but is situated well inside Poland, and the papal document clearly asserts that the frontier followed the course of the Oder as far as Schinesne. This can only apply to the city on the left bank of the mouth of the Oder, *i.e.* Stettin (Szczecin) which Mieszko I had taken from the Ratarians(6). It was the obvious thing for the Pole to do to gain possession of this city, if he did reach the mouth of the Oder at all, which is as good as proved. Stettin was more than a stronghold of the Ratarians whence they could threaten Mieszko's territories in Pomerania ; it was a trading centre the occupation of which was a valuable asset to any owner.

What makes the delineation of the Polish frontiers more reliable is the exclusion from the document of the territories lying between the Upper Bug and the Carpathians with the Red Cities and Przemysl. It had been lost by Mieszko in 981, the year it was occupied by the Russians of Kiev. But it is clear from the Donation that Silesia and the province of Cracow came into Poland's possession after 981 and before 992, the year of Mieszko's death, probably between 987 and 990.

---

(6) The name Schinesne is one of the most debated words in any medieval document. Cf. the different interpretations in Stasiewski, loc. cit., pp. 49. sq. We are of opinion that the best arguments proving that Schinesne stands for Stettin come from the famous Slavonic philologist A. Brückner, in his study—" Boleslaw Chrobry," *Slavia Occidentalis* (1928), vol. 7, pp. 65-79. As the old Polish name for Stettin was Schitno or Szczytno and as Gnesen was seemingly known in the Xth century by the name of Gnezdun, there seems to be little doubt left about the identification of Schinesne with Stettin. The town was of all Mieszko's possessions the most exposed to danger from pagan Slavonic tribes and its possession was essential to the security of the north-western frontier of Mieszko's Poland, so that one can quite understand why he singled it out for special mention in his *Donatio*. To enable the reader to test my interpretation, I submit here the Latin text of the document as published by Wolf von Glanvell, loc. cit., p. 359 : Item in alio tomo sub Johanne XV papa Dagome iudex et Ote senatrix et filii eorum Misica et Lambertus, nescio cuius gentis homines, puto autem Sardos fruisse, quoniam ipsi a IV iudicibus reguntur, leguntur beato Petro contulisse unam civitatem in integro quae vocatur Schinesne, cum omnibus suis pertinentiis infra hos affines, sicuti incipit a primo latere longum mare, fine Bruzze usque in locum, qui dicitur Russe et fine Russe extendente usque in Craccoa et ab ipsa Craccoa usque ad flumen Oddere recte in locum, qui dicitur Alemure, et ab ipsa Alemura usque in terram Milze, et a fine Milze recte intra Oddere, et exinde ducente iuxta flumen Oddera usque in predictam civitatem Schinesne.

ABBREVIATIONS USED IN THIS BOOK

A.S. Acta Sanctorum of the Bollandists.
Bonn. Corpus Scriptorum Historiae Byzantinae, also called the Byzantine Corpus of Bonn.
C.C.H. Český Časopis Historicky (Czech Historical Review).
F.R.B. Emler, J. Fontes Rerum Bohemicarum, Prague, 1871.
M.G.H. Monumenta Germaniae Historica.
—— Auct. Ant. Auctores antiquissimi.
—— Dipl. Diplomata.
—— Ep. Epistolae.
—— S. Scriptores.
—— S.N.S. Scriptores, Nova Series.
—— S. in us. schol. Scriptores in usum scholarum.
M.P.H. Monumenta Poloniae Historica. Ed. Bielowski. Lwów, Kraków, 1864-93.
Hist. Zeitschr. Historische Zeitschrift, München.
Kwart. Hist. Kwartalnik Historyczny, Lwów.
S.R.H. Scriptores Rerum Hungaricarum, vol. I, II, Budapest, 1938-40.
Teubner. Bibliotheca Teubneriana, Leipzig.
P.G. Migne, Patrologia Graeca, 140 volumes, Paris, 1844-65.
P.L. Migne, Patrologia Latina, 221 volumes, Paris, 1844-64.

BIBLIOGRAPHY

SOURCES

Abramovich, D. J. Zhitiya Svyatykhs Muchenikov Borisa i Gleba, (The lives of the saintly martyrs Boris and Gleb), in *Pamyatniki Drevnerusskoy Lit.* vol. II, St. Petersburg, 1916.
Adamus Bremensis. *Historia Ecclesiastica.* ed. L. Weiland, M.G.H.S. VII, 1846, pp. 280-389.
Adhemar of Chabannes, Historia Francorum, *M.G.H.S.* IV, pp. 113-148 (ed. G. Weitz).
Albericus Monachus. Trium Fontium Chronica. ed. P. Scheffer-Boichorst, *M.G.H.S.* XXIII, pp. 674-950.
Alfred the Great. Bosworth, J. *A Description of Europe and the Voyages of Ohthere and Wulfstan*, written in Anglo-Saxon by King Alfred the Great, London, 1855.
Annales Altahenses Maiores, ed. W. Giesebrecht, Pertz, *M.G.H.S.* XX.
—— Bertiniani. Ed. Pertz, *M.G.H.S.* I.
—— Cracovienses Breves, ap. Pertz, *M.G.H.S.* XIX, pp. 664-666 (ed. R. Röpell, W. Arndt).
—— Cracovienses Capituli, *M.G.H.S.* XIX, pp. 582-607, (ed. Tidem).
—— Cracovienses Vetusti, *M.G.H.S.* XIX, pp. 577, 578, (ed. Tidem).
—— Einhardi. *M.G.H.S.* I, pp. 135-218.
—— Fuldenses, *M.G.H.S.* I, pp. 343-415.
—— Hildesheimenses. *M.G.H.S.* III.
—— Juvavenses Maiores. ed. H. Bresslau, 1934, *M.G.H.S.* XXX, pars 2.
—— Kamenzenses. ed. R. Röpel, W. Arndt, *M.G.H.S.* XIX, pp. 580-582.
—— Lamperti. *M.G.H.S.* III.
—— Mechovienses. *M.G.H.S.* XIX, p. 668 (ed. R. Röpell, W. Arndt).
—— Polonorum, *M.G.H.S.* XIX, pp. 612-656 (ed. R. Röpell, W Arndt).
—— Quedlinburgenses. *M.G.H.S.* III, pp. 22-69, 72-90.
—— Ratisbonenses. ed. Wattenbach, *M.G.H.S.* XVII, pp. 579-590.
—— Rudberti S. Salisburgensis. *M.G.H.S.* IX, pp. 758-810.
—— Sazavae. *F.R.B.* II.
—— Virdunenses. *M.G.H.S.* IV (ed. G. Waitz).
—— Xantenses. *M.G.H.S.* II, pp. 219-235.
Annalista Saxo. Chronicon, ed. G. Waitz, *M.G.H.S.* VI, pp. 542-777.
Anonymi Gesta Hungarorum. ed. A. Yakubovich, 1937, *F.R.H.* I.
Anonymus Gallus. Chronicae Polonorum, *M.P.H.* ed. A. Bielowski, Lwów, 1864, vol. I, pp. 301-481.
Archangelsky, A.S. *Pamyatniki Drevney Pisimennosti*, 1884.
Arnoldus. De S. Emmerano, *M.G.H.S.* IV.
Auctarium Garstense. *M.G.H.S.* IX, pp. 561-569 (ed. Wattenbach).
Bakri. *Kitab al-Masalik. . .*, Excerpts in English translation, see Bibliography, Macartney, C. A., *The Magyars. . .*, pp. 189-190, 192-208.
Beneshevich, V. N. *Sbornik Pamyatnikov po Istorii Tserkovnago Prava* (Collection of documents on the history of canon law), Petrograd, 1914, vol. I.
Bernonis Abbatis Augiensis Epistolae, *P.L.*, vol. 142.
Bibliotheca Hagiographica Latina, Bruxelles, Société des Bollandistes, 3 vols., 1898-1911.
Boris and Gleb. See Abramovich, D. J.
Bielowski, A. Epitaphium Chrabri Boleslai. *M.P.H.* I.
Böhmer, J. F. and Will, C. *Regesten zur Geschichte der Mainzer Erzbischöfe.* Innsbruck, 1877.

Böhmer, J. F. *Regesta Imperii*, Innsbruck, 1893, (vol. II).
Book of Degrees. Stepnaya Kniga. *Poln. Sobranie Russk. Lietop*, vol. XXI, 1908.
Bosworth, J. *A Literal Translation of King Alfred's Anglo-Saxon Version of the Compendious History of the World by Orosius*, London, 1855.
Brunonis. Vita Quinque Fratrum, ed. R. Kade. *M.G.H.S.* XV, 2.
Bruno. Epistola Brunonis, *M.P.H.* I, pp. 224-228.
Bruno of Querfurt. Passio S. Adalberti, *F.R.B.* I, pp. 266-304.
Burchardi Wormacesis Episcopi Decretorum Libri XX. *P.L.*, vol. 140, col. 537-1058.

Canaparius, J. Vita et Passio S. Adalberti. *F.R.B.*, I, pp. 235-265.
Capitularia Regum Francorum. Ed. A. Boretius, V. Krause, 1897, *M.G.H.* Leges II.
Cedrenus, G. *Historiarum Compendium.* Bonn, vol. II.
Christianus. Vita S. Venceslai. *F.R.B.*, I. J. Pekar, *Die Wenzels und Ludmila Legenden und die Echtheit Christians*, Prag, 1905.
Chronicon Pictum Vindobenense. Ed. A. Domanovszky, *S.R.H.* I.
Chronicum Hungarico-Polonicum. Ed. J. Deér, *S.R.H.*, II, 1938.
Codex Diplomaticus Aevi Saxonici. Ed. J. M. Kemble, London, 1839-1847.
Codex Traditionum S. Emmeramensium. B. Pez, *Thesaurus Anecdotum Novissimus*, Augsburg, 1721-3, t.I.
Constantinus Porphyrogenetus. *De Administrando Imperio.* Bonn.
—— *De Caeremoniis Aulae Byzantinae.* Bonn, vol. I, II.
—— *De Thematibus.* Bonn.
Cornelius Tacitus. See Tacitus.
Cosmas Pragensis. Chronicae Bohemorum Libri III, ed. B. Bretholz, *M.G.H.S.N.S.* II, Berlin, 1923.
Cross, S. H. The Russian Primary Chronicle. *Harvard Studies in Philology and Literature*, vol. XII, 1930.

Dalimil. Czech Chronicle, *F.R.B.*, III, 1882 (ed. J. Jireček).
Daniel, Abbot. See de Noroff, A. and Wilson, C. W.
Deusdedit. *Collectio Canonum.* ed. P. Martinucci, Romae, 1869 ; Ed. V. Wolf von Glanvell, Paderborn, 1905.
Diplomata Ottonis I. *M.G.H.* Dipl. (ed. Th. Sickel, 1879-1884).
Diplomata Ottonis III. *M.G.H.* Dipl. II (1893).
Duchesne, L. *Liber Pontificalis.* Paris, 1892.

Edrisi. . .Géographie d'Edrisi. *Recueil de Voyages et de Mémoires*, ed. P. A. Jaubert ; published by the Société de Géographie, t.V, VI, Paris, 1824 etc. Cf. also Tallgren, A.M. and Tuulio, O. J.
Emler, J. *Fontes Rerum Bohemicarum.* Prague, 1871.
Endlicher, S. *Rerum Hungaricarum Monumenta Arpadiana*, St. Gallen, 1849.
Epitaphium Chrabri Boleslai. Ed. A. Bielowski. *M.P.H.* I.
Ephraem S. Caillau, A. B., *S. Patris Nostri Ephraem Syri Opera*, Parisiis, 1842, Commentarius in Genesim, vol. I.

Florentii Wigormiensis. *Chronicon.* Ed. B. Thorpe, London, 1848.
Fredegarius Scholasticus. Historia Francorum, *P.L.* vol. 71. *M.G.H.S.* Rerum Merovingiarum, II.
Friedrich, G. *Codex Diplomaticus et Epistolaris Regni Bohemiae*, Prague,1905-1917, vol. I.

Gardizi. Zayn al-Akhbar, Excerpts in English transl., see Macartney, C. A., *The Magyars.* . . pp. 189-200, 203-215.
Granum Catalogi Praesulum Moraviae. See Loserth, J.
Gelzer, H. Ungedrukte und ungenügend veröffentlichte Texte der Notitiae Episcopatuum, *Abhandlungen der Phil. Philol. Kl. d. Bayerischen Akademie*, vol. XI, München, 1901.
Georgius Monachus. *Chronicon.* ed. De Boor, Leipzig, 1904. Slavic version, ed. V. M. Istrin, *Khronika Georgiya Amartola*, Leningrad, 1920-30, 3 vol.
Gerbert. Lettres de Gerbert, published by J. Havet, *Collection des Textes pour servir à l'Etude et à l'Enseignement de l'Histoire*, Paris, 1889.
Gregorius S. Turonensis, Historia Francorum, *M.G.H.S.* Rer. Merov. I.
Gumpoldus Mantuanus. Vita S. Wenceslai, *F.R.B.* I.
Goetz, L. K. Kirchenrechtliche u. Kirchengeschichtliche Denkmäler Altrusslands. *Kirchenrechtliche Abhandlungen* (ed. u. Stutz), Hefs. 18, 19. Stuttgart 1905.

Harkavy, A. *Skazaniya Musulmanskikh Pisatelei o Slavyanakh i Russkikh* (Reports by Moslem writers about the Slavs and the Russians). St. Petersburg, 1870.
Hartwig. Legenda S. Stephani Regis, ab Hartvico episcopo conscripta, ed. E. Bartoniek, *S.R.H.* II, pp. 400-440 (1938).
Harvararsaga. Ed. S. Bugge, *Det Norske Oldscriftselskabe Samlinger*, vol. VIII, Christiania 1865.
Heimskringla. Snorre Sturlason, *Heimskringla*, ed. E. Monsen, A. H. Smith, Cambridge, 1932

320

Helmoldus. Chronica Slavorum, *M.G.H.S.* XXI. F. J. Tschan, *The Chronicle of the Slavs by Helmold, Priest of Bosan.* Translation, Introduction and notes, London, Milford, 1935.
Henry II. Abaldi Episcopi Traiectensis, Vita Henrici II, imperatoris. *M.G.H.* IV, pp. 679-695 (ed. D. G. Waitz).
Henry II. Adalberti Diaconi Vita S. Henrici Imperatoris, ed. Pertz. *M.G.H.* IV, pp. 799 sq.
Herodotus. See Niebuhr, B. G.
—— *Historiarum Libri* IX, ed. H. Kallenberg, Leipzig (Teubner), 1886-87.
Hieronymi. Commentaria in Ezechielem. *P.L.*, vol. 25.
Hudud al-Alam. See Minorsky, V.
Humbertus Cardinalis. Liber adversus Simoniacos, *M.G.H.* Libelli de Lite, I (ed. F. Thaner).
Huntingdon. Henrici Archidiaconi Huntingdon Historia Anglorum, *P.L.*, vol. 195.

İbrahim ibn Jacub. G. Jacob, *Arabische Reiseberichte*, Berlin, 1927. Cf. also F. Westberg.
Idrisi. See Edrisi and Tallgren-Tuulio, O. J.
Inscriptiones Antiquae Orae Septentrionalis Ponti Euxini, ed. V. Latyshev, Petropoli, 1890.
Ivan, S. Historia B. Ivani, *F.R.B.* I, pp. 111-120.

Jaffé, P. *Bibliotheca Rerum Germanicarum.* Berolini, 1864.
—— *Regesta Pontificum Romanorum.* Leipzig, 1885.
John XII. Decreta Joannis XII Papae, *P.L.*, vol. 133.
Jordanes. De Origine Actibusque Getarum (Getica). *M.G.H. Auct. Antiq.* V, pp. 52-138 (ed. Th. Mommsen).

Krachkovsky, J. & Vasiliev, A. Histoire de Yahya-ibn-Sa'id d'Antioche. *Patrologia Orientalis*, .vol. XXIII. Paris, 1932.

Lampertus Hersfeldensis. Annales, *M.G.H.S.* III, V ; *M.G.H.S.* in us. Schol.
Legenda S. Stephani Regis. Legenda Maior et Minor. *S.R.H.* II (1938), (ed. E. Bartoniek).
Liber Pontificalis. See Duchesne.
Liudprand of Cremona. *Antapodosis.* English translation by F. A. Wright, *The Works of Liudprand of Cremona*, London, 1930, *M.G.H.S.* III.

Relatio de Legatione Constantinopolitana, *M.G.H.S.* III.

Malalas, J. *Chronographia*, ed. Dindorf Bonn, 1831.
Masudi. See Marquart, I.
Matilda of Suabia. Letter to Mieszko II, *M.P.H.* I.
Maurus. Legenda SS. Zoerardi et Benedicti, vol. II, *S.R.H.*, Budapest, 1938, ed. E. Madzar.
Mela. See Pomponius Mela.

Necrologium of S. Gallus Abbey, *M.G.H.* Necrologia, I.
Nestor (Pseudo Nestor). Annals (Povest Vremenykh Let. Russian Primary Chronicle) ed. *Polnoe Sobranie Russkikh Letopisey.* Hypatian version, vol. II, fasc. I (3rd ed. Petrograd, 1923). Laurentian version, vol. I, fasc. I (2nd ed. Leningrad, 1926). English translation, see Cross, S. H. ; see also Russkie Memuary, Shakhmatov, A. H., Foester, R.
Nicephorus Callistus. Ecclesiae Historiae Libri XIV, *P.G.*, vol. 146.
Nikon. Chronicon. Nikonovskaya Letopis. *Polnoe Sobranie Russkikh Letopisey*, vol. IX.
Notitiae Episcopatuum. See Gelzer, H.

Old Slavonic Translations of Latin Works, see A. Sobolevsky.
Ostrogorski, G. *Geschichte des Byzantinischen Staates.* München, 1940.
Origo Gentis Langobardorum. ed. G. Waitz in *M.G.H.S.* Her. Lang. pp. 2-6.
Otloh. Vita S. Wolfkangi. *A.S.*, Novembris, vol. I, pars I, pp. 565-583.

Panov, V. See Nestor and Russkie Memuary.
Passio S. Adalberti. *F.R.B.* I, pp. 231-234. Cf. Die von Papst Silvester II edierte Passio S. Adalberti, ed. Kolberg, A., *Zeitschrift für die Geschichte und Altertumskunde Ermelands* (1879) vol. VII.
Paulus Diaconus. Historia Gentis Langobardorum, *M.G.H.S.* Her. Lang. (ed. L. Bethmann, G. Waitz).
Perdrizet, P. *Le Calendrier de la Nation d'Allemagne de l'Ancienne Université de Paris*, Paris, 1937.
Plinius Minor. *Naturalis Historia*, ed. C. Mayhoff, Leipzig (Teubner), 1906, I : ed. L. Janus, *ibid.*, 1870.
Photius. In Rossorum Incursionem Homiliae, I-II. ed. A. Nauck, *Lexicon Vindobonense.* St. Petersburg, 1867, pp. 201-232.
Pomponius Mela. *De Chronographia Libri Tres*, ed. C. Frick. Leipzig, 1889 (Teubner).
Povest Vremenykh Let. See Nestor.
Priscus Rhetor. *Historia Gothica. Excerpta e Prisci Historia*, ed. L. Lindorf. Bonn, 1829
Procopius. *De Bello Gallico*, Bonn. Ed. I. Haury, Leipzig (Teubner), 1905.

Ptolemy. *Claudii Ptolomaei Geographia*, ed. C. Müllerus. Paris, 1883, 1901. Ed. Noble, Leipzig, 1843.
Pulkava. Chronica Bohemorum, ed. G. Dobner, *Monumenta Historica Bohemiae*. Prague, 1764-85, vol. III, pp. 72-290.

Ravennatis Anonymi *Cosmographia et Guidonis Geographica*, ed. M. Pinder & C. Parthey. Berlin, 1860.
Regino Prumiensis. Chronicon, *M.G.H.S.* I ; M.G.H. in us. schol. Ed. F. Kurz, 1830.
Registrum Gregorii VII. E. Caspar, *Das Register Gregors* VII. Berlin, 1920 (Epistolae Selectae ex Monumentis Germaniae Historicis, vol. 2).
Russian Annals. See Nestor.
Russian Primary Chronicles. See Nestor.
Russkaya Pravda. New edition under the supervision of B. D. Grekov, by V. P. Lyotiniov, N. F. Lavrov, M. I. Tikhomirov, G. L. Geyermans, G. E. Kochin. *Akad. Nauk, Instit. Istorii.* Moscow, 1939.
Russkie Memuary. Dnevniki Pisma i Materialy, published by the Acad. *Drevnierusskie Letopisi*, vol. I. Moscow-Leningrad, 1936, (V. Panov's Russian translation of Nestor).
Rusta, Ibn. *Kitab al-Alak an-Nafisa.* Excerpts in English transl., see Macartney, C. A., *The Magyars.* . . , pp. 191-215.

Septuagint. Lee Brenton, L.C. *The Septuaginta Version of the Old Testament translated into English.* London, 1844.
Socrates. Historia Ecclesiastica. *P.G.*, vol. 67.
Stephen S. Vita S. Stephani Sugdaeensis, ed. Vasilievsky, V. G., *Trudy*, vol. III.
Strabo. *Geographica*, ed. Meinecke. Leipzig, (Teubner), 1852, 1853.

Tabari. *Annales.* Excerpts in Russian transl., See Harkavy, pp. 74-76.
Tacitus. *De Origine et Situ Germanorum*, ed. E. Koestermann, Leipzig (Teubner), 1936.
—— *Historiarum libri*, ed. E. Koestermann. Leipzig (Teubner), 1936.
Thangmar. Vita S. Bernwardi, *M.G.H.S.* IV, pp. 757-782.
Theotmar. Epistola Theotmari Juvavensis ecclesiae archiepiscopi et aliorum episcoporum Bavarensium ad Johannem P. IX scripta a. 900, *P.L.* vol. 131, pp. 34-38.
Theophanes Confessor. *Chronographia*, ed. Bonn. ed. De Boor, Leipzig, 1883-85.
Theophanes Continuatus, ed. Bekker, Bonn, 1838.
Thietmar. Chronicon, Thietmari Merseburgensis episcopi, *M.G.H.S.N.S.* IX, ed. R. Holtzmann (1935).
Translatio S. Godehardi. *M.G.H.S.* XII.

Urbani II. Epistolae et Privilegia. *P.L.*, vol. 151, col. 283-558.

Vajs, J. and Vašica, J. Literárni památky o sv. Václavu a sv. Ludmile (Collection of Old Slavonic literary records on S. Wenceslas and S. Ludmila), *Sbornik Starosl. Pamiâtek.* Praha, 1929.
Venantius Fortunatus. Carmina, *M.G.H. Auct. Antiq.* IV.
Vladimir S. See V. J. Sreznevsky.
Vladimir Monomakh. See Ivakin, M.
Vita S. Bartholomaei Cryptoferratensis, *P.G.* 127.
—— S. Bernwardi. See Thangmar.
—— S Burchardi episcopi, ed G Waitz, *M G H S* IV
—— S Clementis Ochridensis, *P G* vol 126
—— S Romualdi, auctore Petro Damiano, *P L* , vol 144.
—— Constantini (S. Cyril), Vita Methodii. French translation in F. Dvornik, *Les Légendes de Constantin et de Méthode vues de Byzance.* Prague, 1933.
—— S. Wolfkangi auctore Othlone, *A.S.* Nov. II, I, pp. 565-583.

Wenceslas S. Slavonic Legends of S. Wenceslas, cf. J. Vajs and J. Vašica.
—— See Gumpold, Christianus, J. Pekař.
—— First Slavonic Legend, see M. Weingart.
Widsith. K. Malone, *Widsith* (Methuen Old English Library). London, 1936.
Widukind. Chronica Saxonum, *M.G.H.S.* in us. schol. (ed. P. Hirsch, H. E. Lohmann). German translation by Hirsch, *Widukinds Sächsische Geschichten.* Leipzig, 1931.
Wiponis. Gesta Chuonradi II ceteraque quae supersunt opera, ed. H. Bresslau, *M.G.H.S.*XI.
Wolpherii. Vita Godeshardi Episcopi, ed. Pertz, *M.G.H.S.* XI, pp. 196-218.

Yahya of Antioch. Vasiliev, A., Histoire de Jahya-Ibn-Sa'id d'Antioche, *Patrologia Orientalis*, vol. XXIII, Paris, 1932.

Zacharias Rhetor. Historia Ecclesiastica, transl. by K. Aehrens and G. Krüger—*Die sogenannte Kirchengeschichte des Zacharias Rhetor*, Leipzig, 1899 (Teubner).

GENERAL.

Abraham, W. *Organizacya Kościoła w Polsce do połowy wieku* XII, Lwów, 1893.
Arne, T. J. La Suède et l'Orient, *Archives Orientales,* vol. VIII, 1914.
Aubin, H. Die Ostgrenze des alten Deutschen Reiches, *Histor. Vierteljahrschrift,* vol. 28, 1933.

Bachmann, A. Böhmens Staatsrechtliche Beziehungen, *Deutsche Arbeit in Böhmen.* Berlin, 1900.
Baethgen, F. Zur Geschichte der ältesten Deutsch-Polnischen Beziehungen, *Altpreussische Forschungen,* 13. Jahrh. 1936.
Balzer, O. *Genealogia Piastów* (Genealogy of the Piasts). Cracow, 1896.
Barraclough, G. Medieval Germany (*Studies in Medieval History,*) vol. I, Oxford, 1938.
—— *The Origins of Modern Germany,* Oxford, 1946.
Baumgarten de, N. Généalogies et Mariages Occidentaux des Rurikides Russes du Xe au XIIIe s., *Orientalia Christiana,* No. 35, 94. Rome, 1927, 1934.
—— Olaf Tryggwison, Roi de Norvège, *Ibid.,* No. 73, 1931.
—— Aux Origines de la Russie, *Orient. Christ. Anal.,* No. 119, 1939.
—— S. Vladimir et la Conversion de la Russie, *Orient. Christ.* vol. XXVII, 1932.
Birkenmajer, J. *Bogurodzica Dziewica.* Lwów, 1937.
—— Zagadnienia Autorstwa " Bogurodzicy " (The Problem of the Authorship of the Hymn " Bogurodzica.") Gniezno, 1937.
Bloch, R. Verwandschaftliche Beziehungen des Sächsischen Adels zum Russischen Fürstenhause im XI. Jh., *Festschrift, A. Brackmann.* Weimar, 1931.
Bodyansky. *O Vremeni Proiskhozhdeniya Slavyanskikh Pismen* (Date of the Invention of the Slavonic Alphabet). Moscow, 1855.
Bogusławski, W. *Dzieje Słowiańszczyzny Północno-Zachodniej* (History of the North-western Slavs), 4 vol. Poznań, 1887-1900.
Böhmer, J. F. & Will, C. *Regesten zur Geschichte der Mainzer Erzbischöfe.* Innsbruck, 1877.
Bonkáló, A. Die Ungarländischen Ruthenen, *Ungarische Jahrbücher,* vol. I, 1921.
Brackmann, A. Anfänge der Slavenmission und die Renovatio Imperii des Jahres 800. *Sitzungsberichte Preuss. Akad.,* Berlin, 1931.
—— Die Anfänge der Abendländischen Kulturbewegung in Osteuropa und deren Träger. *Jahrbücher für Geschichte Osteuropas,* vol. III, 1938.
—— Die Erneuerung der Kaiserwürde im Jahre 800, *Geschichtliche Studien für A. Hauck,* Leipzig, 1916.
—— *Deutschland und Polen,* München, Berlin, 1933 (cf. *also Kwart. Histor.,*1934. The Polish Answer to the above).
—— Der Streit um die Deutsche Kaiserpolitik des Mittelalters, *Velhagen u. Klasings Monatshefte,* vol. 43, 1929.
—— Die politische Bedeutung der Mauritius-Verehrung im frühen Mittelalter, *Sitzungsber., Preuss. Akad.,* Phil. Hist. Kl., vol. XXX, 1937.
—— Der Römische Erneuerungsgedanke und seine Bedeutung für die Reichspolitik der Deutschen Kaiser, *Sitzungsber. der Preuss. Akad. Hist. Phil. Kl.,*1932.
—— Die Anfänge des Polnischen Staates, *ibid.,* 1934.
—— Reichspolitik und Ostpolitik im frühen Mittelalter, *ibid.,* 1935.
—— Kaiser Otto III und die Staatlichen Umgestaltungen Polens und Ungarns, *Abhandl. der Preuss. Akad.,* 1939.
—— *Magdeburg als Hauptstadt des Deutsches Ostens.* Leipzig, 1937.
Brady, C. *Legend of Ermanaric.* University of California Press, 1943.
Braun, F. Russland und die Deutschen in Alter Zeit, *Germanica, E. Sievers zum 75. Geburtstage.* Halle, 1925.
—— Das Hist. Russland im Nord. Schrifttum d. X-XIV Jhd., *Festschrift E. Mogk,* Halle, 1924
Brandenburg, E. Problem um die Kaiserin Gisela, *Berichte über die Verhandlungen d. Sächs. Akad., d. Wissensch. Phil.-Hist. Kl.* vol. 80, Leipzig, 1928.
Bresslau, H. Die Schlacht auf dem Lechfelde, *Hist. Zeitschr.,* 1906, vol. 97.
—— Zu den Urkunden König Stephans von Ungarn, *Archiv für Urkundenforschung,* vol. VI, 1918.
—— *Jahrbücher des Deutschen Reiches unter Konrad II,* 2 vols. Leipzig, 1884, 1879.
—— Die ältere Salzburger Annalistik, *Sitzungber,. d. Preuss. Akad.,* Phil. Hist. Kl., 1923.
Bretholz, B. Mähren und das Reich Herzog Boleslavs II. von Böhmen, *Archiv für Oesterreichische Geschichte,* vol. 82, Wien, 1895.
—— *Geschichte Böhmens und Mährens bis zum Aussterben der Przemysliden.* Leipzig, 1912.
Brewitz, V. Kaiser Otto III, *Volk und Rasse,* vol. XIV, 1939 (München).
Brook, Z. N. *A History of Europe from 911 to 1198.* London, 1938.
Brückner, A. Bolesław Chrobry (Boleslas the Great), *Slavia Occid.,* vol. 7, 1928.
—— Fälscher an der Arbeit, *Jahrbücher für Geschichte Osteuropas,* vol. II, 1937.
Bryce, I. *The Holy Roman Empire.* London, 1887.
Buczek, K. Pierwsze Biskupstwa Polskie (First Polish Bishoprics), *Kwart. Hist.,* vol. 53, 1938.

Bury, J. S. The Treatise " De Administrando Imperio", *Byzant. Zeitschrift,* vol. XV, 1906.
—— Early History of the Slavonic Settlements in Dalmatia, Croatia and Serbia. Constantine Porphyrogennetos, De Adm. Imp. Chapters 29-36, *Texts for Students,* No. 18, London, 1920.
Buxton, D. R. *Russian Medieval Architecture,* Cambridge, 1934.

Caillau, A. B. *Sancti Patris Nostri Ephraim Syri Opera,* Parisiis, 1842, vol. I. (Commentarius in Genesim).
Carlyle, R. W. & A. J. *A 'History of Medieval Political Theory in the West.* London, Edinburgh, 1903-1936.
Cartellieri, A. Otto III, Kaiser der Römer, *Judeich-Festschrift* Weimar, 1929.
Cessi, R. Il Costituto di Constantino, *Rivista Stor. Ital.,* vol. 48, 1931, pp. 155-176.
Chadwick, N. K. *The Beginnings of Russian History.* Cambridge, 1946.
Chaloupecky, V. Radla-Anastasius, *Bratislava,* vol. I, 1927.
—— Slovenské Diecese a tak řečená apostolská práva (Slovak Bishoprics and the so-called Apostolic Rights), *Bratislava,* vol. II, 1928.
—— Stare Slovensko, Bratislava, 1923 (*Spisy Filos. Fak. University Komenského,* vol. III).
—— Česká hranice východní koncem XI. stoleti (Czech Eastern Boundaries at the end of the XIth century), *Czech Hist. Rev.* vol. XXXII, 1926.
—— Československé dejiny (Czechoslovak History), *Czech Hist. Rev.,* vol. XXVIII, 1922.
Chambers, R. W. *Widsith. A Study in Old English Heroic Legend.* Cambridge, 1912.
Cibulka, J. Václavova Rotunda sv. Vita (Wenceslas' Rotunda of S. Vitus), *Svatováclavsky Sbornik,* Praha, 1934.
Cook, S. H. Ibn Fadlan's Account of Scand. Merchants on the Volga in 922, *Journal of Engl. a. Germ. Philol.,* vol. XXII, 1923.
Cross, S. H. The Scandin. Infiltration into Early Russia, *Speculum,* vol. XXI, 1926.
Czekanowski, J. *Wstęp do Historji Słowian* (Introduction to Slav History). Lwów, 1927.
—— Zróżnicowanie etnograficzne Polski w świetle przeszłości (The Ethnographical Differentiation of Poland in the light of the past), *Proceedings of the Polish Academy,* vol. XI, Cracow, 1935.
—— The Racial Structure of Silesia, *Baltic and Scandinavian countries,* vol. III, Toruń Gdynia, 1937.

Da Costa-Louilet, Germaine. Y eut-il des Invasions Russes dans l'Empire Byzantin avant 860 ? *Byzantion,* vol. XV, 1940-41 (New York), pp. 231-248.
Dahlmann, F. E. *Geschichte von Dänemark,* vol. I, Hamburg, 1840.
Dannenbauer, H. Zum Kaisertum Karls des Grossen und seiner Nachfolger, *Zeitschrift für Kirchengeschichte,* vol. 49, 1930.
Dawson, Ch. *The Making of Europe.* London, 1932.
Delahaye, H. De S. Wolfgango, *A.S.,* Nov. vol. II, part I,
Deér, J. *Heidnisches und Christliches in der Altungarischen Monarchie.* Szeged, 1934.
Diehl, Ch. *Manuel d'Art Byzantin.* Paris, 2nd ed., 1926.
Dietrich, R. *Die Polenkriege Konrad II und der Friede von Merseburg.* Giessen, 1895.
Doeberl, M. *Entwicklungsgeschichte Bayerns.* München, 1906.
Doenniges, S. W. *Jahrbücher d. Deutschen Reichs unter Otto I.* Berlin, 1839.
Duda, F. *Rozwój terytorjalny Pomorza Polskiego* (Territorial Evolution of Polish Pomerania) Cracow, 1909.
Duchesne, L. *Les Premiers Temps de l'Etat Pontifical.* Paris, 1898. Engl. Transl. by A. H. Mathew, London, 1908.
Dümmler, E. *Pilgrim von Passau und das Erzbistum Lorch.* Leipzig, 1906.
—— *Kaiser Otto der Grosse.* München, 1876.
Dyakonov, A. P. Izvestiya Pseudo-Zacharii o drevnikh Slavyanakh, *Vestnik drevney Istorii, Institut Istorii Ak. Nauk SSSR.* Moskva, 1939.
Dvorak, M. Prispevek k životopisu sv. Vojtiecha (Contribution to the Biography of S. Adalbert), *Czech Hist. Rev.,* vol. IV, 1898.
Dvornik, F. *S. Wenceslas, Duke of Bohemia,* Prague, 1929.
—— Les Slaves, Byzance et Rome au IXe siècle, Paris, 1926 (*Travaux de l'Institut d'Etudes Slaves,* vol. 4).
—— Les Légendes de Constantin et de Méthode vues de Byzance. Prague, 1933 (*Byzantinoslavica, Supplementa,* vol. I).
—— The First Wave of the Drang nach Osten, *Cambridge Historical Journal,* vol. VII, No. 3, 1943.
—— *National Churches and the Church Universal.* London, 1944.
—— *The Photian Schism. History and Legend.* Cambridge, 1948.
—— The Kiev State and its Relations with Western Europe. *Transactions of the R. Hist. Society,* vol. XXIX, 1947.

Eckhart, F. *Introduction à l'Histoire Hongroise.* Paris, 1923.
Eck, A. En relisant Porphyrogénète, *Melanges Bidez.* Bruxelles, 1934.
Ediger, Th. *Russlands älteste Beziehungen zu Deutschland, Frankreich und der Röm. Kirche.* Halle, Dissertation, 1911.

Eichengrün, F.   Gerbert (Silvester II) als Persönlichkeit, Leipzig, Berlin, 1928.   *Beiträge zur Kulturgesch. des Mittelalters und Renaissance*, vol. 35.
Eichmann, E.   Königs-und Bischofsweihe, *Sitzungsber. d. Bayer. Ak. Phil. Hist. Kl.*   München 1928.
Erdmann, E.   Der Heidenkrieg in der Liturgie und die Kaiserkrönung Ottos I, *Mitteilugnen des Oester. Instituts für Geschichtsforschung*, vol. 46, 1932.
Evans, J.   *Monastic Life at Cluny* 910-1157.   Oxford, 1931.

Fischer, F. M.   Politiker um Otto den Grossen, *Hist. Studien*, Heft. 329, Berlin, 1938.
Florovsky, A. V.   *Chekhi i vostochnye Slavyane. Ocherki po Istorii Checho-Russkikh otnosheny X-XVIII vv.* (The Eastern Slavs and Czechs.   Essays on the History of Czecho-Russian Relations during the Xth-XVIIIth centuries).   Prague, Slovansky Ustav, 1935.
Foerster, R.   Die Entstehung der Russischen Reichsjahrbücher, *Jahrbücher für Geschichte Osteuropas*, vol. I, 1936.
Franke, W.   Romuald von Camaldoli und seine Reformtätigkeit zur Zeit Ottos III, *Hist. Studien*, Berlin, Heft 107, 1913.
Freeman, E. A.   *The History of the Norman Conquest of England*.   London, 177.
Friedrich, G.   O Privilegiu Papeže Jana XV (The Privilege of Pope John XV) *Czech Hist. Rev.*vol. XI, 1905.
Frisius.   *De Episcopatu Kiovensi eiusque Praesulibus Brevis Commemoratio*.   Warsaw, 1763.
Fritz, F.   Gottesgnadentum und Widerstandsrecht im Früheren Mittelalter, *Mittelalter- lische Studien*, vol. I, Leipzig, 1914.
Fritzler, K.   *Zwei Abhandlungen über Altrussisches Recht ; Die sogenannte Kirchenordnung Jaroslavs ein Denkmal Russischen Germanischen Rechts*.   Berlin, 1928.

Gasquet, A.   *De l'Autorité Imperiale en Matière Religieuse à Byzance*.   Paris, 1879.
—— *L'Empire Byzantin et la Monarchie Franque*.   Paris, 1888.
Gay, J.   L'Italie Méridionale et l'Empire Byzantin, *Biblioth. des Ecoles Francaises d'Athènes et de Rome*, vol. 90, Paris, 1904.
Geidel, H.   Alfred der Grosse als Geograph, *Münchener Geographische Studien*, vol. XV, 1904.
Gesenius, G.   *Thesaurus Linguae Hebraicae et Chaldeae Vet. Test.*   Lipsiae, 1843-1853.
Geza de Francovichova.   Contributi alla Scultura Ottoniana in Italia.   Il Puteale di S. Bartolomeo all'Isola di Roma, *Bolletino d'Arte del Ministero del'Educazione Nationale*, V, 1936, pp. 207-224.
Giesebrecht v. W.   *Geschichte der Deutschen Kaiserzeit*.   Braunschweig, 5th ed., 1881.
Giesebrecht, H. L. Th.   *Wendische Geschichten aus den J.* 780-1182, 3 vol. Berlin, 1843.
Gieysztor, A.   Władza Karola Wielkiego w opinii współczesnej (The Power of Charlemagne in the opinion of his Age), *Rozprawy Histor. Tow. Nauk.* Warszawa, 1938.
Golubinsky, E.   *Istorya Russkoy Tserkvi* (History of the Russian Church).   Moscow, 1901, vol. I.
Görlitz, S.   Beiträge zur Geschichte der Königlichen Hofkapelle im Zeitalter der Ottonen und Salier, *Histor. Diplom. Forschungen*, Bd. I, Weimar, 1936.
Grégoire, H.   La Légende d'Oleg et l'Expédition d'Igor, *Bulletin de la Classe des Lettres, Acad. Royale de Belgique*, I, 43, pp. 80-94.
—— L'Habitat Primitif des Magyars, *Byzantion*, vol. XIII, 1938, pp. 262-278.
—— L Origine et le Nom des Croates et des Serbes, *Byzantion*, vol. XVII, 1944-45.
Gregorovius, F.   *Geschichte der Stadt Rom im Mittelalter*.   Stuttgart, Berlin, 1903-1908, 5th ed. English translation : see Hamilton, G. H.
Grekov, B. D.   Kievskaya Rus (Kievan Russia), *Akademiya Nauk SSSR, Institut Istorii*, Moscow, Leningrad, 1939.
Gumplowicz, L.   *Chorwaci i Serbowie* (The Croats and the Serbs).   Warsaw, 1902.
—— Die Politische Geschichte der Serben und Kroaten, *Polit. Anthrop. Revue*, 1903.
Gumowski, N.   Szkice Numizmatyczno-Historyczne z XI wieku (Numismatic and Historical Essays on the XIth century) Poznan, 1924 *Tow. Przyj. Nauk, Kom. Hist.* t.III, ser. 2.
Gudzy, N.   *Khrestomatiya po Drevney Russkoy Literature XI-XVII vekov* (Chrestomathy of Old Russian Literature from the XIth to the XVIIth century).   Moscow, 1938.
—— Biskupstwo Kruszwickie w XI w. (The Bishopric of Kruszwica in the XIth century). *Tow. Przyj. Nauk, Kom. Hist.* tom II. ser. 3. Poznan 1921.

Haller, J.   *Das Papsttum, Idee und Wirklichkeit*.   Stuttgart, 1937.
—— *Tausend Jahre Deutsch-Französicher Beziehungen*, 4th ed. Stuttgart 1939, (English translation by Dora von Beseler : *France and Germany. The History of One Thousand Years*.   London, 1932).
—— *Das Altdeutsche Kaisertum*.   Stuttgart, 1934.
—— *Der Eintritt der Germanen in die Geschichte*.   Berlin, 1938.
Halphen, L.   La Cour d'Otton III à Rome, *Mélanges d'Archéologie et d'Histoire*,Paris-Rome, 1905, vol. XXV.
Hamilton, G. H.   *History of the City of Rome in the Middle Ages*.   London, 1900-9.
Hartmann, L. M.   *Geschichte Italiens im Mittelalter*.   Leipzig, 1897-1915.

Hampe, K. *Herrschergestalten des Deutschen Mittelalters.* Leipzig, 1939.
—— Kaiser Otto III und Rom, *Histor. Zeitschr.*, vol. CIL, 1929.
Harkavy, A. I. *Skazaniya Musulmanskikh Pisateley o Slavyanakh i Russkikh* (Reports by Moslem writers on the Slavs and the Russians). Moscow, 1870.
Hartmann, L. M. *Geschichte Italiens im Mittelalter.* Gotha, 1897-1915.
Hauck, A. *Kirchengeschichte Deutschlands.* Leipzig, vol. I and III, 4th ed., 1904, 1906 ; 5th vol. 1900-1920. vol. II (2nd ed. 1900).
Hauptmann, L. Die Herkunft der Kärntner Edlinge. *Vierteljahrschrift für Sozial u. Wirtschaftsgeschichte*, vol. XXI, (1928).
Hauptmann, L. Kroaten, Goten und Sarmaten, *Germanoslavica*, vol. III, 1935.
—— Seoba Hrvata i Srba (Migrations of Croats and Serbs), *Yugosl. Istor. Casopis* vol. III, (Yugoslav Historical Review), 1937.
—— Karantanska Hrvatska, (Carinthian Croatia), *Zbornik Kralja Tomislava.* Zagreb, 1935.
—— Prihod Hrvatov (Arrival of the Croats), *Strena Buliciana.* Zagreb, 1924 ; reprinted in Croat in Zbornik Kralja Tomislava, *Opera Academiae Scientiarum et Artium Slavorum Meridionalium separatim edita*, vol. XVII. Zagreb, 1925.
Hefele, C. J. von—Leclercq, H. *Histoire des Conciles.* Paris, 1907 etc.
Heidemann, von, O. *Margraf Gero.* Brunswick, 1860.
—— *König Konrad I.* Jena, 1922.
Heil, A. Die Politischen Beziehungen zwischen Otto dem Grossen und Ludwig von Frankreich (936-954), *Hist. Studien*, Heft 46, Berlin, 1904.
Heimpel, H. Bemerkungen für die Geschichte König Heinrichs des Ersten, *Berichte über die die Verhandlungen der Sächs. Ak. der Wissenschaft*, Leipzig, 1937. Bd. 88, Heft 4.
Heinzel, R. Uber die Hervararsaga, *Sitzungsberichte of the Vienna Academy, Hist.-Phil. Kl.*, vol. 114, 1887.
Heldmann, K. Das Kaisertum Karls des Grossen, Theorien und Wirklichkeit, *Quellen und Studien für Verfassungsgeschichte des Deutschen Reichs in Mittelalter und Neuzeit*, B. VI, H.2, Weimar, 1928.
Hennig, R. Die Missionsfahrt des Hl. Adalbert ins Preussland, *Forschungen für Preuss. und Brandenburgische Geschichte*, vol. 47, 1935.
Henry II. Zeitschrift zum 900. Todestage Kaiser Heinrichs des Zweiten, *Heimatsblätter*, vol. VI, Bamberg, 1929.
Hirsch, P. Widukinds Sächsische Geschichten, *Die Geschichtschreiber des Deutschen Vorzeit*, Bd. 33, Leipzig, 1931.
Hirsch, S. v., Bresslau, H., Usinger, R., Pabst, H. *Jahrbücher des Deutschen Reichs unter Heinrich II*, 3 vols., Leipzig, 1862, 1864, 1874.
Hoffman, H. Karl der Grosse im Bilde der Geschichtsschreiber des frühen Mittelalters, *Histor-Studien*, Heft 137, Berlin, 1919.
Hofmeister, A. Die Heilige Lanze ein Anzeichen des alten Reichs, Breslau, 1908. (*Untersuchungen für Staats und Rechtsgeschichte*, ed. Gierke, No. 96), Heft 96.
—— Das Leben des Bischofs Otto von Bamberg von einem Prüfeninger Mönch, *Die Geschichtschreiber Deutscher Vorzeit*, vol. 96, Leipzig, 1928.
—— *Deutschland und Burgund im Früheren Mittelalter.* Leipzig, 1914.
Holinka, R. Sv. Svorad a Benedikt (SS. Zoerard and Benedict), *Bratislava*, 1934.
Holtzmann, R. Die Urkunde Heinrichs IV für Prag vom Jahre 1086 (*Archiv für Urkundenforschung*, Bd. 6), Berlin, 1918 (*Festschrift für H. Bresslau*).
—— *Kaiser Otto der Grosse*, Berlin, 1936.
—— Böhmen und Polen im 10. Jahrh,. *Zeitschrift des Vereins für Geschichte Schlesiens*, vol. 52, 1918.
—— Der Weltherrschaftsgedanke des Mittelalterlichen Kaisertums 'und die Souveränitat der Europ. Staaten, *Histor. Zeitschr.*, vol. 159, 1939, pp. 250 sq.
Homan, B. *Magyar Törtenet* (Magyar History), Budapest, 1928.
—— King Stephen the Saint, *Archivium Europae Centro-Orientalis*, vol. IV, 1938.
Homburg, O. Ein Denkmal Ottonischer Plastik in Rom, *Jahrbücher der Preussischen Kunstsammlungen*, vol. 57, 1936, pp. 130-140.
Howarth, H. The Spread of the Slavs, Part IV, *Journal of the Anthropological Institute of Great Britain and Ireland*, vol. XI; 1882.
Hruby, A. Původni Hranice Biskupství Pražského a Hranice ríše české v. 10. století. (The original frontiers of the diocese of Prague and the frontiers of Bohemia in the Xth century). Review of Hruby's study by Chaloupecky in *Czech Hist. Rev.* vol. XXXIII, 1927.
Huber, A. *Geschichte Oesterreichs.* Wien, 1829.
Hybl, F. Bruno Quertfurtsky, *Czech Hist. Rev.* vol. IV, 1898.
Hrushevsky, M. *A History of the Ukraine* (ed. by O. J. Frederikson). New Haven, 1941.
—— *Geschichte des Ukrainischen Volkes.* Leipzig, 1906.
Hrusovsky, F. Boleslav Chrabry a Slovensko (Boleslas the Great and Slovakia), *Sbornik ·J. Skultétyho*, 1933.

Ivakin, I. M. *Knyaz Vladimir Monomakh i ego Pouchenie* (Duke Vladimir Monomakh and his Instruction). Moscow, 1901.

Jagic, V.   Ein Kapitel zur Geschichte der Südslavischen Sprachen, *Archiv für Slavische Philologie*, vol. XVII, 1895.

Jakobson, R.   *Nejstarši Duchovní Písně česke* (Oldest Czech Religious Hymns), Prague, 1929.

—— Die Reimwörter Czech-Lech, *Slav. Rundschau*, vol. X, 1938.

—— The Beginning of Nat. Self-Determination in Europe.   *The Review of Politics*, vol. VII, (1945).

Janko, I.   O puvodu jméńe Bratislava (Origin of the Name Bratislava), *Czech Hist. Rev.*, t.XXXIII, 1927, pp. 347-351.

Jedlicki, M. Z.   La Création du Premier Archévêché Polonais, *Revue Hist. du Droit Francais et Etranger*, 1933.

—— Die Anfänge des Polnischen Staates, *Hist. Zeitschrift*, vol. 152, 1935.

—— Stosunek prawny Polski do Cesarstwa do 1000 r. (Poland's Legal Relations with the Empire till the year 1000), Poznań, 1939.   *Poznańskie Towarz. Przyjaciół Nauk, Kom. Hist.*, t.XII, Zesz. 2.

Jireček, H.   *Antiquae Bohemiae usque ad exitum s.XII Topographica Historia.*   Wien, Praguis 1843.

Jireček, J.   Staroslovanské životy sv. Ludmily a sv. Jvana, (Old Slavonic Biographies of S. Ludmila and S. Ivan).   *Časopis Musea král. Českeho*, vol. XXXV, (1862).

Jireček, K.   *Geschichte der Serben.*   Gotha, 1911.

Jugie, M.   Les Origines Romaines de l'Eglise Russe, *Echos d'Orient*, vol XXXVI, 1937.

Kaindle, R. F.   *Beiträge zur Aelteren Ungarischen Geschichte.*   Wien, 1893.

—— Zur Geschichte des Hl. Adalbert, *Mitteilungen des Instituts f. Oesterr. Geschichtsforschung*, vol. XIX, 1898.

Kalousek, J.   Uber den Umfang des Böhmischen Reiches unter Boleslas II ; *Sitzungsberichte d. k. Böhm. Gesellschaft der Wiss.*   1883, vol. XXXII.

Kampers, F.   Rex et Sacerdos, *Histor. Jahrbuch*, vol. XLV, 1295.

Karacsonyi, J.   *Szent-Istvan Király Oklevelei es a Szilvester Bulla.*   Budapest, 1891.

Kawerau, S.   Die Rivalität Deutscher und Französischer Macht im 10. Jh., *Jahrbuch der Gesellschaft für Lothringische Geschichte und Altertumskunde*, 1910.

Kehn, P.   Urkundenbuch des Hochstiftes Merseburg, *Geschichtsquellen der Provinz Sachsen*, Bd. 36; 1889.

—— Das Erzbistum Magdeburg und die erste Organisation der Christlichen Kirche in Polen, *Abhandl. des Preuss. Ak. der Wissensch.*   Berlin, 1920.

—— *Die Urkunden Otto III.*   Innsbruck, 1890.

Kern, F.   Gottesgnadentum und Widerstandsrecht im Früheren Mittelalter, *Mittelalterliche Studien*, vol. I, Leipzig, 1914 ; English transl. by S. B. Chrimes, *Kingship and Law in the Middle Ages*, (Studies in Medieval History) Oxford, 1939.

Kendrick, R. D.   *A History of the Vikings.*   London, 1930.

Kętrzyński, S.   Kazimierz Odnowiciel (Casimir the Renovator), *Rozprawy of the Cracow Acad.*, *Hist .Phil. Cl.*, 1899.

Kętrzyński, W.   Najdawniejsze Żywoty św. Wojciecha i ich autorowie (The Oldest Biographies of S. Adalbert and their authors) ; *Proceedings of the Acad. of Cracow*,t.43.

—— *Granice Polski w. X. w.* (Poland's Frontiers in the Xth century), *Ibid.* vol. 26.

—— *O Zaginione Metropolie z czasów Bolesława Chrobriego*, (The Vanished Metropolitan Sees of the time of Boleslas the Great).   Warsaw Univ. Histor. Institute. vol. I. (1947).

Kirchberg, I.   Kaiseridee und Mission unter den Sachsenkaisern und den Ersten Saliern von Otto I bis Heinrich III, *Hist. Studien*, Heft 259, Berlin, 1934.

Kissling, W.   Das Verhältnis zwischen Sacerdotium und Imperium nach den Anschauungen der Päpste von Leo dem Grossen bis Gelasius I (440 496), *Görresgesellsch., Veröffentl. d. Sekt. f. Rechts u. Sozialwiss.* vol. XXXVIII, 1921.

Klebel, E.   Herzogtümer und Marken bis 900, *Deutsches Archiv für Geschichte des Mittelalters*, vol. II, 1938.

Klich, E.   *Polska terminologia Chrześciańska* (Polish Christian Terminology), Poznań, 1927.

Klippel, A.   Die Völkerrechtlichen Grundlagen der Deutschen Königsrechte in Italien, *Hist. Studien*, Heft 140, Berlin, 1920.

Knabe, L.   Die Gelasianische Zweigenwaltenlehre bis zum Ende des Investiturstreites, *Hist. Studien*, Heft 292, Berlin, 1936.

Koch, H.   Byzanz, Ochrid und Kiev 987-1037, *Kyrios*, (Berlin), vol. III, 1938.

Kochinim, G. E.   *Pamyatniki Istorii Kievskogo Gosudarstva IX-XII vv.* (Documents relating to the History of Kievan Russia of the IXth-XIIth centuries), Leningradsky Gosudarstvenny Universitet. Leningrad, 1936.

Koczy, L.   Thietmar i Widukind (Thietmar and Widukind), *Kwart. Histor.*, vol. II, 1936, pp. 656-676.

—— *Polska a Skandynawia za Pierwszych Piastów* (Poland and Scandinavia under the first Piasts), Poznan, 1934.

—— Jomsborg, *Kwart. Hist.* vol. XLVI, 1932.

Kölmel, W.   Rom und der Kirchenstaat im 10.u.11.Jh. bis in die Anfänge der Reform, *Abhandl. zur Mittl. u. neuren Geschichte*, 78 Heft, Berlin, 1935.

König, E.   Zur Vorgeschichte des Namens " Russen," *Zeitschrift der Deutschen Morgenländischen Gesellschaft*, Band 70, 1916.
Kostrzewski, J.   Reports on Important Excavations, *Baltic Countries*, vol. I, Toruń, 1935.
—— Biskupin.   An Early Iron Age Village in Western Poland, *Antiquity*, vol. XII, 1938, pp. 311-317.
Kozłowski, L.   Kultura Łużycka a problem pochodzenia Słowian (Lusatian Culture and the Problem of the Origin of the Slavs), *Memorial of the IVth Congress of Polish historians in Poznań*, Lwów, 1925.
—— Mapy Kultury Łużyckiej (Maps of Lusatian Culture), *Kwart. Hist.* vol. XL, Lwów, 1926.
—— *Wenedowie w zródłach historycznych i w świetle kartografii prehistorycznej* (The Venedae in historical sources and in the light of pre-historic cartography), Lwów, 1937.
Kraus, A.   Christe ginado a Hospodine Pomiluj ny (The Hymns Christe ginado and Hospodine Pomily ny), *Proceedings of the Royal Scient. Assoc. of Bohemia*, Prague, 1898.
Krofta, K.   Kurie a církevní správa Zemí českých v době předhusitské (The Curia and the ecclesiastical administration of Bohemia in the period prior to the Hussite days), *Czech Hist. Rev.*, vol. X, 1904.

Łabuda, G.   Magdeburg i Poznań (Magdeburg and Posen), *Roczniki Hist.*, vol. XIV, 1938.
Łaguna, S.   Pierwsza wieki Kościoła Polskiego. (The First Centuries of the Polish Church) *Kwart. Histor.* (1891), vol. V.
Laehr, G.   Die Konstantinische Schenkung in der abendländischen Literatur des Mittelalters bis zur Mitte des 14. Jh., *Historische Studien*, H. 166, Berlin, 1926.
—— Die Anfänge des Russischen Reiches, *ibid.*, Heft 1897, Berlin, 1930.
Larson, L. M.   *Canute the Great*.   New York, London, 1912.
Lauer, Ph.   Robert I et Raoul de Bourgogne, rois de France (923-936), *Bibl. de l'Ecole des Hautes Etudes*, Paris, 1910, Sc. Hist. et. Phil. vol. 188.
—— *Le Régime de Louis IV d'Outre-Mer*, Paris, 1900, *ibid.*, vol. 127.
Laurent, V.   Aux Origines de l'Eglise Russe.   L'Etablissement de la Hiérarchie Byzantine, *Echos d'Orient*, vol. XXXVIII, 1939.
Läwen, G.   Stammesherzog und Stammesherzogtum, *Neue Deutsche Forschungen, Abteilung für Mittelalterliche Geschichte* Bd. I, Berlin, 1935.
Leclère, L.   A propos du Couronnement de l'an 800, *Mélanges P. Fredericq*, Bruxelles, 1909.
Ledit, J.   Russie, *Dict. de Théologie Cathol.*, vol. XIV, Paris, 1939.
Leib, B.   *Rome, Kiev et Byzance à la fin du XIe siècle*.   Paris, 1924.
Le Quien.   *Oriens Christianus*.   Paris, 1740.
Lesêtre, H.   *Saint Henri*.   Paris, 1897.
Lewicki, A.   Mieszko II, *Rozprawy, Cracow Academy. Cl. Hist. Phil.*, vol. V, 1876.
Lintzel.   Heinrich I und das Herzogtum Schwaben, *Histor. Vierteljahrschrift*, 1929.
—— Zur Geschichte Ottos des Grossen, *Mitteil. d. Oesterr. Institutes für Geschichte*, vol. 48, 1934.
Lippert, J.   *Sozialgeschichte Böhmens in Vorhussitischer Zeit*.   Wien, 1896.
Löher, F.   König Konrad I und Herzog Heinrich von Sachsen, *Abh. d. Bayr. Ak.* München, 1857.
Łoś, J.   *Początki piśmiennictwa polskiego*.   Lwów, 1922.
Loserth, J.   Der Sturz des Hauses Slavnik, *Abh. f. Oesterr. Geschichte*, Bd. 65, 1895.
—— Das Granum Catalogi Praesulum Moraviae, *Archiv f. Oesterr. Geschichte*, vol. LXXVII, 1892.
Loserth, J.   Studien zu Cosmas von Prag, *Archiv für Oesterreichische Geschichte*, vol. 61, Wien, 1880, pp. 1-32.
—— Der Umfang des Böhmischen Reiches unter Boleslav II, *Mitteilungen des Instituts f. Oesterr. Geschichtsforschungen*, vol. II, 1881.
Lot, F.   *Les Invasions Barbares*, 2 vols. Paris, 1937.
—— Le Règne de Hugues Capet et la Fin du Xe siècle, *Bibliothèque de l'Ecole des Hautes Etudes*, vol. 147, Paris, 1903.
—— *Les Invasions Germaniques*.   Paris, 1934.
—— Les Derniers Carolingiens, Paris, 1891.   *Bibl. de L'Ecole des Hautes Etudes,* vol. 87.
Łowmiański, H.   The Ancient Prussians, Toruń-London, 1936 (*The Baltic Pocket Library*).
Łoziński, G.   La Russie dans la Litérature Française du Moyen Age, *Revue des Etudes Slaves*, vol. IX, 1929.
Luchaire, A.   Les Premiers Capétiens, in E. Lavisse's *Histoire de France*, I, II, 2, Paris, 1901.
Ludat, H.   Mieszkos Tributpflicht bis zur Warthe, *Archiv für Landes and Volksforschung*, 1938.
Lüdtke, F.   *Heinrich I, der Deutsche*.   Leipzig, 1934.
Luschin von Ebengreuth, A.   *Geschichte der Stadt Wien*.   Wien, 1897. vol. I, ed. H. Zimmermann and published by the Altertumsverein zu Wien.
Lüttich, R.   Ungarnzüge in Europa im 10. Jh., *Histor. Studien*, Heft 84, Berlin, 1910.

Macartney, C. A.   *The Magyars in the Ninth Century*.   Cambridge, 1930.
—— Studies on the Early Hungarian Sources, *Ostmitteleuropaeische Bibliothek*, No. 18, 21, Budapest, 1938, 1940.

Macurek, J. *Dejiny Madarů a Uherskeho Státu* (History of the Magyars and of Hungary). Praha, 1934.
—— Dějiny vých. Slovaníů (History of the Eastern Slavs). Prague, 1946.
—— Východní Dejepisectví (Historiography of the East). Prague, 1947.
Manitius, M. *Geschichte der Lateinischen Literatur des Mittelalters.* München, I—III, 1911-1931, vol. II, 1924.
Miklosich, F. *Die Slavischen Elemente im Magyarischen*, 2nd ed. by L. Wagner, Wien, Teschen, 1884.
Manojlovic, G. Studie o spisu " De Administrando Imperio " cara Konstantina VII Porfirogeneta (Study on the work " De Adm. Imp." of the Emperor Constantine Porphyrogenetus VII), *Rad Jugoslav. Akademije*, vol. 187.
Marquart, I. *Osteuropäische und Ostasiatische Streifzüge.* Leipzig, 1903.
Maschke, E. Der Peterspfennig der Polen und der Deutsche Osten, *Königsberger Historische Forschungen*, Bd. 5, Leipzig, 1933.
Meillet, A. & Vaillant, A. *Le Slave Commun.* Paris, 1934.
Michel, A. Der Josefsche Kaiser Heinrich II, *Theol. Quartalschr.* vol. XCVIII, 1917.
Minasi, G. *S. Nilo di Calabria.* Naples, 1892.
Minorsky, V. F. Hudud al-Alam. The Regions of the World—A Persian Geography 383 A. D.—982 A. D., *E. J. Gibb Memorial Series.* New Ser. No. II, London, 1937.
—— Rus.*The Encyclopedia of Islam*, vol. III, (Leyden, London, 1936).
Nikkola, I. Avarica, *Archiv für Slavische Philologie*, vol. XLI, 1927.
Mommsen, T. *Studien zum Ideengehalt der Deutschen Aussenpolitik im Zeitalter der Ottonen und Salier.* Berlin, 1930.
Moravczik, G. Byzantine Christianity and the Magyars in the first period of their Migrations. *American, Slavonic and East Eur. Review*, vol. V, (1948).
Moshin, V. A. Varyago-Russkoy Vopros, *Slavia*, vol. X, 1931, pp. 109-136, 343-379, 501-537.
Much, R. Ascriburgion Oros, *Zeitschrift für Deutsches Altertum*, vol. 33, 1889.
—— Widsith, *ibid.*, vol. 62, 1925.
Mueller, H. *Das Heilige Kaiserpaar Heinrich und Kunegunde*, Steyl, 1903.

Nachtigal, R. Donesi k zgodovini vprasanja o imenu Hrvat (Contributions to the History of the Problems concering the name of the Croats), *Etnolog*, Ljubljana, 1937-1939, vol. X-XI.
Niebuhr, B. G. A Dissertation on the Geography of Herodotus. *Researches into the History of the Scythians, Getae and Sarmatians*, Oxford, 1830.
Niederle, L. O Počátcích Dejin zemí Českých (Early History of the Czech Lands), *Czech Hist. Rev.* 1900.
—— *Slovanské Starožitnosti* (Slavonic Antiquities). Prague, 1904-1924.
—— Manuel de l'Antiquité Slave, Paris, 1923. *Manuels de l'Institut d'Etudes Slaves*, vol. I.
—— Počátky Karpatské Rusi (Origins of Carpathian Russia), *Věstnik Narodopisnéhio Musea*, Prague, 1922.
Norden, W. Erzbischof Friedrich von Mainz und Otto der Grosse, *Hist. Studien*, Heft 103, Berlin, 1912.
Noroff de, A. *Pélérinage en Terre Sainte de l'Igoumène Russe Daniel au Commencement du XIe siècle.* St. Petersbourg, 1864.
Novák, J. B. L'Idée de l'Empire Romain et la Pensée Politique Tchèque au Moyen Age, *Le Monde Slave*, vol. II, 1925.
Novotny, V. *Ceské Dejiny* (Czech History), vol. I, 2, Prague, 1912.

Orel, D. Hudebnî prvky svatováclavské (Musical Materials Connected with S. Wenceslas), *Svatovácl. Sbornik*, vol. II, Prague, 1937.
Orlov, A. S., Adrianov-Perets, V. P., Gudzy, N. K. Istoriya Russkoy Literatury, vol. I, Moscow-Leningrad, 1941, (*Akademiya Nauk SSSR Institut Literatury*).
—— Drevnaya Russkaya Literatura XI-XVI vv. (Ancient Russian Literature of the XIth-XVIth centuries) Moscow-Leningrad, 1937 (*Akademiya Nauk SSSR, Nauchno-Populyarnaya Seriya*).
Ostir, K. K Predslovanski etnologiji Zakarpatja (Contribution to the pre-Slavonic Ethnology of the Lands beyond the Carpathians), *Etnolog*, I, 1926-1927.
Ostrogorsky. Vladimir i Bizantia, *Vladimirskii Sbornik*, Beograd, 1938.

Palacky, F. *Geschichte von Böhmen*, Prag, 1836-1867.
Peisker, J. The Asiatic Background, *Cambridge Medieval History*, vol. I, pp. 323-360 (1911).
—— The Expansion of the Slavs, *ibid.*, vol. III, pp. 418-460 (1913).
Pekař, J. K Sporu o Zakladací Listinu Biskupství Prazskeho (A contribution to the controversy on the Foundation Charter of the bishopric of Prague), *Czech Hist. Rev.* vol. X, 1904.
—— Die Wenzels und Ludmila Legenden und die Echtkeit Christians, Prag. 1906.
—— Sv. Václav (S. Wenceslas), *Svatovaclávsky Sbornik*, 1934, vol. I.
Piekosinski, F. *Rycerstwo Polskie Wieków Średnich* (Polish Knighthood in the Middle Ages). Cracow Academy, 1896.
Pirenne, H. *Mohammed et Charlemagne*, Paris-Bruxelles, 1931. English translation : Mohammed and Charlemagne, by B. Miall, London, 1939.

Platonor, S. J. *History of Russia* (translated by E. Aronsberg), London, 1925.
Pogodin, A. Epigraficheskie Sledui Slavyanstva (Epigraphic documents on the Slavs), *Russ. Filol. Vestnik*, 1901, vol. XLVI.
—— Les Rodsi : un Peuple Imaginaire, *Revue des Etudes Slaves*, t.XVII, 1937.
Polivka, J. Evangelium Nikodemovo v Literaturách Slovanskych (Nicodemus' Gospel in Slavonic Letters), *Časopis Českého Musea*, t.64, 65, 1890.
Poole, L. Burgundian Notes, *Engl. Hist. Review*, XXVI, 1911 ; XXVII, 1912 ; XXVIII, 1913.
Pothast, A. *Bibliotheca Historica Medii Aevi*. Berlin, 1896.
Potkanski, K. Kraków przed Piastami (Cracow before the Piasts), *Proceedings of the Polish Acad., Phil. Hist. Cl.* vol. IX, Cracow, 1897.
—— Postrzyżyny u Słowian i Germanów (The cutting of boys' hair among Slavs and Germans). *Proceedings of the Polish Acad., Hist. Phil. Cl.* series II, vol. VII, Cracow, 1905.
Pourpardin, R. Le Royaume de Bourgogne (888-1038), Paris, 1937. *Bibl. de l'Ecole des Hautes Etudes, Sc. Hist. et Phil.* vol. 163.
Priscuś. *Historia Byzantina*, Excerpta de Legationibus Gentium ad Romanos, ed. Bonn.
Priselkov, M. D. Ocherki po Tserkovno-politicheskoy Istorii Kievskoy Rusi, X-XII vv., St. Petersburg, 1913 ; *Zapiski of St. Petersburg University*, vol. CXVI.
—— Russko-Vizantiyskie Otnosheniya (Relations between Russia and Byzantium), *Vestrnik, Drevney Istorii, Institut Istorii Akad. Nauk SSSR.*, 1939, vol. 3, pp. 98-109.
Prévité-Orton, C. W. Italy and Provence, 900-950. *English Hist. Review*, vol. 32, 1917.
Ptaśnik, J. *Dagome Iudex*, Cracow, 1911.

Radig-Elbing, W. *Heinrich I, der Burgbauer und Reichsgruender*, 1937.
Ramous, F. Praslovensko Kaseg " Edling " (The Primitive Slav Name of Kaseg-Edling), *Rasprave znanstv. drustva za human. vede*. Ljubljana, 1925.
Réau, L. *L'Art Russe des Origines à Pierre le Grand*, Paris, 1922.
Riezler, S. Die Landnahme der Baiuwaren, *Sitzungsber. d. Bay. Ak. d. Wissensch. Phil. Hist. Kl.* 1920, München, 1921.
—— *Geschichte Bayerns*, Gotha, 1878, I.
Roepell, R. Geschichte Polens, Hamburg, 1840.
Rosen, W. R. *Imperator Vasily Bolgaroboytsa*, (The Emperor Basil Boulgaroktonos). St. Petersburg, 1883.
Rosenstock, X. X. E. *Königshaus und Stämme in Deutschland zwischen 911 und 1250*. Leipzig 1914.
Rostovtzeff, M. *Iranians and Greeks*. Oxford, 1922.
Rudnicki, M. Dyskusja na temat nazwy Śląska (Discussion on the subject of the name of Silesia), *Slavia Occidentalis*, vol. XVI, 1938.
Runciman, S. *A History of the First Bulgarian Empire*, London, 1930.
Rus, J. Slovanstvo in Vislanski Hrvatje 6 do 10 stoletja (The Slavs and the Croats on the Vistula from the VIth to the Xth century), *Etnolog*, vol. V-VI, 1933.
—— *Kralji Dinastije Svevladicev*(Kings of an autochthonous dynasty), Ljubljana, 1931.

Šafařik (Schafarik), P. J. *Slavische Altertümer* (transl. from the Czech by Mosig von Aehrenfeld), 2 vol. Leipzig, 1843, 44.
Salle de Rochemaure, Duc de la. *Gerbert (Silvestre II)*, Paris-Rome, 1921.
Sante, W. Die Deutsche Westgrenze im 9. and 10. Jh., *Hist. Aufsätze A. Schulte gewidmet*, Düsseldorf, 1927.
Sappok, G. Die Anfänge des Bistums Posen und die Reihe seiner Bischöfe von 968-1498, *Deutschland und der Osten*, Bd, 6, Leipzig, 1937.
—— Polen, Reich und Pommern im 10. Jh., *Jahrbücher für Geschichte Osteuropas*, II, 1937.
Schäfer, D. Die Ungarnschlacht von 955, *Sitzungberichte der Preuss. Ak. Phil. Hist. Kl.*, Berlin, 1905.
Schiffmann. Die Zollurkunde von Raffelsteten, *Mitteilungen des Instituts für Oesterr. Geschichte*, vol. XXXVII, 1917.
Schlumberger, V. G.L' *Epopée Byzantine à la fin du dixième siècle, Jean Tzimisces I*, vol. I, Paris, 1896 ; vol. II, 1900.
Schoene, C. *Die Politischen Beziehungen zwischen Deutschland und Frankreich in den Jahren 953-980*, Berlin, 1910.
Schramm, P. Kaiser, Rom und Renovatio, *Studien der Bibl. Warburg*, vol. XVII, Berlin, 1929.
—— Kaiser, Basileus und Papst in der Zeit der Ottonen, *Hist. Zeitschr.*, vol. 129, 1929.
—— *Die Deutschen Kaiser und Könige in Bildern ihrer Zeit*, Berlin, 1928.
—— *Der König von Frankreich. Das Wesen der Monarchie vom 9. zum 16 Jh.*, Weimar, 2 vols., 1939.
—— Die Krönung in Deutschland bis zum Beginn des Salischen Hauses, *Zeitschr. der Savigny Stiftung*, vol. 55, Kan. Abt. XXIV, Weimar, 1935.
Schranil, I. *Die Vorgeschichte Böhmens und Mährens*, Berlin, 1928.
Schubert v. H. Der Kampf des Geistlichen und Weltlichen Rechts, *Sitzungber. der Akad. Heidelberg, Hist. Phil. Kl.*, 1927.

Schulte, W.   Die Gründung des Bistums Prag, *Historisches Jahrbuch*, Bd. I, München, 1901
Schulze, E. O.   Die Kolonisierung und Germanisierung der Gebiete zwischen Saale und Elbe, *Preisschriften der Jablonowskischen Gesellschaft, Hist.-Nationalökonom. Sect.* No. XX, Leipzig, 1896.
Schünemann, K.   Die Deutschen in Ungarn bis zum 12. Jh., *Ungarische Bibliothek*, I, vol. 8, Berlin-Leipzig, 1923.
Scheinfurth, P.   *Geschichte der Russischen Malerei im Mittelalter*, Haag, 1930.
Semkowicz, W.   Geograficzne podstawy Polski Chrobrego (Geographical foundations of Poland under Boleslas the Great) *Kwart. Hist.* t.39, 1925.
Shaytan, M. E.   Germanya i Kiev v XI v. (Germany and Kiev) *Letopis Zanyatyj Postoyannoy istoriko-arkheograficheskoy Komissyi*, I, vol. XXXIV, Leningrad, 1927.
Shahmatov, A. H.   *Razyskaniya o Drevneyshikh Russkikh Letopisnykh Svodakh* (Researches on the Oldest Collections of Russian Chronicles), St. Petersburg, 1906.
—— Povest Vremmenyikh Let i yego Istochniki (The Russian Primary Chronicle and its Sources), *Trudy Otdela Drevne-Russkoi. Lit. Ak. Nauk. SSSR.*
Shlyapkin, I. A.   *Zhurnal Ministerstva Narodnago Prosveshchenya*, 1884, No. 12.
Sickel, Th.   *Das Privilegium Ottos I für die Römische Kirche vom Jahre 962*, Innsbruck, 1883.
Simák, V.   Vicinus Subregulus r. 936, *Czech Hist. Rev.* vol. XXVII, 1912.
Skalsky, G.   Denár sv. Vojtiěcha (The denarius of S. Adalbert), *Czech Numismatic Review*, vol. V, 1929. Cf. also *Czech Hist. Rev.*, vol. 45, 1939, Mv. 104, 371.
Smirnov, A. P.   Ocherki po Istorii drevnikh Bulgar, (Essays on the History of the Bulgars), *Trudy Gosudarstvennogo Istoricheskogo Museya*, vyp. XI, *Sbornik Statey po Arkheologii SSSR.*, Moskva, 1940, pp. 55-136.
Sobolevsky, A.   Russko-Skifskie Etyudy (Russo-Scythian Studies), *Izvestiya Otd. Russ. Jazyka i Slov.*, 1921, vol. XXVI.
—— Tserkovno-Slavyanskiya Teksty Moravskago proiskhozhdeniya (Church Slavonic texts of Moravian origin), *Russky Filologichesky Vestnik*, 1900, No. I.
—— Studü k Khronologii Drevneyshikh Tserkovno-Slavyanskikh Pamyatnikov (Chronology of the oldest Church Slavonic literary works), *Izvestiya*, vol. XI, 1906, No. 2.
—— Muchenie Papy Stefana po Russkomu spisku XV veka (The martyrdom of Pope Stephen after a Russian work of the XVth century), *Izvestiya*, vol. X, No. I.
—— Muchenie sv. Apollinariya Ravenskago, (The Martyrdom of S. Apollinarius of Ravenna). *Izvestiya*, vol. VIII, 1903, No. 2.
—— Zhitie prepod. Benedikta Nursyskago po Serbskomu spisku XIV veka (The Life of S. Benedict of Nursia after a Serbian work of the XIVth century, *ibid.*
—— Muchenie sv. Vita v drevnem Tserkovno-Slovyanskom perevode. (The Martydom of S. Vitus in an old translation into Church Slavonic), *Izvestiya Otd. Russk. Yazyka i Slovesnosti Imp. Ak. Nauk*, vol. VIII, 1903, Book I.
—— Russiya Molitvy s upominaniem Zapadnykh Svyatykh (Russian Prayers that mention western saints), *Sbornick Otd. Russk. Yazyka i Slovesnosti Imp. Ak. Nauk*, t. 88, No. 3, St. Petersburg, 1910.
—— Iz oblasti drevney Tserkovno-Slavyanskoy propovedi (From the field of Old Church Slavonic homiletics), *Izvestiya*, vol. XI, 1906.
—— Materialy i Isledovaniya v oblasti Slavyanskoy Filologii i Arkheologii (Materials and Studies from the field of Slavonic Philology and Archeology), *Sbornik Otd. Russk. Yazyka i Slov. Imp. Akad. Nauk*, t.88, No. 3, 1910.
—— Neskolko redkikh molitv iz Russkago Sbornika XIII veka (Some rare prayers from Russian XIIIth-century Collections). *Izvestiya*, vol. X, 1905.
Soloviev, A.   He exo Rosia, *Byzantion*, XIII, 1938.
Speransky, M. N.   *Istoria Drevney Russkoy Literatury* (History of Ancient Russian Literature), Moscow, 3rd ed., 1920.
Spuler, B.   Ibrahim ibn Ja'Qub, Orientalische Bemerkungen, *Jahrbücher für Geschichte Osteuropas*, vol. III, 1938.
Sreznevsky, V. J.   Pokhvala Vladimiru (In Praise of S. Vladimir), *Zapiski Imp. Ak. Nauk*, S.VIII, vol. I, 1897.
Stasiewski, B.   *Untersuchungen über die Quellen für die Aelteste Geschichte und Kirchengeschichte Polens*, Breslau, 1933.
Stender-Peterson, A.   Die Varägersage als Quelle der Altrussischen Chronik. *Aelta Jutlandica*, vol. VI, (1934).
—— Zur Bedeutungsgeschichte des Wortes voeringi. *Acta Philol. Scandinavica*, vol. VI, (1934).
Steinen von der, W.   Kaiser Otto der Grosse, *Heilige und Helden des Mittelalters*, vol. V, Breslau, 1928.
Stengel, E. E.   *Den Kaiser macht das Heer*, Weimar, 1910.
—— *Der Entwurf des Kaiserprivilegs für die Römische Kirche 817-962*, *Hist. Zeitschr.*, vol. 134, 1926.
Stenton, E. M.   Anglo-Saxon England, *Oxford History of England*, 1943.
Stevenson, E. L.   *Geography of Claudius Ptolemy*, translated into English with introduction by I. Fosher, New York, 1932.
Stutz, U.   The Proprietary Church as an Element of Medieval German Ecclesiastical Law, in Barraclough's *Studies in Medieval History*, Oxford, 1938, vol. II, pp. 35-70.
—— *Die Eigenkirche als Element des Mittelalterlich-Germanischen Kirchenrechtes*, Berlin, 1895.

Sulimirski, T. *Poland and Germany*, London, 1942.
—— *Najstarsze Dzieje Narodu Polskiego* (Early History of the Polish Nation), London, 1934.
Suvorov, N. S. *K voprosu o Zapadnom vliyanii na drevnee Otechestvennoe Pravo* (Western influences on ancient Russian Law), Jaroslavl, 1892.
—— *Sliedy Zapadnokatolicheskago Tserkovnago Prava v Pamyatnikakh Drevne-Russkago Prava* (Traces of western Catholic canon law in the monuments of ancient Russian law), Jaroslavl, 1888.

Tallgen, A. M. & Tallgren-Tuulio, O. J. Idrisi, La Finlande et les autres Pays Baltiques Orientaux ; *Studia Orientalia*, vol. III, Helsingfors, 1930.
Tellenbach, G. Römischer und Christlicher Reichsgedanke in der Liturgie des Frühen Mittelalters, *Sitzungsber. der Ak. Heidelberg, Phil. Hist. Kl.*, 1934.
—— Otto der Grosse, *Neue Deutsche Biographie*, ed. W. Andreas and W. v. Scholz, vol. I, 1934.
—— Königtum und Stämme in der Werdezeit des Deutschen Reiches, *Quellen und Studien zur Verfassungsgeschichte des Deutschen Reiches*, Bd. 7, Heft 4, Weimar, 1939.
Thompson, J. W. *Feudal Germany*, Chicago, 1926.
Thomsen, V. *The Relations between Ancient Russia and Scandinavia and the Origin of the Russian State*, Oxford, London, 1877.
Thoss, A. *Heinrich I, der Gründer des Ersten Deutschen Volksreiches*, Goslar, 1936.
Tobler, T. *Bibliographia Geographica Palaestinae*, Leipzig, 1867.
Tungar, A. *De l'Histoire Profane dans les Actes Grecs des Bollandistes*, Paris, 1874.
Tuulio, O. J.-Tallgren & Tallgen, A. M. *Du Nouveau sur Idrisi, Studia Orientalia*, vol. VI, Helsingfors, 1936.

Uhlirz, K. *Geschichte des Erzbistums Magdeburg unter den Kaisern aus dem Sächsischen Hause*, Magdeburg, 1887.
Uhlirz, M. Die Italienische Kirchenpolitik der Ottonen, *Mitteilungen des Instit. für Oesterr. Geschichtsforschung*, Bd. 48, 1934.
—— Das Deutsche Gefolge Kaiser Ottos III in Italien, *Gesamtdeutsche Vergangenheit, Festgabe für H. von Srbik*, 1938.
Uspensky, F. I. Znachenie pokhodov Svyatoslava v Bolgariyu (The Meaning of Svyatoslav's Expeditions into Bulgaria), *Vestnik Drevney Istorii*, vol. 4, 1939, pp. 91-96.

Vaczy von, P. *Die Erste Epoche des Ungarischen Königstums*. Pecz Fünfkirchen, 1935.
Vaillant, A. Les " Lettres Russes " et " La Vie de Constantin," *Revue des Etudes Slaves*, 1935, t.XV.
Varges, W. *Das Herzogtum, Aus Politik und Geschichte*, Gedächtnisschrift für Georg von Below, Berlin, 1928.
Vasilev, V. V. History of the Byzantine Empire, *Univ. of Wisconsin Studies on the Soc. Sc. and Hist.*, No. 13, 14, Madison, 1928, vol. I.
Vasica, J. *Bedřich Bridel Život sv. Irania* (Frederick Bridel, The Life of S. Irania), Praha. Břevnov, 1936 (Opus Dei, vol. II).
Vasiliev, A. The Goths in the Crimea. *Monographs of the Medieval Academy of America*. vol. II. (Cambridge Mass., 1936).
—— The Russian Attack on Constantinople in 860, *ibid.* vol. XII, (1946).
Vasilievsky, V. I. K Istorii 976-986 godov (Contribution to the history of the years 976-986), *Trudy*, 1909, vol. III.
—— Vizantya i Pechenegi, *Trudy*, vol. I, St. Petersburg, 1908.
—— Drevnyaya Torgovlya Kieva s Regensburgom (Early trading between Kiev and Regensburg), *Zhurnal Minist. Narodn., Prosv.* 1888, vol. VII.
Vernadsky, G. Goten und Anten in Südrussland, *Südostdeutsche Forschungen*, vol. III, Leipzig, 1938.
—— *History of Russia (Ancient Russia)*, New Haven, Yale University Press, vol. I, 1943.
—— The Status of the Russian Church during the first half century following Vladimir's Conversion, *The Slavonic and East Eur. Rev.* (1941), vol. XX, (The Slav Year-Book), pp. 295-314.
Voigt, H. G. Der Verfasser der Römischen Vita S. Adalberti, *Sitzungsber. d. Böhm. Gesellsch. d. Wissenschaften*, 1903.
—— *Adalbert von Prag*, Berlin, 1898.
—— *Brun von Querfurt, Mönch, Eremit, Erzbischof der Heiden und Märtyrer*, Stuttgar, 1907.
Voigt, K. *Staat und Kirche von Konstantin dem Grossen bis zum Ende der Karolingerzeit*, Stuttgart, 1936.

Wachowski, K. Slowiańszczyzna Zachodnia (Western Slavs), *Studia Hist.* vol. I, Warsaw, 1902.
Waitz, G. *Jahrbücher des Deutschen Reichs unter König Heinrich I*, Berlin, 1863.

Wasmer, M.   *Untersuchungen über die ältesten Wohnsitze der Slaven — Die Iranier in Südruss-land*, vol. I, Leipzig, 1923.
—— *Die Urheimat der Slaven*, Breslau, 1926.
Wattenbach, W.—Holtzmann, R.   *Deutschlands Geschichtsquellen im Mittelalter*, vol. I, Berlin, 1938.
—— Zur Frage der Przemysliden Rundkirchen (Round Churches from the time of the Przemyslides), *Kyrios*, vol. II, 1937.
—— Methodius und die Mährer, *Jahbücher für Geschichte Osteuropas*, vol. II, 1937.
Weingart, M.   Byzantské Kroniky v Literatuře církevněslovanské (Byzantine Chronicles in Slavonic Ecclesiastical Literature), *Publications of the Fac. of Phil. of the University of Bratislava*, 1922-1924.
—— Review of Vajs' and Vašica's Collection of Old Slavonic Literary Records on S. Wences-las and S. Ludmila, *Byzantino-Slavica*, vol. II, 1930.
—— Vznik první české duchovní písně (Origin of the first Czech Religious Hymns), *Byzan-tino-slaviça*, vol. II, 1930.
—— První Česká Cirkevně Slovanská Legenda o sv. Václavu (First Czech Church Slavonic Legend of S. Wenceslas), *Svatovácl. Sborničk*, vol. I, 1934.
—— *Bulhaři a Cařihrad před tisíciletim* (Bulgars and Constantinople 1000 years ago), Prague, 1915.
Weingartner, L.   *Vereinigung Burgunds mit dem Deutschen Reiche unter Konrad II*, Brüun, 1880

Westberg, F.   Ibrahim-ibn-Ja'kubs Reisebericht über die Slavenlände, *Memoires de l'Acad. Impér. des Sc.*, St. Petersburg, 1899.
—— Zur Wanderung der Langobarden, *Memoirs of the St. Petersburg Imp. Acad. of Sciences, VIIIth Series, Hist. Phil. Cl.*, (1904), vol. VI, No. 5.
Widajewicz, J.   Poważe w dokumencie biskupstwa praskiego z r 1086 (The region of the Vag in the documents of the diocese of Prague), *Pozn. Tow. Przyj. Nauk, Historical Commission*, tome XI, No. 4, 1938.
—— Licicaviki Widukinda (The Licicaviki in Widukind's Chronicle), *Slavia Occident.*, vol. VI, Poznan, 1927.
Widajewicz, J., Wichmann.   *Poznańskie Towarzystwo Przyjaciol Nauk* (Society of the Friends of Science in Poznań), *Histor. Commission*, Poznań, 1933.
Wienecke, E.   Untersuchungen zur Religion der Westslaven, *Forschungen zur Vor-und Frühgeschichte*, Heft 1, Leipzig, 1940.
Wilman, R.   *Jahrbücher des Deutschen Reiches unter der Herrschaft Ottos III*, Berlin, 1840.

Wilson, C. W.   Pilgrimage of the Russian Abbot Daniel in the Holy Land, 1106-1107, London, 1888.   *The Library of the Palestine Pilgrim's Text Soc.* vol. IV.
Winterswyl, L. A.   *Otto der Grosse und das Erste Reich der Deutschen*, Berlin, 1937.
Wojciechowski, T.   *Szkice Historyczne IX. wieku* (Historical Sketches bearing on the IXth century).   ed. St. Zakrzewski, Warszawa, 1925.
Wojciechowski, Z.   Mieszko and the Rise of the Polish State, Toruń-Gdynia-London, 1936. *Baltic Pocket Library.*
—— The Territorial Development of Pomerania, *Baltic Pocket Library*, London, 1936.
—— *Ustrój polit. ziem Polskich w czasach przedpiastowskich* (Political Organisation of Polish Lands in the days preceding the Rise of the Piast Dynasty), Lwów, 1927.
Woodruff, D.   *Charlemagne*, London, 1934.

Zakrzewski, S.   Opactwo św. Aleksego i Bonifacego na Awentynie (The Abbey of S. Boniface and Alexius on the Aventine), *Rozprawy of the Polish Acad. Hist. Cl.* v. 43.
—— *Boleslaw Chrobry Wielki*(Boleslas the Brave, the Great), Lwów-Kraków, 1925.
—— Geograf Bawarski, The Bavarian Geographer, *Archiwum Naukowe*, Lwów, 1917.
—— Najdawniejsza Bulla dla Polski (The Oldest Bull concerning Poland), *Archiwum Nau-kowe*, Lwów, 1921.
—— *Mieszko I jako budowniczy państwa Polskiego* (Mieszko I, Builder of the Polish State), Warszawa, 1921.
—— Zródla i Literatura o czasach Chrobrego (Sources and Literature about the Times of Boleslas the Great), *Kwart. Hist.* vol. 39, 1925.
—— Vychodni Hranice Privilegia Pražskeho (The Eastern Boundaries of the Prague " Privi-legium "), *Sbornik Bidluv*, Prague, 1928.
Zeisberg, H.   Otto III und Boleslaw I von Polen, *Zeitschr. für die Oesterr. Gymnasien*,vol. XVIII, 1867.
—— Die Oeffentliche Meinung im XI. Jh. über Deutschlands Politik gegen Polen, *Zeitschrift für Oesterr. Gymnasien*, 1868, vol. XIX, pp. 83-100.
—— Misecoll Polnischer Christlicher Beherrscher, *Sitzungsber. d. Ak. Hist. Phil. Kl.* Wien, 1867.
Zibert.   *Bibliografie Česke Historie* (Bibilography of Czech History), Prague, 1902.

Zlatarski, V. N.   Die Besiedelung der Balkanhalbinsel durch die Slaven, *Revue Intern. des Et. Balkaniques* (1936), vol. II.

Zupanic, N.   Harimati, studija k problemu prvobitnih Hravatov (The Harimati, a study on the problem of the primitive Croats), *Etnolog*, vol. I, 1926-1927.

—— Znacenje nekih starih geogr. i etnickih imena (The significance of some old geographical and ethnical names in the Balkan Peninsula), *Etnolog*, vol. V, 1933.

—— Prvi nosilci etn. imen Srb, Hrvat, Ceh in Ant (The first bearers of the names—Serb, Croat, Czech and Antes), *Etnolog*, vol. II, 1928.

—— The Serb Settlement in the Macedonian Town of Srbciste in the VIIth century.   The ethnological and social implications of Constantine Porphyrogenetus' account of the Serbs and the Croats, *Etnolog*, vol. II, 1928.

—— Bela Srbija (White Serbia), *Narodna Ltarina*, vol. I, 1922.

—— Dobrovskega naziranje o Sporih in poznejsa mislenja o hjinl (Dobrovsky's opinion on the Spori and later ideas about them), *Sbornik J. Dobrovsky*, Praha, 1929.

—— Der Anten Ursprung und Name, *Actes du IIIe Congrèss International des Etudes Byzantines*, Athens, 1932.

—— Reka Erak (The Erak River), *Etnolog*, vol. IV, 1930.

—— Srbi Plinija i Ptolemeja (The Serbs of Pliny and Ptolemy), *Zbornick J. Cviji*, Belgrad, 1924.

—— Prvobitni Hrvati (The Primitive Croats), *Zbornik Tomislava, Opera Acad. Scient Slavorum Meridionalium*, I, XVII, Zagreb, 1925.

—— Zngoenfa Carevnega atributa v imenu " Crvena Hrvatska " (The Meaning of the Colour Attribute in the name " Red Croatia "), *Etnolog*, vol. XI, Ljubljana, 1938, pp.355-376.

336

Book of Ceremony, *see* Constantine Porphyrogennetos.
— — Degrees, 173, 175.
Boris and Gleb, SS, brothers of Svyatopolk, 176, 216, 217, 247.
— biographers of, ·178, 238 ; Life of, " *Chtenie*," 176.
Boris, Michael, Bulgarian Khagan, 16.
Borzivoy, Duke of Bohemia, 21, 98.
Bosporan, kingdom, 281.
Bosphorus, (=Byzantium), 1, 42, 65, 149, 270.
Bossuta, Polish Archbishop, 198.
Botulf S., Abbot of Ikanhoe, 243, 244.
Boz, King of the Antes, 281.
Bozena, legend of, 205.
Brackman, A., German historian, 49.
Bralin on the Spree, *see* Berlin.
Brandenburg, 28, 85 ; Diocese of, 51, 73 ; Bishop of, 206 ; March of, 262, 264, 266.
Bratislava, 206.
Brenner Pass, 37.
Breslau, 234 ; diocese of (Vratislava), 142.
Brezalauspurc, 206.
Britain, 11.
British Isles, 171.
Brno, 2.
Brodek, (=Furtel), S. Wenceslas' church in, 232.
Bruckner, A., historian, 274.
Brunabar, capital of the Havelians, 28.
Bruno, Bishop of Augsburg, 195, 201, 202.
Bruno, son of Duke of Carynthia, 121.
— of Querfurt, missionary monk and biographer of S. Adalbert, 133, 134, 161, 163, 196-203, 228 ; Mission to Sweden, 213 ; mission to Kiev, 201, 216 ; martyrdom, 134, 212, 214 ; letter to Henry II, 182, 202-204 ; " *Passio S. Adalberti*," 25, 100, 102, 112, 114, 115, 117, 124, 152, 155, 160-163, 165, 182 ; " *Life of the Five Brothers*," 197, 200, 211.
Brunswick, 14.
Brzetislav, Odalrich's son, 214, 220-222, 226-234.
Brzevnov, Benedictine Abbey at, 113, 162-164.
Buda town, 263.
Budech, Latin school at, 125.
Budyshin, (=Bautzen) Peace Treaty at, (in 1018), 208, 214, 216.
Bug, river, as boundary of Slav settlements, 12, 13, 53, 60 ; as a frontier of the Moravian Empire, 18, 292 ; as frontier of White Crotia, 286 ; as boundary of the Diocese of Prague, 78, 81, 89 ; as a trade route between the Baltic and the Black Sea, 277 ; tribes living along, 282 ; Vladimir's conquests towards, 92.
Buga, White Crotian princess, 268.
Buislaw (=Boleslas I of Bohemia), 80.
Bulgaria, 3, 15, 214, 242, 252 ; contact with Frankish empire, 1, 16 ; conflict with Byzantium, 6. 16, 113, 282 ; conflict with Kievan Russia, 89, 90 ; Slavonic liturgy in, 173 et seq., 236, 241, 242.
Bulgarian, autonomy of —church, 176, 177 ; —manuscripts, 236, 242 ; —origin of the Croats, 273 ; Bulgarian Patriarchate of Ochrida, 170, 174, 175, 177 ;

refugees in Kiev, 173, 236, 246 ; —Slavs, 214 ; —State in Southern Russia 89, 90, 149, 284.
Bulgarians (Bulgars), the, Danubian —5, 17, 19, 80, 83, 89, 90, 173, 256, 275, 281, 282, 288, 291 ; Volga —5, 61, 63, 89, 90, 169, 259, 283.
Burchard, Duke of Saxony, 23.
— II. Duke of Suabia, 23, 24, 31.
— Bishop of Worms, 219
Burdach, K., German historian, 49.
Burgundiab, land, of, 206.
Burgundian kingdom, 227.
Burgundians, the, 1, 47, 281, 284.
Burgundy, 4, 24, 35, 39, 47, 314.
Burgwarde system, 26, 33, 129.
Businc in Moravia, 206.
Butzu, Magyar dignitary, 150.
Buzhanians, the, 258, 282.
Byzantine Church, 149, 176, 177, 236, 255 ; —civilisation, 21, 124, 125, 170, 237, 239, 240, 253, 256, 259 ; historians, 279 et seq. ; missionaries, 4, 17, 18.
Byzantines, the, 7, 15, 38, 45, 65, 90, 136, 150, 171, 174, 202, 237.
Byzantium, — *passim*.
Bzanec, 206.

Cachin tribe, (=Czechs), 271.
Calabria, battle of in 982, 7, 85, 136.
Calendar of the Russian Orthodox Church, 244.
Calocza, Archbishopric of, 166.
Canalitans, the, 291.
Canaparius, S. Adalbert's biographer, 100, 102, 104, 105, 112, 114, 120, 121, 123, 133, 134, 165.
Canute the Great, 213, 220, 225, 226.
— S., 243, 284.
Capet Hugh, 24.
Carenthania, 291.
Carinthia, 289, 290.
Carlellieri A., German historian, 49.
Carloman, 303.
Carolingian Dynasty, 5, 22, 23, 24, 34, 41, 46 ; empire, 33, 136, 149, 241.
Casimir the Great, King of Poland, 259, 264.
Casimir the Renovator, 227, 228, 234, 235, 254.
Catalonia, 138.
Caucasians the, 276.
Cecilia S. (=Kalikyia), 244.
Cedrenus, Byzantine chronicler, 68.
Celestine S., 244.
Celtic tribes, *see* Boii, Celts, Gauls.
Celts, the, 13.
Charlemagne, his revival of Western Christian Empire, 1-7, 16, 27, 231, 232, 262, 291, 293 ; destroys Avar Empire, 17, 294 ; converts Bavaria, 20 ; tradition of, 31-35, 49, 122, 123, 136, 139, 140, 158, 181-183, 203 ; political theories of, 3, 39, 41-47, 140, 145, 147, 188.
Charles III, King of West Francia, 23, 24, 39.
— IV, of Bohemia, 264.
Chernigov, 258, 259.
Cherven, *see* Czerwien.

Frankish Chronicles, 20, 291, 292.
— Church, 128.
— Culture, 16.
— Empire, 2 et seq., 16 et seq., 28 ; disintegration of, 22, 42.
— Nobility, 45.
— tradition, 22, 23.
Franks, the, expansion of, 1 et seq., 11, 16 et seq. ; penetration into South-Eastern Europe, 16, 17, 93, 128, 292, 296 ; influenced by Roman tradition, 42 et seq., 257 ; conflict with White Serbia, 287, 291 ; relations with Slavs, 296, 298, 302.
Fredegar, Frankish historian, 284, 285, 287, 291.
Frederick II, of Germany, 260.
— Archbishop of Mainz, 33, 34, 36, 37.
French culture, 2.
Frisia, 23.
Frisians, the, 24.
Fritzlar, election at (in 918), 23.
Friuli, 1.
Fulda, Slavonic settlements in, 14 ; Abbot of, 50 ; Annals of, see Annales.
Furtel, see Brodek.

Gaihani, Arabian traveller and writer, 201.
Galicia, 258-260, 265, 277, 286, 298 ; Eastern—91, 285, 303 ; Western—285, 303 ; origin of name, 258.
Gallen St., 244.
Gallus Anonymus, Polish chronicler, 52, 71, 131, 142, 198, 214, 247, 249, 253.
Gardisi, Arab writer, 271.
Gaudentius, see Radim-Gaudentius.
Gaul, 1, 11, 20, 45, 139, 180, 183, 284.
Gauls, the, 314.
Gaushof, F. L., German historian, 49.
Gdansk, see Dantzig.
Gebhard, Bishop of Prague, 77-79.
Geiza (Geyza), S. Stephen's father, 149, 150, 152, 155, 159, 162, 164.
Gelasius, Pope, 141, 189.
Genghis Khan, 260.
George Podiebrady, 265.
George the Monk, chronicler, 237.
George, Metropolitan of Kiev, 176, 178, 179.
Georgia, 259.
Gerard, Bishop of Toul, 101, 127.
Gerbert of Aurillac, see Sylvester II, Pope.
Germanic tribes, see Angles, Anglo-Saxons, Bavarians, Burgundians, Danes, Franks, Frisians, Goths, Heruls, Lango-bards (Lombards), Lotharingians, Mar-comans, Norsemen (Nordic tribes), Ostrogoths, Rugii, Quades, Saxons, Scandinavians, Suabians, Swedes, Thuringians, Vandals and Vikings.
Germanicus of S. Spas, Abbot, 179.
Germans, the, passim.
Germany, passim.
Gesenke Forest (Jeseniky Yosurfjoll), 284.
Giecz, 229.
Gierke, O. von, German historian, 49.
Giesebrecht, W. von, German historian, 49.
Giselbert, son of Reginar of Frisia, 24.
Giseler, Archbishop of Magdeburg, 186.

Glagolitic alphabet (" Glagolitsa "), 17, 252, 312.
— Fragments of Kiev, 246, 247, 250.
— Fragments of Vienna, 247.
Glatz, county of, see Kladsko.
Godard S., 248.
Godehard S., biographer of, 200.
Godwine's expedition to Denmark, 225, 226.
Gog, ruler of Magog, 305-307.
Golden Horde, see Kipchak.
Gostomysl, Obodrite prince, 245.
Goswin, Canon of Mainz, 243.
Gotha, Slavonic remnants on the site of, 14.
Goths, the, in Spain, 1, 3, 7, 47 ; migrate from Scandinavia to the Black Sea, 63, 64, 130, 277, 279 ; Empire of 265, 281 ; conflict with the Huns, 273, 274, 285.
Gnesen (=Gniezno), 8, 53 ; S. Adalbert's stay in, 124 ; grave of S. Adalbert in, 131, 133 ; Otto III's visit to, 142-145, 148 ; captured by Brzetislav, 228-230 ; crowning of Wenceslas II in, 263 ; controversy over Gnesen-Schinesne, 318 ; Archbishopric of, 144, 147, 165, 198, 200, 228.
Graeco-Byzantine culture, 18, 237.
Graeco-Roman civilisation, 128, 183, 236.
Graeco-Slavonic culture and literature, 7, 18, 21, 71, 97, 103, 126, 127, 166, 251, 252, 256 ; see also Greek tradition and influence.
Gran, see Esztergom.
Granum Catalogi praesulum Moraviae, 99.
Greece, 104, 168, 239, 287.
Greek Cities in Russia, 277 ; Holy Fathers, 238 ; missionaries, 67, 128, 250 ; Greek and Russian ecclesiastical Rule, 238 ; tradition and influence, 171, 177, 183, 218, 233, 239.
Greeks, the, 12, 89, 128, 169, 170, 172, 177, 253.
Gregoire, H., 274, 288.
Gregory V, Pope, 121.
— VII, Pope, 103, 126, 156-158.
— the Great's sermons in Slavonic liturgy, 245, 246.
— of Tours, S., 44.
Grunwald, battle of (in 1410), 265.
Gumpold, Bishop of Mantua, 126.
— author of Latin Legend of S. Wen-ceslas, 246.
Guncelin, 190.
Gunhild, Canute's daughter, 220.
Gunter, H., German historian, 49.
Gunther, German hermit, 199, 200, 220, 226.
Gylas, ruler of East Hungary, 150, 221.
Gytha, wife of Vladimir Monomakh, 254.

Habsburg, dynasty, 266.
Hadrian I, Pope, 43.
Hadrian II, Pope, 17.
Hahn, L., German historian, 49.
Halberstadt, diocese of, 59, 79.
Halicz, town in Galicia, 258, 259.
Haller, J., German historian, 49.

Ivan, S., hermit of Bohemia, 245.
Ivan the Terrible, Tzar of Russia, 267.
Iwein, see Unwanus.

Jacob, monk, panegyrist of S. Vladimir, 67, 68, 172, 178, 238 ; " Skazanie," 176.
Jadwiga (Hedvig) of Anjou, Queen of Poland, 264.
Jagello, Grand Duke of Lithuania, King of Poland, 264, 465.
Jagellon Dynasty, 265, 266, 281.
Jagic, V., 274.
Jahna (=Meissen), capital of the Sorabs, 28.
Jaromir, brother of Boleslas III of Bohemia, 192-196, 204, 205, 226.
Jerome, S., 306, 309.
Jerusalem, 103, 104, 175, 237.
Jews, the, 62, 81, 105, 106, 169.
John VIII, Pope, 17.
— IX, Pope, 22, 150.
— XII, Pope, 41, 60, 73.
— XIII, Pope, 73 et seq.
— XIV, Pope, 174.
— XV, Pope, 102, 110, 111, 174, 175, 315.
— Sobieski, King of Poland, 266.
— the Baptist, 246.
— S. Chrysostom, 238.
— II, Metropolitan of Kiev, 176-178, 238.
— Tzimisces, 89, 90.
— of the Mangled Fingers, 140, 141.
— the Usurper, 305, 306.
— missionary brother, 200 : see also Bruno's Life of the five Brothers.
Jordan, First Polish Bishop of Poznan, 72-74.
Jordanes, 279-281, 306, 310.
Josurfjöll (Jeseniky), see Gesenke Forest.
Jrvab (Jravt, Khurdab), Slavonic capital, 271, 272.
Judaism, Khazars converted to, 169.
Judith, wife of Brzetislav, 220, 221.
Justinian, 1.

Kalikyia (Cecilia) S., 244.
Kalokyres, Nicophorus' ambassador, 89.
Kama river, 61.
Kazenz, see Kosentzes.
Kehr, P., chronicler, 148.
Kelagast, 282.
Kernaka, see Organa, 288.
Khagan, Bulgarian, 15, 16 ; of the Khazars, 62, 63, 169 ; of the Avars, 282.
Khazaria, 62, 63, 169.
Khazars, the, 5, 60, 61-66, 149, 169, 201, 202, 271, 273, 305, 311-313.
Kherson, 171-173, 175, 177, 178.
Khoruntanians, the, 301.
Khurdab, see Jrvab.
Kiev, 5, 6, 8, 60 ; occupied by Norsemen, 64 et seq., 81, 88 et seq., 130 ; Christian penetration to, 167 et seq., 202, 210, 213 ; occupied by Boleslas the Great, 216, 317 ; cultural importance of, 236-261 ; incorporated into Poland, 265 ; competes with Poland for Galicia, 298 et seq., 318 ; Metropolis of, 66, 178 ; transferred to Moscow, 265 ; see also Ukrainians.

Kipchak (Empire of the Golden Horde), 260.
Kladsko (Glatz), county of, 92, 108.
Klukas, 268.
Koenig, E., 307.
Kolberg (Kolobrzeg), bishopric of, 142.
Konigsberg, 131, 132.
Koros river, 201.
Kosentzes (Kazenz), Croatian chieftain 268, 289, 290.
Kotzilis, Frankish prince, 269.
Krivichians, the, 13, 280, 298.
Kumans, the, 258, 260.
Kunigunde, Henry II's wife, 218.
Kunegunde, daughter of Otto, Margrave of Meissen, Igor's wife, 254.
Kurt, Bulgarian ruler mentioned in the Immenik, 288.
Kurzim, prince of, 93.
Kutroguri, tribe of, 284.
Kuver, Avar governor in Pannonia, 288, 289.
Kuvratos, Bulgarian Khagan, 273, 287-289.
Kuyavians (=Mazovians), 212.

Ladislas the Bald, of Hungary, 253.
— the Short, King of Poland, 264.
Ladoga Lake, 62, 63.
Lambert(us), see Mieszko II.
Lampertus, Bishop of Cracow, 251.
Langobardorum Origo Gentis, 284.
Langobards, the, 284, 285 ; see also Lombards.
Latin, culture, 2 ; —rite, 4, 250, 251 traditions, 233, 257, 258 ; Latin Legends of S. Wenceslas, see Christian Strakhvas and Gumpold ; Latin school at Budech, see Budech ; also see under: Roman.
Latvian lands, 265 ; tribes, 129, 130.
Laurentius, Monk of Monte Cassino, 104.
Lausitz, see Lusatia.
Lebusa, Battle of (in 932), 30.
Lechfeld, battle of (in 955), 5, 37, 39, 51 69, 71, 88, 93, 107, 149, 222, 252.
Lemusians, the, 92.
Lenzen, battle of (in 929), 30.
Leo, S., cult of in Kievan Russia, 243, 244.
— III, Pope, 1, 42, 43, 45.
— IX, Pope, 127.
— III (Isauricus), Iconoclast Emperor, 43.
— VI, Byzantine Emperor, 66.
— Abbot of Rome, 104, 105.
— of Vercelli, Bishop, 140, 142.
Leszek, legendary ancestor of Mieszko I, 52.
Levy Hradec, first church in Bohemia, 21, 98.
Libice, residence of the Slavnik Dukes, 95, 97, 112, 116 et seq., 162, 264.
Libutius, Bishop of Mainz, 69.
Licikaviki (=Poles), 54, 55.
Lignica (Lignitz), battle of (in 1241), 260.
Linus S., Pope, 243.
Lithuania, 264, 265.
Lithuanians, the, 129, 130, 265.
Liudolf, Duke of Suabia, Otto I's son, 35, 37, 41.
Liutici, see Veletians.
Liutpold, Duke of Bavaria, 23.

Liutprand, Bishop of Cremona, chronicler, 35.

Lobelos, Croatian chieftain, 268.

" Logothet of the Dromos," Archives of, 268.

Lombards, the, 1, 7, 47, 314 ; *see also* Langobards.

Lombardy, 1, 6, 7, 23, 31 et seq.

Lorraine, 127.

Lothar, Son of Hugh of Lombardy, 35, 36.

Lotharingia, 23, 33, 35.

Lotharingians, the, 22, 23.

Louis the Pious, Frankish Emperor, 45, 63.
— II, Frankish Emperor, 45.
— the German, 4, 17, 292, 303.
— the Child, 19, 22.
— IV, King of France, 32, 34, 35.
— of Anjou, Hungarian King of Poland, 264.
— Jagellon, King of Bohemia, 265, 266.
— of Burgundy, 39.

Lovat river, 66, 281.

Lublin Union, (in 1569), 265.

Lubush district, 264.

Lucas and Elias, Bishops of Novgorod, 238.

Luchanians, the, 258, 282.

Lucy S., 244.

Ludmila S, Borzyvoy's wife, 7, 21, 25 ; cult of, 242, 248.

Lusatia (Lausitz, Lusace), 190, 204, 208, 223, 264, 284, 294

Lusatian culture, 12.

Lusatians, the, 14, 55, 56.

Lutta river, 310.

Luxemburg dynasty, 264, 266.

Lwow, 260.

Lyakhs (=Poles), 90, 307.

Madeconian dialect, influence on Old Slavonic scriptures, 238.

Magak, King of the Valinians, 238.

Magdeburg, 14, 95 ; Archbishopric of, 6, 59, 60, 70, 72 et. seq., 95 et seq., 127, 148, 182, 197, 199, 201, 228 ; Benedictine Abbey and School, 95, 100, 242 ; jurisdiction of, 60, 72, 73, 75, 147

Magnus S., 243.

Magog, land of, 307, 309.

Magri town, 194.

Magyars, the, 4 et seq. ; invasion of, 21, 26, 28 et seq. ; defeated in the battle of Lechfeld, *see* Lechweld, 64 ; converted to Christianity, 148 et seq., 249 ; cut contact between West Europe and Byzantium, 183, 184, 247 — driven West by the Pechenegs, 201, 202, 311 ; infiltrate from the Danube towards the Carpathian Mountains, 214, 221 ; break up the Moravian Empire, 234, 241, 242, 257, 297, 299, 303 ; relations with the Croats (White Croatia), 268, 269, 302, 304 ; *see also* Onogeurs, Ostyaks, Ukeri, Voguls.

Mainz, 44, 77, 121-123, 163, 244 ; coronation rite of—, 46 ; Reichstag in (in 1085), 77 ; Archbishop of, 37, 101, 102, 232 ; Archbishopric of—, 49, 82, 113, 151.

Malmfrid, daughter of Monomach, 254.

Mammas S, Church of—in Constantinople, 67.

Manchu tribes, 282.

Marchfeld, battle of (in 1278), 263.

Marcomans, the, 14, 20.

Marcus Aurelius, 2.

Marianus S, Abbot of Regensburg, *Life of*, 248.

Margaret S, Cult of in Kievan Russia, 244.

Marquart, 302.

Martin S., of Tours, 243, 244 ; grave of, 123 ; Abbey of in Gran, 159-164.

Martina S, cult in Kievan Russia, 244.

Marvan Kalif, 311.

Mary S, Church of in Cracow, *see* Felicitas and Adauctus SS.
— Monastery of in the Slavonic Province, 163-165.
— daughter of Vladimir, 254.

Maslav of Mazovia, 234.

Massagetes, *see* Misoch.

Ma'sudi, Arab chronicler, 270, 271, 273, 283, 291, 300-302.

Mathilda, Duchess of Lotharingia, 218, 253.

Matilda, second wife of Henry I, 32.

Matthaeus, missionary brother, 200 ; *see also* Bruno's *Life of the five Brothers*.

Mauritius S, Abbey of, 60 ; Spear of, 146, 203.

Maurus S, grave of, 123.
— of Pecz, Bishop, 151.

Maxim S, Abbey of — in Trier, 60.

Mayolus, Abbot of Cluny, 101, 127.

Mazovia, 234.

Mazovians (Kuyavians), the, 53, 212.

Mazurians Lakes, 130.

Mecklenburg-Schwerin, 28, 208.

Meillet A., 275.

Meissen, 28, 86, 92, 99, 190, 208, 264; Diocese of, 73, 74 ; *see also* Jahna.

Merians, the, 298.

Merseburg, 33, 52, 155, 190, 191, 197; Diocese of, 73, 74, 207.

Meseritz (Międzyrzecz), 124, 161, 196 Abbey of, 163.

Meshech, *see* Misoch.

Mesheqqod (=Mieszko), 80.

Mesia, 151, *see* Moesia.

Methodius S, *see* Cyril and Methodius SS; disciples of—, 128, 241 et seq. ; Legend of, 21, 150, 242, 246, 292.

Mezamir, 282.

Michael S, Church of in Kiev, 239.
— I, Byzantine Emperor, 42.
— III, Byzantine Emperor, 17, 65.
— Bishop of Regensburg, 79, 80.
— Michael of Gurgen, Russian Bishop, 178.

Międzyrzecz, *see* Meseritz.

Mieszko I (Mesheqqod, Missica), Duke of Poland—ancestors of, 6, 16, 52, 88 ; unites Polish tribes into a Central European State, 8, 16, 51, 119, 209, 235, 257, 304 ; first clash with German Empire over Pomerania, 6, 51-54 ; introduces Christianity into Poland, 6, 7, 70-72 ; founds the Bishopric of Posen, 72, 74, 144 ; organises a regular standing army, 52, 131, 290 ; pays tribute to Emperor Otto for lands between the Baltic and the river Warta, 54-59, 74 ; co-operates with the Germans

in fighting against the Veletians, 55-59, 87, 204 ; marries Dubravka daughter of Boleslas I of Bohemia, 70-72 ; relations with Bohemia, 70 et seq., 85-87, 92 ; war with Bohemia over Cracow, 106-110, 193; attends the Reichstag of Quedlinburg, 83, 87; backs Bavarian revolt against Otto II, 84, 86 ; relations with Danes and Scandinavians, 87, 88, 213 ; sends embassy to Rome, 74-77, 144 ; offers Poland to the Holy See of Rome, *see Dagome Iudex* document ; relations with Russia, 88 et seq., 259, 300 ; death of, 112, 299.
— II (Lambertus), 205, 206, 218 et seq., 235, 253, 254.
Miliduch, Serbian Duke, 291.
Milsko, 190.
Milzi, Sorbian tribe, 196, 316.
Minorsky, V., 271.
Miracula S. Demetrii, 288.
Misoch (Massagetes, Meshech), prince, 305-309.
Missica, *see* Mieszko I.
Mistivoi, Duke of the Obodrites, 86.
Mitislav, Duke of the Obodrites, 208.
Mlada, daughter of Boleslas I, of Bohemia, 75-77, 84.
Moesia, Roman province of, 308.
Mohammed, 5
Mohammedanism, 169 ; *see also* Islam.
Mohammedans (Moslems, Musulmans), the, 3, 15, 81, 169, 260.
Mohra (Mora Alemure) river, 316.
Moimir I, Moravian Duke, 17, 19, 53.
— II, 19, 21, 251, 296.
Moimirs, dynasty 3, 19, 293.
Moldavia, 265.
Molitva na diavola, Russian transcription of a prayer against the Devil, 244.
Mongols, the, invasion of, 171, 239, 259-260, 281, 282.
Monte Cassino, Benedictine Abbey, 104, 113, 197.
Mora, *see* Mohra river.
Morava river, as boundary of the Moravian Empire, 3 ; Valley of—as a trade route, 64 ; Slav settlements in the valley of, 116, 296, 301 ; Czech penetration crosses the, 154, 221 ; Scythian invasion along the, 277.
Moravia (Great Moravia, Moravian Empire), *passim;* dukes of, 4, 17, 19, 21, 53, 293.
Moravian Church, 19, 21, 150, 251 ; diocese, 77, 82, 98, 99, 151, 157 ; Bishop, 81.
Moravians, the, 20, 21, 53, 64, 183, 213, 214, 234, 270, 291, 301.
Moschoi, Scythian tribe, 307.
Moscow, 259, 265.
Moses, S., 252.
Moskva river, 259.
Moslems, *see* Mohammedans.
Mstislav, Duke of Kiev, son of Vladimir Monomakh, 238, 254, 258.
Muchlo, Croatian chieftain, 268.
Mulde river, 33.
Mundzucus, Attila's father, 306.
Munich, Imperial Archives of, 78.

Musokios, Slavonic chieftain, 283.
Musulmans, the, *see* Mohammedans.

Naccon (Nâqûn), Duke of the Obodrites, 80.
Narentanians, the, 291.
Naum, S., S. Methodius' disciple, 126.
Nemsi, *see* Nimpsch.
Neophyt of Chernigov, Russian bishop, 178.
Nereditsa, church in Novgorod, 239.
Nestor, monk of Pechersky Monastir, 176, 238 ; author of *Chtenie*, 176 ; also of the Life of Theodosius Pechersky and of S. Mstislav of Kiev, 238.
— Annals of (Russian Primary Chronicle, Chronicle of Kiev), *see* Annales.
Nicephorus Phocas, Byzantine Emperor, 89.
Nicetas of Belogorod, Russian bishop, 178.
Nicholas, S., church of in Teschen, 250.
Niemen river, 130, 277.
Nikon, chronicler, 167, 168, 173, 175, 179.
Nilus, S., Greek Abbot of Valleluce, 104, 105, 120, 125.
Nimpsch (Nemsi), siege of (in 1017), 207.
Nitra, 2, 17 ; diocese of 128, 151, 153.
Nizhni-Novgorod, 259.
Nogat canal in the Vistula delta, 133.
Nord-Thüringen, 57.
Norman invasion, 3, 22.
Normandy, Duchy of, 35.
Norsemen, the, 5, 22, 52, 60 et seq. ; *see also* Scandinavians and Vikings.
Norway, 171, 220, 225, 243.
Notec river, 54, 59.
Notkerius of Liege, 121.
Novgorod (Novgorod-Pskov), 5, 61 et seq., 88, 90, 130, 170, 172, 217, 239, 240, 258-260, 280, 281.

Obodrites, the, 14, 28, 30, 33, 47, 51, 56, 82, 208.
Ochrida, *see* Bulgarian Patriarchat.
Octar, Attila's uncle, 306.
Oda, fourth wife of Boleslas the Great, 218.
— (Ote), second wife of Mieszko I, 85, 107, 224, 315, 316.
— Svyatoslav's wife, 254.
Odalrich (Udalrich), Bohemian Duke, 192-195, 204-206, 220 et seq.
Oder river, German expansion towards the, 5, 30, 51, 55-57, 262 ; Polish expansion over and to the mouth of the, 8, 55-58, 70, 76, 88 ; Slavonic settlements along the, 12, 54, 85, 86, 118, 210, 235 ; as a frontier of Poland, 16, 53-59, 74, 316, 318 ; Germanic tribes in the neighbourhood of the, 13 ; Nordic settlements at the mouth of the, 52, 88, 226 ; Sarmatian penetration reaches the, 285.
Odoacer, 284.
Oka river, 61, 259.
Olaf, S., 243.
— Tryggvason, 171.
— Skotkonung of Sweden, 213.
Oldenburg, bishop of, 208 ; diocese of, 51

Oleg of Novgorod, Igor's father, 66, 298-300, 302.
— Svyatoslav's son, 90.
Olga (Helen, Helga), wife of Igor, 67-69, 89-91, 172.
Olomouc, 264.
Olympus Mount, 287.
Onogours, the, 149.
Organa, (Ernik, Irnik, Kernaka), Bulgarian chieftain, 287, 288.
Orosius' *History of the World*, 272.
Ossentians, the, 310.
Ostmark (Austria), 92, 93, 222, 233, 303.
Ostrogoths, the, 281.
Ostyaks, the, 149.
Ota, *see* Oda Mieszko's wife.
Othlo's " *Collection of Visions*," 233.
Othlon (Othloh), biographer of S. Wolfgang, 77, 79, 82, 150.
Othloh of S. Emmeran in Regensburg, author of the Life of SS Columban and Gall, 243.
Otrik, Rector of Magdeburg Episcopal school, 95, 97.
Otto I, Roman Emperor of the German Nation,—revives Charlemagne's Empire 6, 32, 33, 39 et seq., 123, 136 et seq., 181 et seq., 268, 302 ; crushes the Magyars, 5, 37, 51, 71, 88, 149, 241, 291 ; conquests and plan for converting Slavonic lands, 6, 7, 47 et seq., 59, 60, 86, 95, 129, 138, 158, 199 ; relations with Poland, 7, 54 et seq., 70, 71 ; receives tribute from Mieszko I, 54-59, 74 ; relations with Bohemia, 29, 33 et seq., 71 et seq., 89, 94, 98 ; expedition to Italy, 35, 36, 41, 57, 77, 136 ; intervention in France, 35, 36 ; relations with Papacy, 35, 36, 39 et seq., 72 et seq. ; grants the *Privilegium Ottonianum* to Pope John XIII, 41, 188 ; coronation in Rome, 41 ; holds Reichstag at Quedlinburg in 973, 80, 83, 91, 167 ; interior policy towards other German dukes, 34 et seq., 83 ; relations with Russia, 60, 68-70, 91, 95, 167, 179.
— II, German Emperor, — interventions in Italy, 7, 85, 120, 167 ; relations with Bohemia, 79, 82, 99, 101 ; relations with Bavaria, 81 et seq. ; sends mission to Russia, 168, 179, 183 ; death in Calabria, 7, 85, 86, 136, 138, 147.
— III, German Emperor, — his conception of a Christian Empire, 8, 122, 123, 136 et seq., 180 et seq., 197 et seq., 209 et seq., 262 ; *Renovatio Imperii Romanorum*, 8, 123, 139, 143-145, 179, 180, 182, 184, 185, 187, 189, 252 ; election of, 86 ; struggle with the Veletians, 85 ; Alliance with Mieszko I, 87, 109 ; relations with Bavaria, 99 ; alliance with Boleslas the Great, 115, 142 et seq., 190-191, 199 ; pilgrimage to Gnesen, 142-145, 148 ; friendship with S. Adalbert, 8, 120 et seq., 133, 135, 142, 181, 242 ; visits to Rome, 120, 121, 174 ; relations with Pope Sylvester II, 8, 120, 138, 140-143, 180, 188, 189, 197, 199, 212 ; relations with Hungary, 149 et seq. ; relations with Russia, 169, 179 ;

friendship with Bruno of Querfurt, 197, 198 ; death of and its consequences, 183, 184, 198 ; Otto's ideals forfeited by Henry II, 185 et seq., 202, 209 et seq.
— of Saxony, 22.
— of Schweinfurt, Duke of Suabia, 220.
— Mieszko II's brother, 224, 226.
— Margrave of Meissen, 254.
Ottoman Turks, 265.
Ottonian Renaissance, 122, 183.

Pannonia, 2, 3, 14, 17, 19, 79, 128, 149, 151-153, 158, 269, 272, 282, 286, 288, 289.
Papacy, *see* Holy See, *also* Rome.
Paris, 35, 156.
Passau, Bishopric of, 151.
Passio S. Adalberti Martyris, by anonymous author, 124, 131, 132, 163.
Patzianks, *see* Pechenegs.
Paul, Archbishop, incumbent of Kherson, 178.
Paulus Diaconús, Langobardian chronicler, 284, 285.
Pavia, 36, 101, 187.
Pechenegs, the, 4, 89, 90, 201, 202, 216, 217, 258, 269-271, 298, 311.
Pechersky Paterik, *see* Chronicles.
Peene river, 33.
Pelasgians, the, 275.
Pereum Monastery near Ravenna, 197, 199.
Pereyaslav, 90, 258.
Persian Geographer, 271, 272.
Persians, the, 15, 286, 311.
Perun, Slavonic deity, 173.
Peter Damian S, 197, 212 ; — 's biography of St. Romuald, 199.
Peter and Paul SS, 246.
— Stephen's successor in Hungary, 233, 234.
— of Pereyaslav, Russian bishop, 178.
Pezinek, *see* Pozsony.
Philagatos, Anti-Pope, 211.
Photius, Byzantine Patriarch, 65, 176, 255.
Photius' Council (in 879-880), 178.
Piast, legendary founder of the Piast dynasty, 52.
— dynasty, 19, 52, 53, 92, 94, 107, 108, 111, 116, 118, 119, 131, 204, 224, 234, 235, 263, 264-266.
Pilgrim, Bishop of Passau, 150, 151, 156, 251.
Pilsen, 113.
Pippin, Charlemagne's father, 41, 183, 245.
— II, 146, 231.
Plato, 183, 238.
Pliny the Elder, 14, 279, 280.
Po river, 31.
Pogodin A., 274.
Polabians (Elbe Slavs), the, 52, 85, 115, 129, 138, 145, 147, 181, 223.
Poland, *passim*.
Polanians, the, 53.
Poles, the, (Lyakhs, Licikaviki) *passim*.
Polianians, the, 13, 298.
Polish, — annals, *see* Gallus.
Pomerania, 54 et seq., 83 et seq., 107, 128, 131, 146, 225, 226, 234, 262, 264, 265, 318 ; division into Eastern and Western —, 56 et seq., 147.

M.

Roxolani, the (Rosomani, Rogas, Rukhs-As), 308-312.
Rudolph of Habsburg, 263.
Rudolph II, King of Burgundy, 24, 31, 32, 35.
Rugas (Ruotsi, Ruas), *see* Rhos.
Rugii, tribe — 284 ; — land 303, 304.
Rukhs-As, *see* Roxolani.
Rurik (Roerek), chief of the Norsemen, 62, 65.
Rus, *see* Rhos.
Russia, *passim* ; origin of name : Finnish ? —62, 63, 305 ; Sarmatian ?—305-315.
Russian—Church, 177, 178, 236, 242, 244, 247, 255 ; —Primary Chronicle, (Russian Annals) *see* Annals of Nestor ; —MSS., 243-246 ; —Literature, 237-239 ; —Collection of XII Century, 242 ; " *Russkaya Pravda,*" first Law Collection, 238-255 ; —Slavs, 13, 280.
Russians, the, *passim.*
Ruta river, 272.
Ruthenians the, (Ukrainians), 13, 194, 214.
Ryazan town, 259.

Saale river, 7, 13, 14, 27, 28, 30, 33, 56, 270, 273, 285, 291, 292.
Saewulf, chronicler, 237.
Saint-Basle, Synod at (in 991), 120.
Salian Dynasty, 219.
Salis town, 194.
Sallust, 48.
Salzburg, Archbishop of, 17, 151; diocese of, 82.
Samland, part of Prussia, 131, 132.
Samo the legendary, 15, 288, 291.
San river, 107, 272, 277, 285.
Sandomierz, 53, 88, 107, 272, 304 ; Archbishopric of, 199, 228.
Saqulab (=San river) 272.
Saracens, 7.
Sardinia, 315-317.
Sarmatian tribes, 13, 15, 63, 64, 91, 274, 276-280, 285, 305, 310, 314 ; *see also* : Alanes (Alans), Antes (Anthaibs, Antsai, Ants-as, Assaioi), Belochrobați, Chorvatin, Croats, Hrvat (Horithi), Iasi, Iranians, Milzians, Ossentians, Pelazgians, Persians, Roxolani, Saracens, Scythians, Serbs, (Sorabs, Sorbians, Surbin, Surpe), Spalei (Spali, Spori), Tiberenoi, White Croats, White Serbs, Yazigians ; *also* Appendices I, II and IV, pp. 268, 277, 305.
Sava river, 14, 16, 19, 272, 288.
Saxon Dynasty, 7, 37, 94, 95, 100, 136.
Saxons, the, 2 and seq., 17, 22, 23, 48, 84, 87, 122, 158, 182, 186, 200, 206, 210, 215, 227.
Saxony, 7, 23 et seq., 55, 83, 94, 186, 195, 204, 219, 223, 244.
Sazava, Abbey of, 233, 247.
Scandinavia, 11, 69, 90, 130, 170, 244, 259.
Scandinavians, the, 3, 5, 61, 64, 68, 69, 130, 170, 213, 305, 311-313, 315 ; *see also* Norsemen and Vikings.
Scanza Island, 310.
Schaefer D., German historian, 49.
Schinesne, *see* Stettin.

Schleswig March, 28, 30, 220.
— diocese, 50.
Schneider F., German historian, 49.
Schramm P. E., German historian, 163, 187, 189.
Shrove Tuesday Banquet (in 1003), 193.
Schweinfurt, 220, 221.
Schwerin, *see* Mecklenburg.
Sclaveni (=Slavs), 279.
Sclavinia, 119, 234.
Scotland, 220.
Scots Mission, 20.
Scythia (=Slavonia), 180.
Scythian invasion, 13, 14, 277.
Scythians (Scyths, Iranians), 12-14, 63, 64, 277, 285, 305 et seq.
Selpuli, the, 55.
Semkowicz W., Polish historian, 206.
Serbia (Serblia), 269, 287 ; *see also* White Serbia.
Serbs (Sorabs, Sorbians, Surbin, Surpe), the, 13, 14, 15, 19, 28, 30, 48, 56, 57, 86, 92, 227, 242, 256 ; 268 et seq., 285 et seq. 301, 311 ; non-Slavonic origin of the—, 273 et seq.; migration from Saale-Elbe District to Dalmatia, 269 et seq.; *see also* White Serbs.
Sereth river, 201.
Severians, the, 13, 258, 298, 311.
Seversk town, 258.
Severus, Bishop of Prague, 229, 233.
Sicily, 2, 43, 260.
Siegfried, Apostle of the North, 213.
Sigismund of Luxemburg, son of Charles IV, 264.
Sigrid Storrada (Swientoslawa), daughter of Mieszko I, 88.
Sigurd of Denmark, 254.
Sikko, murderer of S. Adalbert, 133.
Silesia,—as part of White Croatia, 13, 286, 296 ; included in the Moravian Empire, 18, 296 ; as part of Bohemia, 72, 88, 229, 230, 232, 263 ; as property of the Slavnik Dukes, 92, 108 ; included in the diocese of Prague, 78 ; in Polish hands, 107, 192, 193, 234, 318 ; as part of the Antes empire, 284, 285 ; annexed by Prussia, 262 ; Slavonic exodus from, 294 ; in the hands of Kievan Russia, 300, 303.
Silesians, the, 8.
Silistria, Siege of (in 971), 90.
Simargl (Bird-dog Senmuro), a pagan Slav deity, 280.
Simeon, *see* Symeon the Great.
Sirians, the, 308.
Sirmium (Sriem), 272, 288 ; diocese of, 17 ; Archbishop of, 128.
Slavitah, Bohemian chief, 292.
Slavnik Duke, Adalbert's father, 94-97.
Slavniks Dynasty in Bohemia, 21, 25, 92 et seq., 121, 137, 155, 160 et seq., 193, 195, 264, 293.
Slavonia, 50, 180.
Slavonic—dioceses; 59, 64, 68, 69 ; —language, 3, 17, 20, 173 ; —letters, 3, 21, 22, 125-127, 170, 173, 233, 236, 245 et seq., 257 ; —liturgy, 17 et seq., 71, 97, 125-128, 170, 173, 233, 236, 246, 247, 249, 250, 252, 253, 257 ;—liturgy of the

Vladivoj, Czech Duke, 193.
Vladislav Jagello, see Jagello.
Vladislav II, King of Hungary and Bohemia 265.
Vladislav III, King of Poland, 266.
Vltava river, 3, 64, 277.
Voguls, the, 149.
Voight, H. J. biographer of Bruno of Querfurt, 213.
Vojtiekh, see S. Adalbert.
Volga Bulgars, see Bulgars.
Volga river, 5, 15, 61, 69, 89, 90, 201, 259, 281, 283.
Volhynia, 258-260, 265.
Volhynians, the, 258, 282, 283.
Volinians, the, 57.
Voproshchanie of Kirik, 238.
Vracen, Moravian Bishop, 81.
Vratislav, father of S. Wenceslas, 21, 25.
Vratislav Duke, Brzetislav's successor, 77, 233.
Vratislava (Breslau), diocese of, 142.
Vrshovici family, 113-117, 192, 193.
Vsevolod, Yaroslav's son, 254, 258.
Vyatichians (Viatichians), the, 13, **169**, 258, 280, 283, 298,
Vyshehrad, castle of, 193, 195.

Wagiri, the, 14, 33, 47, 51.
Waic, (=Stephen I), 157.
Waitz G., German historian, 49.
Warta river, 5, 53, 54, 55, 59, 74.
Wawel Castle, 250.
Wenceslas S., 7, 25-30, 71, 75, 80, 125, 126, 304 ; Legends and biographies of, 84, 93, 104, 105, 112, 118, 126 ; cult of—, in Russia, 242-246 ; in Croatia, 247, 248, 250.
Wenceslas II, Czech King of Poland, 263, 264.
Wenceslas III, 263, 264.
Wenceslas IV, 264.
Werben on the Elbe, 226.
Wernz F. X., German historian, 49.
Western Pomerania, see Pomerania.
White Croatia, 13, 18, 64, 81, 88, 91-93, 107, 108, 119, 199, 247, 249-251 ;see also Appendices I, II and III.
White Lady, Geiza's wife, see Beleknegini.
White Russia, 264.
White Russians, the, 13, 265.
White Serbia, 119, 230, and Appendices I, II and III.
White Serbs, 269.

Wiching, Bishop in Nitra, 128, 150.
Wichman, count, Herman Billung's brother, 34, 54-57, 70.
Widsith, Old English poem, 284.
Widukind of Corvay, Saxon chronicler, 27-29, 32, 33, 36, 39, 48, 54-57, 71, 129.
Wilhelm, Archbishop of Mainz, 59, 79.
Willebald, chronicler, 237.
Willigis, Archbishop of Mainz, 81, 121, 123.
Windin (Winden), (=Serbs in Old Germanic), 295.
Wippo, biographer of Conrad II, 223, 227.
Wirinhar, Thietmar's nephew, 205.
Wislawudu (Vistula-Oder Forest), 284.
Wisle (=Vistula), 273.
Witizla, Bohemian Duke, 293, 296.
Wolfgang S. Bishop of Regensburg, 79, 80, 82, 150.
Wollin (Iomsburg), 52, 87, 88, 129, 226.
Wrytsleof (Wyrtgeorm), King of the Wends, 225.

Xantenses Annales, see Annales.

Yaropolk, Svyatoslav's son, 90, 91, 167, 168, 172.
Yaroslav the Great (The Wise), son of Vladimir the Great, 176, 178, 216, 217, 22?, 234, 238, 239, 253-255, 258.
Yaroslavl, town, 259.
Yazingians, the, 308, 310.

Zacharias, the Rhetor, 305, 307, 309, 310, 311.
Zachlumians, the, 291.
Zara, 16.
Zbislava, wife of Boleslas III of Poland, 254.
Zehde, battle of (in 972), 58.
Zeisberg H. German Historian, 49.
Zeitz, diocese of, 73, 74, 85.
Zemusil (Ziemusil, Ziemomysl), Theodoric's (Dietrich's) son, 226, 234.
Zhupanies (=counties), 269, 290.
Zhupans, the, 273.
Ziemomysl, Legendary ancestor of Mieszko, I, 16, 52, 88.
Ziemovit, Legendary ancestor of Mieszko I, 52.
Zistibor, Serbian prince, 292.
Zlichanians, the, 93.
Zuarazitz, Veletian deity, 203.
Zubur Duke, 154.
Zupanic N., Yugoslav historian, 275.

Dvornik, Francis, 1893–
     The making of central and eastern Europe. With a new introduction
and notes to the text by the author. 2d. ed. [Gulf Breeze, Fla.] Academic International Press, 1974.

     xxix, 350 p. maps. 26 cm. (The Central and east European series,
vol. 3)

     "In some ways the continuation of my book *Les Slaves, Byzance et
Rome au IXe siècle* published in Paris in 1926."

     Errata slip inserted.

     Bibliography: p. 319-334.

     1. Central Europe—Hist. I. Title

DR36.D9 1974   943.022   73-90780
ISBN: 0-87569-023-8

ERRATA

p. 17, line 10: *Moimir* not Rastislav

p. 41, note 2: *Bedeutung* not Berufung

p. 52, note 32: *968* not 969

p. 76, note 95, line 4: *fiercest* not fiereist

p. 77, note 96: *November* not Novembrer;
part not pars.

p. 78, note 98, last sentence: *Boleslas I*
not Boleslas II

p. 91, line 37: *Kiev* not Kief

p. 92, line 18: *felt* not ielt; line 27, *it*
not at

p. 101, note 10, line 3: *monastery* not
convent

p. 134, line 21: *monastery* not convent

p. 151, line 13: *Andrew* not Andreas

p. 154, line 20: *eleventh* not twelfth

p. 157, note 58: *768* not 7678;
XXX not XXXi

p. 202, line 4: *968* not 965

p. 222, line 8 : *Conrad* not Henry

p. 239, line 34: *40* not 400

p. 249, note 52: *in* Russian

p. 251, line 6: *898* not 889

p. 271, note 8: *Witukinds* not Witukinodo;
read notes 13 and 14 in reverse order.

p. 289, line 38: *kazenz* not karenz

p. 291, note 51: *214* not 124

p. 293, note 56: *21* not 11

p. 294, note 60: *269* not 268

p. 298, note 2: *Bonn* not Bran

p. 299, note 8: *Buliciana* not Bubliciana

p. 306, note 6: *Ant.* not Hist.

p. 308, notes 10 and 12: *Meineke*
Meiricke and Meine; note 14:
Koestermann not Koester, M
Mann; *Mayhoff* not Maryhoff.

p. 313, note 31: line 12: *vol. 23*
not vol. V. 23

p. 322, line 12: *Lyotimov* not
Lyotiniov

p. 325, line 4: *vol. 23* not 1. 43,

p. 326, line 31: *Festschrift* not
Zeitschrift

p. 328, line 22: *189* not 1897;
line 45: *LXXXVIII.* not LXX-
VII

p. 331, line 20: *pp.* not Mv.

p. 332, line 21: *Tougar* not Tungar;
line 39: *Ivana and Ivan* not Irania

p. 333, line 6: add *Weidhaas, H.*

p. 334, line 10: *Starina* not Ltarina;
line 11: *mišlenja o njich.* not mislenja o hjinl; line 20: *Značenje
Barevnega* not Zngoenfa Carevnega